...ight be formed. — The greater
...t of it is already reclaimed —
...it.

...cleared and in cultivation,
...tlemans seat.

...hould be sub-divided, it might
...f the River.

Map
of
General Washington's Farm,
of
MOUNT VERNON
from
A Drawing transmitted by
the General

Road to Alexandria 9 Miles from Mt Vernon.

E

Scale

100   200   300

E

R
I
V
E
R

Field Nº 7
120 Acres

Field Nº 5
132 Acres

Field Nº 4
132 Acres

Field Nº 6 — 150 Acres

R I V E R

Orchards, Grass Lots, &c.

84 Acres

Clover Lot
12 Acres

Clover Lot
10 Acres

Clover Lot
10 Acres

F A R M

Field Nº 1 — 130 Acres

C

Common Pasture about
212 Acres

Field Nº 2
110 Acres

Field Nº 3
125 Acres

D

A

C.

R
I
V
E
R

LITTLE HUNTING

The Papers of
George Washington

Frontispiece: GW honored the request of Anne Willing Bingham in sitting for portrait artist Gilbert Stuart in 1796. The oil-on-canvas likeness was to be a gift to the marquis of Lansdowne and came to be known as the Lansdowne Portrait. (National Portrait Gallery, Smithsonian Institution; acquired as a gift to the nation through the generosity of the Donald W. Reynolds Foundation)

The Papers of George Washington

Jennifer E. Steenshorne, *Director and Editor in Chief*

David R. Hoth, *Senior Editor*

William M. Ferraro, *Senior Associate Editor*

Thomas E. Dulan and Benjamin L. Huggins
Associate Editors

Adrina Garbooshian-Huggins, Dana J. Stefanelli,
and Jeffrey L. Zvengrowski
Assistant Editors

Jennifer E. Stertzer
Director, Center for Digital Editing (CDE)

Erica Cavanaugh
Research Editor, CDE

Presidential Series
20

1 April–21 September 1796

David R. Hoth and William M. Ferraro, *Editors*

UNIVERSITY OF VIRGINIA PRESS
CHARLOTTESVILLE AND LONDON

This edition has been prepared by the staff of
The Papers of George Washington
sponsored by
The Mount Vernon Ladies' Association of the Union
and the University of Virginia
with the support of
the National Endowment for the Humanities,
the National Historical Publications and Records Commission,
the Packard Humanities Institute (through Founding Fathers Papers, Inc.),
and the Florence Gould Foundation.

UNIVERSITY OF VIRGINIA PRESS
© 2019 by the Rector and Visitors
of the University of Virginia
All rights reserved

First published 2019

The paper used in this publication meets the minimum requirements of
ANSI/NISO Z39.48-1992 (R 1997) (Permanence of Paper).

Library of Congress Cataloging-in-Publication Data
Washington, George, 1732–1799.
  The papers of George Washington, Jennifer E. Steenshorne, ed.
  Presidential series vol. 20 edited by David R. Hoth and William M. Ferraro.
  Includes bibliographical references and indexes.
  Contents: v. 1. September 1788–March 1789—[etc.]—v. 20.
1 April–21 September 1796
    1. United States—Politics and government—1789–1797.
2. Washington, George, 1732–1799—Correspondence.
3. Presidents—United States—Correspondence.
I. Steenshorne, Jennifer E.; Hoth, David R.; Ferraro, William M.
II. Presidential series.   III. Title.
E312.72 1987b   973.4'1'092   87-410017
ISBN 0-8139-1103-6 (v. 1)
ISBN 978-0-8139-4304-6 (v. 20)

Front endpapers: "A map of General Washington's farm of Mount Vernon from a drawing transmitted by the General," in *Letters from His Excellency General Washington, to Arthur Young, Esq. F.R.S., containing An Account of His Husbandry, with a Map of His Farm; His Opinions on Various Questions in Agriculture; and Many Particulars of the Rural Economy of the United States* (London, 1801). [This illustration was based on a sketch enclosed in GW to Young, 12 Dec. 1793.] Library of Congress, Geography and Map Division.

Back endpapers: [L'Enfant] Plan of the City of Washington in the Territory of Columbia . . . [as drawn by Andrew Ellicott and engraved by Samuel Hill of Boston in 1792]. Library of Congress, Geography and Map Division.

Contents

NOTE: Volume numbers refer to the *Presidential Series.*

Illustration

Map

Introduction

By the period covered in volume 20 of the Presidential Series (1 April–21 Sept. 1796), GW had entered the last year of his presidency and was looking toward retirement. That prospect focused attention on shaping a farewell address. After exchanging ideas and drafts regularly with Alexander Hamilton, GW presented his farewell address to the public in *Claypoole's American Daily Advertiser* (Philadelphia) for 19 September. GW's ideas inspired widespread comment upon their appearance, and the document remains an important statement of guiding principles for the United States.

Advice in the farewell address reflected GW's experience with the controversies surrounding the Jay Treaty of 1794. After the House of Representatives finally agreed on 30 April 1796 to pass the laws necessary to fund that treaty's provisions, GW vigorously began its implementation. The promised transfer of British-held frontier posts to the United States immediately improved relations with Great Britain. More harmony arose when Robert Liston, the new British minister, arrived in May and showed welcome responsiveness to American concerns over the impressment of U.S. seamen and the safety of neutral shipping. To GW's disquietude, despite legal and administrative steps forward, these longstanding issues remained stubbornly intractable because British ship captains persisted in their old ways.

Better relations with Great Britain created increased tensions with France. Hamilton warned GW that the French government intended to send a new minister with authority to annul that nation's treaties with the United States and that French warships intended to seize American vessels carrying goods to England. James Monroe, U.S. minister to France, received a formal French complaint about America's failure to live up to its treaty obligations with France and about the new U.S. treaty with Great Britain. Tench Coxe, commissioner of the revenue, forwarded similar complaints to GW that originated with Vicomte de Rochambeau. A crisis neared when a French privateer seized the merchant ship *Mount Vernon* shortly after it had cleared Philadelphia. Diplomatic tensions with France exacerbated political divisions within the United States. The *Aurora General Advertiser* (Philadelphia) and other newspapers critical of GW's policies printed justifications of the ship's seizure and hinted darkly at more serious repercussions. The discovery of a letter from Monroe that suggested his sympathies lay with the opposition party prompted his recall. GW took pains to ensure that Monroe's replacement, Charles Cotesworth Pinckney, would properly represent U.S. policies to the French government in Paris.

Reports that French leaders had sent Victor Collot to examine American fortifications and spread disaffection along the western frontier further complicated relations between France and the United States. Concerns that the French might obtain New Orleans from Spain subsided when Spanish officials arrested Collot and his companions, preempting American plans to seize Collot and his papers.

A treaty with Algiers signed on 5 Sept. 1795 also required consideration. An impatient dey, the ruler of Algiers, demanded promised funds and threatened to abrogate the treaty if they were not forthcoming in a timely manner. GW's reassurances and the promise of an extra frigate, which would have to be constructed, eased the problem for the moment, but concerns remained over the treaty's stability. In a happy development, a treaty with Spain signed on 27 Oct. 1795 received GW's final proclamation in early August 1796 without drama.

Indian relations dominated the domestic scene. U.S. commissioners negotiated with the Seven Nations of Canada in New York and with the Creeks in Georgia. Settler intrusions on Cherokee lands elicited a letter from Secretary of War James McHenry to the Tennessee governor, and GW directed Secretary of State Timothy Pickering on 1 July to consult with other cabinet secretaries and initiate action on surveying the Cherokee boundary to remove "the pretext of ignorance." McHenry oversaw reorganization of the Indian department in the South. His instructions to the new Cherokee agent, Silas Dinsmore, and the new superintendent, Benjamin Hawkins, reveal much about the government's Indian policy. Additional insights can be gained from an address to the Cherokee Nation issued over GW's signature on 29 Aug. and from the process of revising the initial version of the address.

The army also generated some correspondence. McHenry submitted plans for adjusting the officer corps to conform with a new law fixing the military establishment. Various courts-martial came up for review, and Gen. James Wilkinson's charges against commanding general Anthony Wayne provoked consternation. Regular troops replaced less reliable militia in Georgia to promote peace and protect both Indians and white settlers.

The many complexities involved with construction of the Federal City remained worrisome for GW. He communicated with the city's commissioners most frequently on finances, especially their effort to obtain a loan for construction needs. Other correspondence pertained to building codes, personnel matters, and the rule that the commissioners reside in the city.

Federal appointments, as always, consumed time and caused exas-

peration. In addition to assignments needed to fulfill Jay Treaty stipulations and Monroe's replacement as minister to France, GW had to find
a new minister to Great Britain after Thomas Pinckney indicated his
desire to leave that post. Among other appointments, GW struggled
most with securing a surveyor general after the eminently qualified
Simeon DeWitt declined the office.

Real estate ventures loomed largest in GW's private affairs. He received numerous inquiries about the western lands he had advertised
for sale in February. He also completed a sale of one Pennsylvania tract
and sorted out problems with payments due on another transaction.
He took great interest in reports about the collection of rents for his
land in western Virginia.

As head of his extended family, GW was asked to approve the marriage of his niece Harriot Washington. He took this task seriously
enough to investigate the groom's career prospects. A complaint about
a small debt owed by his nephew Howell Lewis surprised GW, and irk-
some and mildly embarrassing correspondence transpired before the
debt's settlement.

During the summer months spent at Mount Vernon, GW entertained
many prominent visitors, including the new Spanish minister Carlos
Martinez Yrujo. Harriet Marchant Liston, the wife of the new British
minister, accompanied her husband and wrote colorful accounts to
her uncle in Antigua of her travels and of the Washington family at
home. These descriptions followed her memorable initial impressions
of GW and Martha Washington upon being introduced to them at a
presidential levee. She swooned over GW's "appearance & manners"
and found "his face at the age of sixty three rather pleasing, particularly when he smiles." Believing Martha's figure "short & fat" but "not
with out dignity," Henrietta sought more-flattering words in observing that "her face retains the marks of delicate beauty & her voice is
melody itself" (see Hamilton to GW, 10 May, n.4).

Wanting Mount Vernon to be in prime condition, GW frequently
corresponded with his farm manager, William Pearce, regarding efforts
to prepare the estate for visitors, in addition to discussing the usual topics of crops, construction, accounts, overseers, and slave management.
Learning that Pearce planned to leave his position for health reasons,
GW launched efforts to find his successor. His inquiries resulted in an
exchange of letters with James Anderson, whom GW then hired.

Slavery again enters the volume in correspondence seeking the
return of Martha Washington's servant Ona (Oney) Judge, who had
run away from Philadelphia in May. In a less well-known case, John
Dandridge wished to keep a slave family together by purchasing two
slaves that GW had loaned to Dandridge's mother. GW determined to

let the Dandridges work out a suitable arrangement among themselves as he had no desire to reclaim the slaves.

Other topics discussed in the volume include efforts to assist the imprisoned Marquis de Lafayette, pardons for leaders of the Whiskey Insurrection, federal cooperation with state efforts to enforce quarantines, and GW's decision about which educational institution in Virginia would receive his shares of James River Company stock. There is also the last known exchange of letters between GW and Thomas Jefferson. The subjects split almost evenly between farming and politically motivated newspaper criticisms. Politics eventually drove apart these two great Virginians despite their shared passion for agriculture.

Editorial Apparatus

Transcription of the documents in the volumes of *The Papers of George Washington* is as close as practicable to a literal reproduction of the original manuscripts. Except as noted below, punctuation, capitalization, and spelling of all words are retained as they appear in the original document. Generally, paragraphing is modified only for documents printed in annotations. Dashes used as punctuation have been retained, except when a dash and another mark of punctuation appear together. When absent, the appropriate marks of punctuation have been added at the end of a paragraph.

Misspellings in the original manuscript are corrected (either in brackets or in annotation) if the misspelling makes the word incomprehensible. When a tilde (~) is used in the manuscript to indicate a double letter, the letter has been doubled. GW and some of his correspondents occasionally used a tilde above an incorrectly spelled word to indicate an error in orthography. When this device is used, the editors have corrected the word. In cases where a tilde has been inserted above an abbreviation or contraction, usually in letter-book copies, the word has been expanded. Otherwise, contractions and abbreviations have been retained as written, except that a period has been inserted after an abbreviation when needed. If the meaning of an abbreviation or contraction is not obvious, it has been expanded in square brackets: "H[is] M[ajest]y." Editorial insertions or corrections in the text also appear in square brackets. Angle brackets ⟨ ⟩ are used to indicate illegible or mutilated material; when there is a basis for doing so, conjectural text is supplied within the brackets. Endnotes or the source note will indicate if the text is taken from another version of the document. A space left blank in a manuscript by the writer is indicated by a square-bracketed gap in the text [   ].

Material deleted by the author of a manuscript is ignored unless it contains substantive material, and then it appears in the notes. If the intended location of marginal notations is clear from the text, such notations are inserted at that point; otherwise, they are recorded in the notes. The ampersand has been retained; the thorn (þ in Old English, but by GW's day essentially indistinguishable from the letter Y) is transcribed as "th"; and superscripts have been lowered. The symbol for per (℔) is used when it appears in the manuscript. The dateline has been placed at the head of a document, regardless of where it occurs in the manuscript.

When multiple versions of a document are available, the document closest to the one actually received by the addressee is printed. The other versions have been collated with the selected text, and significant variations are presented in the annotation. Since GW read no language other than English, incoming letters written to him in foreign languages were generally translated for his information. Where this contemporary translation has survived, it has been used as the text of the document. If no contemporary translation has been found, the document in its original language has been used as the text.

All of the documents printed in this volume ultimately will be available in the digital edition of the Washington Papers, as will the original foreign language documents (when otherwise not provided), any documents omitted or not printed in full, and ancillary materials. The reports of GW's farm managers at Mount Vernon, some of which have been printed in previous volumes of the *Presidential Series*, now appear only in the digital edition. Certain routine documents that have been omitted from this volume, such as ships' passes (which GW signed as blank forms to be filled in by customs officials), appointments, and land grants, may be omitted from the digital edition as well. To learn more about the digital edition, visit the website of The Papers of George Washington (gwpapers.virginia.edu) or of Rotunda, the digital imprint of the University of Virginia Press (www.upress.virginia.edu/rotunda).

Individuals mentioned in the text usually are identified at their first substantive mention in each series. The index to each volume indicates where identifications appear in earlier volumes of the *Presidential Series*. Variant names and alternate spellings, for individuals as well as for places, may appear in parentheses in both annotation and index.

In the index, main entries are alphabetized letter-by-letter, with alphabetization interrupted only by either a comma or a parenthesis. Any other punctuation is ignored, as is a letter space. Minor words such as articles, prepositions, and conjunctions are ignored as the first word in an entry, but as interior words they are considered in the alphabetization. Names beginning with Mc or Mac are alphabetized as they appear; however, any name beginning with a variation of saint (St., Ste., Sainte) is alphabetized as though spelled out as "Saint." In subentries, personal names are alphabetized by surname, even though presented in a first-name-last-name format.

GW never used the term *cabinet* when referring as a group to the attorney general and the heads of the State, War, and Treasury departments. However, for the sake of clarity, the editors have used this term to indicate corporate meetings by these individuals, both with and without GW, and to describe documents issued as a result of these meetings.

Symbols and Terms Designating Documents

AD   Autograph Document: a document written in the author's hand but not bearing the author's signature

ADS   Autograph Document Signed: a document both written and signed by the author

ADf   Autograph Draft: a draft written in the author's hand but not bearing the author's signature

ADfS   Autograph Draft Signed: a draft both written and signed by the author

AL   Autograph Letter: a letter written in the author's hand but not bearing the author's signature

ALS   Autograph Letter Signed: a letter both written and signed by the author

D   Document: a document (not a letter) bearing neither the author's handwriting nor signature

DS   Document Signed: a document written in the hand of someone other than the author but bearing the author's signature

Df   Draft: a draft bearing neither the author's handwriting nor signature

DfS   Draft Signed: a draft written in the hand of someone other than the author but bearing the author's signature

L   Letter: a letter bearing neither the author's handwriting nor signature

LS   Letter Signed: a letter written in the hand of someone other than the author but bearing the author's signature

LB   Letters copied into a bound letter-book

[S]   Indication that the author's signature has been cut from the original manuscript

Copy   A contemporaneous handwritten representation made of any version of a letter or other document

Transcript   A non-contemporaneous handwritten representation made of a letter or other document (generally not used or cited unless no other version is available, except in the case of a Sprague transcript)

Sparks transcript   Handwritten transcripts made by Jared Sparks, primarily in support of his 1833–37 edition of GW's correspondence

Sprague transcript   Handwritten transcripts made in the 1820s by William B. Sprague to replace documents he had removed from GW's papers

Repository Symbols and Abbreviations

CaOOA	National Archives of Canada, Ottawa, Ontario
CCamarSJ	Saint John's Seminary, Camarillo, Calif.
CSmH	Huntington Library, Art Collections and Botanical Gardens, San Marino, Calif.
CSmvRRL	Ronald Reagan Library, Simi Valley, Calif.
Ct	Connecticut State Library, Hartford
CtHi	Connecticut Historical Society, Hartford
DLC	U.S. Library of Congress, Washington, D.C.
DLC:GW	U.S. Library of Congress, George Washington Papers, Washington, D.C.
DNA	U.S. National Archives and Records Administration, Washington, D.C.
DSoC	Society of the Cincinnati, Washington, D.C.
FrPMAE	Ministère des affaires étrangères, Archives, Paris, France (photocopies at Library of Congress)
G-Ar	Georgia State Department of Archives and History, Atlanta
G-BW	Booth Western Art Museum, Cartersville, Ga.
GU-HR	University of Georgia, Hargrett Rare Book and Manuscript Library, Athens
GyBrS	Staatsarchiv, Bremen, Germany
ICHi	Chicago Historical Society, Chicago, Ill.
MA	Amherst College, Amherst, Mass.
MAnP	Phillips Academy, Andover, Mass.
MaSaPEM	Peabody Essex Museum, Salem, Mass.
MdAA	Maryland Hall of Records Commission, Annapolis
MDedHi	Dedham Historical Society, Dedham, Mass.
MH	Harvard University, Cambridge, Mass.
MHi	Massachusetts Historical Society, Boston
MiD	Detroit Public Library, Detroit, Mich.
MiU-C	University of Michigan, William L. Clements Library, Ann Arbor
MWiW-C	Williams College, Chapin Library, Williamstown, Mass.
N	New York State Library, Albany
NBuHi	Buffalo and Erie County Historical Society, Buffalo, N.Y.
NHC	Colgate University, Hamilton, N.Y.
NhD	Dartmouth College, Hanover, N.H.
NjMoHP	Morristown National Historical Park, Morristown, N.J.
NjP	Princeton University, Princeton, N.J.
NHi	New-York Historical Society, New York
NN	New York Public Library, New York
NNC	Columbia University, New York, N.Y.

NNGL	Gilder Lehrman Collections, on deposit at the New-York Historical Society, New York
NNPM	Pierpont Morgan Library, New York, N.Y.
PHarH	Pennsylvania Historical and Museum Commission, Harrisburg
PHi	Historical Society of Pennsylvania, Philadelphia
PP	Free Library of Philadelphia, Philadelphia, Pa.
PPAmP	American Philosophical Society, Philadelphia, Pa.
PPL	Library Company of Philadelphia, Philadelphia, Pa.
PPRF	Rosenbach Museum and Library, Philadelphia, Pa.
PWacD	David Library of the American Revolution, Washington Crossing, Pa.
RuSpRNB	National Library of Russia, Saint Petersburg
ScC	Charleston Library Society, Charleston, S.C.
StEdNL	National Library of Scotland, Edinburgh
T	Tennessee State Library and Archives, Nashville
UkLoBM	The British Museum, London, England
UkWC-A	Windsor Castle, Royal Archives, Windsor, England
Vi	Library of Virginia, Richmond
ViFreGWF	George Washington's Fredericksburg Foundation, Fredericksburg, Va.
ViHi	Virginia Historical Society, Richmond
ViMtvL	Mount Vernon Ladies' Association of the Union, Mount Vernon, Va.
ViW	College of William and Mary, Williamsburg, Va.

Short Title List

ABPC.   *American Book-Prices Current.* New York, 1895–2004.

Adams Family Correspondence.   Lyman H. Butterfield et al., eds. *Adams Family Correspondence.* 13 vols. to date. Cambridge, Mass., 1963–.

Allis, *William Bingham's Maine Lands.*   Frederick S. Allis, Jr., ed. *William Bingham's Maine Lands 1790–1820.* 2 vols. Boston, 1954. In *Publications of The Colonial Society of Massachusetts,* vols. 36–37.

Ames, *Works.*   Seth Ames, ed. *Works of Fisher Ames with a Selection from His Speeches and Correspondence.* 2 vols. 1854. Reprint. New York, 1971.

Ammon, *James Monroe.*   Harry Ammon. *James Monroe: The Quest for National Identity.* New York, 1971.

Annals of Congress.   Joseph Gales, Sr., comp. *The Debates and Proceedings in the Congress of the United States; with an Appendix, Containing Important State Papers and Public Documents, and All the Laws of a Public Nature.* 42 vols. Washington, D.C., 1834–56.

Arbuckle, *Pennsylvania Speculator and Patriot.*   Robert D. Arbuckle. *Pennsylvania Speculator and Patriot: The Entrepreneurial John Nicholson, 1757–1800.* University Park, Pa., 1975.

Arnebeck, *Through a Fiery Trial.*   Bob Arnebeck. *Through a Fiery Trial: Building Washington, 1790–1800.* Lanham, Md., and London, 1991.

ASP.   Walter Lowrie et al., eds. *American State Papers. Documents, Legislative and Executive, of the Congress of the United States.* 38 vols. Washington, D.C., 1832–61.

Autobiography of Monroe.   Stuart Gerry Brown, ed. *The Autobiography of James Monroe.* Syracuse, N.Y., 1959.

Bear and Stanton, *Jefferson's Memorandum Books.*   James A. Bear, Jr., and Lucia C. Stanton, eds. *Jefferson's Memorandum Books: Accounts, with Legal Records and Miscellany, 1767–1826.* 2 vols. Princeton, N.J., 1997.

Bemis, *John Quincy Adams and American Foreign Policy.*   Samuel Flagg Bemis. *John Quincy Adams and the Foundations of American Foreign Policy.* New York, 1965.

Binney, *Farewell Address.*   Horace Binney. *An Inquiry into the Formation of Washington's Farewell Address.* Philadelphia, 1859.

Brigham, *American Newspapers.*   Clarence S. Brigham. *History and Bibliography of American Newspapers, 1690–1820.* 2 vols. Worcester, Mass., 1947.

Brock, *Dinwiddie Records.*   R. Alonzo Brock, ed. *The Official Records of Robert Dinwiddie, Lieutenant-Governor of the Colony of Virginia, 1751–1758.* 2 vols. Richmond, 1883–84.

Bryan, *National Capital.*   Wilhelmus Bogart Bryan. *A History of the National Capital: From Its Foundation through the Period of the Adoption of the Organic Act.* 2 vols. New York, 1914–16.

Buel, *Barlow.*   Richard Buel, Jr. *Joel Barlow: American Citizen in a Revolutionary World.* Baltimore, 2011.

Carter, *Territorial Papers.*   Clarence Edwin Carter et al., eds. *The Territorial Papers of the United States.* 27 vols. Washington, D.C., 1934–69.

Cash Memoranda, 1794–97.   Cash + Entries & Memorandums, 29 Sept. 1794–31 Aug. 1797. Manuscript in John Carter Brown Library, Providence.

Chalkley, *Scotch-Irish Settlement.*   Lyman Chalkley. *Chronicles of the Scotch-Irish Settlement in Virginia: Extracted from the Original Court Records of Augusta County, 1745–1800.* 3 vols. 1912. Reprint. Baltimore, 1974.

Chase, *Letters of Barbé-Marbois.*   Eugene Parker Chase, trans. and ed. *Our Revolutionary Forefathers: The Letters of François, Marquis de Barbé-Marbois during his Residence in the United States as Secretary of the French Legation, 1779–1785.* New York, 1929.

Clark, *Greenleaf and Law.* Allen C. Clark. *Greenleaf and Law in the Federal City.* Washington, D.C., 1901.

Cometti, *Verme Journal.* Elizabeth Cometti, trans. and ed. *Seeing America and Its Great Men: The Journal and Letters of Count Francesco dal Verme, 1783–1784.* Charlottesville, Va., 1969.

Correspondence of Barclay. George Lockhart Rives, ed. *Selections from the Correspondence of Thomas Barclay, Formerly British Consul-General at New York.* New York, 1894.

Cronin, *Disappearing Islands.* William B. Cronin, *The Disappearing Islands of the Chesapeake.* Baltimore, 2005.

Dallas. A. J. Dallas. *Reports of Cases Ruled and Adjudged in the Several Courts of the United States, and of Pennsylvania, Held at the Seat of the Federal Government.* vols. 2–4. Philadelphia, 1798–1807.

DeConde, *Entangling Alliance.* Alexander DeConde. *Entangling Alliance: Politics & Diplomacy under George Washington.* Durham, N.C., 1958.

Diaries. Donald Jackson and Dorothy Twohig, eds. *The Diaries of George Washington.* 6 vols. Charlottesville, Va., 1976–79.

Dimon, *American Horses.* John Dimon. *American Horses and Horse Breeding: A Complete History of the Horse from the Remotest Period in History to Date. . . .* Hartford, 1895.

"Diplomatic Journal and Letter Book of Cathcart." "The Diplomatic Journal and Letter Book of James Leander Cathcart, 1788–1796." *Proceedings of the American Antiquarian Society,* n.s., 64 (1954): 303–436.

Documentary History of the Supreme Court. Maeva Marcus et al., eds. *The Documentary History of the Supreme Court of the United States, 1789–1800.* 8 vols. New York, 1985–2007.

Dunbar, *Ona Judge.* Erica Armstrong Dunbar. *Never Caught: The Washingtons' Relentless Pursuit of Their Runaway Slave, Ona Judge.* New York, 2017.

Early American Indian Documents. Alden T. Vaughan, ed. *Early American Indian Documents: Treaties and Laws, 1607–1789.* 20 vols. Washington, D.C., Frederick and Bethesda, Md., 1979–2003.

Eisen, *Portraits of Washington.* Gustavus A. Eisen. *Portraits of Washington.* 3 vols. New York, 1932.

Fitzpatrick, *Writings.* John C. Fitzpatrick, ed. *The Writings of George Washington from the Original Manuscript Sources, 1745–1799.* 39 vols. Washington, D.C., 1931–44.

Ford, *Spurious Letters.* Worthington Chauncey Ford. *The Spurious Letters Attributed to George Washington.* Brooklyn, 1889.

Franklin Papers. William B. Willcox et al., eds. *The Papers of Benjamin Franklin.* 42 vols. to date. New Haven, 1959–.

Fraser, *Washingtons.*   Flora Fraser. *The Washingtons: George and Martha, "Join'd by Friendship, Crown'd by Love."* New York, 2015.

General Ledger C.   General Ledger C, 1790–1799. Morristown National Historical Park, Morristown, N.J.

Goebel, *Law Practice of Hamilton.*   Julius Goebel, Jr., ed., *The Law Practice of Alexander Hamilton: Documents and Commentary.* 5 vols. New York, 1964–81.

Griffin, *Catalogue of the Washington Collection.*   Appleton P. C. Griffin, comp. *A Catalogue of the Washington Collection in the Boston Athenæum.* Cambridge, Mass., 1897.

Guillaume, *Comité d'Instruction Publique.*   J. Guillaume. *Procès-Verbaux du Comité d'Instruction Publique de la Convention Nationale.* 6 vols. Paris, 1891–1907.

Hamilton Papers.   Harold C. Syrett et al., eds. *The Papers of Alexander Hamilton.* 27 vols. New York, 1961–87.

Harris, *William Thornton Papers.*   C. M. Harris, ed. *Papers of William Thornton: Volume One, 1781–1802.* Charlottesville, Va., 1995.

Hayes, *Washington.*   Kevin J. Hayes. *George Washington: A Life in Books.* New York, 2017.

Hobson, "Recovery of British Debts."   Charles F. Hobson. "The Recovery of British Debts in the Federal Circuit Court of Virginia, 1790 to 1797." *Virginia Magazine of History and Biography* 92 (1984): 176–200.

Household Accounts.   Presidential Household Accounts, 1793–97. Manuscript, Historical Society of Pennsylvania, Philadelphia.

Jacobs, *Wilkinson.*   James Ripley Jacobs. *Tarnished Warrior: Major-General James Wilkinson.* New York, 1938.

JCC.   Worthington Chauncey Ford et al., eds. *Journals of the Continental Congress, 1774–1789.* 34 vols. Washington, D.C., 1904–37.

Jefferson Papers.   Julian P. Boyd et al., eds. *The Papers of Thomas Jefferson.* 41 vols. to date. Princeton, N.J., 1950–.

Johnston, *Jay Papers.*   Henry P. Johnston, ed. *The Correspondence and Public Papers of John Jay.* 4 vols. New York and London, 1890–93.

Journal of Ellicott.   Robert D. Bush, ed. *Surveying the Early Republic: The Journal of Andrew Ellicott, U.S. Boundary Commissioner in the Old Southwest, 1796–1800.* Baton Rouge, 2016.

Journal of the House.   *The Journal of the House of Representatives: George Washington Administration 1789–1797.* Edited by Martin P. Claussen. 9 vols. Wilmington, Del., 1977.

Journal of the Senate.   *The Journal of the Senate including The Journal of the Executive Proceedings of the Senate: George Washington Administration 1789–1797.* Edited by Martin P. Claussen. 9 vols. Wilmington, Del., 1977.

JPP. Dorothy Twohig, ed. *The Journal of the Proceedings of the President, 1793–1797.* Charlottesville, Va., 1981.

Kappler, *Indian Treaties.* Charles J. Kappler, ed. *Indian Affairs. Laws and Treaties.* 5 vols. Washington, D.C., 1903–41.

Kilbourne, *Society of Cincinnati of Pennsylvania.* John Dwight Kilbourne, *Virtutis Praemium: The Men Who Founded the State Society of the Cincinnati of Pennsylvania.* 2 vols. Rockport, Me., 1998.

Kline, *Burr Papers.* Mary-Jo Kline, ed. *Political Correspondence and Public Papers of Aaron Burr.* 2 vols. Princeton, N.J., 1983.

Knopf, *Wayne.* Richard C. Knopf, ed. *Anthony Wayne, a Name in Arms: Soldier, Diplomat, Defender of Expansion Westward of a Nation; The Wayne-Knox-Pickering-McHenry Correspondence.* Pittsburgh, 1960.

Kohn, *Eagle and Sword.* Richard H. Kohn. *Eagle and Sword: The Federalists and the Creation of the Military Establishment in America, 1783–1802.* New York and London, 1975.

La Rochefoucauld, *Voyage.* La Rochefoucauld-Liancourt. *Voyage dan Les États-Unis d'Amérique, Fait en 1795, 1796 et 1797.* 8 vols. Paris, 1799.

Latrobe, *Journal.* Benjamin Henry Latrobe. *The Journal of Latrobe: Being the Notes and Sketches of an Architect, Naturalist and Traveler in the United States from 1796 to 1820.* Introduction by J. H. B. Latrobe. New York, 1905.

Letters and Recollections of George Washington. *Letters and Recollections of George Washington: Being Letters to Tobias Lear and others between 1790 and 1799, showing the First American in the management of his estate and domestic affairs. With a diary of Washington's last days, kept by Mr. Lear.* New York, 1906.

"Letters of Ebeling." William Coolidge Lane, ed. "Letters of Christoph Daniel Ebeling To Rev. Dr. William Bentley of Salem, Mass. and to other American Correspondents." *Proceedings of the American Antiquarian Society,* n.s., 35 (1925): 272–451.

"Letters of Rumsey, Inventor." "Letters of James Rumsey, Inventor of the Steamboat." *William and Mary Quarterly,* 1st ser., 24 (January 1916): 154–74; 25 (July 1916): 21–34.

List of Patents. *Letter from the Secretary of State Transmitting a List of All Patents Granted by the United States, the Acts of Congress Relating Thereto, and the Decisions of Courts of the United States Under the Same.* U.S. Congress. House. State Dept. 21st Cong., 2d sess., H.R. Doc. 50. Washington, D.C., 1831.

Lodge, *George Cabot.* Henry Cabot Lodge. *Life and Letters of George Cabot.* 1878. Reprint. New York, 1974.

Madison Papers. William T. Hutchinson et al., eds. *The Papers of James Madison, Congressional Series.* 17 vols. Chicago and Charlottesville, Va., 1962–91.

Miller, *Diaries of Gouverneur Morris.* Melanie Randolph Miller et al., eds. *The Diaries of Gouverneur Morris: European Travels, 1794–1798.* Charlottesville, Va., 2011.

Miller, *Treaties.* Hunter Miller, ed. *Treaties and Other International Acts of the United States of America. Vol. 2, 1776–1818.* Washington, D.C., 1931.

Morgan, *Dauphin County.* George H. Morgan. *Centennial. The Settlement, Formation and Progress of Dauphin County, Pennsylvania, from 1785 to 1876.* Harrisburg, Pa., 1877.

Mount Vernon Accounts, 1794–1797. Manuscript Mount Vernon Accounts, 6 Jan. 1794–19 Jan. 1797. Library of Congress, George Washington Papers.

Munson, *Alexandria Hustings Court Deeds, 1783–1797.* James D. Munson, comp. *Alexandria, Virginia: Alexandria Hustings Court Deeds, 1783–1797.* Bowie, Md., 1990.

Nelson, *Wayne.* Paul David Nelson. *Anthony Wayne: Soldier of the Early Republic.* Bloomington, Ind., 1985.

New-York Directory 1796. John Low, *The New-York Directory, and Register, for the Year 1796.* New York, 1796.

Niemcewicz, *Vine and Fig Tree.* Julian Ursyn Niemcewicz. *Under Their Vine and Fig Tree: Travels through America in 1797–1799, 1805, with Some Further Account of Life in New Jersey.* Translated and edited by Metchie J. E. Budka. Elizabeth, N.J., 1965.

North, *Travel Journals of Henrietta Liston.* Louise V. North. *The Travel Journals of Henrietta Marchant Liston: North America & Lower Canada, 1796–1800.* Lanham, Md., 2014.

Pa. Constitution. *The Constitution of the Commonwealth of Pennsylvania.* Philadelphia, 1790.

Paltsits, *Farewell Address.* Victor Hugo Paltsits. *Washington's Farewell Address: In facsimile, with transliterations of all the drafts of Washington, Madison, & Hamilton, together with their correspondence and other supporting documents.* New York, 1935.

Papers, Colonial Series. W. W. Abbot et al., eds. *The Papers of George Washington, Colonial Series.* 10 vols. Charlottesville, Va., 1983–95.

Papers, Confederation Series. W. W. Abbot et al., eds. *The Papers of George Washington, Confederation Series.* 6 vols. Charlottesville, Va., 1992–97.

Papers, Retirement Series. W. W. Abbot et al., eds. *The Papers of George Washington, Retirement Series.* 4 vols. Charlottesville, Va., 1998–99.

Papers, Revolutionary War Series. W. W. Abbot et al., eds. *The Papers of George Washington, Revolutionary War Series.* 26 vols. to date. Charlottesville, Va., 1985–.

Papers of James Monroe. Daniel Preston et al., eds. *The Papers of James Monroe.* 5 vols. to date. Westport, Conn., and Santa Barbara, Calif., 2003–.

Papers of John Adams. Robert J. Taylor et al., *Papers of John Adams.* 18 vols. to date. Cambridge, Mass., and London, 1977–.

Parry, *Consolidated Treaty Series.* Clive Parry, ed. *The Consolidated Treaty Series.* 231 vols. Dobbs Ferry, N.Y., 1969–81.

Philadelphia Directory, 1796. Thomas Stephens. *Stephens's Philadelphia Directory, For 1796. . . .* Philadelphia, [1796].

Philadelphia Directory, 1797. Cornelius William Stafford. *Philadelphia Directory, For 1797. . . .* Philadelphia, 1797.

Pickering and Upham, *Life of Pickering.* Octavius Pickering and Charles W. Upham. *The Life of Timothy Pickering.* 4 vols. Boston, 1867–73.

Pound, *Benjamin Hawkins.* Merritt B. Pound. *Benjamin Hawkins—Indian Agent.* Athens, Ga., 1951.

Randolph, *Papers of Thomas Jefferson.* Thomas Jefferson Randolph, ed. *Memoir, Correspondence, and Miscellanies, from the Papers of Thomas Jefferson.* 4 vols. Charlottesville, Va., 1829.

Rappleye, *Robert Morris.* Charles Rappleye. *Robert Morris: Financier of the American Revolution.* New York, 2010.

Reminiscences of James A. Hamilton. *Reminiscences of James A. Hamilton; or, Men and Events, at Home and Abroad, during Three Quarters of a Century.* New York, 1869.

Rutland, *James Madison Encyclopedia.* Robert A. Rutland, ed. *James Madison and the American Nation, 1751–/1836: An Encyclopedia.* New York, 1994.

Rutt, *Works of Priestley.* John Towill Rutt, ed. *The Theological and Miscellaneous Works of Joseph Priestley, LL.D. F.R.S &c.* 25 vols. London, [1817–32]. Reprint. New York, 1972.

Sage and Jones, *Hampshire County Records.* Clara McCormack Sage and Laura Sage Jones. *Early Records, Hampshire County Virginia, Now West Virginia, Including at the start most of known Va. aside from Augusta District.* Delavan, Wis., 1939.

Senate Executive Journal. *Journal of the Executive Proceedings of the Senate of the United States of America: From the commencement of the First, to the termination of the Nineteenth Congress.* Vol. 1. Washington, D.C., 1828.

Sims, *Making a State.* Edgar B. Sims. *Making a State: Formation of West Virginia, Including Maps, Illustrations, Plats, Grants and the Acts of the Virginia Assembly and the Legislature of West Virginia Creating the Counties.* Charleston, W.Va., 1956.

Sizer, *Trumbull Autobiography.* Theodore Sizer, ed. *The Autobiography of Colonel John Trumbull: Patriot-Artist, 1756–1843.* 1953. Reprint. New York, 1970.

Smith, *Letters of Delegates.* Paul H. Smith et al., eds. *Letters of Delegates to Congress, 1774–1789.* 26 vols. Washington, D.C., 1976–2000.

Smith, *St. Clair Papers.* William Henry Smith, ed. *The St. Clair Papers.*

The Life and Public Services of Arthur St. Clair: Soldier of the Revolutionary War; President of the Continental Congress; and Governor of the North-Western Territory with his Correspondence and other Papers. 2 vols. Cincinnati, 1882.

Stat.　　Richard Peters, ed. *The Public Statutes at Large of the United States of America, from the Organization of the Government in 1789, to March 3, 1845.* . . . 8 vols. Boston, 1845–67.

Strickland, *Tour in the United States.*　　William Strickland. *Journal of a Tour in the United States of America, 1794–1795.* Edited by J. E. Strickland. New York, 1971. In *Collections of the New–}York Historical Society,* vol. 83.

Tagg, *Benjamin Franklin Bache.*　　James Tagg. *Benjamin Franklin Bache and the Philadelphia Aurora.* Philadelphia, 1991.

Thomas, *Columbia University Officers and Alumni.*　　Milton Halsey Thomas, comp., *Columbia University Officers and Alumni, 1754–1857.* New York, 1936.

Todd, *Life and Letters of Barlow.*　　Charles Burr Todd. *Life and Letters of Joel Barlow, LL.D.: Poet, Statesman, Philosopher.* New York and London, 1886.

Walton, *Vermont Records.*　　E. P. Walton, ed. *Records of the Governor and Council of the State of Vermont.* 8 vols. Montpelier, 1873–80.

Zahniser, *Pinckney.*　　Marvin R. Zahniser. *Charles Cotesworth Pinckney: Founding Father.* Chapel Hill, N.C., 1967.

The Papers of George Washington
Presidential Series
Volume 20
1 April–21 September 1796

From Justus Erick Bollmann

Sir,   [Philadelphia] April the 1t 1796.

When I had the honor to wait on Your Excellency shortly after my arrival in Philadelphia,[1] I took the liberty to mention that I had a friend in Olmütz, who interested himself for Gen. Lafayette;[2] that I had arranged with him a safe correspondence; that he had communicated to me, before I left London, a plan according to which the liberty of Gen. Lafayette might have been procured on the expence of about 3000£ Stg; but, that his friends in London rejected it, partly, on account of the absence of Mr Pinckney, not choosing to take upon themselves the responsability for this money, partly, because they entertained great hopes that the applications of Madame Lafayette would prove successful! And I added at the same time that, my first proposals being thus rejected, I had endeavoured to make Madame Lafayette acquainted with my friend, writing a letter to both of them, in order that he might assist her with his advice!

The day before yesterday I have received of this same friend 3 letters, dated from Olmütz the 17th of October, the 26th of November, and the 10th of December 95., out of which I think it my duty to communicate to Your Excellency the following particulars!

Madame Lafayette went to Vienna so precipitately that she had seen the Emperor before my friend received my last letters, and this prevented his concerting with her any measures that might have supported her application. She was allowed by the Emperor to join the Marquis with her two daughters, but, respecting her request to set him free, he answerd "that this was a complicated affair and that his hands were tied" (que l'affaire etait compliquée et qu'il avait les mains liées lû dessus).

She then left Vienna and arrived in Olmütz the 16th of October, where she was immediately introduced to the marquis, and imprisoned with him, the same as her two daughters, who accompanied her. They are kept very closely and not allowed any communication with their friends, neither personally nor by way of Correspondence!

My friend, however, has succeded in establishing a secret

Correspondence; he gives me hope that soon he will be able to send me some original letters of the Marquis and meanwhile communicates to me an extract of the Marquis's letters to himself, out of which, suppressing what regards Mr Huger and myself personally, I think the following passage will be to Your Excelency particularly interesting.

"We flatter ourselves, write Gen. L.F. and his family, that our two friends will be well received in America; and we likewise think that Mr Bollmann will find in each of the different States, in Congress and in the Executif Government favorable dispositions towards the poor prisonners, whom it is the great point to reclaim. He will convince himself that, if Gen. Washington has not yet done every thing that might be useful to us, it is because the manner in which he may serve us never has been well explained to him yet. And, at all events, Mr Bollmann will not forget that, since 20 years, General Lafayette has been attached to General Washington by all the ties of tenderness, gratitude and respect, which can attach an adopted child to his father. We imagine that his stay in America may be of great utility; he will find there George, our son and brother &c. &c."

Some other accounts of my Olmütz-Correspondent mention, that it is the Influence of the Brittish ministry, and almost that alone what keeps the Marquis in Prison. "He suffers, much less because he was the Hero of the French, than because he took a part in the American Revolution!"

I am ready Sir, if You require it, to lay before Your Excellency the original german letters, which contain the informations and extracts above stated;[3] but, as now the way of correspondence is open, I should particularly be glad were I enabled to make to Gen. Lafayette some communications, calculated to sooth his misfortune by the certainty of friendly compassion, or to fortify his Courage by the prospect of relief![4] I have the honor to be with the highest respect Sir Your Excellency's most obedient and humble servant

J. Erick Bollmann

ALS, MHi: Pickering Papers. Following his signature, Bollmann drew a symbol whose significance has not been determined.

In a letter to Alexander Hamilton dated 13 April, Bollmann reported that Secretary of State Timothy Pickering had called him "to the State Office" on 8 April and related "that the President had some inclination to make a new effort to relieve the Marquis, and desired me at the same time to communicate to him by writing my Ideas on this subject. This occasioned a letter, to the Secretary of State, of which I take the liberty to send You again a Copy, repeating once more that I always shall be very glad if You will enable me to regulate my Conduct with respect to myself as well as to the Marquis, after Your advice!

"It was impossible not to have myself in view when I wrote the 8th paragraph of the inclosed letter, but I am so much convinced of what it asserts being essential and strictly true, that I would have written it exactly the same were I myself entirely out of the question!" (DLC: Hamilton Papers).

Bollmann is referring to a letter he had written Pickering on 10 April with some thoughts "respecting the means that might be used in order to rescue Gen. Lafayette from imprisonment."

First, Bollmann suggested that the British ministry was more responsible for Lafayette's continued imprisonment than was Holy Roman Emperor Francis II.

Second: "The inducements which effect this Conduct of the Brittish Ministry seem to be personal hatred, vengence, and an apprehension lest the Marquis, when arrived in this Country, might embrace the Interests of France and make use of his popularity to alienate the public mind from the Brittish Cause. They are of such a nature therefore as *likely* to continue during the present war, the end of which appears to be far distant, and they *may* continue even beyond this period!"

Third, past applications to the British about Lafayette had been unfruitful, and future applications likely "would prove equally ineffectual."

Fourth, with the emperor dependent on supplies from the British, he was unlikely to order Lafayette's release; "what may be obtained . . . is to induce him to connive at his escape" by easing "the present rigour" of Lafayette's confinement.

Fifth, the United States should, therefore, rely on "*An intermediate interference* . . . and the less this interference is suspected in London, or manifest in Vienna, the more probable it will prove successful."

Sixth, Bollmann named possible intermediaries and urged that "a confidential person" be sent "to Europe with several letters from General Washington, written, in his Character as President of the United States" to influential kings, noblemen, and perhaps to the emperor, to be employed "at the discretion of the Confidential person."

Seventh, a successful effort would require the support "of some very influential Individuals in Vienna" and might "require means which to employ perhaps would be incompatible with the Delicacy of the Executif Chief of a Republic." The confidential person should have an interview with George Washington Motier Lafayette in order to acquire the means.

Eighth, success would "in a great measure depend on the choice" of the confidential agent, who should be known to Lafayette and "well acquainted with the German language and of some connexions in the Country where he is to be send to, because, [of] the necessity of taking various kinds of informations and of maintaining a secret intelligence in Vienna and Olmütz with the friends of the Marquis."

Ninth, even if unsuccessful, the effort would "be highly honorable to the

United States and beneficial to the Marquis. Honorable to the United States—because it is a testimony of their affection, their gratitude; and beneficial to the Marquis—because it increases the Consideration he enjoys in Europe, and comforts him in prison by gratifying his sensibility" (ALS, DLC:GW; copy, in Bollmann's writing, DLC: Hamilton Papers). George Washington Motier Lafayette, whom Bollmann mentioned in his seventh thought, was the teenaged son of the imprisoned marquis and arrived in the United States in late summer 1795.

1. Bollmann arrived at Philadelphia in late January following a failed attempt to engineer Lafayette's escape from Olmütz (see Hamilton to GW, 19 Jan.; see also John Adams to Abigail Adams, 29 Jan., in *Adams Family Correspondence*, 11:151–53).

2. Bollmann probably is alluding to Karl Haberlein, an army hospital surgeon.

3. These letters have not been identified.

4. Bollmann's actions dismayed GW (see his letter to Hamilton, 8 May). For Lafayette's confidence in Bollmann, see La Rochefoucauld-Liancourt to GW, 25 July; see also GW to La Rochefoucauld-Liancourt, 8 August.

From Andrew Parks

Sir   Fredericksburg [Va.] 1st April 1796

Although entirely unknown to you, circumstances relative to your Niece Miss Harriot Washington and myself, makes it necessary for me to trouble you with a Letter, and to give you intimation of what has occur'd between us; I have made my addresses to her and she has refer'd me to You, whose consent I am to acquire, or her objections to a Union with me are I am assur'd insuperable, having therefore no hope of possessing her, unless I should be so fortunate as to obtain your assent, and as my happiness measurably depends upon your determination, I shall endeavour by stating to you my situation and prospects in Life, to merit and induce your approbation, Yet they are such as I fear will not much conduce to your favourable decission; I have lived in Fredksburg for more than three Years, my connexions generally reside in Baltimore, and are mostly rich, I am engaged here in the Mercantile Business and concern'd therein with my Brother in Law Mr McElderry of Balte,[1] my fortune at present does not much exceed three thousand pounds, but with industry and economy I have every expectation of rapidly improving my condition in that respect; to enter into a detail of my family I suppose would be unnecessary, however I shall be in Balte a few weeks hence, and if in the interim you should propose no objection to me I will take the liberty of writing to you again and give you a more particular acct of myself and friends, when it is probable my pecuniary situation may be meliorated.[2] The inclosed Letter from Mrs Lewis, who I solicited to write and say something to you concerning me[3]—I am Sir with infinite respect Yr most Obt Humbe Sert

Andrew Parks

ALS, DLC:GW.

Andrew Parks (1773–1836) lived in Kanawha County, Va., now W.Va., at the time of his death.

1. Thomas McElderry (d. 1810), a Baltimore merchant, married Elizabeth Parks, sister of Andrew, in 1787. McElderry served in the Maryland senate from 1806 until his death.

2. See GW to Parks, 7 April, and Parks to GW, 30 April; see also GW to George Lewis, 7 April.

3. Betty Washington Lewis wrote GW on 27 March: "I am going to address you on a Subject which I am request'd to do by Harriot, there is a young Jentleman in Fredericksburg Paying his addresses to her by the Name of Andrew Parks Merchant in that Town she desires me to inform you that he is her Choice if it meets with your Approbation he is One that is Very much respectted by all his acquaintance he is a sober sedate young man and attentive to Business, he sayes his fortune Does not Exceed three Thousand Pounds but has Expectations of something very handsome, you will receive a Letter from him I Expect with this.

"I have not receiv'd a line from You since I left Town which, Place I was Oblig'd to Quit as I should most sertainly been Rewin'd had I Continew'd there one year more the Place is more agrable to me than the one I left, the Place is Pore but with the advantage of the mill it will be more advantage to me than the other.

"Harriot Joines me in Love to you and my sister Washington" (ALS, ViMtvL).

From George Walton

sir,   philadelphia, 1 April, 1796

The letter enclosed, came under cover to me from General Mathews by yesterday's mail. In opening the latter, the seal of the former was a little injured.[1]

With every consideration of delicacy on my part, and of respect to the Executive of the Union on the other, I make this the occasion to mention, that, by the same mail, as well as by other conveyances, I am advised of such a general derangement of public affairs, and of appointments, in Georgia, I would willingly undertake some federal Employment.

Having long served in the Judiciary of that State, my habits and predilections are in that line; and I should have been content to have been continued on the ground I had left: but I have been excluded from the appointments, and even the Commission, for treating with the Creeks for the Oakmulgie lands, has been filled up anew.[2]

Under this unpleasant prospect, I am induced to offer my services to attend the Running of the Southern Boundary of the United-States, under the spanish Treaty.[3] It is in truth, sir, not my wish to embarrass by this application, as I make it with doubts; and shall be content with the reasons which shall pass it by. Advancing to a declining period of my life, my principal aim in this address is, to place myself in view for service, when a fit occasion shall offer.[4] With sincere attachment & respect, I am, Sir, Yr Obt Sert

Geo. Walton

ALS, DLC:GW.

Following James Jackson's resignation from the U.S. Senate in 1795, Walton filled the vacancy under an appointment until the Georgia legislature elected Josiah Tattnall, who took his seat on 12 April 1796.

1. Walton enclosed a letter from George Mathews to GW dated 7 March: "Having in some degree determined to leave the United States for a time if not forever; and knowing the just respect that is due, & paid to your Signature, I have taken the Liberty of requesting my friend Judge Walton to apply to you for such a Testimonial of my character & conduct in public appointments as Justice may intitle me to. This favor will be gratefully acknowleged" (ALS, DLC:GW; for GW's reply, see his first letter to Mathews, 10 June). The cover letter from Mathews to Walton has not been identified.

2. Walton served as chief justice of Georgia from 1783 to 1786. He again served as a state judge from 1790 until his appointment to the U.S. Senate. The commissioners appointed by Georgia for the upcoming Creek negotiations were James Hendricks, James Jackson, and James Simms. For the negotiations at Colerain in June, see *ASP, Indian Affairs,* 1:586–620.

3. Article II of the 27 Oct. 1795 treaty between the United States and Spain defined the southern boundary between the two powers, and Article III provided that each nation should appoint one commissioner and one surveyor to run and mark the boundary (see Miller, *Treaties,* 319–21).

4. Walton subsequently wrote GW from Augusta, Ga., on 20 Aug.: "I have lately been advised that Judge Pendleton has left this state, and that the office of District-Judge, in this District, will, of course, become vacant. Indeed, I had intimations that this would be the case before, and whilst I was at Philadelphia;

and the letter I took the liberty of writing to you, previous to my leaving that place, had this event in contemplation. Should my application meet your approval, and the nomination take place, my situation in life will be bettered; and I trust, the public and individual Justice be satisfied. My residence will be in Savannah, necessarily, on account of the admiralty supervision.

"I cannot forbear to embrace the present occasion of congratulating the President of the United States on the restoration of that public confidence, so essential in the Government of free states. A confidence that was staggered for the moment by the remains of prejudices deeply imbibed against a Nation during the convulsions of a great Revolution; and which inspired involuntary horrors at any Treaty of Amity with her. But reflection and experience have already opened the doors of Discernment and good sense in the Minds of the people; and the Treaty which has been made is beginning to be considered as an auspicious œra in the history of the United States: by its power of preserving the blessings of Peace, and subduing the prejudices of men.

"Undoubtedly, Sir, I wish you much health. Tranquility will follow of course" (ALS, DLC:GW; see also Nathaniel Pendleton to GW, 30 July, and Joseph Habersham to GW, 10 Aug.).

Robert Morris wrote GW from Washington, D.C., on 13 Sept. 1796: "Altho I am very averse to interest myself about the disposition of Public Offices, yet when the Calls of Friendship operate strongly in favour of a Worthy Man, who is qualified to perform the Duties of the Station aimed at, with reputation to himself & utility to the Public, I find it impossible to resist. And it is upon these principles that I recommend my Old Colleague in Congress, Geo. Walton Esqr. to Succeed Judge Pendleton who I am informed has resigned. Mr Walton has already acted as Chief Justice of the State of Georgia, is deemed a sound good Lawyer and a very Honest Man.

"You are not unacquainted with his Public Services & consequently will give to his claim on that score the weight it deserves, I was long in Congress with him and Witnessed his exertions upon many important occasions during the War" (ALS, DLC:GW).

From Alexander Hamilton

Sir   New York April 2d 1796

The express is this morning gone off with your letter to Young La Fayette. I foresaw when in Philadelphia certain machinations on this subject.[1]

I rejoice in the decision you have come to, in regard to the papers. Whatever may happen, it is right in itself—will elevate the character of the President—and inspire confidence abroad. The contrary would have encouraged a spirit of usurpation the bounds of which could not be foreseen.[2]

If there is time, I should like to have back the paper lately sent to correct prune guard & strengthen—I have no copy.[3] But of the expediency of this the circumstances on the Spot will decide. There is great fitness in the message to the House. I see only one point the least vulnerable, the too direct notice of the debate in the house—which may be attacked as contrary to parliamentary usage. I hear the criticism here among the L——s.[4] But this cannot be very material. Most respectfully & Affectny I have the honor to be Sir Yr very obed. ser.

A. Hamilton

ALS, DLC:GW; copy, DLC: Hamilton Papers.

1. See GW to George Washington Motier Lafayette, 31 March. In referring to "machinations," Hamilton evidently had in mind the congressional resolution offering assistance to young Lafayette (see Lafayette to GW, 28 March, and notes; see also Hamilton to GW, 9 April).

2. Hamilton applauded GW's decision to withhold from the U.S. House of Representatives the instructions given to John Jay and other documents concerning the negotiation of the treaty with Great Britain (see GW to the U.S. House of Representatives, 30 March).

3. Hamilton requested the return of his draft for GW's speech to the House delivered on 30 March (see Hamilton to GW, 29 March, n.1). GW had not used the draft, but suggested that he would hold it in reserve "as a source for reasoning" should the House press its demand (GW to Hamilton, 31 March). Hamilton subsequently wrote GW from New York City on 8 April: "I have done something but not what I intended—The sitting of two Courts & my professional engagements there prevent the execution of my plan—I no longer withold the paper lest circumstances should render it of any use" (ADfS, DLC: Hamilton Papers).

4. Hamilton alluded to the Livingston family.

From Timothy Pickering

Department of State April 2. 1796.

The Secretary of State has the honour to lay before the President of the U. States letters from Mr Adams Colo. Monroe & Mr Bayard, some of which were recd this day.[1]

T. Pickering

ALS, DNA: RG 59, Miscellaneous Letters; LB, DNA: RG 59, GW's Correspondence with His Secretaries of State.

1. The dispatches Pickering received from John Quincy Adams, U.S. minister to the Netherlands, and James Monroe, U.S. minister to France, have not been identified. Monroe's letters dated 6 and 22 Dec. 1795, 26 Jan., and 16 and 20 Feb. were acknowledged by Pickering on 13 June. For those let-

ters on various diplomatic subjects concerning France, but most notably the troubled reaction to the Jay Treaty, see *Papers of James Monroe*, 3:534–36, 547–49, 581–83, 590–91, 594–95). The most recent dispatch received from Adams probably was that dated 1 Jan., which discussed a proposal from Lord Grenville for the arbitration of American claims about ship captures and suggested that it might be the best offer available. Other dispatches that may have been enclosed were dated 5, 15, and 19 Dec. 1795 (all, DNA: RG 59, Despatches from U.S. Ministers to the Netherlands).

In a letter to American agent Samuel Bayard written on this date, Pickering acknowledged the receipt of "many" letters, the most recent dated 6 and 9 Feb. (DNA: RG 59, Diplomatic and Consular Instructions). Those probably were enclosed to GW along with Bayard's letter to Pickering dated 4 Feb., the duplicate of which the secretary of state received on 29 March. In the letter dated 4 Feb., Bayard reported that Thomas Pinckney would soon discuss with Lord Grenville "the principles that must govern the largest proportions of the American appeals" and urge an "early hearing" of the American cases. Noting that the British government "may have wished to be satisfy'd as to the measures that would be pursued by the House of Representatives of the U.S. respecting Mr. Jay's treaty," Bayard commented that the House reply to GW's annual address led him "to believe that we shall experience considerable aid in the amicable adjustment of our contr⟨o⟩versies with G.B. particularly in the settlement of the clai⟨ms⟩ and appeals under my direction." He also reported a favorable decision in the case of the *Relief* and mentioned that he was consulting with Pinckney on other "cases of cost & damage" and would report further.

On 6 Feb., Bayard enclosed to Pickering a memorial that he had sent to the Lords of Appeal. Bayard claimed that the memorial had "an effect that will operate highly in favor of our interests." Hearings on some American cases were to begin on 13 February.

In the letter dated 9 Feb., Bayard enclosed a duplicate of the 6 Feb. letter and added that he and Pinckney would postpone further action on the cases of cost and damage pending further instructions from Pickering. "In the mean time we shall urge on every suitable occasion the hearing & determination of our appeals at as early a day as possible. It is a matter of no small importance to us to obtain decisions on the commercial & political questions involved in our appeals prior to the period of a general peace" (all Bayard letters in DNA: RG 59, Communications from Special Agents).

To William Pearce

Mr Pearce,   Philadelphia 3d April 1796.

Your letter of the 27th Ulto, with a Post[s]cript of the 29th, came duly to hand yesterday.[1]

As I have expectation that by the time this letter will have reached you, a Vessel from Liverpool called the Commerce will have arrived at George Town with eight bushels of the field Pea; as much of the Chiccory as will sow four Acres of land; and eight bushels of the Winter Vetch—for, and on my account,[2] I request you to have the two first sowed as soon as you are able. By looking into some of the farming books I lent you; you will discover what quantity of the Pease to allow to the Acre. If these shd be silent, allow two bushels sowed broadcast: at any rate do not give as much as the English husbandry directs, for the quantity allowed in that country (formerly at least) greatly exceeds ours. I sent for as much Chiccory as would sow four Acres of ground,[3] but not mentioning whether in drils or broadcast, I am unable to give you any particular direction on this head; and therefore must leave it to yourself to judge from the quantity of seed, whether it is designed for four acres broadcast, or four acres in drills that the seed is adequate to. The Vetches must be secured in the Seed loft for fall sowing.

If the Chiccory is as valuable for Soiling horses (that is giving it to them green) as I am told it is; I think it would be desirable to allow a proportional quantity of it to each of the four farms; to be sown as convenient as may be to the stables. As you did not, in enumerating the different places in which Oats were to be sowed, mention any for the ground that was in Potatoes, near the quarter, at Mansion house; I think, if it is yet unsown, it would be a good spot (or as much thereof as is necessary) to sow the Pease in: and I see no reason why clover may not be sown with them, as well as with Oats. If this ground should have been seeded already—sow them wherever you please; and with as little delay as possible. Do the same with the chiccory, as the Season is getting late—& if it continues dry they will come to nothing withou⟨t⟩.

In one of my letters, I mentioned plantg the vacant ground in the Cornfield, at Mansion Ho., with Corn, along with the New ground; but in my next letter, I suggested the idea of putting it in Oats, to avoid letting the other part lying waste, or the expence of a fence.[4] But I leave it to you to do what you think best, or rather what you are able to accomplish. My plan always was, and always will be, to attempt no more than can be executed *well*. and this made me desirous of cultivating all the New ground; being well convinced that it will soon be as bad as ever, if the roots & sprouts are not destroyed by this means.

In one of your late letters, speaking of the damage done by

the Wind, you mentioned its having blown down many Trees:[5] it did not occur to me at that time, that this might have happened to the Trees in the yards, gardens, or Lawns. If this was the case, I hope they were set up again.

If the locust Posts for the circle, are ready, let them be put up. and if you should sell the flour on the terms I have mentioned, take care that the payment is well secured.[6]

Mr Minor has recommended a Mr Darnes, as a Tenant, whom he thinks would preserve my land near Alexandria from the Tresspasses it undergoes; and I have, in the enclosed letter (left open for your perusal) requested him to put the said Darnes on.[7] Let the letter be sent to him that he may certainly get it and let Mr Darnes have the field you speak of, & more ground if necessary, to put a house on. But make your agreement with him in writing; that there may be no mistakes. I should not incline to give him a surety of the place for more than 5, 6, or 7 yrs—for the rest I care not.

Unless I rent my Farms, and I have very little expectation of doing it, for the next year, I shall be indifferent about renting my Mill; unless tempted by a good price: but without letting this be known you may learn from Mr Gill what his friend, or any other, would give for her, for the term of years I have offered her.[8]

Let me know the exact size of the Chimney in the New room, at Mansion house; that is, how wide at the front, and at the back, & how deep at the sides; & whether the sides are of Marble. Let me know also how far the chimney piece projects from the plaistering above it; whether there is a middle part that projects more than the rest; how much, & the width of it, &ca; & what the whole length of the chimney piece at top is, from side to side or end to end.[9] I am your friend and well wisher

Go: Washington

ALS, ViMtvL.

1. Pearce's letter has not been found.

2. For this shipment, see James Maury to GW, 26 Dec. 1795.

3. See GW to Maury, 20 Oct. 1795.

4. See GW to Pearce, 13 and 20 March 1796.

5. This letter has not been found.

6. In GW's letter to Pearce written on 29 Nov. 1795, he suggested that during inclement weather the carpenters should be employed in tasks that could be done indoors, including making "Locust Posts for the circle before the door," probably meaning the front door to the mansion house. In his letter

dated 20 March 1796, he asked Pearce to sell the flour "whenever you can get fifteen dollars pr barrel for it payable in Sixty days."

7. George Minor had written GW on 30 March. The draft for the enclosed letter to Minor is dated 4 April. After acknowledging receipt of Minor's letter, GW continued: "For your kind endeavors to preserve my landed property, on four Mile Run, from depredation, I pray you to accept my grateful thanks accompanied with a request that Mr Darne (whom you have mentioned) may be placed on the Premises with a view to protect it.

"Whatever agreement you and Mr Pearce may make with Mr Darne to effect this purpose, I will abide by, and confirm" (ADfS, DSoC).

8. For GW's offer to lease out the farms and the mill at Mount Vernon, see his advertisement dated 1 February.

9. The "New room" refers to the large room that comprises the north wing of the mansion at Mount Vernon. No reply from Pearce has been found, but in an undated memorandum mostly about the dimensions of the mansion house windows, he wrote: "The Size of the New Room Chimny The hight is Three feet 11 Inches By—4 feet and half an Inch wide" (ViMtvL). In another undated but presumably later memo, GW wrote: "The chimney in the new room from the back to the front of the marble is 2 f. 1 I. The width in front is exactly 4 f. and perhaps 4 I. narrower in the back part. The middle part of the Chimney piece is 9 I: wide—and the 2 ends is 14½ Inches—That is projecting from the Wall" (AD [photocopy], ViMtvL).

Letter not found: from William Pearce, 3 April 1796. GW wrote Pearce on 10 April: "Your letter of the 3d instant . . . was received yesterday."

To James Innes

Dear sir,   Philada 4th april 1796.

Before this can have reached your hands, the gazettes will have announced to you that I have taken the liberty (without a previous consultation) to nominate you, conjointly with Thos Fitzsimons esqe an intelligent merchant of this City, one of the Commissioners for carrying the Sixth article of the treaty lately entered into with G. Britain, into effect. As the nomination is confirmed by the Senate, I hope it will be convenient & agreeable to you to accept the trust; for the duties whereof, & other matters relative thereto the article itself will be sufficiently explanatory.[1]

The compensation will not be less, I conceive, than £1000. sterlg per annum; but as it is not absolutely fixed yet, I cannot speak with more decision on the subject; and request that this letter may not be considered as an official one; but meant only to intimate what has been done, & to know your sentiments thereon; the rest you will receive in due time from the Secy of State.[2] With esteem & regard, &c.

G: Washington

LB, DLC:GW.

    1. A report on the nomination appeared in the *Gazette of the United States* (Philadelphia) for 31 March (see also GW to the U.S. Senate, same date, and n.1). Article VI of the 1794 Jay Treaty with Great Britain called for the appointment of five commissioners to determine the amounts owed British creditors for unpaid debts contracted before the 1783 treaty of peace (see Miller, *Treaties*, 249–51).

    2. Innes replied to GW on 8 April.

To Henry Knox

My dr Sir,   Philada 4 April 1796.

Before this will have reached you, you must have seen in the gazettes that I have taken the liberty (without a previous consultation) to nominate you the Commissioner for ascertaining the true St Croix & the Eastern boundary of the U. States, agreeably to the fifth article of the treaty lately entered into with G. Britain. I hope it will be convenient & agreeable for you to accept the trust, the appointment having been confirmed by the Senate.[1]

As the gazettes will give you in detail a resolution of the House of Representatives, calling upon the President for all the papers (excepting such as might respect pending treaties) relative to that treaty; also the debates thereupon, & my answer, it is unnecessary to repeat them.[2] I am beginning to receive what I had made my mind up for on this occasion—the abuse of Mr Bache & his correspondents.[3] The answer which I have given, is referred to a committee of the whole house for wednesday next;[4] the probable result of which, it is too early yet to predict or even to guess at. These are unpleasant things, but they must be met with firmness. Present me to Mrs Knox & the family in acceptable terms & be assured of the friendship & affecte regard of

G: Washington

P.S. At a proper time, after knowing whether you accept the appointmt or not, you will hear officially from the Secretary of State.[5]

LB, DLC:GW.

1. A report on Knox's nomination appeared in the *Gazette of the United States* (Philadelphia) for 31 March (see also GW to the U.S. Senate, same date). For Article V of the Jay Treaty, see Miller, *Treaties*, 249.

2. For the House resolution adopted on 24 March, see GW to the Cabinet, 25 March, n.1; for the reply, see GW to the U.S. House of Representatives, 30 March.

3. A communication in Benjamin Bache's *Aurora General Advertiser* (Philadelphia) for 1 April dismissed GW's reply to the House as "an ingenious summary of the arguments of the minority in the discussion upon the resolution." His attempt to "lecture" the House about the Constitution was "indelicate, to say the least," and "the House have a right to differ, unless he be proved the oracular expositor of all parts of the constitution." The paper also reported that a correspondent was not surprised that GW had "refused the constitutional and just request of the House of Representatives; for he is of opinion, that those papers were of such a nature, that they could not be disclosed without unmasking the administration in such manner as to produce horror in the mind of every true & virtuous American." The same *Aurora* contained another item: "An Irishman was heard to observe upon reading the answer from the executive to the house that one free people by their exertions in maintaining their liberty had struck the President with wonder, it is to be hoped that another will in the same way make him stare if they do not open his eyes."

The *Aurora* for 2 April printed a satirical letter addressed to GW that expressed "the support and adoration of a Loyal Englishman." The Englishman wrote: "You frowned the Democratic societies into annihilation: you are now committed against the Democratic branch of the Legislature. . . . I hope, sir, you will have more firmness and dignity, than to expose the arcana of State, the sanctum sanctorum, to such an insignificant body. As you have adopted the language of the kings of France, pray adopt their conduct also; and should your subjects in Congress refuse to register your edicts, send them with contempt to 'the obscure corners' from whence they came. You can then summon a bed of justice, composed of the worthy 'successors in form' to the old heads of department.—They will register your decrees without hesitation. . . . If your councils should not be remarkable for their wisdom or sound policy, your debates would not be very tedious, your minorities very formidable, nor would there be that danger of Jacobinism which prevails in such a many headed monster, as a House of Representatives."

4. The following Wednesday was 6 April. On that date the House, by a roll call vote, formed a committee of the whole to discuss GW's message, and after discussion resolved to continue the next day (*Journal of the House*, 8:313–14).

5. Knox replied to GW on 14 April.

To Tobias Lear

My dear Sir, PHILADELPHIA, 4th. April, 1796.

As your letter of the 30th. Ulto. gives me room to expect you here in a few days. I shall do no more than acknowledge the receipt of it, repeat the request contained in a joint letter (written by Mrs. Washington and myself to you) of the 30th. Ulto.—and request, if a vessel from Liverpool called the Commerce, commanded by Capt. Tuttle should have arrived at George Town, that Mr. Pearce may have immediate notice of it, as there will be in it two Sacks of field Peas & some other seeds for me in her, which ought *now* to be in the ground.[1] With sincerity & affection I am—Yrs.

Letters and Recollections of George Washington, 106–7.

1. For the shipment on the *Commerce,* see GW to William Pearce, 3 April.

From George Lux

George Washington [Baltimore, c.4 April 1796][1]

I want words to preface a letter more respectfully to you—It is my pride & boast, that you & my dear Father were intimate, & you have occasionally honoured me with your notice.

I have been ill, am still an Invalid, but have strength to wield a pen to assert, I am *proud of you,* & the stand you have made against a dangerous precedent alarming to future generations of United Columbia—Why should we have a *popular Oligarchy?* In an humble station, as only a Clerk to a Committee of Congress, I have, in early youth, found secrecy necessary in foreign negotiations—Domestic Matters ought to be open & explicit.[2]

Our Government has it's Checks & balances, to ensure liberty & prevent an undue preponderancy of either the Judicial, Executive or Legislative Departments—Sick as I have been, I have not seen many, but the few who have conversed with me unite in approbation of George Washington with

George Lux

ALS, DLC:GW.

1. GW docketed this letter, which was posted at Baltimore, as "received 6th April 1796." Mail usually took about a day and a half to travel from Baltimore to Philadelphia.

2. Lux probably commented on GW's reply dated 30 March to the U.S. House resolution adopted on 24 March requesting that he provide instructions, correspondence, and other documents relating to the Jay Treaty.

From James McHenry

Sir   War office 5th April 1796.

I beg leave to request your Excellency attention to the inclosed draught of a letter to the Governor of Georgia.[1] If it can be returned today it may go by to-morrows mail. With the greatest respect I have the honour to be Sir Your most obt st

James McHenry

ALS, DLC:GW; LB, DLC:GW.

1. Jared Irwin (1750–1818), formerly a state senator from Washington County, had been elected governor by the Georgia legislature in January 1796. He served until 1798. Irwin subsequently presided over the 1798 state constitutional convention, served additional terms in the state senate, and was again governor from 1806 to 1809.

McHenry's letter to Irwin has not been identified, but in Irwin's letter to McHenry written on 23 Sept. 1796, he acknowledged receipt of communications dated 5 and 6 April (G-Ar: Georgia Executive Minutes).

From Hampden-Sydney College Committee

Sir   Virginia, Prince Edward County, April 6th 1796.

Your benevolent intention, as to the appropriation of your interest in the James River Canal Company, being known by a resolution of the last General Assembly of this State;[1] a Board of the Trustees for the College of Hamden Sidney, in this County, have appointed us, in their name, to address you, Sir, in behalf of that seminary.

Hamden Sidney lays claim to considerable local advantages; to enumerate them may be unnecessary—it may be unbecoming in us. How far its pretensions to claim the public patronage, or how far, its central situation, and its being adjacent to an extensive back country, may merit your attention, we cannot say. We beg leave to Mr Madison, Mr Coles, Mr Giles and Mr Venable,[2] who are acquainted with its situation and circumstances; and also to such other gentlemen of your acquaintance, as shall think proper to interest themselves in its behalf.

Hamden Sidney was founded, about twenty years ago, by the liberality of private individuals, and with various success; under many and great difficulties, arising from the want of permanent funds, it has struggled hard to rise into real public usefulness and importance; and still, in this condition it maintains the conflict—In its behalf, we beg leave to solicit your attention and patronage. Should you think this seminary worthy of such attention, your liberality towards it will be gratefully acknowledged: and what, we are sure, will interest you much more, we trust, it will be employed in such a manner, as to answer the end of your benevolent intentions. On behalf of the Board, we beg leave to subscribe ourselves, very respectfully, Sir, Your obedient, Humble Servants,

William Cowan,
Samuel W. Venable,
Richard N. Venable.[3]

L, DLC:GW.

Virginia congressman and Hampden-Sydney trustee Abraham B. Venable sent this appeal along with an undated cover letter that he wrote GW: "This institution is the only one that I know of, on the South Side of James River, below the mountains that has been incorporated. Since its establishment it has been very usefull, but that usefulness has been greatly curtailed by the Scantiness of the funds which they have been able hitherto to procure, being almost intirely dependant on private contributions. If you should think proper to take into consideration the pretentions of this place, in making a distribution of the patronage which you have intended to bestow on institutions of this sort, the Gentlemen who are mentioned in the enclosed letter will be able to give information as to its merits. Doct. Smith who is now the President of the Colledge at Princeton was the founder, and is able to give particular information with respect to it" (ALS, DLC:GW).

GW replied to Venable on 26 April, acknowledging receipt of this letter and adding, "it would be uncandid not to inform you, that a Seminary West of the blue Mountains will be preferred by me, to one below it, in behalf of which, to appropriate the Shares I hold in the James River navigation.—And that, the Governor of Virginia will be informed of the particular one so soon as a little more information will enable me to decide thereon" (*The Edwin Babcock Holden Collection: Rare Americana, Mezzotints, Etchings Examples of the Old Masters and Fine Engravings of All Periods* [New York, 1910], item 2684).

1. For GW's desire that a gift of shares in the James River Company be used to support a university in the Federal City and the resolution of the Virginia legislature requesting him to appropriate the shares to a school in western Virginia, see GW to Robert Brooke, 16 March 1795, and n.2 to that document, and Brooke to GW, 9 Jan. 1796, n.2.

2. James Madison, Isaac Coles, William B. Giles, and Abraham Venable then served as Virginia congressmen.

3. William Cowan (c.1751–1806), a lawyer, represented Lunenberg County in the Virginia House for three sessions between 1793 and 1800. First elected as a Hampden-Sydney trustee in 1784, he served on the board from 1790 until his death.

Samuel Woodson Venable (1756–1821), a Prince Edward County planter and merchant, served on the board from 1782 to 1821, acting as clerk from 1788 to 1806.

Richard N. Venable was a Hampden-Sydney trustee from 1792 to 1837.

From Robert Lewis

Spring Hill Fauqr County [Va.]

Hond Uncle,   April 6th 1796

I am duly favored with the receipt of your letter of the 10th of March (in reply to mine of the 17th of February[)] with its several inclosures—Why so long ⟨on⟩ the road and getting to your hands, I am unable to say, unless it proceeded from the neglect of a Gentleman who took charge of it and promised to leave it at the Post Office. We have no regular Post Rider in this part of the Country, altho' there are several who pretend to it—The conveyance is at any rate uncertain—You desire to know "to whose care letters are to be directed since my Mother has left Fredericksburg["]—I know of no person that I wou'd so soon confide them to as Mr James Lewis—Attorney at Law Fredericksburg—If directed to his care, particular attention will be paid to them and a speedy conveyance given.[1]

I can offer but few other reasons for not paying what money I have in my hands of yours to Mr Pearce, or into the Bank of Alexandria, than what before urged in my last letter, Vizt The Replevy Bonds becoming due Apl Court when they will either be paid or Judgments must go against the tenants—The expectation of getting something out of the late Sheriff who collected in Muse's time,[2] and a certainty of my going to Alexandria, as soon as I finish planting my corn—I can assure you the money which I have collected is now in my desk—I have never made any use of it at all, unless it was by your order, or for your use— It was a ridiculous Idea I had adopted, that you would be better pleased to receive your money in a lump annually, than to draw it from me in small parcels—However, as it is your wish I should pay the money to Mr Pearce, or deposit it as soon as collected in the Bank of Alexandria, it shall be done—I shall start at farther-est for one or the other place by the 12th To Mount Vernon I expect—It will give me an opportunity of conversing with Mr Pearce whose advice I have found extremely beneficial to me as a Young Farmer.

Your Advertisement [I] have fixed up at the Court House;[3] it being the most publick place in this part of the Country—I have also seen the Papers which were sent to you by Mr Ariss[4]—The business has not wanted attention—The dispute is for about one eighth of an acre which Mr McCormick holds—There is also an old grudge—As to McCormicks getting a road thro' his yard it is a chimera of the brain—No Court of Justice to gratify an ill natured Man would direct a publick road thro' a gentlemans yard to gain a hundred and fifty yards; as it is not more than that distance around, as the road now runs, and has run for eight or ten years—Mr Ariss wishes to involve me in a Law suit with McCormick, which can derive you no advantage or credit to Mr Ariss; as he has suffered McCormick to have quiet possession many years—The Man has thro' ignorance placed his fence on your land and I believe there may be ten or twelve feet of his Barn over your line.

I received a letter about three days ago from Mr Pearce, wherein he mentions that you were willing, I should take the Jack Compound upon certain conditions—I am extremely obliged to you for the offer, and wou'd most willingly have accepted it, was the season not so far advanced[5]—Most people hereabouts wou'd be glad to get into the breed of Mules, but they have either sent their Mares to some Horse or other, or engaged them—If Agreeable and convenient, I should be glad to take him the next Spring—If I could get him here by February Court I am sure some profit might be derived from him.

A Servant going to Fredericksburg, and who carries this, hur-ries me to conclude—You will therefore excuse incorrectness and haste.

Mrs Lewis offers her Affectionate and respectfull regards to you & my aunt—I remain your much obliged and affectionate nephew

Robt Lewis

P.S. Mrs Haney appears to be in the last stage of a consumption.[6]

R.L.

ALS, ViMtvL. GW replied to Lewis on 17 April.

1. Betty Washington Lewis had moved to Mill Brook farm on the Po River about thirteen miles south of Fredericksburg, Va., in late 1795.

James Lewis, Jr. (died c.1802), apparently was a young attorney just starting his career.

2. Battaile Muse, Lewis's predecessor as the rental agent for GW's lands in Berkeley, Fauquier, and Frederick counties, acted in that capacity from 1785 through 1791. In a "Memo of Arrears of Rents due in Fauquier County under Execution" that he delivered to Lewis on 8 Dec. 1791, Muse referred Lewis to Deputy Sheriff William Bronaugh in regard to the collections (ViMtvL).

3. The advertisement dated 1 Feb. 1796 offered Mount Vernon's farms for lease and GW's western lands for purchase.

4. The papers from GW's tenant John Ariss that were enclosed with GW's letter to Lewis of 10 March have not been identified.

5. William Pearce's letter has not been identified. For the suggestion that a jackass might be sent to Robert Lewis, see GW to Pearce, 13 and 27 March.

6. For the death of Elizabeth Haynie, see Robert Lewis to GW, 5 May.

To George Lewis

Dear Sir   Philadelphia 7th April 1796

Tuesday's Post brought me a letter from a Mr Andrew Parks of Fredericksburgh, covering one from your mother; both on the subject of overtures of marriage made by the former to your cousin Harriot Washington: which, it seems, depend upon my consent for consummatn.[1]

My sister speaks of Mr Parks as a sober, discreet man; and one who is attentive to business. Mr Parks says of himself, that his "fortune at present, does not much exceed £3000, but with industry & œconomy, he has every expectation of rapidly improving his condition" being concerned with his brother in law Mr McElderry of Baltimore, in Mercantil⟨e⟩ business.

As I am an entire stranger to Mr Parks; to his family connexions, or his connexions in trade; to his mode of living; his habits—and to his prospects in trade; I should be glad if you wd ascertain them with as much precision as you can, and write me with as little delay as you can well avoid.[2]

Harriot having little or no fortune of her own, has no right to expect a great one in the man she marrys: but it is desirable that she should marry a gentleman; one who is well connected, and can support her decently, in the line she has always moved, otherwise she would not find matrimony with a large family &

little means, so eligable as she may have conceived it to be. I am your sincere friend and Affectionate Uncle

Go: Washington

This letter will be accompanied by one to my Sister which I pray you to receive from the Post Office and send to her.[3]

ALS, PHi: Dreer Collection; ADfS, PHi: Washington Manuscripts; LB, DLC:GW. The postscript appears only on the ALS.

1. Tuesday was 5 April. The letter Andrew Parks wrote GW on 1 April enclosed Betty Washington Lewis's letter to GW dated 27 March.

2. See George Lewis to GW, 19 April.

3. A draft of GW's enclosed letter to Betty Washington Lewis, written on this date, reads: "Your letter of the 27th Ulto was enclosed to me by Mr Parks, in one from himself, dated the 1st instt on the same subject.

"Harriot having very little fortune herself, has no *right* to expect a great one in the man she marry's; but if he has not a competency to support her in the way she has lived, in the circle of her friends, she will not find the matrimonial state so comfortable as she may have expected when a family is looking up to her & but scanty means to support it.

"Altho' she has no right to expect a man of fortune, she certainly has just pretensions to expect one whose connexions are respectable, & whose relations she could have no objection to associate with. How far this is, or is not the case with Mr Parks, I know not, for neither his own letter, or yours give any acct of his family nor whether he is a native or a foreigner—& we have his own word only for his possessing *any* property at all altho' he estimates his fortune at £3000. A precarious dependance this when applied to a man in Trade.

"I do not wish to thwart Harriots inclinations if her affectns are placed on Mr Park and if upon the enquiries I shall mak⟨e⟩ or cause to be made into his family & connexions, there shall be found nothing exceptionable in them; that he is, as you say "very much respected by all his acquaintance, sober, sedate, & attentive to business"; and is moreover in good business; I shall throw no impedimts in the way of their marriage, altho' I should have preferred, if a *good* match had not offer'd in the meanwhile that she shd have remained single until I was once more settled at Mt Vernon & she a resident there which, if life is spared to us, will certainly happen to me in ten or eleven months—because then she would have been in the way of seeing much company, and would have had a much fairer prospect of matching respectably than with one who is little known—and of whose circumstances few or none can know much about.

"Having had no business to write to you upon—and being very much occupied by my public duties, are the only reasons why I have been silent. I am persuaded you will enjoy more ease & quiet, & meet with fewer vexations where you now are, than where you did live—It is my sincere wish that you should do so and that your days may be happy—in these Mrs Washington joins with Your most Affecte Brother" (ADfS, PPRF; LB, DLC:GW; see also Betty Washington Lewis to GW, 26 June). For the recent move of GW's sister, see Robert Lewis to GW, 6 April, n.1.

To Andrew Parks

Sir   Philadelphia 7th April 1796
    your letter of the first instt has been duly received. The subject on which it is written is a serious one, and it shall meet, as it deserves, a serious consideration.
    My niece Harriot Washington having very little fortune of her own, neither she, nor her friends, have a right to make *that* (however desirable it might be) a primary consideration in a matrimonial connexion. But there are other requisites which are equally desirable, and which ought to be attended to in a union of so much importance; without therefore expressing at this moment, either assent, or dissent, to the proposal you have made, it is necessary for me to pause.
    My wish is to see my niece happy; one step towards which is, for her to be united with a gentleman of respectable connexions, and of good dispositions; with one who is more in the habit (by fair and honorable pursuits) of making, than in[1] spending money—and who can support her in the way she has always lived.
    As you propose being in Baltimore in the course of a few weeks—I shall not object to the receipt of any further details on this subject, which you may be disposed to give from that place: which, when received, may enable me to write more decisively frome hence, or from virginia when I get there—which will happen, I expect, as soon as Congress shall have closed it's session.[2] I am sir your very Hble servant

Df, DLC:GW; LB, DLC:GW. The draft is in the handwriting of Martha Washington.
    1. GW inserted this word.
    2. Parks replied to GW on 30 April.

From Timothy Pickering

                            Department of State April 7. 1796.
    The Secretary of State respectfully requests the President of the United States to grant him an order on the Secretary of the Treasury for Two thousand dollars, to enable him to continue the payment of the expences attending the procuring of copies of the proceedings of the British Courts of Vice Admiralty in the cases of captures by the armed vessels of that nation.[1]
                                        Timothy Pickering.

ALS, DNA: RG 59, Miscellaneous Letters; LB, DNA: RG 59, Domestic Letters; LB, DNA: RG 59, GW's Correspondence with His Secretaries of State.

Below the signature on the ALS, Pickering wrote an order of this date to Secretary of the Treasury Oliver Wolcott, Jr.: "Pay to Timothy Pickering Secretary of State Two thousand dollars for the purpose above mentioned." No signed order from GW has been found, but the report on contingent fund expenditures enclosed with GW's message to Congress of 15 Feb. 1797 indicates that the requested warrant for $2,000 was issued to Pickering on 6 July (DNA: RG 46, entry 47).

1. In response to complaints from merchants about British ship seizures, the federal government appointed a special agent in late 1794 to represent their interests in the admiralty courts of Great Britain and agreed to absorb expenses connected to those cases (see Edmund Randolph to GW, 23 Oct. [second letter] and 1 Dec. [first letter] 1794, and notes).

From Timothy Pickering

Department of State April 7. 1796.

The Secretary of State has the honour to lay before the President of the U. States, copies of the estimates relative to the treaties with Great Britain, Spain, Algiers & the Indian Tribes northwest of the river Ohio, and a copy of the letter from the Secretary to the President of the Senate & to the Speaker of the House of Representatives, which accompanied those estimates, when he laid the same before Congress, agreeably to the Message of the President of the United States with which he communicated to each House the Treaty with his Catholic Majesty.[1]

Timothy Pickering.

ALS, DNA: RG 59, Miscellaneous Letters; LB, DNA: RG 59, Domestic Letters; LB, DNA: RG 59, GW's Correspondence with His Secretaries of State.

1. Copies of the estimated costs to implement the terms of the indicated treaties, along with Pickering's cover letter dated 31 March, are filed with this letter in DNA: RG 59, Miscellaneous Letters. For a summary of the estimates, see GW to the U.S. Senate and House of Representatives, 29 March, n.3. The copy filed with this letter has clerical errors in the estimates for the Barbary States, understating the Algiers deficiency by $1,000 and the total funds needed by $100,000. The cover letter warned that the estimates were sent "*confidentially*, as part of them respect affairs and pending negociations which in their nature and situation appear to require secrecy."

From James Innes

Dear Sir   Richmond Virginia April 8th 1796

I have the honor, this moment, to receive yr letter of the 4th of this month.

The government of the united States, which I voted for at its adoption,[1] on principles of theory, has been progressively endeared to me by its administration, and practice—From this Consideration, I have been ever anxious to give to it Energy, and Efficacy, by every aid in my power—But at the present Crisis—I feel myself actuated by more than ordinary motives, to manifest my Zeal, that it may forever be executed with Independence, and firmness, on the true basis of its Constitution.

After a request, that you would accept my acknowledgement of the honor you have done me—by recommending me to the trust you mention, I do not hesitate to express my willingness to undertake it. That I may, as soon as possible disentangle myself from every Engagement either official, or professional, I take leave to request, that the Secretary of State will have the goodness to give me the most early Information of the period of time, at which I should hold myself in preparation to enter upon the functions of my new office.[2] with Sentiments, of the most perfect respect, Esteem, and regard, I have the honor to be—yr most obt sert

Jas Innes

ALS, DLC:GW.

1. Innes represented Williamsburg at the 1788 Virginia convention that ratified the U.S. Constitution.

2. Innes evidently had not yet received Secretary of State Timothy Pickering's letter to him dated 6 April: "The President informs me that he has written to advise you of his having nominated you to be a Commissioner for the purpose of adjusting the claims of British Creditors, under the sixth article of the Treaty of Amity, Commerce and Navigation with Great Britain: and the nomination having been approved by the Senate, the President thinks it proper that you should be further informed of the actual State of this business.

"There is every reason to believe that the Government of Great Britain intended to carry the treaty into effect with perfect good faith: but the opposition to it manifested by many citizens of the United States, and their appeal to the House of Representatives to defeat it, cannot but have excited an apprehension in the British Government that such might be the event: We know, by direct official information, that the preliminary arrangements for the delivery of the Posts are suspended, at this moment, on account of the part taken in this affair by the House of Representatives, and that they will continue suspended until their decision shall be known.

"Under these circumstances, it is probable that the Commissioners who are to come from Great Britain will remain there until they shall be advised by the Minister here from that Country that the treaty is in a fair train of execution, by the concurrence of the House of Representatives in making the requisite provisions for that purpose. Hence it is not to be expected that the business of the Commission under the sixth article of the treaty can commence sooner than September or October next, and the pay of the Commissioners will in like manner be suspended.

"In this state of things, should you be inclined to accept the appointment of a Commissioner, it will be expedient to suspend the acceptance, seeing it would vacate the office you now hold under the Government of Virginia. The Commissions, which are made out, will consequently remain in this office, until it is certain that the treaty will be executed, and until the Commissioners on the part of Great Britain shall arrive. . . . P.S. Although you may think it proper to suspend your formal acceptance of the appointment, yet it will be desirable to know that you will accept it, at the time above referred to" (DNA: RG 59, Domestic Letters). Innes, who served as attorney general for Virginia, experienced political and personal complications in accepting this appointment under the Jay Treaty (see his letter to GW, 17 Jan. 1797, DLC:GW).

To the United States Senate and House of Representatives

United States April 8th 1796

Gentlemen of the Senate and of the House of Representatives

By an Act of Congress passed in the 26th of May 1790 it was declared that the Inhabitants of the territory of the United States south of the river Ohio, should enjoy all the privileges, benefits and advantages set forth in the ordinance of Congress for the government of the territory of the United States north-West of the river Ohio; and that the government of the said territory south of the Ohio should be similar to that which was then exercised in the territory north-West of the Ohio; exept so far as was otherwise provided in the conditions expressed in an Act of Congress passed the 2d of April 1790, entitled "An Act to accept a cession of the claims of the State of North Carolina to a certain district of Western territory.["][1]

Among the privileges, benefits and advantages thus secured to the Inhabitants of the territory south of the Ohio, appear to be the right of forming a permanent Constitution and State Government and of admission as a State, by its delagates, into the Congress of the United States on an equal footing with the original States in all respects whatever, when it should have therein Sixty thousand free inhabitants: provided the Constitution and Government so to be formed should be Republican, and in conformity to the principles contained in the Articles of the said Ordinance.

As proofs of the several requisites to entitle this territory south of the River Ohio to be admitted, as a State into the Union, Governor Blount has transmitted a return of the enumeration of its Inhabitants, and a printed copy of the Constitution and form of Government on which they have agreed which with his Letters accompanying the same, are herewith laid before Congress.[2]

Go. Washington.

LB, DLC:GW; Df, DNA: RG 59, entry 142. The draft is in the writing of Secretary of State Timothy Pickering.

1. For the acts of 2 April and 26 May 1790, see 1 *Stat.* 106–9, 123. The Northwest Ordinance adopted on 13 July 1787 is printed as a note at 1 *Stat.* 51–53.

2. The return and William Blount's letters to Pickering dated 28 Nov. 1795 and 9 Feb. 1796 are in DNA: RG 59, State Department Territorial Papers: Territory Southwest of the River Ohio (see also *ASP, Miscellaneous*, 1:146–47). Blount transmitted *The Constitution of the State of Tennessee* (Knoxville, 1796).

From Alexander Hamilton

Sir   New York April 9, 1796

It gives me great pleasure to have the opportunity of announcing to you one whom I know to be so interesting to You as the bearer of this Mr Motier La Fayette. I allow myself to share by anticipation the satisfaction which the Meeting will afford to all the parties—the more, as I am persuased, that time will confirm the favourable representation I have made of the person & justify the interest you take in him.

I have pleasure also in presenting to You Mr Frestal who accompanies him & who more and more convinces me that he is intirely worthy of the charge reposed in him and every way intitled to esteem.[1] With the most respectful & Affectionate Attachment I have the honor to be Sir Your very obed. servt

A. Hamilton

ALS, DLC:GW; copy, DLC: Hamilton Papers.

GW wrote Secretary of War James McHenry on 11 April: "Young Fayette and his friend are with me. Come & dine with them to day at 3 oclock if you are not otherwise engaged" (ALS [photocopy], DLC: James McHenry Papers). McHenry's acceptance of this invitation has not been determined, but Vice President John Adams wrote his wife Abigail from Philadelphia on 13 April about the gathering: "I dined on Monday at the Presidents with young La Fayette and his Preceptor, Tutor or Friend, whatever they call him, whose Name is Frestel. I asked Them with Mr Lear to breakfast with me this Morning and they agreed to come: but last Evening Mr Lear came with a Message from The President, to ask my Opinion whether it would be adviseable for the young Gentleman, in the present Circumstances of his Father and Mother and whole Family and considering his tender Years, to accept Invitations and mingle in Society?—Whether it would not too much interrupt his studies? The Youth and his Friend had proposed these Questions to the P. and asked his Advice, and expressed their own opinion that Retirement would be more adviseable and more desirable.

"I Agreed in opinion with the P. and his Guests and as I had been the first who had invited them, at the P's request agreed to excuse them from accepting my Invitation that they might have it to say as a general Apology that they had accepted none" (*Adams Family Correspondence*, 11:250–51).

1. Political considerations had kept George Washington Motier Lafayette and his tutor, Felix Frestel, from visiting GW in Philadelphia since their arrival in the United States in late summer 1795 (see Lafayette to GW, 31 Aug. 1795, and GW to Lafayette, 22 Nov. 1795 and 28 Feb. 1796; see also Hamilton to GW, 2 April 1796, n.1).

From George Lewis

Dr Sir   Fredericksburg [Va.] 9th April 1796

Your letter of the 28th of last month, acknowledging the receipt of my two last letters, I receiv'd,[1] no information since then has transpired respecting the value of western lands that can be depended upon—It has been asked me by some persons whether you would exchange any of those lands for improved estates (good farms) in this part of the country that might be immediately rented to an advantage, as your terms speak nothing of bartar. I supposed it would not be your wish, should an exchange of this kind be agreable—you can advise me. I shall continue my exertions to purchase Wodrowes land, and have not a doubt could I have gone to Kentucky this month as intended, but I should have secured it[2]—Mrs Lewis's indisposition for sometime past, and no prospect of her mending

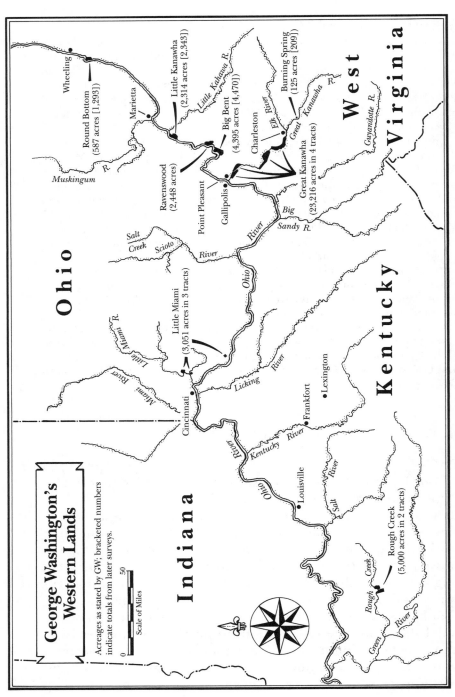

Map 1: GW's western lands occupied an important place in his personal wealth and financial management. He enlisted the help of his nephew George Lewis in trying to sell land he owned on Rough Creek in western Kentucky. (Illustrated by Rick Britton. Copyright

shortly, prevents my goeing this summer, for some dayes past she has been with her Mother in the country, in hopes that a change of air and exercise may be of service.[3] I return'd to town this day, where I received your letter, otherwise it should have been acknowledg'd ere this. I left my Mother and family well yesterday[4]—My love to my Aunt, and accept the sincere respect and esteem of Yr Affectionate Nephew

Go: Lewis

ALS, ViMtvL.

1. GW's letter to Lewis written on 28 March has not been found. Lewis is referring to his letter to GW dated 19 March. The other letter that Lewis references likely has not been found because the next most recent letter from Lewis to GW is dated 24 Oct. 1795.

2. Lewis had pointed out in his letter to GW written on 18 July 1795 that the value of GW's Kentucky lands would be enhanced if a 300-acre tract surveyed for Andrew Wodrow could be purchased. For a summary of GW's unsuccessful efforts to obtain that tract, see Alexander Spotswood to GW, 31 March 1797 (*Papers, Retirement Series*, 1:58–59).

3. Lewis expressed concern about his wife, Catherine, who visited her mother, Mary Willis Daingerfield (1745–1818). The elder woman resided on a plantation called Coventry in Spotsylvania County, Virginia.

4. For the new home of Betty Washington Lewis, see Robert Lewis to GW, 6 April, n.1.

From David Campbell

Territory of the United States South of the River Ohio

Sir   April 10th 1796

It is already known to you that the people of this Territory are taking measures to become a member of the Federal Government by the name of the State of Tennessee. If their wishes are acceded to by Congress, my appointment as one of the Judges for the Territorial Government will cease.[1]

In that event, if you think me a proper person to fill the Office of District Judge for the State of Tennessee I will gratefully accept of the same.[2] I am with verry great Respect Your Obt Servt

David Campbell

ALS, DLC:GW. A notation on the cover indicates that a "Mr Fisk" carried this letter.

1. For Campbell's appointment as one of two judges for the Southwest Territory, see GW to the U.S. Senate, 7 June 1790.

2. Following Tennessee's admission as a state, Campbell again wrote GW on 15 Oct. 1796 seeking nomination as "District Judge" on the basis of prior judicial service performed "with strict attention & fidelity" (DLC:GW). GW instead appointed the other territorial judge, John McNairy.

To William Pearce

Mr Pearce   Philadelphia 10th April 1796

Your letter of the 3d instant, with the Weekly reports, was received yesterday;[1] and I have also seen Mr Lear, who arrived here yesterday about the sametime.

As there is no prospect from the last European accounts (down to the first of March) of Peace; but on the contrary, every appearance of a vigorous prosecution of the War—at least for another Campaign—and they speak (tho' flour is low in some ports) of a *general* scarcity, and rise of it in others; particularly in London:[2] I am not under the smallest apprehension of getting fifteen dollars pr barrel for mine, even at a shorter credit than Six months; but as I wish to have it off my hands, as the warm weather is coming on, which may occasion it to sour, besides being liable to other accidents, I consent to your selling it to Mr Smith for fifteen dollars on a credit of Six months; provided he will give a negociable note, with a good Endorser, on the Bank of Alexandria. But, as there will have been a lapse of time between the conversation you had with Mr Smiths Clerk, & the receipt of this letter, it would be prudent, before you offer him the flour on the above terms, to sound & to discover from him, whether he is still disposed and authorised to make such a contract. and if he is, or if Mr Smith himself shd be returned from New York (which I think highly probable) to see if you could not sell it to him at a shorter credit; but if you cannot, then, and in that case, to dispose of it at a credit of Six months for fifteen dollrs per barrel. get rid of the midlings and Shipstuff also—that the whole may be off your hands.

I am sorry to hear that the only rain (and that a light one) which you have had of late, should be attended with such high & destructive winds to your fences. I fear your Overseers do not see that the fences are well made, by their meeting with such frequent accidents. The winds have been very high here also, but the same disasters have not resulted from them.

You have either misunderstood me, or I must have expressed myself very odly about the Jacks, for I never had any idea of parting with more than one of them; and left or intended to leave it, to you and Peter, to determine whether that one should be Compound, or the Knight of Malta, not intending to use the young Jack at all, this Season; or if any, at least very sparingly. As the Season is now, or soon will be far spent, you had better part with neither; unless one of them is actually gone, or engaged to go to Mr Lewis.[3]

Keep a little good Hay for my h⟨or⟩ses, as I should prefer old to new for the⟨m⟩ and may, tho' I do not expect it, be at M⟨ount⟩ Vernon before June.

I hope the Gardener tried the Graffs altho' the Season was late, as they were of a peculiar kind of apple.[4]

I wish the end may be better, than you represent the beginning, of your fishery to be; as continual bad seasons would be discouraging. I am Your friend

Go: Washington

ALS, ViMtvL.

1. Pearce's letter and reports have not been found.

2. *The Philadelphia Gazette & Universal Daily Advertiser* of 9 April printed a report from Glasgow, Scotland, dated 1 March: "The general features of all the intelligence which has been received from the Continent for some weeks past, have been strongly indicative of an immediate re-commencement of hostilities between the Imperialists and the French." With the nations unable to agree on territorial adjustments, "all hopes of Peace have . . . entirely vanished. Both armies have been considerably augmented." Other reports in the paper stated that "vigorous preparations are making on both sides for the renewal of hostilities" and "that a fifth Campaign is once more to crimson, perhaps with deeper hue, the desolated plains of Europe."

The same newspaper printed news from London, dated 23 Feb.: "The report from the corn market of yesterday is extremely alarming; wheat has greatly advanced in price; and flour . . . has risen ten shillings a sack!" The paper also reported that in Paris "tumults had taken place in consequence of the advanced price of provisions in general."

3. For GW's previous instructions about the jacks, see his letters to Pearce written on 13 and 27 March.

4. About the apple grafts, see GW to Pearce, 9 March.

Letter not found: from William Pearce, 10–13 April 1796. GW wrote Pearce on 17 April: "Your letter of the 10th instt with a Postcript three days later, came to hand."

From William Vans Murray

Sir,   112. Spruce St.[1] [Philadelphia] 11. Apl 1796.
I find from the atto[r]ney of this district that Randal is in a course of being judicially try'd this time in the Circuit Court—& that I am to be a witness.[2] You will I am sure Sir pardon the solicitude that leads me to request of you that the Proceeding may be stopped—After having done what I conceived my duty demanded of me, & after having encountered many little circumstances extremely painful to my feelings in the doing my duty as a member, I should feel myself in a Situation infinitely painful to me in again appearing in this affair—& appearing if at all, as I must in the world's eye, as a Prosecutor. If I might be permitted to make a remark, I would observe that what the house has done amounts to every thing desireable in an example that was at once to assert the dignity of the House, and yet avoid the appearances of rigour—That example can not be repeated on a Scale equally great in a Jury Trial—nor can greater publicity be given to it—The appearance too, Sir, of a Second punishment will not perhaps add any thing to the score of government. As I have been so personally concerned in brin[g]ing Randal to one punishment I should feel very grateful if any further proceeding could be arrested before the grand Jury present him.[3] I am with the Sincerest respect Sir Your most obedient Sert
W. V. Murray.

ALS, DLC:GW.

1. Mary Jones, a widow, kept a boarding house at 112 Spruce St. (*Philadelphia Directory, 1796*, p. 98).

2. The U.S. district attorney for Pennsylvania was William Rawle. For the case of Robert Randall, essentially charged with an attempt to bribe congressmen, see his memorial to GW of 14 January.

3. Randall reputedly had approached several congressmen, including Murray of Maryland and William Loughton Smith of South Carolina, with offers of lands or money to support a land grant memorial. Murray and Smith had served on a seven-man committee that recommended an investigation. The two congressmen subsequently submitted written statements and testified. The House of Representatives found Randall guilty of contempt and held him in custody for week. The payment of fees secured his discharge. Murray, who supported Randall's release, had opposed a resolution to interrogate Randall about congressmen open to his scheme (see *Journal of the House*, 8:58, 62–64, 72–76; *Annals of Congress*, 4th Cong., 1st sess., 166–68, 176–77, 183, 200–205, 207–8, 244).

Later on this date, Murray again wrote GW: "I have conversed with Mr Smith of South Carolina who unites with me in wishes that a Noli prosequi may be made" (ALS, DLC:GW).

To Gilbert Stuart

Sir,   Monday Evening 11th Apl 1796.
I am under promis⟨e to⟩ Mrs Bingham,[1] to set for you tom⟨or⟩-row at nine oclock; and wishing ⟨to⟩ know if it be convenient to you that I should do so, and whether it shall be at your own house,[2] (as she talked of the State House) I send this note to you, to ask information—I am Sir Your Obedient Servt
Go: Washington

ALS (photocopy), National Records of Scotland, Edinburgh. A later writer inserted material at damaged portions of the letter. These characters are shown in angle brackets.

A certificate dated 23 March 1823 that appears below this letter and includes Stuart's signature indicates that GW sat for the portrait "now owned by Samuel Williams, of London." The accuracy of that certificate has been questioned (see Eisen, *Portraits of Washington*, 1:56).

Born in North Kingstown, R.I., Gilbert Stuart (1755–1828) attained renown as a portrait artist.

1. Anne Willing Bingham (1764–1801), a daughter of Thomas Willing, had married William Bingham in 1780. She became known for the political influence of her social gatherings at her palatial home in Philadelphia.

The Binghams had commissioned Stuart to paint a full-length portrait of GW for presentation to the marquis of Lansdowne (see frontispiece).

2. GW addressed the cover of the ALS to Stuart at "Chesnut Street."

From Richard Graham

Sir   Arch Street No. 129 [Philadelphia] April 12 1796.
At the request of a very worthy Young Gentleman, Lieutenant Charles Lewis, I take the liberty to enquire of you if the Land late the property of Col. George Mercer was included in the Mortgage that Col. Mercer made to Mr Paine of London—or in any other Mortgage that might have come to your knowledge[1]— Lieut. Lewis is now in Fredericksburgh on a bargain for that Land with the Executors of Mr James Mercer—if he makes the purchase the Land will be immediately settled which will be a

great benefit to that part of the Country; as it runs I think about twelve or fourteen miles on the River.

Your Excellency will I hope excuse this freedom—With due respect I am Sir Your most obedt Servt

Richd Graham

ALS, DLC:GW. No reply to this letter has been identified.

GW noted that George Washington Craik, a son of his longtime friend James Craik, began as private secretary on this date (see *Diaries*, 6:222). Craik (1774–1808) briefly practiced law in Alexandria, Va., before becoming GW's secretary. He remained about a year in the position.

1. For the complicated financial affairs of George Mercer, see GW's statement concerning Mercer's estate, 1 Feb. 1789, and notes.

From Bartholomew von Heer

Philada 12th April 1796.
in Eighth street near Vine street

The petition of Bartholomew Von Heer Humbly sheweth

That your petitioner having contributed his part to the funds of the Society and that from his deranged and unfortunate circumstances in business and his reduced situation as well as from a long and tedious bodily indisposition he is without the means of acquiring the Common Necessaries of life and is therefore constrained to apply for a part of the bounty of the Institution and he would humbly hope that he may be considered as entitled to a participation of the bounty of the Society and which he never would claim but from necessity he doth therefore humbly pray that you may be pleased to consider his situation and that relief may be afforded to him in his present condition and your petitioner will pray &ca.[1]

Bartholomew Von Heer

ALS, DNA: RG 59, Miscellaneous Letters. The petition was addressed "To the President and Members of the Society of Cincinati of the United States"; the cover was addressed to GW.

1. "The Standing Committee of the Cincinnati Society of Pennsylvania" adopted a resolution on 16 April to give Heer $20 ("Minutes of the Pennsylvania State Society of the Cincannati from July 4, 1789 to June 14, 1815 inclusive," p. 261, in Archives of the State Society of the Cincinnati of Pennsylvania, on deposit at DSoC).

From James McHenry

Sir   War office 12 April 1796

I beg leave to lay before you a letter from Mr Seagrove which I received this morning,[1] and one from Mr Price, the factor or agent for the trading house at Colerain with a draught of answers thereto.[2] If you can spare time to look over them, I can receive your instructions at Any hour as the vessel is to sail to-day.[3] I have the honour to be with the most perfect respect Sir Your most ob. & hble st

James McHenry

ALS, DLC:GW; LB, DLC:GW.

1. The letter from Creek agent James Seagrove has not been identified.

2. The letter from Edward Price has not been identified, but McHenry replied to Price on this date: "I have received your letter of the 24th of February ultimo. Your remarks on the mode that has been prescribed for carrying on the Indian trade with the public goods appear to me judicious and pertinent. The difficulties of Supplying them without intermediary white traders had occurred, but they were not deemed insurmountable. It was, at least, hoped that the Indians might be gradually induced to a freer intercourse and more intimate friendship, by becoming generally the Sellers of their own peltry, and buyers of the articles they wanted in return.

"As this Subject is important, you will be pleased to give to it further attention, and to communicate the result of your observations & reflexions. In the mean while, it may be expedient to give such small credits to the traders who may be recommended to you by Mr Seagrove, or those in whom you can confide, as may prevent present inconveniencies, 'til such time as a permanent arrangement can be taken in the premises.

"The Sloop William, which carries supplies for the troops, and Stores for the commissioners to hold the treaty with the creeks, is ordered to return as soon as you can ship the peltry and Skins you may have on hand" (DNA: RG 75, Letters to Factors).

3. Philadelphia newspapers for 16 April reported the departure for St. Marys, Ga., of the *William.*

From the Commissioners
for the District of Columbia

Sir   [Washington] City 13th April 1796.

Our Principal surveyor Mr Freeman has applied to us to recommend him to an Appointment for laying out the Lines under the direction of General Knox:[1] His good Conduct whilst in public Employment entitles him to our Recommendation & We with pleasure give it. Mr Freeman wou'd be usefull to us in the City for some Months yet, but We cannot blame his seeking a just Occasion to advance his fortune. We have found him steady, sober, & attentive to business & believe him to be very much a master of the Business he professes.[2]

We forbear to say any thing respecting the affairs of the City, presuming our Letters to Mr White on that subject are communicated to you.[3] We have the honor to be with great Respect Sir Yr mo. obt servts

Gusts Scott

William Thornton

LS, DLC:GW; LB, DNA: RG 42, Records of the Commissioners for the District of Columbia, Letters Sent.

1. Henry Knox had been appointed as the U.S. representative on the commission created by Article V of the Jay Treaty to determine the St. Croix River boundary with Canada (see Miller, *Treaties*, 249). Knox declined the appointment.

2. See Thomas Freeman to GW, this date.

3. Since their last letter to GW, dated 17 March and transmitted with their letter to Alexander White written on 18 March, the commissioners had written letters to White dated 22, 24, and 29 March and 5 and 12 April (all DNA: RG 42, Records of the Commissioners for the District of Columbia, Letters Sent). The letter written on 22 March noted that the construction of public buildings would not commence as soon as weather might permit and mentioned the possibility of a lawsuit to settle the financial obligations of Robert Morris.

On 24 March the commissioners continued discussion of their problems with Morris and lamented the lagging hotel lottery that had halted progress on that facility. "Money alone is wanting" to resume construction of public buildings during the summer. "Without 8 or 10,000 Dollars," the commissioners surmised, "it will be impossible to set seriously to Work."

On 29 March the commissioners questioned whether the city should be charged for the attorney general's opinion on the case arising from negotiations with Morris. They also enclosed to White "the present state of the President's house—We think the covering ought to be of slate; & that the second story ought to be finished, plain & without mahogany—The best, or principal story may be finished, as proposed, with plain mahogany Doors & that the stair case should be of Wood—We wish you to lay the statement before the President & to take, his opinion, if he chooses to give one, & in the mean time, we have directed Hoban to act as if the measures proposed were adopted." White wrote the commissioners from Philadelphia on 6 April that he had laid their letter dated 29 March before GW, who "said he did not think the difference of expense between Mahogany and pine Doors an object sufficient to authorise a change, he gave no opinion, and it did not occur to me to ask him, respecting the roof and Stair Case" (DNA: RG 42, Records of the Commissioners for the District of Columbia, Letters Received).

On 5 April, the commissioners wrote White about news of the House passage of the bill to guarantee a loan for the Federal City. A loan of $60,000 or $70,000 with the payment of the next installment by Morris and John Nicholson "would probably carry us through the season. We see no prospect of obtaining money here—& unless aid can be obtained from Phila. or New York Banks, we know not where to look for an immediate supply. There can be no doubt that the Bill past by the house of Representatives, if concurred in by the Senate & president, will give a great additional Value to the property here, & may perhaps prevent the necessity of our seeking any other Loan . . . In the present state of the Treasury (which is 1300 Dollars worse than nothing) we dare not hazard commencing active operations on the buildings—should our funds be insufficient at the end of a month, to pay off the Stone setters, Brick layers &c., they would assuredly disperse, & might not be collected again, during the season." Discussion on the finances of Morris and Nicholson and Samuel Blodget, Jr.'s hotel concluded the letter. White informed the commissioners on 8 April that he had written Morris and Nicholson the previous day, "having first obtained the Presidents approbation." Hearing that "there are a number of Gentlemen going to Washington, some with a view of purchasing—I mentioned this to the President who agrees with me that we ought to sell should any offers be made." In his letter dated 7 April to Morris and Nicholson, White wrote: "My Colleagues have requested me to press in the most earnest manner the immediate payment of your Arrears—and to learn from you what reliance they may have on future payments particularly that the time for which is fast approaching—The Crisis is too impo[r]tant for us to pass over without an effort on our part—the payment of your Arrears and of your next instalment with punctuality, would enable us to go on with spirit till money could be procured from other Sources, but without money the Works must cease, and there is none from whence we have a right to demand aid." To meet their payments, White urged Morris and Nicholson to sell lots at a private sale (both letters, Records of the Commissioners for the District of Columbia, Letters Received).

Writing to White on 12 April, the commissioners expressed pessimism about finances, with little hope of raising money until a loan guarantee passed Congress. "Every thing is at a stand and must remain so until 10 or 12000 Dollars can be raised—The prospect of raising it here, is very gloomy except it can be extracted from Morris & Nicholson." They also noted Henry Lee's interest in purchasing about 100 lots for a price lower than a desirable figure.

From Thomas Freeman

Sir   Surveyor's Office City of Washington apl 13th 1796
    The active and interesting operations in my department in this City, being now verging to a close, & the salary annexed thereto

being but a bare support, I feel it a duty incumbent on me to seek the most early opportunity of judiciously changing my present situation—to this end, my first object would be that business wherein my services would be most useful & best rewarded.

The ascertaining & adjusting the Western limits, and bounds of the United States as contemplated in the late Treaties, will require, industry, perseverence, & much Mathematical knowledge—my services in that department would, I flatter myself be acceptable—Permit me therefore to offer my self to your consideration in the arrangement of that business, and should I be so fortunate as to succeed to an appointment therein I shall gratefully endeavour to deserve your confidence[1]—By the inclosed letters you will perceive that I make this application under the sanction of the Commissioners of the City of Washington.[2] I have the Honor to be, with great respect Sir, your most obedient humble Servant

Thos Freeman

ALS, DLC:GW.

1. Articles IV and V of the 1794 treaty with Great Britain called for boundary surveys of the northern Mississippi River and the St. Croix River. Article III of the 1795 treaty with Spain called for a survey of the southern boundary between the United States and the Spanish colonies (see Miller, *Treaties*, 248–49, 320–21). For Freeman's nomination under the latter treaty, see GW to the U.S. Senate, 21 May, and to the Commissioners of the District of Columbia, 30 May.

2. Freeman enclosed the commissioners' letter to GW written on this date and former commissioner Thomas Johnson's letter to GW dated 12 February. Johnson reported that Freeman "came strongly recommended to the Commissioners and whilst I acted supported the Character he brought with him which, I have no Doubt, he still maintains. I have had occasional Conversations with him on the surveying Business in the City and think him uncommonly well informed and ready—his platting too does him very great Credit—I believe sir he may be depended on" (ALS, DLC:GW).

From Timothy Pickering

Department of State April 13. 1796. 6 o'clock p.m.

The Secretary of State respectfully lays before the President of the United States letters from Colo. Humphreys from No. 24. to No. 29th—the numbers 27. 28 & 29 with inclosures, the Secretary has not been able to examine and arrange till now—they were received yesterday.[1]

T. Pickering

ALS, DNA: RG 59, Miscellaneous Letters; LB, DNA: RG 59, GW's Correspondence with His Secretaries of State.

1. These letters from David Humphreys to Pickering, and their enclosures, are found in DNA: RG 59, Despatches from U.S. Ministers to Spain. Humphreys, who then served as minister to Portugal and chargé d'affaires to the Barbary States, wrote number 24 in Lisbon on 18 Dec. 1795, and it was docketed as received on 8 April 1796. Not having sent a letter for some time because no vessels sailed "owing to the extreme badness of the weather," Humphreys "enclosed letters of the 5th & 11th of Octr from Mr [Joseph] Donaldson, together with the List of Consular Presents for Algiers & some observations on the subject." Humphreys judged it "essential for counteracting intrigues, removing undue impressions & preserving Peace, that Consuls should be appointed without loss of time for all the Barbary States with which we may be in Amity." He complained about his workload, lack of assistance, and low salary. Humphreys also returned some papers "which have become useless, in consequence of M. Skjöldebrand's having declined accepting the Consulship for Algiers, & of the apparent incompetence of Captn Heissel to execute in a proper manner the functions of the Consulate for Morocco."

Number 25, dated 31 Dec. 1795, has not been identified, but Humphreys alluded to it when he wrote number 26 from Lisbon on 11 Jan. 1796. His number 26 also reads: "The only intelligence I obtain from Algiers, is, that Mr Donaldson was confined to his bed by a complication of disorders, among which the gout & dysentery were the most prevalent. I hope no fatal consequences will ensue. But, in all events, it appears to me, the necessity of having a Consul named for that Regency becomes everyday more pressing." Humphrey closed with the plans of the prince and princess of Brazil to travel "in order to have a personal interview with the King & Queen of Spain."

When he wrote number 27 from Lisbon on 23 Jan., Humphreys enclosed two letters received from Donaldson, one from Philip Sloan, and one from Robert Montgomery: "From the two former you will learn the measures which have been taken with respect to Tunis & Tripoli; and what ground there is for hoping that a Truce will be observed. From the two latter you will be informed that there are other Dispatches on their way from Algiers for me; and that the State of Affairs in Africa is not so favorable as could be wished. To what this general report of the unfavorable state of affairs alludes, I am unable to determine. But, when I consider the impatience, fickleness, avarice & want of respect for public opinion, which are said to constitute a part of the Character of the Dey of Algiers; I must own I can never be without apprehensions of receiving disagreeable intelligence from thence. I am particularly sorry to hear that Mr. Donaldson has fallen into discredit with him; as well as that the health of Mr Donaldson continues to be so much impaired as to operate on his conduct, in such a manner as to induce Mr Philip Sloan to decline acting any longer under his orders. For I consider Sloan's assistance as Interpreter of considerable importance." Humphreys also enclosed a letter dated 23 Dec. 1795 from Joel Barlow, who was leaving Paris for Alicante, Spain, where he promised to improve the situation. Humphreys feared his own communications might be less frequent because the price "of most Articles of the produce of the U.S. is now so much higher in other Countries of Europe than in this Kingdom, that few or no vessels arrive here from thence. Consequently few or none will depart from hence for the U.S. for some time to come."

Humphreys wrote number 28 in Lisbon on 31 Jan.–4 Feb.: "Mr Montgomery has not arrived here with the expected Dispatches from Algiers; nor have I received any intelligence from Barbary since my letter to you of the 23d inst." Bad weather had greatly affected shipping, including the British fleet with troops bound for the West Indies. News had come from Paris that French and Austrian generals had concluded a truce to negotiate a peace, and signs indicated that the British government also might be preparing for peace negotiations.

Humphreys wrote number 29 in Lisbon on 6 Feb.: "At length Mr Montgomery has arrived (last night) with the long expected Dispatches from Algiers. His Journey has been retarded by heavy rains, bad roads, & swelled Rivers rendered impassable by the loss of Bridges. The vessel which is to carry this letter sails immediately, so that I have only time to copy the letter from the Dey of Algiers & that from Mr Donaldson to me. I enclose herewith the Copy of the Dispatch from the former; and the original letter from the latter." The dey's letter to Humphreys dated 4 Jan. expressed dissatisfaction over the lack of news regarding U.S. ratification of the Algiers treaty completed in early September 1795 and doubts over Donaldson's authority to negotiate that instrument. He wanted Humphreys to "immediately dispatch a Courier" to explain the delay or risk "fatal consequences." Written from Algiers on 3 Jan., Donaldson's letter to Humphreys noted the dey's demand and warned that the "Capricious" and "Avaricious" ruler might make peace with Portugal and turn against the United States.

From Oliver Wolcott, Jr.

Treasury Departmt April 13th 1796.
The Secretary of the Treasury respectfully submits to the consideration of the President of the United States sundry documents relative to a proposal for making five chains for the use of the Beacons & Buoys in Charleston & Delaware bays.[1]

It is the opinion of the Secretary that it will be for the interest of the United States to contract for the chains upon the terms specified in the proposal.[2] All which is respectfully Submitted.

Oliv: Wolcott Jr
Secy of the Treasy

LB, DLC:GW.

1. Letterbook copies of enclosed papers can be found in DNA: RG 26, Lighthouse Deeds and Contracts. They included Matthew Van Dusen's letter dated 9 April to William Allibone, in which he agreed to furnish three chains for the Delaware River within six weeks for ten pence per pound; and Allibone's letter dated 11 April to Tench Coxe, commissioner of the revenue, enclosing Van Dusen's letter and adding in a postscript that he had "agreed with Mr Van Duzen for the two Chains for So. Carolina on the same terms." Coxe transmitted the papers to Wolcott on 12 April.

2. GW approved the contract on this date (see *JPP*, 334, and Coxe to Wolcott, 12 April).

From Henry Knox

My dear Sir   Boston 14 April 1796.
I have received your kind favor of the 4th instant.

I shall always regret every circumstance which may obstruct a compliance with your wishes public or private.[1] The appointment of Commissioner would mar most effectually my plans for the Summer, and which are now in an expensive train of execution.[2]

There is another circumstance which I confess confidentially, has a considerable influence on my mind, in declining the appointment. I am directly and collaterally very much interested in the lands of the district of Maine.[3] I am impressed with the opinion that our claims are not well founded. But the people of this State have their expectations buoyed up on the subject. Any decision therefore contrary to their wishes may be liable to wrong constructions, not only against me as interested but against the executive for appointing such a person.

It would seem upon closer reflection most proper, that a person not of this state should be appointed as Commissioner. My mind lately has fixed upon Colonel Wadsworth but I do not know whether he would accept. Judge Sullivan would make a very proper agent, and advocate for the U. States.

I have however in a private letter to Colonel Pickering mentioned[4] that under certain circumstances the appointment might stand as it is for the present. Not that I desire it, but merely as it might be expedient to have an ostensible appearance on the part of the executive of a readiness to execute the treaty.[5]

The great Mass of the people of New England, I verily beleive 9/10ths approve of yr reply to the house of representatives, as truly wise and unanswerable.[6]

The abuse of certain[7] newspap⟨ers⟩ produces no other effect than indignation.

No cheif Magistrate ever possessed in a greater degree the affection and respect of the people than you do. I am my dear Sir with perfect attachment and respect Your humble Servant

H. Knox

ALS, DLC:GW; ADf, NNGL.

1. GW had offered Knox an appointment as one of the commissioners created under Article V of the Jay Treaty to determine the river boundary between Maine and Canada.

2. At this point on the draft, Knox wrote and struck out a line. He then penned material omitted from the ALS: "I shall have sixty workmen employed during the summer, in errecting Mills, and other buildings and opening slate and marble quarries, and makeing lime and bricks. These and other things are exper[i]ments to raise a revenue while my lands are gradually selling at the le[a]st market prices."

3. Knox had inherited a fifth of the Waldo Patent in Maine, a tract of approximately 170,000 acres. He also had engaged in large land purchases and speculations with William Duer and William Bingham (see Allis, *William Bingham's Maine Lands*, 1:38–45, 80–92, 521–676; 2:677–761).

4. Knox inadvertently omitted this word, which is taken from his draft.

5. In his private letter to Secretary of State Timothy Pickering written on this date, Knox explained: "A multitude of Workmen whom I have employed for the present year, and who will require my actual presence effectually prohibit my acceptance of the appointment.

"If however it should be certain that circumstances would prevent any call for actual services this year, and a new appointment at present should be in any degree embarrassing to the executive, I should have no objection to the appointment remaining as it is until the next winter, and then to accept or decline as circumstances of a private nature should dictate. But if this idea should not comport entirely with the views of the President, then please to consider my public letter as definitive" (MHi: Pickering Papers).

6. Knox is referring to GW's message dated 30 March to the U.S. House of Representatives asserting executive privilege to withhold diplomatic correspondence.

7. On his draft, Knox inserted this word to replace "the Jacobinnal," which he struck out.

To Joseph Priestley

April 14th 1796

The President U.S. has, agreeably to his promise,[1] caused the Laws of the U. States "to promote the progress of useful arts &c." to be examined; and finds that the last act passed on this subject, vizt on the 21st of Feby 1793 (repealing the first act of the 10th of April 1790), confines the granting of patents to citizens of the United States.[2] The first act of the 10th April 1790 does not appear to have limited this right to any particular description of persons; and why it is thus confined in the second, the President can, at this time, see no good reason; but he will take occasion to enquire into the cause of this limitation; & if it should not appear improper, to relinquish it, he can have no doubt of the disposition of the Legislature to make such alteration in the existing law as will give to the U.S. the advantage which may arise from the useful inventions or improvements of foreigners, as well as of our own Citizens.

LB, DLC:GW.

1. No previous correspondence on this subject has been found. GW likely made the promise in conversation with Priestley, who arrived in Philadelphia on 11 Feb. for a series of Sunday lectures commencing on 14 Feb. (see *Discourses Relating to the Evidences of Revealed Religion, Delivered in the Church of the Universalists, at Philadelphia, 1796* [Philadelphia, 1796]). Soon after his arrival, Priestley spent about two hours with GW at tea: "He invited me to come at any time, without ceremony" (Priestley to Theophilus Lindsey, 12–15 Feb. 1796, in Rutt, *Works of Priestley*, 1 [part 2]: 330–34; quote on 332).

2. For these acts, see 1 *Stat.* 109–12, 318–23. The new restriction appears in section 1 of the later act.

From Abraham Small and John Thompson

s⟨ir⟩   Philadelphia April 14, 1796

We hope we do not take an unpardonable Liberty by endeavouring to get the proposals herewith enclosed, into your hands for perusal.[1]

If you, Sir, will have the Goodness to look them through, they will fully explain the motives which have guided us, and the views we have in the completion of our Undertaking.

We are conscious of having made a successful effort to raise the most useful of all the Arts, to the same summit of excellence in America—from which she has in Europe long drawn forth general admiration.

Whilst we are endeavouring to bring to perfection that Art from which mankind derive all they know—which has ever been the Guardian of Liberty, nothing can be more natural than our Wish that the name of Washington, should be first among our Patrons.

Our Prayer is, that your Excellency will look at so much of our performance as we have finished—we hope it will then speak for itself. We, are with the utmost Deference, Your Excellency's Most humble servants

Abrm Small
John Thompson

LS, DLC:GW.

Abraham Small (1765–1829) and John Thompson (d. 1805) were Philadelphia printers.

1. The enclosed proposals have not been identified, but their subject is evident from an advertisement placed in Philadelphia newspapers later in April. The version rendered in the *Aurora General Advertiser* for 22 April reads: "*SPECIMEN OF* Elegant Printing. JOHN THOMPSON & ABR. SMALL . . . inform those who admire, and would wish to encourage any improvement in those Arts which are an ornament to a State; that after much expence and great attention, they have printed for public inspection, the First Number of their HIGHLY FINISHED Hot-Pressed Bible, Which they believe to be the most beautiful production of its nature, hitherto seen.

"Similar Works in Europe have for some years been liberally patronized—they have had an honourable place in the Libraries of Men of Taste: The present production is an attempt to show, that in America, Works CAN be executed, in every respect equal to the efforts of Trans-Atlantic genius. . . .

"It claims patronage as being wholly American—the paper, by far the best ever used here for printing, is made within a few miles of this city—the types, which are truly beautiful, are also American—and the whole apparatus, for Hot-Pressing, has been procured from different parts of the Union:—It is also the cheapest HOT-PRESSED *BIBLE* ever printed in any country. . . .

"It is proposed to deliver the whole in Forty Numbers, at One-Half Dollar each—one of which will be completed every two weeks."

For the completed project, see *The Holy Bible, containing The Old and New Testaments: Together with the Apocrypha; Translated out of the Original Tongues . . .* (Philadelphia, 1798).

From Oliver Wolcott, Jr.

Treasury Department April 14th 1796.
The Secretary of the Treasury respectfully submits to the consideration of the President of the United States, a Letter from the Commissioner of the Revenue, accompanied with an account of fifteen hundred & sixty two gallons of oil purchased at New York for the use of the Lighthouse establishment.[1]

As it appears that this Oil has been obtained on terms favorable to the United States, the Secretary is of opinion that it will be adviseable to confirm the purchase.[2] All which is respectfully submitted.

Oliver Wolcott Jr
Secy of the Treasy

LB, DLC:GW.

1. Tench Coxe had written Wolcott on 12 April: "A purchase of oil has been made by the Superintendent of the New York Light House, upon very favorable terms agreeably to the account hereunto annexed. You will be pleased to submit the same to the Presidents consideration" (DNA: RG 26, Lighthouse Letters). The account has not been identified.

2. On this date, GW approved the purchase of "Spermaciti Oil" for $1,425.58 (*JPP*, 334).

From Oliver Wolcott, Jr.

Treasury Department April 14th 1796
The Secretary of the Treasury respectfully submits to the consideration of The President of the United States a Letter from the Commissioner of the Revenue of the 12th Instant enclosing the copy of a Contract entered into by the Collector of Wilmington with Isaac Davis for the stakeage of Cape Fear river in North Carolina.[1]

The Secretary is of opinion that it will be for the interest of the United States to confirm the said Contract. All which is respectfully submitted.[2]

Oliver Wolcott Jr
Secy of the Treasy

LB, DLC:GW.

1. In his letter dated 12 April, Tench Coxe notified Wolcott that he had written James Read, collector at Wilmington, N.C., the previous September

about the 1796 contract for stakeage. Coxe also wrote: "The enclosed papers No. 1. 2. & 3 have been this day received from him, you will be pleased to submit them to the President. The same business was done in 1791 for 85 Dollars, Tho it is presumed that the Buoys since authorized by law will diminish the number of stakes in the most expensive places, yet it does not appear probable that a new Contract could be effected on better terms" (DNA: RG 26, Lighthouse Letters).

Coxe enclosed a note from a pilot named Isaac Davis written at Smithville, N.C., on 12 Dec. 1795, and proposing to "undertake the Stakeage of the River Cape Fear and keep it in repair for the year 1796" for $100. Coxe also enclosed the contract entered into by Davis and his securities with Read (both items, DNA: RG 26, Lighthouse Deeds and Contracts). When Coxe wrote Read on 15 April, he acknowledged a letter from Read to him dated 25 March, which presumably was the third enclosure. Coxe then reminded Read to seek proposals earlier to obtain better prices "as well as to save the trouble of explanations to the President when a contract is not made in due time" (DNA: RG 26, Lighthouse Letters).

2. GW approved the agreement on this date (see the contract with Davis, and *JPP*, 334).

From Christopher Myers

City of Washington [D.C.]
M[a]y it Please your Excellency   April 15th 1796

I should have written long before this time were it not, that the substantial matter on which I could wish to give a clear opinion upon, has not in My mind come into that digested form so as to be perfect in representation.

I feel how much I trifle with your time, but fearfull, that a continued scilence may give cause for thoughts prejudicial to that respectfull gratitude I hourly feel—I have taken the liberty of addressing myself to your Excellency—and to return you my thanks for the introduction you have given me to Mr Lear[1] whos communications on the Potomac navigation [h]as been of real and essential service to me.

Mr Lear will have communicated to your Excellency the substance of the various reports I have made on the subject of the River, and future plans of operation—having met with the approbation of the Board of directors[2]—My constant end[ea]vour shall be the bring[ing] to perfection this great national concern.

I am proud in the Idea of having to execute an object originally formed by your Excellency and which has been so Long in contemplation.[3]

Permit me to add to my gratitude My prayers, that your Excellency may long continue to exersize that strenght of mind so benificial to your countrys prosperity and Wellfare. I have the honor be M[a]y it please your Excellency—Your most Obliged and humble Servant

C. Myers

LS, DLC:GW.

1. See GW to Tobias Lear, 26 Dec. 1795.

2. Meeting at Georgetown, D.C., on 5 April, the directors of the Potomac Company ordered a "Monthly Report & Sundry papers" from Myers "deposited with the Treasurer" (DNA: RG 79, Proceedings of the Board of President and Directors of the Potowmack Company 1785–1800).

3. For a summary of GW's early involvement with the Potomac Company, see GW to Thomas Jefferson, 29 March 1784, and n.1 to that document (*Papers, Confederation Series*, 1:237–41).

From Timothy Pickering

Department of State April 15. 1796.

The Secretary of State begs leave to inform the President of the United States, that the patent for Benjamin Tyler is destined to be carried to him by Mr Strong, who will leave town to-morrow morning by three o'clock.[1] If the President should find time to attend to it before this evening, the Secretary will then have the honor to receive it at the President's house.[2]

Timothy Pickering

ALS, DNA: RG 59, Miscellaneous Letters; LB, DNA: RG 59, GW's Correspondence with His Secretaries of State.

1. "Mr Strong" probably was Caleb Strong, U.S. senator from Massachusetts, who began a leave of absence on 18 April (*Journal of the Senate*, 8:156). A notice in the *Columbian Centinel* (Boston) for 7 May 1796 reported his return to Philadelphia.

Benjamin Tyler (1733–1814) operated a number of different mills in Claremont, New Hampshire.

2. GW on this date signed Tyler's patent (now numbered X109) for "a new and useful improvement, in the mode of cleaning Wheat, Rye, Buck-Wheat, and all other kinds of grain" (see also *JPP*, 334).

From James Ross

Sir   Philadelphia 15. april 1796

By this days post I learn that Charles Morgan is dead. The report says that he died on his way home from Kentuckey. Colo. Ritchie who purchased your lands upon Millers Run in Washington County is desirous that the lines should be run & the quantity Ascertained as soon as possible.[1] I suggest to you the propriety of writing to Colo. Presly Neville on this subject, he is now at Pittsburgh, & by enclosing to him the courses and distances, mentioned in your patent, he can go upon the ground & execute the Survey without delay.[2] Colo. Ritchie States that he will at all events pay a Sum equal to what may be supposed due upon the first of June & make the necessary arrangements afterwards, Should it be inconvenient to you, or impracticable to accomplish the Settlement sooner.

Enclosed is a check for the money paid by Colo. Shreve & I will wait upon you to morrow morning before the Post goes out to know what Answer I shall send to Colo. Ritchie.[3] With perfect respect I have the Honour to be Sir your most obedient humble Servant

James Ross

LS, DLC:GW.

1. Ross had negotiated an agreement to sell GW's Millers Run tract in Washington County, Pa., to Matthew Ritchie (see Ross to GW, 20 Aug. 1795). For further developments in this transaction, see Indenture with Matthew Ritchie, 1 June 1796; Alexander Addison to GW, 4 July; GW to Addison, 8 July; and Ross to GW, 18 August.

2. GW wrote Presley Nevill on 16 April: "I have, as you probably may have heard, sold my land on Millers run to Colo. ⟨Ritchie⟩. This land was to be re-surveyed, and to be paid for by the acre, agreeably to what it shall *actually* measure. This re-survey was to have been made by Mr Charles Morgan, of whose death I have just heard, from Mr Ross (one of your Senators) who has advised me to commit this business to you.

"May I then request the favor of you to make, or cause to be made by some accurate artist, this Survey, at as convenient a moment as it can be ex⟨e⟩cuted. The cost of the Survey, and incidenta⟨l⟩ expences I will pay, or cause to be paid, upon demand.

"The courses & distances of the tract (copied from the Patent) are enclosed; as also the quantit⟨y⟩ therein mentioned: but having good reasons to believe that the *real*, will exceed the *nominal* amount I preferred selling by the former" (ALS [letterpress copy], DLC:GW; LB, DLC:GW; the letter-book copy is incorrectly dated 10 April).

Nevill replied to GW from Pittsburgh on 22 April: "I have this moment been honored with your Excellency's letter of the 16th Inst. and will with the greatest pleasure attend to the business therein mentioned; I am but just arrived at Home, having taken Virginia in my route, but I believe the Information relative to the death of Mr Chas Morgan is not true, at all events the Survey shall be made with accuracy as soon as I can give Colo. Ritchie Notice, (supposing it will be agreable to him to be present,) and the Plot or Draft transmitted to your Excellency, as soon as conveniently may be" (LS, DLC:GW).

3. Israel Shreve paid money due on his purchase of GW's Washington's Bottom tract in Fayette County, Pa. (see GW to Shreve, 14 Jan. and 21 Feb. 1795, and Shreve to GW, 7 Feb. 1795). An entry in GW's cash accounts for 15 April 1796 records the receipt from Ross of $1,160, "part of the second payment for the Land sold the sd Shreve . . . deposited the said sum in the hands of Mr Washington Craik the 22d of April to pay the Contingent expences of the family" (Cash Memoranda, 1794–97; see also GW to Ross, 11 June 1796).

From Vincent Redman

Collectors office Port of Yeocomico [Va.]
Sir   16th April 1796
I beg yr permission to resign my Office, & I therefore inclose my Commissions as Collector & Inspector at the Port of Yeocomico on the Potomac.

When honor'd with these appointments I received them with gratitude, nor shou'd the small salary ass[i]gn'd by Congress as a compensation for my Trouble been of itself a reason Sufficient to induce my present application, but the Inconvenience of my family residence b⟨ein⟩g 16 Miles from the Port, & the consequent necessity of employing a Deputy will plead my excuse for my resignation.[1]

My Deputy was (for six months past) and now is Mr James A. Thompson a resident on the river Yeocomico, his attentive assiduity claims my warmest thanks, and as Mr Thompson is anxious for this appointment, I use the freedom Sir, to mention his Name as my Successor & to add that an application to the Heads of Departments will do Justice to the oppinion Therein express of Mr Thompson,[2] I beg leave Sir, to assure you of my respect, esteem & gratitude & have the honor to be Sir, Yr Mo. Obt Servt
                                              Vincent Redman

ALS, DNA: RG 59, Miscellaneous Letters.

Vincent Redman, who served as an officer of the Richmond County, Va., militia during the Revolutionary War, was appointed collector at Yeocomico in 1789 and inspector of the same port in 1792. He lived in the upper district of Lunenberg Parish in Richmond County.

1. Section 54 of "An Act to provide more effectually for the collection of the duties imposed by law on goods, wares and merchandise imported into the United States, and on the tonnage of ships or vessels," approved 4 Aug. 1790, granted to the collector at Yeocomico a salary of $100 and fees (1 *Stat.* 145, 172). For the boundaries of the Yeocomico district, see 1 *Stat.* 34, 150.

2. On 4 May, GW nominated James A. Thompson to be collector and inspector at Yeocomico (L[S], DNA: RG 46, entry 52; copy, DLC:GW). The Senate ordered that this nomination "lie for consideration" on this date before consenting on 5 May (*Senate Executive Journal*, 206–7). Thompson served until his death, probably in 1803 (see *Jefferson Papers*, 41:684).

From Burwell Bassett, Jr.

Dear Sir   Eltham [Va.] April 17th 1796

As it is always agreable to find others interested in the wellfare of those to whom we are attached I trust it will not be unpleasant to you that I take the liberty to adress you relative to those poor little orphans your and my nephews, and their sister.[1] The goodness of Mr Lears heart will no doubt bind then like a father to them and was it not for the interference of his business in no ones hands could they do better. In his letters to me he seems to expect the boys will remain with him if this is your wish I shall acquiesce but could wish that Charles was to be with me as after the present summer I shall be living in Williamsburg which will afford every advantage of education if in the earlier stages thereof there be any thing material except the care of an interested friend to guard him against the snares of vice.[2]

I shall write to Mr Lear on this subject by the next mail. With respect and esteem your obt Sert

Burwell Bassett

ALS, DLC:GW. GW replied to Bassett on 24 April.

1. Bassett is referring to George Fayette Washington, Charles Augustine Washington, and Anna Maria Washington, the children of George Augustine Washington, who died on 5 Feb. 1793, and Frances "Fanny" Bassett Washington. The widow married Tobias Lear in 1795, but she died in late March 1796.

2. Charles Augustine Washington, born in 1791, was the youngest of the siblings.

To Robert Lewis

Dear Sir,   Philadelphia 17th April 1796
   Your letter of the 6th Ulto has been duly received;[1] & this will
go under cover to Mr Pearce;[2] as, from the tenor of it, it is not
unlikely you may be at Mount Vernon about this time.

   You do not seem to understand me yet, relative to the mode
of paying my rents. I neither want every driblet, as it is received,
sent to Mr Pearce or deposited in the Bank of Alexandria; nor
the *whole* withheld untill all are collected. My idea on the subject
is simply this. On the first of January in every year, *all* the Rents
become due. On some other certain day (if not paid) they are
destrainable. It is presumable then, that between those periods
you will have visited the Tenants, or given them notice that the
Rents *must* be paid in *that* time; or distress will be made, and it
is expected that *such* collections as are made in that time will
be paid, as above, for my use; for *after that,* if you withhold the
money, so collected untill the tardy tenants pay; or it can be recovered in a court of Justice, I may lie out of it a considerable
time—you run a hazard in keeping it by you—while no one is
benefitted by the collection.

   I did not know how the matter betwen Mr Airess & McCormick
stood. I wanted nothing more than my right; and this, if possible,
by fair & amicable means. I never litigate (if it can possibly be
avoided) on my own account, and sure I am I will not (knowingly
do it) to gratify the prejudices, or passions of any other.

   As to the Jack, as it is now too late to send him to you for the
present season, there will be time enough between this & the
next, to decide on the best disposition of him. Present my best
wishes, in which your Aunt unites, to Mrs Lewis and be assured
of the sincere friendship and affectionate regard of Your Uncle
                                   Go. Washington

Sparks transcript, MH.
   1. GW is referring to Lewis's letter dated 6 April.
   2. GW enclosed his letter to Lewis in one he sent to William Pearce on this
date.

To William Pearce

Mr Pearce   Philadelphia 17th April 1796.

Your letter of the 10th instt with a Postcript three days later, came to hand in due course of Post.[1]

I am sorry to hear that Maria continues unwell—& that Charles Washington was siezed with a fever: Let them want for nothing, and whenever it is needful get Doctr Craik to attend them.[2]

It would be unlucky, as my crop of Wheat last year turned out but indifferently, and the prospect of a good one this year, bad; if I should have missed the best Market for flour. If there ever was *good* cause for flour's selling for fifteen dollars per barrel, hitherto; there is none, that I know of, for the fall in the price of this article now, for all accounts from Europe agree, that the Crops of Wheat are very short, & the apprehensions of the Want of bread, great. Under these circumstances I am at a loss to what to ascribe the reduced price; & therefore will keep mine up for the price mentioned in my last; until I have better evidence than appears to me at present, for this fall. but authorise you, as I did in my last, to take Mr Smiths offer, if you cannot obtain better terms.[3]

If a good occasion offers, I will make some enquiry of Mr Christie into the character of Mr Joseph Gallop, and his brothers;[4] not that I expect there is any chance of agreeing with them; first, because I do not want the Land and Negros to go together. and 2dly because 2000 bushels of Wheat pr ann. for River farm is very little more for the land, Negros & Stock, than what I ask for the land alone; as there is 1207 acres within the present fences, of ploughable ground. I knew, that by fixing the Rent in Wheat (while it bore so high a price) would make it appear high; but I believe no reasonable person expects, when Peace is established, that it will be more than a dollar. and if it was more, that the trouble or expence in raising it would be greater. Besides, as Wheat is a staple article, it will be the standard or regulating price of other articles: and is equal & just, for both Landlord and Tenant; for otherwise, if instead of a bushel & half of wheat pr acre, I was to set a dollar & half, and the former should rise, by degrees, to 25/; and other things (which I might have occasion to buy) in proportion; a money rent, under such circumstances, would be ruinous to *me*; on the other hand, if it was at £5 pr Bushel, the Rent (for the reason already mentioned, namely, that it costs the Tenant no more to raise it) would not be oppressive to him; & even if it were to be bot if the price of a Cow, a sheep, or a hog bore a proportionate price, the difficulty in paying for it would not be greater than if it was at 6/ and the price of other articles was governed thereby.[5]

Are all the repairs to the Mansion and other houses completed? If the windows in the Corn & hay lofts, over the Stables, and on the back side, are not put in, I request they may be; as both lofts and Stables wants Air exceedingly.

If Mr Robt Lewis has not been to Mt Vernon, keep the enclosed until his arrival—but if he has been there & gone, let it go to the Post Office,[6] I am Your frd &ca

G. Washington

ALS, ViMtvL.

1. Pearce's letter has not been found.
2. GW's niece Anna Maria Washington and nephew Charles Augustine Washington were at Mount Vernon (see Tobias Lear to GW, 30 March).
3. See GW to Pearce, 10 April.
4. Joseph Gallup (born c.1769) was a tenant farmer on Spesutie Island in Harford County, Md., which fell in the congressional district of Gabriel Christie. At least three of Gallup's brothers also lived in Maryland: Oliver (b. 1754), Charles (b. 1759), and Gilbert (1761–1832).
5. The Gallups apparently responded to GW's advertisement to lease the Mount Vernon farms (see Advertisement and Lease Terms, both 1 Feb. 1796).
6. See GW to Robert Lewis, this date; see also Pearce to GW, this date, and n.1 to that document.

From William Pearce

Sir   Mount vernon april 17th 1796

I have Recevd your Letter of the 10th Instant with Respect to the price of Flour It sells In alexandria for a 11 or 12 dollars ℔ Barrell at most for cash and I beleve some Gives 13 Dollars ℔ Barrell on a Creddit of 60 days—Mr Smith has Returnd from New york and I have Sounded him on the subject of buying yours at 15 Dollars ℔ Barrell at the c[r]edit he offered to take it at before he went from home But he sais he would not buy flour now at that price at a Creddit of 6 months—and the most he would give now on that Creddit would be 14 dollars ℔ barell for superfine and 13 [1]/2 Dollars ℔ Barrell for fine.

Mr Robert Lewis has been here and has paid Into my hands £169.17.6 and said he should Leave a draft In alexandria for £40 more. but That I have not yet Recevd[1]—he sais it will not sut him to take the Jack Compound as it was too Late In the season before he got notice of it.

The weather still keeps dry we have not had any rain yet to do any good. thare was a small shour Last friday eve[n]ing which only Lasted for a few minutes[2] I fear that all the wheat barly & oats will be all Ruined with the Drouth. you mention that you ware affraid that the fences ware not put up well or Elese they would not have blown down so often but I can assure you that they ware well made and I do not think you will dislike them when you see them But the wind was so Voilent hard that they could not possable stand aganst it all the Nieghbourhood shared the same fate.

The appearon[c]e for Catching herring Is better Than It was but we have not Caught Scarcely any shad—and I do not beleve many will be Caught here this season. and we have an Exelent Seine and a Greater Length of Rope those say who are used to the fishery than they Ever saw used here before.

Miss Marriah washington & her brothers are all well now— when I wrote you befor Charles was ve[r]y Sick but he is now quite Recovred. I am with the Greatest Respect Sir you[r] Humb. Servt

William Pearce

ALS, DLC:GW. Pearce enclosed with this letter a farm report for 10–16 April (DLC:GW).

1. Pearce recorded the first payment in an account entry dated 15 April and the second in an undated entry immediately following (Mount Vernon Accounts, 1794–1797, p. 72). Robert Lewis had arrived at Mount Vernon "just at dark" on 12 April and left on 13 April, after having taken Pearce's receipt for the money (Robert Lewis Diary, March-July 1796, ViMtvL).

Lewis wrote GW from Alexandria, Va., on 21 April: "Having occasion to lay in a parcel of herrings for the use of my negro's which brought me into the neighbourhood of this place, I thought proper to bring with me what money I had of yours in my possession—One hundred and sixty nine pounds, seventeen shillings and six pence I deposited with Mr Pearce at Mount Vernon & forty pounds with Mesrs Bennett & Watts of this place, agreeable to the request of Mr Pearce—Making in all £209.17.6—There are some few rents behind still in replevy bonds which will be paid in the course of the next month. They compose the greatest part of the Rental—Mr Ariss in particular pays sixty pounds per ann: which is very small, considering what an extensive farm he holds, and is ever the last man to pay. With love to my Aunt I remain your dutifull and Affectionate nephew" (ALS, CSmH). Lewis recorded his payment to Bennett and Watts under this date in his diary (ViMtvL).

Charles Bennett (d. 1839) and John Watts (d. 1808) sold dry goods and general merchandise from the Bennett and Watts store at the corner of King and Fairfax streets in Alexandria until the partnership dissolved in 1805.

2. The previous Friday was 15 April.

From John Jay

private
Dear Sir   New York—Monday 18 Ap. 1796

You can have very little Time for private Letters, and therefore I am the more obliged by the one you honored me with on the 31 of last month. I was not without apprehensions that on Enquiry it might not appear adviseable to gratify Mr Pickman's wishes; for altho' Integrity and amiable manners are great, yet they are not the only Qualifications for office.[1]

Your answer to the Call for Papers, meets with very general approbation here.[2] the prevailing Party in the House of Representatives appear to me to be digging their political Grave. I have full Faith that all will end well; and that France will find us less easy to manage than Holland or Geneva.

the Session of our Legislature is concluded, and nothing unpleasant has occurred during the course of it.[3] I think your measures will meet with general and firm Support from the great majority of this State—there is no Defection among the Fœderalists—as to the others they will act according to Circumstances—These contentions must give you a great Deal of Trouble, but it is apparent to me that the conclusion of them, like the conclusion of the late war, will afford a Train of Reflections which will console and compensate you for it. attachment to You as well as to my Country urges me to hope and to pray that you will not leave the work unfinished. Remain with us at least while the Storm lasts, and untill you can retire like the Sun in a calm unclouded Evening. may every Blessing here and hereafter attend You.[4] I am Dr Sir your obliged & affectte Servt

                                       John Jay

ALS, DLC:GW; ADf, NNC.

1. Benjamin Pickman had sought appointment as a commissioner under the Jay Treaty (see Jay's first letter to GW, 14 Dec. 1795, and notes 1 and 2 to that document).

2. See GW to the U.S. House of Representatives, 30 March.

3. The nineteenth session of the New York legislature ran from 6 Jan. to 11 April.

4. GW replied to Jay on 8 May.

From Charles Lee

Sir   Philadelphia 18th April 1796

I have conversed with Mr Rawle on the petition of Daniel Hamilton for a pardon of his offence and on the petition of Daniel Leet and others for a general pardon of all those concerned in the late western insurrection to whom the clemency of government has not yet been extended.[1]

We concur in opinion that so long as any offender keeps himself out of the power of that court to which he is properly amenable, he is not to be deemed a fit object of mercy. Daniel Hamilton is of this description. Having fled the justice of that court before whom he is triable he remains in Kentucky and from thence sends his petition. Perhaps in that state he beleives he is personally safe from the just power of the United States, and therefore is not affraid to make known the place of his abode. However this may be; as it is known where he is to be found and that he is within one of the states, and consequently within the arm of justice of the United States, he ought to be within the jurisdiction & power of the circuit court of Pennsylvania for the purpose of a fair trial and until he is so he ought not to be pardoned.

It is in the power of the judge of Kentucky district to issue his warrant for apprehending and removing him from that state to this; and that this may be done a copy of the indictment should be sent to the judge which accompanied with proof of the identity of Daniel Hamilton, will authorize his apprehension and removal.

Relative to the petition for a general pardon the principle above stated is deemed applicable and is corroborated by another, namely befor any person is pardoned *he* should himself condescend to solicit it.

I cannot think it expedient under these circumstances to cease the prosecution against Daniel Hamilton, or at this time generally to pardon those who have heretofore been excepted.[2] With the most perfect respect I am Sir your most obedient humble servant

Charles Lee

LS, DLC: Pennsylvania Whiskey Rebellion Collection.

1. In an undated petition to GW apparently drawn between June and September 1795, Daniel Hamilton wrote: "Being informd that their is Bill found against him for adding and assisting in the Disturbences of the four western Countys" of Pennsylvania and "Placeing the Utmost Confydence in the Meshuers goverment heald out to Us and Expecting Pardon their from your Petitioner did most Chearfully sighn your ammesty himself and was an instrument of geting Maney others to sighn also all which was done within the time Prescribed by proclamation." Moreover, he "was in kentuck at the Commsment of" the disturbances, although he admitted that after his return to Pennsylvania he "unhapely ingaiged in that Unhapey affair." Expecting "the Benefit of the Ingaigements made By the Commissioners and the proclamation of your Excelency dated the 2⟨5⟩ of September Last and trusting That the Publick faith will Be observed," Hamilton prayed "that a Nolleprosequi of the Inditement now Dipending against him May be Directed to Be Enterd By the attorny of the United States" (DS, DLC: Pennsylvania Whiskey Rebellion Collection).

Daniel Leet and others had written GW on 3 Dec. 1795. Lee drafted a response for GW on 24 April 1796 that almost certainly was not sent: "I have received and considered your petition bearing date the third day of last december for a general pardon of all those concerned in the late western insurrection who having fled from the public justice have not been comprehended in any act of Amnesty. While citizens accused of crimes or misdemeanors are endeavouring to elude a fair trial by the laws of the land, absconding or otherwise keeping themselves from the power of the court to which most properly they are amenable they seem not entitled to the clemency of government; and more especially when that clemency is not solicited by the offenders themselves. Under these circumstances they, in whose behalf you have been led by motives of compassion to intercede, are not deemed now to deserve the forgiveness of their country" (Df, in Lee's writing, DLC: Pennsylvania Whiskey Rebellion Collection). When Secretary of State Timothy Pickering wrote the petitioners on 8 July to convey GW's opinion, he generally followed the wording of Lee's draft (DNA: RG 59, Domestic Letters).

2. Lee again wrote GW on 25 April: "Though a written answer to the Petitioners in favor of the insurgents not yet pardoned, has been thought proper, there is not the same reason for a written answer to be given to Daniel Hamilton; & circumstanced as he is, he does not deserve one. A verbal communication to any of his friends that may enquire of the matter, that he is not deemed a fit object of mercy while a fugitive from justice, is all that can be expected of government: In this way it has been mentioned by me on one occasion already.

"Nothing stated by A. Brodie appears to be within the cognisance of the government of the United States; and consequently his applications will not admit of any kind of notice" (ALS, DLC: Pennsylvania Whiskey Rebellion Collection).

From Duncan McLaren

Sir   Raehill [Scotland] Aprill 18th 1796

Doubting not but it will appear Strange and great presumtion in me who are a mean Mechanic to trouble Such a great man with my writing from a Foreign Country and having no title to any favour from you: yet I hope in hearing my Claim you will in Some measure excuse me; I was bred a Mason and taught in the differant branches of that trade Such as Stone Cuting and building Stones and bricks; I was employed eight years building Bridges and Canales and Sixteen building Houses the most part of which time I was employed in building a House to the Earl of Hopetoun on his estate in Annandale; and now about finished:[1] I have a great inclination to go to America and by reason of my large family I am unable to pay for our passage without Some help. By often hearing of your Character induced me to aply to you for help that if you needed one of my trade or Could help me to employment the[n] you would Cause to write or Speak to a Captain of a Vessel that trades from your Country to this Country to bring me over and I and my family will be at your Disposal till what money you lay out be paid with reasonable interest and my family will be willing to work at what you think best till the money be Paid; If you think proper to incourage me to Come I will bring letters from the Earl of hoptoun and other Gentlemen to testify my Character and my ability in the diferent branches of the Mason trade and you will find that what I write is real; and if you be pleased to grant this favour I will Surely ever look on you as my benefactor; This ruinous war is greatly hurt this Country and although a peace was made we are afraid it is the beginning of our troubles by reason of the enormous burdens that we are under this is part of the reason why So many emigrate to that hapy Country of which So much is Spoke of; and that free nation who is So much envied. May you Sir live long to See the good effects of that government that you was So much an instrument of bringing about.

This letter Come to you with a Mason that has wrougt long with me and if he Can he is to deliver it with his own hand and however employs him will find him a very worthy man and deserves to be trusted with any kind of mason work.[2] Sir I am your mot obdt mot Huble Servt

Duncan McLaren

N.B. If you think proper to Cause to write Direct to me Mason to the Earl of Hopetoun at Raehill near Moffat North Britain. D. McL.

ALS, DNA: RG 59, Miscellaneous Letters.

1. James Hope-Johnstone (1741–1816) served as a military officer during the Seven Years War. He became 3d earl of Hopetoun in 1781, and in 1792, he inherited the estates of George Johnstone, 3d marquis of Annandale, adding the Johnstone to his name. Between 1784 and 1796, he served several years as a representative peer of Scotland in the British House of Lords.

2. John Currie wrote GW from New York on 6 July, enclosing this letter and adding: "Should you think proper to favor him with an Answer, I beg you would be so good as put it under cover to John Currie Stone Mason, to the care Mr John Charters Bartley [Barclay] Street New York, & I will forward it him directly" (ALS, DNA: RG 59, Miscellaneous Letters).

To the United States Senate

Gentlemen of the Senate   United States April 18th 1796.

I nominate John McIntosh to be Collector and Inspector of the Revenue for the Port of Brunswick, in the State of Georgia,[1] in the room of Christopher Hillary deceased: and

Stephen Skinner to be Surveyor and Inspector of the Revenue for the Port of Hartford in the State of North Carolina, in the room of Josiah Murdaugh resigned.[2]

Go: Washington

LS, DNA: RG 46, entry 52; LB, DLC:GW.

The Senate ordered that these nominations "lie for consideration" on this date before confirming them on 19 April (*Senate Executive Journal*, 205). "By Order of the President U.S.," George Washington Craik signed an announcement of the appointments on that same date (ADS, DLC:GW).

1. John McIntosh (c.1755–1826) served as an officer in both the Revolutionary War and the War of 1812. He acted as collector until 1800.

2. GW had given Josiah Murdaugh a recess appointment as surveyor for the port of Hertford, N.C., in August 1791; he was confirmed by the Senate in November of that year. Murdaugh resided in the Edenton District of Perquim-

ans County, where he apparently experienced financial troubles in 1794 and 1795 and landed in jail for debt (see *State Gazette of North-Carolina* [New Bern], 6 June 1794 and 21 May 1795).

Stephen Skinner, also of the Edenton District, remained surveyor and inspector until 1816.

From Tobias Lear

My dear Sir,   [Philadelphia] Tuesday Morng 19th Apl 96

Could I beleive, for a moment, that you thought my Opinions were grounded on interested motives, or influenced by party views, I should blush to appear before you; but having long known the liberality of your mind, I have never hesitated to declare my sentiments to you, without reserve, on such points as occasionally occurred between us; and I am pleased to think that you do not esteem me less for this openness, even when our opinions have not coincided with each other.

I have, however, since our conversation last Evening, been much distressed, lest the manner in which I then expressed myself should not have been done with that respect and deference which my heart always pays to you: And I shall not feel at peace with myself 'till I am assured of your forgiveness; for to lose that place which I flatter myself I have held in your esteem, would now be the most painful occurrence that could happen to your devoted & most affectionate friend

Tobias Lear.

ALS, DLC:GW.

From Joseph Leech

Sir   Newbern North Carolina 19th April 1796

The Inhabitants of the Town of Newbern hope they may stand excused for any forwardness, or indiscretion which may appear in this address, if the[y] convey to you expressions of gratitude and approbation, as the only return your fellow Citizens have the power of making for the hard and in some instances, vexatious burden, which their affections and confidence have placed upon you.[1]

We consider, Sir, that your having refused to comply with the resolution of the House of Representatives of the 24th March, upon the ground you have taken, among the most signal acts of service which your eminent Virtues & Talents have rendered your Country;[2] as the influence of your examples, may prolong the date of the Constitution, many ages beyond what might have been the short period of its' existence, had you admitted the principle, and yielded to the requisition of the House—It is the pride and the boast of every enlightened American, that the principles which have been associated in the composition of our most excellent Constitution, have eminently qualified it to extend the most perfect liberty, security and protection, to every rank and condition of life, and they, who know how to appreciate such a blessing, cannot see any act, that may have the most remote tendency to rob them of it, without alarm, nor behold any exertion to preserve it, but with emotions of gratitude.

In addition, suffer us to express the warmest wishes which grateful hearts can feel for your welfare, that it may be the happiness of America, long to experience the Wisdom of your influence in the management of affairs; and that you may long enjoy that satisfaction which the confidence and gratitude of a happy People is capable of conferring.[3] In behalf of the Citizens of the Town of Newbern I have the Honor to be with The most profound Respect Sir Your most obedient and very humble Servant

Joseph Leech Ch[airma]n

LS, DLC:GW; LB, DLC:GW.

Joseph Leech (1720–1803) was a New Bern businessman and a militia officer. Active in politics, he held numerous local and state elected offices. Leech participated in the 1788 and 1789 conventions called to consider the federal constitution.

1. Leech enclosed the proceedings of a meeting held on 19 April that passed three resolutions. The first fully approved "the firm and independant temper with which the President of the United States has withstood a compliance with the resolution" of 24 March requesting papers regarding Jay Treaty negotiations. The second called for an address "expressive of the gratitude and admiration with which every Individual present feels himself agitated, on the recollection of the virtues, integrity, and real love of Country, which determined the President to resist the Resolution of the House, in support of our most excellent Constitution, and in preservation of the liberty, tranquillity and happiness, which as long as the harmony of it's balances remains undisturbed, it is calculated to ensure us." The third expressed regret "that so much of the public time and Treasure should be consumed in a discussion, which a candid

resort to the Constitution in the first instance, might possibly have prevented" (DS, DLC:GW; LB, DLC:GW).

2. Leech is referring to GW's message to the U.S. House dated 30 March. For the resolution adopted on 24 March, see GW to the Cabinet, 25 March, n.1.

3. GW replied to Leech on 5 May: "I have received from you the address and resolutions of the inhabitants of the town of Newbern, passed at their meeting on the 19th of April, noticing the call of the House of Representatives for the papers relating to the negociation of the treaty with Great-Britain, and my answer to that call.

"A sacred regard to the constitution, and to the best interests of the United States as involved in its preservation, having governed my conduct on that occasion, the consciousness thereof would at all times have furnished me with strong ground of satisfaction: but it gives me real pleasure to find that conduct approved by my fellow-citizens; and the kind and affectionate terms in which the approbation of the inhabitants of Newbern has been conveyed to me, are peculiarly grateful, and demand my cordial acknowledgements. These I beg you to express to them, with my sincere thanks for their earnest wishes for my welfare" (Df, in Timothy Pickering's writing, DLC:GW; LB, DLC:GW; GW wrote the dateline and docket on the draft). Secretary of State Timothy Pickering probably supplied the draft to GW on 20 May, and GW chose to backdate the reply (see Pickering's second letter to GW on that date).

From George Lewis

Dr Sir   Fredericksburg [Va.] 19th April 1796

Mrs Lewis's indisposition has detained me in the country for eight dayes past,[1] which prevented my getting your letter of the 7th Inst. untill to day, otherwise it would have been immediately acknowledged.

With respect to Mr Parks, he is a young Man in the Mercantile line, appears industrious and attentive to his buisness. I have known him for twelve months past, and from his conduct since living in this place has been countenanced and respected by the first characters in town and neighbourhood—he has alwayes been spoke of as connected in trade with his Brother in law at Baltimore,[2] but in what proportion, I am not able to ascertain, but conjecture (from his mode of doing buisness) that he has been altogether in the commission line, his selling for ready money, and having never been engaged in the purchase of produce and makeing his remitances altogether in money, convinces me that I am not wrong in my conjecture—as to his family I am told, his Father is an industrious farmer in Maryland with a small property, from whom he can have no expectation,[3] in short his marrying Harriot at this time would be madness in the extreme, at all events, I think it would be well to put it of[f] untill your return to Virginia, by which time you can have an opportunity of being better acquainted, with Mr Parks's prospects in life, and give them time to reflect seriously on what they are about, at present I conceive it has been an inconsiderate step on both sides.

Mr Parks is a young Man of good talents and discovers a disposition to do well, and I have not a doubt with industry but he may in a short time acquire the means to support a family, at present, I really think it would be unwise in them to attempt it—Your letter to my Mother was taken from the post office by her directions, before I came to town[4]—and forwarded to her at Mr Carters in culpeper county, where she and Harriot now are, and have been for these ten dayes past—my love to my Aunt.[5] I am with the utmost respect Yr Affectionate Nephew

Go: Lewis

ALS, ViMtvL.

1. See Lewis to GW, 9 April, and n.3 to that document.
2. The brother-in-law was Thomas McElderry.
3. John Parks (d. 1812) fathered five children.
4. Lewis is referring to GW's letter to Betty Washington Lewis dated 7 April (see GW to George Lewis, same date, n.3).
5. GW acknowleged this letter from Lewis when he wrote his nephew on 28 April.

From Alexander Robertson

Honoured & Dear Sir   Newyork 19 April 1796

Stand Unmoved in the Integerity of your Heart on the Solid Ground in Which Our Divine Master has placed You as President of the United States See with Wondour how A Wise Providence is Carr[y]ing on the Plan in Disposeing of all the Distractions that take place in our National Afairs how the plans formed by Wicked & Desginneeing Men are Overturned and made to Work for the General Good I can See it clearly by that Party in the National Assembly who have combined to Overset our happie Goverment and Oppose the Treaty entred into with Britian the good effects of which has Already been experenced in the keeping this Country in Pace and out of a Destructive Warr The Good effects of there Wicked plan is this The Whole Contenent is alarmed with there Conduct and particulary the Mercantile Intrest in whose hands the principal Wealth of the Country are Lodged and are the Springs of its circulation have Judged it prudent to Stop Trade and not Exporte or Insure property only for Sea Risque to Europe This has had Such an effect on the Mind of the publick that provisions of every kind have fallen from 15 to 20 per Cent in Value Nothing but a publick alarm Such as the present could have brought about Such a change in the price of Provisions for the Good of the poor So that this is one Good end the present Wicked Men have brought about contrary to there Intention and No doubt our Gracouse God will also frustrate all there other wicked Schames and make them Work for the Good this Country and they Shall have Shame and Disgrace for that part they have Acted You have the Aprobation and the prayers of the Godly for your Suport Aproveing of the line your conduct and you have Nothing to fear from the plans of Wicked Men our God will carry you Honourably through and I hope Crown you with better Honours then this poor World can give Belive me to be with great regard Your Most Obedent & very Humb. St

Alexander Robertson

N.B. The Merchants & Traders this City have had a Meeting this day at Coffiee House To Send a Petition to Congress to Adopt the Treaty & make provision for it with G. Britian[1] which petition will be as respectable One as has been ever before Congress as our demecrates now hang there Head very low.

ALS, DLC:GW.

Alexander Robertson (c.1733–1816) was a New York City merchant and stockholder in the Bank of North America and the Bank of New York. He contributed to several civic and charitable organizations. For Robertson's letter to James Madison dated 15 April 1796 supporting the Jay Treaty, see *Madison Papers*, 16:327–28; see also Robertson to Albert Gallatin, 27 April 1796 (NHi).

1. The *American Minerva; An Evening Advertiser* (New York) for 19 April printed the address to the U.S. House of Representatives adopted at this meeting in the Tontine Coffee House: "We the undersigned Merchants Traders and other Citizens of the City of New-York being of the number of your constituents and deeply interested in the issue of every public measure that can affect the essential interests of our Country, find ourselves impelled by that consideration to address you on the subject of certain resolutions now depending

in your House respecting the Treaty made with Great Britain, which fill our minds with very serious apprehensions, which have already given occasion to very serious embarrassments and which in our opinion threaten very extensive and complicated evils—the whole magnitude of which it is not easy to foresee or to calculate.

"Whatever difference of sentiment may at any time have existed among us respecting particular public measures, yet on this occasion and at this time, we all unite in one opinion—and that opinion is, that the above mentioned Treaty ought to be provided for, and executed on the part of the United States with punctuality and good faith."

Regardless of the distribution of authority among the branches of government, "no existing considerations are of sufficient weight, to render it adviseable to refuse making provision for the execution of the said Treaty." Indeed, "compleat execution of the Treaties with Great-Britain, Spain and Algiers . . . appears to us a point of the greatest consequence to this young and rising Country—affording a prospect of durable peace; and of an uninterrupted progress to that maturity and strength, which will enable us to defy the enmity of foreign Powers, without those immense sacrifices which War in our present situation, must inevitably produce."

From John Keon

Carrick on Shannon [Ireland] 20th April 1796
When Elevated Characters are Solicited to grant the request of their Humble Petitioners the abuse of time and words wasted in Compliments Eulogiums &ca to the great annoyance of the Petitioned in my mind deserves reprehension—From your Excellency's general character in these Realms without any such frippery or parade I take leave to call on your Excellencys Humanity if possible to direct me. I think the year 1775 or shortly before the troubles in that Country commenced there lived in Buck's County and Province of Pensylvania a Peter Keon (Brother to my father Bartholomew) a Magistrate and Counsellor at Law as stated by his Letter; a widower shortly after his Marriage with a Miss Cartland who died without Issue and in right of whom Peter her Husband Inherited a property to a considerable amount, Six or Eight hundred a year, she was an orphan but the Daughter of a Gentleman of distinction and as I understand she was under the Guardianship of her uncle by the Father, who refused his consent to the Marriage consequently after her decease he disputed Peter's title to said property but Peter defeated him and established his claim of course. From

the date of the Letter which I allude to or the happy restoration of Peace to that Country not a word heard from him, a Circumstance the more alarming as being remarkable for his attachment to his family. He was then forty years of age and upwards of fine person and manly appearance. If he died without Issue the probability is (no Kinsman of his near him to dispute their title) that his Wife's Connections reassumed the property, granting in one Instance that they have a right to it, yet if the fact is that they are in possession your Excellency may admit that his Heir at Law or next of Kin shoud share in the prosperity which attended his adventures; and if not the whole, to get a part. In vain have I referred to many Characters many ways and means for Information but the manly Idea of hazarding an application to your Excellency may be more prosperous and prove of service and Consolation to me and Peter's Connections if thro the medium intended any discovery shall be made—If your Excellency ordered a few Lines directed "Carrick on Shannon County Leitrim Ireland" no doubt they woud be most gratefully acceptable to me a Man who adores Honor and Humanity in any person and may it please your Excellency with the utmost deference Have the Honor to be Your Excellency's Humble Petitioner & Servt

John Keon M:D.

ALS, DLC:GW.

From Edward Carrington

Dear Sir   Richmond April 22. 1796

The late Votes of the House of Representatives which have just reached us, and from which it appears that appropriations are not entended to be made for giving effect to the Treaty between the U. States and Great Britain, have in my opinion brought our political maladies to a crisis.[1] The disorganizing machinations of a faction are no longer left to be nourished and inculcated on the minds of the credulous, by clamorous demagogues, while the great mass of Citizens, viewing these, as evils at a distance, remain inactive. The consequences of a failure of the Treaty are too plain, and too threatening to the unparalleled happiness and prosperity we enjoy, not to excite alarm in the minds of all who are attached to peace & order—this class of Citizens will now come forward & speak for themselves, and will be found to compose the great body of the community—I may possibly be mistaken—I however feel a confidence in an opinion, that the sense of Virginia to the purpose, will shortly be extensively expressed, in public meetings and by Petitions—A meeting of the people of this City, will take place on Monday next, for the purpose of expressing their opinions on the pending measures, and setting on foot a Petition or remonstrace, to the House of Representatives, thereon.[2] From what I can learn from various parts of the Country I verily believe that similar measures will be adopted, at least, in many Counties.[3] Feeling as I do, a strong conviction that the intelligence contained in this letter is well founded, I have indulged myself in the satisfaction of communicating it to you, and hope that events will realise it.[4] with unalterable attachment and confidence I have the Honor to be Dear Sir Your Most Ob. st

Ed. Carrington

ALS, DLC:GW. The cover of this letter is marked "(Private)."

1. Carrington most likely referred to two resolutions that passed the U.S. House of Representatives on 7 April in response to GW's assertion of executive privilege in withholding documents related to the Jay Treaty. The first claimed that "when a treaty stipulates regulations on any of the subjects submitted by the constitution to the power of Congress, it must depend for its execution, as to such stipulations, on a law or laws to be passed by Congress; and it is the constitutional right and duty of the House of Representatives, in all such cases, to deliberate on the expediency or inexpediency of carrying such treaty into effect, and to determine and act thereon as in their judgment, may be most conducive to the public good." The second held it as unnecessary "to the propriety of any application from this House to the Executive for information desired by them, and which may relate to any constitutional functions of the House, that the purposes for which such information may be wanted, or to which the same may be applied, should be stated in the application" (*Journal of the House*, 8:316–20; quotes on 316–17).

2. For the meeting in Richmond on Monday, 25 April, see Carrington to GW, 27 April.

3. In April and May, the U.S. House of Representatives officially received petitions in support of appropriations to implement the Jay Treaty from the towns of Alexandria, Fredericksburg, and Norfolk, as well as Fairfax, Frederick, King William, and Westmoreland counties (*Journal of the House*, 8:360, 369–70, 375–76, 401). Meetings representing Williamsburg and the counties of Accomack, Augusta, Northampton, Loudoun, and Prince William also sent the House resolutions favoring appropriations (*Gazette of the United States*

[Philadelphia], 17, 18, and 21 May; *Columbian Mirror and Alexandria Gazette* [Va.], 3 and 10 May).

4. GW replied to Carrington on 1 May.

From Charles Lee

Sir,   Philadelphia 22 April 1796

There is reason to believe unless the Congress during their present Session shall make some addition to the fees or emoluments now allowed to the Attornies of the United States in the several Districts,[1] that some of the most useful of those Officers will resign and their vacancies I fear it will be found impossible to fill with fit persons. None but eminent Counsel ought to be called to those Offices, and I am persuaded that on their present establishment they ought rather to be rejected than accepted by such Characters; and more especially in the larger States in which Courts are necessarily held by the District Judge at various places distant from the residence of the Attorney as occasions require. I beg leave therefore to suggest the propriety of allowing to each District Attorney a small Salary to be apportioned to the trouble and service that may reasonably be expected in each State in addition to the fees and emoluments now established by Law. These though small, will defray many of the necessary contingencies in the transaction of their duties, and will render the Offices more acceptable when if not profitable they will not expose the Citizens who take them to expences that are not reimbursed.[2] With the most profound respect I am Sir Your most obedient Servant

Charles Lee

Copy, DLC:GW; LB, DLC:GW.

1. For the fees and compensation allowed district attornies, see section 3 of "An Act for regulating Processes in the Courts of the United States, and providing Compensation for the Officers of the said Courts, and for Jurors and Witnesses," passed on 8 May 1792 (1 *Stat.* 276–77).

2. GW submitted this letter to the U.S. Senate and House of Representatives on 28 April with the following message: "Herewith I lay before you, a letter from the Attorney General of the United States relative to compensation to the Attornies of the United States in the several districts; which is recommended to your consideration" (copy, DLC:GW). The House referred the matter to a committee of three that reported on 25 May, but no further action was taken (*Journal of the House*, 8:371, 486).

From Charles Carroll of Carrollton

Dear Sir   Annapolis 23d April 1796

The principal surveyor in the city of Washington has applied to me to recommend him to be appointed to lay out, under the direction of general Knox, the boundary lines between the United States and Canada, & has transmitted to me an authenticated copy of a letter from the Commissioners to you recommending him to that appointment. My recommendation can add but little, if any, weight to that of the Commissioners; however I can with truth say from my experience & knowledge of Mr Freeman that he deserves the character given of him by those gentlemen.[1]

Mr Richard Sprigg Junr is elected a Representative in the room of Mr Duvall.[2] The citizens of this town have instructed him to vote for the appropriations to carry into effect & operation the british treaty—In this measure our citizens were nearly unanimous. It being county-court week several respectable persons from the county were present at the meeting; all of them approved of instructing and would willingly have signed the instructions, but not being citizens of Annapolis, it was thought improper: I believe they will be signed by almost every influential character in the county to whom these or similar instructions may be presented.[3]

The proceedings of the H. of Representatives have excited a very general alarm amongst us, thinking as we do, that they have a strong tendency to involve this country in a war, a measure deprecated by every well wisher to it.

Removed from the scene of action, and having no correspondence with any members of either branch, I am totally at a loss to account for the motives of the Majority. Do they wish to engross all power to themselves, & to destroy the checks & balances established by the Constitution? does a blind & inveterate hatred to G.B., and an inordinate & impolitic predilection for France influence their conduct? Is it the real interest of this country, that either of those powers should obtain a decided superiority over the other? does not our tranquility depend on their remaining pretty equally balanced? Pardon, Sir, if they are improper, these questions, & sentiments; they are the overflowings of a mind deeply agitated by the present very important Crisis. What can the Representatives expect, if the treaty remains unexecuted on our part? another treaty more favorable? surely they Can not entertain a reasonable hope of such an event: and yet I see no alternative between setting on foot another treaty to resettle matters already settled by a treaty already made, but not executed, or going to war with G.B., or of tamely & ignominiously submitting to the continued detention of the posts, & part of our territory, & farther depredations in, & obstructions to our commerce.

On your steadiness & wisdom, Sir, on the firmness & Judgment of the Senate, combined with the exertions of all good citizens, & principally on that kind Providence, which has hitherto preserved us, wisely for our deliverance from the dangers which now hang over us.[4]

I beg a tender of my respectful compliments to Mrs Washington and remain with Sentiments of the highest respect & regard Dr Sir Yr most obdt hum. Servant

Ch. Carroll of Carrollton

ALS, PHi: Gratz Collection.

1. See Thomas Freeman to GW, 13 April, and n.2 to that document.

2. Gabriel Duvall resigned as U.S. representative in March to become a judge of the Maryland General Court.

Richard Sprigg, Jr. (c.1769–1806) of Prince Georges County, who had served in the Maryland House and Senate, took his seat in the U.S. House of Representatives on 5 May 1796. Sprigg served until 1799 and again from 1801 to 1802, when he resigned to take a Maryland judicial post.

3. The U.S. House of Representatives received on 28 April a petition from inhabitants of Annapolis "praying, that the laws necessary for carrying into effect, with good faith, the treaty lately made between the United States and Great-Britain, may be enacted" (*Journal of the House*, 8:369). The *Gazette of the United States* (Philadelphia) for 29 April 1796 reported the petition "signed by 164 persons."

4. GW replied to Carroll on 1 May.

To Burwell Bassett, Jr.

Dear Sir   Philadelphia 24th Apl 1796

Your letter of the 17th inst: was received yesterday. With you, I sincerely regret the death of your amiable Sister; but as it is one of those events which is dispensed by an allwise and uncontroulable Providence; and as I believe no person could be better prepared to meet it, it is the duty of her relatives to submit, with as little repining as the Sensibility of our natures is capable of.

Mr Lear is now in this City—& before the receipt of your letter we had had some conversation respecting the disposition of the children. At first, he seemed unwilling to part with any of them—but upon more mature reflection yielded to the propriety of your having Maria.[1] And as he has engaged a tutor, and was on the point of taking his own Son home,[2] it was concluded that the boys should remain with him until my re-establishment (next March) at Mount Vernon; when some new arrangement might be made.

It was always my intention, as you probably may have understood, to take Fayette under my immediate care, but as they are now bereft of father and mother it would be best, I conceive, and more grateful to *their* feelings to keep them together, in whatsoever situation they may be placed—for this reason, as I have mentioned before, the ultimate decision relative to them may be postponed until I bid adieu to public life; when I will advise with you and Mr Lear on their future destination and shall readily acquiesce in any plan which shall appear most conducive to their permanent[3] interest, & advantage. With compliments to Mrs Bassett and esteem & regard for yourself I am—Dear Sir Your Obedient Servt

Go: Washington

The Children at present are all at Mount Vernon.

ADfS, ViMtvL; LB, DLC:GW.

1. Anna Maria Washington, born in 1788, was the oldest among her siblings.

2. Tobias Lear's only child from his first marriage, which ended with his wife's death in 1793, was Benjamin Lincoln Lear, born in 1791.

3. GW inserted "permanent" on his draft to replace "substantial." Neither word appears in the letter-book copy, which reads "their, interest & advantage."

From Thomas Law

Dear Sir. Baltimore 24 April [1796][1]

I took the liberty of introducing Mr Barry at Mount Vernon, he now waits upon you to inform you of Eliza's health, & of our mutual happiness.[2]

We regret very much that the business of Congress has caused so long a detention of Mrs Washington & you from your retirement & comfort—& are very anxious to wellcome you home.

I remain With much respect & unfeigned esteem & affection Yrs
mt Sy & Obly

Thomas Law

ALS, DLC:GW.
    1. The year is taken from the docket.
    2. This visitor probably was James Barry, a Baltimore merchant with business
interests in the Federal City.
    Law had married Elizabeth Parke Custis on 21 March 1796 (see GW to Law,
10 Feb., and to Custis, 21 March; see also GW and Martha Washington to Law,
28 March).

To William Pearce

Mr Pearce,   Philadelphia 24th April 1796.
    I am sorry to find by your letter of the 17th instant, accom-
panying the reports of the preceeding week, that the drought
continued; and that the prospect for good crops of small grain
was so unpromising. I should hope, however, that they cannot
be so much injured yet, as not to be recovered by seasonable
weather. If the grain stands sufficiently thick on the ground, I
shall not regard the backwardness of it, occasioned by the want
of rain; running much into straw is no service to the grain.
I had flattered myself (until your letter was received) that the fine
rain which fell in these parts on Saturday the 16th instant, had
extended to you. The alteration occasioned by it, both in grain &
grass in the neighbourhood of this city, is very great indeed.
    I wish, as your prospect for grain is discouraging, that it may, in
a degree, be made up in a good fishing season for Herrings; that
for Shad, must, I presume, be almost, if not quite over.
    As I can see no permanent cause for the fall, in the price of
flour, and believe it will rise again; I am not, at this time at least,
disposed to take less for mine than has been mentioned in my
former letters to you:[1] but continue to advise me, always, of the
Alexandria price of this article; that I may know better how to
govern myself.
    I expected Mr Robert Lewis's collection would have amounted
to more than £169.17.6 and the promised draught for forty
pounds, which you had not, at the time of writing, received.
This, and other money, except for current expences, had better

be deposited in the Bank of Alexandria, as a place of security; & from whence it can be drawn when wanted.[2]

Since the receipt of your letter of the 10th,[3] I have seen Mr Hughs, to whom Joseph Gallop & his brothers are tenants, on Spesusa Island.[4] He speaks of them in favorable terms; as honest, industrious men, and good farmers. But it is somewhat extraordinary that the one who was with you, should entertain an idea of giving no more than 2000 bushels of Wheat as a rent for River farm, with all the Negros and Stock thereon; when, for 450 acres *only*, (about the half of Spesusa Island, for Mr Hughs says they have no more ground tho' they are allowed the use of the Marsh for their Cattle to run upon) they pay him annually *1200* bushels of Wheat and *1500* bushels of Indian Corn: and before these men had it, the same part rented for 30/ pr Acre. This, reckoning two bushels of Indian Corn for one of wheat, makes 1950 bushels of the latter, or more than four bushels of it to the acre; without labourers, or stock of any kind furnished by him. It is true that the Land on the Island is good, and there is an advantage in the Marsh, as a range; but these are far short of compensating for the difference between Six pecks of wheat, which is all I ask as rent pr acre for mine, and 17⅓ pecks which (allowing 2 bushls of Corn for one of wheat) he gets for his. I fixed mine at a moderate rent because I wanted to induce good farmers to settle thereon—and would wish to see them thrive, which would enable them to do justice to, and improve the premises; which will be a primary object with me.

What prospect have you for fruit this year? Has it sustained any injury yet from the frosts? Have you altered the fields No. 2 & 3 at Dogue run, agreably to the line of stakes set up while I was last at home. Is your Lucern seed sown? and how does that, the Chiccory, and Clover seed come up.

I am glad to hear that Maria and Charles have got well again.[5] I wish you health and am Your friend

Go: Washington

ALS, ViMtvL.

1. See GW to Pearce, 10 and 17 April.

2. On 6 May, Pearce deposited at the Bank of Alexandria $695.70, equivalent to £208.15. The remainder of the sum received from Robert Lewis is charged as "By a Loss in gold—By weight" (Mount Vernon Accounts, 1794–1797, p. 72).

3. Pearce's letter to GW of 10–13 April has not been found.

4. The ironmaster Samuel Hughes had purchased Spesutie Island in 1779 (see Cronin, *Disappearing Islands*, 23).

5. GW is referring to his niece and nephew Anna Maria and Charles Augustine Washington.

Letter not found: from William Pearce, 24 April 1796. GW wrote Pearce on 1 May: "Your letter of the 24th Ulto has been received."

From Isaac Levan

Philada April 26th 1796

The Subscriber being willing to serve his Country humbly offereth himself as superintendant at one of the trading Posts to be establish'd in the Indian Country the inclos'd Recommendation is therefore respectfully submitted to his consideration.[1]

Isaac Levan

ALS, DLC:GW.

1. The enclosure has not been identified. Levan sought a position under "An Act for establishing Trading Houses with the Indian Tribes," approved 18 April (1 *Stat.* 452–53).

William Wilson wrote GW from Harrisburg, Pa., on 18 July: "The Memorial of William Wilson most respectfully sheweth

"That your Memoralist has for many years been in the Mercantile Line and being now fixed with his Family in the Back Settlements of Pennsylvania and desireous of an Industrious Active Life—Requests that your Execellency amongst your Appointments to Persons in Trust for the Trade between the United States and the Indian Nations, may be pleased to Commission your Memoralist, upon the Recommendations and Security to be offered to your Excellency's Satisfaction.

"That such an Appointment will be thankfully acknowledged and punctually attended to by your Memorialist" (ADS, DLC:GW). Below Wilson's signature, seven prominent citizens of Dauphin County, Pa., subscribed their names to a statement, which is in the same handwriting as Wilson's memorial: "We the Subscribers being well acquainted with William Wilson Esquire and Knowing him to be in the Mercantile Line of Buisiness for a Number of years past, holding now a Commission as a Magistrate beg leave to recommend him as a Confidential Person suitable and well qualified to Superintend one of the Public Stores in the Indian Trade."

Major Swiney wrote GW from Harrisburg on 28 July: "The memorial of Major Swiney Sheweth, that your Memorialist from long practice and intense observation, both of foreign and domestick trade, hath acquired a competent knowledge of both; and as it is judiciously appointed by Goverment, that

houses in different parts of the frontier of the Union should be stored with Merchandize suitable to the use of Indians. Your Memorialist conscious of the rectitude of his own intentions, and looking up with an humble degree of confidence to Your Excellency, would request an appointment to superintend one of these Stores; flattering himself by his assiduity, to promote the genuine intention contemplated by your Excellency in recommending those kind of publick warehouses, that after trial, your Memorialist would render to the publick as faithful, and as satisfactory accounts of the trust reposed in him, as those who may have a train of signatures to recommend them.

"Your Memorialist would further beg leave to observe that the support of a family chiefly consisting of boys, stimulates him in some measure to make this request, being possessed of an opinion that your Excellency may encourage the honest exertion of a man endeavouring to support and educate a family by industry: and however excentrick this application to some might appear without a long appendage of recommendation, which your Memorialist intentionally declines to exhibit, as he conceives it tacitly dictating to your Excellency, who ought, or ought not to be the proper objects of your choice in the above business. He will only add, that he is acquainted with the quality of Peltry & Fur; and should he through the philanthropy of your Excellency have an appointment of one of those Stores, he will for thaithful performance of the trust reposed in him, pledge to Your Excellency, his three sons, namely George Washington, Montgomery, and Franklin, all advanced in liturature as far as any of their respective age in the States, and he Your Memorialist; has sanguine hopes, that at a future period they will in some degree, emulate the ever memorable characters whose names they bear" (ALS, DLC:GW). Below Swiney's signature, John Andre Hanna and John Kean signed a statement: "We know Major Swiney, the above Memorialist, And think unreserved confidence may be placed in him." The oldest son, George Washington Swiney, was about thirteen years old.

Major Swiney (d. 1799) emigrated from Ireland to escape taxation sometime before 1792 (see Swiney to GW, 25 Oct. 1792). Apparently jailed for supporting the Whiskey Insurrection, he later moved from Harrisburg and drowned at Nescopeck Falls, Pa. (see *Claypoole's American Daily Advertiser* [Philadelphia], 21 June 1799, and Morgan, *Dauphin County*, 212).

For another aspirant, see John Lee to GW, 19 September.

From Edward Carrington

Dear Sir   Richmond April 27. 1796

The meeting of the people of this City & vicinity, of which I did myself the Honor to inform you a few days ago, as being in agitation,[1] took place the day before yesterday, the 25th Inst. and the enclosed paper of Davis of this date, contains the proceedings of the day, also a very correct statement of the manner in which they were conducted.[2] While I enjoy the satisfaction of being enabled to give you this evidence of the popular sentiment, expressed in a very numerous meeting, in opposition to the declaration of a thin one in the same place on a former occasion, I feel it incumbent on me, on the score of exhibiting the true complexion of our political situation to apprise you that the Enemies of the Treaty, or rather of Government, are putting in practice every art and effort to obtain subscriptions to a counteracting paper—as a sample of the means they descend to for the purpose of imposing on the people at a distance, I also enclose a paper of Dixon of yesterday (the 26th), in which, under the Richmond head, you will find a Representation of the proceedings of the day which exhibits, by the suppression of truth, a most absolute falshood.[3] The Resolutions annexed to his representation are those mentioned in Davis's paper as proposed by the opposers of the Treaty, and were eventually rejected by the adoption of that which they were offered in opposition to, yet, from the representation, it would appear that the one really carried by a considerable majority was not even listened in the meeting—corresponding committees you see are announced by that party, & there will doubtless be great activity on that side, while, unfortunately, as usual, great lassitude will prevail on the other. I trust & hope they will not succeed, but under such circumstances evil is certainly to be apprehended. there never was a crisis at which the activity of the Friends of Government was more urgently called for—some of us here have endeavoured to make this impression in different parts of the Country—the events of a few days will shew how successfully. I shall endeavor to give you as frequent & correct information as events shall enable me,[4] and have the Honor to be, with unfeigned attachment Dear Sir Your Most Obedt Humble servt

Ed. Carrington

P.S. the statement in Davis's Paper is I believe a little incorrect as to School Boys & apprentices Signing the Petition of the supporters of the Treaty—how it is on the other side I know not.

ALS, DLC:GW.

 1. See Carrington to GW, 22 April.

 2. Augustine Davis (c.1752–1825) printed *The Virginia Gazette, and General Advertiser* (Richmond). According to the account that paper published on

27 April, "a very numerous meeting of the inhabitants of the City of Richmond and its vicinity" approved "by a large majority" this resolution: "That the peace, happiness, and welfare, not less than the national honor of these United States depend, in a great degree, upon giving, with good faith, full effect, to the treaty lately negociated with Great-Britain."

The same newspaper reported that former Jay Treaty opponent Henry Banks presented the supportive resolution. "He observed that while the treaty was unratified, disliking some of its parts, he thought himself justifiable in opposing it, but after it had received all the constitutional sanctions of a law of the land, he conceived it to be a violation of national faith to defeat its operation, and from the present circumstances of affairs, he thought it the true interest of the nation that it should be carried into effect . . . The opponents made a proposition that no person should be permitted to sign the measures to be adopted but those qualified to vote for a Representative—it was observed by the other side that instructions should be signed by freeholders only, but that every citizen had a right to petition, and might with propriety sign it. These preliminaries being understood some amendments were proposed to the resolution, and other resolutions offered by the opposers to the treaty, but they barely ensued without the question being put upon them . . . the arguments were lengthy, and towards the conclusion warm, and some small disorder appeared in the meeting, but, upon a call of order it subsided . . . the question was put on the resolution proposed by Mr. Banks, and was carried by a majority I think of about five to three—It might be more or it might be less, but the majority was so evident that it was admitted."

The same newspaper then reported that the clerk had read a petition to the U.S. House of Representatives (also printed in the *Gazette*), but "the minority" interrupted the proceedings to announce that "they should lay a paper, containing their sentiments, upon the table, for the signature of those who chose to sign, and the other side might do the same—They also gave notice that they would open committees of correspondence. The meeting was now more numerous than I ever saw one at this place upon similar occasions—it consisted of inhabitants of the town, of the county, and most of the adjacent counties, and of strangers—After the votes were taken, many went off without signing on either side—but both sides of the question I have reason to believe, were signed by some of every description of citizens above, and by the young gentlemen students of law, school boys, apprentices, &c and many signatures were obtained on both sides out of doors after the meeting broke up." In consequence, Davis doubted "whether their numbers of subscribers be a fair criteria to judge of the sense of the meeting."

3. John Dixon (1768–1805), the son of Virginia printer John Dixon, Sr. (d. 1791), published a number of newspapers in Richmond between 1791 and 1799.

Dixon's newspaper at this time was the *Richmond Chronicle.* The 26 April 1796 issue included this item: "Yesterday, at the instance of some friends to the British Treaty, a Meeting, (on short notice) was held at the Capitol in this City, when a Resolution was proposed, expressing the wish of the People, that Congress would carry that Treaty into full effect, without any reservation as

to Constitutional impediments:—In opposition to that Resolution, the following were offered, and subscribed by a vast number of the Meeting, and are
now circulated thro' this City and county of Henrico, for the subscription of
all those who concur in the sentiments therein expressed, and who are willing to leave the Representatives of the People in Congress to the free exercise of their Rights, till they shall be explained or altered in a Constitutional
mode."

The same newspaper then printed three resolutions: "That no reason, as
yet presents itself to justify an apprehension that those Representatives will
abuse the confidence of their Constituents, or will be unmindful of the great
interests of their Country. . . . That when any difference may arise between the
co[-]ordinate departments of government respecting their several functions,
it is unsafe for the people to decide between them, except in those Constitutional modes, which combining a just representation of the people, with the
means of free enquiry and of full information, will be most likely to ensure
the Peace of our Country and the improvement of its Constitution. . . . That
it is not necessary or expedient, at this time, for the People of this District to
offer any Instructions to their Representatives in the Congress of the United
States, and that they do firmly rely, that he will heartily co-operate with the
Representatives of the good People of these States in Congress, to preserve
the sacred Principles of the Constitution, and to promote the best Interests of
our common Country."

4. See Carrington to GW, 9 May.

To George Lewis

Dear Sir,   Philadelphia 28th April 1796
Not knowing where to direct to your Brother Howell, I put my
letter to him, under cover to you—and leave it open for your
perusal. to be sealed before delivery.[1]

I have not the least knowledge of Mrs Dubarry—or the circumstance she relates—but, if her claim is just, I hope your
Brother has more honor than to keep her out of it.[2]

Your letter of the 19th has been duly received—I hope Mrs
Lewis's health is restored—My best wishes are offered for it in
which your Aunt joins[3] with Dear Sir Your Affecte Uncle
                                                Go: Washington

ALS, PHi: Dreer Collection.
1. GW's letter to Howell Lewis has not been found, but see notes 2 and 3,
below.
2. Anne Louise Beekman (1775–1802) married Louis (Lewis) Chodkewiez
(Chodkewicz) of Poland at New York in July 1793. After his death at Philadelphia in October of that year, she married in 1794 Jean (John) Marie DuBarry

(d. 1830), a merchant originally from France, but most recently from Saint Domingue.

Anne Louise DuBarry sought payment of a debt that Howell Lewis owed her first husband. She wrote GW from Philadelphia on 28 July: "the 13th of Last month I had the honour of writing to you. I Directed my Letter to you at Philadelphia not knowing you had Left that place and being yet without an answer I fear my Letter is Lost as Likewise the note of Mr Howell Lewis which I took the Liberty of encloseing to you. immediately upon the Receipt of the Letter you honourd me with dated the 15th of may I rote to Mr Lewis but not having Received any answer and not knowing of any oppertunity of passing his note to him except by addressing myself to you induced me again to trouble you wich Liberty I hope you will pardon if your honour will be so good as to favour me with a Line you will be pleased to Direct to No. 56 Lombart Street Phila." (ALS, DNA: RG 59, Miscellaneous Letters). DuBarry's letter to GW dated 13 June and the enclosed note have not been found. GW's letter to DuBarry dated 15 May also has not been found.

GW replied to DuBarry on 3 Aug.: "Your letter of the 28th of July came to my hands by the last Post. The other, which you allude to, was presented to me at Wilmington as I passed through that place, abt the middle of June. I did not answer it; for in truth I had not time; nor did I know where to direct a letter to you.

"As soon as I arrived at this place, I sent your letter (wch I received at Wilmington) to Mr. Howel Lewis, informing him that his note was in my hands; & that I would receive the money & transmit it to you. I have heard nothing from him since, but his Brother in Fredericksburgh (to whose care I sent the letter) wrote me, that Howell had gone (on a journey) into the upper Country.

"If I should receive the money on your note, before I leave this, it shall be paid to you when I return to Philadelphia; which will be by the first of September; If I should not, I shall return the note, and you must pursue legal measures to obtain payment as I can have no further Agency in the Business" (ALS, in private hands). GW's letter to Howell Lewis has not been found, but it probably was the one enclosed with his letter to George Lewis dated 27 June. The letter that George Lewis sent GW also has not been found.

GW then wrote Bartholomew Dandridge, Jr., from Mount Vernon on 5 Aug.: "The enclosed letter from a Mrs A. L. Dubarry (whom I never saw in my life) and one from Major George Lewis, will shew you what is to be done with the hundred Dollar note enclosed in the letter of the latter.

"By the continuance of the Mail that brought Major Lewis's letter to me I inform'd the above named Mrs Dubarry that I had wrote to Howell Lewis as soon as I got to Mount Vernon, but had heard nothing from him; that I should return his note to her, when I got back to Philadelphia; and that, she must have recourse to a Court of Justice; as I cd have no further Agency in the business.

"I request that you would immediately find her out (by the direction in her own letter); Shew her Major Lewis' letter; & take her receipt for the money you pay. Howell Lewis's note was given to a Mr Chodkewiez the former husband of Mrs Dubarry; it may be proper therefore, that some enquiry be made after her *present* one, at the time you pay the money; that caution may be observed.

But as she appears to be in distress, by her manner of writing, let there be no delay in the payment. The note of hand for this money is dated 21st of March 1793 and ought, in my opinion to have been discharged with interest; and so I shall write Major Lewis.

"Enclosed also, you will find another letter to me from One Wilhelm Louis Wernecke, with the answer (open) wch Mr Craik by my direction has given— Seal & contrive it to him, if you can find where he lives" (ALS, ViHi: Robert Traylor Papers).

Dandridge replied to GW from Philadelphia on 10 Aug.: "Your letter of the 5 inst: with its enclosures was received yesterday forenoon. Agreeably to your direction I waited on Mrs Dubarry in the afternoon, shewed her Major Lewis' letter, and paid her the $100 which it covered, as you will see by her rect now enclosed. I thought it best (& she did not object to it) to take her rect in full— the Interest, if Mr Lewis thinks proper to allow it, can be paid her notwithstanding. Her present husband M. Dubarry was with her during my visit—he is a man of genteel appearance. I also found the lodgings of Mr Wernecke, & was informed by the lady of the house that he had gone to Virginia a few days ago, to look after the Estate which he has been in pursuit of. I retain the letter for him therefore, supposing it of no consequence that he should have it" (ALS, DLC:GW; see also Wilhelm Louis Wernecke to GW, 24 July, and notes 3 and 4 to that document). Dandridge enclosed a copy of the receipt given Anne DuBarry on 9 Aug.: "Received of Mr Howell Lewis of Virginia, through the hands of B. Dandridge one hundred Dollars; being in full discharge of a note of hand dated the 21st of March 1793 given by said Lewis to my former husband Mr Chodkewiez" (DLC:GW).

3. George Lewis replied to GW from Fredericksburg, Va., on 4 May: "The last post brought me your letter of the 28th of last month, covering one with other papers to my Brother Howell, which I delivered. he express'd much concern that you should have been applyed to on the buisness contained and conceived it to be a rude attempt, to exact from you money which they might have had, and has ever been ready provided a proper application had been made for it, I think he observed, that he had passed a note or bond for the money which he wished to have got, before he would pay any order, that the note was originally given to some man who had transfered it to others, that by paying the money without getting his note, he might be placed in a disagreable situation, however he is determin'd to forward the money immediately, by some person going to Philadelphia.

"Mrs Lewis is returned to town, but still in bad health, we shall leave this so soon as our district court terminates (which is now setting) for Mr Carters in Culpeper county, in hopes that the ride and change of air will contribute in restoreing her to health again—she joins me in love and best wishes to my Aunt" (ALS, ViMtvL).

George Lewis subsequently wrote GW from Fredericksburg on 1 Aug.: "The inclos'd bill of one hundred dollars was sent me yesterday by my Brother Howell, with a request that I should forward it to you, He is much concerned that you should have been so troubled in this buisness—Your letter informing him, of his note being in your possession; did not reach him in Culpeper untill some few dayes since, otherwise he observes, the money should have been forwarded without delay.

"Please tender my love to my Aunt" (ALS, ViMtvL). GW's letter to Howell Lewis has not been found, but the note almost certainly was the one that Anne DuBarry sent GW (see n.2 above).

George Lewis again wrote GW from Fredericksburg on 7 Aug.: "Last evenings post brought me your letter acknowledging the receipt of my letter of the first instant with a bank note of one hundred dollars on Acct of my Brother Howell—his absence prevents my saying any thing with respect to the interest, which he certainly ought to have consider'd when he forwarded the principal, he is at present over the ridge with his family. by the first opportunity, I shall make acquainted with the contents of your last letter.

"Mrs Lewis unites in best wishes to you and My Aunt" (ALS, ViMtvL; the cover of this letter is marked "Free" and "Dumfries 10th August"). GW's letter to George Lewis has not been found.

To the United States Senate

Gentlemen of the Senate   United States April 28th 1796

I nominate Thomas Nelson to be Attorney for the United States in the District of Virginia,[1] vice Alexander Campbell, who has resigned that Office.

G: Washington

LB, DLC:GW.

1. The Senate ordered that Thomas Nelson's nomination "lie for consideration" on this date before consenting on 29 April (*Senate Executive* Journal, 205–6). He served as federal district attorney for Virginia until his death in 1803.

To Tobias Lear

My dear Sir   Philadelphia 29th April 1796

Yesterday's Post brought me the letters which had arrived in the Commerce, Captn Tuttell; enclosing Invoice and Bill of lading for the long expected Seeds (which by the bye have cost me at least four times as much as I expected).[1]

The Invoice and Bill of lading are now sent to you, lest from the want of them, any difficulty or delay should arise on account of the duties[2] and they are accompanied with an earnest request that the packages may be forwarded to Mr Pearce with as little delay as possible the season for sowing the Peas and Succory being already far advanced. The Winter vetch cannot be sown before Autumn.

If you incline to try some of these Seeds at your farm you are very welcome to part of each sort.[3] When the purposes for which Mr Murrays letter, Invoice & Bill of lading are sent, are answered be so good as to return them to Dear Sir Your Affectionate Sert

Go: Washington

P.S. If the Seeds should, before the arrival of this letter, have been sent to Mount Vernon, I pray you to contrive the one[4] by some safe conveyance to Mr Pearce. And Washington request you will send the letter he has written to his Sister Peter. It relates to their Carriage & some other matters entrusted to his enquiries.[5]

ALS, ViMtvL: Storer-Decatur Collection; ADfS, owned (1970) by CCamarSJ; LB, DLC:GW. Lear docketed the ALS as received on 4 May. The draft and letter-book copy do not include the last two sentences of the postscript.

1. The enclosures evidently included James Maury's letter to GW dated 26 Dec. 1795. *The Columbian Mirror and Alexandria Gazette* (Va.) for 28 April 1796 reported the arrival at Alexandria of the brig *Commerce* from Liverpool, England.

2. An entry under 15 May in Lear's account with GW in General Ledger C records a cash payment of 11 pounds and 10 shillings "for freight of 4 Bags & 1 Cask from Liverpool in the Brigantine Commerce."

3. George Augustine Washington had established at GW's urging what became known as "Walnut Tree Farm," a 360-acre tract on Clifton's Neck at the northeast corner of River farm (see GW to George Augustine Washington, 25 Oct. 1786, in *Papers, Confederation Series*, 4:307–10). After Lear married Frances "Fanny" Bassett Washington, George Augustine Washington's widow, GW arranged a life lease of the farm to the couple, dated 21 Sept. 1795 (DS, owned [1996] by John H. Freund, Armonk, N.Y.).

4. GW wrote "this letter" instead of "the one" on his draft, almost certainly referring to the letter (not found) that he wrote William Pearce on this date.

5. The letter from George Washington Parke Custis to Martha Parke Custis Peter has not been identified.

Letter not found: to William Pearce, 29 April 1796. GW wrote Pearce on Sunday, 1 May: "I wrote you on friday last."

From Andrew Parks

Sir   Baltimore 30th April 1796

I have had the honour to receive your Letter of the 7th Instt, and pursuant thereto, I have communicated within a few days, that I have been here; the Subject, to my friend Mr McElderry, on which I am so materially interested, for your approbation; he has written to the Secretary at War, and given him an oppinion of me, of which, I presume you have, or will, be advertis'd.[1] Mr McElderry, has relinquished his part of the concern, in the business, I have been pursuing, which I shall conduct hereafter on my own Acct, and with industry, and his friendship, I expect will be attended with considerable advantages; this is the only amendment in my prospects, I have it in my power to acquaint you with.[2]

I hope I possess most of the requisites, necessary to make your Niece, happy; I have been for several Years, accustomed to Business, which has, I am persuaded, kept me clear of a temper, for vicious dispositions; my connexions, are respectable generally, inasmuch as they are people of Business, and mostly in good circumstances. I have described to your Niece, as nearly as I could, what my Situation would afford, in the style of living; which wd not be more than genteel, and comfortable, this she sais, will perfectly satisfy her, and render her happy, provided you can think it sufficient. I am Sir with infinite respect Yr very Hbl. Sert

Andrew Parks

ALS, MH: Jared Sparks Collection.

1. Thomas McElderry wrote James McHenry on 11 April: "I received your favour of the 6th Mentioning Andw Parks's request to the President, it is the first I have heard of his having such intentions As to his character and Sircumstance I will briefly state them to you, On the failure of his Father in the year 92 being rendered unable to do any thing for his son I took him into Partnership and established him in Business at Fredericksburg and from what I have heard as well as from my own observation he has conducted himself in a verry proper manner and has gaind the esteem of the People generaly, his engaging in Business for himself before he was Nineteen years of age, and conducting it with so much propriety and reputation, induces me to believe he will make a good Husband, much more promising than many of the Virginian Gen[t]lemen with their large Landed Estate and Negroes, He commenced Business in June 92 and on the 16th of September 93 I went to Fredericksburg and took an acct. of his goods when it appear'd he had clear'd 1106£.10s.0 after paying all expences and verry little outstanding debts for his plan is to sell for ready money, since which he has been doing a good Business but I have been so ongaged here that I could not spare time to take an acct. of his stock nor has it been done to my knowledge since so that I cannot explain exactly what he may be worth at this time.

"You will perceive by what I have already done for Mr Parks my Desire of serving him, whether the match contemplated may be a prudent one for him I can not pretend to judge or advise you know I am not much a friend to great Parade or extravagant manner of Life if his Connection would have that tendancy (which I hope Not) it might not be so happy—He is to be here in a few days to lay in his spring supply of goods I know of no other arrangement he has in contemplation at present It will however give me great Pleasure if I can assist him farther on his changing his state, it is probable the young Lady may have something also which could be beneficialy employed by him as I would not whish him to divide the Profit with me when his capitol is equal to do Business by himself which I trust will soon be the case" (MH: Jared Sparks Collection).

2. The *Federal Gazette & Baltimore Daily Advertiser* for 24 May 1796 printed a notice from McElderry and Parks: "THE Partnership which has subsisted between the subscribers at Fredericksburg, Virginia, under the firm of Andrew Parks and Co. was dissolved on the 2d Instant, by mutual consent."

From Thomas Marshall

Sir   [c.April 1796]

I received yours of the 6th of Feby with a duplicate of your other of the 2d of Jany last. The latter I had previously received. If age & infirmaty will not be a sufficient excuse for my not sooner acknowledgeing that honor, I fear I must remain culpable for really I have no better to offer. For tho' I am not more than one year older than you are I am much farther gone than my wishes lead me to hope you are.

Major Lewis will be much more proper to confide the sale of your rough Creek lands to than myself, as he will be on the spot. I have not been able to procure more particular information respecting the quallity of that land than I formerly wrote you,[1] tho' I expect it every day, as a Gentleman who has it in his power has promis'd me to make the necessary enquiry & inform me.

I now can only say that settlements in that quarter encrease rapidly and consiquently the price of Lands increase in the same proportion. Lands of the first quallity in this part of the country are now selling (unimproved) from 40/ to £3 pr Acre & I see no good reason why lands of the same quality may not rise to an equal price there as here when the settlement is equally full.

I thank you for the kind notice you take in your PostScript of having seen my son John & am happy to hear of his being well.

I now send your terms of sale to one of the Lexington Printers & have ordered a publication of them agreable to your directions.[2] Give me leave to assure you Sir that it is with the greatest pleasure I shal⟨l⟩ recieve & execute any future request with

whic⟨h⟩ you may think proper to honor me. I have the honor
to be with the most respectfu⟨l⟩ esteem Sir Your most obedient
servant

T. Marshall

ALS, DLC:GW. GW endorsed this letter as received on 30 April 1796.
   1. See Marshall to GW, 12 Aug. 1795.
   2. GW's advertisement of his western lands, dated 1 Feb. 1796, appeared
in the *Kentucky Gazette* (Lexington) for 23 April (extra) and 14 May.

To Edward Carrington

(Private)
Dear Sir,   Philadelphia 1st May 1796.
   With much pleasure I received your letter of the 22d ulto; and
if the sense of the great body of Citizens in Virginia should be
expressed in the manner you seem to expect, it would give me,
and I believe I might add every friend to order and good government throughout the United States, very great satisfaction: More
so than similar sentiments from any other State in the Union;
for people living at a distance from it know not how to believe
it possible, that its Representatives both in the General & State
Legislatures can speak a language which is repugnant to th⟨e⟩
Sense of their Constituents; especially too, as they seem to give
the tone to all the States south of them.
   Whatever my own opinion may be on this, or any other subject, interesting to the Community at large, it always has been,
and will continue to be, my earnest desire to learn, and to comply, as far as is consistent, with the public sentiment; but it is on
great occasions *only*, and after time has been given for cool and
deliberate reflection, that the *real* voice of the people can be
known.
   The present, however, is one of those *great* occasions; than
which, none more important has occurred, or probably may
occur again, to call forth their decision. And to them the appeal is now made. For no candid man, in the least degree acquainted with the progress of this business, will believe for a
moment, that the *ostensible* dispute, was about papers[1]—or that
the British Treaty was a *good* one, or a *bad* one; but whether there
should be a Treaty at all without the concurrence of the house
of Representatives: which was striking at once, & boldly too, at

the fundamental principles of the Constitution; and if it were established, would render the Treaty making Power not only a nullity, but such an absolute absurdity, as to reflect disgrace on the framers of it: for can any one suppose, that they who framed, or those who adopted that Instrument, ever intended to give the power to the President & Senate to make Treaties (and declaring that when made & ratified, they should be the Supreme law of the land)[2] and in the same breath place it in the powers of the house of Representatives to fix their Veto on them? unless apparent marks of fraud or corruption (which in equity would set aside any contract) accompanied the measure, or such striking evidence of National injury attended their adoption as to make War, or any other evil preferable. Every unbiassed Mind will answer in the Negative.[3]

Whence the source, and what the object of all this struggle is, I submit to my fellow citizens. Charity would lead one to hope that the motives to it have been pure. Suspicions, however, speak a different language—and my tongue, for the present, shall be silent. Such further information on this head (or any other similarly important) which may come to your knowledge—and your leisure and inclination may enable you to give—will be very acceptable[4] to Dear Sir Your Obedt & Obliged Servt

Go: Washington

ALS, ViMtvL; ALS (letterpress copy), DLC:GW; LB, DLC:GW.

1. GW is referring to the House resolution adopted on 24 March requesting papers about the Jay Treaty (see GW to the Cabinet, 25 March, n.1). GW denied the request in his message to the U.S. House of Representatives, 30 March.

2. The power to make treaties is stated in Article II, section 2, of the Constitution. Treaties are declared supreme law in Article VI.

3. GW reiterated these points in his letter to Charles Carroll of Carrollton on this date.

4. Carrington replied to GW on 9 May.

To Charles Carroll of Carrollton

(Private)

Dear Sir,　　　　　　　　　　Philadelphia 1st May 1796.

Your favor of the 23d Ultimo has been duly received. With respect to the application of Mr Freeman, I shall do, as I always have done on similar occasions, and what I am sure you will approve of—namely to lay the recommendations of applicants by, until the hour comes when nominations are to be made; and then, after reference to them, and an attention to other circumstances (which is often essential) prefer those who seem to have the greatest fitness for the Office.

Accompanying the information of the Election of Mr Sprigg, and the Instructions with which he was charged, you propound several interesting questions; such as I am persuaded your own good sense, after a resort to the debates on the important points which have been discussed, will leave you at no loss to solve: Few, however, I believe, acquainted with the proceedings in the Ho. of Representatives, conceive that the *real* question was, whether the Treaty with G: Britain was a *good* or a *bad* one; but whether there should be a *Treaty at all* without the concurrence of that house;[1] and taking advantage of the partialities in favour of one Nation and of the prejudices against that of another with the aid of such unfavorable interpretations as they were disposed to give to some parts of the Treaty it was conceived that, no occasion more suitable, might ever occur to establish the principle & enlarge the powers they aimed at. On this ground therefore it was resolved to attempt, at *every* hazard, to render the Treaty making power a Nullity without their consent: nay worse to make it an absolute absurdity; Such as could not fail to reflect disgrace upon the understanding, & wisdom of those who framed, but on those also who adopted the Constitution, from the inconsistency of giving a Power to the President & Senate to make Treaties (and when made and ratified, declaring them to be the Supreme law of the land)[2] and in the same instrument to vest a power in the house of Representatives: to fix their veto[3] upon it unless bribery and fraud was apparent in the transaction (which in equity wd annul any contract) or ruin was so self evident as to make war, or any evil, preferable to the execution.

With respect to the *motives* wch have led to these measures, and which have not only brought the Constitution to the brink of a precipice, but the Peace, happiness & prosperity of the country into eminent danger, I shall say nothing—Charity tells us, they ought to be good. but suspicions say they must be bad. At present, my tongue shall be silent.[4]

Every true friend to this Country must *see*, and *feel*, that the

policy of it is not to embroil ourselves with any Nation whatsoever; but to avoid their disputes & their politics; and if they will
harrass one another, to avail ourselves of the Neutral conduct
we have adopted.[5] Twenty years peace, with such an increase of
population and resources as we have a right to expect; added to
our remote situation from the jarring powers, will in all probability enable us, in a just cause to bid defiance to any power
on earth. Why then should we—prematurely embar⟨k⟩[6] (for the
attainment of trifles comparatively speaking) in hostilities—the
issue of which is *never* certain—always expensive—& beneficial
to a few only (the least deserving perhaps) whilst it must be distressing & ruinous to the great mass of our Citizens. But enough
of this—the people must decide for themselves and probably
will do so, notwithstanding the vote has gone in favor of the appropriations by a majority of 51. to 48 as the *principle* and *assumption of power* which has been contended for remain although the
consequences by the *present* decision probably will be avoided.
With esteem & regard I am—Dear Sir Your most Obedt Se⟨r.⟩

Go: Washington

ALS (letterpress copy), ViMtvL; LB, DLC:GW.
    1. For the Jay Treaty debate in the U.S. House of Representatives, see *Annals
of Congress*, 4th Cong., 1st sess., 426–783.
    2. See Article II, section 2, and Article VI of the Constitution.
    3. This word is "vote" in the letter-book copy.
    4. GW expressed similar thoughts in his letter to Edward Carrington on
this date.
    5. See Neutrality Proclamation, 22 April 1793.
    6. GW wrote over the letterpress in several places, apparently to clarify faded
or blurred text. At this place, "embark" appears to have been the original
word, but GW's rewriting is not clear. The word is rendered as "embarrass" in
the letter-book copy.

From Joseph de Maisonneuve

Romain motier Canton of Berne[1]
mr President,   in Switzerland 1st May 1796
    M. The Grand Master of Malta, my sovereign, ⟨or⟩ders me to
transmit the inclosed Letter to your Excellency.[2]
    In fulfilling this duty, I venture mr President to renew the re-
spectful solicitations which I have already had the honor of presenting to you in order to obtain from your goodness the favor

which the Grand master of malta has been pleased to request for me.[3] I am, with the most profound respect Your Excellency's most obt & very humble servt

The Commander of Maisonneuve

Translation, DNA: RG 59, Miscellaneous Letters; ALS, in French, DNA: RG 59, Miscellaneous Letters.

1. Romainmôtier (now Romainmôtier-Envy) is a village in the Swiss Canton of Vaud, which was in 1796 part of the Canton of Berne.

2. François Marie-des-Neiges Emmanuel de Rohan-Polduc (1725–1797) served as grand master of Malta from 1775 until 1797.

Maisonneuve enclosed a letter from Rohan-Polduc to GW dated 25 Feb. 1796. As translated by George Taylor, Jr., of the State Department, that letter reads: "I have observed by the dispatches written to me by the Commander of Maisonneuve, that your Excellency appeared impressed with the assurances which I charged him to give you of my dispositions and wishes to establish between the government of the United States and my Order, when circumstances should permit, relations of reciprocal friendship and utility, founded on a treaty of alliance in which the political and commercial Interests of the two Powers should be respectively fixed and guaranteed.

"I had also already occupied myself on this subject by the ministry of my chargé d'affaires in france, who on my part, made overtures to Mr Monroe Minister Plenipotentiary of the United States at Paris. I had on the other hand engaged M. le chevr de Tousard who has the honor of being personally known to your Excellency, to open this matter to you; but important considerations Sir which will not have escaped your sagacity, have intervened to the suspension of all negotiation in this respect, until a general peace, shall have succeeded to the war now afflicting and desolating Europe. It will therefore be at that epoch, and after the signature of the Treaty of alliance to be made between the United States and my order, that I shall with pleasure see your Excellency name for your minister or Consul near me, the Commander of Maisonneuve who earnestly desires that place and who appears to me in every respect worthy of the Confidence with which you may be pleased to honor him. I shall at the same time fix my choice upon the member of my order who will be charged to go and reside near your Excellency and the Congress over whom you preside with so much wisdom.

"I pray you to believe that my eagerness, for an establishment, so interesting as the one in question to the security and prosperity of the commerce of the United States in the mediterranean, is as unlimited as the high consideration and distinguished sentiments—with which I am, sir, Your Excellency's Most affectionate friend & servant" (translation, filed at 25 Feb., and ALS, in French, filed at 1 May, DNA: RG 59, Miscellaneous Letters). GW replied to Rohan on 18 Feb. 1797 (DNA: RG 59, Credences; see also Timothy Pickering to GW, 19 Feb. 1797, in DNA: RG 59, Miscellaneous Letters).

3. Maisonneuve's previous letters to GW have not been found, but for their subject, see Pickering's second letter to GW dated 28 Sept. 1795 and notes 3 and 4.

To William Pearce

Mr Pearce, Philadelphia May 1st 1796.

Your letter of the 24th Ulto has been received,[1] and I am sorry to find by it that the drought still continued with you. On this day week there was a very good rain here, and on wednesday following[2] a great deal fell; but the weather has been windy, cold and disagreeable ever since—notwithstanding which, the Grain and grass in these parts look extremely well.

I am glad to find that you were, at the date of your letter, so near the completion of Corn-planting; and hope, if you have had the late rains, that it will have come up well, for I think this happens best when it is planted dry, & rains come after.

I wrote you on friday last (and put the letter under cover to Mr Lear) informing you, that the Seeds were arrived at last; at George Town:[3] and expressing an earnest wish that the Peas & Chiccory might be got into the ground as soon as possible and that the Peas, as they were of two distinct sorts—might be seperately, and distinctly sown. I wished also, that the Chiccory might be sown as convenient to the Stables at the different farms, as fit ground could be obtained; as it was designed to be cut and fed green to the work horses. The Winter vetch must be carefully preserved till autumn, as that is the season for sowing it.

I am sorry to find that flour continues to depreciate in price; but the present cause for this is, the dispute in the House of Representatives respecting the provisions for carry the British Treaty into effect; which has, for sometime past, occasioned a suspension in purchasing, shipping, & the Insurance of all sorts of property: but as the discussion is now brought to a close, it is to be hoped, and expected, that matters will recover their former tone again. At any rate, I will risque there getting worse, rather than take the present Alexandria price for my flour: but I repeat what I have said in former letters, that I will take 15 dollars, at 6 months credit.[4]

By a letter which I received from Mr Robt Lewis (dated in Alexandria, the 21st of last month) he informs me that he had left for, and on my acct, in the hands of Messrs Bennett & Watts, of that place, the Sum of Forty pounds; which it would be proper you should receive, and place it with the sum he paid into your own hands.[5]

I am surprized to find by the Reports so few calves produced from my stock. Does it proceed from indifferent Bulls, or the Want of them. Be it either, or from any other cause, a remedy should be applied. and I wish the same with respect to the Rams, as the number of my Lambs are not equal to what they formerly were.

I would have you again stir up the pride of Cyrus; that he may be the fitter for my purposes against I come home; sometime before which (that is as soon as I shall be able to fix on the time) I will direct him to be taken into the house, and clothes to be made for him. In the meanwhile, get him a strong horn comb and direct him to keep his head well combed, that the hair, or wool may grow long.[6] I wish you well and am Your friend

Go: Washington

P.S. By a Vessel which says she will sail from hence to Alexa. on Wednesday next,[7] I shall send two dozn Windsor Chairs which the Captn has promised to land as he passes Mount Vernon. Let them be put in the New Room.[8]

ALS, ViMtvL.

1. Pearce's letter to GW dated 24 April has not been found.

2. That Wednesday was 27 April.

3. GW's letter to Pearce written on 29 April, evidently enclosed with his letter to Tobias Lear of that date, has not been found. GW had written James Maury on 20 Oct. 1795 about sending these seeds from Liverpool, England.

4. See GW to Pearce, 10 and 17 April 1796.

5. See Pearce to GW, 17 April, n.1.

6. GW intended the slave Cyrus to become "a waiting man" (see GW to Pearce, 13 Dec. 1795).

7. That date was 4 May.

8. GW purchased "24 Ovel Back Chairs" from Gilbert and Robert Gaw of Philadelphia and recorded a payment of $44 in an entry for 14 May 1796 in his household accounts. Most of the chairs were destined for use on the piazza at Mount Vernon.

Letter not found: from William Pearce, 1 May 1796. GW wrote Pearce on 8 May: "I am glad to find by your letter of the first instant, that the rain wch fell here on the 27th Ulto had extended to you."

From James McHenry

Sir.   War office 2 May 1796.

I have the honour to submit several letters & papers from the Governor of the State of New-York for your information and further directions.[1]

As the Government of the State of New-York is desirous that a treaty should be authorised to be held with certain chiefs of the Cohnawagas or seven nations of Canada, now at New York, for the purpose of enabling the State to purchase from them a right or claim which they set up to a parcel of land laying within its limits.[2]

And as the extinguishment of the said claim may tend to preserve a good understanding between these Indians and the United States; and be necessary to the safety and quiet of those persons who have settled or may settle upon the land in question, under the authority of New-York, the desire of the State would seem reasonable and proper.

Should you consider the application in this point of view, I submit the following draught of a message to the Senate for the attainment of its object.[3] With the utmost respect, I have the honour to be, Sir, Your most ob. & hble St

James McHenry
Secy of war

ALS, DLC:GW; LB, DLC:GW.

1. The enclosures probably included the letters from New York governor John Jay to McHenry dated 13, 22, and 28 April (N: Governor's letterbook). Jay wrote from New York on 13 April to ask that GW appoint a commissioner to treat with the Indians concerning a land claim involving the state. He suggested Abraham Ogden or Elisha Boudinot because of their availability and noted: "We are anxious to avoid delay for as these Chiefs are now here, it is very desireable that so good an opportunity of treating with them may not be lost." In the other two letters, Jay discussed the Indian delegation's credentials and a misplaced letter of authority purportedly left with GW (probably referring to the letter from the Seven Nations chiefs to GW of 4 Feb.). Jay wrote on 28 April: "If the President is content to proceed, I am—if he should hesitate, the Interpreter and One of the Chiefs will return and obtain a New Instrument—but this will consume much time, and they are very impatient to finish their Business and go Home in order to attend and assist at Some Great Council Fire soon to be held." Jay added that Jeremiah Wadsworth would be an excellent commissioner.

2. Wadsworth had spoken to members of the Seven Nations during treaty negotiations at Fort George, N.Y., in September 1795 and described the claimed land as beginning at a creek called Thaenlawgeontale on the south side of the Saint Lawrence River, "about Ten miles below Buck Island and Supposed to be the Northern Boundary of the Lands ceded by the Oneidas and thence by a direct Line to the nearest Branch of Hudsons River—Thence down that River to the Shortest distance from the Half way Brook between Fort George and Fort Edward. Thence to the Half way Brook—Thence down the Half way Brook and Wood Creek to Lake Champlain—Thence Thro Lake Champlain to the Boundary Line between the United States and the King of Great Britain—Thence along the said Boundary Line to the River St Lawrence—and Thence Up the River St Lawrence to the place of Begining" (CtHi: Jeremiah Wadsworth Papers).

3. GW wrote the Senate on this date: "Sometime last year Jeremiah Wadsworth was authorized to hold a treaty with the Cohnawaga Indians, stiling themselves the seven Nations of Canada, to enable the State of NewYork to extinguish by purchase a claim which the said Indians had set up to a parcel of land lying within that State. This negociation having issued without effecting its object; and the State of NewYork having requested a renewal of the negociation; and the Indians having come forward with an application on the same subject, I now nominate Jeremiah Wadsworth to be a Commissioner to hold a treaty with the Cohnawaga Indians, stiling themselves the Seven Nations of Canada for the purpose of enabling the State of NewYork to extinguish the aforesaid Claim" (LS, DNA: RG 46, entry 52; copy, DLC:GW). The enclosed draft has not been identified, but GW may have signed the draft document to create the LS, which is in the handwriting of War Department clerk Nathan Jones. The Senate received this message on 3 May and ordered that it "lie for consideration" before approving Wadsworth's nomination on 4 May (*Senate Executive Journal*, 206).

GW then wrote McHenry on Thursday, 5 May, at 1:00 P.M.: "Having but this moment returned from a ride, I could not hand the enclosed to you sooner. As an expression therein stood, it might have embarrassed the Commissioner. What the Indians might deem a *good* price, & be well content to receive, he might judge inadequate; and thereby, so tied down, might mar the Negociation. To see that the business is conducted *fairly*, and with candour is enough" (ALS, PHi: Etting Collection). GW apparently returned a draft of the instructions to Wadsworth as commissioner to negotiate with the Caughnawaga Indians. McHenry sent final instructions to Wadsworth on this date that authorized him "to hold a treaty with the said Indians, their deputies or Chiefs, at sch time and place within the State of NewYork, as may be fixed on by the Governor of the said State.

"The sole object of this treaty is to enable the State of NewYork to extinguish by purchase the right to the land in question; you will take care therefore, that the negociation for this purpose, between the Agents of the State of NewYork, and the said Indians or their Deputies, be conducted with such candour and fairness as to preclude all reasonable ground of complaint hereafter on the part of those Indians. The compensation and all expences connected with the Treaty, are to be paid and satisfied by the State of NewYork" (CtHi: Jeremiah Wadsworth Papers; see also GW to the U.S. Senate, 17 May).

From the Batavian Republic

[The Hague, 3 May 1796]
To the President of the United States of America.

Since we have deemed it prudent for our service to recall the Citizen Peter Francis Van Berckel heretofore Resident with the United States of America, it has been our first care to choose a proper person to transact & execute our Business with you, and for which we could not appoint a more fit person than the Citizen R. G. Van Polanen, in whose qualifications for representing the same character with the U.S. of America we place the fullest confidence.[1] We hope that you will be satisfied with him, especially as he will renew the assurances of the high esteem we feel for you and for the United States of America—and of our wish and desire to cultivate a close friendship and correspondence with you for the reciprocal benefit of our respective Governments.

We pray you will give the Citizen Van Polanen a favorable Audience, and give full credence to all his transactions done for us and in our name, as though done by ourselves. In which we shall think ourselves much obliged, and we shall endeavour to shew by every oppy how much we are inclined to render you and the United States every desirable service. With which we conclude, recommending you to the protection of Almighty God.

Done at the Hague the 3rd May 1796 the second year of Batavian Liberty &c.

(signed) D. C. De Leeuw ⟨Sc.⟩
Ter ordonnantie van Dezelve
F. v. Leyden[2]

Translation, DNA: RG 59, Communications from heads of foreign states, ceremonial letters; ALS, in Dutch, DNA: RG 59, Communications from heads of foreign states, ceremonial letters.

1. Roger Gerard Van Polanen (1757–1833) served as minister until recalled in 1802. For his official reception, see Timothy Pickering to GW, 29 Aug. 1796; see also Pickering's second letter to GW, 21 July, n.3.

2. Daniel Cornelis de Leeuw (1747–1834), of Utrecht, was president of the

National Assembly from 2 to 17 May 1796. The Dutch phrase could be translated as "by ordinance of him." The translator, not surprisingly, did not know what to make of the second signature and just tried to draw what it looked like.

Frédéric Auguste van Leyden (1768–1821) was secretary of the Committee of Foreign Affairs of the National Assembly.

From Alexander Hamilton

Sir   [New York] May 5. 179[6]

The letter of which the inclosed is a copy contains such extraordinary matter that I could not hesitate to send it to you. The writer is Mr G—— M——. I trust the information it conveys cannot be true; yet in these wild times every thing is possible: Your official information may serve as a comment.[1] very respectfully & affectly I have the honor to be Sir Yr Obed. Ser.

A. Hamilton

ALS, DLC:GW; copy, DLC: Hamilton Papers. Both the ALS and copy are dated 1795, but the enclosure establishes the correct date as 1796.

Hamilton transmitted this letter and its enclosure to Rufus King with a letter written on this date: "After reading seal & hand on the inclosed. If such things are to be you cannot leave the Senate. *Jay* is against it at all events till the European storm is over. We must all think well of this business" (*Hamilton Papers*, 20:160–61).

1. GW replied to Hamilton on 8 May.

Enclosure
Gouverneur Morris to Alexander Hamilton

My Dear Hamilton   London March 4. 1796

I have just now written to the President to communicate some Intelligence lately received from Paris.[1] This I have done in abstract but my correspondent has written to me as follows "The Government here are highly displeased with ours. You may easily guess the Reason. It is come to a very serious pitch. A fleet is to be sent to our shore with a new minister. A definitive answer must be given in 15 days. The Government are to declare to us within a few days that our Treaty with them is annulled.[2] This will put Mr Monroe in a cruel Dilemma—He is already much displeased and a war will probably be the consequence. The British will be glad of this. Perhaps we may have here a Revolution from the Industry of the Jacobins. The Finances are worse than ever. They cannot stand much longer." This letter is dated in Paris the 15th of last month. You may be sure by my communicating it to you that I have confidence in the source.

I have barely stated to the President the intention as to a new Minister.[3] To you I will declare my conviction that this Government cannot stand whether the Monarchy be restored or not.[4] The adherents to the Royal Cause grow dayly more numerous. If I knew decidedly the steps to be taken in aid of them I could tell you almost with certainty whether they would be successful. For the state of that Country now presents sufficient data on which to reason soundly. I need not say to you that if the French Rulers persist in the measures which are abovementioned America will probably be obliged to take part in the War. On a former occasion when they talked somewhat highly, I told them that they would certainly force us into the contest but as certainly it would be against them, let the predilections in their favour be ever so great, because it would be madness in us to risk our Commerce against the Navy of the world. That to join them would do them no good and would do us much evil. *That* time they believed me. What representations Mr Monroe may make, I cannot pretend to divine & much less the effect of them. Supposing however that you should be *driven* to make this election you will naturally weigh not only the naval force but also the financial resources of the opposed powers. The noisy folks with you will undoubtedly be loud on our obligations to France and on the long list of our grievances from England. As to the former I think we should always seek to perform acts of kindness towards those who at the bidding of their Prince stept forward to fight our battles.[5] But would it be kind to support that power which now tyrannizes over France and reduces her inhabitants to unheard of misery? Would it be grateful to mix with—much less to league with those whose hands are yet red with the blood of him who was our real protector? Would it be decent? As to the conduct of Britain towards us, although I see as clearly as others the grounds which we have to complain and can readily account for the resentments which have been excited, yet I give due weight to the causes by which that conduct was instigated— And while in some cases I find it unjustifiable, I cannot consider it as in all cases inexcusable. Provided therefore that our honor be saved, I am so far from thinking that the injuries we have endured should become the source of inextinguishable hatred and perpetual war that I would seek in future good offices the fair motive for consigning them to oblivion.

I have not my Dear Hamilton any such view of our present political machinery as to judge what may be the effect of lofty menace.[6] It is possible after all that the demand may turn on a single pivot that we shall no longer pretend to claim an exemption from seizure for those goods of an enemy[7] which may be found in our ships. If so the case is plain and easy. We slide back to the law of Nations which it is our interest to preserve unimpeached. Probably we shall be called upon for our guarantee of St Domingo[8] & here many curious questions will arise—in the course of which we shall see perhaps some very strange things.[9] It appears certain to me that the French Directory would not risk high language to us, if they had not received previous assurances that the people would force our Government to sacrifice the national interest. Those assurances were I presume given and the present plan proposed while victory seemed yet bound to the French standards, and while you received *official* assurances of the prosperous state of their internal affairs. The scene is now not only changed but almost reversed, & I presume that the language if not the conduct of certain persons will experience a similar change. Adieu &c.

Copy, in Hamilton's writing, DLC:GW. Hamilton made significant cuts to the copy enclosed to GW. See the notes below for comparisons with an incomplete copy in DLC: Hamilton Papers and a letter-book copy in DLC: Gouverneur Morris Papers.

1. See Morris to GW, this date.

2. The correspondent is referring to the Treaty of Amity and Commerce between the United States and France of 6 Feb. 1778.

3. The other copies continue: "His late Declaration as to the existing french Government has prevented me from saying a word to him on a Subject where he has I think committed himself."

4. An additional sentence appears in the other copies: "The People in general are averse to it."

5. The other copies continue: "Nor would I ever permit a frigid Reasoning on political motives to damp those Effusions of Sentiment which are as laudable in a nation as they are decorous to a private Citizen."

6. The other copies continue: "I apprehend that some feeble Counsels will be given: Whether they will be received and pursued you best know and will doubtless act accordingly. What I have to ask is that you would put yourself in

the Way of being consulted. I mean locally, for should you be at a Distance the Time may be too short for Communication."

7. The copy in DLC: Hamilton Papers ends here.

8. Article XI of the 1778 Treaty of Alliance with France bound the United States to "guarantee . . . the present Possessions of the Crown of france in America" (Miller, *Treaties*, 39–40).

9. The preceding three words replace the following text in the letter-book copy: "wise and virtuous Slave Masters contending for the Propriety of general Emancipation with all it's consequent Train of Crimes."

From Robert Lewis

Hond Uncle,   Fredericksburg [Va.] May 5th 1796

Your last letter dated the 17th ultimo, I have this instant received, and as I shall leave town this afternoon, will leave this in the post office for the next mail. My business here was to have ejectments issued against those persons who are in possession of the Land on Accoceek which you were so good as to say I might have, provided it cou'd be come at.[1] All the previous and necessary business has been arranged in order that it might come on against the next District Court for trial—But greatly to my mortification and disappointment, after a good deal of trouble and some little expence; my Counsellers informed me that the Land which you had given me and which you conceived to be your right as Heir at Law to my Grandmothers Estate becomes by the Law of Descents the joint property of yourself and Brothers Heirs[2]—As the property wou'd be divided and sub-divided into so many different parts provided it cou'd be obtained, I have thought proper to relinquish all claim—It being besides a bad cause—or at least a doubtfull one. The only point which gave me any hopes, wou'd have been the testimoney of several very old inhabitants who live in the neighbourhood—Also possession of a small part by a Mr Taylor, who was a tenant to my Grandmother, and who has been for several years past distressed by the party in possession for rent which he never wou'd pay without being forced.

I am sorry to inform you of the death of Mrs Haney—She died on Friday last[3] in extreme pain, and with the most rapid consumption, I believe, that ever was known; having only complained of symptoms of that disorder about two months past—She was truly a religious good Woman and has left a poor unhappy Orphan to deplore her loss—As to Virtue and exemplary conduct the Daughter of Mrs Haney is surpassed by none—And I am really sorry that the avocations of my family will not admit of constant employment for her—Her Mother recommended her to my care and put her under my auspices on her dieing bed, provided you did not point out some other mode more to her advantage—My House is small and it will certainly be attended with some inconvenience, and if no place can be provided for her where she can derive some advantage as well in improvment as profit, she's perfectly welcome to her board—Mrs Lewis has taken considerable trouble to teach her reading—writing, and useful needle work, in which she is very defective. She wants neither capacity or inclination to learn. I have taken the liberty & without your consent to purchase her some few articles which she was much in want of and cou'd not well be delayed to keep up a decent appearance—I have never furnished her with any thing since her coming to my Plantation except what you directed in the first instance;[4] and have always impressed upon her mind in the strongest terms what you requested, in regard to supporting herself—She has made every exertion, I believe, in order to do it, but to no effect—The people of this neighbourhood are uncommonly industrious and do every thing within themselves; of course there is little opportunity of doing much in the way of support, altho' every little, takes off some of the expence. She wou'd make an extraordinary housekeeper, if a place in some genteel family cou'd be procured—Of this, you will be the best judge.[5]

My Mother is at present in Culpepper with my sister Carter who is just delivered of a son[6]—They are both very well I am informed—Present my affectionate regards to my Aunt and believe me your much obliged and affectionate Nephew

Robt Lewis

ALS, ViMtvL.

1. For GW's gift to Lewis of land near the Accokeek ironworks in Stafford County, Va., see GW to Lewis, 29 April 1793.

2. Lewis's advisers misinterpreted "An act directing the course of descents" (1785), amended by "An act to amend the act, intituled 'An act directing the course of descents'" (1790), and "An ACT to reduce into one, the several acts

directing the course of descents" (1792; *Va. Statutes* [Hening], 12:138–40, 13:122–24; *Va. Statutes* [Shepherd], 1:99–101). The last law, which established rules for intestate individuals, did not apply in GW's case because his mother, Mary Ball Washington, had bequeathed to GW in her will "all my Lands on Accokeek Run in the County of Stafford" (20 May 1788, DLC:GW).

3. The previous Friday was 29 April.

4. In a letter dated 22 Feb. 1795, GW had directed Lewis to present Sally Ball Haynie with "a handsome, but not costly gown, and other things which she may stand mostly in need of." Sally's mother, Elizabeth Haynie, was GW's cousin.

5. Sally Haynie found another residence (see Lewis to GW, 26 July 1796).

6. Charles Edward Carter, born on 16 April, died young.

To the United States Senate

Gentlemen of the Senate,　　　　　　　United States May 5. 1796

I lay before you, for your consideration and advice, an explanatory article proposed to be added to the treaty of Amity Commerce and Navigation between the United States and Great Britain; together with a copy of the full power to the Secretary of State to negotiate the same.[1]

　　　　　　　　　　　　　　　　　　Go: Washington

LS, DNA: RG 46, entry 53; copy, DNA: RG 59, entry 142; copy, DLC:GW.

1. GW also enclosed a letter dated 26 March from the British chargé d'affaires at Philadelphia, Phineas Bond, to Secretary of State Timothy Pickering (DNA: RG 46, entry 53). Bond presented a conflict between Article VIII of the 1795 Treaty of Greenville with the northwestern Indians, which required anyone residing with or trading with the Indians to obtain a license from the United States, and Article III of the 1794 Jay Treaty with Great Britain, which promised free passage across territorial boundaries to citizens of both nations and the Indians (see Kappler, *Indian Treaties*, 2:42–43, and Miller, *Treaties*, 246–48). Bond continued that he was "directed to propose on his Majesty's part that an Article should, for that purpose, be added to the Treaty of Amity, Commerce and Navigation, between His Majesty and the United States, so as to form a part thereof, conformably to the Provisions, contained in the 29th Article of that Instrument, by which it shall be declared, that no Treaty, subsequently, concluded by either party with any other State or Nation, whether European or Indian, can be understood, in any manner, to derogate from the Rights of free Intercourse and Commerce, secured by the aforesaid Treaty of Amity Commerce and Navigation, to the subjects of His Majesty, and to the Citizens of the United States, and to the Indians on both sides of the boundary-line; but that all the said persons shall remain at full liberty freely to pass and repass into the Countries, on either side of the said Boundary Line,

and to carry on their trade and commerce, with each other, freely and without restriction, according to the stipulation of the third Article of the said Treaty, which stipulations are, by the said Treaty declared to be permanent." Bond was authorized to negotiate the terms of such an article with a representative of the U.S. government (DNA: RG 46, entry 53).

The explanatory article in part reads: "That no stipulations in any treaty subsequently concluded by either of the contracting parties with any other State or Nation, or with any Indian tribe, can be understood to derogate in any manner from the rights of free intercourse & commerce secured by the aforesaid third Article of the treaty of amity, commerce & navigation, to the subjects of his Majesty & to the citizens of the United States & to the Indians dwelling on either side of the boundary line aforesaid" (DNA: RG 46, entry 53; see also Miller, *Treaties*, 346–48).

The power authorizing Pickering to negotiate is dated 4 May (DNA: RG 46, entry 53; see also *ASP, Foreign Relations*, 1:552).

The Senate voted nineteen to five on 9 May to advise ratification of the article (*Senate Executive Journal*, 207).

To Tobias Lear

Dear Sir   Philadelphia 6th May 1796

This letter will be put into your hands by Mr Volney—who proposes to visit the Federal City.[1] If you are not acquainted with him personally, I am sure you must have a knowledge of his character—his travels & works; I therefore recommend him to your civilities while he remains in the Federal City.[2] I am always and sincerely Yours

Go: Washington

ALS, DLC: Tobias Lear Papers.

Claypoole's American Daily Advertiser for 28 July 1796 printed an item from "A CUSTOMER" to "Mr. Printer" with a purported letter of introduction from GW: "The bearer C. F. VOLNEY, so well known and admired in the literary world, needs no recommendation from GEORGE WASHINGTON, President of the United States." *The Rural Repository* (Leominster, Mass.) for 18 Aug. 1796 identified the printer as "*Mr. Pleasant*," presumably Samuel Pleasants, Jr., editor of the *Richmond and Manchester Advertiser* in Virginia.

1. See Thomas Law to GW, 11 May.

2. Gouverneur Morris had written GW on 29 Oct. 1793 to introduce Constantin-François Chasseboeuf Volney.

From Thomas Pinckney

Dear Sir   London [England] 7th May 1796

Your several favors of the 20th & 20th of February & 5th of March were delivered to me a few days ago by the Captain of the Ship Favorite; the letters which accompanied them have been forwarded in the manner you pointed out; & the printed notification shall be used in conformity to your desire.[1]

Be pleased, Sir to receive my best acknowledgements for the very friendly mode in which you communicate the acceptation of the Spanish Treaty[2]—I derive no small part of the satisfaction I feel on this event from the consideration that it may have had a tendency to diminish rather than to increase the unpleasant circumstances which have attended the exercise of some of your official duties. History has unfortunately so many examples of the rarest merit & most eminent services ill requited, that I was not greatly surprized by the unmerited obloquy with which several of our Gazettes for some time past have teemed: but I confess that though I was not astonished, I was much mortified because my partiality for my Countrymen had induced me to augur better both of their discernment & gratitude: I still however cherish the hope that these disgraceful productions have proceeded from a party scarcely more significant for their numbers, than eminent for their candor, liberality, or patriotism.

I will not fail, whenever a fit opportunity shall offer, to proceed to the full extent of what you have authorized with respect to the Marquis la Fayette[3]—at the present moment I am in expectation of an unofficial answer from Lord Grenville to an application I lately made with the hope of interesting this administration in behalf of our friend: prior communications to the department of State have informed you of my former advances of this nature[4]—& I have proposed this also unofficially & as from myself; assuring the Minister however at the same time that from my knowledge of all circumstances I was certain it would be a measure of a conciliatory and beneficial tendency—Lord Grenville stated that he could not of course give an official answer, but that he would take it into consideration. this is a more favorable answer than I have hitherto received on this subject. I expected to have met his Lordship yesterday, when I hoped to obtain the result of his consideration, but the conference was postponed.

I consider the interference of this Government, with whom we may be supposed to have some influence, as the most probable means of effecting the purpose we desire; but in case of the failure of this attempt whatever I can suggest as the dictate of justice, propriety, liberality & true policy, supported by your personal influence, shall be detailed to the Imperial Envoy. By the latest accounts the confinement of the Marquis continues to be rigorous though the Emperors Minister[5] assures me that he is extremely well treated—his wife & daughters have been permitted to reside with him & as I understand are equally prisoners with himself.

Accept, dear Sir, my best thanks for your kind compliance with my request to retire—I shall in consequence prepare for my return home in the summer, & shall carry with me to my retreat the sentiments of affectionate regard & attachment you have impressed on the mind of Your much obliged & respectful servant

Thomas Pinckney

ALS, DLC:GW; ALS (duplicate), DLC:GW.

1. Pinckney acknowledged GW's advertisement dated 1 Feb. for the lease of his Mount Vernon farms, and GW's letters written on 20 Feb. to the Earl of Buchan, John Sinclair, and William Strickland. For instructions about those documents, see GW's first letter to Pinckney on 20 February.

The captain of the *Favourite* was James Drummond.

2. See GW's letter to Pinckney written on 5 March.

3. See GW's second letter to Pinckney written on 20 February.

4. For some of his efforts on Lafayette's behalf, see Pinckney to Thomas Jefferson, 25 Sept. 1793 (*Jefferson Papers*, 27:151) and Pinckney to Secretary of State, 21 June 1794 (DNA: RG 59, Despatches from U.S. Ministers to Great Britain).

5. Ludwig Joseph Max von Starhemberg (1762–1833), a career diplomat, became the Austrian minister to Great Britain in 1793.

To Alexander Hamilton

(Private & confidential)

My dear Sir,   Philadelphia 8th May 1796.

Your note of the 5th instant accompanying the information given to you by G—— M—— on the 4th of March, came safe on friday. The letter he refers to, as having been written to me, is not yet received; but others from Mr Monroe of similar complexion, and almost of as imperious a tone from that government, have got to hand.[1]

That justice & policy should dictate the measures with which we are threatned, is not to be conceived; and one would think that even folly & madness on their part, would hardly go such lengths, without supposing a stimulus of a more serious nature than the Town meetings, & the partial resolutions which appeared in the course of last Summer & Autumn on ours.[2] Yet, as it seems to be the Æra of strange vicissitudes, & unaccountable transactions; attended with a sort of irresistable fatality in many of them, I shall not be surprized at any event that may happen, however extraordinary it may be; and therefore, it may not be amiss to ruminate upon the information which has been received in its fullest latitude; and be prepared to answer the demands on the extensive scale wch has been mentioned.

What then do you think ought to be said in case G—— M——s information should prove true, *in all its parts*? And what, if the proceedings, & Instructions of the French Directory should not exceed my conjecture; which is, that encouraged by the proceedings of last Summer on the Treaty (as already mentioned) and aided perhaps by communications of influencial men in *this* country, thro' a medium which ought to have been the last to engage in it, that that government *may*, and I believe *will* send out an Envoy extraordinary, with Instructions to make strong remonstrances against the unfriendliness (as they will term it), and the tendency of our Treaty with Great Britain; accompanied probably, and expectedly, with discretionary powers to go farther, according to circumstances, and the existing state of matters when he shall have arrived here. Perhaps these Instructions may extend to a releasement from that part of our Treaty with *them*, which claims exemption from the seisure of Enemies goods in *our* Vessels.[3] Perhaps, to demand the fulfilment of our guarantee of their West India Islds as the most likely means of affording them relief, under the circumstances they labor at present.[4] Perhaps too, to endeavor to render null & void our Treaty with G: Britain. Possibly *all of them*, or the dissolution of the Alliance. But I cannot bring my mind to believe that they seriously mean, or that they could accompany this Envoy with a Fleet, to *demand* the annihilation of the Treaty with G. Britain in fifteen days; or that War, in case of refusal, must follow as a consequence.

Were it not for the unhappy differences among ourselves, *my* answer wd be short & decisive, to this effect. We are an Independent Nation, and act for ourselves. Having fulfilled, and being willing to fulfil, (as far as we are able) our engagements with other nations, and having decided on, and strictly observed a Neutral conduct towards the Belligerent Powers, from an unwillingness to involve ourselves in War. We will not be dictated to by the Politics of any Nation under Heaven, farther than Treaties require of us.

Whether the *present*, or any circumstances should do more than *soften* this language, may merit consideration. But if we are to be told by a foreign Power (if our engagements with it are not infracted) what we *shall do*, and what we shall *not do*, we have Independence yet to seek, & have contended hitherto for very little.

If you have communicated the purport of G—— M——s letter to Mr Jay, I wish you would lay this also before him, *in confidence*, and that you & he would be so good as to favor me with your sentiments, & opinions on both; and on the measures which you think would be most advisable to be taken, in case we should have to encounter the difficulties with which we are threatned: which, assuredly, will have been brought on us by the misconduct of some of our own intemperate people; who seem to have preferred throwing themselves into the arms of France (even under the present circumstances of that Country) to that manly, & Neutral conduct which is so essential, & would so well become us, as an Independent Nation.

Before I close this letter, I will mention another subject; which, tho' in a smaller degree, is nevertheless, embarrassing. This also is communicated in confidence. It respects the wishes of young Fayette, relative to his father. As is very natural, & what might have been expected, he is extremely solicitous that something should be attempted to obtain the liberation of him; and has brought forward several plans (suggested by Doctr Ballman; who, it is to be feared will be found a troublesome guest among us) to effect it.[5]

These will be better understood by the Enclosures now sent,[6] than by any details I could give, when I add to them—the supposition of Fayette & Frestal, that the Doctor is without funds, and will be more embarrassing *to them* the longer he remains here. No mention, however, that has come to my knowledge of his going away.

The result of my reflection on this subject, and which I have communicated to the two young Men, is, that altho' I am convinced in my own mind that Mr La Fayette will be held in confinement by the combined Powers until Peace is established; yet to satisfy them, & their friends of my disposition to facilitate their wishes, as far as it can be done with any propriety on my part; I would, *as a private person*, express in a letter to the Emperor, my wish, and what I believe to be the wishes of this Country towards that Gentleman; viz.—that the liberation of him, conditioned on his repairing hither would be a grateful measure. That this letter I would put under cover to Mr Pinckney, to be forwarded or not, according to the view he might have of its success; after conversing indirectly with the Diplomatic characters of the combined Powers in London. But that I could not, while in Public Office, have any Agency in, or even knowledge of, any projects that should require concealment, or that I should be unwilling to appear openly & avowedly in. That as Doctr Ballman had committed an Act (however meritorious & pleasing it might be to the friends of Mr de la Fayette) which was viewed in a very obnoxious light by the Power in whose possession the prisoner was.[7] Had narrowly escaped condign punishment for it himself. and was released upon the express condition that he should never again appear in those Dominions; that I could neither shew him countenance—nor could I furnish him with money to extricate himself from difficulties (if he was in any)—Seeing but little difference between giving before, or after, to a man who stands in the light he does between that Power & the Executive of the U. States; but that, if he was disposed to quit the latter, I had no doubt, & he might be so assured, that the friends of Mr de la Fayette would raise a sufficient sum to enable him to do this, and to defray his expences since he has been in this Country. What they will say to him, or he do in this matter, I know not.

If you & Mr Jay see no impropriety in such a letter as I have mentioned, to be used at the discretion of Mr Pinckney—I would thank either of you for drafting it. Mr Jay in particular having been in the habit, & better acquainted with the stile and manner of addressing these sort of characters than I am, would be able to give it a better shape. To return the papers now sent, with the draught required, as soon as convenient, would be acceptable to Dear Sir Your Affecte Servt

Go: Washington

ALS (photocopy), NjP: Armstrong Collection.

1. Hamilton's letter to GW written on 5 May, and its enclosure from Gouverneur Morris to Hamilton dated 4 March, reached GW on Friday, 6 May.

Writing Secretary of State Timothy Pickering from Paris on 16 Feb., James Monroe, U.S. minister to France, reported officially that in consequence of the ratification of the Jay Treaty with Great Britain, the Directory considered the French alliance with the United States "as ceasing to exist," and that they would "appoint an Envoy Extraordinary to attend and represent the same to our government." In his letter written on 20 Feb., Monroe reported a subsequent meeting in which he argued against such action by the French government. Charles Delacroix, French minister of foreign affairs, replied "that France had much cause of complaint against us, independently of our Treaty with England; but that by this Treaty, ours with them was annihilated: that the Directoire considered our conduct in these respects as absolutely unfriendly to them" and thought it their "duty" to make the representation. French officials deemed the mode of protest "mild and respectful," but Delacroix would convey Monroe's objections (*Papers of James Monroe*, 3:590–91, 594–95).

2. GW is referring to the many local meetings reporting resolutions in opposition to the Jay Treaty.

3. GW is referring to Article XXIII (originally XXV) of the 1778 Treaty of Amity and Commerce with France (see Miller, *Treaties*, 20–21).

4. Article XI of the 1778 Treaty of Alliance with France bound the United States to "guarantee . . . the present possessions of the Crown of france in America" (Miller, *Treaties*, 39–40).

5. See Justus Erick Bollmann to GW, 1 April.

6. These enclosures have not been identified.

7. GW is referring to Justus Erick Bollmann's effort to help Lafayette escape from prison in fall 1794.

To John Jay

Private
My dear Sir,   Philadelphia 8th May 1796

You judged very right when in your letter of the 18th Ulto you observed I "can have very little time for private letters." But if my friends will put up with the hasty and indigested ones I can write, under such circumstances, there are a few of them (among whom allow me the gratification to place you) with whom I should feel very happy to corrispond: and while I hold my present Office, to learn their sentiments upon any of the important measures which come before the Executive of the United States.

I am *sure* the mass of Citizens in the United States *mean well*; and I firmly believe they will always *act well* whenever they can obtain a right understanding of matters; but in some parts of the Union, where the sentiments of their delegates and leaders are adverse to the government, and great pains are taken to inculcate a belief that their rights are assailed, and their liberties endangered, it is not easy to accomplish this; especially (as is the case invariably) when the Inventors, and abettors of pernicious measures, use infinitely more industry in disseminating the poison, than the well disposed part of the Community do to furnish the antidote. To this source all our discontents may be traced, and from it our embarrassments proceed. Hence, serious misfortunes, originating in misrepresentation, frequently flow, and spread, before they can be dissipated by truth.

These things do, as you have supposed, fill my mind with much concern, and with serious anxiety. Indeed the trouble & perplexities which they occasion, added to the weight of years which have passed upon me, have worn away my mind more than my body; and renders ease and retirement indispensably necessary to both, during the short time I have to remain here.

It would be uncandid therefore, and would discover a want of friendly confidence (as you have expressed a solicitude for my (at least) riding out the Storm) not to add, that nothing short of events—or such imperious circumstances (which I hope & trust will not happen) as might render a retreat dishonorable, will prevent the public annunciation of it in time, to obviate waste, or misapplied Votes at the Election of President and Vice-President of the United States, in December next, upon myself.

I congratulate you on the tranquil Session, just closed in your State, and upon the good dispositions, generally, which I am informed prevail among the citizens thereof. With most friendly sentiments I remain Dear Sir Your Obedt & Affecte Servt
Go: Washington

Permit me, to request the favor of you, to send the enclosed to its Address.[1]

ALS, NNC; ADfS, DLC:GW; LB, DLC:GW. The postscript appears only on the ALS.

1. GW enclosed his letter written on this date to Alexander Hamilton.

From Charles Lee

Dear Sir   Philadelphia 8th may 1796

I have been reflecting on the train of measures to be pursued respecting the western posts which yesterday seemed to meet your approbation. The subject was new to me then, and therefore I hope you will excuse me for presenting to your better judgment the result of mine on the letter proposed to be written to Lord Dorchester. That part of it which is to express an acquiescence on your part in the detention of the posts after the first day of june next and indeed a desire that they should remain in the possession of the british for safe custody until the troops of the United States shall arrive to receive them appears objectionable on two grounds.[1]

1st It is not absolutely necessary, and will imply a concession that the punctual delivery of the posts does not take place, in consequence of delays, neglects or impediments of some kind on the part of the United States or of some department in our government. In itself this proposition may be questioned; but admitting it to be true; I do not perceive the propriety in the present stage of the business of the president's doing any act or using any words which may be interpreted into an acknowledgement, on our part, that the non-delivery of the posts according to stipulation is to be attributed to ourselves. If certain occurrences have produced an impossibi[li]ty on our part to take possession on or before the first of June next; and also a necessity on the part of the british to continue to hold the posts after that period, it will be safest for you to suffer, that impossibi[li]ty and that necessity, to stand upon their own circumstances as they have already happened.

2dly It may be questioned whether the President can be justified in consenting that an *armed force of a foreign nation* shall occupy a post in the *territories* of the United States after the time appointed for the evacuation by a treaty solemnly concluded between the two nations. It is my opinion that such an act cannot be justified under the constitution. If the evacuation is not punctually made in consequence of unavoi[d]able causes or of absolute necessity, it may be excusable on that account and must be submitted to: but this is very different from consenting or desiring that the evacuation should be postponed beyond the day stipulated.

A treaty duly made is obligatory as a law; the execution of the latter cannot be denied or delayed by the president except in particular instances by pardon &c. of offences, so also he cannot dispense with the obligations of a treaty.

But even supposing to request the british governor to hold the posts and take care of them till the arrival of our troops though subsequent to the first day of next june could be justified as a lawful act, yet it seems to be a condescencion on the part of the United states towards the british nation, that will be unpleasing to many, and complained of by some.

Viewing this matter in a more important light than the other gentlemen seemed to have contemplated it, as it may affect yourself, I could not refrain from communicating my sentiments in writing for your more mature consideration.[2] With the most perfect esteem and Respect I remain your most obed. hbl. sert

Charles Lee

ALS, DLC:GW.

1. Article II of the Jay Treaty set 1 June 1796 as the date for the British to have evacuated all military posts within the territorial boundaries of the United States (Miller, *Treaties*, 246).

2. See GW to James McHenry, this date.

To James McHenry

Dear Sir,   Sunday Afternoon 8th May 1796

The enclosed letter presents a serious—perhaps a just view of the subject[1] which has been under consideration—and as I wish in every thing, particularly in matters of foreign relation, to conduct with caution; I request that your letter to the Govr General of Canada; the Instructions to Major Lewis;[2] and all your arrangements respecting the reception of the Posts may accord with the ideas contained therein.[3]

Let the March of the Troops who are to take possession of the Posts be facilitated as much as possible; and let every measure necessary thereto for supplying them on their March, and when there, be concerted without delay.[4] I am, as always Yours

Go: Washington

ALS, G-BW; ADfS, DLC:GW; LB, DLC:GW.

1. GW inadvertently wrote "subjest" for this word.

2. Thomas Lewis (1749–1809), of Virginia, had been a lieutenant during the Revolutionary War and was now a captain in the U.S. Army.

3. GW presumably enclosed Charles Lee's letter to him written on this date.

4. McHenry replied to GW on 9 May.

To William Pearce

Mr Pearce,   Philadelphia 8th May 1796.

I am glad to find by your letter of the first instant, that the rain wch fell here on the 27th Ulto had extended to you.[1] The cold & drying Winds I knew would deprive the plants of some of its good effects; but benefit must have resulted to them notwithstanding. If the frosts which accompanied those Winds have injured the fruit (as you fear) it will be a circumstances much to be regretd altho' not to be avoided.

I wish you had sowed all the Peas as soon as they were received (as the grd was prepared) altho' the season was far advanced, and the Books spoke of February as the proper period for depositing this Crop in the ground. They may not come up another year; but admitting they would do it, and it shall be found that they are A crop worth cultivating, your prospect for getting into a good stock of Seed would have been better by sowing the whole quantity, than an Acre only, & keeping the residue of the Seed until next Spring. Indeed, dry as the weather has been with you, it is a question whether sowing at the time you did was not better than to have done it a month sooner; especially as it is to be hoped that the fine rains which fell here on thursday night and all day friday were general.[2] No alteration, or addition to what you have already done can take place after this letter gets to hand, with either Peas or Chiccory, as the Spring will be too far advanced.[3]

If the clover seed which you sowed did not vegitate, & perish with the drought, it is to be hoped it may yet come to something. It will be unfortunate if it should; not more so on acct of the want of the Crop than on acct of the high price of the seed though both are bad enough.

Did you begin your lane at Dogue run at the 2d gate, next the Overseers house, or at the outer gate, so as to extend it across the Meadow? The last if you had had time, would have been best on two accounts; first by throwing that meadow into two divisions—and 2dly by making both more secure; for the gates being often left open Hogs & other things are frequently getting in and doing injury; and besides, having space enough, the Carts are cutting different tracts which form new gulies; wch would not, nor cannot be the case in a lane.

Let me know the amount of your receipts for Fish sold. I do not want the particulars, but the agregate Sum of what they have fetched, or will fetch, when the money is all received.[4]

If an acct was kept of the times my Coach Mares went to the Jack—particularly when those called Nancy & the blind mare, were covered, let me know it in your next letter. The two whose names are mentioned I am pretty sure are with foal, & I want to know at what time it may be expected they will bring them, that I may regulate their movemt on the Road to Mount Vernon.

It is expected that Congress will rise between the 20th and last of this month. But admitting the fact, it is impossible for me, at this time, to say precisely when I shall be at Mount Vernon. I wish you well and am Your friend

Go: Washington

P.S. Mrs Washington sends a memorandum enclosed which I pray you to have attention given to.[5]

ALS, ViMtvL.

1. Pearce's letter to GW dated 1 May has not been found.

2. The preceding Thursday was 5 May.

3. About the pea and chicory seeds, see GW to Tobias Lear, 29 April.

4. Under 23 April, Pearce recorded £63.17.9 "cash Recvd for fish sold to different persons at the Landing" (Mount Vernon Accounts, 1794–1797, p. 72).

5. The enclosed memorandum has not been identified.

Letter not found: from William Pearce, 8 May 1796. GW wrote Pearce on 15 May: "Your letter of the 8th, with the Reports, are at hand."

From Edward Carrington

Dear Sir   Richmond May 9. 1796

I have been honored with your favor of the 1st Instant, and have the satisfaction of seeing in the papers, the decision of the House of Representatives on the Resolution for carrying into effect the British Treaty.[1] I presume the struggle will not be renewed on the appearance of the Bill—the party in opposition has evidently been weakened by the memorials received before the passage of the Resolution, and this influence is certainly encreasing by the arrivals of other memorials.

With pleasure I can assure you of my confirmation in the opinion which I ventured to communicate to you, as to the will of Virginia on this subject.[2] the apparent certainty of a decision of the question, before the acts of the people could arrive, have prevented their being numerous—enough has however been done to ground an opinion, that the popular wish of the Country is for the execution of the Treaty; nor would it be unreasonable to conclude, that there is a turn as to the general administration.

In mine of the 27th Ult. I suggested the possibility of evil, from efforts of opposition, by means of corresponding committees. the attempt has been made here, under the Guidance of Mr Campbell who, with a few others, nearly self elected assumed the office of a Committee for this place—their circular letters have been dispatched to all quarters; but, so far as we have heard, they met with little attention, and, in some instances, it is known, that they have been treated as presumptuous.

I have already done myself the pleasure of communicating to you, the proceedings of this City & its vicinity—you have also seen in the papers, those of fairfax & Frederick Counties, & the Town of Fredericksburg.[3] the two Counties on the Eastern shore, I am undoubtedly informed have sent to their Representative Mr Page, an instruction to vote for appropriations. Strong Resolutions to the same effect are gone from King William County & the City of Williamsbg and meetings in Fauquier & Berkeley Counties, I have heard have done the same.[4] But the most decisive mark of the popular opinion has been manifested at Petersburg, in a meeting of a great number of Citizens from the neighboring Counties, called for the avowed purpose of censuring the refusal of the papers, & advising the defeat of the Treaty. the history of this business is as follows—the Merchants of that Town, having, on Sunday the 24th of April, Assembled in the Court House, for the purpose of agreeing to an address similar to that of the Merchants of Philadelphia,[5] a number of opposition characters, intruded on them for the purpose of intimidating them, or to over-rule their measures—the merchants withdrew to another place & compleated their business without further interruption; but after the departure of the merchants, the remaining persons organized themselves under a chairman & Secretary, & passed a Resolution for calling a meeting of the neighbouring Counties on the Sunday following (the 1st May)—the enclosed paper contains the proceedings of this Body on the 24th apl which carry on their Face, both the object of the call, & the confidence with which it was made[6]—for good reasons the Petersburg Press, which is in the hands of the Secretary of the first meeting, has never announced the issue of that held on the 1st May[7]—we are however well informed what it was; the Meeting was numerous, & those who called it presumed much on their Strength, having all the orators on their side, who it seems displayed great talents on a proposition for condemning the refusal of the papers— it was opposed by only one plain Man, and on a division was lost. the meeting then passed a Resolution expressive of their desire that the Treaty be executed and quietly adjourned, Sine die. I have been particular in relating this transaction, because it marks, in a striking manner the sense of our Farmers & Planters, who had been called together, under the name of a very popular Man, for an avowed contrary object, and an additional prejudice against coinciding with the Merchants of the place who were subjects of the usual slanders against that class of Man. another circumstance is worthy of consideration while appretiating the issue of this Meeting, as evidencing a change of public opinions generally—the Town of Petersburg & the Counties around it, have been distinguished for zeal & unanimity, in opposition to the government while depending, & its measures ever since its adoption.

I have heard of but one Meeting which issued in a determination against the appropriations—this was at Norfolk where it is said a majority of about ten so determined.[8] I conclude that but little has been done in obtaining subscriptions to the circulating petitions of the opposition, from our having seen nothing of their successes published in the papers.

With pleasure I shall from time to time give you such information as events shall induce me to believe will be useful to you, neither requesting or expecting, any reply, but when it may consist with your leisure and inclination. your leisure can be but little. I have the Honor to be with unalterable attachment & confidence Dear Sir, Your Obt Servt

Ed. Carrington

ALS, DLC:GW.

1. After contentious votes on 30 April, the U.S. House of Representatives agreed to a resolution "that it is expedient to pass the laws necessary for carrying into effect the treaty lately negotiated between the United States and Great-Britain" (*Journal of the House*, 8:378–82).

2. See Carrington to GW, 22 and 27 April.

3. *The Columbian Mirror and Alexandria Gazette* (Va.) for 21 April reported that citizens of Alexandria and its vicinity met twice on 20 April and agreed to support implementation of the Jay Treaty. The same newspaper for 23 April printed their memorial, which ended: "We view the peace of our country as its greatest blessing; and we deprecate any measure that, by defeating a compact which is founded upon the conclusion of former complaints, may open a contention which we are happy to see concluded." A subsequent meeting of "Landholders and Farmers of Fairfax County" approved the memorial and agreed to distribute it for signatures (*Columbian Mirror and Alexandria Gazette*, 30 April).

The Frederick County, Va., meeting at Winchester adopted a petition (with "upwards of 850" signatures) expressing alarm over reports that the treaty might "be impeded or lost for want of such appropriations as may be necessary . . . They, therefore, unequivocally delare, that as they were highly pleased and gratified at the formation of that treaty, entered into, as they conceive, most wisely to continue and promote the happiness of their country, advancing in prosperity with a pace before unexampled in the world, and rapidly encreasing by a well administered government, under the best of constitutions, do most earnestly pray, that no risque may be run by making new experiments, but that the said treaty . . . without loss of time be completed and confirmed, by making such appropriations of monies as may best conduce to this end—and thereby, that all those dangers and confusions which may result from a contrary conduct, may be avoided" (*Columbian Mirror and Alexandria Gazette*, 3 May).

A meeting of Fredericksburg, Va., "merchants and traders" held on 22 April issued a memorial with the opinion "that a further delay of its operations would be injurious to the peace, happiness and prosperity of our country, and a breach of the national faith" (*Federal Gazette & Baltimore Daily Advertiser*, 3 May).

4. The addresses to U.S. Representative John Page from Accomack and Northampton counties, Va., were printed in the *Gazette of the United States* (Philadelphia) for 18 May. The Accomack address, dated 26 April, urged full implementation of the Jay Treaty despite conceding "a power in Congress to

defeat the operation of the treaty by refusing to pass the laws necessary to carry it into effect." The Northampton address, dated 23 April, arose because Page's constituents disapproved of his opposition to the treaty. Addressing him "to exercise an inherent and constitutional right," they sought a "proportional influence" on his future conduct. The constituents enclosed a statement calling the treaty "a politic and necessary measure," condemning "the unremitting efforts of members of Congress to arrest this instrument," demanding "necessary appropriations . . . to render the treaty efficient," and asking that "the constitutional agency of the Federal Legislature with respect to the treaty" be postponed for later consideration.

The Virginia Gazette, and General Advertiser (Richmond) for 4 May printed a memorial from "Freeholders" meeting in King William County, Va., on 25 April to the U.S. House of Representatives that expressed "great anxiety in consequence of the doubts that have arisen as to the execution of the Treaty." The memorialists hoped for no further delay in "giving full and complete operation to the same."

The meeting at Williamsburg on 28 April resolved that the Jay Treaty "ought to be carried into immediate effect" and agreed to an address requesting their congressmen's "utmost endeavors for the attainment of this object" (*Gazette of the United States*, 17 May).

The *Gazette of the United States* for 30 April mentioned a petition in favor of the Jay Treaty "from the citizens of Frederick and Berkeley counties . . . signed by upwards of 400 persons."

5. *The Independent Gazetteer* (Philadelphia) for 20 April printed a memorial from merchants and traders of Philadelphia who met on 15 April. Being "seriously alarmed lest those measures" needed to implement the Jay Treaty "should be further delayed or entirely omitted," the memorialists argued that the restitution of property seized by Great Britain, the safety of U.S. merchant vessels, and the preservation of peace and prosperity depended on the treaty. They urged the U.S. House "that no partial considerations of policy may influence their decision on this important question; but that the faith, the honor, and the interest of the nation may be preserved by making the necessary provisions for carrying the treaty into fair and honorable effect."

6. The enclosure has not been identified, but the *Aurora General Advertiser* (Philadelphia) for 4 May reprinted the proceedings of the 24 April meeting in Petersburg, Va., apparently from a local newspaper or account dated 26 April.

7. The report of the proceedings of the Petersburg meeting on 24 April lists William Prentis as secretary of the gathering that remained after the merchants departed. The secretary of the original meeting has not been identified.

William Prentis (1762–1824) cofounded *The Virginia Gazette, or Weekly Advertiser* at Richmond in 1782. He left that paper in 1785 and published newspapers in Petersburg from 1786 to 1804, at this time the *Virginia Gazette, & Petersburg Intelligencer*. Prentis served four terms as mayor of Petersburg between 1793 and 1806.

8. A meeting of the citizens of Norfolk and Portsmouth, Va., on 26 April approved an address to the U.S. House stating that the Jay Treaty "could not be fully and completely carried into effect without the concurrence of your

house" and their firm persuasion "that the faith, honor, interest, and happiness of the people of the U. States, will not be endangered by withholding the appropriations required to carry the treaty into effect." A resolution to transmit the address won 90 to 83 (*Aurora General Advertiser*, 6 May).

From James McHenry

Sir   9th May 1796.

I have the honour to submit for your inspection a draught of a letter to Lord Dorchester, made out agreeably to the idea presented in the attorney generals letter, which corresponds with the second draught I had the pleasure of reading to you on saturday, and yesterday morning.[1] I beleive it is the safest ground to move upon, and the most correctly constitutional. I have shewn it to Mr Lee & Mr Woolcot who approve of it.

If you should be of opinion that any thing like the inclosed private instruction to Capn Lewis might be useful, I shall correct it and have it ready with the other letters.[2]

I expect the Senate to concur in the additional article to the British treaty to-day, and if you advise it, will dispach Capn Lewis to-morrow.[3]

Mr Murray was out of town yesterday, but is expected to return this morning. I shall see him of course. With the sincerest respect I have the honour to be Sir Your most ob. st

James McHenry

ALS, DLC:GW; LB, DLC:GW; ADf, DLC: James McHenry Papers.

1. Saturday was 7 May. A later draft dated "May" of McHenry's letter to Guy Carleton, Lord Dorchester, governor of the British provinces in North America, is at MiD: James McHenry Papers. McHenry informed Dorchester that "the provisions required, on the part of the U.S., by the [Jay] treaty . . . have been duly made by government," that "detachments from the army of the U.S. are ordered to be put in motion to take possession of the posts to be evacuated," and that Capt. Thomas Lewis "is authorised to receive from your Lordship, and to transmit to those detachments, a duplicate of the orders for their evacuation, and to concur in arrangments relative to this object if such concurrence shall be in any particular necessary." A copy of the letter at CaOOA: Archives Reports 1891 gives 10 May as the date on the final version of the letter. For Dorchester's response, see McHenry to GW, 27 June (second letter).

Attorney General Charles Lee wrote McHenry on this date: "I have added an authority to concur in arrangements in terms not limited to any particular object; because though I do not perceive any instance which shall require a concurrence, yet it is possible that such an instance may occur—It is qualified by adding 'if it be necessary in any instance.[']

"Unless some such authority be given and in some such way it is possible that Capt. Lewis will be the longer delayed in the execution of this business" (DLC:GW).

2. A draft of instructions to Lewis, dated May, is in MiD: James McHenry Papers. McHenry directed Lewis "to proceed to Canada with as much expedition as possible" and deliver the letter to Dorchester. After receiving the evacuation orders and Dorchester's answer, Lewis was to "immediately return to Philadelphia. And as a detachment from West Point will be on its march to Oswego and Niagara you will endeavour to fall in with it on your route and provide the commanding officer with a copy of the orders."

3. For Senate approval of this article on this date, see GW to the U.S. Senate, 5 May, and n.1 to that document.

From Timothy Pickering

Department of State May 9. 1796.

The Secretary of State respectfully lays before the President a letter of March 29th from Governor Blount with the address to him from the General Assembly of Tennessee, which were handed to the Secretary this day by Mr Cocke, a Senator Elect from that government.[1] When the Secretary told Mr Cocke that the letter with its inclosure should be laid before the President, Mr Cocke expressed earnestly his desire that they should also be officially communicated to the Senate; of which the Secretary did not see the necessity, but begs leave to submit to ⟨the⟩ President's decision.

The Governor of that territory being no longer an officer of the United States, the office of superintendent of Indian Affairs will of course cease to be united with that of Governor, according to the act of Congress of the 26th of May 1790;[2] and now be conferred on whomsoever the President, with the advice and consent of the Senate, shall be pleased to appoint.

Timothy Pickering.

ALS, DNA: RG 59, Miscellaneous Letters; LB, DNA: RG 59, GW's Correspondence with His Secretaries of State; LB, DNA: RG 59, Domestic Letters.

1. William Blount wrote Pickering from Knoxville on 29 March that the government of the state of Tennessee had been organized, ending his functions as territorial governor. He would "continue to exercise the office of Superin-

tendant of Indian Affairs" until his departure for Philadelphia in mid-April. The address of the Tennessee general assembly praised Blount's conduct as territorial governor and announced his election as U.S. senator from Tennessee (Carter, *Territorial Papers*, 4:422–23).

William Cocke (1748–1828), a leader in the attempt to establish the state of Franklin in the 1780s, served in the U.S. Senate, 1796–97 and 1799–1805.

2. Pickering is referring to section 2 of "An Act for the Government of the Territory of the United States, south of the river Ohio" (1 *Stat.* 123).

To the United States Senate

Gentlemen of the Senate   United States 9. May 1796
I nominate James McDowell to be Inspector of the Revenue for the sixth survey in the District of virginia vice James Brackenridge resigned.[1]

L[S], DNA: RG 46, entry 52; copy, DLC:GW.

Secretary of the Treasury Oliver Wolcott, Jr., had written GW on 6 May: "The Secretary of The Treasury has the honor to submit to The President, recommendations in favor of several Candidates for the office of Inspector of the Revenue for the 6th Survey of the District of Virginia, vacant by the resignation of James Brakenridge Esqr." (LB, DLC:GW). The enclosed recommendations have not been identified.

1. The Senate received this message on 10 May and confirmed the nomination on 11 May (*Senate Executive Journal*, 207–8).

James McDowell (1770–1835), of Rockbridge County, Va., was a son-in-law of GW's acquaintance William Preston (1729–1783). McDowell's children included a namesake son, who became governor of Virginia, and a daughter Elizabeth, who married Thomas Hart Benton, noteworthy as U.S. senator from Missouri.

From Bartholomew Dandridge, Jr.

my dr sir,   Green briar Court house [Va.] May 10 1796
My last to you was I believe dated at Shippensburg in Pennsylvania.[1] on the morng succeeding its date, I bent my course towards Virga & crossing the Potomac at Wmsport I passed through Winchester, & along up the Shenandoah, & thro Orange County to Charlottsville & from thence to staunton, in the neighbourhood of which I rested a few days. From Staunton I departed with the intention of visiting the country on & at the mouth of

the Kanhawa; but on my arrival here I found this part of the country so pleasant & healthful that I have resolved to tarry in it for some weeks, & for that purpose have taken up my abode at a respectable farmer's about 12 miles from this place towards the Ohio. I have already experienced the good effects of a change of scenee & objects wch had become necessary to me, & hope, if I can have it in my power to spend the summer on this side the ridge, to have my health & tranquility establishe⟨d.⟩ It is still my intention, (if agreeable to you & if you have not provided a person who can answer your purposes better) to return to your service in the fall previous to the meetg of the next Congress. If however, you should not think proper to permit this, I will thank you to let me know it as soon as possible, as in that case I shall be obliged to get into some other business if I can. You may obtain many who are in some respects more capable of doing your business; but I can truly say you will not fin⟨d⟩ one who will be more faithful to your interest, according to my ability. Perhaps you may wish to make use of me in the disposal of your Western Lands. This employment I should prefer far before that which you have been pleased heretofore to honor me with. Many have made inquiries of me respecting it—& all seem to agree in the opinion that it would be greatly favorable to your interest to divide it into small tracts from 2 to 500 acres. I have no doubt if that was done but that from 6 to 8 Dollars per acre might be had for it, accordg to quality & situation. New settlers are daily going to the point & above that place on the Ohio.[2] You will I am persuaded do me the favor to let me hear from [you] as early as you can upon the above subjects, that in case you do not wish to give me any place in your service, I may endeavour to obtain one some where or other. In the last event I must beg of you to enclose me a certificate of the time I lived with you & of my conduct during that time. As I am sure you will do this with strict justice, it will be serviceable to me. a mail arrives at this place only once a fortnight, I cannot therefore expect to hear from you in less than 4 weeks. Be pleased to present my affectionate respects to my Aunt, remember me to Washington, & to accept yourself my prayers for your happiness & prosperity. With sincere esteem & the truest attachment I have the honor to be my dr sir, Yr very h'ble servt

                                                    B. Dandridge

P.S. please to direct to me, to the care of Mr Chas Arbuckle merchant at Lewisburgh, alias G.B. Ct house.[3]

ALS, DLC:GW. GW received this letter on 3 June (see his letter to Dandridge, 5 June; see also GW's first letter to James McHenry, 1 Aug.).

Dandridge again wrote GW from Greenbrier Courthouse, Va., (now Lewisburg, W.Va.), on 1 June: "I wrote to you fully by the last post from this place (I believe of the 15: ulto) informg you of my having wander'd to this place, & my intention to rest here & in this neighbourhood till I could have the satisfaction of hearing from you—'till when I know not what course to take. I take the oppy by a Gentleman sets out in a few moments for Philadelphia (in case my letter by post shou'd miscarry) to repeat my readiness, & indeed wish, to return to your service, to shew you that my quitting it was not dictated by any unworthy motives. I would either return to Philada as soon as the hot months are past; or if you think I can be of service in the dispossal of yr Western Lands, I should be glad to be employ'd in that way. The Gentleman who carries this waits, & I must end with requesting you to present me affectionately to my Aunt, & to Washington" (ALS, DLC:GW; the cover indicates that "Mr Skiles" carried this letter). Charles Arbuckle's father-in-law was Henry Skyles (see n.3 below).

1. This letter from Dandridge to GW has not been found.

2. Dandridge probably was referring to Point Pleasant (now W.Va.) near the junction of the Kanawha and Ohio rivers.

3. Charles Arbuckle (1769–1846) was a son of the frontiersman and Revolutionary War officer Matthew Arbuckle (d. 1781).

From Alexander Hamilton

Sir   New York May 10. 1796

When last in Philadelphia you mentioned to me your wish that I should *re dress* a certain paper which you had prepared—As it is important that a thing of this kind should be done with great care and much at leisure touched & retouched, I submit a wish that as soon as you have given it the *body* you mean it to have that it may be sent to me.[1]

A few days since I transmitted you the copy of a letter I had received from Mr G—— M——.[2]

It is rumoured, that Mr Pinckney Intertains a wish to return to this Country. Give me leave to make known to you, that in such an event, I have ground to believe it would not be disagreeable to Mr *King* to be the successor.[3] I verily believe, that a more fit man for the purpose cannot be found and I imagine Mr King will in every event leave the Senate. Should you think well of his

appointment, I presume he would be disposed by a *previous resignation* to make the way easy to his nomination by you. Considering the strong commercial relations of the two countries it is
truly very important that each should have with the other a man
able and willing to give fair play to reciprocal interests—From
what I have seen of Mr Liston the present Minister of G.B. &
from what Mr Pinckney and others say of him to me—I believe
he will be found a well disposed intelligent and agreeable man.[4]
Very respectfully & affectly I have the honor to be Sir Your obedt
Servant

A. Hamilton

ALS, NN: Alexander Hamilton Papers.

1. Hamilton had visited Philadelphia in February to argue a case before the
Supreme Court. The paper was a draft for GW's farewell address (see GW to
Hamilton, 15 May, and the enclosure to that document; see also Madison to
GW, 20 June 1792, enclosure).

2. See Hamilton to GW, 5 May 1796, and enclosure.

3. See Rufus King to Hamilton, 2 May, in *Hamilton Papers*, 20:151–53.

4. Robert Liston, Great Britain's new minister to the United States, arrived
at New York on 2 May. Liston wrote Phineas Bond, British consul at Philadelphia, from New York on Monday, 9 May: "My intention was to have set out
to-day; but the badness of the weather last night & this morning has determined me to defer my departure till to-morrow. And as the roads are likely to
be a good deal spoiled by the rain, it will probably be thursday morning before
I can have the pleasure of seeing you" (StEdNL: Liston Papers). Liston's wife,
Henrietta, described the trip from New York to Philadelphia in her journal
entry dated 26 May. Apparently having reached their destination on Thursday,
12 May, she continued: "Congress had *not* risen when we arrived, & I felt great
anxiety to see the President. *Washington* has made to himself a *name remarkable*
in Europe, but of peculiar Magic in America. Mr. Liston was introduced by
Mr. Pickering. . . . Mr. Liston delivered his Credentials on a Monday, & Tuesday
being Levee day I accompanied him to the House of the President & was, by
him [Timothy Pickering], presented to Mrs. Washington, she was seated in a
Drawing room alone, & received me with much kindness, her figure, though
short & fat, is not with out dignity, her face retains the marks of delicate beauty
& her voice is melody itself.

"The Gentlemen from the *Levee* crowded to make thier Bows to her. . . .

"After the Levee was over the President came into the room, accompanied
by Mr. Liston. *Washingtons* appearance & manners struck me extremely. Tall,
Majestic & well proportioned, his face at the age of sixty three rather pleasing,
particularly when he smiles. In his air & movements, there was a dignity which
the general coldness of his address did not lesson; to *me* he was *affable* & *kind*
& when we rose to take leave, requested to see us often without ceremony
or reserve" (North, *Travel Journals of Henrietta Liston*, 5–8; quotes on 7–8).

Henrietta Marchant Liston wrote her uncle James Jackson from Philadelphia on 28 May regarding GW, "(or as He is called here the *President*,) I have only time to say that He has paid me every compliment in his power particularly an Invitation to visit him at his House in Virginia which We mean to do" (StEdNL: Liston Papers; see also GW's first letter to James McHenry, 22 July, and n.2 to that document).

From Thomas Law

Dear Sir.   Washington City the 11th May [1796].

Eliza & I were looking at our houses when Mr Volney delivered to me the note of introduction from you,[1] which afforded me the greatest pleasure, it were superfluous to say that every attention will ever be paid to any wishes you honor me with.

Mrs Stuart Miss Custis & Mrs Peters are gone to Virginia; Eliza is quite well as are all her family.

The appropriations for the Treaty & the passing of the guarantee loan Bill in the City have quite revived our drooping spirits.[2] System Œconomy & concentration of force will do more in one Year than the last three or four—Mr Volney is delighted with the situation of the City. Eliza joins with me in requesting that you & Mrs Washington will oblige us with a few days stay. I remain with unfeigned respect esteem & affection yr most Obt H. st

Thomas Law

ALS, DLC:GW.

1. GW had written introductions for Constantin-François Chasseboeuf Volney (see GW to Tobias Lear, 6 May, and the source note to that document).

2. The U.S. House of Representatives resolved on 30 April "that it is expedient to pass the laws necessary" to implement the Jay Treaty (*Journal of the House*, 8:378–82; quote on 379).

The D.C. commissioners had sought a guarantee from Congress to support their efforts to obtain a loan (see GW to the U.S. Senate and House of Representatives, 8 Jan., and n.1 to that document). The desired law "authorizing a Loan for the use of the City of Washington, in the District of Columbia, and for other purposes therein mentioned" was approved on 6 May (1 *Stat.* 461).

From Paul Joseph Guérard de Nancrède

Sir   Boston May 11th 1796

In submitting to your patronage, the inclosed work, we flatter ourselves, that our particular application or its mode, will not be deemed presumptuous or intrusive, when you consider that, although it be acknowledged by those who have read it, one of the most ingenious and moral productions extant, yet there are very few copies of it in america; and as it is the particular province of men of taste in dignified stations, to discountenance the propagation of immoral works, or such as tend to wound the cause of religion or good order, so it is the peculiar satisfaction of men, whose virtues have acquired them unbounded influence, to patronise those productions, which are intended to promote the cause of virtue of science and of submission to the laws.[1]

We presume to sollicit your leave, to inscribe the work to you, sir, and fully sensible of what we ask, and sollicitous to use your patronage to the greatest advantage, our wish is to inscribe it simply to George Washington, President of the united states.[2] With great respect we are sir Your most hble and most obedt Servants

for the publishers   Joseph Nancrede

ALS, DLC:GW.

Paul Joseph Guérard de Nancrède (1761–1841) was a Boston bookseller and printer.

1. Nancrède probably enclosed at least one volume of Henry Hunter's translation of Jacques-Henri Bernardin de Saint-Pierre's *Studies of Nature*, published in five volumes at London in 1796. Nancrède, in partnership with William Spotswood, another printer and bookseller, had proposed an American edition (see *Federal Orrery* [Boston], 5 May).

2. No reply from GW has been found, but Nancrède's desired dedication appeared in the American edition when published in three volumes in 1797. The dedication in the first volume takes the form of a letter from Nancrède to GW dated February 1797. Nancrède expressed hope that he did "not take a disrespectful or unwelcome license. As a member of the human family, he finds a superior gratification, in testifying his respect for a character, equally known and revered among mankind. As an AMERICAN CITIZEN, he feels a sweet satisfaction in paying the tribute of gratitude and veneration, in his power, to the MAN, whom his country delights to honour and to bless, as having eminently contributed to establish her independence, by his military command; to insure her peace and prosperity, by his civil administration; and to enhance her glory, by his public and private virtues."

To James Madison

12th May 1796
The President of the United States requests the Pleasure of Mr
Madison's Company to Dine, on Thursday next,[1] at 4 o'Clock.
An answer is requested.[2]

D (printed with manuscript insertions), DLC:GW.
   1. The next Thursday was 19 May.
   2. No reply has been found, but see *Madison Papers,* 16:355–56.

From Richard Peters

Dear Sir   Belmont[1] [Pa.] 12. May 1796
I have so long waited for the Answers to a Number of Queries,
I proposed to several of our most intelligent Farmers, on the
subject of Manures, & particularly the Gypsum; & have been so
much disappointed in not receiving the requisite Information,
that I cannot longer trespass on your Patience, by detaining Sr J.
Sinclair's Communications which I now return to you.[2] Many
of the Subjects are too amply discussed, to need any Additions.
If any were necessary, American Farmers have made too little
Progress in their Art, to teach those of Europe. Our Stercou-
ries are in a rude state; and but few take any pains to improve
them. Composts are rare. Native Manures, except Lime, Plaister
& River Mud, little sought after. Perhaps I should add that Oys-
ter Shells & Salt Sedge or Grass, are much used, as Manures, on
our Sea Coasts. In the Neighborhood of Cities and Towns, the
Manures produced in them are all used, some well applied, but
generally without much Art or Management. Altho' our Agriculture on our old Lands is much improved, it is yet in its Infancy.
There is so much fresh Land to be had, that the worn Lands are
frequently abandoned to *what is called rest,* or left in the hands of
those who manage them (with however many Exceptions) but
indifferently. The only Subject on which I could reasonably hope
to afford any useful Information, was that of Plaister of Paris. For
this Purpose I proposed the Queries I enclose to sundry of our
Farmers, who appear to be averse from putting their Thoughts
on Paper. I also send you the Answers of a Mr West (Brother to
the celebrated Painter of that Name) who has effected wonder-

ful Changes in his Farm, by Means of this Manure chiefly.[3] His Farm is now a Garden tho' it was a miserable sterile Waste. He is not singular in the successful Use of Plaister. It is now becoming very general, and is always productive of beneficial Effects, in greater or less degrees. Many of our Farmers who are within Reach of the Sea Ports, where they can purchase Plaister, are rapidly getting rich, by means of this Manure.

I must for the present, content myself with sending you the enclosed Answers to the Queries on this Subject. At a future Day, if I find any thing worthy of troubling you with, I will send any further Communications I receive, or Thoughts which are suggested from Conversations with our Farmers or my own Reflections.[4] I am with sincere & respectful Esteem Your Obedt Servt

Richard Peters

I wish it were possible to get one or two Copies of the Surveys and Reports made to the Board of Agriculture of G. Britain. I want one for our Agricultural Society and one for myself. If they were to be purchased I would buy them. If you think it will not be laying yourself under Obligations or involving yourself in trouble I will be obliged to you to desire Sr J.S. to send one or two Copies. If any Expence attends it I will cheerfully pay it.

Copy, DLC:GW. GW's note filed with this document identifies it and the enclosures as copies (see notes 3 and 4 below). He also wrote: "The originals were sent to Sir Jno. Sinclair" (see GW to John Sinclair, 12 June).

1. Belmont, the country estate and mansion of Peters, bordered the Schuylkill River near Philadelphia. The mansion is now within Fairmount Park in that city.

2. Peters returned Robert Somerville's *Outlines of the Fifteenth Chapter of the Proposed General Report from the Board of Agriculture. On the Subject of Manures* (London, 1795), which GW had sent to him on 4 March. He also may have returned *Extracts from the Minutes of the Proceedings of the Board of Agriculture, respecting Mr. Elkington's Mode of Draining; together with Copies of such Papers as have been communicated to the Board upon that subject* (London, 1795), which, like the *Outlines*, had been sent to GW with John Sinclair's letters of 18 July 1795.

3. William West (c.1724–1808) was Benjamin West's elder brother. In addition to farming, he represented Delaware County in the Pennsylvania House for a number of terms during the 1790s.

Peters wrote West: "The Gypsum Plaister of Paris according to a late Analysis of its component parts as declared in an English Work is said to be compounded of a Mineral Acid and a Calcareous Earth. The first an Enemy, the second friendly to Vegetation. According as the one or the other prevails it is said to be good or bad. It is said there to operate on virgin Soils with good

Effect, but not on Grounds which have been long under Cultivation and especially those that have *been limed.* The result of your experience is requested on this particular Point. My Observations do not support this Assertion." He then posed eleven specific questions and finished by encouraging "any miscellaneous Remarks founded on your Experience tho' they may not be immediately applicable to the foregoing Queries." A copy of West's reply is filed with this letter to GW in DLC:GW.

4. A copy of Peters's responses to the eleven questions and his miscellaneous observations is filed with this letter to GW in DLC:GW. Peters noted in his miscellaneous observations: "After all that can be said, we have much to learn on the Qualities and Effects of the Gypsum as it relates to Agriculture. It is a capricious and whimsical Substance" whose effects varied widely. Thoughts about the grinding of plaster and a test of its quality subsequently appear under the date 26 May. These additions presumably came after this letter to GW.

From Timothy Pickering

Sir, Department of State May 12. 1796.

As far as I have been able, I have stated in the inclosed paper the objects which I conceived you wished to consider, as deducible from various letters from our ministers and consuls abroad. There are others of a subordinate nature, or which respect situations which do not demand instant decision; but which will be resumed & pursued as soon as I find relief from the present anguish of my heart.[1]

T. Pickering

ADfS, MHi: Pickering Papers. A later docket on the letter says the date "should be 11th May," but the apparent reference to the death of Pickering's son indicates that 12 May is the correct date.

1. Charles Pickering (1784–1796) died on this date (see Pickering and Upham, *Life of Pickering,* 3:286–89).

Enclosure
Report on Foreign Affairs

Wednesday May 12. 1796.[1] ½ past three o'clock

Mr Pinckney having desired to relinquish his mission and return to America, there will be a vacancy for a minister at London. Mr King has intimated that it would be agreeable to him to succeed Mr Pinckney. At all events, without fixing on the time, Mr King contemplates a relinquishment of his seat in the Senate.

A minister of his abilities & experience & law-knowledge would seem peculiarly desirable at this time for the mission to London. For independent of the general interests of the Union respecting further negociations, the important claims of the citizens for spoliations on their commerce may derive very material support from his interposition with the British ministers, and our commissioners much useful information & advice.

Mr Short having decided on resigning his mission to Madrid, and desired letters of recall, for which he waits at Paris, a vacancy presents at Madrid.[2]

Mr Short says that the allowance of 4500 dollars, the salary to a minister resident, is quite inadequate to the expences of a residence at the Spanish Court. He also represents it as a matter of peculiar importance at that Court that a minister should hold an elevated grade. And as the Spanish minister recently appointed to the U. States, has the rank of minister plenipotentiary, this would seem to enforce the other reasons for giving the like grade to the new minister to go from the United States to that court.[3] Mr Wm Smith of South-Carolina having manifested a desire to be employed in the diplomatic line, he appears extremely well adapted to the service at the court of Spain. A familiar knowledge of the French language, which Mr Smith possesses, would render his communications with that court perfectly easy.

Should the President finally resolve on a change of the minister at Paris, perhaps no man could be found better qualified, there to represent & support the interests of the U. States and its citizens (the latter as well as the former are of great magnitude) than Mr J. Quincy Adams.

Algiers

The gentleman whom Mr FitzSimons consulted as a candidate for the consulate at Algiers, seems to have had no objection to the service, but on the score of *compensation*, which is limited by law to 2000 dollars a year.[4] He speaks and writes French, Spanish & Italian, which would be extremely useful in that employment: but the final enquiry presents some circumstances less propitious—a want of enterprise—and his close connections with the editor of the Aurora.

The result of my reflections on this subject is, that as Mr Barlow has accepted a temporary appointment under the orders of Colo. Monroe & Colo. Humphreys, he should be continued.

He is a citizen of France, as well as of the U. States; and going thither under the patronage of the French Government, he may be very useful, if he shall have arrived in time, to prevent the fatal mischief so much apprehended by a delay in the pecuniary arrangements to fulfil the agreement entered into by Mr Donaldson. Should Mr Barlow be named to the *Senate*, it is doubtful whether he woud be approved: his new religious character & his politics are obnoxious to leading men in the majority of that body.[5] Before a permanent Consul, possessing the requisite knowledge, just political principles, the integrity and the abilities demanded for the maintenance of the interests of the U. States at Algiers, can be appointed, it will probably be necessary for Congress to provide a more ample salary. The discretionary powers of our consul there must be very extensive in a matter the most liable to abuse—the disbursement of large sums of money for which no vouchers can be obtained, and for which it will often be necessary to issue promptly, without waiting particular orders from Government. Probably four or five thousand dollars a year (or the salary of a minister resident) would alone tempt a fit character to accept the office: unless considerable commercial advantages could be connected with it; of which Mr FitzSimons, who has been so good as [to] make enquiry, has yet obtained no satisfactory information.

The appropriation bill for Barbary Affairs has passed the House: as soon as it becomes a law the measures requisite to fulfil the engagements for Algiers may be begun.[6]

At my request, Mr FitzSimons has procured a British Mediterranean Pass, to serve as an exemplar in forming our own; which will serve I suppose for all the Barbary Powers including Morocco, whose emperor, Mr Simpson says, desires our vessels to be so furnished, according to the usage of the European powers.

Morocco

It will be desirable to have a consul for that Kingdom who is acquainted with the customs of the country. Such an one presents in the person of Mr Simpson, who is now our consul at Gibraltar. He is willing to accept the Consulate for Morocco, to reside at Tangier, to which place he says the French have removed their consulate, to avoid the great expences of a residence near the Court. Mr Cabot is personally acquainted with Mr Simpson, and knows him to be a man of worth. His negociation of the recognition of our treaty with Morocco seems to have been very well & very economically conducted. Should a vacancy be thus occasioned at Gibraltar, and no fit candidate immediately present, Mr Simpson could be desired to employ an agent for the service of the Gibraltar Consulate until a regular appointment could be made—in the same manner as he must have done while he was last summer and autumn employed at Morocco.

He says a present must accompany the annunciation of the Consul, and he has given a detail of the articles most acceptable, consisting of military stores.

He says also that a house must be built at Tangier for the American Consul, as is done by the European powers. But we know not the fashion or size suitable for the purpose. The frame and lumber must be sent from America. I have consulted Mr FitzSimons on the subject, who thinks the building were better suspended, to obtain farther information.

Mr Simpson also represents that occasional presents will be indispensable: but that some restrictions will be necessary. These will come into view in forming the instructions for the Consul when appointed.[7]

Naples

John S. M. Matthieu, native of that place, is handsomely recommended for consul there. His own letter of the 14th of January manifests a very competent knowledge of the English tongue. Mr Vanuxem, who has written two letters in his favour, is a French merchant of Philadelphia, who many years since married in New Jersey, and has been carrying on business extensively, & enjoys I believe the reputation of an honest man. His description of the reputation Mr Matthieu acquired at St Domingo corresponds with that given by the French letter inclosed in Mr Bingham's.[8]

Dunkirk

Francis Coffyn, son of the late Consul his father, solicits the appointment of Consul for Dunkirk. He is now acting as such under Colo. Monroe's sanction. He acted as Chancellor in the consulate for his father, and for some time conducted the whole business—during his father's ill health.[9]

Belfast, Ireland

James Holmes, recommended for consul at Belfast, by his fellow citizens, and by General Walter Stewart.[10]

Alexander Montgomery solicits the same office for himself or his brother Hugh. The letter is addressed to Mr Randolph, to whom it seems the writer was personally known during nine years residence at Richmond.[11]

Bremen

There are two applications; neither appears on enquiry to be very satisfactory. I expect information in a day or two of a third; when the whole will be laid before the President.[12]

Hamburg

Complaints have been made by Colo. Monroe against the present Consul, John Parrish, as an agent for the British, and adverse to France: a particular complaint was made for his engaging transports to convey the Emigrants to Great Britain.[13]

I had somehow understood that Mr Parish was a merchant of respectability, & enquired of his character. Mr Robert Morris informs me, that he is a merchant of great wealth and of the most fair & honorable reputation: that in the beginning of our revolution he was the correspondent of the Secret Committee of Congress; and before we had any funds, procured for the U. States articles of essential importance, to the amount of sixty thousand pounds sterling, which most opportunely arrived: that he is now the Chief correspondent of the American Merchants trading to Hamburg; and now has in consequence an agent or partner in this city, to whom Mr Morris referred me for information "deserving attention & credit in what he might say regarding Mr Parrish." This gentleman says the transporting of the emigrants was thus. A considerable number of American Vessels (twenty or thirty) at Hamburg, wanted employment, or to be sold. Mr Parrish informed them of the call for vessels to transport the emigrants. Many readily desired to sell. The business was left with a Clerk of Mr Parrish's. The sales were very advantageous to the American owners. Some of the American masters refused the employment. There was nothing in it repugnant to our treaty with France; which on the contrary provides for the very case—declaring that the enemy soldiers may be taken out & made prisoners—but the vessel to go free.

Mr Parrish is not the English Consul at Hamburg. He does nothing for the British but as a private merchant whose ability integrity & respectability recommend him to the merchants of that nation.

These are all the cases which seem to me in a situation necessary to be immediately decided upon. It has not been possible for me yet to read the entire correspondence of all our ministers. There are some regulations respecting consuls which[14] when digested it might be proper to lay before the legislature at the next session. Whatever remains to be brought into the view of the President, must be the result of further examination.

The distressed situation of my family obliges me to go to them immediately.

T. Pickering

ADS, MHi: Pickering Papers.

1. This date was a Thursday.

2. In his letter of 22 May 1795 to then secretary of state Edmund Randolph, William Short had requested that a leave of absence be made permanent and that letters of recall be delivered by his successor. His letter to the secretary of state dated 30 Oct. 1795 announced his departure for Paris (both, DNA: RG 59, Despatches from U.S. Ministers to Spain).

3. In Short's letters to the State Department dated 30 Aug. and 4 and 16 Sept. 1794, he reported that his official reception at the Spanish court had been delayed by his status as minister resident (all, DNA: RG 59, Despatches from U.S. Ministers to Spain). In his letter written at Madrid on 16 Sept., he reported how an undersecretary had explained that "there were no other Ministers here than those of the second order, and that that order could be only where the Character of Plenipotentiary was given in the letter of credence." As a "mark of regard" for the United States, they finally accepted Short's credential, pending a correction in rank by the president. Short also addressed the inadequacy of his allowance for attendance on the Spanish court, "the most expensive without exception in Europe."

4. Section 5 of "An Act concerning Consuls and Vice-Consuls" imposed this limitation (1 *Stat.* 254–57). The candidate has not been identified.

5. For Joel Barlow's designation as acting consul at Algiers by James Monroe, U.S. minister to France, and David Humphreys, U.S. minister to Portugal and chargé d'affaires to the Barbary States, see Monroe to the Secretary of State, 4 Oct. 1795, in *Papers of James Monroe*, 3:476–78. Barlow was strongly identified with support of the French Revolution. Although a former army chaplain, his association with Thomas Paine opened him to allegations of atheism.

6. The U.S. House of Representatives resolved on 10 May 1796 to appropriate $260,000 "to carry into effect, any treaty already made, and to enable the President to effect any treaty or treaties with any of the Barbary states." A committee reported a bill that passed a second (not final) reading on 12 May (*Journal of the House*, 8:423–24, 433–34). "An Act making further provision for the expenses attending the intercourse of the United States with foreign nations; and to continue in force the act, intituled 'An act proving the means of intercourse between the United States and foreign nations[']" became law

on 30 May (1 *Stat.* 487–88). A previous act, "making an appropriation for defraying the expenses which may arise in carrying into effect the Treaty made between the United States and the Dey and Regency of Algiers," had been approved on 6 May (1 *Stat.* 460).

7. For James Simpson's various remarks, see his letter to the secretary of state, 24 Sept. 1795, in DNA: RG 59: Despatches from U.S. Consuls in Gibraltar.

8. See William Bingham to GW, 9 Jan. 1796, and n.1 to that document.

9. Francis Coffyn, Jr., served as consul at Dunkirk, France, beginning in 1796. For Coffyn's interest in the consulship, see Monroe's letter to him written on 28 May 1795 in *Papers of James Monroe*, 3:314.

10. James Holmes (d. 1832), a Belfast merchant, wrote then secretary of state Edmund Randolph on 10 June 1795 seeking the consulship at Belfast and enclosing a recommendation of the same date signed by 43 "Merchants and Traders resident in the Town of Belfast and Kingdom of Ireland." Walter Stewart wrote a testimonial at Philadelphia on 12 Sept. 1795 that characterized Holmes as "a Gentleman of Strict Honour, Universally respected, of Extensive Capital, & in Every Way Adapted for the Situation of Consul" (DLC:GW). Holmes was appointed consul and retained that post until 1815.

11. Alexander Montgomery wrote Randolph from Belfast on 13 June 1795: "I take the liberty to advise you of my residence here since my return from America in the Year 1792 & of my establishment in partnership with my Brother Hugh, under the firm of Hugh & Alexander Montgomery, and presuming on the Personal knowledge you have of me, I beg leave to request your friendly interference to procure for my Brother or myself the appointment of Consul for the united States of America, at this Town." Rather than a recommendation from Belfast inhabitants, Montgomery believed his "residence at Richmond for nine Years immediately under your own observation" better showed his merits (DLC:GW).

12. The burgomasters and senators of Bremen had written GW on 15 Oct. 1794 to request the recall of Christoph Diedrich Arnold Delius as consul at that place. Christian William Carpzov, a Bremen merchant, subsequently renewed his application (see Frederick Gorrissen to Edmund Randolph, 3 Dec. 1794, and William Temple Franklin to Robert Morris, 1 Feb. 1795, both DLC:GW). Timothy Green wrote Elias Boudinot from New York on 9 Dec. 1795 to urge the qualifications of Bremen merchant Frederic William Schultze (DLC:GW). Frederick Jacob Wichelhausen, also of Bremen, traveled to the United States and received significant backing (see John P. Pleasants to Samuel Pleasants & Sons, 10 May 1796, and Clement Biddle to Pickering, 17 May 1796, both DLC:GW). GW appointed Wichelhausen as consul at Bremen, and he served until 1833.

13. Monroe's letter to Pickering dated 22 Dec. 1795 included a complaint from Charles Delacroix, French minister for foreign affairs, that John Parish was "granting passports for France to British subjects, equipping the emigrants, and acting in all cases as the English agent." Monroe added that Parish's conduct was even "more reprehensible" because he equipped the emigrants "in American bottoms with a view of protecting them under our flag" (*Papers of*

James Monroe, 3:547–49). See also Pickering to GW, 24 May, and n.4 to that document.

14. Pickering inadvertently wrote "when" for this word.

From the Commissioners
for the District of Columbia

Sir   City of Washington, 13th May 1796

In consequence of a correspondence between Mr Scott & Mr Robert Gilmor of Baltimore, and a conversation Mr White had with Mr Gilmor, in his return from Phila., we have judged it expedient, through his means to set on foot a negotiation for a Loan in Holland—Mr Gilmor expressed a very clear opinion that the necessary Sums may be procured at an interest not exceeding 6 percent per Annum, including charges, and possibly, at a Lower rate—For the accomplishment of this business, we have executed a power of attorney to Messrs Wilhem & Jan Willink of Amsterdam—agreeably to a form furnished by Mr Gilmor, varying only, such parts, as were necessary to adopt it to our particular case—We presume it will be necessary, for the President or the Secretary of State to certify under the seal of the United States, that we are the Commissioners designated by the Law, and that an authenticated Copy of the Act of Congress should accompany the power of Attorney—We likewise suppose, that the direction of the President to borrow, should appear in some authentic form; and also, the obligation of the United States, ultimately to make good the loan—For these purposes we have, we have drawn and transmitted an instrument for the signature of the President, should it be approved Mr Gilmor will be in Phila. when this Letter arrives[1]—You will, consequently have an opportunity of conversing with him, & if you judge the measure proper, you can have the advice of counsel, as well as the opinion of Mr Gilmor, as to the mode of carrying it into effect—There will be no occasion of a recurrence to us unless the power of attorney should be deemed defective: in that case, we should wish to have such an instrument prepared for our signature as may be satisfactory.

We have taken the liberty of enclosing a Letter to Mr Gilmor, who is either at Mr Bingham's or Mr Mordecai Lewis's—and who will no doubt wait on you, as soon as he receives the Letter[2]—We are, with respect yrs &c.

sign'd G. Scott

W. Thornton

A. White

It would be agreeable to us that the Attorney General be consulted, at least, so far as the president is to act, rather than rely, solely on our own opinion.

LB, DNA: RG 42, Records of the Commissioners for the District of Columbia, Letters Sent.

1. The commissioners prepared a power of attorney on this date for Dutch bankers Wilhem and Jan Willink that authorized them "to negotiate a Loan in Amsterdam to the amount of five hundred and twelve thousand Guilders, Dutch currency" (DNA: RG 42, Records of the Commissioners for the District of Columbia, Letters Sent). The original form has not been identified, but a copy of a duplicate is filed at 31 May in DNA: RG 42, Records of the Commissioners for the District of Columbia, Letters Received. Robert Gilmor's company acted as agent for the Willinks (see Alexander White to the Commissioners, 2 May, DNA: RG 42, Records of the Commissioners for the District of Columbia, Letters Received).

GW provided the requested certification on 23 May: "Be it Known to all persons to whom these presents shall Come, that I George Washington President of the United States of America, by Virtue of an Act of the Congress of the said United States entitled 'An Act authorizing a Loan for the use of the City of Washington in the District of Columbia, & for other purposes therein mentioned' have directed Gustavus Scott, William Thornton and Alexander White Commissioners appointed under an Act entitled an Act for establishing the temporary & permanent Seat of the Government of the United States, to borrow by themselves or by their Attorney or Attornies Agent or Agents duly empower'd & authorized in the present year one thousand seven hundred ninety & six the sum of five hundred & twelve thousand Guilders of Dutch Currency in Amsterdam at an Interest not exceeding six per Cent per Annum reimbursable at any time after the year one thousand eight hundred and three by Installments not exceeding one fifth of the whole sum in any one year.

"And I do further declare and make known that all the Lots in the said City of Washington (except those now appropriated to public Use) vested in the Commissioners aforesaid or in Trustees in any Manner for the use of the United States are chargeable with the Re payment of all and every Sum or sums of money or Interest thereupon which Shall be borrowed by the said Commissioners under the direction of the President of the United States pursuant to the said first mentioned Act—And I do further declare and make known that if the product of the Sales of all the said Lots shall prove inadequate to the payment of the Principal and Interest of the sums borrowed under the first mentioned Act, That then the Deficiency shall be paid by the United States agreeably to the Terms of the said Loan" (copy, DLC:GW).

2. The enclosed letter to Gilmor written on this date asked him to wait on GW "as soon as convenient" (DNA: RG 42, Records of the Commissioners for the District of Columbia, Letters Sent).

From James McHenry

Sir.   13 May 1796

The Secry of the Treasury has mentioned to me this morning the substance of a communication, which he said he had imparted to you some time since. It respects certain instructions given by Mr Adet to persons who are on their road to the Western Country which affect and may bring into danger the peace and safety of the U.S.[1]

I inclose you papers containing matter apparently connected with this subject; that of the 24 was sent me, perhaps a week ago, by Mr Pickering; those tied together, I had to-day from General Wayne.[2]

When I conjoin with these circumstances, some of a private and others of a public nature, all tending to the same issue, there is too much room for apprehending a serious crisis to be approaching, which it may be proper to have the means to dissipate.

I have said to Mr Woolcot, that I thought such instructions as he mentioned, would justify the President to direct the persons employed to execute them to be seized. If this can be done with propriety, and the instructions be as represented, and can be obtained, their publication, at a fit moment, might be attended with the happiest consequences.

All these things together have made such an impression on my mind that I cannot help mentioning it to you for your own reflexions.[3]

Col. Rochfontaine has changed his request and now prefers a court of Enquiry. I have of course changed the order I had given to General Wayne to accord with his request.[4] With the sincerest respect I am Sir your most ob. st

                                                                  James McHenry

ALS, DLC:GW; LB, DLC:GW; ADf, MiU-C: James McHenry Papers.

1. Secretary of the Treasury Oliver Wolcott, Jr., probably conversed with GW (see Wolcott's statement, 19 May).

2. Charles-Joseph Warin had sent Pickering on 24 March his resignation as an army engineer, written in French (MHi: Pickering Papers). McHenry may have enclosed a translation of Warin's letter. The other enclosures have not been identified.

3. McHenry wrote Gen. Anthony Wayne privately on 25 May: "The President has received information that certain emissaries are employed and paid, to gain a knowledge of our military posts in the Western country, and to encourage and stimulate the people in that quarter to secede from the union, and form a political and seperate connexion with a foreign power." The remainder of the letter identified the emissaries as Victor Collot, Thomas Power, and Warin. It also authorized their arrest and the seizure of their papers (Knopf, *Wayne*, 481–84; see also Charles Lee to GW, 20 May, and McHenry to GW, 2 July, n.4).

4. On 12 May, McHenry wrote Wayne, enclosing charges exhibited against Stephen Rochefontaine by officers of the corps of artillery and engineers. Noting Rochefontaine's desire for a court of inquiry, McHenry directed Wayne to order a court "to sit at West Point" and to "endeavour to form it of unprejudiced and the most enlightened Officers" (Knopf, *Wayne*, 481). An undated document headed "Charges against Lieut. Col. Rochefontaine" listed conduct unbecoming an officer, neglect of duty, incompetence, and "Violating the laws of the United States in public orders" (PHi: Wayne Papers). McHenry's earlier order on this subject has not been identified.

From the Commissioners
for the District of Columbia

sir   City of Washington 14th May 1796

Our Letter of Yesterday, covering the power of attorney to Messrs Willink, will shew you, that we are busily engaged in endeavoring to draw some good effects from the Loan Bill which has cost us so much time & trouble—We beg leave to submit to your consideration, the enclosed advertisement, which, when approved by you, we wish to appear in the public prints at Boston, New York and Phila., as soon as possible—There can be no reason to return them to us, previous to their being inserted in the public prints; when approved by you, we shall immediately proceed to have the advertizement inserted in the public prints here and in the Southern States[1]—We are using our best endeavors to procure some immediate supplies to commence, actively, on the public buildings—We are not yet able to say what will be the result—Morris & Nicholson promise to come forward in the course of the month, but experience will not permit us to place much confidence in their promises[2]—We mean, however, to proceed to advertise their property for Sale on the first of June, agreeably to the notice given them, unless they make their payments, as required—We have the honor &c.

(signed) G. Scott

W. Thornton

A. White

LB, DNA: RG 42, Records of the Commissioners for the District of Columbia, Letters Sent.

1. The advertisement on this date reads: "The Commissioners give notice, that under direction of the President of the U. States they will *immediately* proceed to the Sale of Lots in the said City, and continue the same until they shall have raised a sum sufficient to compleat the Public Buildings, and to repay all sums borrowed or hereafter to be borrowed for that purpose. they will sell on moderate terms, and will give a preference to those who mean to improve— One third part of the price will be expected in hand, and the remainder in two equal annual payments—Or in deferred Stock of the U. States as may best suit Purchasers—Information respecting the situation and prices of Lots may be had at the Commissioners Office in the said City where constant attendance will be given" (DNA: RG 42, Records of the Commissioners for the District of Columbia, Letters Received).

2. Commissioner Alexander White had written Robert Morris and John Nicholson from Philadelphia on 9 May to threaten sale of their lots "as soon as 30 days after the May instalment becomes due" if $12,000 was not paid. Morris and Nicholson replied to White from Philadelphia that same date: "Our inclination to pay the instalments to the Commissioners of the Federal City has more influence over our Conduct, than any other consideration can have.

"We shall therefore make exertions to pay the $12000 you mention within the time prescribed because we believe it to be necessary to progress in the buildings and we think we shall be able to accomplish this payment to Your wish" (both letters, DNA: RG 42, Records of the Commissioners for the District of Columbia, Letters Received).

White's correspondence with Morris and Nicholson resulted from White's conversation with GW on 7 May. White summarized the exchange when he wrote the commissioners from Philadelphia on Monday, 9 May: "Altho: I expect to accompany this letter as [far] as the City of Washington I have supposed there might be a propriety in the whole of my proceedings at this place appearing on your file. And therefore inform you that on Saturday I had a conversation with the President on the affairs of the City in which I submitted to his consideration the following subjects.

"1st Morris and Nicholson

"2d The Sale of Lots

"3d The Roof and Stair Case of the Presidents House

"4th The erecting Buildings for the Executive Departments

"5th The propriety of retaining a Treasurer

"6th The propriety of selling the Freestone Quarry reserving a right to take as much Stone as may be necessary for the Publick Buildings

"In regard to the first he is of opinion, that no further indulgence ought to be granted, and that I should acquaint those Gentlemen with that determination before I should leave the City. . . .

"With respect to the second, he repeated his opinion as formerly expressed as to large Sales but thinks it proper to sell in small quantities to such as mean to improve, and that the money arising from these Sales may be applied to the payment of the interest of the money borrowed, if a Loan shall be made, and the Overplus, if any, invested in the U: States stock to indemnify the Gover[n]ment against the Guarantee, and that this measure should be made as publick as possible, As to the prices at which Lots ought to sell he gave no opinion.

"The roof of the Presidents House, he wishes to be of Slate, if it is within our means, that is, if the expence will not be too great. And if Workmen whose skill and integrity may be relied on can be procured to execute—With respect to the Stair Case, he said he was not well acquainted with such things, but supposed that any Stone other than marble, and a particular kind of marble too would have a very heavy appearance, and that marble would be very expensive, On the whole he appeared to prefer Wood, and intimated very plainly a wish, that such private matters might be conducted without particular applications to him.

"He thinks nothing should be done towards erecting Buildings for the Executive Departments until the Presidents House and Capital are finished, or so far advanced that their seasonable completion may be relied on.

"A Treasurer he thinks a useless Officer in the present state of things—and consequently an unnecessary expense, At the commencement of the business when the Commissioners resided at a distance and seldom met, it might be necessary to have some responsible Person on the spot to receive and pay money but now the Commissioners, always present may deposit the money, when there is any on hand, with the Bank of Columbia and draw it out as wanted.

"The Freestone Quarry he would not agree to sell unless compelled to it by the absolute want of money, as he thinks the value will rapidly rise with the encrease of the City" (DNA: RG 42, Records of the Commissioners for the District of Columbia, Letters Received).

From John Sinclair

Board of Agriculture Whitehall [London]

Sir.   May 14th 1796.

In addition to the paper respecting Manures which I had the honor of forwarding to your Excellency last year, I now beg leave to Subjoin a further Memoir on the Same interesting Subject.[1]

The Board of Agriculture will be highly obliged to your Excellency, if you will please at your leisure to cast an Eye over it, and would recommend it to the attention of your intelligent friends conversant in Such inquiries whose remarks upon it would be highly acceptable. I have the Honor to remain with the greatest Respect Sir Your Excellency's most humble and most obedient servant

John Sinclair

I beg leave also to inclose a Copy of my address to the Board of Agriculture at its last meeting, stating the progress that has been made by the Board in Carrying on the Improvement of the Country during the last sessions.[2] Excuse my making use of a borrowed hand having been of late much troubled with an inflammation in my Eyes.[3]

LS, DLC:GW. For this letter being completed at a later date, see n.2 below.

1. Sinclair enclosed *Additional Appendix to the Outlines of the Fifteenth Chapter of the Proposed General Report from the Board of Agriculture. On the Subject of Manures* (London, 1796). He had enclosed the original *Outlines* with his letters to GW of 18 July 1795.

2. Sinclair evidently added this postscript after 24 May 1796. The four-page printed address filed with this letter in DLC:GW has the title: *Sir John Sinclair's Address to the Board of Agriculture, on Tuesday, the Twenty-Fourth of May, 1796: Stating the Progress that Had Been Made by the Board, during the Third Session since Its Establishment* (n.p., n.d.).

3. GW acknowledged this letter when he wrote Sinclair on 10 Dec. (DLC:GW).

From Oliver Wolcott, Jr.

Treasury Department May 14th 1796.

The Secretary of the Treasury has the honour most respectfully to submit to the President of the United States, certain documents in respect to Sylvanus Walker, Inspector of the revenue for the third survey of the District of South Carolina;[1] by which it appears,

1st. That the said Inspector wants the capacity so necessary to insure a due and correct discharge of the duties attached to his office.

2d. That the said Inspector has subjected the United States

to considerable loss by omitting to enforce the execution of the Laws for creating internal Revenue.

3d. That the said Inspector has neglected to render his accounts at the time and in the mode prescribed, although frequently required so to do by the Supervisor of the District of So. Carolina.

For all which reasons, the Secretary of the Treasury is of opinion that the public Interest indispensably requires, that the said Inspector be displaced from office.

If the President should see cause to remove Sylvanus Walker from the office he now holds, the Secretary would beg leave to mention William Benson as his successor; he being recommended as a person well qualified to discharge the duties of Inspector, by three of the Representatives of South Carolina, whose letter to the Commissioner of the revenue on that subject accompanies the other documents.[2] All which is most respectfully submitted to the Consideration of the President of the United States.

Oliv: Wolcott Jr
Secy of the Treasy

LB, DLC:GW; ADf, CtHi: Oliver Wolcott, Jr., Papers.

1. Sylvanus Walker probably was the man who served in the South Carolina General Assembly, 1785–86, and Senate, 1789–90. He became inspector for the third survey (Abbeville, Edgefield, Greenville, Laurens, Newberry, Pendleton, Spartanburg, and Union counties) in 1791.

The enclosed documents included Walker's letter to Commissioner of the Revenue Tench Coxe written on 2 Jan. and a letter from Daniel Stevens, superintendent of the revenue for South Carolina, to Coxe dated 5 March (both, DNA: RG 59, Miscellaneous Papers). Responding to concerns about delinquencies in his accounts, Walker blamed poor guidance from Stevens, problems with a subordinate, local opposition to enforcement of the laws, and his own "incapability in business." Stevens forwarded Walker's letter to Coxe and added: "It is truly painful to me to call in question any Man's veracity, particularly an Officer under me, or to complain of his inattention and highly criminal errors constantly committed in his Accounts, but sir, as there are several parts of his letter to you, which are palpable falsities, tending to exculpate himself in some measure from the charge of having committed errors in his Accounts and Returns, and to sanction or cloke his neglect, of duties of his Office, by avering it was by my consent or acquiescence, I think it necessarry in the first instance, positively to deny such unjust insinuation." Stevens then detailed Walker's shortcomings and requested resolution of the contentions.

2. William Benson (c.1743–1796) held local offices and represented Spartanburg in the South Carolina General Assembly in 1791.

Congressmen Robert Goodloe Harper, Samuel Earle, and Wade Hampton wrote Coxe on 8 April 1796 to express "a hope that no change may be found Necessary in the appointment" for the third survey, but they agreed that Benson "unites in an eminent degree the qualities that appear to be necessary for the office" (DLC:GW). GW removed Walker and nominated Benson on 17 May. The Senate confirmed that nomination on 18 May (*Senate Executive Journal*, 208). Benson died in July.

Letter not found: to Anne Louise DuBarry, 15 May 1796. In DuBarry's letter to GW of 28 June, she referred to "the Letter you honourd me with dated the 15th of may" (see GW to George Lewis, 28 April, n.2).

To Francis II (Holy Roman Emperor)

To the Emperor of Germany.   Philadelphia 15th May 1796

It will readily occur to your Majesty, that occasions may sometimes exist, on which official considerations would constrain the Chief of a Nation to be silent and passive, in relation even to objects which affect his sensibility, and claim his interposition, as a man. Finding myself precisely in this situation at present, I take the liberty of writing this *private* letter to Your Majesty; being persuaded that my motives, will also be my apology for it.

In common with the People of this Country, I retain a strong and cordial sense of the Services rendered to them by the Marquis De la Fayette; and my friendship for him has been constant and sincere. It is natural therefore, that I should sympathize with him and his family in their misfortunes, and endeavor to mitigate the calamities wch they experience; among which his present confinement is not the least distressing.

I forbear to enlarge on this delicate subject—Permit me only to submit to your Majesty's consideration, whether his long Imprisonment—and the confiscation of his Estate—and the Indigence & dispersion of his family—and the painful anxieties incident to all these circumstances, do not form an assemblage of sufferings, which recommend him to the mediation of Humanity? Allow me Sir! on this occasion to be its organ; and to entreat that he may be permitted to come to this country, on such conditions and under such restrictions, as your Majesty may think it expedient to prescribe.[1]

As it is a maxim with me not to ask, what under similar circumstances I would not grant, Your Majesty will do me the justice to believe, that this request appears to me to corrispond with those great principles of Magnanimity & wisdom, which form the basis of sound policy and durable glory. May the Almighty and merciful Sovereign of the Universe keep Your Majesty under his Protection and guidance.

Go: Washington

ALS (2), enclosed with GW to Thomas Pinckney, 22 May, NNPM; LB, DLC:GW. GW inadvertently omitted the word "persuaded" from one ALS. The substance of the two letters is the same despite differences in punctuation, capitalization, and paragraphing.

1. For background on Lafayette's imprisonment, see Justus Erick Bollmann to GW, 1 April; see also GW to Alexander Hamilton, 8 May.

To Alexander Hamilton

My dear Sir,   Philadelphia 15th May 1796

On this day week, I wrote you a letter on the subject of the information received from G—— M——, and put it with some other Papers respecting the case of Mr De la Fayette, under cover to Mr Jay: to whom also I had occasion to write.[1] But in my hurry (making up the dispatches for the Post Office next morning) I forgot to give it a Superscription; of course it had to return from N: York for one, & to encounter all the delay occasioned thereby, before it could reach your hands.

Since then, I have been favored with your letter of the 10th instt; & enclose (in its rough State) the paper mentioned therein, with some alteration in the first page (since you saw it) relative to the reference at foot.[2] Having no copy by me (except of the quoted part)—nor the notes from wch it was drawn, I beg leave to recommend the draught now sent, to your particular attention.

Even if you should think it best to throw the *whole* into a different form, let me request, notwithstanding, that my draught may be returned to me (along with yours) with such amendments & corrections, as to render it as perfect as the formation is susceptible of; curtailed, if too verbose; and relieved of all tautology, not necessary to enforce the ideas in the original or quoted part. My wish is, that the whole may appear in the plain stile; and be handed to the public in an honest; unaffected; simple garb.

It will be perceived from hence, that I am attached to the quotation. My reasons for it are, that as it is not only a fact that such an Address *was written,* and on the point of being published, but *known also to one or two* of those characters who are now strongest, & foremost in the opposition to the Government; and consequently to the person Administering of it contrary to their views; the promulgation thereof, as an evidence that it was much against my inclination that I continued in Office, will cause it more readily to be believed, that I could have *no* view in extending the Powers of the Executive beyond the limits prescribed by the Constitution; and will serve to lessen, in the public estimation the pretensions of that Party to the patriotic zeal & watchfulness, on which they endeavor to build their own consequence at the expence of others, who have differed from them in sentiment. And besides, it may contribute to blunt, if it does not turn aside, some of the shafts which it may be presumed will be aimed at my annunciation of this event; among which conviction of fallen popularity, and despair of being re-elected, will be levelled at me with dexterity & keeness.

Having struck out the reference to a *particular character* in the first page of the Address, I have less (if any) objection to expunging those words which are contained within parenthesis's in pages 5, 7 & 8 in the quoted part, and those in the 18th page of what follows.[3] Nor to the discarding the egotism (however just they may be) if you think them liable to fair criticism, and that they had better be omitted; notwithstanding some of them relate facts which are but little known to the Community.

My object has been, and must continue to be, to avoid personalities; allusions to particular measures, which may appear pointed; and to expressions which could not fail to draw upon me attacks which I should wish to avoid, and might not find agreeable to repel.

As there will be another Session of Congress before the Political existence of the *present* House of Representatives, or my own, will constitutionally expire, it was not my design to say a word to the Legislature on this subject; but to withhold the promulgation of my intention until the period, when it shall become indispensably necessary for the information of the Electors, previous to the Election (which, this year, will be delayed until the 7th of December).[4] This makes it a little difficult, and uncertain what to say, so long beforehand, on the part marked with a pencil in the last paragraph of the 2d page.[5]

All these ideas, and observations are confined, as you will readily perceive, to *my draft* of the valedictory Address. If you form one anew, it will, of course, assume such a shape as you may be disposed to give it, predicated upon the Sentiments contained in the enclosed Paper.

With respect to the Gentleman you have mentioned as Successor to Mr P—— there can be no doubt of his abilities, nor in *my mind* is there any of his fitness. But you know as well as I, what has been said of his political sentiments, with respect to another form of Government; and from thence, can be at no loss to guess at the Interpretation which would be given to the nomination of him.[6] However, the subject shall have due consideration; but a previous resignation would, in my opinion, carry with it too much the appearance of Concert; and would have a bad, rather than a good effect. Always, & sincerely I am Yours

Go: Washington

ALS, DLC: Hamilton Papers.

1. See GW to Hamilton and to John Jay, both 8 May. The information came from Gouverneur Morris.

2. See n.1 of the enclosure printed below.

3. See notes 5, 6, and 11 of the enclosure printed below.

4. By "An Act relative to the Election of a President and Vice President of the United States, and declaring the Officer who shall act as President in case of Vacancies in the offices both of President and Vice President," the electors were to meet on the first Wednesday in December (1 *Stat.* 239–41).

5. These pencil markings have not been identified on the enclosure printed below. The last paragraph on the second page of that document begins "In this hope."

6. GW alludes to Rufus King. During the Genet controversy in 1793, a defender of Genet asserted that King had no sincere "wishes for the peace and prosperity of France, under any but a monarchical form of government" ("*CATO*—No. I," in *The Diary; or Loudon's Register* [New York], 5 Dec. 1793). For King's nomination as minister to Great Britain in place of Thomas Pinckney, see GW's first letter to the U.S. Senate, 19 May.

Enclosure
GW's Draft for a Farewell Address

Friends and Fellow Citizens

The quotation in this address, was composed, and intended to have been published, in the year 1792; in time to have announced to the Electors of the President & Vice President of the

United States the determination of the former previous to the sd Election but the solicitude of my confidential friends,[1] added to the peculiar situation of our foreign affairs at that epoch induced me to suspend the promulgation; lest among other reasons my retirement might be ascribed to political cowardice. In place thereof I resolved, if it should be the pleasure of my fellow citizens to honor me again with their suffrages, to devote such services as I should render, a year or two longer: trusting that within that period all impediments to an honorable retreat would be removed.

In this hope, as fondly entertained as it was conceived, I entered upon the execution of the duties of my second Administration. But if the causes wch produced this postponement had any weight in them at that period it will readily be perceived[2] that there has been no diminution in them since, until very lately, and it will serve to account for the delay wch has taken place in communicating the sentiments which were then committed to writing and are now found in the following words.[3]

"The period which will close the appointment with which my fellow citizens have honoured me, being not very distant, and the time actually arrived, at which their thoughts must be designating the citizen who is to administer the Executive Government of the United States during the ensuing term, it may conduce to a more distinct expression of the public voice, that I should apprize such of my fellow citizens as may retain their partiality towards me, that I am not to be numbered among those out of whom a choice is to be made.

"I beg them to be assured that the Resolution which dictates this intimation has not been taken without the strictest regard to the relation which as a dutiful citizen I bear to my country; and that in withdrawing that tender of my service, which silence in my situation might imply, I am not influenced by the smallest deficiency of zeal for its future interests, or of grateful respect for its past kindness: but by the fullest persuasion that such a step is compatible with both.

"The impressions under which I entered on the present arduous trust were explained on the proper occasion.[4] In discharge of this trust I can only say that I have contributed towards the organization and administration of the Government the best exertions of which a very fallible judgment was capable. For any errors which may have flowed from this source, I feel all the regret which an anxiety for the public can excite; not without the double consolation, however, arising from a consciousness of their being involuntary, and an experience of the candor which will interpret them. If there were any circumstances that could give value to my inferior qualifications for the trust, these circumstances must have been temporary. In this light was the undertaking viewed when I ventured on it. Being, moreover still farther advanced into the decline of life, I am every day more sensible that the increasing weight of years, renders the private walks of it in the shade of retirement, as necessary as they will be acceptable to me.[5] May I be allowed to add, that it will be among the highest as well as purest enjoyments that can sweeten the remnant of my days, to partake, in a private station in the midst of my fellow citizens, of that benign influence of good laws under a free Government, which has been the ultimate object of all my wishes, and in wch I confide as the happy reward of our cares and labours. May I be allowed further to add as a consideration far more important, that an early example of rotation in an office of so high and delicate a nature, may equally accord with the republican spirit of our Constitution, and the ideas of liberty and safety entertained by the people.

"In contemplating the moment at which the curtain is to drop for ever on the public scenes of my life, my sensations anticipate and do not permit me to suspend, the deep acknowledgments required by that debt of gratitude which I owe to my beloved country for the many honors it has conferred on me, for the distinguished confidence it has reposed in me, and for the opportunities I have thus enjoyed of testifying my inviolable attachment by the most steadfast services which my faculties could render. All the returns I have now to make will be in those vows which I shall carry with me to my retirement and to my grave, that Heaven may continue to favor the people of the United States with the choicest tokens of its benificence; that their union and brotherly affection may be perpetual; that the free Constitution which is the work of their own hands, may be sacredly maintained; that its administration in every department, may be stamped with wisdom and with virtue; and that this character may be ensured to it, by that watchfulness over public Servants and public measures, which on one hand will be necessary to prevent or correct a degeneracy; and that forbearance, on the other, from unfounded or indiscriminate jealousies which would deprive the public of the best services, by depriving a conscious integrity of one of the noblest incitements to perform them; that in fine the happiness of the people of America, under the auspices of liberty, may be made compleat, by so careful a preservation, and so prudent a use of this blessing, as will acquire them the glorious satisfaction of recommending it to the affection—the praise—and the adoption of every Nation which is yet a stranger to it.

"And may we not dwell with well grounded hopes on this flattering prospect; when we reflect on the many ties by which the people of America are bound together, and the many proofs they have given of an enlightened judgment and a magnanimous patriotism.

"We may all be considered as the children of one common Country. We have all been embarked in one common cause. We have all had our share in common sufferings and common successes. The portion of the Earth allotted for the theatre of our fortunes, fulfils our most sanguine desires. All its essential interests are the same; whilst its diversities arising from climate from soil and from other local & lesser peculiarities, will naturally form a mutual relation of the parts, that may give the whole a more entire independence than has perhaps fallen to the lot of any other nation.

"To confirm these motives to an affectionate and permanent Union, and to secure the great objects of it, we have established a common Government, which being free in its principles, being founded in our own choice, being intended as the guardian of our common rights—and the patron of our common interests— and wisely containing within itself a provision for its own amendment, as experience may point out its errors, seems to promise every thing that can be expected from such an institution;[6] and if supported by wise Councils—by virtuous conduct—and by mutual and friendly allowances, must approach as near to perfection as any human work can aspire, and nearer than any which the annals of mankind have recorded.

"With these wishes and hopes I shall make my exit[7] from civil life; and I have taken the same liberty of expressing them, which I formerly used in offering the sentiments which were suggested by my exit from military life.[8] If, in either instance, I have presumed more than I ought, on the indulgence of my fellow Citizens, they will be too generous to ascribe it to any other cause than the extreme solicitude which I am bound to feel, and which I can never cease to feel for their liberty—their prosperity—and their happiness."

Had the situation of our public affairs continued to wear the same aspect they assumed at the time the aforegoing address was drawn I should not have taken the liberty of troubling you—my fellow citizens—with any new sentiment or with a rep[et]ition, more in detail, of those which are therein contained; but considerable changes having taken place both at home & abroad, I shall ask your indulgence while I express with more lively sensibility, the following most ardent wishes of my heart.

That party disputes, among all the friends and lovers of their country may subside, or, as the wisdom of Providence hath ordained that men, on the same subjects, shall not always think alike, that charity & benevolence when they happen to differ may so far shed their benign influence as to banish those invectives which proceed from illiberal prejudices and Jealousy.

That as the Allwise dispensor of human blessings has favored no Nation of the Earth with more abundant & substantial means of happiness than United America, that we may not be so ungrateful to our Creator—So wanting to ourselves—and so regardless of Posterity—as to dash the cup of benificence which is thus bountifully offered to our acceptance.

That we may fulfill with the greatest exactitude *all* our engagements, foreign and domestic; to the *utmost* of our abilities whensoever, and in whatsoever manner they are pledged: for in public, as in private life, I am persuaded that honesty will forever be found to be the best policy.

That we may avoid connecting ourselves with the Politics of any Nation, further than shall be found necessary to regulate our own trade; in order that commerce may be placed upon a stable footing—our merchants know their rights—and the government the ground on which those rights are to be supported.

That every citizen would take pride in the name of an American, and act as if he felt the importance of the character by considering that we ourselves are now a distinct Nation the dignity of which will be absorbed, if not annihilated, if we enlist ourselves (further than our obligations may require) under the banners of any other Nation whatsoever. And moreover, that we would guard against the Intriegues of *any* and *every* foreign Nation who shall endeavor to intermingle (however covertly & indirectly) in the internal concerns of our country—or who shall attempt to prescribe rules for our policy with any other power if their be no infraction of our engagements with themselves, as one of the greatest evils that can befall us as a People; for whatever may be their professions, be assured fellow Citizens and the event will (as it always has) invariably prove, that Nations as well as individuals, act for their own benefit, and not for the benefit of others, unless both interests happen to be assimilated (and when that is the case there requires no contract to bind them together)—That all their interferences are calculated to promote the former; and in proportion as they succeed, will render us less independant. In a word, nothing is more certain than that, if we receive favors, we must grant favors; and it is not easy to decide beforehand under such circumstances as we are, on which side the balance will ultimately terminate—but easy indeed is it to foresee that it may involve us in disputes and finally in War, to fulfil political alliances. Whereas, if there be no engagement on our part, we shall be unembarassed, and at liberty at all times, to act from circumstances, and the dictates of Justice—sound policy—and our essential Interests.

That we may be always prepared for War, but never unsheath the sword except in self defence so long as Justice and our *essential* rights, and National respectability can be preserved without it—for without the gift of prophecy,[9] it may safely be presumed, that if this country can remain in peace 20 years longer—and I devoutly pray that it may do so to the end of time—such in all probability will be its population, riches & resources, when combined with its peculiarly happy & remote Situation from the other quarter of the globe—as to bid defiance, in a just cause, to any earthly power whatsoever.

That whensoever, and so long as we profess to be Neutral, let our public conduct whatever our private affections may be, accord therewith; without suffering partialities on one hand, or prejudices on the other to controul our Actions. A contrary practice is not only incompatible with our declarations, but is pregnant with mischief embarrassing to the Administration—

tending to divide us into parties—and ultimately productive of all those evils and horrors which proceed from faction—and above all

That our Union may be as lasting as time. for While we are encircled in one band we shall possess the strength of a Giant and there will be none who can make us affraid—Divide, & we shall become weak; a prey to foreign Intriegues and internal discord, and shall be as miserable & contemptible as we are now enviable and happy—And lastly—

That the several departments of Government may be preserved in their utmost Constitutional purity, without any attempt of the one to encroach on the rights or priviledges of another—that the Genl & state governmts may move in their propr Orbits—And that the authorities of our own constituting may be respected by ourselves as the most certain means of having them respected by foreigners. On expressing these sentiments it will readily be perceived that I can have no view now—whatever malevolence might have ascribed to it before—than such as result from a perfect conviction of the utility of the measure. If public servants, in the exercise of their official duties are found incompetent or pursuing wrong courses discontinue them. If they are guilty of mal-practices in office, let them be more ex[em]plarily punished—in both cases the Constitution & Laws have made provision, but do not withdraw your confidence from them—the best incentive to a faithful discharge of their duty—without just cause; nor infer because measures of a complicated nature—which time, opportunity and close investigation alone can penetrate, and for these reasons are not easily comprehended by those who do not possess the means, that it necessarily follows they must be wrong; This would not only be doing injustice to your Trustees, but be counteracting your own essential interests—rendering those Trustees (if not contemptable in the eyes of the world) little better at least than cyphers in the Administration of the government and the Constitution of your own chusing would reproach you for such conduct.

As this Address, Fellow citizens will be the last I shall ever make to you, and as some of the Gazettes of the United States have teemed with all the Invective that disappointment, ignorance of facts, and malicious falsehoods could invent, to misrepresent my politics & affections; to wound my reputation and feelings;

and to weaken, if not entirely to destroy the confidence you had been pleased to repose in me; it might be expected at the parting scene of my public life that I should take some notice of such virulent abuse. But, as heretofore, I shall pass them over in utter silence; never having myself, nor by any other with my participation or knowledge, written or published a scrap in answer to any of them. My politicks have been unconcealed; plain and direct. They will be found (so far as they relate to the Belligerent Powers) in the Proclamation of the 22d of April 1793;[10] which, having met your approbation, and the confirmation of Congress, I have uniformly & steadily adhered to—uninfluenced by, and regardless of complaints & the attempts of *any of these* powers or their partisans to change them.

The Acts of my Administration are on Record. By these, which will not change with circumstances—nor admit of different interpretations, I expect to judge & If they will not acquit me, in your estimation, it will be a source of regret; but I shall hope notwithstanding, as I did not seek the Office with which you have honored me, that charity may throw her mantle over my want of abilities to do better—that the grey hairs of a man who has, excepting the interval between the close of the Revolutionary War, and the organization of the new government—either in a civil, or military character, spent five and forty years—*All the prime of his life*—in serving his country, be suffered to pass quietly to the grave—and that his errors, however numerous, if they are not criminal, may be consigned to the Tomb of oblivion, as he himself soon will be to the Mansions of Retirement.

To err, is the lot of humanity, and never, for a moment, have I ever had the presumption to suppose that I had not a full proportion of it. Infallibility not being the attribute of Man, we ought to be cautious in censuring the opinions and conduct of one another. To avoid intentional error in my public conduct, has been my constant endeavor; and I set malice at defiance to charge me, Justly, with the commission of a wilful one; or with the neglect of any public duty, which, in my opinion ought to have been performed, since I have been in the Administration of the government. An Administration which I do not hesitate to pronounce—the infancy of the government and all other circumstances considered—that has been as delicate—difficult—& trying as may occur again in any future period of our history. Through the whole of which I have to the best of my judgment, and with the best information and advice I could obtain, consulted the true & permanent interest of my country without regard to local considerations—to individuals—to parties—or to Nations. To conclude, and I feel proud in having it in my power to do so with truth, that it was not from ambitious views; it was not from ignorance of the hazard to which I knew I was exposing my reputation; it was not from an expectation of pecuniary compensation—that I have yielded to the calls of my country; and that, if my country has derived no benefit from my services, my fortune, in a pecuniary point of view, has received no augmentation from my country. But in delivering this last sentiment, let me be unequivocally understood as not intending to express any discontent on my part, or to imply any reproach on my country on that account.[11] The first wd be untrue—the other ungrateful. And no occasion more fit than the present may ever occur perhaps to declare, as I now do declare, that nothing but the principle upon which I set out—and from which I have, in no instance departed—not to receive more from the public than my expences has restrained the bounty of several Legislatures at the close of the War with Great Britain from adding considerably to my pecuniary resources. I retire from the Chair of government no otherwise benefitted in this particular than what you have all experienced from the increased value of property, flowing from the Peace and prosperity with which our country has been blessed amidst tumults which have harrassed and involved other countries in all the horrors of War. I leave you with undefiled hands—an uncorrupted heart—and with ardent vows to heaven for the Welfare & happiness of that country in which I and my forefathers to the third or fourth progenitor[12] drew our first breath.

Go: Washington

ADfS, N.

1. GW struck out original text at this point: "a few friends who were apprised of my intention, and on whose judgment I did very much rely (particularly in one who was privy to the draught) that I would suspend my determination." Within this passage, GW also struck out a footnote identifying the one who was privy as "Mr Madison."

2. GW wrote this word above "acknowledged," which he did not strike out.

3. The following quotation comes from the draft of a farewell address that James Madison had enclosed to GW with a letter dated 20 June 1792.

4. The reference is to GW's inaugural address, 30 April 1789.

5. The text from this point to the end of the paragraph was bracketed in pencil.

6. The text from this point to the end of the paragraph was bracketed in pencil. The marked text begins on page 7 and ends on page 8.

7. GW inadvertently wrote "exist" for this word.

8. GW is referring to his circular letter to the states from June 1783 announcing his intention to resign from the army. There are numerous variants of this document, including a draft and the Varick transcript dated 8 June in DLC:GW; see also Fitzpatrick, *Writings*, 26:483–96.

9. The preceding three words apparently replaced "spirit of divination," a phrase GW did not strike out.

10. GW is referring to his Neutrality Proclamation of that date.

11. GW bracketed the text from this point to the start of the sentence beginning "I retire" and wrote in the margin: "This may, or not, be omitted."

12. GW wrote this word above "Ancestry," which he did not strike out.

To William Pearce

Mr Pearce,   Philadelphia 15th May 1796.

Your letter of the 8th, with the Reports, are at hand;[1] and I am glad you sowed all the Peas (except the small reserve mentioned in your letter) and the Chiccory; as I think it better than withholding them, until next Seed time. I am glad also that you have got your flour off hand (as warm weather and accidents were against keeping it longer) altho' I am convinced that if I had held it up a month or two longer, I could have obtained a better price; or at any rate the same price on a much shorter credit.[2] Deliver it as soon as possible for two reasons. first, to be exonerated from risque, by fire or otherwise; and 2dly that the day of payment may not be prolonged, by the detention of it in your possession.

I am sorry to hear you speak of no more than *showers* of Rain! On friday the 6th instant it rained here, and throughout the whole of this country, from before six in the morning, until after Seven in the evening without ceasing; and in the best manner possible; & showers have fallen since. Such weather if it had extended to you, although it has been a little cool, must have changed the face of every thing with you; & would have brought on the Oats, Peas & grass seeds of all kinds, finely, as it has done here.

I do not, now, know where to advise you to get supplied with good Rams, unless Mr Gough (near Baltimore) has them for sale. He imports both cattle & sheep, and is curious I am told in the Breed of them; & sells their descendents high. But this ought not to deter you from the purchase of (at least) one good Ram, to go to a score or more of your choicest ewes.[3] from such an experiment and beginning, you might, by the year following, have Rams enough for the whole flock. This method I pursued some years ago to the very great advancement of my breed of sheep.[4]

If Mr Darnes is a man in whose integrity and activity full reliance can be placed, and he will agree to watch, diligently, in order to prevent the depredations which are aimed at my land on four mile run, I will give him a surety of living thereon Rent free during *his* life; and the priviledge of clearing a small, but defined quantity there of: and an agreement conformably to these ideas, you may enter into with him as soon as you please; and the sooner the better.

To What height, has Davis raised the Walls of the Barn at River Farm? Does he raise the shed Walls at the same time? If not, the work will not appear so well united, even with pains & proper attention; and without them, they will have a disjointed look. Do you frame the inside upon the same plan as that of Union farm? I think I directed it to be done so, but cannot speak with certainty.[5]

Let the house in the upper Garden, called the School house, be cleaned & got in order against I return; Glass put in the windows if wanted; and a lock on the door. I canot yet say with certainty when I shall be able to visit Mount Vernon, but *hope* it will be by, or before the middle of June. Have good meats ready for us by that time; & tell the Gardener I shall expect an abundance of every thing in the Gardens; and to see every thing in prime order there, & in the Lawns. I am with best wishes Your friend

Go: Washington

Paschal seems to be pretty regularly reported sick Six days in the Week. What is the matter with him?[6]

ALS, ViMtvL.

    1. Neither the letter nor the reports from Pearce have been found.

    2. Pearce recorded the sale of flour to Alexander Smith under the date

of 24 May. Smith purchased 419 barrels of fine and superfine flour at $15 per barrel and 11 barrels of condemned flour at $14 per barrel for a total of £1930.14, payable in six months (Mount Vernon Accounts, 1794–1797, p. 53). For Smith's desire to delay payment, see GW to Tobias Lear, 16 Nov. (NNGL).

3. Henry Dorsey Gough had written GW about his livestock breeding (see GW to Gough, 4 Feb. 1792, n.1). The *Columbian Centinel* (Boston) for 25 April 1792 printed an item: "A fine breed of *Persian Sheep* is raising in *Maryland*. The original stock is owned by Mr. GOUGH. The Ram Lambs sell for 20 dollars." The *Gazette of the United States, & Philadelphia Daily Advertiser* for 22 Sept. 1796 reported that Gough sold a bull for $200 and four others for $100 or more. For a subsequent offer to purchase sheep from Gough, see GW to Gough, 13 Aug. 1797, and Gough to GW, 17 Aug. 1797, in *Papers, Retirement Series*, 1:295, 302.

4. GW is alluding to his sheep breeding between 1784 and 1788 (see GW to Anthony Whitting, 2 June 1793).

5. With the old barn at River farm in danger of collapse, GW had underway a new brick barn "60 by 30 feet, besides ends and wings, sufficient for stabling 20 working horses, and as many oxen" (Advertisement, 1 Feb. 1796). GW's previous directions, if any, have not been found.

6. Paschal (Pascal), one of the slaves that GW hired from Penelope Manly French in 1786, worked primarily as a ditcher. On a slave list compiled in 1799, he was reported as "lately lost" (*Papers, Retirement Series*, 4:540).

Letter not found: from William Pearce, 15 May 1796. GW wrote Pearce on 22 May: "Your letter of the 15th instt . . . came duly to hand."

To the United States Senate

Gentlemen of the Senate.　　　　　　United States 17th May 1796

An unexpected circumstance having obliged Jeremiah Wadsworth, to decline his appointment of Commissioner to hold a treaty with the Cohnawaga Indians, stiling themselves the Seven Nations of Canada; I now nominate Abraham Ogden Commissioner to hold the said Treaty.[1]

It having become necessary to remove Sylvanus Walker, Inspector of the Revenue for the third Survey in the district of South Carolina, I also nominate William Benson to succeed the said Sylvanus Walker in said Office.[2]

　　　　　　　　　　　　　　　　　　Go: Washington

LS, DNA: RG 46, entry 52; copy, DLC:GW.

The Senate ordered that these nominations "lie for consideration" on this date and approved them on 18 May (*Senate Executive Journal*, 208).

1. See James McHenry to GW, 2 May, and the notes to that document.
2. See Oliver Wolcott, Jr., to GW, 14 May.

From John Gill

Sir.   Alexandria [Va.] 18th may 1796
The Deed which I recd from you for the Tract of Land on Difficult, was put into the hands of my Clerk to get recorded, & by some means or other it has been mislaid & on examination I find has not been recorded—I am therefore at a loss to know the day on which the rent becomes due, & my wish being to pay it punctually I am under the necessity of requesting you to look at the Counterpart which you have & to inform me[1]—I am sorry to give you this Trouble, but the neglect which has happened cannot now be remedied any other way—When you come to Virginia which I understand will be soon, I shall be obliged by your permitting Mr Craik to bring the Counterpart with him that I may have it copied, & executed again in order to have it recorded—With much respect I am Sir Yr mo. obed. servt
                                                          John Gill

ALS, DLC:GW.
1. For information about this deed regarding land along Difficult Run in Loudoun County, Va., see GW to Gill, 17 May 1795, and n.1; and Charles Lee to GW, 18 July 1795.

From Timothy Pickering

                                        Department of State May 18. 1796.
The Secretary of State respectfully lays before the President of the United States a list of names for public offices, in the form of a message to the Senate.[1] The Secretary expected to have added to the list the name of a consul for Bremen: but his doubts as to the person among the candidates entitled to a preference not having been otherwise resolved, he had recourse to Mr R. Morris, who possessed information concerning one of them, & from circumstances could probably obtain immediately information of the others, which he promised to communicate, & which the Secretary expects to receive to-day.
                                                  Timothy Pickering

P.S. George Knox is recommended for Consul at Kingston upon Hull by so many respectable merchants of New-York, as to leave no room to doubt of his fitness, or of the utility of the appointment.[2]

ALS, DNA: RG 59, Miscellaneous Letters; LB, DNA: RG 59, GW's Correspondence with His Secretaries of State.

1. The enclosed list has not been found; it was evidently a draft for GW's second message to the U.S. Senate on 19 May.

2. An undated "Petition of the Merchants, Shipowners, and Masters of Ships trading from the City and Port of NewYork to the Port of Kingston upon Hull in Great Britain, and others," addressed to the president is filed in DNA: RG 59, Letters of Application and Recommendation during the Administration of John Adams. The petitioners asserted that trade between New York and Kingston upon Hull "is very extensive and is rapidly increasing," but complained "That Disputes often arise at Kingston upon Hull between the Masters and Mariners of Ships belonging to the United States—that the Mariners of such Ships often desert—and that Instances not unfrequently occur of their being impressed at Kingston upon Hull aforesaid to the great Inconvenience and Damage of your Petitioners and to the Detriment of the Citizens of the United States in general." Such "Grievances" might be "greatly remedied" by the appointment of a consul, and George Knox, a Kingston merchant "extensively concerned in the Trade," was recommended as "of much Respectability of Character and . . . in every Respect a proper Person."

From Arthur St. Clair

c.18–25 May 1796.[1] "As I feel myself under sensible obligations for the confidence you have always reposed in me, it would be a want of candor and an ill-return if I did not inform you that I have been very much disgusted for a considerable time, and in consequence of treatment from some of the departments, which I persuade myself has never come to your knowledge, but which made such an impression upon me as to determine me to retire from all public service; a resolution which was not carried into immediate execution only from the consideration that it might be construed into ingratitude and disrespect to you, and that the wretched situation of my affairs did not admit of it being carried into immediate execution. That derangement in which they have been, and still are, has been produced by that very conduct of the departments, and the foolish, unbounded confidence I had in the honor and integrity of the Government."

Complains that although he was superintendent of Indian affairs and known to the Indians as such, "for a very long time I have never been made acquainted with any thing respecting them; numbers of them have been called to the seat of Government from time to time, by persons employed by the Secretary of War, without the slightest intimation to me. Persons have been sent to reside among them, in public characters, without my knowledge or concurrence, and who never thought proper to have the smallest communication with me." Defends his earlier negotiations with the Northwest Indians[2] as avoiding war "when they were united and prepared for it," allowing divisions that would prevent their cooperation in the later "unavoidable" war. "The share I had in prosecuting that war, when it did supervene, although very unfortunate, I have no cause to be ashamed of, though the consequences to me have been the same as if the sinister events of it had been produced by my misconduct."[3] When negotiations ended the war, he, the superintendent of Indian affairs, learned of them only through a newspaper printing of Gen. Anthony Wayne's proclamation "commanding the people in my government to abstain from hostilities," a proclamation that should have issued through St. Clair as territorial governor.[4] Since then the War Department had issued orders embodying militia "after they had been disbanded by my orders, without the least intimation to me."

St. Clair's Indian negotiations "involved considerable expense," and the presents for the Indians "were obtained on my private credit." Despite Secretary of the Treasury Alexander Hamilton's assurances that the accounts seemed reasonable, the comptroller "raised an infinity of objections" and insisted that St. Clair apply to Congress, where "so much of them" were rejected "as to leave me saddled with a debt of upwards of six thousand dollars."[5] To raise the money, St. Clair sacrificed "an estate for which the day before I would not have taken twenty-four thousand dollars."

The new land law assigned to the territorial governor "new duties" that "must be attended with considerable expense," for which "no provision" had been made.[6] Moreover, the British surrender of army posts, "which will soon take place," would require the governor to "visit them and set the civil government in motion. That can not be done without a very heavy expense." Detroit, in particular, "is the most expensive place in the world, and to give such impressions as ought to be given on the introduction of a new government over new subjects cannot be done without considerable expense. I am now poor, very poor, and were it proper, which it is not, can not make them from my own funds, and no provision is made for that purpose; besides, I have too much experience of the disposition of Congress and the officers to run any risks of that nature again."[7]

St. Clair's visit to Philadelphia "was rendered necessary by the comptroller, to obtain compensation for my horses." He needed the money because of difficulties in settling his accounts from the 1791 campaign.[8]

Extract ("from a private letter"), Smith, *St. Clair Papers*, 2:390–94.

1. Although the source for this letter dated it "PHILADELPHIA [*Without date*], 1795," it could not have been written before the passage of the land law on 18 May 1796 (see n.6 below), and it apparently was written before GW's message to Congress on 25 May 1796 (see n.7 below).

2. These negotiations resulted in the Treaty of Fort Harmar, 9 Jan. 1789 (see St. Clair to GW, 2 May 1789).

3. St. Clair led an expedition that was defeated by the western Indians on 4 Nov. 1791. During the congressional investigation of his responsibility for that defeat, St. Clair resigned his military commission (see William Darke to GW, 9–10 Nov. 1791, and the source note to that document; and St. Clair to GW, 7 April 1792).

4. The Treaty of Greenville was concluded on 3 Aug. 1795; Gen. Anthony Wayne's proclamation has not been identified. St. Clair issued a proclamation on 25 Aug. 1795 requiring citizens to keep peace with the Indians and "to abstain from injury or molestation to them" (*Centinel of the North-Western Territory* [Cincinnati], 5 Sept. 1795).

5. See "An Act to compensate Arthur St. Clair," approved 31 May 1794 (6 *Stat.* 16).

6. Section 4 of "An Act providing for the Sale of Lands of the United States, in the territory northwest of the river Ohio, and above the mouth of Kentucky river," approved 18 May 1796, provided that "seven ranges of townships" to be surveyed under that act were to "be offered for sale, at public vendue, under the direction of the governor or secretary of the western territory." Section 8 required the governor to keep books recording those sales and to transmit copies of the books to the secretary of the treasury (1 *Stat.* 464–69).

7. On 25 May, GW sent a message on this subject to Congress. Secretary of State Timothy Pickering wrote Winthrop Sargent on 11 Aug. that GW acted "upon the suggestion of Genl St Clair" (Carter, *Territorial Papers*, 2:565–66).

8. St. Clair had arrived at Philadelphia on 3 Feb. 1796. On 9 Feb., the House of Representatives removed from the table and assigned to the Committee of Claims a memorial that St. Clair had submitted in 1794 requesting compensation for horses lost in the 1791 campaign against the Indians. That committee reported a bill on 22 April "allowing compensation for horses, killed in battle, belonging to officers of the army of the United States" (*Journal of the House,*

8:155, 357–58). The resulting act of 12 May 1796 was made retroactive to 4 March 1789 (1 *Stat.* 463).

To the United States Senate

Gentlemen of the Senate,　　　　　United States 19th May 1796.
I nominate

Rufus King, of New York, to be the minister Plenipotentiary of the United States at the Court of Great Britain, in the room of Thomas Pinckney, who desires to be recalled.[1]

David Humphreys, of Connecticut, to be the minister Plenipotentiary of the United States at the Court of Spain; William Short, the Resident Minister to that Court having desired to be recalled.[2]

Go: Washington

LS, DNA: RG 46, entry 52; copy, DLC:GW.

The Senate received these nominations on this date and approved them on 20 May (*Senate Executive Journal*, 209).

1. GW wrote King George III of Great Britain on this date: "Thomas Pinckney who for several years has resided with you as the Minister Plenipotentiary of the United States, having desired to return to America, we have yielded to his request. He will accordingly take his leave of you; embracing that occasion to assure you of our Friendship and sincere desire to preserve and strengthen the harmony and good understanding so happily subsisting between the two Nations, and which will be further manifested by his Successor. We are persuaded, that he will do this in the manner most expressive of these sentiments, and of the respect and sincerity with which they are offered. We pray God to keep you, Great and Good Friend, under his holy protection" (LB, DNA: RG 59, entry 33).

GW again wrote George III from Philadelphia on 7 June: "I have made choice of Rufus King, one of our distinguished citizens, to reside near your Majesty, in the quality of Minister Plenipotentiary of the United States of America. He is well informed of the relative interests of the two Countries, and of our sincere desire to cultivate and strengthen the friendship and good correspondence between us; and from a knowledge of his fidelity, probity and good conduct, I have entire confidence that he will render himself acceptable to your Majesty and to us, by his constant endeavours to preserve and advance the interest and happiness of both Nations. I, therefore, request your Majesty to receive him favourably and to give full credence to whatever he shall say to you on the part of the United States; and most of all when he shall assure you of their friendship and wishes for your prosperity: and I pray God to have your Majesty in his safe, and holy keeping" (copy, DNA: RG 59, entry 33). See also Alexander Hamilton to GW, 10 May, and GW to Hamilton, 15 May.

In a letter of credence to Queen Charlotte Sophia of Great Britain also written on this date, GW explained that his knowledge of Rufus King's "good qualities gives me full confidence that he will so conduct himself as to merit Your esteem and I pray that you yield entire Credence to the assurances which he will give you of Our Friendship" (LB, UkWC-A: Letterbook of Queen Charlotte; LB, DNA: RG 59, entry 33).

2. GW wrote King Charles IV of Spain on 11 June: "The interests of the United States which were committed to the care of William Short, Minister Resident near you for the United States of America, admitting of his absence, and the state of his health requiring a change of climate, he has desired permission to return to America. We have, therefore, yielded to his request. He will accordingly take his leave of you; embracing that occasion to assure you of our friendship and sincere desire to preserve and strengthen the harmony and good understanding so happily subsisting between the two Nations, and which will be further manifested by his successor. We are persuaded that he will do this in the manner most expressive of these sentiments, and of the respect and sincerity with which they are offered. We pray God to keep you, Great and good Friend, under his holy protection" (LB, DNA: RG 59, Credences; copy, ViW: William Short Papers).

Secretary of State Timothy Pickering wrote David Humphreys on the same date: "I have the pleasure to inform you, that the President, with the advice and consent of the Senate of the United States has appointed you their minister plenipotentiary to Spain. But the negociations with the Barbary powers, which were committed to your management, remaining incomplete; and even the peace concluded with Algiers being in jeopardy, the President deems it necessary that you should, for the present, continue the prosecution of those affairs, as well as your ordinary functions of Minister Resident at Lisbon. The progress of the Barbary affairs you will of course from time to time communicate to this Department; These communications will indicate the moment when the public interests will admit your transfer to Madrid . . . In the mean time the new appointment will be to you a grateful evidence of the President's remembrance of your long and faithful services to your Country, and of his continued confidence in your integrity and abilities" (DNA: RG 59, Diplomatic and Consular Instructions; see also GW to Charles IV of Spain, 20 Feb. 1797, in DNA: RG 59, Credences, entry 33). The delay in transferring Humphreys, who did not arrive in Madrid until August 1797, also impacted the appointment of John Quincy Adams as minister to Portugal (see GW's third letter to the U.S. Senate, 28 May).

To the United States Senate

Gentlemen of the Senate,   United States May 19th 1796.
    I nominate
James Simpson, at present Consul of the United States at Gibraltar, to be their consul for the Kingdom of Morocco

John S. M. Matthieu, to be their Consul at the City of Naples.

Francis Coffyn, to be their Consul at Dunkirk

James Holmes, to be their Consul at Belfast in the Kingdom of Ireland.[1]

George Knox, to be their Consul at Kingston upon Hull in England.[2]

Go: Washington

LS, DNA: RG 46, entry 52; copy, DLC:GW.

The Senate received these nominations on this date and approved them on 20 May (*Senate Executive Journal*, 209).

1. For the consulships at Morocco, Naples, Dunkirk, and Belfast, see Report on Foreign Affairs, 12 May, printed as an enclosure with Timothy Pickering to GW, same date.

2. See Pickering to GW, 18 May, and n.2 to that document.

Statement of Oliver Wolcott, Jr.

Philadelphia May 19th 1796

In the latter part of March last, a Gentleman in whose honour & veracity I have entire confidence called upon me at my Office and informed me; that Mr Collot & Mr Varin, with another Frenchman whose name he did not know, were shortly to proceed on a tour through the western parts of the United States;[1] that they were to visit the western parts of Pensylvania, the north western territory, Kentucky, & the South western territory, & that they were to be furnished with Maps & drafts of those Countries; that they were instructed by Mr Adet the French Minister, to observe the posts of the United States on the lakes & elsewhere, & to note all places possessing remarkable natural advantages either for defence or Commerce, that they were to proceed down the Mississipi to New Orleans, & were there *in concert with Officers of the Spanish Government*[2] to ascertain the proper place for a *Depot*; that in their travels they were to ascertain & note the names of the persons of most influence in every town & Village, & were to avail themselves of opportunities of observing the temper of the Country in respect to a political connection with France; that they were to cherish sentiments favourable to such a connection by observing, that the interests of the eastern & western parts of the United States were in collision; that the period was not distant when a separation must take place & that the range of Mountains on this side the Ohio, was the natural boundary of the new Government & that in the event of a separation, the western people ought to look to France as their natural Ally and Protector.

The Frenchmen before mentioned were moreover instructed to use all means in their power, to promote the election of Mr Jefferson as President of the United States.

The gentleman who gave me the information before related said, that I might rest satisfied with its truth, as he had seen the instructions in writing from Mr Adet the French Minister; he moreover said, that the expences of the mission to the western Country were to be born by the French Government.

It is not to be understood that what is herein said of the Instructions, is literally exact, as the gentleman relied on his memory; he said however, that he had seen & read the Instructions but two days before he informed me of their purport as before stated.

I communicated the information immediately to the President, with the name of the Gentleman from whom I received it & took measures for observing the conduct of the Frenchmen, particularly Collot, & am well assured that they left Philadelphia for the westward about the latter part of April—I have reason to believe that they carried Letters from Messrs Gallatin & Findley.

Having conferred this day with the Gentleman who gave me the information before stated, he admitted it to be correctly related in this paper.

Oliver Wolcott jr

ADS, MHi: Adams Papers; ADfS, CtHi: Oliver Wolcott, Jr., Papers.

At the end of the ADS, GW wrote and signed the following statement, dated 24 May: "The Gentleman who gave the aforegoing information to Oliver Wolcott Jr (Secretary of the Treasury) acknowledged, and declared to me, that the whole was correctly stated (except that, he was not absolutely certain, tho' he verily believed, the words contained in a parenthesis in the first page & scored) contains the precise meaning of the Instructions he read, & from whence his knowledge of the fact is derived" (see n.2 below).

1. Charles-Joseph Warin (c. 1770–1796), who had served under Victor Collot as an adjutant general in Guadeloupe, was employed by the War Department as an assistant engineer in 1794. He briefly taught drawing and fortifications at West Point before resigning in March 1796, ostensibly because of poor health.

Secretary of War James McHenry mentioned a third man associated with

Warin and Collot in letters to Gen. Anthony Wayne and Gov. Arthur St. Clair (see McHenry to GW, 13 May, and n.3). Thomas Power, believed to have been born in the Canary Islands of Irish descent, was described as a physician about 35 years of age (see McHenry to Wayne, 25 May, in Knopf, *Wayne*, 481–84; McHenry to St. Clair, May, in Smith, *St. Clair Papers*, 2:395–96). Power, then called a Spanish agent, later emerged as a figure in the Aaron Burr conspiracy trials.

2. GW probably placed parentheses around the underlined text on 24 May.

From George Fitzhugh

Sir   Gloucester County [Va.] 20 May 96

A few days ago, as I promised in my last I shoud do,[1] I took a full view of your Estate in this place; its soil does not altogether answer my expectation, however its situation with the advantages ariseing therefrom will make it a very agreeable little Farm, and as your terms are such that I can conveniently purchase under will esteem it a singular favour you will not dispose of it to any other Person till you see me, which shall be as soon as I hear of your arrival at Mount Vernon.[2]

There is very little Timber, and what there is, is chiefly of Pine; believe me I do not mention this to decry the Land for much Timber was not an object with me, but to inform there has been great damage commited by intruders.[3] With every sentiment of esteem I am very respectfully Sir Your Ob. Hble Sert

George Fitzhugh

ALS, DLC:GW.

1. See Fitzhugh to GW, 28 March.

2. Fitzhugh wished to purchase roughly 400 acres on Back River in Gloucester County, Va., that GW had acquired from John Dandridge in 1789. GW had stated the terms in his letter to Fitzhugh dated 28 Jan. 1796.

3. Fitzhugh again wrote GW from Alexandria, Va., on 16 Aug.: "I intended to have visited you whilst in this Neighbourhood to have complyed with my promise in my last Letter to you but being disappointed in receiving a sum of money that has been long due to me in this place renders it useless as I woud not undertake to make a purchase of your Lands in Gloucester unless it was in my power to pay down the first advance and a certainty of punctuallity in the future payments as required It is a purchase I wish to make & flatter myself shoud you not dispose of it before Novr next it will then be in my power to advance Cash as my debtors give me every Assurance I shall receive payment from them by that time Wishing you every happiness" (ALS, DLC:GW).

Fitzhugh eventually lost interest in purchasing this land (see GW to George Ball, 6 March 1797, n.1, in *Papers, Retirement Series*, 1:7–8).

From Alexander Hamilton

Sir   New York May 20. 1796

A belief that the occasion to which they may be applicable is not likely to occur, whatever may have been once intended, or *pretended* in *terrorem*, has delayed the following observations in compliance with your desire—and which are now the result of conferences with the Gentleman you named.[1]

The *precise form* of any *proposition* or *demand* which may be made to or of the Government must so materially influence the course proper to be pursued with regard to such proposition or demand, that it is very difficult by anticipation to judge what would be fit and right. The suggestions which can be submitted must therefore be very general and liable to much modification according to circumstances.

I. It would seem in almost any case adviseable to put forward a calm exhibition of the views by which our Government have been influenced in relation to the present War of Europe—making prominent the great interest we have in peace in our present infant state—the limitedness of our capacity for external effort—the much greater injury we should have suffered than good we could have done to France—by taking an active part with her—the probability that she would derive more advantage from our neutrality than from our direct aid—the promptitude with which, while all the world was combined against her, we recognised the new order of things and the continuance of our Treaties & before any other power had done so[2]—the danger to which we exposed ourselves in so doing—the fidelity with which we have adhered to our Treaties notwithstanding formal violations of certain parts of them on the other side[3]—our readiness to the utmost extent of our faculties to discharge our debt, without *hesitation in the earliest period of the revolution,* and latterly having facilitated an anticipated enjoyment of the ballance[4]—the zeal and confidence of our Merchants by which they are now creditors for very large sums to France—the patience with which we have seen infractions of our rights—the peculiar nature of the War as it regarded the origin of our relations to France (Quare?) the declaration of the War by France against the maritime powers[5]—her incapacity for maritime effort and to supply our deficiency in that particular so as to render a war not absolutely ruinous to us—the early expectations given to us by her Agents that we were not expected to become parties—the exposed state of our commerce at this time with an immense property of our merchants afloat relying on the neutral plan which they have understood our Government to be pursuing[6] even with the concurrence of France at least without its opposition— the extreme mischiefs to us of a sudden departure from this plan & the little advantage to France from our aid—the *merely peace* views which influenced our Treaty with Great Britain—the nature of that treaty involving no ingredient of political connection reserving the obligation of our prior Treaties the commercial articles terminating in two years after the present war;[7] nothing in it to change the nature of our relations to France. All this will of course require great caution & delicacy so as not to compromit the dignity of this Country or give umbrage elsewhere— and I think observations ought to hold out the idea that under all the circumstances of the case the Government of this Country thought itself at full liberty consistently with its Treaties with France to pursue a neutral plan—and they ought to hold up strongly our desire to maintain friendship with France our regret that any circumstance of dissatisfaction should occur our hope that justice & reason will prevail & preserve the good understanding &c. The conclusion of this prelimenary exposition will be according to the nature of the proposi[ti]on.

If it should claim a renunciation of the British Treaty—The answer will naturally be that this sacrifice of the positive & recent engagements of the country is pregnant with consequences too humiliating and injurious to us to allow us to believe that the expectation can be persisted in by France since it is to require a thing impossible & to establish as the price of the continuance of Friendship with us the sacrifice of our honor by an act of perfidy which would destroy the value of our friendship to any Nation— That, besides, the Executive, if it were capable of complying with a demand so fatal to us, is not competent to it—it being of the province of Congress by a declaration of War or otherwise in the proper cases to annul the operation of Treaties.

If it should claim the abandonment of the articles of the present Treaty respecting free ships free goods &c.[8] the answer may be

That our Treaties with France are an entire work parts of a whole—that nevertheless the Executive is disposed to enter into a new negotiation by a new Treaty to modify them so as may consist with a due regard to mutual interest and the circumstances of parties and may even tend to strengthen the relations of friendship & good understanding between the Two Countries.

If the Guarantee of the West Indies should be claimed[9]—The answer may be—

"That the decision of this question belongs to Congress who if it be desired will be convened to deliberate upon it." I presume & hope they will have adjourned—For to ⟨gain⟩ time is every thing.

The foregoing marks the general course of our reflections— They are sketched hastily because they can be only general ideas—and much will depend on numerous circumstances

I observe what you say on the subject of a certain diplomatic mission. Permit me to offer with frankness the reflections which have struck my mind.

The importance to our security and commerce of good understanding with G. Britain renders it very important that a man *able* and *not disagreeable* to that Government should be there. The Gentleman in question equally with any who could go & better than any willing to go answers this description—The idea hinted in your letter will apply to every man fit for the mission by his conspicousness talents and dispositions—'Tis the stalking horse of a certain party & is made use of against every man who is not in their views & of sufficient consequence to attract their obloquy. If listened to, it will deprive the Government of the services of the most able and faithful agents—Is this expedient? What will be gained by it? Is it not evident that this party will pursue its hostility at all events as far as public opi⟨nio⟩n will permit? Does policy require any thing more than that they shall have no real cause to complain? Will it do, in deference to their calumniating insinuations to forbear employing the most competent men or to entrust the great business of the Country to unskilful unfaithful or doubtful hands? I really feel a conviction that it will be very dangerous to let party insinuations of this kind

prove a serious obstacle[10] to the employment of the best qualified characters. Mr King is a remarkably well informed man—
a very judicious one—a man of address—a man of fortune and
œconomy whose situation affords just ground of confidence—
a man of unimpeached probity where he is best known—a firm
friend to the Government—a supporter of the measures of the
President—a man who cannot but feel that he has strong pretensions to confidence and trust.

I might enlarge on these topics but I have not leisure neither
can it be necessary. I have thrown out so much in the fulness of
my heart & too much in a hurry to fashion either the idea or the
expression as it ought to be. The President however will I doubt
not receive what I have said as it is meant—as dictated by equal
regard to the public interest & to the honorable course of his
administration. I have the honor to be Very respectfully & affecty
Dr sir Yr Obed. ser.

A. Hamilton

ALS, DLC:GW; copy, DLC: Hamilton Papers.

1. Hamilton responded to GW's letter to him dated 8 May.

2. Hamilton wrote in the left margin, opposite the two lines that begin
with "the new order" and end at this point, "I believe this is the fact." For the
decision to recognize the minister of the new French Republic, see GW to the
Cabinet, 18 April 1793, and Minutes of a Cabinet Meeting, 19 April 1793.
See also Thomas Jefferson to Gouverneur Morris, 12 March 1793 in *Jefferson
Papers*, 25:367–70.

3. Gouverneur Morris, when U.S. minister to France, had protested that
the French decree of 9 May 1793 allowing the seizure of neutral vessels carrying provisions to an enemy port violated the 1778 Franco-American Treaty of
Amity and Commerce (see *ASP, Foreign Relations*, 1:364, 377–78). For a summary of the vacillating French response, see *Jefferson Papers*, 26:70–71. For additional protests in 1794 regarding French violations of the treaty, see James
Monroe to Edmund Randolph, 15 Sept. and 7 Nov. 1794, in *Papers of James
Monroe*, 3:73–77, 141–45.

4. Hamilton had proposed conversion of the foreign debt of the United
States into a domestic debt in his 16 Jan. 1795 report on public credit (see
Hamilton Papers, 18:46–148). "An Act making further provision for the support
of Public Credit, and for the redemption of the Public Debt," signed into law
on 3 March 1795, authorized that conversion (1 *Stat.* 433–38). By January
1796, the Treasury Department reported the liquidation of the French debt
(see *ASP, Finance*, 1:380–81).

5. France declared war on Great Britain and the Netherlands on 1 Feb. and
on Spain on 7 March 1793.

6. Hamilton is referring to GW's Neutrality Proclamation of 22 April 1793.

7. The reservation that nothing in the Jay Treaty was to "be construed or operate contrary to former and existing Public Treaties" appears in Article XXV. The two-year limitation applied to Article XII concerning trade with the West Indies; other articles were to run for twelve years from the exchange of ratifications (Miller, *Treaties*, 254–55, 262, 264).

8. Article XXV (XXIII after two articles were suppressed) of the 1778 Treaty of Amity and Commerce with France explicitly stipulated that "free Ships shall also give a freedom to Goods" (Miller, *Treaties*, 20–21).

9. Article XI of the 1778 Treaty of Alliance with France bound the United States to "guarantee . . . the present possessions of the Crown of france in America" (Miller, *Treaties*, 39–40).

10. Hamilton wrote "obstable" for this word.

From Charles Lee

20th May 1796

The Attorney General having considered the information contained in Mr Wolcott's note of the 19th instant most respectfully reports.

That it affords reasonable ground to believe that the Republic of France has serious expectations to obtain from the King of Spain all or a part of his territories on the continent of North America, and contemplating a separation in government of the Western from the Eastern parts of the United States has commenced her plan of operations to facilitate and produce that event, and that Collot, Warin and another person are employed and paid by France and have received the instructions from Mr Adet the minister of France here, the substance of which is therein stated.

Though these instructions from the representation made of them appear to have been digested with much art & caution and relative to some objects not to be reprehensible, yet in their general scope and at least in two particulars they direct a conduct towards the United States that cannot be justified according to the laws of nations.

1st The emissaries are to cherish among the western people sentiments favorable to a political connection of that part of the United States with France by representing that the interests of the Western and eastern parts are in collision, which must soon produce a separation.

2dly They are to use all means in their power to promote the election of Mr Jefferson as President of the United States.

As to the first, it cannot be denied that an Ambassador who sets on foot dangerous projects, tending to disturb the domestic tranquility of that nation where he resides, who endeavours to excite discontents, and to foment discord, who recommends a political separation of one part of a nation from the other and a political connection of that part with his own state in all such instances commits offences, for which his recall might be demanded or for which he might be dismissed, or if the safety of the injured nation made it indispensable in extreme cases, for which he might be arrested and sent to his own country even under custody. For this doctrine reference may be made to Vattel, Book 4. Ch. 7 Sections 93 to 101—See also B. 2 Ch. 4 Sec. 56.[1]

The United States being a nation composed of many independent members united under one government, it is especially dangerous to their tranquility and union and consequently to their independence (for on their union rests their independence) for a foreign minister to interfere so far in their internal politicks as to endeavour to effect a dismemberment, and therefore such practices ought to be discovered checked and prevented by all just and lawful means.

As to the second particular, "If any intrude into the domestic affairs of another nation and attempt to influence its deliberations they do it an injury" Vattel B. 1, Ch. 4 Sec. 37[2]—It is the violation of this principle that forms one of the complaints of France against Great Britain in the present day.

Therefore for the minister of the republic of France to endeavour by means of emissaries secretly maintained and dispersed at public expense to trouble the tranquility of the republic of America, by alienating the affections of one part from the other and endeavouring to effect a disunion, or to interfere in the election of the supreme executive officer, is contrary to every principle of honor and justice.

The next enquiry must be, what are the measures which the executive should now pursue respecting this subject.

There being a possibility and perhaps a probability of detecting and seizing the instructions to Collot, Warin and their associate in their own possession, it becomes the duty of the executive to use all lawful means to obtain them: if obtained they will furnish evidence completely satisfactory of the designs of the French Minister against whom at this time there does not seem any necessity of proceeding upon the information of Mr Wolcott. To this end Governor St Clair should be furnished with a copy of that information signed by Mr Wolcott: So authenticated it may be presumed to obtain credit with any person acquainted with the situation and character of Mr W. who shall read it.

If the emissaries or either of them happen to be found within the territory northwest of the Ohio, some credible person should make an affidavit before a judge or justice of the peace in that district to the purport following viz. that he has reason to believe and does believe that [   ] Collot [   ] Warin & [   ] are persons sent, paid, charged and instructed by Mr Adet minister Plenipotentiary from the republic of France near the United States, to set on foot and bring about a separation of the western from the Eastern parts of the United States, and also to interfere in the ensuing election of the president of the United States by promoting the election of Thomas Jefferson to that office; & also that he believes by searching their trunks and packages they will be found possessed of such instructions or other writings evidencing that they are emissaries from the minister of France aforesaid for effecting nefarious and injurious purposes against the Union and tranquility of the United States and against the continuance of the present government of the territory northwest of the Ohio.

Upon an affidavit of this sort may be issued a *special* warrant to arrest the persons and seize the packages therein described and to bring them before a justice of the peace to be examined and dealt with according to law.

If after examination nothing appears against them, they are to be discharged.

But if any papers are found shewing any unlawful designs or employment, copies are to be taken by the justice, certified by him and kept in his care, and the originals are also to be certified by him and any other person present and sent to the Governor who is to transmit them by a safe conveyance to the president, retaining copies in his possession. If no overt acts of a criminal nature can be proved against any of them in that country, they may be dismissed, unless there be good cause to require them to give surety for their future good behaviour of which the civil magistrate must judge.

In all events the Governor should communicate to the President whatever shall be the result of the examination.

If any of them come within the reach of the military power, they may be apprehended as suspected persons and examined by orders from the Commander in chief who also will transmit the result of his enquiries to the President.

Charles Lee

ADS, MHi: Adams Papers.

Presumably after Lee's opinion, Secretary of War James McHenry wrote a letter dated May to Northwest Territory governor Arthur St. Clair: "The President has had information which affords strong ground to believe that there are certain persons employed and paid to visit the Western country for the purpose of encouraging the people of those parts to secede from the Union, and form a separate connection with a foreign power. . . .

"It is thought that they will be very open in their conversations, that they will be easily traced by those apprised of their project, and that an overweening confidence in the success of their mission may originate circumstances upon which to ground a legal procedure for the seizure of their papers.

"You will perceive that it is important to such a seizure that they should have no reason to suspect, from ill-timed inquiries or measures, that they are discovered. You will, of course, keep your knowledge of their errand and designs to yourself, and trust it only to those who may be necessary to the plans you may adopt, and at the moment when it confidently may be used to effect its successful execution. . . .

"I have only to add that these persons are believed to be in possession of papers which it is considered of great importance to obtain, and I have to request, if procured, that copies be made of them, and attested, as well as the originals, by yourself or some other person, and forwarded by safe conveyance to the President" (Smith, *St. Clair Papers*, 2:395–96; see also McHenry to Anthony Wayne, 25 May, in Knopf, *Wayne*, 481–84).

1. Lee cited Emmerich de Vattel's multivolume work on international law, published in English as *The Law of Nations; or Principles of the Law of Nature: Applied to the Conduct and Affairs of Nations and Sovereigns*, 2 vols. (London, 1759), and widely reprinted. For Book 4 ("Of the Restoration of Peace, and of Embassies"), chapter 7 (*"Of the Rights, Privileges and Immunities of Ambassadors, and other Public Ministers"*), sections 93 ("How the foreign minister is to behave"), 94 ("How he may be corrected, first, with regard to common faults"), 95 ("2d. For faults committed against the prince"), 96 ("Right of ordering away an ambassador who is guilty, or justly suspected"), 97 ("Right of checking him by force, if he behaves as an enemy"), 98 ("Of an ambassador forming dangerous plots and conspiracies"), 99 ("What is allowable against him, according to the exigency of the case"), 100 ("Of an ambassador who should attempt the prince's life"), and 101 ("Two remarkable instances concerning the immunities of public ministers), see 2:148–55. For Book 2 ("Of a Nation considered relatively to others"), chapter 4 (*"Of the Right to Security, the Effects of the Sovereignty, and the Independence of Nations"*), section 56 ("How it is permitted to enter into the quarrel between a sovereign and his subjects"), see 1:139.

2. Section 37 ("No foreign power has a right to interfere") falls within Book 1 ("Of NATIONS considered in themselves"), chapter 3 (*"Of the Constitution of a State, and the Duties and Laws of the Nation in this Respect"*). See Vattel, *Law of Nations*, 1:19.

From Timothy Pickering

Department of State May 20th 1796

The Secretary of State respectfully lays before the President of the U. States three papers of nominations.[1] To that respecting the Spanish treaty he wished to have added a name for a commissioner for the spoliations: but is not satisfied about a suitable character.[2] He has examined the Constitution of Pennsylvania & by that, the office of Mayor of Philadelphia, which comprehends the office of a judge, is incompatible with the office of a Commissioner under the U. States; and the Mayor's office, considering that it may probably be continued in Mr Clarkson for some years, would be preferable to that of Commissioner for the Spanish spoliations. Perhaps it may be left to withhold the nominations for the Spanish treaty until the Commissioner for spoliations may be found.[3] Mr Latimer informs me there is not a man at Wilmington whom he can recommend.

Mr Dexter wishes to consider till to-morrow morning, before he decides on the office of district attorney for Massachusetts: he will then write me a line.[4]

T. Pickering

ALS, DNA: RG 59, Miscellaneous Letters; LB, DNA: RG 59, GW's Correspondence with His Secretaries of State.

1. The enclosed papers have not been identified, but they presumably were drafts for GW's two letters to the U.S. Senate written on this date and his letter to the U.S. Senate dated 21 May.

2. Pickering is referring to the commissioner to be appointed under Article XXI of the 1795 treaty with Spain (see Miller, *Treaties*, 335–37).

3. Article II, section 8, of the Pennsylvania constitution of 1790 in part reads: "No member of Congress from this state, nor any person holding or exercising any office of trust or profit under the United States, shall, at the same time, hold or exercise the office of Judge, Secretary, Treasurer, Prothonotary, Register of Wills, Recorder of Deeds, Sheriff, or any office in this state, to which a salary is by law annexed" (*Pa. Constitution*, 10–11). Despite constitutional concerns, Philadelphia mayor Matthew Clarkson received the nomination as commissioner to decide spoliation claims (see GW to the U.S. Senate, 21 May).

4. No pertinent letter from former Massachusetts congressman Samuel Dexter to Pickering has been identified. For the eventual nomination to fill this position, see Pickering to GW, 24 May, and n.2 to that document.

From Timothy Pickering

May 20. 1796.

The Secretary of State respectfully returns the papers from Newbern, with the draught of an answer which seemed to him pertinent to the occasion.[1]

Mr Smith thinks it would by no means suit Mr Izard to undertake the St Croix business.[2] In conversing afterwards on the subject with Mr King, Mr Cabot & Mr Ames, and looking over all the States eastward of Pennsylvania, no character appeared so eligible as David Howell of Providence, Rhode-Island.[3] He was some years a member of the old Congress—has been a judge of the supreme court of Rhode Island, and is now a practising lawyer. Govr Bradford & Mr Bourne have no doubt of his readiness to accept the trust.[4] And all agree in opinion of Mr Howells integrity, abilities, great learning & perseverance in whatever he undertakes.

The doubt I suggested to Mr Strong, he communicated to Mr King, who is decidedly of opinion that the *Agent* to manage the St Croix business must also be nominated to the Senate.[5] The candidates who are thought best qualified are Theophilus Parsons of Newburyport, & James Sullivan, now the Atty Genl of Massachusetts.[6]

T. Pickering

ALS, DNA: RG 59, Miscellaneous Letters; LB, DNA: RG 59, GW's Correspondence with His Secretaries of State.

1. New Bern, N.C., residents had favored GW's handling of the Jay Treaty (see Joseph Leech to GW, 19 April, and n.3 to that document).

2. Pickering probably alludes to South Carolina congressman William Loughton Smith and Ralph Izard, U.S. senator from that state.

3. Pickering consulted with U.S. senators Rufus King of New York and George Cabot of Massachusetts as well as Massachusetts congressman Fisher Ames. The congressman had spoken in the House of Representatives on 28 April arguing for full implementation of the Jay Treaty (see GW to Thomas Pinckney, 22 May, and n.2 to that document).

4. Pickering refers to William Bradford, U.S. senator from Rhode Island, and Benjamin Bourne, a congressman from that state.

5. Pickering presumably contacted U.S. senator Caleb Strong of Massachusetts.

6. Article V of the 1794 Jay Treaty with Great Britain required commissioners to determine "what River was truly intended under the name" St. Croix River in the 1783 treaty of peace. The article called for these commissioners to deliver their records to agents who would "manage the business on behalf of the respective Governments" and reach a "final and conclusive" decision (Miller, *Treaties,* 249). For nominations under this article, see GW to the U.S. Senate, this date (first letter).

Letter not found: from Gustavus Scott, 20 May 1796. GW wrote Scott on 25 May: "Your favor of the 20th inst: came to hand yesterday."

To the United States Senate

Gentlemen of the Senate,   United States 20th May 1796.
    I nominate,
David Howell, of the State of Rhode Island, to be the Commissioner on the part of the United States, for the purpose of ascertaining the River St Croix, agreeably to the fifth Article of the treaty of Amity, Commerce and navigation, between the United States and Great Britain, in the room of Henry Knox, declined.[1]
James Sullivan, of Massachusetts, to be the Agent on behalf of the United States to manage the business of the fifth Article of the Treaty of Amity, commerce and navigation between the United States and Great Britain.[2]
Frederick Jacob Wichelhausen, to be the Consul of the United States at the City of Bremen.[3]

                                    Go: Washington

LS, DNA: RG 46, entry 52; copy, DLC:GW.
    1. See Henry Knox to GW, 14 April.
    2. For nominations under Article V of the Jay Treaty, see Secretary of State Timothy Pickering's second letter to GW on this date.
    3. The Senate received these three nominations on this date and confirmed them on 21 May (*Senate Executive Journal,* 210–11).
    GW announced the consular appointment on 21 May: "Know Ye, that reposing special Trust and Confidence in the Abilities and Integrity of Frederick Jacob Wichelhausen of Bremen, I have nominated and by and with the Advice and Consent of the Senate do appoint him Consul of the United States of America for the Port of Bremen; and do authorize and empower him to have and to hold the said office and to exercise and enjoy all the Rights, Preemi-

nences, Privileges and Authorities to the same of Right appertaining, during the pleasure of the President of the United States for the time being. He demanding and receiving no Fees or Perquisites of Office whatever, which shall not be expressly established by some Law of the said United States: And I do hereby enjoin all Capitains, Masters and Commanders of Ships and other Vessels armed or unarmed sailing under the Flag of the said States, as well as all other of their Citizens to acknowledge and consider him the said Frederick Jacob Wichelhausen accordingly. And I do hereby pray and request all Powers and Authorities therein and thereover to permit the said Frederick Jacob Wichelhausen fully and peaceably to enjoy and exercise the said office without giving or suffering to be given unto him any molestation or trouble, but on the contrary to afford him all proper countenance and assistance, I offering to do the same for all those who shall in like manner be recommended to me by the said Powers and Authorities" (copy, GyBrS). For the acknowledgement, see Burgomasters and Senators of Bremen to GW, 16 Feb. 1797 (DNA: RG 59, Communication from Heads of Foreign States).

To the United States Senate

Gentlemen of the Senate,   United States May 20th 1796.
    I nominate Oliver Bowen, of Georgia, to be Marshal of the district of Georgia in the room of Thomas Glasscock, resigned.[1]
Go: Washington

LS, DNA: RG 46, entry 52; copy, DLC:GW.
    1. The Senate postponed action on Oliver Bowen's nomination on 21 May before consenting on 24 May (*Senate Executive Journal*, 210–11; see also Bowen to GW, April 1789).

From Timothy Pickering

Sir,   Department of State May 21. 1796.
    A demand is presented to me for 1868 49/100 dollars for transcripts of proceedings on American Vessels in the Vice Admiralty Court of Dominica, & other expences connected therewith; and some other smaller demands are depending. I have on hand but 1612 26/100 dollars. I therefore request the Presidents order on the Treasury Department for One Thousand Dollars, to enable me to discharge the above demands and others of like nature as they shall occur:[1] and am very respectfully sir your most obt servant
Timothy Pickering

ALS, DNA: RG 59, Miscellaneous Letters; LB, DNA: RG 59, GW's Correspondence with His Secretaries of State; LB, DNA: RG 59, Domestic Letters.

1. GW wrote Secretary of the Treasury Oliver Wolcott, Jr., on this date: "Pay to Timothy Pickering secretary of state one thousand Dollars out of the proper fund, for the purposes expressed in his Letter of this date hereto annexed" (LB, DLC:GW). Warrant 6108 for that purpose was issued on 23 May (see the report of expenditures enclosed with GW to the U.S. Senate and House of Representatives, 15 Feb. 1797, in DNA: RG 46, entry 47).

To the United States Senate

Gentlemen of the Senate,   United States May 21st 1796
    I nominate
Matthew Clarkson, of Pennsylvania, to be the Commissioner on the part of the United States, agreeably to the 21st article of the Treaty of Friendship, limits and navigation between them and his Catholic Majesty, to examine and decide the claims of the Citizens of the United States for losses sustained in consequence of their vessels and cargoes having been taken by the subjects of his Catholic Majesty during the late war between France and Spain.[1]
Andrew Ellicott, of Pennsylvania, to be the Commissioner and
Thomas Freeman of the District of Columbia, to be the Surveyor, on the part of the United States, to run and mark the southern boundary of the United States, which divides their territory from the Spanish Colonies of East and West Florida;[2] agreeably to the second and third articles of the treaty of friendship limits and navigation between the United States and his Catholic Majesty.[3]

Go: Washington

LS, DNA: RG 46, entry 52; copy, DLC:GW.
    The Senate ordered that these nominations "lie for consideration" on this date before consenting on 24 May (*Senate Executive Journal,* 210–11).
    1. For Article XXI of the 1795 treaty with Spain and deliberations regarding this nomination, see Timothy Pickering's first letter to GW on 20 May, and notes 2 and 3 to that document.
    2. See Commissioners for the District of Columbia to GW, and Thomas Freeman to GW, both 13 April; see also GW to the commissioners, 30 May.
    3. Article II of the Spanish treaty defined the boundary "by a line beginning on the River Mississipi at the Northermost part of the thirty first degree of

latitude North of the Equator, which from thence shall be drawn due East to the middle of the River Apalachicola or Catahouche, thence along the middle thereof to its junction with the Flint, thence straight to the head of St Mary's River, and thence down the middle there of to the Atlantic Occean." Article III required the two countries to appoint commissioners and surveyors "to run and mark" the boundary (Miller, *Treaties*, 319–21; see also Pickering to GW, 14 and 15 [first letter] Sept.).

To the Commissioners for the District of Columbia

Gentlemen,   Philadelphia 22d May 1796

Your letters of the 13th and 14th instant have been duly received, and the Attorney General of the United States having given his opinion relatively to the Powers of Attorney; And having pronounced the proceedings to be accordant with the Act for Guaranteeing the Loan; matters have been arranged with Mr Gilmore for execution, and the Papers, agreeably to your desire, will be forwarded to Holland.[1]

A duplicate of the Power of Attorney to Messrs Wilhem & Jan Willink, is necessary to guard against the delay which would result from a miscarriage of the original.[2] In short, as the vigorous prosecution of the Works depend upon the facility with which the Loan is obtained, no risk that can be avoided ought to be left to chance: For fatal indeed would it be to the operations in the City if a disappointment, or any considerable delay should take place. And here let me add—If I had been called upon for an opinion relative to this loan before arrangments were made with Mr Gilmore, I should, under my present view of the subject, have given a decided opinion against placing the *whole* of the sum, authorized to be borrowed in one year, upon this issue; if any part thereof could have been obtained in this country within, or not exceeding, the Provisions of the Law.

In all probability it will be *six months* before the result of the application in Holland will be known. This may, & from the peculiar state of things in that country tis not unlikely will be, unfavorable. What is to be done in that case? and what in the meantime? You have declared, yourselves, that you do not place much confidence in aids from Messrs Morris & Nicholson, & point out no other specific resources. Notwithstanding these sentiments, I am unwilling to obstruct a measure which I presume you have considered in all its relations & chances, & have therefore given facility to your plan; wishing heartily that it may be attended with success.

The year 1800 is approaching by hasty strides; The friends of the City are extremely anxious to see the public Works keep equal pace therewith.[3] They are anxious too on another account—namely—that the Commissioners should *reside in the City* where the theatre of the business lies. This was, and is, my opinion. It is the principle, and was declared to be so at the time; upon which the present establishment of the Commissioners was formed; that, by being on the spot, and giving close attention to the operations, they might prevent abuses, or correct them in embryo.[4] It is said, if this had been the case, those defective walls, which to put up, & pull down, have cost the public much time, labour & expence, would never have been a subject of reproach.[5] For these, and other reasons which might be added, it is my decided opinion & expectation that the Commissioners do reside *in the City*. and the nearer they *are* to the public Works the better, & more desirable it will be. I wish this as well on their own account, as on that of the public; because they would have it much more in their power to scrutinize all the movements of men & measures which are under their controul, than it is possible to do at the distance of two or three miles & periodical, or occasional visits. Being on the spot, & seeing every thing that occurs, they would be better enabled to systematize the business & have it conducted with greater œconomy; and finally, would insure to themselves those honors & consolations which flow from the punctual discharge of public trust.

I have sent your advertisement of the sale of Lotts, to the places you have requested; but I beg that it may be unequivocally understood that, I am opposed to the sale of them in large parcels, to Speculators. It might be asked, if this was to happen, and with propriety too, why give these people the profit arising between the wholesale & retail prices, when, if the same means & industry in the disposal, were used by the Commissioners, it would be saved to the public? To sell by single lots, or at most squares, on moderate terms to those who will improve them, appear most eligible to me. particular cases *may* arise, to render a departure from this rule necessary, but such cases must speak for themselves—& the advantages to be derived from them must be evident.

If there are any matters which you are desirous of laying before me, let me request that they may be prepared (if a decision is not required sooner) by the time I shall pass through the City; which is as likely to happen about the middle of next month, as at any period I can name at present. My stay at Mount Vernon cannot be long & I shall have many matters of private concern to attend to while there.[6] With great esteem & regard I am—Gentn Your most Obedt

Go: Washington

ALS, DLC: U.S. Commissioners of the City of Washington records; ALS (letterpress copy), DLC:GW; LB, DLC:GW.

1. GW is referring to "An Act authorizing a Loan for the use of the City of Washington, in the District of Columbia, and for other purposes therein mentioned," approved 6 May (1 *Stat.* 461).

2. About the power of attorney, see Commissioners for the District of Columbia to GW, 13 May, n.1; see also GW to the commissioners, 30 May.

3. Section 3 of "An Act for establishing the temporary and permanent seat of the Government of the United States" tasked the commissioners with providing "suitable buildings" for Congress, the president, and the public offices by the first Monday in December 1800. Section 6 directed that the government be moved to the district on that date (1 *Stat.* 130).

4. For a statement of the principle in relation to William Thornton's appointment as commissioner, see GW to Tobias Lear, 28 Aug. 1794 (first letter). GW's letter to Alexander White on 28 April 1795 offered him appointment as commissioner and indicated residence in the city as a requirement. See also GW to Gustavus Scott, 25 May 1796, and n.5 to that document.

5. Writing Edmund Randolph on 26 June 1795, commissioners Scott and Thornton reported that such "bad work" had been done on some walls of the Capitol that "in Some parts prudence requires they should be taken down" (DNA: RG 42, Records of the Commissioners for the District of Columbia, Letters Sent). GW subsequently reminded the commissioners that their salaries had been raised to promote greater vigilance over such tasks (see Randolph to the D.C. commissioners, 6 July 1795, in DNA: RG 59, Domestic Letters).

6. The commissioners replied to GW on 31 May.

To William Pearce

Mr Pearce,   Philadelphia 22d May 1796.

Your letter of the 15th instt, enclosing the Reports of the preceeding Week, came duly to hand.[1]

I am glad to hear that the weather has been Seasonable of late; but sorry indeed, to find by your letter that the grain & grass has received so little benefit from the rains which have fallen; here, in great abundance. And it is peculiarly unfortunate after giving so high a price for clover Seed, that it should either not have come up, or been destroyed afterwards, by the drought.[2] Has your Corn come up well, & how does it thrive? And how does the Oats—Peas—Chiccory—and other things which have been sown, and planted this Spring come on?

It is much to be regretted, and I do regret exceedingly, that the Honey locusts which have been set out, should have perished— It would seem I think as if I never should get forward in my plan of hedging. With respect to the transplanting of Cedar (or any other evergreen) I am persuaded there is no other sure way of getting them to live, than by taking them up in the winter with a block of frozen earth around the Roots (and as large as it can conveniently be obtained—proportioned to the size of the plant)—This not only gives them their mother earth, but by its adhesion to the principal roots, it nourishes the body until the fibres from the former shoot sufficiently to secure the vegitation & thriftiness of the plant. I transplanted thousands of Pine & Cedar without getting scarcely one to live until I adopted the above method; after which, so long as it was practiced, I never lost one. Witness the pine groves by the Gardens; both of which were planted in this manner, and to the best of my recollection not one of them died: whereas, out of the first planting, just as they now are, not more than two or three of them lived.

I am very sorry indeed to hear of the damage which the family piece of the Marquis de la Fayette has sustained. and am unable to account for it.[3] If the window shutters had been left open, I should have attributed it more to the sun, than to the dryness of the Air.

Ask Peter, if some of the Mares wch I took down with me, when I went alone to Mount Vernon in April of last year, did not go to the Jack at that time? If they did not, their foaling will be much about the time I shall be on the Road which will be unfortunate.

For what purpose is the Well house from the Mansion, carried to Union Farm? Save a plenty of the best Hay of last year for my horses, as I had rather they should be fed upon old, than the Hay of this season, when I come home. I am Your friend

Go: Washington

ALS, ViMtvL.

1. Pearce's letter and the reports have not been found.
2. For the clover seed, see GW to Pearce, 28 Feb., and n.5.

3. GW acknowledged receipt of this portrait and promised to "give it the best place in my House" when he wrote Lafayette on 25 July 1785 (*Papers, Confederation Series*, 3:151–55; quote on 155). A visitor to Mount Vernon in 1798 described its deteriorated condition: "The Mar[quis] in an American uniform is presenting to his wife, who is seated, his son aged 4 also in an American uniform; his two daughters nearly the same age complete the group. The picture is well painted and well composed but the paint has fallen off in many places. The marquise has a broad slash the whole length of the left side of her face, a slash which has deprived her of an eye; the older of the girls is also one-eyed, and the younger has lost the end of her nose" (Niemcewicz, *Vine and Fig Tree*, 96; brackets in source).

Letter not found: from William Pearce, 22 May 1796. GW wrote Pearce on 5 June: "Since my last I have received your letters of the 22d & 29th of last Month."

To Thomas Pinckney

(Private)
Dear Sir   Philadelphia 22d May 1796
   To my letters of the 20th of February and 5th of March, I beg leave to refer you for the disclosure of my sentiments on the subjects then mentioned to you.
   Very soon afterwards, a long, and animated discussion in the House of Representatives relative to the Treaty of Amity, Commerce & Navigation with Great Britain, took place; and continued—in one shape or another—until the last of April; suspending, in a manner, all other business; and agitating the public mind in a higher degree than it has been at any period since the Revolution. And nothing, I believe, but the torrent of Petitions, and remonstrances which were pouring in from all the Eastern and middle States, and were beginning to come pretty strongly from that of Virginia, requiring the necessary provisions for carrying the Treaty into effect, would have produced a decision (51 to 48) in favor of the appropriation.[1]
   But as the debates (which I presume will be sent to you from the Department of State) will give you a view of this business, more in detail than I am able to do, I shall refer you to them. The enclosed Speech, however, made by Mr Aimes at the close of the discussion, I send you; because, in the opinion of most that heard it delivered, or have read it since, his reasoning is unanswerable.[2]

The doubtful issue of the dispute, added to the *real* difficulty in finding a character to supply your place, at the Court of London, has occasioned a longer delay than may have been convenient or agreeable to you. But as Mr King of the Senate (who it seems had resolved to quit his Seat at that board) has accepted the appointment, and will embark as soon as matters can be arranged, you will soon be relieved.[3]

In my letter of the 20th of Feby, I expressed, in pretty strong terms, my sensibility on acct of the situation of the Marquis De la Fayette. This is increased by the visible distress of his Son, who is now with me, & grieving for the unhappy fate of his parents. This circumstance, giving a poignancy to my own feelings, on this occasion, has induced me to go a step further than I did on the letter above mentioned; as you will perceive by the enclosed Address (copy of which is also transmitted for your information) to the Emperor of Germany: to be forwarded by you in such a manner, and under such auspices as, in your judgment, shall be deemed best: or to arrest it, if from the evidence before you (derived from former attempts) it shall appear *clear*, that it would be of no avail to send it.[4]

Before I close this letter, permit me to request the favor of you to embrace some favorable occasion, to thank Lord Grenville, in my behalf, for his politeness in causing a special permit to be sent to Liverpool for the shipment of two sacks of the field Peas, and the like quantity of Winter Vetches, which I had requested our Consul at that place to send me, for Seed; but which it seems could not be done without an Order from government.[5] A circumstance which did not occur to me, or I certainly should not have given it the trouble of issuing one, for such a trifle. With very great esteem & regard I am—Dear Sir Your obedt Servant

Go: Washington

ALS, DLC: Pinckney Family Papers; ALS (duplicate), NNPM; LB, DLC:GW. Pinckney replied to GW on 31 July.

1. The U.S. House of Representatives initially debated the Jay Treaty with Great Britain from 7 March to 7 April (see *Annals of Congress*, 4th Cong., 1st sess., 426–783). Debate commenced on 13 April over a resolution for carrying into effect the treaties with Algiers, Great Britain, Spain, and the Northwest Territory Indians. The House quickly disposed of the other three treaties but debated the Jay Treaty until 30 April, when the indicated vote took place (see *Annals of Congress*, 4th Cong., 1st sess., 939–1292). During April, the House received supportive petitions from several places in Pennsylvania, New Jersey,

and Maryland; New Castle and Kent counties, Del.; New York City, Albany, Lansingburg, and Kings County, N.Y.; Boston, Newburyport, and Salem, Mass.; Providence, R.I.; and Washington, D.C. (see *Journal of the House*, 8:302, 321, 338, 343, 352–54, 358, 359–60, 363, 365–66, 368–70, 373–78). For petitions from Virginia, see the notes with Edward Carrington to GW, 9 May.

2. Massachusetts congressman Fisher Ames had delivered a speech in the House on 28 April advocating Jay Treaty implementation. Ames argued that House refusal to execute a binding treaty negotiated by the president and ratified by the Senate would be a breach of national faith justifiable only if the treaty was "bad, not merely in the petty details, but in its character, principle, and mass" and "the enlightened public" concurred with the determination. Ames found both conditions lacking. As "auxiliary arguments" to fulfill the treaty, he advanced the benefits of the spoliations clause, the protection given frontier settlers by the return of military posts, and the avoidance of war with Great Britain (*Annals of Congress*, 4th Cong., 1st sess., 1239–63; quotes on 1244 and 1257; see also Ames, *Works*, 2:37–71).

3. For Rufus King's nomination as minister to Great Britain, see GW's first message to the U.S. Senate, 19 May, and n.1 to that document.

4. See GW to Francis II, 15 May.

5. About this shipment, see GW to James Maury, 20 Oct. 1795, and Maury to GW, 26 Dec. 1795.

From Cyrus Griffin

Richmond May 23d 1796

Can I hope for pardon Sir if once more I take the liberty to experience your well known Goodness and Indulgence.

upon the resignation of Mr Blair I think it was generally expected that if a Judge was nominated from Virginia the present District Judge would have the preference,[1] unless indeed Mr Marshall or Mr Washington from their uncommon legal Talents. I did not solicit because I thought it unseemly to do so for a man already upon the Bench; it would shew a greediness of disposition not characteristic with the office, and a diffidence that the chief magistrate had forgotten me; but the appointments being made from other states, and as they are Gentlemen of the best abilities in the Law the union are extremely happy and thankful to have the Supreme Court thus ably Completed. And yet it has been now hinted to me that perhaps some objections might lay against my character if it should be in contemplation to appoint another Judge from Virginia when a vacancy shall arrive.

would there, Sir, be any objection to my *moral* character? Indeed I am not sensible of it myself. I do not game. I have not speculated to the amount of one shilling in my life; and I am temperate & retired, confining myself to Books, my Family, and the duties of my station.

would there be any objection to my *political* character? I do not believe there is a more orderly Citizen in the United States. always a sincere friend, and advocate for the present Constitution; a real well wisher and defender of the Administration of Government—particularly in the late Treaty with England.

perhaps I have not Industry for the labour of a Judge? the gentlemen of the Bar will not say so. I hold it impossible for any man to be more assiduous in the stated and special District and the Circuit Courts than I am. I have not lost one day since my Family were brought from new york unless by unavoidable necessity—and I do a great deal of business out of Court; the district is very extensive and myself always upon the spot.

Then it would be for the want of *Talents* to exercise that very important Employment. I hope to Heaven that is the only objection, for I had rather be thought honest and attentive than a man of the most splendid Intellects. however I have determined many Causes of great importance in my Court from which there has not been a single appeal but in two cases to establish points of *practice,* and two others upon the *Jurisdiction* of the Court; none upon the *merits* of a question; the lawyers being perfectly satisfied with the reasons of the Judge. In the circuit Court indeed I gave my opinion that payment of British Debts into the loan office of the state should be considered as valid and here Mr Iredell and myself had the misfortune to differ from a very learned and virtuous Judge, Mr Jay, whom we both revere.[2] I gave my opinion also in another great question the *carriage* Tax, and was unlucky enough to differ from Judge Wilson.[3] I thought the Tax one of the best that could be laid, but it appeared to me not to be done in a Constitutional manner. Most of the Bar were of the same opinion. I was sworn to determine according to the best of my Judgment; but I constantly paid the Tax myself and advised others to do it also. upon both of these two important qu[e]stions I have the honor of according in opinion with a late amiable and able Judge.[4]

I should hope, Sir, that no misrepresentations have been made to you relative to me. I have long known that a Gentleman once high in your Confidence was not a friend of mine, that confidence is deservedly withdrawn, and his conduct shews that I never had occasion to lament his want of friendship.[5] other gentlemen also who stood high in estimation professed a great deal towards me, but having changed their principles, possibly they may have changed their attachments. a Family rising into consequence and who possess very considerable merit I hope are not Enemies of mine, tho early in the Consideration and upon the purest public principle I gave my voice in Congress to recall their Relations from the Courts of Europe.[6] this occasioned great bitterness against me in the elder names. Some reports were also hinted to me.

That I was not active enough in condemning a vessel belonging to a Mr Sinclair and said to be fitting out as a privateer. the case came before the Court upon the day appointed by the District Attorney, 24 witnesses were supœened on the part of the U. States, 22 of them appeared and were Sworn, but their Testimony was not sufficient and the Jury acquitted the vessel without hesitation. as a material witness was absent the attorney obtained a new Trial and after a special Court lately the cause is dismissed unless good reasons can be given at the June Court to reinstate the business. I was fully as active as a Judge ought to be.[7]

another report was circulated that I was determined to Condemn all prizes brought into this district by armed vessels of the above description or fitted in our ports. nothing under the Sun was ever more false. there lives not a Judge upon Earth of more discretion in his office. my opinion upon any qu[e]stion was never known untill given Judicially.

It was said also that I was an advocate for Mr Genet. The only thing I ever said was, upon that subject, "that a man of Mr Genet's understanding could hardly have acted So absurdly and unwarrantably unless he had been thus instructed by his nation, and if his nation had thus instructed him he was bound to obey." when the Instructions were published the points *then* agitated turned out such as I supposed them.[8]

Another matter has been mentioned that I admitted to bail a man charged with opposing the militia draught to be sent against the Insurgent: the Truth is that no witness appeared against him, and I admitted the man to bail in a large amount to be present at the next succeeding Court; the prisoner appeared; and the prosecution was dismissed by the attorney.

A late affair also: a young man by the name of Goosely in the Town of york was surrendered upon my warrant for stealing Bank Bills &c. from the Post-office agreeable to the promises of the assistant post master, upon the surrender by the young man's friends when he might have escaped, upon his delivering up all the money, and upon his making a candid discovery of the particulars of that wicked Transaction, I thought it perfectly right to bail him with good security in the sum of 20,000 dollars.[9]

I beg leave to mention another matter also; some little time ago it was stated to me by Colonel Newton of Norfolk "That he had good grounds to believe certain British agents were purchasing Horses in this Country for the military use of that Government, to be sent against our Allies the French in the West Indies, and that Vessels were getting ready to transport the said Horses." I wrote him for answer that the law of Congress pointed out the mode of proceeding, and that in the first Instance it was not consistent with my Station as Judge to interfere. Mr Oster the french Consul has also written to me upon the subject by way of memorial.[10]

I ought to mention also that I had the imprudence to write to you sir concerning my son John in Europe. poor Fellow! having no Fortune to give him, he being very anxious to be introduced to the public under the present administration, and being convinced myself that he was a young man of an active mind, sensible, and honorable in his demeanor I did venture to write in his behalf, but the letter was hardly gone before I repented and saw the impropriety.[11]

Thus Sir I have taken the freedom to say somewhat relative to myself, only as a sort of *exculpation* if any person whatever has unkindly traduced me, and I defy any man to prove the contrary of what I have now the honor to assert. I know my Innocence and can challenge with Confidence.

That I have faults, that I have follies and deficiencies I do not deny—but I owe to you a thousand obligations, and no man breathing is possessed of a more feeling heart.

"Truth and candour will always estimate the conduct of public men,"[12] and well knowing that I have never laid one Syllable derogatory to your personal or political character I am with a grateful mind & the most profound respect Sir Your very obedient servant

Cyrus Griffin

ALS, DLC:GW.

GW replied to Griffin from Philadelphia on 8 June: "I am sorry, that without being accused, you should think it necessary to go into a lengthy justification of your conduct & principles.

"What the entire design of your letter of the 23d ulto may be, I am at a loss to conceive; and pressed as I have been, and still am, on all sides, in the discharge of my public functions, I have no leizure to enquire. If the object of it (among other things) is to intimate that you have been overlooked in some recent appointments, I can only say, that nominations are made from the best view I am able to take of the cases which come before me. in doing which I have often, if not always, where the appointments are not of a local nature, found it necessary to combine a variety of considerations—none of which, however, has originated from a desire to serve a friend or relation; or a wish to oblige this, or that man—or set of men; but from the best information I can obtain (where I have no personal knowledge) of the fitness of characters to Offices.

"That I may have erred, and in many instances made injudicious nominations, is highly probable: wonderful indeed would it be, if the case was otherwise; but numerous, and chagreening as disappointments may have been to individuals (and abundant they are) I can defy malignancy itself to ascribe partiality, or interested motives to any of my nominations; or omissions, to prejudice or dislike. I have naught therefore, on this score to reproach myself with.

"For the attachment you have professed for my person & Administration, I pray you to accept my best thanks" (ALS [letterpress copy], DLC:GW; LB, DLC:GW). For Griffin's response, see his letter to GW dated 4 July.

1. Griffin, the district judge for Virginia, is referring to the resignation of U.S. Supreme Court justice John Blair.

2. Griffin referenced *Ware* v. *Hylton*, a circuit court decision in June 1793 (see Hobson, "Recovery of British Debts," 189–92; and *Documentary History of the Supreme Court,* 7:210–14).

3. Griffin referenced *Hylton* v. *United States,* decided in the May 1795 term of the circuit court (see *Documentary History of the Supreme Court,* 7:361–65).

4. Griffin may have been referring to Blair.

5. Griffin likely meant former U.S. Attorney General Edmund Randolph.

6. Griffin apparently earned the opposition of the Lee family by supporting an effort to recall Arthur Lee from France in 1779 (see *JCC,* 14:542–43, and Griffin to Burgess Ball, 10 Aug. 1779, in Smith, *Letters of Delegates,* 13:345–47).

7. John Sinclair of Smithfield, Va., owned the *Unicorn,* seized in July 1794 (see Oliver Wolcott, Jr., to GW, 26 May 1795, n.1). Federal district attorney Alexander Campbell wrote Secretary of State Timothy Pickering from Yorktown, Va., on 16 Jan. 1796 about his efforts to condemn the vessel after a verdict given at Williamsburg had been set aside upon appeal: "It is with Concern that I mention to you, that after wasting the whole week, we could procure

no more than two or three of the public Witnesses; tho' more than ten had been summoned. One of those who were absent (a Captain Daughterty) was so material a Witness, that without his testimony I could by no means think of hazarding a trial. I was therefore obliged to move for a Continuance of the Cause, which has been granted, and the trial is respited 'til March." Campbell next complained that through Griffin's decision the vessel had "been permitted to go out of the custody of the Court before the appeal was decided which was to determine whether she had become forfeited to the United States" (DNA: RG 59, Miscellaneous Letters).

8. Griffin presumably alludes to *The Correspondence between Citizen Genet, Minister of the French Republic to the United States of North America, and the Officers of the Federal Government. To which are prefixed, the Instructions from the Constituted Authorities of France to the said Minister. All from authentic Documents* (Philadelphia, 1793).

9. Campbell wrote Pickering from Yorktown on 17 Jan. that Griffin had bailed "Young Goosely . . . I am concerned at this, because I not only do not think the case, under all it's circumstances, was such as authorized the admission of bail; but I am persuaded that the public will be much dissatisfied about it" (DNA: RG 59, Miscellaneous Letters). A jury acquitted John Goosely on 27 May (see *Documentary History of the Supreme Court*, 3:128).

10. For reports about this incident, see Pickering's second letter to GW on 30 Jan. and its enclosure; see also Pickering to GW, 6 February. Griffin's correspondence on the subject has not been identified.

11. See Griffin to GW, 7 Feb. 1794.

12. Griffin may have quoted GW's reply to Frederick County, Va., citizens, dated 16 Dec. 1795 (see Pickering to GW, same date, n.1).

From Timothy Pickering

May 24. 1796.

The Secretary of State respectfully lays before the President of the U. States—the draught of

A message to Congress on the subject of Genl St Clair's letter—[1]

Message to the Senate naming a district attorney for Massachusetts—[2]

A letter to Mr Pinckney[3]—and

A letter to Mr Parrish, Consul of the U. States at Hamburg.[4]

Timothy Pickering

ALS, DNA: RG 59, Miscellaneous Letters; LB, DNA: RG 59, GW's Correspondence with His Secretaries of State.

1. These documents involving Northwest Territory governor Arthur St. Clair

have not been identified but presumably related to GW's message to the U.S. Senate and House of Representatives dated 25 May.

2. GW's message to the Senate of this date reads: "I nominate Harrison Gray Otis, of Massachusetts, to be the Attorney of the United States for that District" (LS, DNA: RG 46, entry 52; copy, DLC:GW). The Senate received the message on 25 May and approved the nomination on 26 May (*Senate Executive Journal,* 212). Harrison Gray Otis declined the office (see Oliver Wolcott, Jr., to GW, 20 June, postscript, and Pickering to GW, 22 June).

3. GW returned Pickering's letter to Thomas Pinckney, minister to Great Britain, with his approval on 25 May (*JPP,* 337). Pickering's letter, dated 23 May, covered diplomatic developments with Spain, matters related to implementation of the Jay Treaty, and the process for settling small spoliation claims with Great Britain. He concluded: "Mr [Rufus] King expects to sail for London in June; and he is very desirous to meet you there. If no pressing object requires your departure at an earlier day, the President will be well pleased that you should await his arrival, and personally communicate to him whatever you shall deem material to the interests of the United States for him to know. Relying that this arrangement will be agreeable to you, Mr King will himself be the bearer of your letter of recall.

"I do not know what has been the former practice of the ministers of the United States but it really appears as proper as important that your whole correspondence relative to the affairs of the United States with the British Government and with this Department should be delivered over to your successor, whose acts and negociations must have a frequent and necessary reference to and connection with your own. I am therefore instructed by the President to desire you to tran[s]fer them accordingly" (DNA: RG 59, Diplomatic and Consular Instructions).

4. Pickering probably enclosed a draft of his letter to John Parish dated 2 June: "Complaints have been received at this office, originating with American Citizens, of your partiality to the British, and direct unfriendliness to the French Republic." Pickering specified the complaints and excused Parish's conduct, but he reported it still "expedient . . . to remove the cause of complaint. As Consul, you represent the American *Government.* But the President of the United States as the chief Administrator of that Government, desires that his *conduct* may appear as impartial as his *principles.* I am therefore directed to inform you, that a change is proposed in the Consulate of Hamburg. The President will endeavor to fill the place with an American citizen. But until a Successor shall notify to you his appointment, you will be pleased to continue to exercise your functions as Consul." Pickering assured Parish that the change did not reflect on his "integrity" or "mercantile reputation. You will still enjoy here the respect to which these qualities entitle a man, and that consideration which by your early services to this Country you have acquired" (DNA: RG 59, Diplomatic and Consular Instructions; see also the Report on Foreign Affairs, 12 May, and n.13, printed as an enclosure with Pickering to GW, same date).

Alexander Hamilton had written Secretary of War James McHenry from New York on 1 June with thoughts on handling Parish, whom he believed a victim of favoritism toward the French. Hamilton wanted Parish "superseded, with a kind letter to him. I do not write to *Pickering* or the *President* because I am not regularly possessed of the information. But I hope you will attend to the matter, even if at the expense of being a little officious" (*Hamilton Papers*, 20:212–14).

From James Madison

Philada May 25. 1796

Mr Madison presents his respectful compliments to the President, and begs to mention the wish of Joseph Nevil Esqr. (late a member of the House of Representatives)[1] to be taken into consideration in the appointment of Surveyor, under the law for the sale of lands N. West of the Ohio.[2] He takes the liberty also of inclosing a letter from General Posey, expressing his wishes with respect to an appointment, which Mr M. does not think it proper to withold, altho' the precise object of them, may not correspond with the arrangements of the law.[3]

AL, DLC:GW.

1. Joseph Nevill (Nevil; 1730–1819) represented Hampshire County in the Virginia state legislature for several terms between 1773 and 1781 before serving one term in the U.S. House of Representatives, 1793–95.

2. For this law, approved on 18 May 1796, see 1 *Stat.* 464–69. In a letter touching several subjects, Nevill had written Madison on 8 Dec. 1795: "I expect Congress will pass a law this Session for the sale of the lands on the Northwest of the River Ohio, and as that of a Surveyor has been my principle Occupation ever since I grew up I would wish to be appointed to one of the Districts" (*Madison Papers*, 16:160–61).

3. Madison enclosed Thomas Posey's letter to him dated 21 Nov. 1795: "I have some reason to Suppose that the ensuing Congress will establish a Land Office on the northwest side of the Ohio; Should such a regulation take place, an Appointment to the Office would suit me extremely, could I meet the Approbation of the President and Senate. I am well convinced that my abilities are fully adequate to the Office, and my exertions should be such, as to endeavor to discha[r]ge the duties of the office with propriety agreeable to the nature of the business. I shall esteem myself singularly obliged, if you will mention me to the President as a candidate for the Appointment. Had I any reason to suppose that I could get the Appointment I would immediately arrange my business in such a manner as to settle on the Northwest side of the Ohio instead of Kentucky" (DLC:GW). For subsequent consideration of Posey, see GW to John Marshall, 15 July.

To Gustavus Scott

Sir,   Philadelphia 25th May 1796
   Your favor of the 20th inst: came to hand yesterday.[1]

   I have neither received, nor heard of an Address from the Proprietors of the Federal City. Nor do I know any more of Mr Law's sentiments relative to the concerns of it, than I do of Tippo Saib's.[2] The ideas conveyed in my last to the Commissioners (dated the 22d) are not of recent adoption. They are as old as the change which took place in the establishment of the Commissioners; and were the cause of that change. A combination of causes have brought them more actively, and pointedly into view than heretofore: among which, and not the least to be regarded, are the remarks which were made during the discussion of the Guarantee Bill, even by its friends (not so much in, as out of the house)—the indispensable necessity for close attention, & great exertion in all those to whom the business is entrusted; with an eye to the strictest œconomy, under the best systems that can be formed.[3]

   You cannot, I am persuaded, be entirely unacquainted with the remarks which have been made on the want of œconomy, and due attendance to the operations which are carrying on by those who are entrusted with the management of it. Nor, acquainted as *you are* with the jealousies, & contracted views of the Proprietors, can the utmost circumspection, and the minutest attentions in the Commissionrs to all the wheels that are in motion, and to all the persons who move them, appear unimportant. Consequently, wherever the scene of business is, there also should be the principal actors. And 'till this happens, the Jealousies between the upper & lower end of the City will not subside, nor will the injurious consequences flowing from them, cease. Nor indeed will it be believed, be the fact as it may, that while the Commissioners, or the major part of them (with the subordinate Agents) reside in George Town, that the concerns of the City will be conducted uninfluenced, and to the best advantage— We may dispise public opinion, and these kind of reports as we please—but they are not less injurious on that account. The time is very short in which a great deal for the reception of Congress is to be done; and no means, or exertion should be wanting to accomplish it.[4] It would be ineligable, & highly impolitic to bring any new proposition before Congress, before the Government is fixed there.

I do not precisely know what the late Secretary of State may have written with respect to the alternative allowed the Commrs to reside in the City, or *George Town*[5] But it is a fact known to every one who ever heard me express a sentiment on the subject, that it has been decidedly in favor of the former; and that nothing but necessity, arising from the want of accomodation, could justify the latter. Nay more, it is known to the first Commissioners, that I not only coincided in opinion with them, that a house, situated between the two principal buildings should be built for their accomodation, but actually approved a plan for the purpose.[6] Why it was laid aside, unless their going out of Office, or the want of funds occasioned it, I am unable to say.

I have been thus particular, that you may see what my opinion *uniformly* has been; that it has not proceeded from any recent movements in the City (which were unknown to me, before your letter came to hand)—and that it has appeared more necessary & has been more pointedly mentioned, since I find that the *friends* of the City, and I presume the Community at large, conceive (as I have always done) that the measures which have been suggested, are useful & proper. With esteem & regard I am Sir Your Obedet Servant

Go: Washington

ALS, anonymous donor; ALS (letterpress copy), DLC:GW; LB, DLC:GW.

1. Scott's letter has not been found.

2. This address, dated 24 May, has not been identified, but GW later acknowledged its receipt on 1 June (see GW to Alexander White, 5 June). Some hint of Thomas Law's sentiments come from notes that he wrote at a much later date: "The President's house was advanced rapidly and the Capitol was only above ground and the foundation was so bad that it was to be undone and commenced again. In short Mr. Stoddert, Secretary of Navy, and the majority of the Commissioners and the bank being George Town men, resolved to have Congress meet in the President's house or in George Town College and to make the progress of the West End tend to counteract that of the Capitol.

"General Washington having been informed of these injurious ideas in the Commissioners and being displeased at witnessing the slow advancement of the Capitol ordered the Commissioners to live in the city and to encourage persons to build for the accommodation of Congress" (Clark, *Greenleaf and Law*, 255).

Tipu Sultan (Tippoo Sahib; 1750–1799), also known as the Tiger of Mysore, ruled Mysore in India from 1782 until his death. He was known for his conflicts with Great Britain.

3. GW especially is referring to debate in the House of Representatives on 31 March over a "bill authorizing a Loan for the City of Washington" (*Annals of Congress*, 4th Cong., 1st sess., 825–40; quote on 825–26; see also GW to the U.S. Senate and House of Representatives, 8 Jan. 1796, and Thomas Law to GW, 11 May, n.2).

4. This concern worried GW (see his letter to the Commissioners for the District of Columbia, 22 May, and n.3 to that document).

5. Secretary of State Edmund Randolph mentioned residence in Georgetown or the city "as necessary" when he wrote Scott on 18 Aug. 1794 to offer appointment as commissioner (DNA: RG 59, Domestic Letters).

6. Daniel Carroll, then a D.C. commissioner, had written then Secretary of State Thomas Jefferson on 16 April 1792 that the commissioners "concluded to build a House for their Office and accomodation in the City near the place called the Church Square, being not far from the Center and nearly equidistant on the way between the Presidents House and the Capitol" (*Jefferson Papers*, 23:428–29). The commissioners contracted for the work on 7 June 1792 (see DNA: RG 42, Records of the Commissioners for the District of Columbia, Proceedings).

To the United States Senate and House of Representatives

United States May the 25th 1796.
Gentlemen of the Senate and of the House of Representatives,

The Measures, now in operation for taking possession of the posts of Detroit and Michilimackinac, render it proper, that provision should be made for extending to those places and any others alike circumstanced the civil authority of the north western territory. To do this will require an expence, to defray which the ordinary salaries of the Governor and Secretary of that territory appear to be incompetent. The forming of a new County or new Counties[1] and the appointment of the various Officers, which the just exercise of Government must require, will oblige the Governor & Secretary to visit those places and to spend considerable time in making the arrangements necessary for introducing and establishing the Government of the United States. Congress will consider what provision will in this case be proper.[2]

G: Washington.

Copy, DLC:GW; copy, DNA: RG 233, entry 26, Journals; copy, Sotheby's, *Fine Manuscript and Printed Americana* (sale 6618, 7 Nov. 1994), 158.

1. The copy in RG 233 renders the preceding five words as "new country, or new countries."

2. The House of Representatives received the message on this date and referred it to a committee of three. An order discharged the committee on 1 June, and no action was taken regarding "an additional allowance to the governor and secretary" of the Northwest Territory in this Congress (*Journal of the House*, 8:485–86, 533).

From Alexander White

Sir   Martinsburg [Va., now W.Va.] 25th May 1796

Agreeably to my expectation I left Philada on Monday the 9th instant and arrived at Washington the ensuing Wednesday; the measures adopted to avail ourselves of the guarantee of Congress have been communicated by the Board,[1] but my Colleagues seemed in a state of suspense respecting the commencement of the Works, having no assurance on which they could rely of obtaining the means of carrying them on—I felt much chagrine that at this critical period when the Eyes of the World were drawn a fresh towards the City by an event considered as favourable to it, that so unpleasant a prospect as a total stop to the buildings should be held up, and expressed this chagrine with reference to the supineness of the many wealthy men interested in the City, in terms of perhaps too much asperity—it however produced a request, that I would remain 'till a meeting of the Proprietors could be had, to which I readily agreed, and on tuesday 17th instant several Gentlemen met, and after a good deal of conversation and some propositions, which it is unnecessary to repeat, they agreed in the course of 30 days to advance on the credit of the City Funds from 12 to 20,000 dollars, if so much should be necessary for immediate operations—On Wednesday the Board met and directed the works to commence on the Walls of both Houses on Monday last, with all the force we can command, giving a considerable preference in point of numbers to the Capitol.

When I was honoured with my present appointmt it was not expected, that I could immediately remove my Family to the City, but the time which has since elapsed might then be thought sufficient to make the necessary arrangements: the fact however is otherwise. I have not during that whole time had one week to consider and dispose of my private affairs. My property has become more deranged and my business accumulated by my necessary absence from the Courts of March and April⟨.⟩ A great clamour is raised in the City respecting the non-residence of the Commissioners; though I accepted the Office with reluctance[2] I do not now wish to resign I could not place myself in the situation I left, and to which I was perfectly reconciled, but I will not continue in Office without making known the conduct I mean to pursue; All I can do is, to place my property here in a situation which will render it productive, or at least save it from destruction in my absence; to purchase one or more Lots in the City; to build as fast as I can raise money to carry on my buildings; and when I finish a House to make it the place of my residence; in the mean time to pay all possible attention to the business of the City, consistent with prior engagements, which engagements I shall discharge as soon as possible, and in which I expect considerable aid from a Nephew lately come to the Bar[3]—Should holding my Office under these circumstances be agreeable I shall continue my exertions to promote an object, in which from various causes I feel myself deeply interested, if not, I shall hold myself ready to resign whenever the President shall make known his Sentiments; the sooner this takes place the more agreeable; as my future Arrangements will in many respects depend on it.

I expect this letter will reach you the 3d of June—An Answer by the Post which leaves Philada the next morning will find me at my own House near Winchester—but if it should not be convenient to write so soon, please direct to me in Washington where I expect to be the 12th of June I am really sorry to give you this trouble, but I thought a clear understanding necessary to avoid censure in future.[4] I am with Sentiments of the highest respect and most sincere regard Sir Your most Ob. Servt

Alexr White

ALS, DLC:GW. "Private" is written on the cover of this letter.

1. See Commissioners for the District of Columbia to GW, 13 and 14 May.

2. For White's hesitant acceptance of the appointment as commissioner, see his letters to GW dated 11 May and 8 and 22 June 1795.

3. White had several nephews.

4. GW reported receipt of this letter on 3 June when he replied to White on 5 June.

From Richard Clarkson

Sir   Durham [England] 26 May 96

I hope your goodness will pardon me the trouble of this address, the reason for which I sincearly lament by the advice of my attorney Geo: Pearson Esqr: of this place, I gave a power of attorney to Mr. C: Richmond a native of this neiborhood (he being then here) who lives at Baltimore maryland impouring him to receive for me what was due from the will of the late Mr Colvill the Business I need not repeat to you Sir—the last letter from him was of 13th July 1794 from which time neither his friends here, nor I, have reced any acct from him, which occations me much Surprize under so long & so disagreable a Suspence Sir, it is not unnatural to Suppose the worst—indeed Sir I fear he is Dead, for I do not suspect his Veracity in the Least, his professions of friendship were Generous & disinterested, which assur'd him my entire Confidence as also Mr Pearsons—if he is living, I think he ceartainly wo'd have wrote long ere now—what I have to beg of you Sir is that your Goodness will so far Condesend as favr me with an answr[1] & if Mr R: is alive or not which will ad to the Obligations already recd by sir Yr Most Hbe Servt

Richd Clarkson

P.S. permit me Sir to give you a transcript of what Mr Richmond gave me respecting the Business in his last letter of the above Date—he says, my friend Philip Richard Fendall Esqr. of Alexandria with whom your papers are—informed me a few days before I wrote to my Brother that his Neibor Mr Kieth had been applied to by him on the Subject of your Legacy—and that Mr Kieth answer'd—the Lawsute hat been brought to issue and a remainder found due to the residuary Legatees the last Summer; but that the money had not been paid to the Executer Genl Washington—that when the General received it, the money would be placed in the hands of the Chancellor of the State of Virginia, by whom the merits of the Several Claims wo'd be desided upon—thus the matter at present rests and I am Convinced that no delay which can be avoided will be caused by the

President—it has been a troublesome and unprofitable Business to him and I know he wishes it out of his hands as soon as posable, you may rely upon my doing every thing within my power to bring the affair as far as you are concern'd to an issue & give you the Erliest Notice.[2]

ALS, DLC:GW.

1. No reply to this letter has been found.

2. Clarkson's attorney George Pearson wrote GW on 12 May 1797 about his client's claim on the Thomas Colvill estate and the involvement of Christopher Richmond. In his reply to Pearson dated 15 Sept., GW discussed the estate settlement and referred him to a notice published in the *London Gazette* (see *Papers, Retirement Series*, 1:137–39, 360–61). For the notice, see GW to Rufus King, 25 Aug. 1796, n.1.

From James McHenry

Sir.   War office Thursday afternoon [26 May 1796]

Mr Liston has this moment favoured me with the inclosed letter.[1]

If you have time to look over the draught of the letter to Capn De Butts, and can return it to-day I shall endeavour to get him dispached to-morrow.[2] I have the honour to be Sir with the highest respect Your most ob. st

James McHenry

ALS, DLC:GW; LB, DLC:GW. The docket reads "May 27th 1796" on the ALS, and the letter-book copy shows the same date, which was a Friday.

1. The enclosure from British minister Robert Liston has not been identified.

On 25 May, Liston and his wife had dined with GW as his guests. Henrietta Marchant Liston described the invitation in her travel journal entry for 26 May as "a compliment commonly paid to a Foreign Minister on his *first* arrival." She continued: "This Entertainment though sombre & formal had an air of Magnificence. There was a Plateau ornamented with French figures, two Courses of French cookery served up in the American style & a Desert. . . . The President during dinner drinks Wine with every Lady, & with most of the Gentlemen. He gives no toast *after dinner*. Though this was not a scene of animation or hilarity, it pleased me upon the whole by a look of respectability & perfect propriety" (North, *Travel Journals of Henrietta Liston*, 8–9).

2. The enclosed draft has not been identified, but Capt. Henry De Butts was being sent to Detroit to hire vessels for the transport of troops and equipment to that post and Fort Michilimackinac (see McHenry to Anthony Wayne, 29 May, in Knopf, *Wayne*, 484–85).

From William Deakins, Jr.

Dear Sir　　　　　　　　　　Geo. Town [D.C.] May 27th 1796

I find some of the City Proprietors, have or Intend to remonstrate to you the Necessity of the Commissioners' living in the City[1]—there is no doubt it would be more agreeable, if the Commissioners lived at the public Buildings, but it cannot be an Object of so much Consequence as to cause the removal of good Men from the Office, Doctr Thornton has agreed to remove to the City, & Mr Scott is Erectg buildings for his Accomodation Near the City Line & within one Mile of the Presidents Square, his Situation will be as Convenient as if he was settled on the Eastern Branch or in the City Near the Stone Bridge,[2] I think him a Valuable Commissioner, perhaps equal to any one that has yet been in the appointment, Mr White is also a Valuable Man Neither of these Gentleman will agree at present to settle in the City. if Mr Whites family should agree to remove No doubt they will settle in the City. but Mr Scott will never remove—from the Improvements he is now Making at so heavy an Expence the proprietors seem to Ask what is unreasonable, the Change of Commissioners or at least two of them, would be a serious Evil, it would derange the whole business of the City and thousands would be lost by such an Event. Scott is well Calculated for making Contracts & seems to have a perfect Knowledge of the Value of Work & Meterials the Contracts for the public buildgs have been made on much more favorable terms, than Contracts made by private Individuals who are laying out their own Money. It may be thought that my situation as Treasurer may give me a Bias in favor of the Commissioners, or that my Office as Treasurer may be an Object. I can with truth say Neither has any Influence on my Mind. I beleive I have lost more than I have gain'd by the Commission. I have frequently been largely in Advance for the City to prevent a discharge of the hands at a time when great Injury would have been done, & these Advances happened at times when I could have laid out my Money in produce & Cleared a profit of ten pCt in 60 days—& in all the Negotiations with the Banks for the Accomodation of the City I pledged my private Estate, otherwise the Money could not have been borrowed, the Bank of Maryland as well as the Bank of Columbia refused to discount my Notes as Treasurer of the City of Washington, however as I expect there will not now (as soon as the loan is Negotiated)[3] be any difficulty as to Money Maters when this happens, I shall probable resign my office into other hands, It may be an Object to others it is no Object to me—and as my residence is in Geo. Town the proprietors may be better pleased if this offi⟨ce⟩ is put in other hands, & if any Intimati⟨on⟩ of such a desire should come to you through the proprietors, I wish you to tell them that they may be gratified, I do not know they have any such wish but if they should I wish to set them at ease—I have frequently taken the Liberty to Communicate to you my Sentiments on public Matters that has come under my knowledge & I hope it will not be thought Improper,[4] I am with Every Sentiment of Respect & Esteem—Dear Sir Your Obt Servt

Will. Deakins Junr

ALS, DLC:GW.

1. This address, dated 24 May, has not been identified, but it came to GW's attention on 1 June (see GW to Alexander White, 5 June; see also GW to Gustavus Scott, 25 May).

2. William Thornton would move from a property near 32d and M Street in Georgetown to a property on F Street near 13th, not far east of the location for the president's house (see Bryan, *National Capital*, 1:288; Harris, *William Thornton Papers*, xlix, lxx).

Gustavus Scott occupied a property in Georgetown near Rock Creek just north of the Federal City boundary. Deakins probably meant the stone bridge over Rock Creek completed in 1793.

3. Deakins is alluding to "An Act authorizing a Loan for the use of the City of Washington, in the District of Columbia, and for other purposes therein mentioned," approved on 6 May 1796 (1 *Stat.* 461).

4. GW replied to Deakins on 6 June.

From Timothy Bloodworth

Sir   Philadelphia May 28th 1796

Pleas to indulge the freedom of Mentioning to the President of the United States, Mr Hugh Williamson, as a Carrecter quallifyed to fill the Station of Surveyer General for No: Wst Territory. his scientific information, Moral Carracter, & known application, Needs no Comment. With every expression of Esteem, & respect, due to exalted Merrit. I have the Honor to be Sir. Your Most Obedient Humble Servant

Timothy Bloodworth

ALS, DLC:GW.
   Timothy Bloodworth (1736–1814) served as a senator from North Carolina, 1795–1801.

To the United States Senate

Gentlemen of the Senate,   United States May 28th 1796.
I nominate,
Ebenezer Tucker, of New Jersey, to be Collector and Inspector
   of the Revenue for the District of Little Egg harbour in that
   State.
Roger Boyce, of Maryland, to be collector and Inspector of the
   Revenue for the district of Havre de Grace, in Maryland.[1]
Asa Andrews, of Massachusetts, to be collector and Inspector of
   the Revenue for the District of Ipswich in Massachusetts.[2]
                                                  Go: Washington

LS, DNA: RG 46, entry 52; copy, DLC:GW.
   The Senate received these nominations on this date and approved them on
30 May (*Senate Executive Journal*, 212–13).
   1. Roger Boyce (d. 1811) continued as collector until his death.
   2. Asa Andrews (1762–1856), a graduate of Harvard College, was removed
from this post in 1829.

To the United States Senate

Gentlemen of the Senate.   United States May 28th 1796
   I nominate Simeon De Witt, of New York, to be Surveyor
General.[1]

                                                  Go: Washington

LS, DNA: RG 46, entry 52; copy, DLC:GW.
   1. Simeon DeWitt (1756–1834), who had served as geographer of the Continental army, was at this time surveyor general of New York.
   The Senate received this nomination on this date and consented on
30 May (*Senate Executive Journal*, 212–13). DeWitt declined the appointment
(see Timothy Pickering to GW, 27 June, n.2, and GW to Pickering, 1 July; see
also GW to John Marshall, 15 July).

To the United States Senate

Gentlemen of the Senate   United States 28th May 1796
  I nominate John Quincy Adams, at present Minister Resident of the United States at the Hague, to be their Minister Plenipotentiary at Lisbon.[1]

Go: Washington

Copy, DLC:GW.
  1. The Senate received this nomination on this date and consented on 30 May (*Senate Executive Journal*, 212–13).
  John Quincy Adams never served as minister to Portugal. For his continuance as minister to the Netherlands, see Timothy Pickering to Adams, 11 June, in DNA: RG 59, Diplomatic and Consular Instructions. President John Adams nominated his son as minister to Prussia on 20 May 1797 (see *Senate Executive Journal*, 240; see also GW to John Adams, 20 Feb. 1797, in MHi: Adams Papers, and Bemis, *John Quincy Adams and American Foreign Policy*, 86–89).

To the United States Senate and House of Representatives

United States 28th May 1796
Gentlemen of the Senate and of the House of Representatives.
  The extraordinary expenses, to be incurred in the present year in supporting our foreign intercourse, I find will require a provision beyond the ordinary appropriation, and the additional twenty thousand dollars lately granted.[1]
  I have directed an estimate to be made, which is sent herewith, and will exhibit the deficiency, for which an appropriation appears to be necessary.[2]

Go: Washington

LS, DNA: RG 46, entry 47; copy, DNA: RG 59, entry 142; copy, DNA: RG 233, entry 28; copy, DLC:GW.
  1. The ordinary appropriation was $40,000. For the additional $20,000, see section 2 of "An Act making further provision for the expenses attending the intercourse of the United States with foreign nations; and to continue in force the act, intituled 'An act providing the means of intercourse between the United States and foreign nations,'" delivered to GW on this date and approved on 30 May (1 *Stat.* 487–88; see also *Journal of the House*, 8:455, 510; and *Journal of the Senate*, 8:289–90).
  2. The enclosed "Estimate of the sums necessary for defraying the expenses

of foreign intercourse, for the year 1796," signed by Secretary of State Timothy Pickering, estimated $36,000 for ministers plenipotentiary at Paris, London, Madrid, and Lisbon; $18,000 for outfits at the latter three cities; $5,400 for four secretaries; $5,600 for salaries of ministers returning home; $3,000 for contingent expenses of ministers; and $20,000 "Probable expenses of obtaining papers and prosecuting the claims of our citizens for spoliations on their Commerce." Given the $60,000 appropriation and a deduction of $4,500 for the half-year difference between the salaries of two ministers plenipotentiary and two ministers resident, there remained a deficit of $23,500 (DNA: RG 46, entry 47).

To defray "the extraordinary expenses . . . for foreign intercourse," section 3 of "An Act making further appropriations for the year one thousand seven hundred and ninety-six," approved on 1 June, appropriated "a sum not exceeding" $23,500 (1 *Stat.* 493).

Letter not found: to Alexander Hamilton, 29 May 1796. Hamilton wrote GW on 1 June: "Your letter of the 29th was delivered me."

To William Pearce

Mr Pearce,   Philadelphia 29th May 1796.

No Mail beyond Baltimore (Southerly) was received at the Post Office in this City yesterday; consequently, I got no letter from you; what may have been the cause I know not, unless the considerable falls of rain which happened here during last week, may have rendered the waters between Alexandria and Baltimore (if they extended so far) impassible.

You have never mentioned in any of your late letters, nor has it occurred, at the time of writing mine, to ask, whether a Pipe of Wine, & box of Tea, which was sent from this place for Mount Vernon, had arrived, and in what condition. It was in March, or the beginning of April they left this—And another Vessel with Windsor Chairs and sundry other Articles for the same place, have been gone from hence long enough to have heard of their arrival 'ere this. These occurrences ought always to be noticed in your letters, to relieve one from the suspense which otherwise follows.[1] Before we leave this, we shall send several other matters round, but whenever they are shipped you shall have notice thereof that they may be taken from Alexandria so soon as they arrive there; at which time procure a groce of good Porter to be taken down along with them. In the meantime, have a few

Bottles of Porter there, & some wine for particular company, who may be *particularly* recommended to you by myself: among these Mr Aimes, a respectable member of Congress (travelling for his health) will, I expect, be one, as he proposes to set out from hence for the Federal City about the middle of this week, and is one I wish to be well treated, while he stays. I have requested Mr Lear to shew him the way down to Mount Vernon.[2]

Is Maria and the two boys at that place now, or where are they?[3] No mention has been made of them for sometime. When (from present appearances) will your early Wheat be ready to cut? and how does that, and the other small grain, Peas, & grasses come on? What was done with the Seed saved from the India Hemp last Summer? It ought, *all* of it, to have been sown again; that not only a stock of seed sufficient for my own purposes might have been raised, but to have dissiminated the seed to others; as it is more valuable than the common Hemp.[4]

Congress talk of rising about the middle of this week; but there is no dependance on it. In about ten or twelve days after the Session closes, it is likely I shall commence my journey homewards:[5] as soon as I can fix the day, I will advise you of it.

I have several times spoke concerning a necessary for the Quarter People, at Mansion house; and once or twice shewed Thomas Green the precise spot to place it—viz.—in the drain that leads from the old brick kiln back of the Well, towards the gully leading towards the gate; that, having this advantage the offensive matter might be washed off by the Rain water that collects in the gutter. I wish you would have this done before we come home that the yard of the Quarter may be always clean & Sweet. If the old necessary on the brow of the Hill can be moved with more ease than building a new one, let it be done, as it is not only useless where it is but is an eye-sore. Order the other two to be ⟨well cleaned &⟩ kept in good order. During my stay at Mount Vernon I expect much company there, and of the most respectable sort. it would be pleasing to us therefore to find everything in nice order. I wish you well and am your friend

Go: Washington

ALS, ViMtvL.

1. For the pipe of wine from Madeira, see John Marsden Pintard to Bartholomew Dandridge, Jr., 27 Feb., and n.1. For the chairs, see GW to Pearce 1 May, and n.8.

2. GW's request to Tobias Lear about Massachusetts congressman Fisher Ames has not been found, but see GW to Thomas Pinckney, 22 May, and n.2.

GW wrote Ames on Tuesday, 31 May: "As it may not be convenient for you to call upon me before your departure for the Federal City, and if it was, I might be otherwise engaged at the moment; I hand you the enclosed letters: not meaning by doing so, to avoid the pleasure of seeing you before you set out. and then, as now, to wish you an agreeable journey, and the perfect restoration ⟨of⟩ your health . . . P.S. If you do not leave the City before Thursday, let me ask the favor of your company at Dinner that day, 4 Oclock" (ALS [photocopy], MDedHi; ALS [photocopy], NN: George Washington Papers). When Ames wrote Thomas Dwight from Philadelphia on 30 May, he indicated his intention to "leave this city for the south on June 2d, unless Congress should linger in their seats. I reckon three weeks for the journey" (Ames, *Works*, 1:194–95).

3. Lear's stepchildren—Anna Maria Washington, George Fayette Washington, and Charles Augustine Washington—had been staying at Mount Vernon since early April.

4. GW had sent his gardener a few seeds of East India hemp in spring 1793 and wanted to accumulate a supply by saving seed from repeated sowings (see GW to Howell Lewis or Pearce, 6 Jan. 1794, and to Pearce, 24 Feb. and 10 Aug. 1794, and 5 March 1795).

5. The congressional session ended on Wednesday, 1 June. GW left Philadelphia for Mount Vernon on 13 June (see his letter to David Humphreys, 12 June).

Letter not found: from William Pearce, 29 May 1796. GW wrote Pearce on 5 June: "I have received your letters of the 22d & 29th of last Month."

From James Anderson (of Scotland)

Honoured Sir   Cotfield near Edenburgh 30th May 1796
   Your respected favour of the [   ] Feby was transmitted to me by Mr Pinckney about a week ago, since which time I have felt uneasy lest you may have thought I neglected to return an answer, in time, to the letter you alude to dated in December last, which never has yet reached me.[1] I shall regret, if in consequence of that circumstance, any thing that could have depended upon me shall have been neglected—But little is it in my power to be of the service I wish on any occasion!

   I never in my life experienced this inability more strongly than at present, for, I fear the circumstances of the two countries are relatively such as to bar all hopes of my being able effectually to forward your views. This does not proceed so much from any political arrangements, or legislative regulations here, as from the situation of individuals respecting enterprises of the kind proposed: for things are much changed from what they were a few years ago, in that respect. At the period to which I allude, many respectable sober-minded persons of moderate fortune had their eyes directed to the American states as a country in which there was a greater prospect of rendering a small stock a foundation of a moderate independance that might be enjoyed in peace and tranquillity than elsewhere; but in consequence of the reports that have been circulated by a few individuals who have returned; corroborated by letters that have been received in all parts of this country by the relations of many who have remained, the desire of emigrating, among persons of the above description has died almost entirely away, and it is now only found to prevail to a considerable degree among persons of another description, who I should be very sorry to recommend to your notice.

You must be sufficiently informed from other quarters, that there exists in this country (and I fear in other countries also) a small, but violent party who are highly discontented with the present form of our government. As this government, however, is firmly supported by a vast majority of the thinking people in all parts of the country, they find their efforts to change it so ineffectual as to have excited a rage in their minds that prompts them to wish for a change of situation. Of this class of emigrants many have of late years found their way into America, little I fear to its profit—and more are still desireous of going thither; nor do I know that ever any effort has been made by government to restrain them. Among persons of this description, were I to search for them I have no doubt but some would be found who would gladly close with any proposals that could be offered on your part—but my regard for you is too sincere ever to permit me to think of such a thing. I have watched this class of men for several years past, and barring a few persons of very mean intellectual powers, I have reason to believe that the whole party derives its existence from embarassment of circumstances, or an inordinate desire for rule, frequently, among persons of even large property originating from the same source. There are many men ⟨in⟩ every country who choosing to live in a stile beyond that to which their funds can easily reach, feel private embarassments that the world in general does not perceive—

this naturally tends to sour the mind, and to make it dwell with satisfaction on the gloomy side of every object, so that it at last becomes so exceedingly disposed to discontent, that every hint which touches on that string produces a forcible effect and they become at last seriously convinced that nothing good exists around them—Had the same person never felt the embarassment which gave the first gloomy biass to the mind, that biass would never have been experienced—On the contrary if the cheering sensation that results from easy circumstances had prevailed, content and satisfaction would have been the natural tendency of the mind. Whether these remarks are just or not, it is a certain fact that nine out of ten of the disaffected party here are men of dissipated manners, or such as are in needy circumstances neither of which would be proper for your purpose. Among the class of respectable opulent farmers, who in this part of the country at present form a very valuable part of the community, none are to be found, who would move even to a few miles distan⟨ce⟩ from their native place without very high encouragement indeed—And if such men were to go to America they would aim at becoming proprietors of land themselves, the purchase price of which is so much lower than in this country as strongly to impress their mind with that idea—But among this class of men at present for the reasons above given, few are to be found who have their views turned towards America.

Before the war there was another class of men who without ever intending to leave this island had begun to purchase great tracts of land there, as a mercantile speculation, with a view to sell them out again in smaller allotments. But the immoderate profits that monied men can now derive from their capital by speculating in the funds here; has entirely driven all the ready cash of the nation into that vortex, so as for the present to put a stop to every idea of entering into distant speculations of any sort—Besides, the laws of some of the states lay bars in the way of such attempts and an idea begins to prevail here that the tenure by which such property is held is less secure than it was once imagined to be, which must have a tendency to repress similar enterprises, as it will probably have an effect also upon the state of your public funds. From all these considerations my hope of being able effectually to cooperate in forwarding your views by no means corresponds with my wishes, which occasions a regret so strong that it perhaps makes me also more desponding than I ought to be. Should that prove to be the case, nothing will more add to my happiness in life—for next to enjoying tranquillity of mind myself there is nothing could be more pleasing to me than to think that I could be in any respect instrumental in augmenting the tranquillity and enjoyment that you have so good a right to expect. I shall do my best to put the papers you have entrusted to me into the hands of such persons as I think have the best chance of doing service—under the cautions you have, with your usual liberality recommended.[2] I regret however, that from my inferior station of life, and the narrow sphere in which I move, that I can have less in my power than others might have had. The only thing that I can command in this case is my best wishes and these shall never be wanting.

I am glad you approve the principle of the iron bridge. The calculations have been sufficiently accurate to prove beyond a doubt that in every case the charge must be greatly below that of a stone bridge—And that in some cases it could not amount to one tenth part of the sum—But these are particulars that are not at present of sufficient importance to require your attention.[3]

I have used the freedom to request the favour of Mr Pinckney to transmit to you an additional volume of Essays relative to Agriculture and Rural affairs (bei⟨ng the thi⟩rd) just now published by me, which I beg the favour of you to ho⟨nour⟩ with your acceptance[4]—Should a time ever arrive when you could be permitted to direct your undisturbed attention to objects of that nature you would find it a source of much enjoyment—But at present objects of greater magnitude call for your attention. This volume gives a view of some of the internal arrangements in Britain, that are not, I presume, very generally known abroad. I have the honour to be, with the most respectful esteem Sir your most obedient Hule Servt

Jas Anderson

ALS, DLC:GW.

1. See GW to Anderson, 24 Dec. 1795 and 15 Feb. 1796.

2. With his letter written on 15 Feb., GW enclosed to Anderson handbills of his advertisement dated 1 Feb. 1796 that offered to lease the farms at Mount Vernon.

3. Anderson discussed the construction of iron bridges in his letter to GW dated 15 Sept.–3 Oct. 1795.

4. GW acknowledged receipt of the third volume of Anderson's *Essays Relating to Agriculture and Rural Affairs* (Edinburgh, 1796) in his letter to Anderson of 7 April 1797 (see *Papers, Retirement Series*, 1:79–82; see also Thomas Pinckney to GW, 12 Feb. 1797, DLC:GW).

To the Commissioners for the District of Columbia

Gentlemen,   Philadelphia 30th May 1796.

As no Mail southward of Baltimore was received at the Post Office in this City on Saturday;[1] and as you may not have understood by my letter of the 22d instt, that the duplicate of the Power of Attorney to Messrs Wilhem and Jan Willink was required to be forwarded *through me*, I address this to you, in order to remove the doubt if any there be; as copies of the other papers are ready, and only waiting *your* duplicates to be dispatched.

In consequence of your recommendation of Mr Freeman, he was nominated, and by the advice & consent of the Senate has been appointed, Surveyor for running the Territorial line between the United States and Spain,[2] at the rate of (*)[3] dollars pr annum.

This service cannot commence before the Ratification of the Treaty by Spain is received; and the Commissioner and Surveyor on the part of that Power are known, & ready to proceed.[4] It will not therefore interfere with any Services *you* may require, and *Mr Freeman* can render, until he is called upon to execute this business; which, probably, will not be before Autumn. At which time the Commissions will issue.

His request was to be employed in settling the Northern boundary between the United States and Great Britain, but the appointment of the Surveyors for that purpose is left to the Commissioners, who are to decide ultimately; I did not incline therefore to bring forward the name of any one for this service, even to our own Commissioner.[5] With esteem & regard I am— Gentlemen Your obedient Servant

Go: Washington

ALS, DLC: U.S. Commissioners of the City of Washington records; ALS (letterpress copy), DLC:GW; LB, DLC:GW.

The commissioners (Gustavus Scott and William Thornton) replied to GW from the "City of Washington" on 3 June: "We have the honor of your favor of the 30th Ulto & have communicated to Mr Freeman, that part of it which respects him—We now enclose a Duplicate copy of our power of attorney to Messrs Willinks—Should it be necessary, we can easily forward a Triplicate, executed by a full board" (LB, DNA: RG 42, Records of the Commissioners for the District of Columbia, Letters Sent). The duplicate power of attorney, signed by Scott and Thornton, was notarized on this date (DNA: RG 42, Records of the Commissioners for the District of Columbia, Letters Received).

1. The previous Saturday was 28 May.

2. Thomas Freeman wrote GW on 3 June: "Being this day informed by the Commissioners of the City that I have been appointed *Surveyor* for running the Territorial Line between the United States and Spain; I take the liberty to return my most grateful acknowledgements for your attention to me in that appointment, for which I shall hold my self in readiness, and hope that by a faithful discharge of the duties of that office to merit the confidence reposed in me" (ALS, DNA: RG 59, Miscellaneous Letters; see also Commissioners for the District of Columbia to GW, 13 April, and GW to the U.S. Senate, 21 May).

3. The asterisk references a note at the bottom of the page: "I *believe* of 1500$."

4. Article III of the 1795 treaty with Spain called for each country to appoint one commissioner and one surveyor to meet within six months of ratification (Miller, *Treaties*, 320–21).

5. For Freeman's request, see his letter to GW dated 13 April. Article V of the Jay Treaty empowered the appointed commissioners "to employ such Surveyors or other Persons as they shall judge necessary" (Miller, *Treaties*, 249).

From Tobias Lear

My dear Sir,   Washington May 30th 1796

I have this moment returned from Berkley County where I have been detained much longer than I expected on account of the difficulties raised by the Wagers; because the land was not taken possession of on the first of April, agreeably to contract.[1] These I have at last surmounted, and have received possession for the United States; but the deeds are not yet executed, as one of the parties is in Philada. The money, of course, is not yet paid. They have, however, obligated themselves to have the deeds ready by the first of july.[2] The Court have not yet decided on the Saw-mill tract; but have engaged to do it in the August term. I have taken possession of that, so far as to have any use of it or the Saw mill that may be wanted for the United States in the mean-time.

You will have the goodness, my dear Sir, to let Mrs Washington know that I can procure no dble refined Sugar in this quarter, but at a price higher than in Philadelphia, and therefore have not purchased any.

I intend tomorrow to visit my little folks, who, I hear, are well. I expect my son Lincoln here in the course of a week or ten days, with a young man who is highly recommended as a tutor.[3] I expect my mother will come on with him and pass the summer with me.

Mr Pearce informed me, the day before I sat off up the Country, that Mr Smith had agreed to take your flour @ $14, on a Credit of 6 Months, which I think was doing very well with it;[4] for it is now down to 9½ dollars Cash—and very dull. Upwards of 40,000 barrels are in Alexandria, and no demand abroad to justify shipping even at 9 dollars. Large quantities are still in the Country, and coming in daily. I was detained at Harpers ferry from tuesday 'till saturday last,[5] during which time upwards of forty boats passed by and sailed from thence, loaded with flour, each carrying from 100 to 120 barrels. The wheat and other grain in the part of the Country where I have been look remarkably well—and there is more in the ground than was ever before known in one year. The rains which have been falling almost incessantly for 6 days past may injure the Crops; but, without such an event, they will be the largest ever known. The early wheat, and the common which was sown early, will receive most injury.

The people throughout the Country where I have been (and I have travelled pretty extensively for 2 weeks past) appear highly satisfied with the treaty having gone into effect, and if the British give up the posts according to stipulation, I see nothing to interrupt the happiness of our Country. Should they not do it, there will be but one voice in the community.[6]

I shall have the honor to write to you by the next, or following post and hope soon to have the happiness to see you in this quarter.

I have not yet heard from Mr B. Bassett since I wrote to him from Philadelphia. I shall write to him again, and should he not come or send for Maria before I get my boys fixed I shall have her attended to with them.

Please to make my best & most affectionate Respects acceptable to Mrs Washington—and my kindest regards to my good friends Mr Fayettee, Mr Frestel and Washington.[7] With the purest respect & most perfect attachment I have the honor to be, My dear Sir, Your grateful & affectionate friend.

Tobias Lear.

ALS, DLC:GW.

1. For the initial agreement reached on 22 Feb. to purchase land for an arsenal at Harper's Ferry, Va., see Lear to GW, 23 Feb. and 30 March, and n.1 to the latter.

2. By an indenture completed on 15 June, five members of the Wager family conveyed to the United States an island in the Potomac River ("Containing Twenty Acres more or Less") and a "parcel of Land . . . Commonly known by the name of Harpers ferry Tract" (with the exception of a specified six acres). The Wagers also received the privilege to operate a public ferry across the Shenandoah and Potomac rivers (DNA: RG 156, Letters Received). Additional documents related to the conveyance accompanied the indenture, most notably an acknowledgement (dated 15 June) that GW had paid the Wagers through Lear "Seven Thousand and Sixteen Dollars and two thirds of a Dollar" and a notice of the deed being recorded on 24 July 1797.

3. For Lear's stepchildren from his second marriage and son from his first marriage, see Burwell Bassett, Jr., to GW, 17 April, and n.1 to that document, and GW to Bassett, 24 April, and n.2 to that document.

4. For Alexander Smith's flour purchase, see GW to William Pearce, 15 May, n.2.

5. The previous Tuesday through Saturday was 24–28 May.

6. Article II of the Jay Treaty stipulated that British evacuation of posts on U.S. territory take place by 1 June 1796 (Miller, *Treaties*, 246).

7. GW replied to Lear on 3 June.

From John Sinclair

Sir   Whitehall [London] 30th May 1796

Being unfortunately much troubled with an Inflammation in my Eyes, I beg Your Excellency will have the Goodness to excuse the Liberty I take, in making use of a borrowed Hand.

The Session of the Board of Agriculture has closed for this Year, and I am now preparing to go to Scotland, which hurries me much; but I could not think of leaving this Town, without having the Honour of acknowledging the Receipt of Your obliging Letter of the 20th of February, with the Inclosure.[1] I regret much that any Circumstance should have prevented for the present (but I hope that some time or other it will be effected) the establishing of that Agreement so interesting to Humanity, and from which all Nations must derive such Benefit, but, I hope that Your Excellency will have it in View, whenever a proper Opportunity occurs.[2]

We have printed an additional Appendix to the Chapter on Manures, on which we should be glad to be favored with the Remarks of the intelligent Farmer to whom the former Paper on that Subject was given.[3] We are now carrying on a Set of Experiments, under the Directions of Dr Fordyce, which I trust will clear up the Doctrine of Vegetation and Manures.[4] The Queries respecting Live Stock, Copies of which are also sent, will, I trust, throw much Light on that important Department in Husbandry.[5]

I take the Liberty at the same time of sending to Your Excellency Copies of my Address to the Board, explaining the Progress we have made during the last session; also specimens of the Manner in which we acknowledge the Receipt of Communications, and return Our Thanks to those who merit them.[6]

I am glad to hear that Your Excellency preserves good Health, and if you wish to enjoy Tranquillity and Ease, as you cannot expect that Satisfaction in America where even at Mount Vernon you would be perpetually applied to on Matters of Business, I hope you will excuse me expressing my Hopes and Wishes, *that you would think of spending at least one Year of Tranquillity and Ease in England,* where, I am sure, you would be received in a Manner highly flattering and agreeable, by all Ranks and Descriptions of People, and by none with more Respect and Regard than by Him, who has Honour to subscribe himself, Your Excellency's faithful and obedient Servant

John Sinclair

N.B. I hope that a very beneficial Intercourse will be established between America and Great Britain, in the article of oil Cake—I have ordered the Bookseller to send Your Excellency two Sets of the corrected County Reports, as they come out,[7] and he will settle regarding the Price with his Correspondent in America. I think that there cannot be too many of those Reports circulated there—I shall write to Your Excellency from Scotland respecting the Farms on the Mount Vernon Estate.

LS, DLC:GW.

GW acknowledged this letter when he wrote Sinclair on 10 Dec. (DLC:GW).

1. GW had enclosed his advertisement dated 1 Feb. to lease Mount Vernon farms and sell his western lands.

Sinclair subsequently wrote GW from Whitehall on 11 Sept.: "I do not much like the present aspect of Europe, and have some thoughts, incase of accidents, to secure an asylum for my family in america. The Revolution of France, now confirmed, will probably occasion Revolutions in other Countries, and it is not impossible, even here, where, though the government is good, yet it is ill administered. Indeed what else could be expected from surrendering the administration of the affairs of a great country, to inexperienced boys, such as Pitt and his companions, to lawyers, like Dundas & Wedderburn, who are men of information and abilities in the line of their own profession, but were not trained up to be regular statesmen; and having nobody to look up to, incase of their dismission, but such *characters* as Fox and Sheridan, who have talents, particularly those of an oratorical nature, but from their dissipation, their extravagance, their pecuniary difficulties, and in some respects, their vicious conduct, never can acquire, the confidence of the people, and who have not application enough for public business; With a load of debts and taxes on the country almost unsupportable, and yet increasing every year; without any bounds to our public expences, and our public credit not a little shook; and joined to all these untoward circumstances at home, with so formidable an enemy abroad as France, *an armed nation*, ably governed, within a few hours sail of us, these points united, furnish but a gloomy prospect, to a thinking native of this country.

"I should be glad to be favoured with your opinion, respecting a purchase in America, on a moderate scale, from 2 to £3000. you wrote me that you had some farms to let in the neighbourhood of Mount Vernon. Have any of them a tolerable good house, and instead of letting them on a short lease, would you grant, what in Scotland is called a *feu*, a species of perpetual lease, at a rent not augmentable, or would you sell them out right, as they seem to be in an eligible part of the country. If either plan would be acceptable, have the goodness to mention the terms" (ALS, DLC:GW).

Alexander Wedderburn (1733–1805), first baron Loughborough, served as lord chancellor of Great Britain from 1793 to 1801.

Richard Brinsley Sheridan (1751–1816), the dramatist, allied in Parliament with Charles James Fox to argue that the French had a right to form their own government and that Great Britain should recognize the result.

2. Sinclair is referring to his *Plan of an Agreement among the Powers in Europe, and the United States of America, for the Purpose of rewarding Discoveries of general Benefit to Society* (London, 1795), which he had enclosed with his letters to GW of 18 July 1795.

3. The *Additional Appendix to the Outlines of the Fifteenth Chapter of the Proposed General Report from the Board of Agriculture. On the Subject of Manures* (London, 1796) was in GW's library at his death (Griffin, *Catalogue of the Washington Collection*, 90).

4. George Fordyce (1736–1802), a London physician, graduated from the University of Edinburgh. He wrote on medicine, chemistry, and mineralogy as well as agriculture.

Fordyce printed his proposal for the experiments as *Plan for Ascertaining the Effects of the Different Sorts of Manures in Promoting Vegetation* (London, 1795).

5. Sinclair sent *Queries Relating to Live Stock* (n.p., n.d.). GW held three copies in his library (see Griffin, *Catalogue of the Washington Collection*, 89).

6. For this address, see Sinclair to GW, 14 May 1796, postscript and n.2 to that document.

7. For citations to the Board of Agriculture county surveys in GW's library at the time of his death, see Griffin, *Catalogue of the Washington Collection*, 92–95.

Sinclair had played a pivotal role in the establishment of the Board of Agriculture in 1793 as an association in Great Britain to promote scientific agriculture.

From William Strickland

Sir   London May 30th 1796.

By the civility of Mr Pinckney in seeking me out in this place, I had the honor of receiving your letter a few days since, & am consequently enabled to acknowledge the receipt of it by the Packet which will be made up tomorrow. I am extremely happy in being favoured with your recollection & should an opportunity present itself of being of service to you in making known to any one, who, as you state it, may have resolved on transplanting himself, the terms on which you propose disposing of your property or any other particulars connected with it, which may have come to my knowledge, I shall seize it with pleasure; but I am apprehensive that the power to be of service, may fall far short of the inclination; According to observations I have made both here & in America; of all classes of people, the farmer appears most rarely to emigrate & they who do emigrate, to have often other than good motives for it. The cause of this is easily assigned; of all the different professions in this country the farmer is the most respected, enjoys the greatest number of comforts, distinctions, & immunities & possesses the most property; he is moreover from habit or principle strongly attached to the soil on which he has been brought up, & to the country that places him in a station of so much respectability, & is according to his views & station in life in my opinion better circumstanced here than in any other country I have seen; it is therefore not to be wonderd at that so few people of this description should quit it; I therefore despair of meeting with such respectable characters, as I ought to introduce to you or you would choose to receive; but chance may throw them in my way.[1] This statement of mine has been frequently controverted in America, but I am sure your liberality will allow me to state an opinion founded on much observation, and which has been confirmed by the few gentlemen from America (& I wish for the sake of both our countries that they had been far more numerous) who with decerning eyes have travelled in this country.

The letter with which you have favourd me, affords an opening which I regretted having lost when in America, for making a few agricultural remarks on subjects which struck me during my last year's tour,[2] & which the short time I was in Philadelphia after my return from the southward deprived me of the opportunity of communicating. these I will take the liberty of addressing you upon soon after my return home, when I shall also farther notice your letter, & the paper accompanying it, as naturally connected with the other subject; not having my memorandums with me in London I am not able to enter upon it at present.

I was in hopes of having an opportunity, when in America, of introducing to your acquaintance a particular Friend of mine, who crossed the Atlantic with me, but who not having been in Philadelphia during that period, it never occurred. The person I allude to is Mr Miles Smith now residing at Ross Hall near New-Brunswick in N: Jersey, which estate he has purchased. Mr Smith is a gentleman of good family & connections in the county of York, with whom I have been intimately acquainted the greatest part of my life, & I take the liberty of mentioning him to you because, exclusively of his being an estimable character in every point of private life, he is by far the best practical farmer on a great scale of any gentleman with whom I ever was acquainted, & particularly in every branch of agriculture connected with the Plough or Sheep, & was looked up to as such by his whole neighbourhood, & nothing can more fully prove his intelligence than a most beautifully cultivated estate, which I remember not many years since little better than a wilderness, of which he still keeps the occupancy in his own hands, in Yorkshire. It appears to me that Mr Smith could not be in any part of the United States which I have seen, without being able to suggest much for the improvement of it; but as Mr S: has unfortunately lost his wife, since I returned to this country, & is left with a numerous young family, it is possible he may be under the necessity of returning home again; Such a character I am confident I need not apologise for mentioning to you, having observed the patronage you have always extended to the meritorious stranger, & your desire of communicating with all those who could be of service to your country. I will add that Mr Smith has not had the slightest intimation of my intention of mentioning his name to you, in order to avoid any expectation on his part or inconvenience on yours, & that I shall not for the same reasons hereafter notice it to him.[3]

By a letter I received some time since from Mr Wadsworth of Connecticut, I was sorry to find, that of some seeds in part the same as those I took the liberty of presenting to you, few had grown, probably from having received damage on Shipboard, tho I had taken what care of them I was able; should yours have succeeded no better, there could no longer be any doubt of the fact & I should be desirous of being informed of it that I might have an opportunity of replacing any you would point out, or would allow me to substitute in their place;[4] give me leave to add that I could experience no greater satisfaction, than in being of any service to you in my power in this country, or in executing any commission with which you would charge me; it would be the slightest return I could make for the civilities & attentions I received from you when in America, which I shall ever remember with pleasure & gratitude.

The Board of Agriculture are steadily pursuing the object of their institution, with every prospect of this country & perhaps others, reaping much advantage from it, as I convey to you, along with this letter a parcel and a letter which Sr John Sinclair has this day put into my hands; I need say nothing more on this subject.[5] I beg you will make my best respects to Mrs Washington & that you will believe me to be with the truest esteem & respect Sir Your very obedient, Humble Servant

Wm: Strickland

P.S. My direction (should it at any time be required) is W: S: York England.

ALS, DLC:GW.

1. GW's letter to Strickland dated 20 Feb. had sought his assistance in leasing Mount Vernon farms. It also enclosed GW's related advertisement dated 1 February.

2. Strickland kept a journal during his travels (see Strickland, *Tour in the United States*).

3. Miles Smith (1756–1838) and his family arrived with Strickland at New

York on 20 Sept. 1794. Smith had purchased Ross Hall, a property in Piscataway Township, Middlesex County, N.J., in 1792, and he occupied that estate until his death. His first wife, Jane Legard Smith (1756–1795), was a daughter of Sir Digby Legard (1729–1773) of Ganton Hall in Yorkshire, England.

4. In his reply to Strickland dated 15 July 1797, GW wrote that his seeds "shared the same fate that Colo. Wadsworths did" (*Papers, Retirement Series*, 1:253–59; quote on 256).

5. See John Sinclair to GW, this date, and n.7.

To the United States Senate

Gentlemen of the Senate, United States May 30th 1796.

I nominate Silas Talbot, of New York and John Trumbull, of Connecticut, Agents for the purpose of obtaining the release of impressed american citizens and others sailing under the protection of the american flag, and to execute the other duties prescribed for such agents by the act of congress passed on the 28th of the present month, entitled "An Act for the relief and protection of american seamen."[1]

I nominate Jacob Mayer, a native citizen of Pennsylvania, to be consul of the United States at the port of Cape François and its dependences in the Island of St Domingo.[2]

Go: Washington

LS, DNA: RG 46, entry 52; copy, DLC:GW.

The Senate received these nominations on this date and consented on 31 May (*Senate Executive Journal*, 213).

1. This law also directed the agents "to render an account of all impressments and detentions whatever, from American vessels, to the executive of the United States" (1 *Stat.* 477–78). John Trumbull declined his appointment (see Trumbull to Timothy Pickering, 27 Aug., in Sizer, *Trumbull Autobiography*, 194–95).

Maryland congressman Gabriel Christie wrote GW from Philadelphia on 3 June: "By an Act which passed the last legislature of the United States it's contemplated that an agent for the Releff & Protection of American Seamen will be appointed to reside in Great Britain Should the President of the United States think me qualify'd to fill that trust and would honour me with the Appointment it shall be executed to the best of my ability" (ALS, DLC:GW).

2. Jacob Mayer (d. 1802) was a merchant who resided at Cap Français.

Sharp Delany had written Secretary of State Timothy Pickering on 20 May: "Mr Jacob Mayer who will have the Honour of delivering this note—has resided for a considerable time at Cape Francois—a considerable number of the Merchants of this City, informs him it would be of great benefit to them in having a Consul resident at the Cape for the North side of Hispaniola—

Mr Mayer is well known to the Merchants—and I beg leave to mention him as long known to me as an industrious intelligent Young Gentleman—and I make no doubt of his capability for the Office" (DLC:GW). Andrew Bayard wrote Pickering on the same date to repeat his recommendation of Mayer for consul made "in a conversation a few days ago." Bayard presented Mayer "as a person well qualified for the appointment from his long residence in Cape Francois & from his acquaintance with the principal Officers of the government in that quarter as well as from his general knowle[d]ge of the business of the Island, both as it respects the American & French Citizens" (DLC:GW). Twelve Philadelphia merchants and firms signed a recommendation docketed 28 May that lamented frequent "inconveniences and delays in their business for want of an American Consul, or some representative of the United states to whom the American masters of vessels may resort for advice and assistance." The signers desired Mayer as "a Native Citizen of Pennsylvania" (DLC:GW).

Mayer was removed as consul in 1800 (see Pickering to George Cabot, 16 June 1800, in Lodge, *George Cabot*, 275–78).

From James Francis Armstrong

Sir   Trenton [N.J.] May 31st 1796

I beg leave to bring before your mind that, if a vacancy in any office in your appointment, for which you may judge me fit, should occur, you would consider me as a candidate. The Secretary of the Treasury will detail the motives upon which I found my request.[1] I have the honour to be—Sir, your most obedient Servant

James F. Armstrong

ALS, DLC:GW.

James Francis Armstrong (1750–1816), a Princeton graduate and former Continental army chaplain, served as pastor of the Presbyterian church in Trenton from 1787 until his death.

1. Armstrong also wrote Secretary of the Treasury Oliver Wolcott, Jr., from Trenton on this date: "The continuance of the rainy weather almost the whole of the time I was in Philadelphia so increased the force of my rheumatick indisposition that I was under the necessity of leaving the city without having an opportunity of speaking with you as I wished—I hope therefore you will excuse the liberty I take of making you acquainted with my business by letter— During more than a twelve month past I have laboured under a rheumatick complaint which has not yeilded to any medical prescription—thro the winter I have been confined mostly to my house, & for some months past my Breasts & lungs have been so much affected by the disorder that I have been obliged to decline preaching altogether—Necessity therefore compels me to apply to some person near the President to advocate my cause with him to procure

me some small office which may help to support my family most of them yet small & helpless—deprived as I am in the course of providence of supporting them as I have hitherto done with comfort & reputation and in a way which I still sincerely wish to finish my course in life . . . My choice of a friend in this case has fallen upon you—the trouble attending it will be all your own—I can promise nothing else—I have also enclosed a note to the President, which you will please to deliver if you think it not improper after sealing it. . . . Please to keep this a secret until I see you" (CtHi: Oliver Wolcott, Jr., Papers).

From the Commissioners
for the District of Columbia

sir— City of Washington 31st May 1796

We have this day, the honor of your Letter of the 22nd of this month, which was detained on the road by the late heavy rains—The Duplicate of the powers to Mesrs Wilhem & Jan Willink, we should not fail to forward by the next post, but as the original was signed by Mr White, it will be more in order to have his signature to the Copy—It shall be our first business, on his arrival, which we expect will be in few days—Your objection to placing the whole Sum authorized to be borrowed in one Year, upon the issue of a negotiation in Holland; which, under existing circumstances, may be ineffectual, we likewise had under consideration, but the result was—if we could borrow money here, it might be repaid upon the successful issue of the Dutch negotiation and we should thus run no risk of interrupting our operations—Under this Idea, we have proceeded, & have obtained an accommodation from some of the proprietors of the City—They agreed to offer their notes at the Bank of Columbia for $12,000 for the use of the City of Washington, for 2 months, to be repaid from the first receipts of the Commissioners after taking up the notes passed in their own private capacity, to the amount of 20,000 Dollars—3,000 Dolls. have been obtained and loaned to the City.[1]

We opened the Works on the 23rd Ulto—and although the Weather has been uncommonly wet and unfavorable, yet we have made a very great progress, and we hope that no just cause of complaint, can possibly exist—It is not unknown to us that some unthinking persons have attributed the mal-construction of the foundation-Wall of the Capitol to the want of attention

on the part of the Commissioners—but if they had visited and
walked over the Walls three times a day, it would not have been
possible to prevent imposition where men are resolved to practice it, and the Commissioners had reliance on the Work, not
only from the Character the undertaker then enjoyed;[2] but also
on the care and attention of the Superintendant[3]—Many dis-
advantages are attributed to the non-residence of the Comms.
in the City—We lament that any person could expect us to live
there, before houses are prepared for accommodation—some
of the board have always said, that they mean to remove thither
as soon as even decent houses could be had—The proprietors
have not been active in their preparations, otherwise, this cause
of their complaint would not now exist. The board are disposed
to do every thing in their power, not only to give satisfaction to
the public, but also, to obtain the approbation of those whose
knowledge of their affairs may enable them to judge more justly
& truly of their conduct—Your wishes with respect to the Sale
of Lots, we are happy to have anticipated—We know it to be
a principle which you have constantly inculcated to encourage
individuals disposed to build & settle & to discourage large speculations—Such principles we have made the constant rule of
our conduct, and we think it the only certain mode of disposing
of the public property to advantage, except our necessities may
require a certain departure from this established rule—In such
a case, however, we should act with caution, and consider the
evidence of its advantages, as requisite to our justification—If
the situation of the Bank of the United states is such, as to afford any prospect of success—We think it would be prudent to
endeavor to obtain 20 or 30,000$ through that channel—We
think 10,000$ ℔ month, with our other funds, might do, during
the building season—Some conversation on this subject, passed
between Mr White & the Secy of the Treasy—Would Mr Wolcott
interest himself with the Directors, it might have a good effect—
The sum wanted ought to be repaid out of the first receipt under the Loan—& an advance of 10,000$ ℔ month could not be
sensibly felt, by the Bank—We have written to Genl Stewart, one
of the Directors, for information on the state of the Bank—no
answer has yet been received[4]—Any thing that may [be] deemed
worthy of your attention, and which may escape us, at present,

we shall not fail to lay before you, when We have the happiness to welcome you to this place.[5] We are Sir &c.

Signed—G. Scott

W. Thornton

LB, DNA: RG 42, Records of the Commissioners for the District of Columbia, Letters Sent.

1. For an earlier report on this agreement, see Alexander White to GW, 25 May.

2. The undertaker in late June 1795 was Cornelius McDermott Roe (d. 1807), a stonemason and bricklayer from Ireland who had been employed at Mount Vernon in the 1780s.

The commissioners had approved Roe's proposal for masonry work at the Capitol in 1794 (see entry of 15–24 April 1794, DNA: RG 42, Records of the Commissioners for the District of Columbia, Proceedings). They later sued Roe for the cost of repairs (see Arnebeck, *Through a Fiery Trial*, 571).

3. The supervisor was either Collen Williamson, who had been hired to oversee the stonemasons, or James Hoban, who then exercised responsibility over construction at both the Capitol and the President's House.

4. The commissioners (Gustavus Scott and William Thornton) had written Walter Stewart on 24 May: "Your early and steady attachment to the City induces us to write to you on a subject, in the present state of affairs, very important to us—While we feel great pleasure in the new energy & spring given to the City by the guarrantee of a Loan, by Congress, it is of great consequence to lose no time in progressing with the public buildings—This, without money, is impossible—no aid has hitherto been drawn from Messrs Morris & Nicholson that can be called effectual; and our proceedings must be languid until money is procured some where—We look with some degree of hope, if not confidence, to the Bank of the United States, and as one of the Directors of that Bank, we request you to endeavor to obtain us a loan of 15 or 20000 Dollars—if only for 6 or 8 months—We are trying the effect of a loan abroad, & have every reason to believe, that from July, we shall soon be able to do something; that neither of these can supply the wants of the moment, and the summer months ought not to pass away in Idleness—Operations are commenced on the public buildings, & we are exerting every means in our power to continue & to encrease them—Could 15 or 20,000 Dolls. be procured in 30 & 60 days from the Bank of the United States—We hope there would be no occasion for further aid this season & that the money could, at all events, be repaid in the course of 6 or 8 months—We beg the favor of you to get the fullest information you can, on this subject, & to communicate to us as early as possible, the result" (DNA: RG 42, Records of the Commissioners for the District of Columbia, Letters Sent).

5. GW replied to the commissioners on 10 June.

From James McHenry

Sir.   Tuesday afternoon [31 May 1796]
    If you see no objection to the inclosed letter in answer to
Mr Hawkins received to-day it may be sent by to-morrows mail.[1]
I have the honour to be Sir with sincere regard Your ob. st
                                              James McHenry

ALS, DLC:GW; LB, DLC:GW. The ALS is docketed 31 May 1796, which
matches the date on the letter-book copy.
    1. Neither the enclosed letter to Benjamin Hawkins nor the one to which it
responded has been identified.

From Timothy Pickering

                                              May 31 [1796]
    The Secretary of State has the honor to inclose a letter from
our Consul at Cadiz, with one for the President.[1]
    The secretary recollects a Colo. Tatem's calling on him last
summer. He said he had been formerly in the southwestern
territory—talked about very valuable maps of the U. States or
some of them which he had made and was making; but needed
pecuniary aid to complete & publish his plans—he might have
intimated a hope of governmental aid.[2]
                                              T. Pickering

ALS, DNA: RG 59, Miscellaneous Letters; LB, DNA: RG 59, GW's Correspondence with His Secretaries of State. The year appears on the docket of the ALS
and is consistent with Pickering's position as secretary of state.
    1. The consul at Cadiz was Joseph M. Yznardi (also called Joseph Yznardi,
Jr.). The enclosed letters have not been identified.
    2. Pickering may have been referring to Howell Tatum, who was a lieutenant
colonel of Davidson County militia in Tennessee and served as a topographical
engineer under Andrew Jackson during the War of 1812.

From Alexander Hamilton

Sir   New York June 1. 1796
    Your letter of the 29th was delivered me by Mr King yester-
day afternoon.[1] I thought I had acknowleged the Receipt of the
paper inquired for in a letter written speedily after it—or in one

which transmitted you a draft of a *certain letter* by Mr Jay.[2] I hope this came to hand.

I am almost afraid to appear officious in what I am going to say; but the matter presses so deeply on my mind that fearing you may not recollect the situation of the thing and that it may happen not to be brought fully under your eye, I cannot refrain from making the suggestion to you. It regards a Bill which I am told has lately passed the two houses of Congress authorising a sale of *Bank Stock* for paying off a sum due to the Bank[3]—You will perceive by the 8th and 9th Sections of the Act intitled "An Act making further provision for the support of public Credit and for the Redemption of the public Debt" passed the 3d of March 1795 that the dividends of the Bank Stock are appropriated to the Sinking Fund with all the force and solemnity of which language is capable[4] and that to divert them in the manner proposed (and this too without any substitute in the act which so diverts) will be a formal express and unequivocal violation of the public faith—will subvert the system of the Sinking Fund and with it all the security which is meant to be given to the people for the Redemption of the Public Debt, and, violating the sanctity of an appropriation for the public Debt, will overturn at once the foundation of Public Credit. These are obvious and undeniable consequences, and though I am aware that great embarrassments may ensue to the Treasury, if the Bill by the objection of The President is lost and no substitute for it takes place towards the reimbursement of the Bank—Yet I am sure no consequences can ensue of equal moment from the rejection as from the principle of the Bill going into execution. All the Presidents administration has effected for establishing the Credit of the Country will be prostrate at a single blow—He will readily make all the necessary comments upon this position. It grieves my heart to see so much shocking levity in our Representative Body. Most respectfully & Affecty I remain Sir Yr very Obed. Ser.

A. Hamilton

ALS, DLC:GW; copy, DLC: Hamilton Papers. "(Private)" is written on the cover of the ALS.

1. GW's letter dated 29 May has not been found.

2. The paper evidently was the draft of GW's farewell address transmitted with his letter to Hamilton of 15 May. No previous acknowledgement by Hamilton has been found. John Jay's draft letter has not been identified, but it most

likely was for GW's letter to Francis II (Holy Roman Emperor) of 15 May. In his letter to Hamilton written on 8 May, GW had asked that he or Jay provide such a document. Hamilton's letter to GW transmitting Jay's draft has not been found.

3. Section 3 of "An Act making provision for the payment of certain Debts of the United States" stated that "it shall be lawful for the commissioners of the sinking fund, if they shall find the same to be most advantageous, to sell such and so many of the shares of the stock of the bank of the United States, belonging to the United States, as they may think proper; and that they apply the proceeds thereof to the payment of said debts, instead of selling certificates of stock, in the manner prescribed in this act" (1 *Stat.* 488–89). GW had approved the act on 31 May.

Hamilton had written Secretary of the Treasury Oliver Wolcott, Jr., on 30 May: "I perceive Congress are invading the Sinking Fund system. If this goes through & is sanctionned by the President the fabric of public Credit is prostrate & the Country & the President are disgraced. Treasury Bills & every expedient however costly to meet exigencies must be preferable in the event to such an overthrow of system" (*Hamilton Papers*, 20:204–5).

4. For this act, see 1 *Stat.* 433–38; especially, 434–35, for sections 8 and 9.

From Elizabeth Willing Powel

Dear Sir   [Philadelphia] Wednesday June 1st 1796

Feeling myself incapable of nourishing an implacable Resentment; and in conformity with your better and dispassionate Judgment I have after maturely considering all that passed Yesterday, determined to dine with you Tomorrow, when I will endeavor to meet your Ideas with Fortitude.[1] With Sentiments of Respect & Affection I am Sir Your sincere Friend

Eliza. Powel

ALS, DLC:GW; ALS, ViMtvL. The ALS at DLC has a cover with GW's docket; the ALS at ViMtvL was most likely a retained copy or draft.

1. For the possibly romantic dimensions of Powel's friendship with GW, see Fraser, *Washingtons*, 288, 340, 350–51.

Indenture with Matthew Ritchie

1 June 1796. In consideration of $12,000 paid by Ritchie, GW and Martha Washington convey to him "A CERTAIN TRACT or piece of Land Situate lying and being in Washington County in Pennsylvania aforesaid formerly Augusta County in the State of

Virginia on the Waters of Millers Run, One of the Branches of Shirtee Creek which is a Branch of the Ohio River and bounded as follows: to Wit,

"BEGINNING at a white Oak standing on the North side of Millers Run a Branch of Shirtee, thence North three hundred and Nineteen Poles to a white Oak, West Seven hundred and forty Poles to a Spanish Oak standing on the North side of a Hill South Six hundred and thirty Poles to a white Oak standing on the South side of a Hill, East seven hundred and forty Poles to a stake standing between two Sycamores and North Three hundred and eleven Poles to the BEGINNING." The tract of 2,813 acres, more or less, is that conveyed to GW in letters patent of Governor Dunmore, dated 5 July 1774.[1] GW's receipt of 1 June 1796 for the $12,000 accompanied the indenture, as did a statement from Judge James Biddle, dated 2 June, that GW and Martha Washington appeared on that date "and in due form of Law acknowledged the above written Indenture to be their and each of their Act and Deed and desired the same might be recorded as such."[2]

Typescript, DLC:GW, ser. 9. The Washington County, Pa., recorder of deeds certified the typescript on 22 June 1922 as a true copy from a record entered into the deed book on 10 Aug. 1796.

1. The patent is recorded in Vi: Land Office Patent Book 42 (1773–74), 516; see also James Ross to GW, 20 Aug. 1795, and Sims, *Making a State*, 135–36.

2. James Biddle (1731–1797), a cousin of Clement Biddle, served as president judge of the court of common pleas for the First District of Pennsylvania (Philadelphia County) from 1791 until his death.

Proceedings of the Sinking Fund Commissioners

[1 June 1796]

At a Meeting of the *Commissioners* of the *Sinking Fund*, at the office of the Secretary of the Treasury on the first day of June 1796.

Present, The Secretary of State, the Secretary of The Treasury The Attornay General.

A Report of the Secretary of the Treasury dated May 31st 1796, respecting the measures proper to be adopted by this Board, for the due execution of the Act entitled "An Act making provision for the payment of certain Debts of the United States"[1] was read; and is as follows—To wit

The Secretary of the Treasury respectfully reports to the Commissioners of the Sinking Fund,

That the following sums of the capital or principal of the public debt, already have or will become due and payable in the course of the present year, the reimbursement of which according to law is to be made under the superintendence of the Commissioners of the Sinking fund—vizt

To the Bank of the United States,

Three instalments of a Loan of 400,000 dollars obtained pursuant to an act entitled "an act for raising a further sum of money for the protection of the frontiers & for other purposes," passed on the 2d day of May 1792[2]	300,000.
Two instalments of a Loan of two millions of dollars obtained pursuant to an act passed on the 18th day of December 1794 for that purpose[3]	200,000.
Two Loans of 500,000 dollars each obtained pursuant to an act making appropriations for the military & naval establishments & for the support of Government passed on the 3d of March 1795[4]	1,000,000.
A Loan of 500,000 dollars obtained under the 1st section of the act for the support of public credit & for the redemption of the public Debt, passed on the 3d of March 1795[5]	500,000
Two instalments of the Loan of 2,000,000 of dollars obtained pursuant to the act for incorporating the Bank of the United States[6]	400,000.
An instalment of a Loan of 800,000 dollars obtained pursuant to an act passed on the 21st day of February 1795, for the expenses of foreign intercourse[7]	200,000.

To the Bank of New York for amount of a loan obtained pursuant to an act passed on the

20th of March 1794 for expenses of foreign
Intercourse[8]   200,000.

To Creditors in Holland for, An instalment of
one million of Guilders due on a Contract
dated June 11. 1782[9]   400,000.

Amounting in the whole to $5,000,000.
five Millions of Dollars.

That by an Act passed during the present session of Congress
entitled "An Act making provision for the payment of certain
debts of the United States" the Commissioners of the Sinking
Fund are authorised with the approbation of The President of
the United States to obtain the said sum of five millions of Dollars upon Loan, by creating a funded stock transferable at the
Treasury & Loan offices respectively bearing Interest at six per
centum per annum payable quarter yearly, which stock at the
said rate of Interest is to remain fixed & irredeemable until the
close of the year 1819 and to be redeemed thereafter at the pleasure of the United States.

That the Creditors of the United States before mentioned may
pursuant to the said act subscribe to the said Loan & receive the
said Stock in payment of their respective demands, or the Commissioners of the Sinking fund may cause certificates for the said
stock to be constituted & sold in the United States or elsewhere,
applying the proceeds thereof to the payment of said demands,
provided that not more than two millions five hundred thousand
Dollars of the said Stock be sold under par: or the said Commissioners may sell the shares of the stock of the Bank of the
United States, belonging to the United States, in lieu of selling
the funded stock before mentioned, if in their judgments sales
of the said Bank shares will be most advantageous to the United
States.

Upon this recital of facts The Secretary of the Treasury represents, that dividends upon the Stock of the Bank of the United
States, have been for several years, made at the rate of four per
Centum half yearly; that there is a reasonable prospect that
future dividends will be declared at the same rate; that by a resolution of the President & Directors of the said Bank, the proprietors of the capital Stock thereof residing in Europe are entitled
to receive either in London or in Amsterdam, the half yearly

dividends which may be declared, six months after the said dividends are declared in the United States: in London at the rate of one pound sterling for every four dollars and forty five cents; or in Amsterdam at the rate of one Guilder current money for every forty cents & four mills money of the United States; that the Bank undertakes the risque and expense of remittances at these rates, & therefore that Bank Stock when transferred to a foreigner possesses the essential properties of a Debt contracted in a foreign Country, that it is the policy of the United States not to increase unnecessarily public debt in foreign Countries; that the present price of Bank Stock is no more than twenty seven perCent advance upon the original capital when sold in the United States; that the price in London by the last advices was even considerably below this rate; that sales to any great amount would probably depress the price here to a level with the current price in London, & that for these reasons a comparison between what now is the price of a stock bearing eight pr Centum ℔ annum, with a stock bearing six pr centum pr annum does not afford a correct criterion to guide the choice of the Commissioners upon the alternative contained in the Law; he is therefore of opinion that the Commissioners of the Sinking fund ought to attempt to raise the requisite funds upon Loans, or by sales of the proposed new funded stock, and that recourse ought not to be had to the authority to sell the Bank shares belonging to the Ud States except in a case of the utmost emergency, or without the absolute injunction of Law.

The Secretary is moreover of opinion, that the Commissioners ought to be restrained from selling the said Bank shares, not only by the improvidence of such a measure, but also by their respect for the principles of public credit, and their duty as Trustees for the Creditors. By an Act of last Session the dividends on the Bank stock belonging to the United States were declared to be *appropriated to the Sinking fund & vested in trust in the Commissioners until the whole of the then present debt of the United States except the three prCent stock should be fully reimbursed & redeemed; the faith of the United States was moreover pledged that the said dividends with the other funds mentioned in the Act should inviolably remain appropriated & vested to be applied to the said reimbursement & redemption.*[10] Under these circumstances the Secretary considers the said dividends as having been compleatly alienated by the Legislature and as cloathed with all the qualities of private property in the hands of the Commissioners who are answerable not only to the United States, but also to the creditors for the faithful discharge of their trust. On these principles the Secretary presumes that the Commissioners will not judge it to be advantageous to the United States to authorise sales of the said Bank stock, & he therefore submits the following resolutions to their consideration.

Resolved that application be made to the President of the United States for his consent & approbation to the opening of a Loan for Five millions of Dollars pursuant to the terms & conditions of the Act entitled "An act making provision for the payment of certain Debts of the United States & for the purposes therein mentioned."

Resolved that if the consent & approbation of The President of the United States be obtained for opening the said Loan, the same be conducted under the direction of the Secretary of the Treasury in manner following—To wit

1st. That the President & Directors of the Bank of the United States be invited to subscribe the whole or any part of the said five millions of Dollars upon condition that so much of the said sum as shall be subscribed & as shall be necessary to satisfy the Loans & Instalments had of said Bank which already have or will fall due on or before the first day of Januy next, shall be applied to that purpose, and upon condition that for such further sums as shall be subscribed, the said Bank will advance & lend an equal amount to be applied in payment of the Loan had of the Bank of New York or the Instalment of foreign Debt which will fall due in the course of the present year.

2d. That in case the said President & Directors of the Bank of the United States shall decline to subscribe the whole sum of Five millions of Dollars, that then the president and Directors of the Bank of New York be invited to subscribe the sum of Two hundred thousand dollars to be applied to the payment of the Loan had of said Bank.

3rd. That for such sum of the Loan of Five millions of Dollars as shall not be subscribed by the President & Directors of the Bank of the United States or the President & Directors of the Bank of New York as before proposed, there be constituted certificates of Stock in the manner authorised by Law, and that the same be sold for account of the United States by the President

& Directors of the Bank of the United States on such terms and pursuant to such directions as shall from time to time be given by the Commissioners of the Sinking Fund, or the Secretary of the Treasury, for that purpose. So however that not more than two millions & five hundred thousand dollars be in any event sold for less than par including Interest thereon to the time of sale.

4th. That the proceeds of all sales of Stock be placed in the Treasury of the United States & forthwith applied to the payment of some part of the capital or principal of the public debt, now due or to become due in the course of the present year, to the Bank of the United States, the Bank of New York or the Creditors of the United States in Holland; and that in the application of the monies so placed in the Treasury, the Secretary of the Treasury have regard to the priorities already established by Law in favor of the Creditors respectively. All which is respectfully submitted by

Treasy Departmt   Olivr Wolcott Jr
May 31st 1796.   Secy of the Treasy

Whereupon, it was resolved that this Board agree to the resolutions proposed in said Report and that a copy of this proceeding be laid before the President of the United States for the purpose of obtaining his consent & approbation to the opening of said Loan of Five millions of Dollars.[11]

Timothy Pickering
Oliv. Wolcott Jr
Charles Lee.

LB, DLC:GW.

1. For this act, approved 31 May, see 1 *Stat.* 488–89; see also Alexander Hamilton to GW, this date, and n.3 to that document.

2. Section 16 of the cited act authorized the president to borrow up to $523,500 (1 *Stat.* 262).

3. See "An Act authorizing a Loan of two million of Dollars" (1 *Stat.* 404).

4. Section 6 of the cited act authorized the president to borrow "any sum or sums not exceeding in the whole, the sums herein appropriated" (1 *Stat.* 439).

5. See "An Act making further provision for the support of Public Credit, and for the redemption of the Public Debt" (1 *Stat.* 433–38; especially 433 for section 1).

6. Section 11 of "An Act to incorporate the subscribers to the Bank of the United States," approved on 25 Feb. 1791, had authorized this particular loan (1 *Stat.* 191–96; especially 196 for section 11).

7. Section 1 of "An Act for the reimbursement of a Loan authorized by

an Act of the last Session of Congress" authorized the Bank of the United States "to lend to the United States, the whole, or any part of the sum of eight hundred thousand dollars (remaining unapplied)" made available under an earlier act (1 *Stat.* 418; see also n.8 below).

8. Section 1 of "An Act making further provision for the expenses attending the intercourse of the United States with foreign nations; and further to continue in force the act intituled 'An Act providing the means of intercourse between the United States and foreign nations'" authorized the president to borrow up to $1,000,000 (1 *Stat.* 345).

9. A translation of the contract dated 11 June 1782 is in DNA:PCC, item 84, and a transcript of the contract (in Dutch with a translation) is in DNA:PCC, item 104. See also "Contract for a Loan with Wilhem & Jan Willink, Nicolaas & Jacob van Staphorst, and De la Lande & Fynje," 11 June 1782, in *Papers of John Adams*, 13:110–16.

10. Wolcott referred to "An Act making further provision for the support of Public Credit, and for the redemption of the Public Debt," especially sections 8 and 9, approved on 3 March 1795 (1 *Stat.* 433–38).

11. The letter-book copy of these proceedings concludes with an indication of GW's approval on 2 June 1796.

To the United States Senate

Gentlemen of the Senate: United States June 1st 1796
I nominate the following persons for appointments in the Army of the United States.
John Wilkins of Pennsylvania to be Quarter Master General vice OHara resigned.
Joseph Philips, Surgeon's Mate in the First Sub Legion to be Surgeon of the third Sub Legion vice Heyward resigned.
David Davis to be Surgeons Mate in the first Sub Legion vice Philips promoted.
Cyrus Dart to be Surgeon's Mate in the Second Sub Legion vice Strong resigned.
Charles Rodes to be Surgeon's Mate in the Corps of Artillerists and Engineers vice Griffith resigned.
Samuel Osborne to be Surgeons Mate in the Corps of Artillerists and Engineers vice Brewster resigned.

Go: Washington

LS, DNA: RG 46, entry 52; copy, DLC:GW.
The Senate received and approved these nominations on this date (*Senate Executive Journal*, 214).

From Jeremiah Claypole

Sir   June 3rd 96—in Hampshire County Virginia

I Propose to pay the President of the United States Eight Dollars pr accre for what is Call'd Round Bottem—on the Ohio river—Provided it will be accepted by the President—or his agant[1] from Your Obedt Humble Servt

Jeremiah Claypole

ALS, DLC:GW.

Jeremiah Claypole (Claypoole, Claypool), the stepson of a plantation owner in Hampshire County, Va. (now W.Va.), sold a "negro woman named Rachel and her children, with their future increase" in 1784 (Sage and Jones, *Hampshire County Records*, 9). Claypole and a partner sold 152 acres in Hampshire County in 1798.

1. GW evidently bargained with Claypole but reached no agreement (see Bartholomew Dandridge, Jr., to GW, 26 Sept. 1796, DLC:GW; see also Archibald McClean to GW, 2 July 1798, and GW to McClean, 6 Aug. 1798, in *Papers, Retirement Series*, 2:364–66, 492–94).

For others interested in purchasing the Round Bottom tract, see Robert McLean to GW, 7 June 1796, and Thomas G. Johnston to GW, 1 Sept. 1796.

To Tobias Lear

My dear Sir,   Philadelphia 3d of June 1796

Your letter of the 30th Ulto was received yesterday. As I expect (nothing new & unforeseen happening to prevent it) to commence my journey for Mount Vernon in ten or twelve days, I shall enter into no details respecting any of the matters touched upon in your letter of the above date.

The chief design of my writing to you by this Post, is to inform you that your good Mother, and lovely son, arrived in this City on Tuesday evening;[1] and left it yesterday about ten oclock on their way to the Federal City. Mrs Lear is very well, & Lincoln as sprightly as ever; but both disappointed at not meeting you here.

It was with great difficulty a Carriage could be procured to take her on; for it so happened, that Congress closed their Session yesterday—that the members were struggling for, and bidding on each other for conveyances—and your Mothers anxious desire to get to you, would not permit her to wait. At length, after some unavailing attempts, Mr Craik succeeded in getting a Carriage & pair of horses, which I hope will take her safe down.

I will send sugar, and some other things from hence.[2] We are all as well as usual, and join in best wishes for you. with sincere esteem & regard I am Your Affectionate

Go: Washington

P.S. A Mr Prescot attends Mrs Lear & Lincoln.[3] And it is not unlikely, as the weather is cool, but that they may be with you as soon as this letter as the Post does not travel on Sunday.

I did not know until after the Post had left the City on Wednesday, that Mrs Lear was in it, or expected; or you should have been advised of the circumstance by the Mail of that day.

ALS, CSmH.

Lear replied to GW from Washington, D.C., on 6 June: "Your kind letter of the 3d instant has been duly received. I am happy to inform you that my honored Mother and dear boy reached this place in safety last evening. Words cannot express, my dear Sir, the gratitude which I feel for the repeated instances of your goodness to me. The kind attentions shewn by yourself and your good Mrs Washington to my mother & son have made a deep impression on my mind, and the reiterated marks of parental regard which I have experienced from you both puts it out of my power to make proper acknowledgements for them. May heaven bless you with the choicest of its favours!

"I am happy to find that we may so soon expect the satisfaction of seeing you in this quarter, where I hope you will experience a little repose from the arduous & anxious business in which you have been so long engaged.

"My mother informs me that she receivd one hundred dollars from you to defray her expenses &c. to this place. Expecting to meet me in New York she did not take with her more money than was necessary to carry her on there. This will be duly accounted for by me. My journey & detention up the Country prevented my going to New York to meet her.

"My dear little folks at Mount Vernon are in fine health. I shall get them up this week & Mr Prescott will take charge of them here.

"My mother desires that her best respects & most grateful acknowledgements may be presented to Mrs Washington & yourself—to which I add mine—and my best regards to my good friends with you.

"The wheat looks very fine. Your's exceeds any in this part of the Country, and unless an accident happens to it now, the Crop will be great. With the most grateful & affectionate heart" (ALS, DLC:GW; see also n.3 below). GW recorded the $100 supplied Mary Stillson Lear as a loan in his cash accounts under 3 June (Cash Memoranda, 1794–97). He also recorded the sum in his account with Tobias Lear in General Ledger C.

1. The previous Tuesday was 31 May.

2. A payment of $46.64 for loaf sugar from Isaac & Edward Pennington, Philadelphia sugar refiners, was recorded in GW's household accounts for this date.

3. The chaperone may have been Benjamin Prescott, who later advertised

in the *Alexandria Advertiser* (Va.) for 25 Sept. 1797, and in subsequent issues of that newspaper, that during his absence in the West Indies he had authorized Lear to "transact his business."

From David Lenox

Sir   Philada 3d June 1796

I have till now deferred making application to you on behalf of a Man to whom I conceive myself indebted for life, from the consideration that it might be improper while the fate of others were undetermined, as well as the consideration of troubling you during the Session of Congress.

The Person Sir who is the object of my addressing you, is a certain Benjamin Parkinson who was concerned in the late Insurrection in the Western Counties of Pennsylvania, this Man at the evident risque of his life, threw himself between me and a Banditti when they had presented their Riffles at only a few yards distance and would inevitably have destroyed me but for his interference,[1] if proof of the circumstance should be wanting I refer to Colonel Presley Nevill who was with me at the time, as well as evidence produced on the trials of the Insurgents in the possession of the District Attorney. Circumstanced as I am Sir I need only appeal to your own breast where I am confident I should stand convicted were I to omit doing every thing in my power to obtain this mans pardon. I therefore now step forward to solicit it, I solicit it Sir as (at the time) holding an Office under Government, and I humbly solicit it from the motive of gratitude to the Man, firmly believing that he is convinced of his error & will in future conduct himself as a good Citizen. I beg leave only to add that my request is unsolicited by any person whatever, and I fond[l]y hope I shall not be disappointed in obtaining this act of justice to myself.[2] With the greatest respect I am Sir Your Most Obedt Servt

D. Lenox

ALS, DNA: RG 59, Petitions for Pardon; ALS (retained copy), PHarH: Lukes-Lenox Papers.

1. For a brief account of Lenox's confrontation with insurgents in July 1794, see Alexander Hamilton to GW, 5 Aug. 1794, and n.47.

2. GW referred to Lenox's application when he pardoned Benjamin Parkinson on 3 March 1797. For a facsimile of GW's signed pardon, see *Historical*

Magazine of Monongahela's Old Home Coming Week: Sept. 6–13, 1908 (Mononga-hela, Pa., 1908), 96.

From Timothy Pickering

Department of State June 3d 1796.
The Secretary of State respectfully lays before the President of the United States a note from Mr Liston, his Britannic Majesty's Minister plenipotentiary, with copies of two letters, one from Lord Dorchester, the other from the Sheriff of Montreal; and expresses his concurrence with Mr Liston in the opinion, That while the reciprocal delivery of murderers & forgers is expressly stipulated in the 27th article of our treaty with Great Britain, the two Governments are left at liberty to deliver other offenders, as propriety and mutual advantage shall direct. That it will there-fore be expedient to express this opinion to the Governor of Vermont, in order to procure the arrest & delivery of Barnes.[1] Ld Dorchester's information respecting James Clarkson Freeman is correct—He was convicted of forgery in Jersey, broke jail, and fled to Canada, some four or five years since.[2]

Timothy Pickering

The Attorney General has just called, and thinks the opinions expressed to be correct.

ALS, DNA: RG 59, Miscellaneous Letters; LB, DNA: RG 59, GW's Correspon-dence with His Secretaries of State; LB, DNA: DG 59, Domestic Letters.

1. The enclosed circular letter from Guy Carleton (Lord Dorchester) to U.S. governors, dated 31 March, reported that Ephraim Barnes, indicted for highway robbery and horse stealing, and James Clarkson Freeman, indicted as an accessory to the horse stealing, had escaped from the jail at Montreal. Carleton asked their return "in order that they may be brought to Trial." Brit-ish minister Robert Liston wrote Pickering on 27 May that Vermont governor Thomas Chittenden "denied complying with that demand, from an idea he is not authorized so to do by the late treaty between Britain and the United States." Liston then advanced the interpretation of Article XXVII of the Jay Treaty that won Pickering's support (Walton, *Vermont Records*, 4:485–86; see also Miller, *Treaties*, 263).

The enclosed letter from the Montreal sheriff has not been identified, but according to Pickering's letter to Chittenden dated 3 June, it reported the Vermont governor's "disposition to deliver up the offenders, Barnes and Freeman, who had broken Jaol and fled from Canada, if to be found in your Government, provided the treaty between the United States and Great Britain did not oppose it. I have consulted the Attorney General of the United States on this point; and stated our concurring opinion to the President, That Mr Liston's ideas on this subject are perfectly correct. The reciprocal delivery of murderers and Forgers is positively stipulated by the 27th Article of the treaty; the conduct of the two Governments with respect to other offenders is left, as before the treaty, to their mutual discretion: but this discretion will doubtless advise the delivery of culprits for offences which affect the great interests of society.

"The President approves of this opinion, and of the communication of it to your Excellency" (DNA: RG 59, Domestic Letters). Pickering's letter to Chittenden enclosed a copy of Liston's note dated 27 May (see also Pickering to Liston, 3 June, in DNA: RG 59, Domestic Letters).

Edward William Gray (1742–1810), a merchant who held several government appointments, served as Montreal sheriff.

2. Pickering appears to have referenced erroneously the case of Clarkson Freeman (see Abraham Freeman to GW, 5 Sept. 1793).

To James McHenry

[4 June 1796]

Return the enclosed as soon as Mr Ross (under strong injunctions) have read it—Never put papers, improper to be seen, under a cover sealed with a Wafer—At any time, but especially when wet, the contents m⟨ay⟩ be seen and the cover closed ⟨mutilated⟩ without suspicion, or appearan⟨ce⟩ of being opened.

G: W——n

ALS (photocopy), DLC: James McHenry Papers. McHenry wrote a note dated 4 June 1796 at the bottom of the letter: "This enclosed the information given by Mr Wolcott respecting Collot Waren &c.—which I communicated to Mr Ross."

McHenry presumably communicated with James Ross, U.S. senator from Pennsylvania. For Victor Collot and Charles-Joseph Warin, see McHenry to GW, 13 May, notes 2 and 3, and Statement of Oliver Wolcott, Jr., 19 May; see also McHenry to GW, 2 July, n.4, and 10 July, n.1.

To James McHenry

Dr Sir,   Saturday ½ past 12 [4 June 1796]

If it is not too late for Fenno's Paper of this Afternoon, an extract from Chapins letter, respecting the removal of the artillery, Stores &ca from Niagara, to the other side of the River (British side) might afford pleasing information.[1] I presume there can be no doubt of its authenticity. Yrs always

Go: W——n

ALS, PHi: Dreer Collection. The letter's date derives from the publication of the suggested extract (see n.1 below).

1. John Fenno's *Gazette of the United States* (Philadelphia) for 6 June printed an "Extract of a letter from a gentleman in Canandarqua, dated May 18th, 1796. 'The British are making every preparation to leave Niagara, and have already dismounted their cannon, and moved some of their military stores on their own side of the river, into a new magazine which they have built.'" Israel Chapin, Jr., had written McHenry on 18 May, and the extract came from that letter. A copy of Chapin's letter is in NHi: Henry O'Reilly Collection.

To Bartholomew Dandridge, Jr.

Dear Sir,   Philadelphia 5th June 1796

The letter you left with Mr Kitt—the one you wrote from Shippensburgh and another from Greenbriar Court house dated the 10th Ulto have all been recd.[1]

It can excite no ⟨*illegible* t⟩hat the ⟨*illegible*⟩, the manner, and other cir⟨cumstanc⟩es attending your departure from this place, was not more displeasing than it was surprising: not only to me, but to every one else; and opened the door for variety of conjectures; some of them you may be sure not favorable; and more or less s⟨o⟩ according to the knowledge People had of you. All this is natural, and what you must have made your mind up for.

For myself, as I always entertained a good opinion of your honor and honesty, vexation at being left in the manner I was in the midst of busy, and perplexing scenes, without a moments intimation of the event, or knowing where to apply for aid, was all the impression, injurious to you, that it made upon me.

It was sometime and after much enquiry for a character in whose discretion and ⟨a⟩ttachment I could place entire confidence, before Mr Washington Craik (who had returned to Virginia) occurred to me. He is now with me as my private Secretary, & will, I expect Continue in that Office ⟨*illegible*⟩ remain in the Administration of the government.[2]

You may remember that the Suggestion in your letter from Greenbrier, with respect to the mode of dividing and disposing of my lands on the ⟨we⟩stern waters is an event which I told you would be likely to happen, and might find you employment, after your Services in the line you ⟨were⟩ was terminated; but that I wanted first to try if I could not make a sale of them in the ⟨*illegible*⟩. I must now wait till September, to see the result of my advertisemant,[3] after which if offers to my liking have not come forward, I shall proceed to lay off and sell my lands on the Ohio and its waters in the manner you suggest; and am very well inclined to put the business into your hands, and allow you the profits arising from the management thereof, allowing a Commission upon the Sales, which is to embrace the expence of laying off the Lots. Yourself, which you may soon learn to do.

⟨If⟩ you remain in the mind you were, at the date of your letter of the 10th Ulto; which did not get to my hands until the 3d instant, it will be necessary for me to see, or at least to have a direct communication opened with you, on the first of September; that the business may be fully arranged, and a plan devised for the prosecution of it.

On Monday the 13th I expect to leave this City for Mount Vernon; but as well ⟨as⟩ to meet the offers which may be made me, as to attend to the business of the Public (from which I cannot be absent longer) it is my intention to return to this place again (alone) before the day above mentioned. By, or before which, give me all the information you can, in writing, if I shd not see you, of the value of my lands, or rather, from what you can collect from others, what they would sell for, divided into any sized lots to suit the purchasers.

Your Aunt and Washington join me in affectionate regard for you,[4] and I am Your sincere friend

Go: Washington

P.S. As it may be of Service to you, and ⟨to me⟩ also, I enclose a print of my Advertisement.

ALS (letterpress copy), NN: Washington Papers.

1. Neither the letter Dandridge left with Frederick Kitt nor his letter from Shippensburg, Pa., has been found.

2. For George Washington Craik's start as GW's private secretary, see Richard Graham to GW, 12 April, source note.

3. See GW's advertisement of 1 February.

4. GW wrote Secretary of War James McHenry from Mount Vernon on 1 Aug.: "(Private) . . . This letter will be presented to you by Mr Dandridge,

who has rejoined my family and proceeds to Philadelphia in order to facilitate the recording of my loose files.

"As he left my family a little suddenly, I thought it necessary to mention this matter to you, lest *that* circumstance should be ascribed to unworthy motives; none of which I have to charge him with, as I always had, and still have, a high opinion of his honor and integrity" (copy [facsimile], DLC: James McHenry Papers; see also GW to John Dandridge, 11 July, and to Oliver Wolcott, Jr., 1 Aug.).

From Gouverneur Morris

Private

My dear Sir   London 5 June 1796

It is now some Time since I received your kind Letter of the 4 March accompanying a Copy of that which you did me the Honor to write on the 22d Decr. The Original of this last has never yet reached my Hands. On that to which it is principally a Reply[1] I must give you a Clue which for sundry Reasons I could not send in due Season. It was written to bear the Inspection of Ld G—— &ca &ca—I did fully expect to have made my Reply to these Letters in Person but I am suddenly called on by some indispensible Circumstances to take a Journey into Switzerland and my Sense of Propriety induces me to make the long and inconvenient Circuit by Hamburg in Preference of the short cut thro France.[2] There is a Clause in your Letter of the 22d Decr which begins thus "To this Catalogue may be added &c: &ca as also"[3] Now if the Parties there alluded to be not speedily removed it will be *only* because the Means of providing for them do not easily present themselves and they cannot with Propriety be turned adrift. I have recommended *Englishmen* as the most fitting Characters. I cannot write fully about this or indeed any Thing else having hardly a Moment to myself and not knowing how this Letter is to go.

I send herewith one to the Secretary of State which I leave open and pray you my dear Sir to cast your Eye over it then all will be put right if it be not so already.[4] I must not close this Letter however short without the tedious Repetition how important I conceive it to be that you should continue in Office. Would you require a very strong Reason indeed? You Yourself shall give it from the last four Months of our History, and I will freely consent to your Retirement when you can designate a Successor who will *truly* hold the Sentiments and pursue the Conduct mentioned in yours of Decr. But even then you ought to consider that it is not given to every Man to bend the Bow of Ulysses, whatever may be his Wishes or Intentions.[5] And you well know that Weight of Character is in arduous Circumstances quite as useful as Strength of Mind. God grant you long Life and Good Health; the Rest you will take Care of Farewell—I am ever yours

Gouvr Morris

ALS, DLC:GW; LB, DLC: Gouverneur Morris Papers.

1. GW's letter to Morris dated 22 Dec. 1795 replied to one Morris had written on 3 July 1795 that reported a conversation with Lord Grenville, British secretary of state for foreign affairs.

2. Morris left London for Hamburg on 7 June 1796, but military operations apparently prevented travel through Switzerland. He instead went through Berlin and Dresden (see Miller, *Diaries of Gouverneur Morris*, 279, 327, 346, 348).

3. GW had complained in this passage about the "ungracious & obnoxious characters" Great Britain sent as consular agents to the United States.

4. Morris wrote Secretary of State Timothy Pickering on this date to explain his enclosed financial account with the federal government subsequent to 1 July 1794 (see DLC: Gouverneur Morris Papers).

5. In Homer's *Odyssey*, book 21, Penelope, the wife of Ulysses, burdened with suitors, agrees to accept the one who can string the bow of Ulysses and shoot an arrow through twelve axes arranged in a line. After all fail, Ulysses returns in disguise, passes the test, reveals himself, and kills the suitors. GW evidently owned a translation of the *Odyssey* (see Griffin, *Catalogue of the Washington Collection*, 485).

To William Pearce

Mr Pearce,   Philadelphia 5th June 1796.

Since my last I have received your letters of the 22d & 29th of last Month—The first came to hand on Tuesday, the other on Saturday, as usual.[1]

On Wednesday last Congress closed their Session; but there is yet a good deal for me to do, before I can leave the Seat of the Government. My present expectation however is, that I shall be able to do this on tomorrow week: but as this is not certain, and as I shall travel slow, to avoid what usually happens to me at this season—that is—killing, or knocking up a horse; and as we shall, moreover, stay a day or two at the Federal City, it is not likely we shall arrive at Mount Vernon before the 20th, or 21st of this month.[2]

In a few days after *we* get there, we shall be visited, I expect, by characters of distinction;[3] I could wish therefore that the Gardens, Lawns, and every thing else in, and about the Houses, may be got in clean & nice order. If the Gardener needs aid, to accomplish as much of this as lyes within his line, let him have it; & let others rake, & scrape up all the trash, of every sort & kind about the houses, & in holes & corners and throw it (all I mean that will make dung) into the Stercorary and the rest into the gullied parts of the road, coming up to the House. And as the front gate of the Lawn (by the Ivies) is racked, and scarcely to be opened, I wish you would order a new one (like the old one) to be immediately made—and that, with the new ones you have just got made, and all the boarding of every kind that was white before, to be painted white again. If Neal and my own people cannot make the front gate, abovementioned, get some one from Alexandria to do it—provided he will set about & finish it immediately. This must be the way up to the House.

Let the Rooms in the Servants Hall, above & below, be well cleaned; and have the Beds & bedsteads therein put in order; after which have a good lock put on the door of the west room, above, and order Caroline, or whoever has the charge of those rooms, to suffer no person to sleep, or even to go in to it, without express orders from her Mistress or myself. Let exactly the same things be done with the Rooms over the Kitchen; as there will be a white Cook with us that will require one of them;[4] and the other may also be wanted for some other Servants, or use—it being likely, there will be a call for all these places and things. And I hope, especially as there is no Ice to keep fresh meats, that you will have an abundant supply for the demands that will probably be made thereon during our stay at home. And besides, will ascertain from the Butcher in Alexandria, the stated days on which Beef and Veal are killed; that we may know what dependence to place on him—Tell the Gardener, I shall expect every thing that a Garden ought to produce, in the most ample manner.

There may be many other things necessary to be done, as well for appearance as use, that do not occur to me at this momt but as you can judge from what I have said, what my wishes are, I have no doubt but that you will contribute all you can to accomplish them; and give the *whole* as neat & clean an appearance as they are capable of.

About the time you were employing a joiner to do the North end of the House, I directed Venetian blinds to be made, and painted green, for all the windows on the West side of the House, & mentioned the manner in wch I thought it best to execute them: but have never been informed what, or whether any thing has been done in consequence of it.[5] The omitting to give information of what *has,* or what *cannot* be done in consequen[ce] of such requests, often throws me into a disagreeable Suspence, and frequently occasions me to write often on the same subjects. I am equally ignorant whether the dormant windows are yet put into the stable, & Corn lofts; both of which, for the purpose of Air, is indispensably necessary; besides adding to the appearance of the building.[6]

Take care to keep a sufficiency of Oats, and the best of your old Hay on hand. I shall have Eight or ten horses of my own *with me,* and there will be *many others* with visitors.

You had better, I conceive, get the midlings and ship-stuff off your hands at what they will fetch; as the weather is getting warm, & the flour may turn Sower. Unless you want the money for current expences, it might be sold on such a credit as to receive payment on the same day your demand upon Smith, for the other flour, will become due, so as to have the whole at once. This credit may enhance the price, and will be (if the money is not wanted for the purposes beforementioned) no disadvantage to me in giving it.[7]

I hope, at your last shearing, there was a complete cull, & seperation of all the old, scabby & disordered Sheep. I do not know how to account for the weekly loss you sustain, in this species of Stock, unless it be by keeping such poor and diseased sheep in the flocks as contaminate others.

I have no doubt but that you will endeavor so to arrange matters, as to keep your grain, & Hay harvests from interfering as much as possible with each other; and this too without either suffering, by standing too long, if it can possibly be avoided. Begin the former as soon as it can be cut without loss.

If Miss Nelly Custis should apply to you for a Cart to Transport her Trunk and other things from Doctor Stuarts to Mount Vernon—let it be sent as soon as applied for, and something to cover and secure the contents against Rain—in case any should fall while they are on the Road.

I perceive Mrs Washington's Memm herewith sent contains nearly the same requests that are made in this letter—but I send it notwithstanding.[8] I wish you well and am Your friend

Go: Washington

P.S. Direct your next letter to me, to be left at the Post Office in Baltimore till called for. If I set off according to my present expectation, I shall, probably lodge in that Town on thursday Night; which is the Night the Mail of that day from Alexandria reaches that place.[9]

ALS, ViMtvL.

1. GW most recently had written Pearce on 29 May. Pearce's letters to GW dated 22 and 29 May have not been found. GW received the former on Tuesday, 31 May, and the latter on Saturday, 4 June.

2. GW was at Mount Vernon on 22 June (see GW to James McHenry, that date).

3. GW anticipated visits from British minister Robert Liston and his wife Henrietta as well as from Massachusetts congressman Fisher Ames (see Alexander Hamilton to GW, 10 May, n.4, and GW to Pearce, 29 May, and n.2 to that document; see also GW to Timothy Pickering, 29 June, and his second letter to James McHenry, 1 July).

4. GW paid a cook named Gentil wages for nine months from around this time to early March 1797 (see entries for 21 Nov. 1796 and 16 Jan. and 7 March 1797, Household Accounts).

5. See GW to Pearce, 7 Feb. 1796.

6. GW had asked that dormant windows be made for the stable when he wrote Pearce on 5 July 1795.

7. In the entry for 9 June 1796, Pearce recorded that Andrew Jamieson and Robert Anderson had purchased 30 barrels of midlings and 40 barrels of ships stuff for £167.17.11. They paid $100 cash and the remaining $464.70 by a note payable in sixty days (Mount Vernon Accounts, 1794–1797, p. 53).

8. Martha Washington's memorandum has not been found.

9. GW arrived in Baltimore on Thursday, 16 June, and departed the next morning (see Oliver Ellsworth to GW, 19 June, n.1).

To Alexander White

(Private)
Dear Sir,   Philadelphia 5th June 1796
    Your Letter of the 25th Ultimo from Martinsburgh, did, as you
expected, come to my hands on the 3d instant; but not untill the
Mail of that day was dispatched, consequently the Post of tomorrow will be the first, by which I can reply to the contents of it.
I wish, *very much indeed*, that you could make it convenient, and
agreeable to yourself, family & business; to remain in the City
Commission; and that you would prosecute to the end, the good
work you have begun. I sincerely believe that this is the wish *of all*
who know you, and are true friends to that place; and very sorry
indeed should I be, if the absence, and attention necessary for
your private concerns (which Your Letter does not sufficiently
define, to enable me to form a correct judgment) should be
found incompatible with the duties which are expected from the
Commissioners.
    It is unnecessary, I am sure, for me to[1] remark to you (on
general ground, & reasoning) the necessity there is for the closest attention, & the most vigorous exertion of the Commissioners to push this work on: But independent of *general* considerations, a particular occurrance has happened, lately wch makes
me, more than ever, wish you to devote as much time as possible
to this business. It is this.
    It is not entirely unknown to you: I believe that I have been
hinting in pretty broad terms to your Colleagues, that I did not
conceive that the trust reposed in them could be satisfactorily
executed while they remained at a distance from the scene of
action, and held periodical meetings only; & that, where there
was inattention, or remissness in the head, it would be found to
extend itself to all the Members; Not perceiving that these hints
had all the effects that was intended. Finding from the discussion of the Guarantee Bill in Congress that serious charges were
laid against the œconomy in carrying on the business[2]—knowing
that there was no way so effectual to prevent, or to correct errors while they were in embryo, as a close inspection into them
while they were in a progressive state; and no measure so likely
to remove jealousies as a residence of the Commissioners *in the
City* I did on the 22d ulto when acknowledging the receipt of

their Letters of the 13th & 14th relative to the loan in Holland, give it as my decided opinion to that Board, that this event, for the reasons I assigned, ought to take place; and the nearer they could fix, conveniently, to the principal theatre, the more agreeable it would be.

Thus much happened before I receivd any advice of what was transacting in the City; but on the 1st instant was handed to me an Address from the Proprietors thereof, dated the 24th preceeding, requesting me to *do* what I had actually *done,* and which I find is not at all pleasing to Mr Scott.[3] How it may be to Doctor Thornton I know not, having heard nothing from *him* on the Subject.

I have given you these details (in a private letter) that you may see at one view what my situation & wishes are; and the necessity there is for my preserving consistency—at least in a degree. I shall touch upon no other parts of your letter, at this time; but that you may have a dble chance of receiving these sentiments soon, this letter shall be forwarded to Winchester, and a duplicate lodged in the Post Office in Washington, that if you miss the first, the other may be found there on your arrival.

On other subjects I will converse with you when we meet in the Federal City, where it is probable I shall be about the 18th instant, if nothing (at present unforeseen) happens to prevent it. With sincere esteem & regard I am—Dear Sir Your Obedient Servt

Go: Washington

ALS (letterpress copy), DLC:GW; LB, DLC:GW. The first page of the letterpress copy is missing and has been replaced by a copy.

1. The letterpress copy begins with this word.

2. See GW to Gustavus Scott, 25 May, and n.3 to that document.

3. For earlier references to this unidentified address, see William Deakins, Jr., to GW, 27 May, and n.1 to that document.

To William Deakins, Jr.

Dear Sir: Philadelphia 6th June 1796

Your letter of the 27th Ulto has been duly received. Before I knew, or had heard of any movement in the Federal City, among the Proprietors thereof, I had, in answering some dispatches

from the Commissioners, given it to them as my clear and decided opinion, that those who were entrusted with the affairs of
the City ought to be residents thereof.[1] It is & has always been my
opinion. It was the principle upon which the new establishment,
and compensation took place;[2] and what I have always expected
would happen, as soon as accomodations could be provided.
To assign all the reasons for this opinion, which have weight in
my mind, would run me into prolixity, unnecessarily; as few of
them can have escap'd a reflecting man. One however, you may
recollect I brought to your view upon a former occasion; when
you suggested a residant of George Town for a Commissioner.[3]
although that case may not apply *quite* as strongly to any ⟨of⟩ the
present commissioners, yet it *does apply*, and in *that* degree, is injurious; as you see by the effects, & the complaints.

The time in which a great deal is to be done, is short. In the
discussion of the Guarantee Bill, all the Faupaus which have
been committed—all the neglects, inattentions, and want of
the close & constant scrutiny of those to whom the business was
intrusted, have undergone severe animadversion. It has been
said, that if the Commissioners, & those who had been receiving compensations from the public, had been on the spot, the
abuses which the principal building had sustained could not have
happened—that they would have perciev'd the errors in their
origin, & would have correct'd them, as fast as they arose.[4] In a
word, that there can be no œconomy without a close inspection,
nor a close inspection by men at a distance, &ca &ca—Knowing
these things as I do; and how much depends upon execution, it
behoves me, while I have any thing to do in the business, to attend to measures and not merely to the convenien⟨ces of⟩ those
who are to execute them. If the two can be blended, it is well—
but the first is, & must be, the primary consideration.

Nothing, pointing directly to yourself (Office I mean) has
been said further, than while the Agents, and principal Officers
of the City reside out of it & in G. Town, the attraction *is* where
it *ought not to be*, were the interest of the former, and the accomodation of Congress (when the Government moves to it) as they
ought, to be the primary object. I write in haste, the Post hour
being at hand, but can assure you that I am—Sir Yr Obedient
Servt

Go: Washington

ALS (letterpress copy), DLC:GW; LB, DLC:GW.

1. See GW to the Commissioners for the District of Columbia, 22 May.

2. On the increased compensation for the current D.C. commissioners, see GW to Tobias Lear, 28 Aug. 1794 (first letter).

3. See GW to Deakins, 17 May 1795.

4. GW is referring to the walls of the Capitol (see GW to the Commissioners for the District of Columbia, 22 May 1796, and n.5; see also GW to Gustavus Scott, 25 May, and n.3 to that document).

From Timothy Pickering

Sir,   Department of State June 6. 1796.

The inclosed papers were sent to me by the Secretary of the Treasury. The wrapper, on which is written the opinion of Mr Harrison, the Auditor, gives a concise & just statement of the case on which John Skinner Esqr. late Marshall of North Carolina founds his claim of compensation. His demand is for 900 dollars, being a commission of *three* per cent on 30,000 dollars, the sum illegally taken from a Spanish vessel.[1] The Secretary of the Treasury thinks a commission of 1½ ℔cent sufficient: I am of the same opinion. Had the sum been under adjudication in court, & *condemned*, the Marshall would have been intitled to his 3 ℔cent, for receiving & paying over. But altho' the money was seized by the Collector of the Customs, as having been *illicitly landed*, yet it is not to be imagined that it could have been *condemned*; the Spanish vessel from which it was so illicitly taken & landed, having been captured by a French privateer unlawfully fitted out; and therefore the landing the money can be considered only in the predicament of money or goods so landed by pirates or robbers, whose unlawful acts ought not to prejudice the rightful owners of the property. I presume then that if the case had been brought before the proper judge, he would have acquitted the money seized & ordered it to be restored. In this event, the judge, agreeably to another clause of the same act of Congress, would have determined what compensation should have been allowed to the Marshall for the "custody" of the money:[2] and it appears improbable that he would have allowed more than one and a half per cent, at which rate his compensation would amount to 450 dollars.

The *Deputy Marshall* had the *actual* custody of the money, and by his own affidavit has received "198 dollars for his particular expences & trouble in guarding & taking care of the same."[3]

If the compensation proposed be approved of by the President, I will pay it, charging the same to the fund appropriated for the contingent expences of government.[4] All which is respectfully submitted.

Timothy Pickering

ALS, DNA: RG 59, Miscellaneous Letters; LB, DNA: RG 59, GW's Correspondence with His Secretaries of State; LB, DNA: DG 59, Domestic Letters.

1. The enclosed papers have not been identified, but Secretary of the Treasury Oliver Wolcott, Jr., had written Pickering on 4 June transmitting "sundry papers" related to the case that arose after the French privateer *Aimée Marguerite* captured the Spanish brig *San Josef* (CtHi: Oliver Wolcott, Jr., Papers; see also Richard Dobbs Spaight to GW, 21 Oct. and 19 Dec. 1793, 8 Feb. 1794 [first letter], and 15 March 1794).

2. Section 3 of "An Act for regulating Processes in the Courts of the United States, and providing Compensations for the Officers of the said Courts, and for Jurors and Witnesses," approved 8 May 1792, awarded the marshal "for selling goods and vessels condemned, and receiving and paying the money, three per cent." Section 4 of the act directed that the marshal "shall have the custody of all vessels and goods seized by any officer of the revenue, and shall be allowed such compensation therefor as the court may judge reasonable" (1 *Stat.* 275–79; quotes on 276–77).

3. Deputy marshal John Blakely's affidavit has not been identified.

4. Pickering wrote Wolcott on 7 June that GW had approved "the allowance you proposed" and the $450 payment could be made "at any time" (DNA: RG 59, Domestic Letters).

From Jacques-Philippe-Auguste Dursus

Mr President   Brunswick [Germany] 7th June 1796

The honor I had to serve under your Command during the Campaign of 1780, 1781 & 1782, the misfortunes which oppress me are the titles on which I dare claim the kindness of your Excellency. Having left France my Country almost five years since, and having a very faint hope at least a very remote one of ever being able to return, I desire very much to live in a Country to the Government of which the confidence of the People & their respect for your virtues have called your Excellency. fully convinced of your generous sensibility, I dare flatter myself that you will willingly afford some assistance to an unfortunate Gentleman who is upon the brink of experiencing the horrors of the most dreadful misery. Your Excellency deign to assist me with your kindness since I had the honor to dine with you & to be presented to you after the siege of York where I had been wounded by the late Marquis de Chatellux then major General of the Army. I pray you to permit me to lay before you my condition during the Revolution in France & my conduct since that unhappy epoch.

Having entered at the age of sixteen years in quality of second Lieutenant in the service of his most Christian Majesty in 1774 in the Regiment of Infantry called Soissonnois I performed with this Regiment the Campaign which Rochambeau did under the command of your Excellency. on my return to France I obtained in 1784 the grade of Captain in this Regiment which I did not quit until the arrestation of king Lewis the sixteenth & the suspension of the exercise of Royalty, I went at that epoch to join the Army which had been collected by the Princes his Brothers & I served under their Command the Campaign of 1792 since that epoch I have served no more. and I have lived successively in England the Netherlands & Germany. I could prove to your Excellency by my Commissions Certificates & passports the truth of all that I have the honor to relate to you, and these are the proofs which I cannot annex to my letter, since these titles are indispensibly necessary to me & which it is impossible for me to part with, that I dare implore your Excellency to grant the permission which I have the honor to ask of him to be able to live in the United States, to solicit your kindness to provide me a place in the Troops, or if that is impossible some other employment which will enable me to live, & which you shall judge proper, being deprived of all my fortune by the Revolution I shall bring in America nothing more than a profound respect for the Laws of the Country & for the Chief of the Government & my great desire of becoming useful to my new Country.

After having laid before your Excellency what was my condition during the Revolution of France & what has been my conduct since my emigration, I presume to repeat again my prayer that you will grant me your protection & your kindness & I assure you of my lively & respectful acknowledgement. I am with profound respect Your Excellency's very hble & very Obdt Servant

Dursus
Captain in the service of
his most Christian Majesty

Persuaded that your Excellency will willingly honor me with an answer, I pray you earnestly to remit it to Mr f. A. Muhlemberg Esqr.[1] to be forwarded to Mr William Wilmerding of Brunswick who will send it to me.[2]

Translation, DLC:GW; ALS, in French, DLC:GW. The ALS is docketed: "recd 10th Octr 1796." No reply has been found.

Jacques-Philippe-Auguste Dursus (1758–1828) accurately describes his military service. He returned to France in 1802.

1. Pennsylvania congressman Frederick Augustus Muhlenberg served as Speaker of the House.

2. Dursus may have been referring to William Wilmerding (Christian Wilhelm Wilmerding; 1762–1832). Born in Brunswick, Germany, Wilmerding moved in the 1780s to New York, where he kept a looking-glass store and served as secretary of the German Society. Wilmerding returned to Brunswick in 1795, but business reverses brought him back to New York by 1799.

From Robert McLean

Dear Sir   Union Town [Pa.] 7th June 179[6][1]

I have lately been down the Ohio River and among others have taken a View of a tract of your Land Situate on the East Side of the Ohio River above Bakers Station and below Grave Creek Generally known by the Round Bottom[2]—I have a desire to become a purchaser—And would beg the favour of you, Sir to inform me as soon as convenient "by Letter directed to the Care of Alexander MClean of Union Town Esquire"[3] the lowest terms you will accept of—I am interested in the information, as I wish to turn my Eye to another object if I cannot acceede to your terms.[4] I am Sir with due Regard your Excellencies most Obt Humble Servant

Robert MClean

P.S. I live on Monongahela River about 3 Miles below the Mouth of Georges Creek.

ALS, DLC:GW.

1. McLean wrote "1795," but GW docketed the letter as "7th June 1796," which seems the more likely date.

2. Baker's Station, also known as Cresap's Fort, was a blockhouse erected in the 1780s at the head of Cresap's Bottom in what is now Marshall County, West Virginia. It is about three miles down the Ohio River from current McKeefrey.

Grave Creek enters the Ohio River from the West Virginia side just below Moundsville.

3. Alexander McClean (1746–1834), a surveyor, completed the boundary between Virginia and Pennsylvania in 1782–83. Before the formation of Fayette County, McClean represented Westmoreland County in the Pennsylvania legislature and was appointed county lieutenant in 1782. From late 1783 until his death, he was register and recorder for Fayette County.

4. No reply to Robert McLean's letter has been found. For others interested in purchasing the Round Bottom tract, see Jeremiah Claypole to GW, 3 June, and Thomas G. Johnston to GW, 1 September.

To Henry Knox

My dear Sir, Philadelphia 8th June 1796

I would not let Mr Bingham (who says he is about to visit you) depart without acknowledging the receipt of sevl letters from you;[1] and offering Mrs Knox & yourself my sincere condolence on your late heavy loss. Great, and trying as it must be to your sensibility, I am persuaded after the first severe pangs are over you both possess fortitude enough to view the event as the dispensation of Providence, and will submit to its decrees with Philosophical resignation.[2]

The footing on which you placed the non-acceptance of the Commission for ascertaining the true St Croix, was such, as to leave no hope of your embarking in that undertaking after the arrival of the Commissioner from Great Britain, and his readiness to proceed therein was announced.[3] I therefore nominated, and Mr Howell (of Rhode Island) by the advice & consent of the Senate, is appointed in your place; and Mr Sullivan is designated to prepare the business for them.[4]

Mr Bingham is so well versed in the Politics of this place, and South of it. & so well acquainted with all the movements in both houses of Congress, that it would be a work of supererogation in me, to give you the details. To him then I refer you, for such relations as are interesting.

On Monday next,[5] if not prevented by occurrances yet unforeseen, I shall commence my Journey for Mt Vernon; but shall, myself, be returned to this City again before the first of September; not chusing to be longer absent from the Seat of Government. My best wishes, in which Mrs Washington unites, are tendered to Mrs Knox, your self & family; and with sincere friendship, and affectionate regard, I am always Yours

Go: Washington

ALS (photocopy), DLC: Papers of Thomas J. Clay; ALS (letterpress copy), ICHi; LB, DLC:GW. Only the second page of the letterpress copy has been found.

GW wrote William Bingham on "Thursday Morning," 9 June: "The President presents his compliments to Mr Bingham. Takes the liberty of troubling him with the care of the enclosed letter to General Knox; and of wishing him, Mrs Bingham and the Party, a pleasant journey, and Safe return.

"Recollecting that Mr Bingham, some days ago, was making some enquiries on the subject of Manures, and having had several Copies of a propd Report sent to him by Sir John Sinclair, the Presidt asks Mr Bingham's acceptance of one copy of the said Report" (AL, NjP: De Coppet Collection). GW likely enclosed Robert Somerville's *Outlines of the Fifteenth Chapter of the Proposed General Report from the Board of Agriculture. On the Subject of Manures* (London, 1795), which evidently had been sent with John Sinclair's letters to GW of 18 July 1795. For the travel of Bingham and his party northwards later in the month, see Knox to Bingham, 20 June, and Bingham to David Cobb, 28 June, in Allis, *William Bingham's Maine Lands*, 2:760–64.

1. Knox had written letters to GW dated 28 Jan., 21 Feb., and 14 April 1796.

2. Two of Knox's children, Augusta Henrietta and Marcus Bingham, had died in late April from throat disorders (see Bingham to Knox, 12 May, in Allis, *William Bingham's Maine Lands*, 2:750–52).

3. GW is referring to Knox's letter of 14 April.

The British commissioner to determine the true St. Croix River under Article V of the Jay Treaty was Thomas Henry Barclay, who learned of his appointment at New York on 10 May and then visited Philadelphia (see Barclay to Lord Grenville, 30 May, in *Correspondence of Barclay*, 47–48).

Thomas Henry Barclay (1753–1830) was a lawyer in New York before serving as a Loyalist officer during the Revolutionary War. He subsequently emigrated to Nova Scotia and held office as speaker of the assembly in that province. Barclay became British consul general at New York in 1799.

4. See GW to the U.S. Senate, 20 May (first letter).

5. The next Monday was 13 June.

From Timothy Pickering

June 8. 96

The Secretary of State has examined with as much attention as the time would permit, the several acts of the late session of Congress, & noted the points requiring the acts or directions of the President of the U. States, which notes are respectfully laid before him.[1]

The Secretary also presents the draught of instructions for the person who is to go to London to aid the Commissioners on spoliations. Mr Samuel Cabot was contemplated as the Agent.

Mr FitzSimons & the Committee of Merchants have seen his recommendations—they know of no person whom they can recommend in preference: Mr FitzSimons entirely approves of him, & thinks it fortunate that he will undertake.[2]

T. Pickering

ALS, DNA: RG 59, Miscellaneous Letters; LB, DNA: RG 59, GW's Correspondence with His Secretaries of State.

1. See Acts Requiring Presidential Action, c.8 June, printed as an enclosure to this letter.

2. Samuel Cabot (1759–1819), a Boston merchant, was a younger brother of George Cabot, U.S. senator from Massachusetts. The draft of Pickering's instructions has not been identified, but he wrote final instructions to Cabot dated 29 June: "It has been represented to the President of the United States, that the Commissioners who are to examine and decide on the claims of American citizens for losses and damages sustained by the illegal capture and condemnation of their vessels and other property, under colour of authority or commissions from his Britannic Majesty, will find perhaps insuperable difficulties in adjusting the accounts and liquidating the charges, unless assisted by a person well versed in the commerce of the United States. With a view to obviate these difficulties, and to expedite the proceedings of the Commissioners, by which the citizens of the United States may obtain more speedy satisfaction for their losses; the President of the United States has determined on the appointment of such an agent, in the character of an Accountant; and has selected you for this employment. It is understood that it will meet your acceptance, and that you will be able soon to embark to attend the Commissioners in London.

"In executing the trust thus confided to you, it is expected, that under the direction of the Commissioners, you will inspect the documents in every case which shall be brought before them; arrange them in the fittest order for their examination; critically review all the items in the accounts, and when the charges appear to you too high or too low to note the same with your opinion of the charges that would be just and equitable; and state the accounts in the most convenient form for the final decision of the Commissioners. These are the general ideas entertained of the services you are to render in aid of the Commissioners. The whole board, it is presumed, will concur in the opinion of their utility; and in prescribing more particularly the duties you are to perform. But if the Commissioners on the part of Great Britain shall choose to consider you merly as an Agent of the United States, to exhibit and support the claims of their citizens, you will act accordingly, exercising your own discretion to effect a just and equitable settlement of their demands.

"The trust thus committed to you is so important, by the magnitude of the property it embraces, as to require your unremitting attention; and from the testimonies given of your talents and industry, the President feels a confidence that his expectations and those of his fellow citizens whose interests are thus committed to your care will be fulfilled." Cabot also was empowered to examine "certain claims of British subjects . . . in the same manner as in the case of the American claims." As compensation, he would receive $3,000 the first year and subsequently $2,500 annually, with the higher initial "allowance . . . being in consideration of the expenses you must incur in preparing for this service and in performing your voyage to London" (MHi: Pickering Papers; see also GW to Pickering, 9 June).

Enclosure
Acts Requiring Presidential Action

[c.8 June 1796]

Act may 17th 1796—empowers the President to appoint Superintendants of the Light house to be erected on Cape Cod.[1]

Act may 17th 1796—empowers the President to approve of the locations of certain lands granted to Ebenezer Zane.[2]

Act may 18th 1796, empowers the President to appoint a Surveyor General—also an agent to join in the direction of the sales of land to be made at Pittsburg—The President to fix the compensation of the Assistant Surveyors, Chain Carriers and axe men, not to exceed in the whole 3 dollars per mile.[3]

Act may 19th 1796, Boundary line according to treaties with the Indians to be marked under direction of the President—a Superintendant to be appointed for granting licences to reside among the indians—Sect. 7th Temporary agents to reside among them.[4]

Act may 27th 1796, The President to give directions to certain officers concerning Quarantine.[5]

act may 28th 1796, directs the president to appoint two or more agents concerning Seamen.[6]

act 1 June 1796, form of Passports for ships to be approved by the President.[7]

act 28th may 1796, President to make allowance of compensation to inspectors relative to duties on Carriages.[8]

act 31 may—President empowered to borrow 324,539 dollars 6 cents.[9]

act 31 may President to approve of the loan of 5 millions of dollars.[10]

no. 45—June 1. Passports for Ships & vessels—form to be approved by the President.

no. 46—regulating grants of land &c. to the Moravians.

47. admission of the State of Tennessee.

48—making appropriation to satisfy certain demands attending the late insurrection &c.

49. *drawback.*

50—further appropriations for 96.

51—*President to borrow 650,000 dollars.*

52—relief to owners of Stills.[11]

53—to indemnify the estate of the late Genl Greene.[12]

No. 13. Date April 18. Agents for Indian Trading Houses.[13]

No. 12. date Apl 8. The President to approve of the Contract for building a light house on Baker's Island, near Salem.[14]

No. 14. April 20. The president to authorize to be sold such of the perishable materials provided for the frigates as shall not be wanted to complete three of them—& other materials to be safely kept for further use.[15]

No. 21. May 6. To direct the loan for the city of Washington.[16]

No. 22. May 6th. To authorize the building or purchasing of revenue cutters; & to order to be sold such as are unfit for service.[17]

D, DNA: RG 59, Miscellaneous Letters. This document immediately follows Pickering's letter to GW dated 8 June and was docketed by Pickering as "The Atty General's Notes on the Acts of Congress." Attorney General Charles Lee wrote the first portion of the document, with the remainder in Pickering's writing (see n.10 below).

1. See "An Act authorizing the erection of a Lighthouse on Cape Cod, in the State of Massachusetts" (1 *Stat.* 464).

2. See "An Act to authorize Ebenezer Zane to locate certain lands in the territory of the United States northwest of the river Ohio" (6 *Stat.* 27).

3. See sections 1, 6, and 10 of "An Act providing for the Sale of the Lands of the United States, in the territory northwest of the river Ohio, and above the mouth of Kentucky river" (1 *Stat.* 464–69).

4. See sections 1, 7, 13, and 20 of "An Act to regulate Trade and Intercourse with the Indian Tribes, and to preserve Peace on the Frontiers" (1 *Stat.* 469–74).

5. See "An Act relative to Quarantine" (1 *Stat.* 474).

6. See sections 1 and 2 of "An Act for the relief and protection of American Seamen" (1 *Stat.* 477–78).

7. See section 1 of "An Act providing Passports for the ships and vessels of the United States" (1 *Stat.* 489–90).

8. See section 12 of "An Act laying duties on Carriages for the conveyance of persons; and repealing the former act for that purpose" (1 *Stat.* 478–82).

9. See section 5 of "An Act making further provision for the expenses attending the intercourse of the United States with foreign nations; and to continue in force the act, intituled 'An act providing the means of intercourse

between the United States and foreign nations'" (1 *Stat.* 487–88). GW had approved this act on 30 May.

10. See section 1 of "An Act making provision for the payment of certain Debts of the United States" (1 *Stat.* 488–89). Lee's writing ends here (see source note above).

11. GW approved the preceding eight acts on 1 June, and the numbers match the chapter numbers in 1 *Stat.* 489–94. The text associated with numbers 46–50 and 52 was later bracketed in the manuscript, probably because those measures did not specify presidential duties.

12. See "An Act to indemnify the estate of the late Major-General Nathaniel Greene, for a certain bond entered into by him during the late war," approved on 1 June (6 *Stat.* 28). The nine words following the number also were bracketed on the manuscript.

13. See section 2 of "An Act for establishing Trading Houses with the Indian Tribes" (1 *Stat.* 452–53); see also Isaac Levan to GW, 26 April, and n.1 to that document.

14. See "An Act authorizing the erection of a Lighthouse on Baker's Island, in the state of Massachusetts" (1 *Stat.* 452).

15. See section 3 of "An Act supplementary to an act entitled 'An act to provide a Naval Armament'" (1 *Stat.* 453–54).

16. See "An Act authorizing a Loan for the use of the City of Washington, in the District of Columbia, and for other purposes therein mentioned" (1 *Stat.* 461; see also GW to the Commissioners for the District of Columbia, 22 May).

17. See sections 3 and 4 of "An Act making further provision relative to the Revenue Cutters" (1 *Stat.* 461–62).

To Timothy Pickering

Sir,   Philadelphia 9th June 1796

The Instructions for Mr King, herewith returned, appear to me to be proper. To them, however, I think might be added a desire that he should attempt to remove any doubts which may arise in the construction of the [   ] article relative to our Trade ⟨with⟩ the East Indies; and to get relieved if it be practicable from the restrictions on our Vessels going from thence with their Cargoes to China.[1]

I shall not impede the forwarding the other Instructions to the Accou[n]tant, for the British Spoliations—as they are now drawn. At the sametime I cannot forbear observing that I think £500 St⟨erling⟩ would have been ample compensation for such a character.

1st Because no such Officer was conceiv⟨ed n⟩ecessary by the

Ne⟨goc⟩iators of the Treaty; nor provided for in the estimate to Congress.

2d Because among other inducements to the appointment of Mr Gore—his supposed knowledge of Commerce was one (a legal & Commercial character being deemed necessary for the purposes of the Commission)—Why then it may be asked, seek for the latter character in an Accountant of *new creation* uncontemplated by the Treaty? and this question more than probable will be accompanied with the charge of favouritism to the wishes of the person designated and his friends—and—

4th Because our Secretaries of Legation are not allowed half what is proposed to be given as compensation to this Accountant.[2]

Go: Washington

ALS (letterpress copy), DLC:GW; LB, DLC:GW. A transcription made in 1866 from the letter sent Pickering shows no significant variation from the letter-press copy (MHi: Pickering Papers).

1. Pickering prepared final instructions dated 8 June for Rufus King, the new U.S. minister to Great Britain: "As the whole correspondence between the Department of State and Mr Pinckney are to be delivered over to you, I beg leave to refer you to the instructions given to him, whether originally or in the course of that correspondence, for information and direction, so far as they may be pertinent to the present state of things." The instructions then covered several trade and commercial aspects of the Jay Treaty before turning to the matter GW raised for clarification. "Doubts have been suggested relative to that part of the 13th Article of Mr Jay's treaty which declares, that the vessels of the United States shall not carry any of the articles exported by them from the British Territories in the East Indies, to any port or place except to some port or place in America, *where the same shall be unladen.* The doubt on this passage is, whether after they shall be thus unladen they may be reexported to Europe, or elsewhere. Further, it is said that 'such regulations shall be adopted by both parties as shall from time to time be found necessary to enforce the due and faithful observance of this stipulation.' The doubt on this passage is whether the two parties are to *concur* in these regulations . . . or are they separately to be formed, by the laws of the respective Governments. It will be expedient to have these doubts removed, with any others which a revision of the treaty shall bring into view.

"While the 'coasting trade of those British Territories' in the East Indies, shall continue to be exclusively reserved to the British, an attempt may be made to gain for us a participation in the trade between the British Territories and those of any other powers in that part of the world.

"These, Sir, are the subjects which on this occasion have occurred as proper to engage your attention in your negociations with the British Government. Doubtless in the course of these negociations other proper topics of discussion will present themselves, which you will be pleased to communicate, with your ideas thereon, to this Department, to be laid before the President for his information and consequent directions" (DNA: RG 59, Diplomatic and Consular Instructions; see also Miller, *Treaties*, 255–56, and GW's first message to the U.S. Senate, 19 May, and n.1 to that document).

2. For these instructions to Samuel Cabot, see Pickering to GW, 8 June, n.2.

To the Commissioners for the District of Columbia

Gentlemen   Philadelphia 10th June 1796.

Your letters of the 31st Ulto and 3d Instant, came to hand by the same Mail, on tuesday last.[1]

The Duplicate of the Powers to Messrs Willink's, have been handed over, for the purpose of transmission. Triplicates, signed by a full board may not be amiss. I will receive them however at the City.

I am very glad to hear that you have re-commenced your operations on the public buildings: exceedingly is it to be wished, that you may be able to proceed therein with vigour. I much question whether *any* of the Banks in *this* City are to be relied on for a loan. The reason for this, needs no explanation. I shall, however, mention the matter to the Secretary of the Treasury; and what I can do, consistently with my official character, may be relied on. If, as I expect to do, I should receive money for some of my Western Lands which have been sold, I will (though it will be little more than a drop in the Bucket) pay the *whole* sum due from me for the lots I hold in the City; and request that the account (agreeably to the terms of Sales) may be made out accordingly, against my arrival.[2] In the last Instalments, I conceive I have been charged more than was due: this, if true, can be rectified by having recourse to the dates of the Sales, times of payment, and the sums paid. Mr Morris, I am informed, talks of visiting the City in the course of next week. You, probably, have better data than I possess, to form an opinion of the certainty of it, and the result.[3]

Thinking it probable that I shall be in the Federal City the latter end of next Week—provided nothing new occurs, I shall only add that with great esteem and regd I am—Gentlemen Your most Obedt Servant

Go: Washington

ALS, DLC: U.S. Commissioners of the City of Washington records; ALS (letter-press copy), DLC:GW; LB, DLC:GW.

1. The previous Tuesday was 7 June. For the letter from the commissioners to GW dated 3 June, see GW to the commissioners, 30 May, source note.

2. GW paid $1,294 in cash on 19 June to "the Treasurer of the City of Washington, in full of all my Instalments for Lots." His record of this payment added: "This sum exonerates me from any further Calls on accts of Lots purchased" (Cash Memoranda, 1794–97).

3. Robert Morris promised such a visit (see D.C. commissioners to GW, 22 June, and n.2 to that document).

From John Fairfax

Morgintown [Va., now W.Va.] June the 10th 1796
To his honour the presadant of the united States, Sir from the Intermit aquntance and good treatment I Recvd from the famaly I have always felt my self very Singerly a tacht to the famaly & have long felt a grate desire to hear how your Honour and Mrs washington has don but more a Speshally the Latter from the Good treatment and perlite Behavour I have Ever Recvd from her ladiship the hole time of my Continuance In servis[1] also how Master george and Miss Nelly has Don.

as for my part I have purchast me a tract of land Near morgintown and for the time I have Been On It I Can venter to Say I have one of the most hansomest farmes that Can bee found about In this part of the Cuntry I have got Som Beautifull Meadow well taken with timmothy I find this Cuntry generelly Speeking to Be very Nacherel to grass of Different kinds and the finest Cuntry for Rasing Stock I have Ever Seen.

from your honour's Advertesment I perseve Sir you are Inclined to Sell your Cornorway land,[2] Should that Be the Case If your honour will Be pleased to a Sist me a little, By Giving Som Indulgance for a part of the money I wish to purch[ase] of your honour and Becom a Sitasen of that Cuntry.

I know It is In your honour's power to a sist me a litle and with out Ingering your honour which Should It Be the Case that you Should Consider me that far I Should Ever Conseave my self under athousand Complements to your honour for Such a faver.

It may Be that your honour may Incline to Setle a farm on Som part of that land In order to Rase stock If Sir you should have any

Inclinashen to Send out a few hands to that Cuntry and Can Repose that much Confidance in me to Commit them to my Cear I Shall Indeavour to use Every Exershen in my power to permote your honours Interest or Should you Incline Sir to have your lands laid off in lots for the Conveanance of purchersers I Can a Commodate that matter for your honour as I have Made my self a quanted with that Branch Sence I Left your honour.

Sir pleas to Send me an answer as quick as Conveanant Either By the post or By Col. Jackson of harason County[3] and pleas to Inform me your termes and your price pr acer, also When your honour Expects to be at mount varnon as I wish to Com down at that time.[4]

pleas to presents my Compleme⟨nts⟩ to Mrs washington and the famaly. So I Remane your honours most Obeadant and very humble Servant

John Fairfax

ALS, DLC:GW. For the probable forwarding of this letter, see Burgess Ball to GW, 1 July.

1. Fairfax oversaw GW's Mansion House farm from the fall of 1784 to December 1790.

2. GW's advertisement of 1 Feb. included four tracts along the Great Kanawha River among lands offered for sale.

3. George Jackson (1757–1831) served as a congressman from Virginia, 1795–97 and 1799–1803.

4. Nothing has been found to indicate that GW pursued Fairfax's propositions, but Fairfax stayed overnight at Mount Vernon on 2 Nov. 1799 (see *Diaries*, 6:373).

To George Mathews

Dr Sir,   Philada 10th June 1796

The best, indeed the *only* excuse I can make for having so long delayed complying with the request of your favor written the 7th of March is, that when it came to hand (which was not speedily after its date) the business of the session pressed so heavily on me, that I had but little leisure for other attentions; and by laying it by, to be taken up at a more convenient moment, it, in a jumble with other papers was overlooked, until a revision, after the adjournment took place, brought it to view again.

This apology I thought due to you, at the same time that it

gives me another occasion to express my good wishes towards you, & regret that any circumstances should arise that have, even for a moment, encouraged the idea of relinquishing your country forever.[1] With great esteem & regard I am Dr Sir &c.

G: Washington

LB, DLC:GW.

Mathews had written GW on 7 March requesting a testimonial (see George Walton to GW, 1 April, n.1). GW supplied this testimonial in a second letter to Mathews on this date: "You inform me that you have it in contemplation to leave the United States for a time, if not forever. . . .

"I know, sir, and with pleasure bear testimony to your patriotism, & to your bravery in action in the defence of the rights & liberties of your Country. In the offices you have held, military & civil, I believe you have manifested that fortitude, prudence & integrity, which entitle you to the praise of having deserved well of your Country" (LB, DLC:GW).

1. Mathews replied to GW from Oglethorpe County, Ga., on 19 Aug.: "I do myself the honor of acknowledgeing the receipt of your polite & friendly letter of the 10th of June with the testimonial inclosed, for which you will please to accept my thanks.

"When I encouraged the idea of leaving the United States, it was at a time when my mind was fully impressed, with the ungratefull reward, I had received from the State of Georgia, for faithful Servises, and not having a prospect of domestic retirement, it put me on contemplating how I should dispose of the Eve of life Many of my friends pursude me aganst Such a measure and your observations have with me their full weight.

"Those reasons have in some measure induced me to relinquish the object I had in view, and to Solicit, you Sir for Some appointment under the federal Government, that will give me employ and Support. from a resolution of the Senate, I observe there is a Governor to be appointed for the Natchy District on the Mississipi. Could the President think me qualified, for the office, I would accept it with gratitude, & my best endeavours would be made to Discharg the duties of the trust" (ALS, PHi: Gratz Collection; Sprague transcript, DLC:GW). Mathews referenced a Senate resolution considered on 20 May that did not become law (see *Journal of the Senate*, 8:274–76).

From Matthew McAllister

Sir,   Savannah June 10th 1796.

I have reason to suppose the Judge of this District purposes resigning provided a more eligible situation shall present itself.

Should that event take place, or any other by which the office he holds may become vacant, I beg leave to suggest my inclination to succeed him, in case it shall meet your approbation.[1]

This intimation, Sir, would certainly have been withheld but from a conjecture that it may have been suggested I do not wish to hold that Appointment even should I have been considered competent to the duties of it.

My inclination in this respect has not been mentioned to any of the Gentlemen who represent this State in Congress—it is therefore the more probable some other person may be recommended to nomination—At the same time I flatter myself that none of the Gentln would do more than urge his particular friend.

If necessary Sir, I must beg leave to refer you to the Judges of the Supreme Court of the United States who have had occasional opportunities of forming opinions in regard to my fitness or otherwise for the Office—to none of whom nor to any person in Congress have I communicated my present desire. With sentiments of the highest respect and regard, I have the honor to be Sir Your most obedient Servant

Matthew McAllister

ALS, DLC:GW.

1. After learning that Nathaniel Pendleton had decided to resign as district judge for Georgia, McAllister again wrote GW from Savannah on 25 July: "Lest my former Letter should not have been received, I again beg leave to repeat my wish should it meet your approbation.

"If necessary Sir, I Must refer you to the Judges of the Supreme Court of the United States who have occasionally been this way" (ALS, DLC:GW; see also Pendleton to GW, 30 July, and Joseph Habersham to GW, 10 Aug.). Unsuccessful in his application, McAllister alleged corruption and improper influence when he wrote GW on 25 Oct. (CtHi: Oliver Wolcott, Jr., Papers).

From James McHenry

Sir.   10 June 1796[1]

This inclosed letter has been procured by Dr Williamson who knows the hand writing. It is written by a Msr Cole Montflorence, a french man who held a commission under the State of North Carolina early in the revolution war.[2]

The letter to Governor Blount by the same person I understand is gone to Tenessee.

It would seem that Montflorence had his information at Paris.

The reflexions which he makes upon it appear however to be his own.

It may be well enough to have the hand writing compared with any letters that may be in the Secy of States office from Monroe, notwithstanding its supposed resemblance to Montflorences. The Secy can return it to me. My fever is increasing. With great respect I have the honor to be Sir your obt

James McHenry

ALS, MiU-C: James McHenry Papers.

1. McHenry may have misdated this letter. GW's reference of it to Secretary of State Timothy Pickering is headed "Thursday ½ after 2 'Oclock," which, if accurate, would have been 9 June. Pickering replied to both McHenry and GW on 10 June. Lacking definitive evidence, both this letter from McHenry to GW and GW's letter to Pickering have been dated 10 June.

2. See James Cole Mountflorence to Thomas Blount, 8 March, printed as an enclosure to this letter.

Enclosure
James Cole Mountflorence to Thomas Blount

Dr Sir   Bordeaux [France] 8th March 96

This Government is much displeased with Mr Jay's treaty, and it is confidentially reported that Mr Adet is recalled, that Colo. Vincent who was emploied last year by the president for the fortification of New-York is to replace him[1]—he is to sail with the fleet bound to the West India, that he is to demand preremptorily a new treaty between the United States & france, or a Rejection of the Treaty with England, that he is not to negociate, but to give only fifteen Days for an explicit answer, and on a Refusal from our Government to leave immediately Philadelphia & repair to the Islands, from whence it is supposed that hostilities will immediately be directed against us—I think it my duty to give you those important and alarming Informations, that you may make Such ⟨use⟩ of them as you may think proper for the Interest of our Country, I will observe tho, that notwithstanding that I candidly believe that such are the present Sentiments of the Directory, yet as their politics have been constantly wandering, they may adopt other measures before the Sailing of the fleet; for I cannot conceive it to be the Interest of france especially at this Juncture to commence hostilities with us; they could get nothing by it, & the Consequence would be the immediate loss of all their Colonies, Strengthening the British forces in the Islands Increasing the British Interest in the United States, alienating from france their partisans in our Country, diminishing their Supplies & Revenues, & add a vast number of brave and intelligent Seamen to the British fleet already too powerful for their Enemy—these Considerations make me still hope that they will abate something from their above Intentions, Intentions which Every Symptom here does manifest—It is proper however that our Government should be informed therewith and be on their Guard—may I request you to mention me to Govr Blount to whom I will write by next Vessel very fully—My best Respects to M. J. G. Blount. I have the Honor to be very respectfully Sir

N.B. William Blound recd a Letter from the same Gentleman dated at Paris 23rd March—The Contents the same as above with the Addition That another Minister had been named after Col. Vincent and that he was not to come but a 3rd or 4th Nomination would be made. The Writer of the Letter had gone from Paris to Burdeaux immediately before he wrote the above Letter.[2]

ALS, MiU-C: James McHenry Papers. For consideration of this communication, see Cabinet to GW, 2 July.

1. Charles-Humbert-Marie Vincent (1753–1831), a military engineer who fled Saint Domingue after the 1793 revolt, was appointed in April 1794 to oversee the fortifications at New York. He then returned to France in August 1795. Vincent's suspicious contacts detered his being named minister to the United States. He went back to Saint Domingue and eventually associated with Toussaint L'Ouverture. See Christian Schneider, "Le colonel Vincent, officier du génie à Saint-Domingue," *Annales historiques de la Révolution française*, no. 329 (July-Sept. 2002), 101–22.

2. The postscript is in a different handwriting, probably that of Hugh Williamson. The letter from Mountflorence to William Blount has not been identified.

To Timothy Pickering

Thursday ½ after 2 'Oclock [Friday, 10 June 1796][1]

Colo. Pickering will attend to the Suggestion of Mr McHenry, & then return the letter, directed to Colo. T. Blount back, as requested.[2]

If there are any authorities which can be consulted on the remonstrance of Mr Vear, it might be well to have recourse to them. The opinion I gave was from what I conceive to be consistent with propriety and us⟨*mutilated*⟩ but, though I have no reason to ⟨*mutilated*⟩ it, it is always best to tread on g⟨rou⟩nd that will support them.[3]

Go: Washington

ALS, MHi: Pickering Papers. Pickering replied to GW on this date.

1. For this date, see James McHenry to GW, 10 June, n.1.

2. GW is referring to James Cole Mountflorence's letter to Thomas Blount dated 8 March, printed as an enclosure with McHenry to GW, 10 June. Pickering wrote Secretary of War James McHenry on 10 June: "I inclose your letter to the President covering that of Montflorence, whose handwriting we have in this office. He is the Chancellor to Mr Skipwith, the Consul Genl of the U.S. at Paris! & one of the clerks *thinks* he once acted as secretary to Mr Monroe! or was employed in copying his letters, some of which came to this office. So no doubt the anonymous letters have been written *in concert.* . . . The President wishes you to dine with him to-morrow (Saturday) at 3 o'clock. Capt. O'Brien is to dine with him" (MiU-C: James McHenry Papers). Fulwar Skipwith apparently considered serving as James Monroe's secretary at the beginning of his tenure as U.S. minister to France (see Aaron Burr to Monroe, 5 June 1794, in *Papers of James Monroe*, 3:5).

3. When Pickering responded on 10 June to an unidentified letter from Spanish chargé Josef Ignacio de Viar dated 6 June, he promised "due inquiry" into a complaint about Capt. Zebulon Pike, who commanded at Fort Massac. Pickering then continued: "In the mean time Sir, I will observe to you, that Captain Pike sustains the reputation of a judicious and prudent officer, of a disposition to conciliate, not to insult, but who at the same time knows how to do his duty.

"I will also observe, that Fort Massac was established to guard the passage of the Ohio, and consequently that Captn Pike must have had orders to be vigilant, and suffer no vessels to pass, at least no armed vessels, until they had given an account of themselves." Seeing a vessel "ascending the Ohio on the *opposite shore*, indicating an intention to pass Fort Massac unnoticed," Pike required "in the usual military stile, that the armed vessel should approach his Fort and show that she was a friend, in pursuit of a lawful business. For although a flag of truce is to protect the bearer *yet it is only to protect when it approaches, in the most direct and proper manner, the nearest guard or post.* This is a plain military rule, hardly to be dispensed with, and when there is the appearance of a design to evade it, the officer commanding the guard or post would be culpable in the extreme if he did not stop the flag" (DNA: RG 59, Domestic Letters).

From Timothy Pickering

Sir   [Philadelphia, 10 June 1796]
    I inclose draughts of instructions for Mr Trumbull and Colo.
Talbot. The latter will not be able to sail for the West Indies until
about the 20th of July. Reflecting on Mr Trumbull's situation in
England, and the nature of the service to be performed there, I
have not a doubt but that 2500 dollars will be a satisfactory compensation. I mentioned to his brother Jonathan £500. Sterling,
who did not suggest that this would form an objection. Mr Trumbull in England, while ingaged in his agency, *will still be in the
way of his private pursuits.* Colo. Talbot engages *solely for the public
service,* in a more expensive scene, and where the risque of life is
not inconsiderable. If the President approves of this distinction,
the sums proposed in the instructions will remain. Then there
will be 500 dollars left to answer any contingency, or to forward
to one or the other agent as shall be needful.[1]
    I have recd this morning a *design* for our Mediterranean pass-
ports from Mr Blodget, which with a British passport accompany
this.[2] A draught of a letter to Mr Viar is also submitted.[3] With the
greatest respect I am sir your obt servt
                                            Timothy Pickering

    Montflorence, who wrote the anonymous letter, is the Chan-
cellor to Skipwith, the Consul of the U.S. at Paris! we have his
handwriting in the office.[4] I have invited Capt. OBrien to dine
to-morrow with the President, & will invite the Secretaries.[5]

ALS, DNA: RG 59, Miscellaneous Letters; LB, DNA: RG 59, GW's Correspondence with His Secretaries of State.
    1. For the appointment of John Trumbull and Silas Talbot as agents to aid
American seamen, see GW to the U.S. Senate, 30 May, and n.1. Trumbull
eventually declined his appointment.
    Pickering's draft instructions have not been identified, but he prepared
similar instructions, both dated 9 June, for Talbot (sent to the West Indies)
and for Trumbull (sent to Great Britain; both documents in MHi: Pickering
Papers). Pickering's instructions to Talbot read: "The President desiring to
avail the United States of your Services, has with the advise and consent of the
Senate, appointed you one of their Agents, for the purposes expressed in the
act for the relief and protection of American Seamen. . . .
    "The particular duties of the Agency being designated in the Act itself, little
more remains, by way of instruction, than to hint at the mode of performing
those duties, and to express to you the earnest desire of the President that

you will use great diligence and perseverence in your endeavours to effect the humane and interesting objects of your appointment.

"You will correspond with such persons in the different Islands as you shall judge proper, to obtain the requisite information to enable you to administer relief and protection to our citizens and others. . . .

"More effectually to fulfil the objects of your appointment, you will find it necessary personally to visit at least the principal ports and places where American Seamen are impressed or detained, your inquiries will indicate these; And nothing is to be confided to others which it will be practicable for you to accomplish yourself.

"You will keep this Department constantly advised of the state of the business committed to your care; more especially when obstacles occur to retard or prevent your affording our Seamen the expected relief and protection, in order that proper representations may be made to the Government whose officers or subjects continue the oppression of which we complain. . . .

"That our Seamen once relieved may not again be exposed to impressment, they should be furnished with certificates in a form which the British Officers and impress-gangs will respect. . . .

"It will be proper to tender your respects to the commanding Officer on each station and in each port, to make known the authority under which you act, and to endeavor to form a just and friendly arrangement for the liberation of our Seamen. While great firmness will be necessary in pursuing the proper measures for relieving our Seamen, much prudence and mildness in the manner will be indispensable. Resentment unnecessarily excited, may refuse what cool judgement would yield to a becoming solicitation.

"You will be allowed for your services and for your personal expenses, including your voyages and journies a compensation at the rate of three thousand dollars a year.

"Every necessary disbursement of money to obtain the liberation of an impressed or detained seamen, and in providing for the support of such of them as shall be sick or disabled, will be allowed you. In providing for the sick or disabled, care must be used to prevent impositions. . . .

"On the subject of expenditures, you will take notice that the whole appropriation for this service is limited to fifteen thousand dollars a year: Hence it will be necessary that your part of the expenditures do not exceed two thousand dollars a year; it is presumed they will not rise to that sum, exclusively of your salary. . . . P.S. The above limitation of your expenditures to two thousand dollars is for the purpose of leaving in the hands of the Executive the means of providing for a third Agency: but you will from time to time transmit to this Office a statement of your disbursements; and if necessary, and the fund will admit of it, additional funds will be furnished" (see also Pickering to GW, 12 June, n.1). Pickering's instructions for Trumbull directed that he correspond with consuls for information and that he advise regularly with the U.S. minister to Great Britain.

2. The enclosed design and passport have not been identified. Article IV of the Treaty of Peace and Amity with Algiers, signed on 5 Sept. 1795, directed that within eighteen months, U.S. merchant vessels needed passports to obtain

the promised safe passage from Algerine warships (see Miller, *Treaties*, 299–300). Samuel Blodget, Jr., then in Baltimore, had sent a design to Pickering with a letter of 5 June 1796, in which he warned "that the inclosed sketch is not sufficiently correct for the engraver unless he may be able to design himself" (DNA: RG 59, Miscellaneous Letters; see also Pickering to GW, 16 Aug.).

3. The draft has not been identified, but Pickering wrote Josef Ignacio de Viar on 10 June (see GW to Pickering, same date, n.3).

4. See James Cole Mountflorence to Thomas Blount, 8 March, printed as an enclosure with James McHenry to GW, this date.

5. The *Gazette of the United States* (Philadelphia) for 8 June reported the arrival in Philadelphia on 7 June of Capt. Richard O'Bryen, "who was 12 years in captivity at Algiers." For O'Bryen, see his letter to Mathew and Thomas Irwin, 20 Dec. 1788, printed as an enclosure with Mathew Irwin to GW, 9 July 1789; see also GW to David Humphreys, 12 June 1796, and to the Dey of Algiers, 13 June.

From Oliver Wolcott, Jr.

Treasury Department June 10th 1796

The Secretary of the Treasury has the honour most respectfully to represent to the President of the United States;

That by an Act entitled "An act making further provision for the expenses attending the intercourse of the United States with foreign Nations, and to continue in force the Act entitled 'an act providing the means of intercourse between the United States & foreign nations,[']" passed on the 30th of May 1796, The President of the United States is empowered to borrow a sum not exceeding Three hundred & twenty four thousand five hundred & thirty nine dollars and six Cents at an interest not exceeding six per centum pr annum, reimbursable at the pleasure of the United States; & it is made lawful for the Bank of the United States to lend the same.[1]

That by another Act entitled, "an act making appropriations for the support of the military & naval Establishments for the year one thousand seven hundred & ninety six," passed the first of June 1796, the President of the United States is empowered to borrow of the Bank of the United States which is authorised to lend the same, or of any body or bodies politic, person or persons, any sum or sums not exceeding in the whole, six hundred and fifty thousand Dollars at an interest not exceeding six prCent.[2]

The Secretary begs leave further to represent that as the product of the ordinary revenue will be inadequate to the demands for the current service, he therefore requests the permission of the President to borrow the several sums specified in the said acts, and he accordingly transmits two forms of Powers for that purpose.[3] All which is most respectfully submitted.

Olivr Wolcott Jr
Secy of the Treasy

LB, DLC:GW.

Wolcott again wrote GW on 11 June: "The Secretary of the Treasury has the honor to transmit to the President of the United States the enclosed papers announcing the resignation of Thomas Jones Collector for Hampton, received this day" (LB, DLC:GW). The enclosed papers have not been identified. For the replacement collector and inspector of the revenue at Hampton, Va., see Wolcott to GW, 20 June, and n.4.

1. For this act, see n.9 to Acts Requiring Presidential Action, c.8 June, printed as an enclosure with Timothy Pickering to GW, 8 June.

2. See 1 *Stat.* 493–94.

3. GW provided Wolcott with two warrants on this date (one for each act named in this letter) that empowered the secretary of the treasury or his authorized agent to borrow the specified sums (both LB, DLC:GW).

To James Ross

Dear Sir, Philadelphia 11th June 1796.

I should not have given you the trouble of receiving a letter from me at this time, but for the purpose of explaining a mistake which in a degree implicates you.

Two or three days ago a person (whose name I did not ask) called upon me to pay me, at the request he said of Colo. Shreve, £100 on account of the Land he had purchased of me.[1] I told him I would not receive money from that Gentleman in driblets; that nothing less than the *whole* Second payment, which was £600 & inter[es]t, would be received; and that, if I was thus trifled with by Colo. Shreve, I would have recourse to other means to obtain a more punctual compliance with our bargain.

This reply produced a further offer, to the amount I think, in the whole of £300; but conceiving as I did, at that moment, that the *whole* second Instalment was due, I refused this sum also. Nor was it before this morning it occurred to me, that in April last, you paid me Eleven hundred and Sixty dollars in part of this Instalment.[2]

Having made this discovery too late to rectify it with the person who was charged with a payment, by Colo. Shreve, and having authorised that person to inform him that nothing short of the whole sum due, would content me; I feel it incumbent on me to give you this explanation of the matter; and through you, (if an occasion should present) of making it known to Colo. Shreve.

I think it not improbable that the person I allude to (not knowing his name) with the aid of the 1160 dollars received from you, would have paid the whole sum due on the second instalment with interest agreeable to the Articles; for he is a purchaser from Shreve, of part of the Tract, at a price very considerably advanced.

Not knowing whether Mr Chas Morgan is living or dead, or what has been done relatively to the Rents which was due on the Land, will you permit me, to request the favor of you, to ask him (if in being) or Colo. Shreve, when I am to receive it. I am in the same predicament with respect to the Rents of the Land on Millers run, & shall be equally obliged by your enquiries concerning it whenever it shall fall in your way.[3] With very great esteem & regd I am—Dear Sir Your Obedt Servt

Go: Washington

P.S. For the government of those who may have business to transact with me, I add, that on Monday or Tuesday[4] next, I shall leave this City for Virginia;[5] that I shall return to it again *myself* before the first day of September; and shall remain here until the middle or 20th of the Month.[6]

G.W.

ALS, owned (1985) by Jay I. Kislak, Miami, Fla.; ALS (letterpress copy), NN: Washington Papers; LB, DLC:GW. The letter-book copy has a number of minor variations from the ALS, probably resulting from the poor quality of the letterpress copy. The most substantive differences are reported in notes 3 and 4 below.

1. For Israel Shreve's purchase of GW's Washington's Bottom tract in Fayette County, Pa., see Ross to GW, 3 Aug. 1795, and notes.

2. See Ross to GW, 15 April, and n.3 to that document.

3. The previous seven words do not appear on the letterpress or letter-book copies.

GW continued to pursue payment from Shreve and rents from other tenants (see GW to Ross, 12 Nov., NjP: Armstrong Collection).

4. The preceding two words do not appear on the letter-book copy.

5. GW started for Mount Vernon on Monday, 13 June (see his letter to David Humphreys, 12 June).

6. GW wrote from Philadelphia on 23 Aug. (see his letter to Jeremiah Wadsworth, that date, found at Wadsworth to GW, 12 June, n.2). For his last late-summer letter addressed from Philadelphia before his departure for Mount Vernon, see GW to the Commissioners for the District of Columbia, 18 September.

To David Humphreys

(Private)

My dear Humphreys   Philadelphia 12th June 1796.

I could not suffer Capt: OBrian to return without carrying along with him, a testimony of my continued friendship and regard for you, in a few lines.[1] In the diction of which, I must be concise: for a long and interesting Session of Congress, which only closed on the first instt, and many laws which require immediate attention & execution;[2] added to a preparation for a journey to Mount Vernon (tomorrow) for a little relaxation from the unpleasant Scenes which have been, and are continually presenting themselves to my view—will not, however well disposed I might otherwise be, permit me to be profuse in my declaration.

From the Office of State, you will receive every thing that relates to public concerns; and the Gazettes (which I presume will accompany the dispatches) will give you a pretty good idea of the state of Politics, and Parties in this country; and will shew you, at the sametime (if Bache's Aurora is among them) in what manner I am attacked for persevering, steadily, in measures which, to me, appear necessary to preserve us (during the conflicts of the Belligerent powers) in a state of tranquillity. But these attacks, unjust, and as unpleasant as they are, will occasion no change in my conduct;[3] nor will they produce any other effect in my mind than to increase the solicitude which, long since, has taken fast hold of my breast, to enjoy, in the shades of retirement, the consolation of believing that I have rendered my country every service to which my abilities were competent—not from pecuniary or ambitious motives, nor from a desire to provide for *any* one farther than their intrinsic merit entitled them to; and surely not with a view to bring any of my own relations into Office.

Malignity, therefore, may dart its shafts, but no earthly power can deprive me of the consolation of *knowing* that I have not, in the whole course of my Administration (however numerous they may have been) committed an *intentional* error.

Whenever you shall think with the Poet, or Philosopher "that the Post of honor is a private Station"[4] and may be disposed to enjoy yourself in my shades—I do not mean the shades below—where, if you put it off long—I may be reclining, I can only repeat that you will meet with the same cordial reception at Mount Vernon, that you have always found at that place; and that I am, and always shall be, Your sincere friend, & Affectionate Servt

Go: Washington

P.S. Mrs Washington who keeps her health as well as usual presents her best wishes to you. Betsey Custis is married to Mr Law (who was, I believe, in this Country when you were here last) an English Gentleman but last from the East Indies, of considerable fortune, and lives in the Federal City. Patcy you know was married 'ere you left us, to Mr Peter's—Nelly has spent the last Winter with her mother—Washington grows fast—& We have just heard that all Doctr Stuarts family are well.[5]

ALS, NNGL; LB, DLC:GW. Humphreys replied to GW on 1 Jan. 1797 (DLC:GW).

1. For Capt. Richard O'Bryen, see Timothy Pickering to GW, 10 June 1796, n.5.

2. See Acts Requiring Presidential Action, c.8 June, printed as an enclosure with Pickering to GW, 8 June.

3. GW may have referenced Letter III from "PAULDING" to Benjamin Franklin Bache, who edited the *Aurora General Advertiser* (Philadelphia). Paulding's letter, which appeared in the *Aurora* for 9 June, claimed that the Jay Treaty had "given the French Republic a sufficient inducement to treat us with severity" because it gave "evident advantages to Great Britain at the expence of the French Republic" and "thus violated our neutrality." Paulding averred that American neutrality had been "a fraudulent one. . . . Indeed nothing but the universal sentiment of enthusiastic affection displayed by *the people* of the United States" towards France "could have subdued the Machiavelian policy" displayed in the questions that GW posed to the cabinet in his letter of 18 April 1793. GW's letter, Paulding concluded, "has stamped upon its front in characters brazen enough for idolatry itself to comprehend, perfidy and ingratitude. . . . For the honor of the American character & of human nature, it is to be lamented, that the records of the United States exhibit such a stupendous monument of degeneracy. It will almost require the authenticity of holy writ to persuade posterity, that it is not a libel ingeniously contrived to

injure the reputation of 'the saviour of his country.'" GW continued to follow this anonymous critic (see his letter to Timothy Pickering, 18 July, and n.2 to that document; see also Tagg, *Benjamin Franklin Bache*, 280–81).

4. GW quoted from act 4, scene 4, of Joseph Addison's play *Cato*: "When vice prevails, and impious men bear sway, The post of honour is a private station."

5. See Thomas Law to GW, 11 May.

From Timothy Pickering

Sir, Sunday Evening [12 June 1796]

Reflecting on the proposed application to Mr Liston respecting our seamen impressed in the West Indies, I thought a more effectual mode than a conversation, would be to address him by letter. While in the country to-day, I draughted the inclosed for that purpose.[1] I also sketched a letter to Mr Adet on the subject of the piratical privateer which has captured one of our ships, and in effect blocked up the Delaware. It is formed on the *reports* of the case—the *facts* when ascertained will doubtless make alterations necessary. The sketch I will make legible to present to you in the morning,[2] at as early an hour as will suit your convenience, after sun-rise. I am very respectfully, sir, your obt servant

T. Pickering

ALS, DNA: RG 59, Miscellaneous Letters; LB, DNA: RG 59, GW's Correspondence with His Secretaries of State. The letter-book copy supplies the date.

1. Pickering's draft has not been identified, but his letter to British minister Robert Liston, dated 25 June, enclosed a copy of the "Act for the relief and protection of American Seamen" and depositions exemplifying "the oppression practised on American citizens impressed by the Officers of his Britannic Majesty, sometimes at Sea, but more frequently in the ports of the West Indies. I am possessed of many such depositions, collected within a short period, and more are daily coming in.

"The design of the present letter is to request your interposition, to give facility and efficacy to the measures proposed by Congress to remedy the evil here refered to. . . .

"You will observe that one of the agents required by the act of Congress to be appointed, is to reside in Great-Britain. There, so near the sources of power great abuses, I trust, are seldom practised, But the West-Indies, so remote from the correcting hand of government, appears to have been the scene of unexampled cruelties. And altho' certificates sanctioned by the same solemnities as the Ships' papers may generally have been admitted as evidence of citizenship, yet sometimes they have been utterly disregarded. In other cases, where certificates have been lost, or by the improvidence of our seamen never obtained, all other reasonable proofs of citizenship have been rejected.

"With a view to seek relief for such suffering citizens, the President of the United States has appointed Silas Talbot Esquire to repair to the West Indies. . . . But the attempt may not succeed, unless your aid be interposed; unless your letters to his Majesty's officers give our agents access to them; and unless your representations shall procure a proper attention to the rights of American citizens. And I am sure that your sympathy for suffering humanity, your respect for the rights of a foreign nation to which you are the accredited minister, and your desire to promote its harmony with your own, will prompt you to afford the requested interposition; and in a case of such urgency, regardless of unessential forms, persuade you to give your aid in any way which absolute impropriety does not forbid (DNA: RG 59, Notes from the Department of State to Foreign Ministers and Consuls in the United States; see also GW to the U.S. Senate, 30 May, and n.1, and Pickering to GW, 10 June).

2. Pickering wrote French minister Pierre-Auguste Adet on 13 June: "The merchants of Philadelphia are extremely alarmed by the conduct of a small Privateer called the Flying Fish, bearing, it is understood, a commission from the French Republic. It is said she has been lying in this port for some time, preparing for sea: and it seems that after inquiring and observing what valuable vessels were to sail for foreign ports, she sailed herself to the Capes of the Delaware, and not far from thence lay in wait for the vessels she had marked for her prey. Accordingly, on the 9th instant, she seized on the Ship Mount Vernon . . . within two hours after the pilot had left her, and within about six leagues of Cape Henlopen; took possession of all her papers, and forced the master, mate and all her crew, save two men to leave her; and under these circumstances she was sent—they know not whither! . . .

"Such conduct has more the appearance of an act of piracy than of the lawful procedure of an armed vessel regularly commissioned by your Republic. Other vessels were on the point of leaving the Delaware Bay; but witnessing or hearing of this outrage, have put back, and returned up the river for safety. . . ."

Pickering added that even should there be "any just ground to believe" the *Mount Vernon* "to be the property of an enemy of the French Republic," the master and mate ought to have been allowed to remain on the ship to represent the owners at adjudication.

"I have only further to express to you, Sir, the President's reliance that if you are possessed of any information on the subject of this letter, you will communicate the same with the candour and frankness due from the representative of a friendly and allied nation. . . . P.S. The public solicitude is so great on this subject, and so many vessels are in consequence detained, you will permit me to request a speedy answer" (DNA: RG 59, Domestic Letters). For Adet's reply, dated 14 June, see Pickering to GW, 22 June, and n.1 to that letter; see also Oliver Wolcott, Jr., to GW, 20 June, and GW to Pickering, 24 and 27 June.

To John Sinclair

Sir,   Philadelphia 12th June 1796

A long, and interesting Session of Congress—which did not close until the first day of this month—and the Laws which required to be carried into execution promptly; will, I am persuaded, be admitted as a reasonable excuse for my not writing to you since the 20th of Feby last, agreeably to assurances then given. But what apology can I offer *now*, that I am about to give you the result of the enquiries you requested me to make, when it will be found to fall so far short of what you might have expected, from the time which has been taken, to render it?

Your wishes on this head, I communicated to Richard Peters Esqr.; who is one of the most intelligent, and best practical, as well as theoretical farmers we have; with a desire that he would advise with others, and condense their observations in a summary Statement.[1] Why this was not done—and why *he* could do no more—you will find in his own, original letter, with the questions and answers therein enclosed.[2]

To Mr Peters's experience with respect to Gypsum as a manure, let me add the following, as an unequivocal evidence, that it has no effect on stiff—heavy land—that does not absorb, or permit the water on the surface, occasioned by super abundant falls of Rain or Snow, to penetrate quickly; which is the case, generally, with the Soil of my Estate, at Mount Vernon. The experiments, & proof to which I allude, were made eight or nine years ago; at the rate of from one to twenty bushels of the Plaster of Paris to the acre (among other things, to ascertain the just quantum to be used)—I spread it on grass grounds, and on ploughed land. On the latter, part of it was ploughed in; part harrowed in; part scratched in with a light bush; while another part lay undisturbed, on the surface. All with Oats, in the Spring. But it had no more effect, in *any* instance—*then*, or *since*, than so much of the earth it was spread over would have had, if it had been taken up & spread again.[3]

If any thing should hereafter occur on this, or any other subject, which I may think worthy your attention, in this interesting branch of your pursuits, I shall not fail to communicate them to you;[4] being with very geat esteem, respect & consideration Sir, Your most Obedt, and very Hble Servt

Go: Washington

ALS, UkLoBM: Add. MSS 5757; LB, DLC:GW; ADfS (letterpress copy), DLC:GW. The second and third pages of the letterpress copy are faded and mostly illegible. Although there is only one minor word change (repeated in the letter-book copy), the first page is evidently not a press of the ALS.

1. See GW to Richard Peters, 4 March.

2. See Peters to GW, 12 May, and n.4.

3. GW experimented with plaster of paris (gypsum) as fertilizer in 1785 (see the entries for 8, 15, 18–19, and 25 April, 9 May, 29 Oct., and 6 Nov. in *Diaries*, 4:115, 120, 123, 127–28, 136, 215, 219–20).

4. Sinclair replied to GW on 10 September.

From Jeremiah Wadsworth

Dear Sir   Hartford June 12th 1796

Yesterday I purchased for you a Black Guelding Eight Years old fifteen hands high a good pacer both slow & fast.[1] his trot not so good, but fast—I wish I could say he was handsome but that rarely belongs to this breed, but he carries well & when moveing has a decent appearance—he Cost one hundred & thirty Dollars. he has always been used to a plain snaffle Bit. I can every monday send him by a carefull Man who rides Post thro Litchfield to New York so as to arrive their on Wednesday. to that place you can send a Boy in the Stage with a Saddle & Bridle to ride him to you. I should send him tomorrow to be left at a stable just at the Ferry Stairs in New York to be delivered your order but fearing you may be absent from Philah. I shall keep him untill I hear from you—if we live two or three Years I hope to furnish you with a perfect Narraganset as I have two fine Mare Colts one of which when old enough you shall have.[2] I am with great sincerity your most obedient Humble Servant

Jere. Wadsworth

ALS, DLC:GW.

1. GW had requested a Narragansett horse (see his letter to Wadsworth, 11 Feb., and n.2 to that document).

Developed in Rhode Island, the Narragansett pacer was a breed of saddle horse noted for speed, endurance, and an easy gait. It disappeared around 1800. For an account of the breed's history, see Dimon, *American Horses*, 52–55; see also Charlotte Carrington-Farmer, "The Rise and Fall of the Narragansett Pacer," *Rhode Island History* 76 (2018): 1–38.

2. GW replied to Wadsworth from Mount Vernon on 26 June: "Your letter of the 12th instt found me at this place; having left Philadelphia on the 13th.

"I thank you for the purchase of a Naraganset on my Acct; and pray, unless a good and safe opportunity shd offer, by which he could be sent to my Stables in Philadelphia (by the same hand) that you would commit him to the care of some honest farmer in your neighbourhood (to be well fed) until my return to the Seat of Government; which will happen before the last of August. Whatever expence is incurred for the feed—pasturage—& care of him, shall be paid the moment the account of them is presented.

"On, or before my arrival in Philadelphia (if the above event should not take place previous thereto) I will request him to be sent on in the manner you have suggested, and will forward a servant to meet him at New York; being apprised of the day he will be there.

"It may happen, though it is not within the chances, that some person (in whom you could confide) having business in the Federal City, or Alexandria, might find it convenient to ride him there, rather than travel in the Stage; should this happen, it would suit me better than either of the former modes.

"You have made a cheaper purchase than I expected; and if there is any person in this part of the Country, or Philadelphia to whom you would have the hundred & thirty dollars paid, it shall be immediately done; or if you would have it in promisary Bank notes of the United States, under cover of a letter, that sum shall be transmitted to you, in this manner, by the first Post after I receive the advice.

"If I should not be embarked on some other Journey, two or three years hence, I shall remember your promise to furnish me with a Naraganset of your own raising. My best respects are presented to Mrs Wadsworth and the family" (ALS, Ct: Joseph Trumbull Papers).

GW subsequently wrote Secretary of the Treasury Oliver Wolcott, Jr., from Mount Vernon on 18 July: "Private . . . Let me request the favor of you to pay (out of the money I left in your hands) One hundred and thirty dollars to Mr Thos McEwen, agreeably to the direction contained in the enclosed letter from Colo. Wadsworth to me; and take his receipt for the same on the back of the letter.

"Colo. Wadsworth was obliging enough to offer me a Naraganset of his own breeding—which he thought would be fit for use in two or three years—this I accepted, provided I was not in the prosecution of a journey to the Land of Spirits (before that time) in which he might be of no service to me" (ALS, CtHi: Oliver Wolcott, Jr., Papers; see also GW's first letter to Wolcott, 13 June, and Wolcott to GW, 23 July). The enclosed letter from Wadsworth to GW has not been found.

Thomas McEuen (McEwen; c.1765–1822) worked as a broker in Philadelphia. He later represented the city in the Pennsylvania legislature.

GW later wrote Wadsworth from Philadelphia on 23 Aug.: "Be so good as to inform me of the precise time, and at what place in the City of New York, the horse you were so obliging as to procure for me can be delivered; and a person shall be there in order to receive him: and the sooner, the more convenient it will be for me.

"Let the account of his expences for feed & pasturage; and whatever you shall agree to give the Post Rider (or whoever brings him to New York) for his trouble, & the expence of doing it, be mentioned in your letter; and the person who goes for him shall be furnished with money to pay the whole. The One hundred and thirty dollars—the cost of him, has, as I presume you have been advised, been paid to —— agreeably to your desire. My best respects attend Mrs & Miss Wadsworth" (ALS, CtHi: Washington Letters and Papers).

Wadsworth replied to GW from Hartford on 27 Aug.: "your favor of the 23d came so late last night, that there was no possibility of replying by the same Post: otherwise your Horse would have been at New York on Wednesday evening, of next week. as it is he will be there on the evening of Wednesday the 7th of September—at Powels Stable about twenty Yards from the Ferry Stairs on the North River. the charges on the Horse are as under and may be paid to Thos McEwen & Co. Chesnut street Philadelphia as it is possible your servant may not meet with the post—Mrs & Miss Wadsworth beg your acceptance of their respectfull compliments and pray you to present them to Mrs Washington . . . one of my Yearling mare Colts of the Narraganset breed is very handsome and will be for you when fit to ride " (ALS, DLC:GW). The postscript with this letter showed charges for "10 Weeks Hay & Grass" at £1; 8 bushels of "Oats 2/6" at £1; and "Post to New York 3 doll." The charges totaled £2.18, or $9.67. A record in GW's household accounts under 6 Sept. indicates payment of this sum to McEuen.

To the Dey of Algiers

[Philadelphia, 13 June 1796]
To the most Excellent and most Illustrious Hassan Bashaw Dey of the City and Regency of Algiers.

By the late arrival of Captain O'Brien from Lisbon,[1] with letters from Colonel Humphreys, I have received the painful intelligence that the money stipulated by Joseph Donaldson Junior when he concluded a treaty with you in behalf of the United States, has not yet been paid.[2] This disappointment I extremely regret; because of the many inconveniences arising from so long a delay; and more especially as it has led you to doubt, sometimes, whether the said Donaldson was authorized to negotiate the treaty, at other times whether the United States were sincere in their engagements. I have therefore written this letter, and signed it with my own hand, and caused it to be sealed with the great Seal of the United States to make known to your Excellency the certainty of the said Donaldson's authority to negotiate the treaty, & to form the stipulations which he entered into in my name, as President of the United States of America, and in the name of the Citizens of the United States, with your Excellency the Dey of Algiers, your Divan and subjects, on the 21st of the Luna of Safer 1210, corresponding with the 5th of September 1795. I further make known to you, that timely provision was made, and adequate funds lodged by the Secretary of our treasury, in London, for the fulfilment of all those engagements; and that all the delays of payment which have happened have arisen from causes as unexpected as they are unexampled. The great, the opulent city of London, whose commerce surpasses that of any other City in Europe, and whose abundant wealth has supplied the largest portion of the money with which Great Britain and her allies have carried on their present war, was deemed the surest depository of the funds of the United States. But it has happened that the immense supplies so furnished by that City, together with certain circumstances for some months past peculiar to her commerce, have produced the singular event, that the money necessary to perform Mr Donaldson's engagement, when demanded, could not be procured: altho' the great mercantile house in whose hands the funds of the U.S. had long before been lodged, had assured Colonel Humphreys that they should at any time be ready to pay his draughts.[3] The singular facts here stated will account to your Excellency for the disappointments you have experienced. But if this or any other untoward event should still longer delay the payments, nevertheless I desire you to rest assured that the United States are faithful to all their engagements, and will perform those made with you as before mentioned in their behalf. As a farther testimony thereof the treaty formed with your Excellency, your Divan and Subjects, by Mr Donaldson, and confirmed by Colonel Humphreys, was in due time after the receipt of it here, ratified by me, with the advice and consent of the Senate of the United States, according to the rule prescribed in the Constitution of our Government. Still more to testify our liberality as well as our good faith, & our sincere desire to maintain peace and friendship with your Excellency, your Divan & Subjects, I have given directions to have built, & equipped, with as much expedition as the case will admit of, such a frigate as, in consideration of the delays which we all regret, Messieurs Donaldson & Barlow have promised should be finished.[4] With these assurances I close this letter;[5] praying God to have your Excellency in his holy keeping, and to crown your life with length of days, felicity & honour. Written at Philadelphia the thirteenth day of June 1796.

Go. Washington
By the President of the United States of America
Timothy Pickering
Secy of State

Copy, PWacD: Sol Feinstone Collection, on deposit at PPAmP; LB, DNA: RG 59, Credences. The copy is signed as such by State Department clerk George Taylor, Jr.

1. For Capt. Richard O'Bryen's arrival in Philadelphia, see Timothy Pickering to GW, 10 June, n.5.

2. O'Bryen apparently carried a letter from David Humphreys, minister to Portugal and chargé d'affaires to the Barbary States, to Secretary of State Pickering dated 25 April. That letter is known only from a letter Humphreys wrote Pickering from Lisbon on 26 April, which begins: "I had yesterday the honour of addressing a letter to you by Captn O'Brien stating the extremely perilous situation of our affairs with respect to Algiers, and desiring to learn by your answer, as expeditiously as possible, the explicit determination of our Government, on the stipulation made by Messrs Barlow & Donaldson, for presenting a frigate of 36 Guns to the Dey of Algiers" (DNA: RG 59, Despatches from U.S. Ministers to Spain).

3. For details about the difficulty with funds sent John & Francis Baring and Co. of London, see their statement of 29 Aug. in *ASP: Foreign Relations*, 1:556–58.

4. Joel Barlow and Joseph Donaldson, Jr., had written Humphreys from Algiers on 5 April about the frigate promised to the dey (see *ASP, Foreign Relations*, 1:554–55; see also Pickering to GW, 22 June, and n.6; James McHenry to GW, 7 and 16–17 July; and GW to McHenry, 13 July).

5. *The Independent Gazetteer* (Philadelphia) for 2 July printed an item: "The United States brig Sophia, sailed a few days ago from this port for Europe.— She is to touch at Lisbon, for a short time, and from thence proceed to Algiers. We learn that the Sophia has on board the means of fulfilling the terms of our Treaty with the Dey and Regency of Algiers, for which purpose she was dispatched by the Executive with Capt. O'Brien on board."

Letter not found: from Anne Louise DuBarry, 13 June 1796. DuBarry wrote GW on 28 July: "the 13th of Last month I had the honour of writing to you" (see GW to George Lewis, 28 April, n.2).

From Abijah Hart

Sir,   New York June 13. 1796

Having some years ago addressed you through my friend Mr Hillhouse on the Mint establishment without success,[1] I feel a diffidence now; which nothing but the hope of serving you could surmount—I have a Ship now loading for Lisbon, which will sail on sunday next—My Brother Wm Hart will go out in her on business for me—he has a Letter of Introduction from Dr Dwight President of Yale College, to the American Minister Col. Humphreys—& is a young man who will be happy to convey any Commands to that Minister,[2] as he will feel himself much honoured by such an Introduction from the President of the United States. I am &c.

Abijah Hart

ALS, DNA: RG 59, Miscellaneous Letters.

Abijah Hart (1764–1829) was a New York merchant. He underwent bankruptcy in 1800 and joined the mercantile firm Vanderbilt, Hart & Hicks. That firm dissolved in 1802, and Hart again took bankruptcy protection in 1803. He spent his later years farming in Connecticut.

1. See Hart to GW, 21 April 1792.

2. The letter from Timothy Dwight to David Humphreys has not been identified.

William Hart (1772–1836) graduated from Yale College in 1792. Initially associated with his brother's business, he spent most of his life as a teacher in Connecticut.

Timothy Dwight (1752–1817), a Congregationalist pastor and man of letters, served as president of Yale College from 1795 until his death.

To Oliver Wolcott, Jr.

Dear Sir,   Philadelphia 13th June 1796

Enclosed you have Bank Bills to the amount of Five hundred Dollars. From this fund I pray you to furnish Mr Frederick Kitt, my Household Steward with *weekly* sums as his occasions require—say from th[i]rty to 40 dollars according to circumstances. It will enable you also to pay the duties on two Pipes of Wine wch I understand is in the Ganges for and on my Acct. As this Wine is in dble cases—I had rather, as it will be to be removed again pay for the *whole* quantity, the inner Pipes originally contained, than have them uncased for the purpose of measuring

the pres[en]t cont[en]ts.[1] With sincere esteem & regard I am—
always yrs

G. Washington

ADfS, MH: Jared Sparks Collection.

GW also wrote three notes to Wolcott on this date directing payments to Secretary of State Timothy Pickering. One was for $1,000 "to be applied by him in defraying the expenses attending the procuring copies of the proceedings of the british Vice admiralty courts in the cases of british spoliations committed on the commerce of the United States." Another was for $5,000 "to be applied by him pursuant to the act of Congress, entitled 'an act for the relief & protection of American seamen,' to the payment of the compensation of the Agents therein mentioned for their services & the incidental expenses attending the performance of the duties imposed on them by that Act" (see also Pickering to GW, 10 June, and n.1 to that document). A third was for $1,000 "out of the sum appropriated to defray the Contingent charges of Government, to be applied by him to that use" (all LB, DLC:GW).

1. For the shipment of two pipes of wine aboard the *Ganges*, see John Marsden Pintard to Bartholomew Dandridge, Jr., 17 July 1795, and notes 1 and 2; see also GW to Wolcott, 24 June 1796 (second letter). *The Philadelphia Gazette & Universal Daily Advertiser* for 2 June reported the arrival of the *Ganges* on the previous evening "from Bengal, in 92 days."

From Tench Coxe

Sir   Philadelphia June 14. 1796

I have the honor to inclose to you a translation of a letter lately received by me from Genl Rochambeau, the younger.[1] During his late residence in Philadelphia, he often manifested to me a concern for the preservation of harmony between the two countries; and just before his departure he expressed some apprehensions of the reverse, at least so far as feelings were concerned, on the side of France.[2] As I have always thought that the cardinal principle of the present extended war, was the checking of representative Government, I have ever treated misunderstandings between those whose governments are not hereditary as peculiarly injurious to us & them—and I felt great sollicitude that France & Holland should not proceed hastily upon grounds of jealousy, suspicion or opinion to any measures of unkindness or inconvenience. General Rochambeaus exchange, for the purpose of being employed, was understood to have taken place, and I felt anxious to obtain thro him some ideas of what was thought by his countrymen on both sides of the Atlantic. The substance of what I learned here, I communicated to Col. Pickering to whom I shall shew the original of the enclosed letter. I have no view in troubling you with this communication, except that of passing to the proper centre information, which may be useful, and I beg you to indulge me in the expression of a desire to receive no communication from you in return, as I wish to preclude every idea of obtrusion.

It will be agreeable to me, if this matter lies with yourself and the Secretary of State, as to the writer & receiver of the letter from Paris. I have the honor to be Sir your most obedient Servant

Tench Coxe

ALS, DLC:GW; copy, PHi: Tench Coxe Papers.
1. See Vicomte de Rochambeau to Coxe, 7 Feb., printed as an enclosure to this letter.
2. Donatien-Marie-Joseph de Vimeur, vicomte de Rochambeau, went to the United States on parole after surrendering Martinique to the British in March 1794. He left the country after his exchange in November 1795.

Enclosure
Vicomte de Rochambeau to Tench Coxe

Paris the 18. Pluviose 4th year &ca (Feby [7]th 1796)[1]

you have some time since recd from me, Sir, a letter which I wrote to you from Havre on my arrival—I promised to write again as soon as my residence at Paris should enable me to communicate some details, which might be interesting to you & to the country which you inhabit—I proceed to keep my promise.

That, which I wrote you before, is but too true—the same sentiments no longer unite our two nations. I find no more among the french, that cordial attachment to the Americans, which they had after the close of the last war. I have endeavoured to ascertain the causes of this coolness, and, I think, I have had occasion to observe that the principal are those that I am about to communicate.

1st The drawing near of the Government of the U.S. to England—a power always the enemy [(]or at least the Rival of France) at the instant when it seemed to draw itself, or, in effect, did draw itself from the Republic.

2dly The ratification of the last treaty of Amity, commerce &

navigation concluded by Mr Jay occasioned principally by the intercepting of a Dispatch more than indiscreet from a french Minister.[2]

3dly The Stock Jobbing on the Exchange of Paris, which is kept up by a great number of your countrymen, who speculate for their benefit in the depreciation of the Assignats—or who lend their names to that scandalous traffic.

4thly The acknowledged bad faith of certain of your sellers of Lands, who have disposed of dry rocks to some of my countrymen, as fertile & well watered Lands.

5thly The Avidity of your merchants, and the numerous complaints of the refugees from our colonies who complain bitterly that they have been defrauded by those to whom they have confided the wrecks of their property.

These, Sir, are the sources of the evils, which it is desireable to cure—such is the situation of things, which becomes still worse, when your vessels arrive in our ports with provisions, which they desire to sell enormously dear, in order to go in ballast to England, carrying thither our corn to procure from thence manufactures to suit the taste of the Americans.

You must be convinced, that if these reproaches are founded, they must create a lively sensation—they must make a deep impression upon a people, haughty & victorious, who believe themselves to be abandoned by those from whom they have a right to claim more than mere amicable communications, but always insignificant in their results.

It is known too, and with astonishment, that the Americans have withdrawn themselves from France just at the time, when the french revolution had taken a republican character, and when the revolutionary government had been established there. But, Sir, who was it that first set before us the example of our conduct, if it was not the Americans themselves—who was it that blended legally the legislative & executive powers in the first Congress? It was the Americans—who first established her committees: This also was done by your countrymen. Who persecuted spoiled, and banished the Tories of the new world: It was still the Americans: and yet the americans were not, as we are, pressed by the armies of all the powers of Europe—and they too had a powerful ally. These truths, which we sometimes dissemble, are of the utmost importance, and ought to meet some consideration. Yes, Sir, if we have advanced towards liberty after the manner of your fellow citizens, the French have had the same wrongs to arrive at republican government.

It is my real attachment to the mutual prosperity of the two Countries, which causes me to present to you the unfavorable side of the picture—I know that the language of truth often offends But it is necessary that the truth should be known, in order to find palliatives, or, what is much better, a perfect remedy.

I have seen Mr Monroe—I have dined at his house, and several times in his company—He enjoys that consideration, which is due to the Minister of a free people, one of our most ancient Allies, but not the most energetic. It appears in short, that his Situation, without being doubtful, is at least sometimes embarrassing, and that the french government observes attentively the course of the American government, or that the measure of the confidence of the first will be according to the unequivocal propositions of a prompt (or ready) Union, sincere & durable.

I must remark, that I have no station in which to write you thus—and that I am influenced solely by the desire, which you have manifested to remove, if it were possible, the unfavorable impressions to which the ratification of your last treaty has given birth. my best respects to your family—You know the degree of my Attachment &ca for you

Dtn Rochambeau

Translation, DLC:GW. What appears to be a draft translation is in PHi: Tench Coxe Papers.

1. The translator wrote "6th," but 1796 being a leap year, 18 Pluviose (year 4) fell on 7 February.

2. Rochambeau is referring to a British-intercepted dispatch dated 31 Oct. 1794 from French minister Jean Antoine Joseph Fauchet that led to the resignation of Secretary of State Edmund Randolph after coming to GW's attention (see Timothy Pickering to GW, 31 July 1795, n.3).

From James McHenry

Sir   War office 14 June 1796.

I have the honour to lay before you the proceedings and sentence of a court-martial on Lieut. Simon Geddis, and several papers and letters connected therewith.[1]

Lieut. Geddis having prayed for a new trial, I shall wave any remarks upon his case, and confine myself to the reasons which favour such an application.

It is declared, in the articles of war, vz. Art. 1. for the administration of justice, that, "General courts-martial may consist of any number of commissioned officers from *five* to *thirteen*, inclusively; but they *shall not consist of less than thirteen* where that number can be convened *without manifest injury to the service.*"[2]

This article discovers great solicitude that general courts-martial should consist of the highest number of members it prescribes; and implies very strongly, that every number *inclusively* between five and thirteen, is to be sought for, and prefered to that of five. It does more. It expresly precludes *five* members from being considered as a constitutional general court-martial, whenever *thirteen* can be convened, without manifest injury to the service.

A general court martial therefore, which should consist of five members only, could not be held to be legal, unless it should be evident that more members could not have been added, so as to approach it to thirteen without manifest injury to the service.

Viewing the question in this aspect, it might be proper, that the fact should be ascertained, whether the situation of the garrison or corps at West-Point, (at the time when the court tried Lt Geddis) was such, as to render a limitation of its members to five an indispensible measure.

If upon inquiry it should emerge, that the situation of things at that time would have admitted of the higher number, or a nearer approach to the highest, a new trial may be considered as a necessary consequence.

I would submit therefore the propriety of returning the proceedings to the commandant of the corps at West Point, with instructions to make the necessary investigation, and grant a new trial, if it should appear to him, that a greater number of members than five might have been convened at that time, "without manifest injury to the service.["][3] I have the honour to be with the greatest respect, Sir your most obt st

James McHenry

ALS, DLC:GW; LB, DLC:GW.

Maj. Anne-Louis de Tousard wrote George Washington Motier Lafayette from West Point, N.Y., on this date to ask his intercession with GW on behalf of Lt. Simon Geddes, Tousard's brother-in-law (DLC:GW).

1. A court-martial at West Point on 12 May consisting of five officers had sentenced Geddes to be dismissed from the service. The enclosed documents have not been identified, but they probably included a letter Geddes wrote McHenry on 8 June with complaints about the proceedings and a request for a new trial. Geddes also asked McHenry "to lay this letter & my Defence together with the Charges before the President of the United states . . . you must excuse this Scrawl as I have wrote in a great hurry and am indesposed" (DLC: James McHenry Papers).

2. For the adoption of this article of war on 31 May 1786, see *JCC*, 30:316.

3. GW replied to McHenry on 22 June. McHenry subsequently recommended a pardon for Geddes when he wrote GW on 26 July. For his eventual compliance, see GW to McHenry, 1 (second letter) and 12 Aug., and McHenry to GW, 8 Aug., n.2.

From James McHenry

Sir. War office 15 June 1796.

Since closing my letter of yesterday I have received the annexed from Majr Cushing whom I had previously directed to join the army.[1]

If he has made a fair statement of his case, some indulgence may be proper. If on the contrary, he has misrepresented it, he is unworthy of any and unfit for a soldier. At any rate, I presume that he has motives and reasons which he has not expressed.

Should you direct me to indulge him would it not be right to limit his furlough. This while it would give him an opportunity to reestablish his health, would oblige him on its expiration, either to a performance of his military duties at camp, or a resignation, and at the same time, avoid any appearance of rigour.

I expect in a few days to have the scheme for the new arrangement of the army ready to lay before you.

As it is no ways necessary that this letter should be made a record of, I take the liberty to hope that you & Mrs Washington got safe to Mount Vernon and feel a little repose.[2] May you always be happy is the sincere wish of Sir your most respectful & ob. st

James McHenry

ALS, DLC:GW; LB, DLC:GW; ADf, MdAA: James McHenry Collection.

1. The annexed document from Maj. Thomas Humphrey Cushing has not been identified.

2. GW replied to McHenry on 22 June.

From Alexander Hamilton

Sir   [New York, c.16 June 1796]

I have received information this morning of a nature which I think you ought to receive without delay—A Mr *Le Guen*, a Frenchman, a client of mine and in whom I have inspired confidence, and who is apparently a discreet and decent man, called on me this morning to consult me on the expediency of his becoming naturalized, in order that certain events between France and the U. States might not prejudice him in a suit which I am directed to bring for him for a value of 160,000 Dollars[1]—I asked him what the events to which he alluded were—He made me the following reply under the strictest injunctions of confidence. "I have seen a letter from *St Thonax*[2] to Mr *Labagarde* of this City—informing him that a plan was adopted to seize all American vessels carrying to any English Port provisions of any kind to conduct them into some French Port, if found to be British property to condemn them, if American, to take them on the *accountability* of the Government—adding that he must not thence infer that it was the intention to make war upon the U. States—but it was with a view to retaliate the conduct of Great Britain, to keep supplies from her, and to obtain them for themselves, and was also bottomed on some political motives not necessary to be explained. That it was also in contemplation when Admiral Richery arrived, if the Ships could be spared to send five sail of the line to this Country." Fearing he said that this might produce a rupture between the two Countries he had called to consult me on the subject &c.[3]

I asked his permission to make the communication to you—He gave me leave to do it, but with the absolute condition that the knowlege of names was on no account to go beyond *you* and *myself.* I must therefore request Sir that this condition be exactly observed[4]—He has promised me further information.

I believe the information, as well because the source of it under all the circumstances engages my confidence, as because the thing appears in itself probable—France wants supplies and she has not the means of paying & our Merchants have done creditting.

It becomes very material that the real situation should as soon as possible be ascertained & that the Merchants should know on what they have to depend. They expect that the Government will ask an explanation of Mr Adet & that in some proper way the result will be made known.

It seems to become more and more urgent that the U. States should have some faithful organ near the French Government to explain their real views and ascertain those of the French— It is all important that the people should be satisfied that the Government has made every exertion to avert Rupture as early as possible.[5] Most respectfully & Affect. I have the honor to be Sir Yr Obed. serv.

A. Hamilton

ALS, DLC:GW; copy, in GW's writing, DLC:GW; copy, DLC: Hamilton Papers. GW docketed the ALS: "without date But recd the 23. June 1796." The cover of the ALS was addressed to GW at Philadelphia, which he had left for Mount Vernon on 13 June (see GW to David Humphreys, 12 June). Secretary of the Treasury Oliver Wolcott, Jr., then at Philadelphia, began a letter to Hamilton on 17 June: "I have your Letters of the 15th. & 16th. instant—that for the President will go on by the next mail" (*Hamilton Papers*, 20:230–33). The dating presumes that Wolcott referred to this letter. GW enclosed the copy in his writing in a letter to Secretary of State Timothy Pickering dated 24 June (see also GW to Wolcott, same date). He wrote at the top of that enclosure: "Copy— (given in confidence, and to be returned to G.W.)." He wrote at the bottom of the same copy: "This letter has no date; but came by the Post of Wednesday, to Alexandria, under cover from The Secretary of the Treasury."

1. The merchant Louis Le Guen (c.1757–c.1830), a native of St. Malo, France, came to New York in 1794. At the July 1796 term of the New York Supreme Court of Judicature, Hamilton instituted action in Le Guen's suit against Isaac Gouverneur, Jr., and Peter Kemble. For the cases involved in the dispute among these men over the handling of goods that Le Guen brought to New York, see Goebel, *Law Practice of Hamilton*, 2:48–164. Le Guen's applications for citizenship apparently never succeeded (see Le Guen to Hamilton, 13 July 1799, in *Hamilton Papers*, 23:263–65; and Le Guen's petition to Richard Peters, sworn on 31 Aug. 1810, when he resided in Philadelphia, in DNA: RG 21, Naturalization Petitions for the Eastern District of Pennsylvania).

2. Hamilton placed an asterisk here to reference a marginal note that reads "Santhonax." Léger Félicité Sonthonax, formerly among the French commissioners governing Saint Domingue, recently had returned to the island as one of several special agents sent to reassert French control.

3. The letter from Sonthonax has not been identified, but "A CITIZEN" sent to John Fenno a different summary of what was surely the same letter. Fenno printed it in his *Gazette of the United States* (Philadelphia) for 20 June. That summary expanded on the political motives and explained that mer-

chants "who have so zealously supported" the Jay Treaty "should see that there
are two sides to the question, and that by temporizing with our enemy, they will
not enjoy that full exemption from the inconveniences of war which they have
promised themselves. It is also essential that we should support our friends in
America, by fulfilling their predictions of evil from the treaty." The French
republic did not desire "a final rupture" with the United States, "and we have
no fears that it will come to an open breach with us. Notwithstanding the coalition between PITT and WASHINGTON, we are well assured by our confidential
friends that the attachment of the American people to the French nation will
oblige the government to be passive, and that if its folly should prompt it to a
r[u]pture with us, there will be more to put on the tri-coloured cockade, than
to join the standard of the hypocritical Washington." A copy of that newspaper,
with a manicule directing attention to "A CITIZEN's" letter, is in DLC:GW.

The recipient of the letter most likely was Peter Delabigarre (d. 1807), a
New York City merchant.

Admiral Richery's fleet remained on station at Cadiz, Spain, until August
1796, and then operated off Newfoundland before returning to France that
November.

Joseph de Richery (1757–1799), a career officer in the French navy, had
been promoted to admiral in early 1796.

4. On the copy of this letter in his writing, GW rendered as blanks all the
names and the sum involved in the lawsuit.

5. GW replied to Hamilton on 26 June.

From Oliver Ellsworth

Sir,   Baltimore June 19 1796.

I had the misfortune to pass you & Mrs Washington without
knowing it.[1] You will be pleased, however, to accept of my wishes
that your present retreat may be undisturbed, and that you may
know, for a few days at least, how much more happifying it is to
converse with the works of nature than with the wiles of man.
In the mean time I believe you may rest assured that the publick mind, as well Southward as elsewhere, is pretty tranquil, and
much more so than it would have been had our Country been
dishonored and exposed by a violation of her faith.[2] But one
game more of the present System remains, and that respects the
next quadrennial election, and is to be played only on condition
that the electors are restrained in the objects of th[e]ir choice.
I have the honor to be Sir, with the highest respect Your most
obedient and most humble Servt

                                          Oliver Ellsworth

ALS, DLC:GW.

1. On his return from attending circuit courts in southern states, Ellsworth presumably passed GW on the road south of Baltimore (see Ellsworth to Abigail Ellsworth, 20 March, in *Documentary History of the Supreme Court*, 3:99,101).

The *Maryland Journal, & Baltimore Advertiser* for 17 June printed an item on GW's arrival in Baltimore the previous day "at the *Fountain Inn*" with "his LADY, G. W. M. LAFAYETTE, and suite. In the evening he was waited on, and congratulated by a number of the most respectable characters; a general satisfaction was expressed by the Citizens of Baltimore on the arrival of this illustrious man.

"He leaves town this morning on his way to Mount Vernon." GW then stopped at Bladensburg, Md., and the Federal City (see the entries for 17–19 June 1796 in Cash Memoranda, 1794–1797).

2. Ellsworth is referring to the failed effort in the House of Representatives to refuse funding for implementation of the Jay Treaty.

From Thomas Jefferson

Dear Sir   Monticello [Va.] June 19. 96.

In Bache's Aurora of the 9th inst. which came here by the last post a paper appears which, having been confided, as I presume, to but few hands, makes it truly wonderful how it should have got there.[1] I cannot be satisfied as to my own part till I relieve my mind by declaring, and I attest every thing sacred & honorable to the declaration, that it has got there neither thro' me nor the paper confided to me. this has never been from under my own lock & key, or out of my own hands. no mortal ever knew from me that these questions had been proposed. perhaps I ought to except one person who possesses all my confidence as he has possessed yours.[2] I do not remember indeed that I communicated it even to him, but as I was in the habit of unlimited trust & counsel with him, it is possible I may have read it to him. no more: for the quire of which it makes a part was never in any hand but my own, nor was a word ever copied or taken down from it, by any body. I take on myself, without fear, any divulgation on his part. we both know him incapable of it. from myself then or my paper this publication has never been derived. I have formerly mentioned to you that, from a very early period of my life, I had laid it down as a rule of conduct never to write a word for the public papers. from this I have never departed in a single instance: & on a late occasion when all the world seemed to be writing, besides a rigid adherence to my own rule, I can say with truth that not a line for the press was ever communicated to me by any other: except a single petition referred for my correction; which I did not correct however tho the contrary, as I have heard, was said in a public place, by one person through error, thro' malice by another. I learn that this last has thought it worth his while to try to sow tares between you & me, by representing me as still engaged in the bustle of politics, & in turbulence & intrigue against the government. I never believed for a moment that this could make any impression on you, or that your knolege of me would not overweigh the slander of an intriguer, dirtily employed in sifting the conversations of my table, where alone he could hear of me, and seeking to atone for his sins against you by sins against another who had never done him any other injury than that of declining his confidences. political conversation I really dislike, & therefore avoid where I can without affectation. but when urged by others, I have never concieved that having been in public life requires me to bely my sentiments, nor even to conceal them. when I am led by conversation to express them, I do it with the same independance here which I have practised every where, and which is inseparable from my nature. but enough of this miserable tergiversator, who ought indeed either to have been of more truth or less trusted by his country.[3]

While on the subject of papers permit me to ask one from you. you remember the difference of opinion between Hamilton & Knox on the one part & myself on the other on the subject of firing on the Little Sarah, and that we had exchanged opinions & reasons in writing. on your arrival in Philadelphia I delivered you a copy of my reasons in the presence of Colo. Hamilton. on our withdrawing, he told me he had been so much engaged that he had not been able to prepare a copy of his & General Knox's for you, and that if I would send you the one he had given me he would replace it in a few days. I immediately sent it to you, wishing you should see both sides of the subject together. I often after applied to both the gentlemen but could never obtain another copy. I have often thought of asking this one or a copy of it back from you, but have not before written on subjects of this kind to you. Tho' I do not know that it will ever be of the least importance to me yet one loves to possess arms tho' they hope never to have occasion for them. they possess my paper in my own handwriting. it is just I should possess theirs. the only thing amiss is that they should have left me to seek a return of the paper, or a copy of it, from you.[4]

I put away this disgusting dish of old fragments, & talk to you of my peas & clover. as to the latter article I have great encouragement from the friendly nature of our soil. I think I have had both the last & present year as good clover from common grounds which had brought several crops of wheat & corn without ever having been manured, as I ever saw in the lots around Philadelphia. I verily believe that a field of 34. acres sowed on wheat April was twelvemonth has given me a ton to the acre at it's first cutting this spring. the stalks extended measured 3½ feet long very commonly. another field a year older, & which yielded as well the last year, has sensibly fallen off this year. my exhausted fields bring a clover not high enough for hay, but I hope to make seed from it. such as these however I shall hereafter put into peas in the broadcast, proposing that one of my sowings of wheat shall be after two years of clover, & the other after 2. years of peas. I am trying the white boiling pea of Europe (the Albany pea) this year till I can get the hog pea of England which is the most productive of all. but the true winter vetch is what we want extremely. I have tried this year the Caroline drill. it is absolutely perfect. nothing can be more simple, nor perform it's office more perfectly for a single row.[5] I shall try to make one to sow 4. rows at a time of wheat or peas at 12. I. distance. I have one of the Scotch threshing machines nearly finished. it is copied exactly from a model Mr Pinckney sent me, only that I have put the whole works (except the horse wheel) into a single frame moveable from one field to another on the two axles of a waggon. it will be ready in time for the harvest which is coming on, which will give it a full trial.[6] our wheat & rye are generally fine, and the prices talked of bid fair to indemnify us for the poor crops of the two last years.

I take the liberty of putting under your cover a letter to the son of M. de la Fayette, not exactly knowing where to direct to him.[7] with very affectionate compliments to Mrs Washington I have the honor to be with great & sincere esteem & respect Dear Sir your most obedt & most humble servt

Th: Jefferson

ALS, DLC:GW; ALS (letterpress copy), DLC: Jefferson Papers. GW replied to Jefferson on 6 July.

Jefferson revealed his thoughts on GW and politics more clearly when he wrote James Monroe, U.S. minister to France, on 10 July: "The campaign of Congress is closed. Tho' the Anglomen have in the end got their treaty through, and so far, have triumphed over the cause of republicanism, yet it has been to them a dear bought victory. It has given the most radical shock to their party which it has ever recieved: and there is no doubt they would be glad to be replaced on the ground they possessed the instant before Jay's nomination extraordinary. They see that nothing can support them but the colossus of the President's merits with the people, and the moment he retires, that his successor, if a Monocrat, will be overborne by the republican sense of his constituents, if a republican, he will of course give fair play to that sense, and lead things into the channel of harmony between the governors and governed. In the mean time, patience" (*Jefferson Papers*, 29:147–48).

1. Jefferson is referring to the questions in GW's letter to the cabinet of 18 April 1793 quoted in an anonymous publication criticizing GW and his administration (see GW to David Humphreys, 12 June, n.3).

2. Jefferson is referring to James Madison.

3. Jefferson commented on Henry Lee. A footnote with this letter in an early edition of Jefferson's correspondence reads: "Here, in the margin of the copy, is written, apparently at a later date, 'General H. Lee'" (Randolph, *Papers of Thomas Jefferson*, 3:330–32; "H. Lee" appears in the left margin beside this paragraph in the letterpress copy). For a contention that Jefferson wrote falsely, see *Observations on the Writings of Thomas Jefferson, with Particular Reference to the Attack They Contain on the Memory of the Late Gen. Henry Lee. In a Series of Letters, by H. Lee, of Virginia* (New York, 1832), 5–20.

4. For the exchange, see Cabinet Opinion on the *Little Sarah* [*Petite Démocrate*], 8 July 1793, and n.8; Memorandum from Alexander Hamilton and Henry Knox, same date; and Jefferson to GW, 11 July. The men disputed whether measures should be taken to detain a vessel allegedly being armed at Philadelphia to serve as a French privateer.

GW subsequently wrote Jefferson from Philadelphia on 28 Aug. 1796: "As soon as I returned to this City, and had waded through the Papers, and other matters wch were laid before me on my arrival, and claimed my earliest attention, I recollected the request in your letter of the 19th of June, and herewith enclose copies of the Papers agreeably to that request" (ALS, DLC: Jefferson Papers; LB, DLC:GW; Jefferson docketed the ALS: "recd Sep. 9").

5. Jefferson praised a seed drill that he obtained from John Taylor of Caroline (see Taylor to Jefferson, 1 June and 15 Aug. 1794, in *Jefferson Papers*, 28:93–96, 112–13).

6. Jefferson's threshing machine followed a model received from Thomas Pinckney (see Pinckney to Jefferson, 10 June 1793, in *Jefferson Papers*, 26:249–50; and Bear and Stanton, *Jefferson's Memorandum Books*, 2:935).

7. Jefferson had written George Washington Motier Lafayette on this date "to express to you the satisfaction with which I learn that you are in a land of safety where you will meet in every person the friend of your worthy father

and family. Among these I beg leave to mingle my own assurances of sincere attachment to him, and my desires to prove it by every service I can render you. I know indeed that you are already under too good a patronage to need any other . . . But I pray you to remember that should any occasion offer wherein I can be useful to you, there is no one on whose friendship and zeal you may more confidently count" (*Jefferson Papers*, 29:126–27; see also Alexander Hamilton to GW, 9 April). Young Lafayette had traveled with GW to Mount Vernon (see Oliver Ellsworth to GW, this date, n.1).

From Oliver Wolcott, Jr.

Sir,   Philadelphia June 20th 1796.

The enclosed Letters have been received by me & the Secretary of State in consequence of the death of Mr Gorham, supervisor of Massachusetts.[1] The Inspectors of Surveys are John Frothingham of the province of Maine, Jonathan Jackson of Newburyport & Leonard Jarvis of Boston. The two last with Mr Davis the present Comptroller are mentioned as Candidates.

Mr Jarvis's application does not appear to be supported; he is said to be much engaged in land speculations; his political principles are opposed to the administration of the Government, & the manner in which he has executed the office of Inspector, though not censurable so far as has come to my knowledge, has not indicated extraordinary zeal or ability. Mr Davis or Mr Jackson would I have no doubt, either of them, do justice to the appointment, & either of the persons would be free from any public objection—The appointment would suit Mr Davis who proposes to remove to Boston: Mr Jackson's claims are however of a peculiar nature. he has served long in the same department, & much of the time for a moderate compensation. the degree of order which has existed in the Revenue Department in the District of Massachusetts is much owing to his exertions. the office now vacant seems therefore to be a just object of expectation by him, and a proper reward of his merit. The force of Mr Jackson's claims are fairly admitted by Mr Davis, and though, as before mentioned the office *in itself* would be desirable, yet he feels a delicacy in being the Competition of Mr Jackson.

In case the President should appoint Mr Jackson to be supervisor—Genl John Brooks & Leonard Vassal Berland are offered as candidates for the office of Inspector.[2] I am not personally acquainted with the qualifications of these gentlemen; but from the enclosed recommendations it would appear that either of them would discharge the office with diligence & ability.

If Genl Brooks shall be appointed Inspector, Colo. Saml Bradford is warmly recommended as a proper character to fill the office of Marshal.[3]

In consequence of the recommendation of Colo. Carrington, concurring with those laid before the President in support of Mr Kirby, a commission has issued in his favor as Collector for the District of Hampton.[4]

Mr Steele has signified his acceptance of the office of Comptroller & will be here about the first of the ensuing month; he desires me to express to The President assurances of his gratitude, & of faithful exertions to merit the confidence reposed in him.

Since the President's absence I have carefully enquired into the circumstances of the capture of the Mount Vernon by a French privateer, & I have reason to believe this to be a true state of the case, which I communicate for the President's information.[5] The ship was built by Mr Murgatroyd a respectable merchant of this City—it was reported about the wharves some time since, that she was sold to Mr Duncanson. Mr Duncanson actually applied for a quantity of Rum to be shipped on board this vessel. On finding however that the vessel could not be registerred in his own name, as he had not been naturalized, some new arrangement took place with Mr Murgatroyd, in consequence of which the ship was to remain Mr M.'s property, *until her arrival in England*.[6] The Cargo, though shipped in the names of Messrs Willings & Francis,[7] I strongly suspect to be Mr Duncanson's property, & that of other Englishmen not naturalized. It is suspected, tho' this is but suspicion, that even the ship is not at Mr Murgatroyd's risque. It is certain that he has underwritten two thousand Dollars in this same vessell. This however is a delicate point, because if the Ship is in whole or in part owned by british subjects, Mr Murgatroyd must have violated the Law, if not been guilty of perjury.[8] His general character would strongly repel suspicions of this nature, yet I find he is suspected, even by candid men, of disingenuous conduct. I must therefore consider it as doubtful, to say no more, whether the Mount Vernon was not lawfully captured. In a public point of view, it would be happy if this were to appear to be the case, as it would obviate some suspicions of an unfriendly disposition on the part of France. The complexion of Bache's paper is calculated however to keep up alarm; it seems to be an object to be preparing the public mind for some new line of conduct, contrary to our Treaty & distressing to our Commerce. If Bache's paper is considered as indicating the designs of the French Government, we are to expect that british property on board our vessells will be captured, & that no englishmen will be considered as American citizens who have been naturalized since the commencement of the present war; perhaps they may proceed so far as to take all vessels bound to or from English ports.[9] Of this however I perceive no indications except what are founded on reports which I cannot trace to any authentic source.

The Democrats, or at least some of them, have been predicting that the French would soon manifest their resentment against the Government. they say as we permit the british to take our vessels, the French have a right to adopt the same line of conduct. If the French Minister has powers for the purpose & can be influenced by our people, there are enough here who would rejoice in any misfortunes which wou'd produce discontents, & thus render the Government odious. If another capture under circumstances less justifiable than those attending the Mount Vernon, were to happen, the case would in my opinion be serious—even at present there are good reasons for apprehension.[10] I have the honor to be &c.

Oliv: Wolcott Jr

Note. I am just informed that Mr Otis declines the appointment of District Attorney. On a former occasion I mentioned Mr Davis as a suitable character.[11] I have no doubt but he would execute the office with ability & that the appointment wou'd give satisfaction. I have however heard nothing from Boston, & I do not write in consequence of any intimation from Mr Davis at this time.[12]

LB, DLC:GW.

1. The enclosed letters have not been identified. Nathaniel Gorham, supervisor of revenue for Massachusetts, had died on 11 June.

2. Leonard Vassall Borland (1759–1801) was a Boston merchant.

3. Samuel Bradford (c.1759–1818), then deputy marshal, previously had been recommended for marshal (see GW to Benjamin Lincoln, 14 Aug. 1791, n.1). Bradford later served as sheriff of Suffolk County, Massachusetts.

4. Following this recess appointment, GW nominated William Kirby for collector and inspector of the revenue at Hampton, Va., on 21 Dec., and the Senate confirmed the nomination the next day (see *Senate Executive Journal,* 216–17; see also Wolcott to GW, 10 June, source note). President Thomas Jefferson removed Kirby "for delinquency in accounts" (List of Appointments and Removals, circa May 1802, in *Jefferson Papers,* 33:668–70). None of Kirby's recommendations have been identified.

5. The *Flying Fish* had captured the *Mount Vernon* (see Timothy Pickering to GW, 12 June, and n.2 to that document).

6. Philadelphia merchant Thomas Murgatroyd (c.1747–1817) previously had been a partner in the firm Rundle and Murgatroyd.

William Mayne Duncanson (d. 1812) came to the United States from India with Thomas Law in 1794 and settled at the Federal City. As a partner in the firm Duncanson and Ray, merchants at Philadelphia and the Federal City, he bought the *Delaware* and renamed the ship *Mount Vernon.* Upon the firm's dissolution in 1797, Duncanson pursued other mercantile and real estate ventures in the Federal City. For correspondence and biographical details, see Allen C. Clark, "William Mayne Duncanson," *Records of the Columbia Historical Society* 14 (1911): 1–24.

7. Thomas Willing, his son Thomas Mayne Willing, and his nephew Thomas Willing Francis conducted the Philadelphia merchant firm Willings & Francis.

8. See "An Act concerning the registering and recording of ships or vessels," 31 Dec. 1792 (1 *Stat.* 287–99).

9. Such arguments appeared in a letter from "A CITIZEN" to Benjamin Franklin Bache printed in the *Aurora General Advertiser* (Philadelphia) for 14 June 1796. "The late capture of the ship MOUNT VERNON by the French privateer FLYING-FISH, has excited just alarms, and apprehensions, and given much room for speculation—It does not appear as yet upon what grounds this capture was made, nor whether it was authorized by the constituted authorities of the French Republic. The dispositions of France towards us are sufficiently known to convince us that it is neither their wish nor their interest to engage in hostilities with this country, but from the dissatisfaction and evident disgust which they have manifested at our late treaty with Great Britain and other acts of our government, we ought to be on our guard against such measures (short of actual hostility) as their resentment might induce them to pursue.—By merely enforcing their *existing laws* respecting the navigation of neutral vessels, they have it in their power greatly to distress the navigation and commerce of the United States." A CITIZEN submitted "for publication with a few explanatory notes and observations, a translation of the Regulation of the 21st July 1778, concerning the navigation of neutral vessels, which, having never been repealed I understand is still considered as a part of the laws of France and has only been suspended in practice during the present war out of respect to neutral nations and particularly to the United States." In his commentary, A CITIZEN highlighted the clause that allowed France to abandon "the principle *free ships make free goods,* if the same was not recognized within a limited time by the other Belligerent powers" and the clause that refused to recognize "the naturalization of their enemies in a neutral country in time of war."

The *Aurora General Advertiser* for 17 June printed under the heading "COM-MUNICATION" a commentary on citizenship: "*A British subject cannot renounce his allegiance.* This is the law of Great Britain and this is the practice. If an Englishman cannot dispense with his allegiance . . . he ought to be considered as a subject of that monarchy, let his residence be where it might, and let his pretended citizenship be here or elsewhere. . . . If this view of the subject is a just one, the name of American citizen ought not to be a protection to the property of a British subject; for certainly if Great Britain claims him as her own, the French Republic have no right to dispute the point. Principles of common justice (retribution out of the question) would then justify the French Republic in considering as British property, every thing held by any man who emigrated to this country from Great Britain since the peace."

The *Aurora General Advertiser* for 20 June also reprinted "From the (N.Y.) ARGUS" an item on the Jay Treaty: "We have made it lawful for the captains of British cruisers to carry in our vessels on bare *suspicion* of having enemy's property on board. This authorizes the French to do the same; although no[t]hing in our treaty with that nation gives them this privilege, yet giving it to Britain gives it equally to them." Referencing "the most favoured nation" clause in Article II of the 1778 Treaty of Amity and Commerce with France, that nation enjoyed "every favour we have granted the British in our late treaty . . . and it appears they mean to avail themselves of it." Moreover, since a British court "lately" ruled "that all British subjects, who came to this country since the declaration of independence, as well as those who were here before, but who remained in their lines, are bona fide British subjects. This, no doubt, the French will readily agree to, and seize our vessels and property where-ever they find them" (see also Miller, *Treaties*, 5).

10. Wolcott developed his views on the capture of the *Mount Vernon* in correspondence with Alexander Hamilton, whom he had written on 14 June: "If more seizures shall be made, or if Mr Adet shall not give a satisfactory explanation, I do not see but that Mr. M[onroe] *must* be recalled & a special confidential Minister sent. A short time will enable us to judge. I shall be glad to know your opinion of what is to be done—if a Minister is sent, who should it be?" (*Hamilton Papers*, 20:220–22). Hamilton replied to Wolcott from New York on 15 June: "From some recent information which I have obtained here, I have scarcely a doubt that the plan of the French is—1 to take all enemy property in our Ships contrary to the Treaty between the two Countries 2 to seize and carry in all our vessels laden with provisions for any English Port. Among this all that they choose to think enemy property will be seized & for the residue they will promise to pay."

"The state of things is extremely serious. The Government must play a skilful card or all is lost. . . .

"Moreover the Government must immediately set in earnest about averting the storm. To this end a person must be sent in place of Monroe." Hamilton suggested Charles Cotesworth Pinckney, John Marshall, Henry William De-Saussure, Bushrod Washington, James McHenry, and Richard Peters, deemed "eligible in different degrees—either of them far preferable to Monroe. . . . PS After turning the thing over and Over in my mind I know of nothing better that you have in your power than to send McHenry. He is not yet obnoxious to the French and has been understood formerly to have had some kindness towards their Revolution. . . . He is at hand & might depart immediately & I believe he would explain very well & do no foolish thing. Though unusual, perhaps it might be expedient for the President to write himself a letter to the Executive directory explaining the policy by which he has been governed and assuring of the friendship. But this would merit great consideration. Our measures however should be prompt" (*Hamilton Papers*, 20:223–24). In his reply to Hamilton, written at Philadelphia on 17 June, Wolcott explained matters regarding the *Mount Vernon* in a manner similar to the letter he wrote GW on this date. Wolcott then continued: "Mr. Adet I understand has written to Colo. Pickering that the Privateer was Commissioned by the French Government of Sn. Domingo, *but that he is ignorant what the orders of the Privateer are, or what orders the French directory in the West Indies are authorised to give in respect to Neutral Vessells.* This answer is neither satisfactory nor the contrary—it is nothing—except that it leaves ground to suspect that the West India Directory possess some discretionary authority, which may be used to distress us, if circumstances should render it expedient. What now gives me more concern than the capture, is the compliance of Baches paper, which is I think calculated to prepare the public mind, to expect a new course of conduct by the French, contrary to our Treaty, & distressing to our Commerce.

"I have for some time been inclined to think that Mr. Munroe ought to be recalled, but as others have doubted, & as the thing was not demonstrable I have not urged it, every event shews however new reasons for believing, that we must stop the channells by which foreign poison is introduced into our Country or suffer the government to be overturned—at all hazards the attempt must be made" (*Hamilton Papers*, 20:230–33; see also Pickering to GW, 22 June, and n.1 to that document). Wolcott again wrote Hamilton on 28 June: "Though the capture of the Mt. Vernon is not a decided evidence that the French mean to contravene their Treaty with the U.S., yet other circumstances render it possible—a confidential character in France is therefore necessary. I do not think any of the persons mentioned by you would undertake the mission, some I know will not." Wolcott asked Hamilton for his opinions on William Loughton Smith, U.S. senator from South Carolina, and John Quincy Adams, recently nominated as minister to Portugal (*Hamilton Papers*, 20:242–44; see also GW to the U.S. Senate, 28 May).

11. For the nomination of Harrison Gray Otis as district attorney for Massachusetts, see Pickering to GW, 24 May, n.2. Wolcott's prior recommendation of John Davis has not been identified. For consideration of Davis, see GW to Wolcott, 4 July, found at GW to Wolcott, 6 July, n.1; and Pickering to GW, 26 July. GW nominated Davis on 21 Dec. (see GW to the U.S. Senate, that date, DNA: RG 46, entry 42).

12. GW replied to Wolcott from Mount Vernon on Friday, 24 June: "Your Letter of the 20th Instant with its enclosures was brought to Alexandria by the Post of Wednesday.

"I have no difficulty in deciding on the following appointments, & commissions may issue accordingly.

"Jonathan Jackson, to be Supervisor of Massachusetts; vice Nathal Gorham, deceased.

"John Brooks to take the place rendered vacant by the removal of Jona. Jackson—and

"Samuel Bradford, to be Marshal of that District, if Brooks accepts the Inspectorship, now held by Jackson.

"I am equally disposed to appoint Mr Jno. Davis, District Attorney of that State, in case of the non-acceptance of it by Mr Otis—& provided his professional knowledge (of which I am no judge & never heard much) is supposed to be competent to the duties, & his residence such as will enable him to discharge them with convenience to the call upon the Office.

"Of this date I have written to the Secy of State on an interesting subject, requesting him to deliberate with you & the Secretary of War on the purport of the Communication, & to transmit me the result. To this letter & its enclosure I shall refer you" (LB, DLC:GW; see also Pickering to GW, 22 June, and GW to Pickering, 24 and 27 June).

From the Commissioners for the District of Columbia

sir   Washington, 22nd June 1796

The board, pursuant to your request, have had under consideration the propriety of permitting the erecting of wooden buildings in the City, & enclose you the result—should you be of opinion that the proposed suspension should take place, they have forwarded a sketch of the form which appears to them to be proper.[1]

We are happy to have it in our power to inform you, that a letter has been received from Messrs Morris & Nicholson, strengthe[n]ing the hope of their soon being down with a considerable supply of Cash[2]—Not altogether relying on their promises, we have written to the Secretary of the Treasury and to the President and Directors of the Bank of Columbia, making propositions for a temporary Loan, to neither of which Letters, we have yet received an answer.[3] We have the honor to be With Sentiments &c.

G. Scott
W. Thornton
A. White

LB, DNA: RG 42, Records of the Commissioners for the District of Columbia, Letters Sent.

1. GW approved the form and returned a signed executive order dated 25 June when he replied to the commissioners on 26 June. GW likely requested an allowance to erect wooden buildings in conversation with the commissioners on 19 June, when he spent the day at the Federal City (see Oliver Ellsworth to GW, 19 June, n.1).

2. Robert Morris and John Nicholson wrote Alexander White on 13 June that "as we are preparing for our Journey to the City of Washington you may rely that one or both of us will set out in the course of this Week and bring with us the means of making a handsome payment to the Commissioners" (DNA: RG 42, Records of the Commissioners for the District of Columbia, Letters Received).

3. The commissioners wrote Secretary of the Treasury Oliver Wolcott, Jr., from Washington, D.C., on 20 June: "We are informed by the President of the United States that he has had some conversation with you on the subject of aiding us with money, through the agency of the Bank of the United States for the purpose of erecting the public buildings in this City—At his desire, we now apply for more particular information: should the proposed purchase of the lately created 6 ⅌ cent Stock, take place at what rates would it sell in small quantities, say 3 or 4000 Dolls. weekly, or 10, 12 or 15000 Dollars ⅌ month? And what will be the nature of the security required by the Bank, for the repayment? . . . We wish for a speedy communication of your sentiments, the affairs of the City requiring immediate supplies, should we fail in this, there ought to be no delay in pursuing other measures" (DNA: RG 42, Records of the Commissioners for the District of Columbia, Letters Sent).

Wolcott replied to the commissioners on 27 June that no stock sales had "yet been made, nor can any judgement be formed how extensive the applications will be; there is no probability however that the whole sum of Two Millions & an half will be applied for, on the first of July—The price which the Stock will command in the Market is a matter of uncertainty; the late intelligence from Europe announcing the recommencement of hostilities will depress the price lower than it otherwise would have been, perhaps it may prevent the sale of any considerable sum at present—It will be most safe for the Commissioners to wait until after an experiment has been made by sales in the Market; when the present value of the Stock must be ascertained—If however the Commissioners choose to become purchasers in the first instance, their application may be made either here or at the Office of Discount & Deposit at Baltimore.

"I do not find any probability of being able to obtain a direct Loan from the Bank of the United States, as the means of that Institution are inadequ⟨ate⟩ to the demands of the Merchants of this City" (DNA: RG 42, Records of the Commissioners for the District of Columbia, Letters Received).

The commissioners wrote the president and directors of the Bank of Columbia on 21 June: "The gentlemen of your board are too well informed of the finances of the City Not to know, that we have, for some time, been strugling with great difficulties on that score." After discussing their prospects for money from The Netherlands and reviewing their relationship with the bank (to whom they owed "about 42,000 Dollars"), they proposed to borrow

$58,000 at 6 percent interest "to be paid to us in four equal monthly instalments—the first payment to be made on the first day of Augt & so monthly, until the whole sum shall be paid—The whole of our debt of 100,000 Dollars to the Bank to be secured by note, to bear an Interest of 6 ℔ cent & payable 6 months after date, & to be endorsed to your satisfaction. . . .

"This is intended as a proposition to the Bank for consideration, & we do not wish any measures to be taken, until we hear from the Secretary of the Treasury" (DNA: RG 42, Records of the Commissioners for the District of Columbia, Letters Sent).

To James McHenry

Sir,   Mount Vernon 22d June 1796.

Your letters of the 14th & 15th instant have been received, but not in time to have been answered by the Post of Monday last; being then on my Journey to this place.[1]

The ground on which you place the compliance with Lieutt Geddes's request, appears to be the best the nature of the case is *now* susceptible of; and for that purpose, I return the Proceedings of the Court Martial and other Papers relative thereto, that they may be forwarded to the Commandant at West point.

As Major Cushing founds his application for a furlough (among other reasons) on his having been on duty ever since he entered the service in the Year 1791—and because he was permitted to visit his friends in the Eastern States I think he ought to be endulged in a *reasonable* absence from the Army; counting the time he has spent in Philadelphia as part of it—although it was Not the place to have effected the last of the objects beforementioned; and surely not the best for restoring health, that had been debilitated by a severe intermittant last autumn; (another reason he has assigned in favor of the indulgence he solicits).[2]

I forgot to obtain a certified copy from the Office of State (with the Seal annexed) of the Act Guaranteeing the loan for the use of the Federal City—and another respecting (if I recollect rightly) the authenticity of the Commissioners appointment both of which were deemed necessary to accompany the Power of Attorney to Messrs Willinks.[3] Let these be sent to me by the return Post, & I will cause triplicates to be forwarded from hence to those gentlemen in order to insure the arrival of one sett.[4]

ADf, DLC:GW; LB, DLC:GW.

1. The previous Monday was 20 June. For GW's travel to Mount Vernon, see his letter to David Humphreys, 12 June, and Oliver Ellsworth to GW, 19 June, n.1.

2. McHenry had written Maj. Thomas Humphrey Cushing on 30 May that GW would not grant a further extension of his furlough without additional inquiry: "I have submitted to the President your letter of yesterday and the complaint which it includes relative to Major General Wayne. . . .

"Were it to be permitted to Officers holding military commissions to withdraw from duty upon every representation of dissatisfaction with their commander on apprehension that if present with the Army they would be neglected in the distribution of commands or from a fear that their General would act towards them contrary to the regulations of the Army and a sound direction; were I say such reason to be considered as sufficient to obtain furloughs it would inevitably lead to a state of things which must soon destroy any army.

"You will perceive therefore in this answer of the Presidents, those principles of discipline and subordination which it is his duty to enforce and that of every officer to practice" (PHi: Wayne Papers). Cushing's letter of 29 May has not been identified.

3. For the requested act authorizing a loan, see GW to the Commissioners for the District of Columbia, 22 May, and n.1 to that document; for the power of attorney, see the commissioners to GW, 13 May, n.1, and GW to the commissioners, 30 May, and the source note to that document.

4. McHenry acknowledged this letter when he wrote GW on 27 June.

From Timothy Pickering

Sir,   Department of State June 22. 1796.

I have the honor to inclose a translation of Mr Adet's letter relative to the capture of the ship Mount Vernon. It seems to be studiously reserved. Besides the case in question, my letter invited a frank & candid communication of any information on the subject. Whatever orders the Directory may have given to their new Commissioners gone to St Domingo, relative to neutrals trading with the enemies of the French Republic, it is plain such new orders could not have been furnished to the privateer called the Flying Fish, which, from the information I have received, left St Domingo, and was even probably in the port of Philadelphia, when those Commissioners arrived in the West Indies.[1]

We have heard of no more captures by the Flying Fish; and her capturing and retaining the ship Mount Vernon seems likely to have been done in expectation of eventually proving her to be

British property, of which a number of circumstances, currently reported, induce the suspicion, in the minds of many people.[2]

yesterday I received a letter from Mr DeWitt: He suspends his decision on the appointment to the office of surveyor general, until he should come to the seat of government, for which he proposed to set off by the *next stage.* His letter is dated the 14th at Albany.[3]

Harrison Gray Otis who was appointed District Attorney for Massachusetts, declines accepting the office. Mr Wolcott says that Mr Davis, the Comptroller, would be gratified by an appointment to that office, when he quits the office of comptroller.

The death of Mr Gorham, supervisor of Massachusetts, presents Mr Jonathan Jackson, now an inspector in that department, as a candidate for the vacant office. He is so well known to you, either personally or by former recommendations of gentlemen who knew his worth, that no new testimonies in his favour seem necessary.

General John Brooks, the present marshall of that district, desires to succeed to Mr Jackson's office: and Colonel Samuel Bradford, now the deputy marshall, who resides at Boston, and has to universal acceptance, done nearly all the business of the Marshall, desires to succeed General Brooks. The general, as well as Judge Lowell, speaks of Colo. Bradford in terms of perfect approbation.[4]

Captain OBrien remained here several days longer than I expected.[5] When I pressed his departure last week I found he was waiting for some spare topmasts & yards which were making. Yesterday at one o'clock I delivered him his dispatches for Colo. Humphreys, and he was to sail before the evening. Mr Humphreys the naval constructor and Mr Fox are making calculations & forming a draught of the proposed frigate, without which proper directions for building her cannot be given.[6] The greater part of the timber sufficiently seasoned may probably be collected from the various public yards.[7] I am with the highest respect sir your most obt servant

Timothy Pickering

ALS, DNA: RG 59, Miscellaneous Letters; LB, DNA: RG 59, GW's Correspondence with His Secretaries of State; LB, DNA: RG 59, Domestic Letters.

1. Pickering had written French minister Pierre-Auguste Adet on 13 June (see Pickering to GW, 12 June, n.2). Adet replied to Pickering on 14 June; his

letter reads in translation: "I have received the letter you did me the honor to write me relative to the seizure of the Ship Mount Vernon, by the French privateer flying-Fish.

"I am vexed, sir, not to have it in my power to give you the information you request of me. I cannot say whether the privateer which is certainly a vessel commissioned by the Republic and come from St Domingo to this port, has or has not acted conformably to orders which have been transmitted to her; I do not know the instructions given by the Directory to its Commissioners in the Colonies, nor do I know what conduct it has prescribed to them to cause to be observed by the armed vessels under their orders, in regard to neutrals trading with the enemies of the Republic. It is impossible for me, at this moment, to furnish you with precise explanations. I shall, therefore, write to the colonies to obtain them, and I will immediately transmit to you what shall come to my Knowledge, as well as to this point as concerning the event which is the object of your letter" (DNA: RG 59, Miscellaneous Letters).

In late January 1796 the Directory appointed a commission of five agents—Léger Félicité Sonthonax, Julien Raimond, Pierre Leblanc, Marc Antoine Giraud, and Philipe Roume—to reassert French control over Saint Domingue. The commissioners arrived at Cap Français on 11 May.

2. See Oliver Wolcott, Jr., to GW, 20 June, and notes 6, 9, and 10.

3. Simeon DeWitt's letter has not been identified, but see GW to the U.S. Senate, 28 May (second letter).

4. For the officials mentioned in the previous three paragraphs, see Wolcott to GW, 20 June, especially notes 11 and 12.

5. For Capt. Richard O'Bryen, see Pickering to GW, 10 June, and n.5.

6. For the frigate intended for the dey of Algiers, see GW to same, 13 June, and n.4 to that document.

Josiah Fox (1763–1847) trained as a shipwright in Great Britain before coming to the United States in 1793. He was employed as a War Department clerk in 1794 with the understanding that he would assist Joshua Humphreys design frigates for the U.S. Navy (see Henry Knox to Fox, 16 July 1794, in MaSaPEM: Josiah Fox Papers). Fox officially became a naval constructor in 1798 and remained involved with public and private shipbuilding until about 1811, when he moved west and eventually settled at Colerain, Ohio.

7. GW replied to Pickering on 27 June.

From John Dandridge

Dr Sir,   New Kent [Va.] June 23: 96

I cannot help saying that I am sorry to be obliged sometimes to trespass on the little time that you have to spare from attending to the many cares which your public & private affairs must ingage you in; but I will not aggravate my trespass by a tedious apology.

Being about to remove some distance from where I now

live, & being possessed of the wives & children of Frederic and George two of the Slaves lent by you to my mother, they will be separated unless I can purchase them of you: I will therefore thank you to say whether I can have them & at what prices. They sold each at £60—under your execution & I suppose both about 31 or 32 years of age. A boy called Burwell now about 14 yrs old & another called pleasant about 11 or 12 yrs old have been raised by relations in my Family, & these I shall also be glad to purchase in the same way if you have no objections.[1]

My mother shall not be injured by parting with them as I will take care to compensate her for the use of them.[2] I am respect-fully yr obt Sert

J. Dandridge

N.B.
Burwell sold @ £22.10
pleasant @ 13.10

ALS, DLC:GW.

1. For the loan of slaves to Mary Burbidge Dandridge, see GW to John Dandridge, 2 Oct. 1791. The slaves had belonged to Mary's husband, Bar-tholomew Dandridge, Sr., but following his death came into GW's possession to satisfy a debt (see GW to Burwell Bassett, Jr., 3 Feb. and 9 March 1788, in *Papers, Confederation Series*, 6:78–79, 149; see also Ledger B, 280).

2. GW replied to John Dandridge on 11 July.

To Timothy Pickering

Sir,   Mount Vernon 24th June 1796.

The information contained in a letter of which the enclosed is a correct copy, (with the reservation only of names, agree-ably to the request of the writer) may serve as a comment upon the conduct of the Owner of the Privateer Flying Fish; and as a developement also of the intentions of the French government so far as it relates to the Commerce of the United States with Great Britain.[1] The communications in the last numbers of the Aurora (that I have seen) afford still further evidence of this system, and are calculated most evidently to prepare the public mind for this event, at the sametime that they labour to make it appear that the Treaty with that Country is the cause of such conduct in France.[2]

The source from whence the information is derived, cannot,

as to its authenticity & knowledge of facts, be doubted; of course if the persons thro' whom it has passed to the reciter, are not mistaken in their details, the mos⟨t⟩ entire credit is to be given to the Account.

Under these impressions, and the serious aspect they present, it is my request that you, and the Secretaries of the Treasury and War would meet—Consult the Treaties—the Laws of Nations & of the United States, which have any relation to the subject—and, after mature deliberation, to Report to me your opinions of the measures which you conceive ought to be adopted under such information and circumstances—particularly

1st. Whether immediate explanation should be asked on this subject from the Minister of the French Republic, in Philadelphia—And in that case (which I am inclined to think is right) to proceed without delay, of sending to me, to make the requisition accordingly: unless from the tenor of the answer to the letter you had draughted before I left Philadelphia respecting the Capture of the Mount Vernon, it should, in your judgments, be rendered unnecessary.[3]

2d Whether there is power in the Executive, and in that case, whether it would be expedient in the recess of the Senate to send an Extra: character to Paris to explain the views of this Government, and to ascertain those of France. and in the affirmative of these, to suggest for my consideration the names of such persons as, in your opinions, are best qualified to subserve these purposes.

I shall expect to hear fully from you on this interesting subject; and shall only add that, if in the investigation of it my presence in Philadelphia is deemed necessary—or if any other occurrence should require my return before the time I had allotted for it, I can, and will set out for that place so soon as I am advertised of the necessity.[4]

Go: Washington

ALS, MHi: Pickering Papers; ADf, DNA: RG 59, Miscellaneous Letters; LB, DNA: RG 59, GW's Correspondence with His Secretaries of State. The ALS reached Pickering on 28 June (see n.4 below).

1. For the enclosure, see Alexander Hamilton to GW, c.16 June. For the *Flying Fish*, see Pickering to GW, 12 June, n.2.

2. See the communications presented at Oliver Wolcott, Jr., to GW, 20 June, n.9.

3. Pickering had written French minister Pierre-Auguste Adet on 13 June (see Pickering to GW, 12 June, n.2). For Adet's reply on 14 June, see Pickering to GW, 22 June, n.1.

4. Pickering replied to GW from Philadelphia on 1 July: "I communicated to the Secretaries of the Treasury & War your confidential letter of the 24th instant, on the day of its arrival, which was on the 28th. We have since been considering the subject, and by the next post will present to you our opinions and the reasons on which they are founded. In the mean time I am authorized to say, that we think the President of the United States has not the power to originate the appointment of a minister extraordinary to France; and that the recall of Mr Monroe, by creating a vacancy, can alone authorize the sending of another minister to that country. On the expediency of this change we are agreed; and I am desired to mention it, together with the following names of gentlemen for the office, to be considered with others which may occur to you; in order that if the reasons we shall have the honor to lay before you shall appear sufficiently weighty to induce the change, time may be gained in making the choice. The names are those of Patrick Henry & John Marshall of Virginia, & of Charles Cotesworth Pinckney & William Smith of South Carolina. The Secretary of War mentioned besides, Charles Caroll of Carolton.

"At present we see no necessity of interrupting your repose or views in your retirement to Mount Vernon: Should any events appear to us to render necessary or expedient your return to the seat of government, we shall not fail to state the same for your consideration" (ALS, DNA: RG 59, Miscellaneous Letters; ALS [letterpress copy] MHi: Pickering Papers; LB, DNA: RG 59, GW's Correspondence with His Secretaries of State). For the promised opinion, see Cabinet to GW, 2 July; see also Wolcott to GW, 20 June, and n.10, and 1 July; and James McHenry to GW, 2 July.

To Oliver Wolcott, Jr.

Private

Dear Sir   Mount Vernon 24th June 1796.

If in the opinion of Judges, it is thought best for my India wine to remain undisturbed where it now is, I am content it should remain there. I had, however, directed Mr Kitt (my household Steward) to learn when it would be ready for landing; and to have it brought up, and Stored in my own Cellar; where it would not only have been safe, but would also have remained undisturbed; which may not be the case in a Merchants Cellar which is continually receiving, and disgorging its liquors; and frequently removing one Cask to get at another.[1]

You will perceive by the copy of a letter which goes from me to Colo. Pickering by the Post of tomorrow from Alexa. that, be the circumstances of the Mount Vernon as they may—there is strong ground to believe the French mean to continue the practice of siezing our Vessels in their Commerce with Great Britain. It is the Buzz of the Democrats; and the Aurora is, evidently, preparing the Public mind for the event as the *natural* consequence of the ratification of the British Treaty.[2]

This measure will merit serious consideration—and close investigation; and I hope it will meet with them accordingly, that the decisions of the Government may be wise, temperate & consistent. With very great esteem & regard I am—Dear Sir Yr affecte

Go: Washington

ALS, CtHi: Oliver Wolcott, Jr., Papers.
    1. For this wine, see GW to Wolcott, 13 June, and n.1.
    2. The letter brought to Wolcott's attention was a copy of Alexander Hamilton to GW, c.16 June, enclosed with GW to Timothy Pickering, this date.

From Thomas Mifflin

Sir.   Philadelphia 25. June 1796.

In consequence of a representation from the Inspectors of the Health-Office of the Port of Philadelphia,[1] I have exercised the power vested in me by the laws of Pennsylvania, for imposing a Quarantine on all vessels arriving from the West-India Islands; and I have the honor to inclose a copy of my Proclamation on that subject for your Excellency's information.[2] I am, Sir, with perfect respect, Your most obedt Hble Servt

Tho. Mifflin

LS, MHi: Pickering Papers; LB, PHarH: Executive Letterbooks. For GW's handling of Mifflin's communication, see his letter to Timothy Pickering, 4 July, and notes 2 and 3.
    1. The Philadelphia health inspectors had passed a resolution requesting the governor to impose a quarantine on the evening of 21 June "in consequence of the Reports which have this day been communicated to the Board, respecting the health of the West India Islands" (PHarH: Executive Correspondence, 1790–99).
    2. Mifflin enclosed a copy of a proclamation issued on 23 June: "Whereas, the Inspectors of the Health Office of the Port of Philadelphia, have reported to me, that an infectious or contagious disease exists in several of the West India Islands, so that the safety and health of the Citizens of Philadelphia require, that a quarantine should be immediately laid, on all vessels arriving in this Port from the said Islands. Therefore . . . any, and every ship or vessel

coming from any of the said West India Islands, shall be stopped and detained in the stream of the River Delaware opposite to the Health Office on State Island, to the intent that the Master or Captain, and all persons on board of such ship or vessel, shall there do, execute, and perform a quarantine of five days, and for such longer term, as the Resident Physician, with the advice of the Consulting Physician, and the Inspectors of the Health Office shall devise and prescribe" (MHi: Pickering Papers).

From J. Basset

Mr President   London June the 26th 1796

a number of observers have already written in a satisfactory manner on North America. but most of those works are unfinished and uncomplete. Mr Ebeling my friend, one of the most distinguished learned men in Germany has undertaken in 1793 the geography and general history of the United-States.[1] struck with the perfection and the powerful interest, which must be inspired by a work, which has already received in Europe the seal of approbation and esteem, I have imposed upon myself the duty of making it known in my own language. travelling and out of my country since ten years I wished to offer to it, in its misfortunes, a masterpiece of litterature, a pattern of administration, and the comforting picture of the prosperity of an Empire which under the Egid of a liberty holy and pure enjoys all the possible perfectibilities of the social contract. reason and justice have inspired me with the desire of dedicating to you sir the result of my work. the citizen who has so gloriously served his country with his sword, his learning, and the example of his civic virtues, will undoubtedly receive with kindness, the picture ingrand of that country so dear to his heart.[2] the two first volumes of the work (which work will be composed of twelve volumes) will appear in the course of this summer.[3] I will have the honor to forward you a printed Copy for yourself, Sir, and some others which I will present to the respectable body of legislators which you preside. I am with the greatest respect Mr President your most humble and just admirator,

signed basset.

Translation, DLC:GW; ALS, in French, DLC:GW.

1. For Christoph Daniel Ebeling's *Erdbeschreibung und Geschichte von Amerika: Die Vereinten Staaten von Nordamerika*, see Ebeling to GW, 10 Oct. 1793.

2. The proposed dedication (in French) and an English translation are with

Basset's letter in DLC:GW. The translation reads: "Europe, since long time, has paid you the tribute owed to the Hero, to the Philosopher, and to the legislator; I offer you one no less precious The picture of your own Country."

3. A plan of the work (in French) and an English translation are with Basset's letter in DLC:GW. The translation reads: "The plan of the work is as extensive as the division of it is simple. it is fixed by each of the united-States: the geography and history are distributed in the following paragraphs." The subsequent list of Twenty-four subjects includes "Geographical extent," climate, soil, waterways, minerals, vegetation, agriculture, wild and domestic animals, fisheries, population, Indians, manners and customs, government, finances, military, religion, education, manufacturing, commerce, and history. The plan also promised "maps corrected by the author" and "an introduction on the four states composing new England." Basset's translation was never published (see Ebeling to Joel Barlow, 16 March 1796, in "Letters of Ebeling," 286–87).

To the Commissioners for the District of Columbia

Gentlemen   Mount Vernon 26th June 1796.

On thursday last[1] I received your letter of the 22d instant, with its enclosures; and should have answered it by the Post of next day, but for many letters which I had to write by that Mail; which prevented my doing it till the succeeding one.

Approving of the proposed Suspension (until the first Monday of the year 1800) of the first and third articles of the terms and conditions declared on the 17th day of October 1791 for regulating the Materials, and manner of buildings & improvements on the lots in the City; I have subscribed, & do now return the Instrument you forwarded to me, and give it as my opinion that the sooner, & more generally it is promulgated, the better, & more advantageous it will be.[2]

I am glad to hear you have receivd fresh assurances of considerable pecuniary aids from Messrs Morris & Nicholson; and especially, that this assurance has occasioned no relaxation in your other endeavors to obtain a loan.

The strong impression I am under of the indispensable necessity of close attention, and great exertion to prepare for the reception of Congress by the year 1800, must, in addition to the propriety of the measure, apologize for my urging again, that those on whom the operation of the works materially depend, may be compelled to take their Stations convenient to the same. It cannot be tolerated, that the Superintendant, and others, whose duty it is to see that every thing moves harmoniously as well as œconomically; and who to effect these ought always to be on the spot, to receive applications & to provide instantaneously for wants, should be at the distance of thre⟨e⟩ miles from the active scences of their employments. The convenience of those who receive compensations from the public, can not—must not—be the primary object of consideration; for sure I am (be the State & condition of the public buildings in the year 1800 what they may) there will not be accomodation for Congress at *that* period within such a distance of the Capitol as to induce a removal, if those whose particular duty it is to be there, and to set an example, hang aloof, and fix the attraction another way. The consequences of such a deficiency, not only to the City, but to George Town, & all the interest thereabouts, is too evident to stand in need of prediction.

If I am urgent on this point, it is from the clearest conviction of the utility of the measure; and not from a desire to incommode one person, or to gratify another. Of this I beg you to be persuaded;[3] as also, that with great esteem & regard I am Gentlemen Your Obedient Servant

Go: Washington

ALS, DLC: U.S. Commissioners of the City of Washington records; LB, DLC:GW; copy, DLC:GW.

1. The previous Thursday was 23 June.

2. GW enclosed an executive order dated 25 June. The order quoted the first article of the regulations of 17 Oct. 1791 that required outer or party walls to be of brick or stone and the third article that set maximum and minimum wall heights. The 25 June order continued: "And whereas, the above recited articles have been found, by experience, to impede the settlement in the City, of mechanicks and others, whose circumstances do not admit of erecting houses of the description authorised by the said Regulations—It is therefore declared" that these regulations be suspended until December 1800 (DS, DLC: U.S. Commissioners of the City of Washington records).

3. The commissioners replied to GW on 29 June.

To Alexander Hamilton

My dear Sir,   Mount Vernon 26th June 1796
Your letter without date, came to my hands by wednesdays Post;[1] and by the first Post afterwards I communicated the pur-

port of it (withholding the names) to the Secretary of State; with directions to bestow the closest attention to the subject, and if the application which had been made to the Minister of France, consequent of the Capture of the Ship Mount Vernon, had not produced such an answer as to supercede the necessity, then to endeavor to obtain such explanation of the views of the French government relatively to our Commerce with Great Britain, as the nature of the case appeared to require.[2]

That the fact is, as has been represented to you, I have very little, if any doubt. Many, very many circumstances are continually happening in confirmation of it: among which, it is evident Bache's Paper, which *receives* and *gives* the tone, is endeavouring to prepare the Public mind for this event, by representing it as the *predicted,* and *natural* consequence of the Ratification of the Treaty with Great Britn.[3]

Let me ask therefore.

Do you suppose that the Executive, in the recess of the Senate, has power in such a case as the one before us—especially if the measure should not be *avowed* by authority, to send a special character to Paris, as Envoy Extraordinary, to give, & receive explanations? And if there be a doubt, whether it is not probable—nay more than probable, that the French Directory would, in the present state of things, avail themselves of the unconstitutionallity of the measure, to decline receiving him? The policy of delay, to avoid explanations, would induce them to adopt any pretext to accomplish it. Their reliance upon a party in this country for support, would stimulate them to this conduct; And we may be assured they will not be deficient in the most minute details of every occurrence, and every opinion, worthy of communication. If then an Envoy cannot be sent to Paris without the Agency of the Senate, will the information you have received, admitting it should be realized, be Sufficient ground for convening that body?

These are serious things; they may be productive of serious consequences; and therefore require very serious & cool deliberation. Admitting, however, that the Powers of the President during the recess, were adequate to such an appointment, where is the character who would go, that unites the proper qualifications for such a Mission; and would not be obnoxious to one party or the other? And what should be done with Mr M—— in that case?[4]

As the affairs of this country in their administration, receive great embarrassment from the conduct of characters among ourselves; and as every act of the Executive is mis-represented, and tortured with a view to make it appear odious, the aid of the friends to government is peculiarly necessary under such circumstances; and at such a crises as the present: It is unnecessary therefore to add, that I should be glad upon the present, and all other important occasions, to receive yours: and as I have great confidence in the abilities, and purity of Mr Jays views, as well as in his experience, I should wish that his sentiments on the purport of this letter; and other interesting matters as they occur, may accompany yours; for having no other wish than to promote the true and permanent interests of this country, I am anxious, always, to compare the opinions of those in whom I confide with one another; and these again (without being bound by them) with my own, that I may extract all the good I can.

Having from a variety of reasons (among which a disinclination to be longer buffitted in the public prints by a set of infamous scribblers) taken my ultimate determination "to seek the Post of honor in a private Station"[5] I regret exceedingly that I did not publish my valedictory address the day after the Adjournment of Congress.[6] This would have preceeded the canvassing for Electors (wch is commencing with warmth, in this State). It would have been announcing *publicly*, what seems to be very well understood, and is industriously propagated, *privately*. It would have removed doubts from the minds of *all*, and left the field clear for *all*: It would, by having preceeded any unfavorable change in our foreign relations (if any should happen) render my retreat less difficult and embarrassing. And it might have prevented the remarks which, more than probable will follow a late annunciation—namely—that I delayed it long enough to see, that the current was turned against me, before I declared my intention to decline. This is one of the reasons which makes me a little tenacious of the draught I furnished you with, to be modified and corrected.[7]

Having passed, however, what *I now* conceive would have been the *precise* moment to have Addressed my Constituents, let me ask your opinion (under a full conviction that nothing will shake my determination to withdraw) of the *next* best time, considering the present, and what may, probably, be the existing state of things at different periods previous to the Election; or rather, the middle of Octr; beyond which the promulgation of my intentions cannot be delayed.[8] Let me hear from you as soon as it is convenient; and be assured always of the sincere esteem, and affecte regard of

Go: Washington

ALS, DLC: Hamilton Papers.

1. See Hamilton to GW, c.16 June. The previous Wednesday was 22 June.

2. GW is referring to Secretary of State Timothy Pickering's application to French minister Pierre-Auguste Adet, 13 June, found at Pickering to GW, 12 June, n.2 (see also GW to Pickering, 24 June).

3. For examples, see Oliver Wolcott, Jr., to GW, 20 June, n.9.

4. James Monroe was the U.S. minister to France.

5. GW quoted loosely from act 4, scene 4, of Joseph Addison's play *Cato*.

6. Congress adjourned on 1 June. GW published his "valedictory" in September (see Farewell Address, 19 Sept., and the accompanying editorial note).

7. See GW's Draft for a Farewell Address, printed as an enclosure with GW to Hamilton, 15 May.

8. Hamilton replied to GW on 5 July.

Letter not found: to Betty Washington Lewis, 26 June 1796. Lewis wrote GW on 5 July: "I receiv'd your Letters of 26th and 29th of June."

From Betty Washington Lewis

My Dear Brother   June 26th 1796

Your letter of the 27th of April[1] I receiv'd and should have answerd it sooner but expecting you in dayly postpon'd writing untill you arriv'd at Mount Vernon, not hearing from you again on Harriots subject, I have been makeing all the enquirey I Could concerning Mr Parks that was in my power I have heard nothing to his disadvantage on the contrary he is respected by all his acquaintance he is A Constant Visitor here and I believe Harriots Affections are plac'd intirely on him, and engag'd so far as this if your consent can be obtaind.

Harriot begs you will pardon her not writing her self but hopes your being fully acquainted with her Sentiments Concerning Mr Parks will be some apology she is not well I believe her anxiety for fear of offending and not gaining your consent has Produc'd this, your long Silence has given her much uneasiness.[2]

My Dear Brother if you have any Mules for sale and can let me have one I will with pleasure pay you the Price of it I am under the necessity of purchaiseing A Work Nag and prefer A Mule.

Harriot Joines me in love and good Wishes for you and my sister Washington[3] and beleive me to be your Affectte Sister

Betty Lewis

ALS, CSmH.

    1. Lewis presumably is referring to GW's letter to her of 7 April, found at GW to George Lewis, same date, n.3. No letter from GW to his sister dated 27 April has been found.

    2. GW's niece Harriot Washington married Andrew Parks on 16 July (see Harriot Washington Parks to GW, 17 July; see also Andrew Parks to GW, 1 and 30 April, and GW to Andrew Parks, 7 April).

    3. Lewis means Martha Washington, her sister-in-law.

To Robert Lewis

Dear Sir,   Mount Vernon 26th June 1796

We arrived at this place on Monday last,[1] where it is probable I shall remain until the middle of August, when public business will require *my* attendance in Philadelphia until towards the end of September.[2] I shall then return to this place again, for Mrs Washington, with whom in the latter part of October I shall make my last journey, to close my public life the 4th of March; after which no consideration under heaven that I can foresee shall again withdraw me from the walks of private life.

I am sorry you have met with so much trouble & difficulty on account of the Land, I presumed I had an indisputable title to, on Accoceek Run; especially as by your information they appear to have been unavailing.[3] It might be well, however, before you give the matter up, to examine my Mothers Will; to see if it is not bequeathed to me in *that.*[4] I ought to have a letter from her, but I do not find it among my Papers at this place, declaratory of her intention of giving it to me; this was often done orally, but the truth is, conceiving it would come to me by descent, I never gave myself any trouble about the Conveyance. When I return to Philadelphia I will examine my Papers there, to see if the letter before alluded to can be found;[5] but even this, with the knowledge of my Mother's intentions of giving it to me, could only establish the *equitable* title; for the legal one wd still be where the Law, or Constitution of the State, has plac'd it. The whole therefore depends upon whether there be any mention of the land in the Will.

I am sorry to hear of the death of Mrs Haney; and will very chearfully receive her daughter the moment I get settled at this place; sooner it would be impossible; because this house will be, as it has been, empty from the time we shall quit it in October, until my final establishment in the Spring. Such necessaries as she needs in the meantime may, however, be furnished her at my expence, and if it is inconvenient for you to retain her in your own house, let her be boarded in some respectable family, where her morals and good behaviour will be attended to; at my expence also. Let her want for nothing that is decent and proper; and if she remains in your family; I wish for the Girls sake, as well as for the use she may be of to your Aunt when she comes here, that Mrs Lewis would keep her industriously employed, *always*, and instructed in the care, and œconomy of housekeeping.

There is another reason against her coming here until I am permanently fixed; and that is, that my house, I expect, will be crouded with company all the while we shall be at it, this Summer, as the Ministers of France, Great Britain and Portugal, in succession, intend to be here—Besides other strangers.[6]

My best wishes, to which your Aunts are united, are presented to yourself & Mrs Lewis—and I remain Your sincere friend & Affecte Uncle

Go: Washington

ALS, ViW: Washington Papers. Lewis replied to GW on 26 July.

1. The previous Monday was 20 June.

2. For GW's return to Philadelphia, see his letter to James Ross, 11 June, n.6.

3. GW begins responding to a letter from Lewis dated 5 May.

4. Mary Ball Washington's will dated 20 May 1788 bequeathed the land to GW (DLC:GW).

5. No letter from Mary Ball Washington to GW matching this description has been found.

6. For GW's anxiety over visitors anticipated at Mount Vernon, see his letter to William Pearce, 5 June, and n.3 to that document.

To George Lewis

Dear Sir, Mt Vernon 27th June 1796

Supposing you are in Fredericksburgh, and not knowing where my Sister, or your Brother Howell is at present, I put the letters for them, and your brother Bob, under one cover to your care[1] and would thank you for letting me know whether you have received them or not.

My best wishes attend Mrs Lewis & yourself in which your aunt joins me. I remain Your sincere friend & affecte Uncle

Go: Washington

ALS (facsimile), James Lowe Autographs, Catalog 25 (1983), item 179. According to an earlier sale notice, GW franked the cover of this letter and addressed it to Lewis "or in case of his absence To—Mrs. Becky [Betty?] Lewis near Fredericksbourgh. Recommd to the care of the Post master at that place" (*The Collector*, no. 9–12 [1969], item C390).

1. See GW to Robert Lewis, 26 June; GW's letters to Howell Lewis and Betty Washington Lewis have not been found.

From James McHenry

Sir, War Office 27. June 1796.

I have the honor to acknowledge the receipt of your letter of the 22d instant with its references.

No. 1. here inclosed contains the documents respecting the meditated loan for the use of the federal City.[1]

No. 2. The last letters received from Brigadier General Wilkinson with copy of my letter of the 7. May referred to in his instructions to Colonel Hamtramck.[2]

General Wilkinson you will observe by this packet has adopted a line of proceeding relative to the British posts different from what my letter suggests.

No. 3. A private letter from General St Clair, a letter from Mr Seagrove and one from Mr Hawkins.[3]

No. 4. Copies of letters to Governor Sevier founded on representations of forced settlements within the Indian boundaries which threaten very serious consequences, and a copy of a letter to the Officer commanding at Tellico appertaining to the same subject &c.[4]

I thought it best to endeavour by gentle expressions to lead the new Governor into a knowledge of his duties; and as the Indian trading houses have been attacked in the Knoxville Gazettes, to touch lightly upon their policy.

No. 5 (A) A formula of the legionary establishment representing it as it now is (B) a Scheme of the legion resolved into four regiments conformably to the Act of Congress "to ascertain and fix the military establishment of the United States.["]

According to this arrangement the Officers of the first Sub Legion become the Officers of the first regiment; those of the Second Sub Legion, the Officers of the Second regiment; those of the third Sub Legion, the Officers of the third regt; and those of the fourth Sub Legion, the Officers of the Fourth regiment, with a few exceptions, resulting from the principle of Seniority which forms the basis of the arrangement.[5]

The Scheme gives the Senior Lieut. Colonel to the first regiment; the second Lieutenant Colonel in rank to the Second regiment; the third Lieutenant Colonel in rank to the third regiment; and the fourth Lieutenant Colonel in rank to the fourth regiment. In like manner, the eight eldest Majors have been numbered from 1 to 8 agreeably to rank. No. 1 and 5 are assigned to the first regiment No. 2 & 6 to the Second regiment No. 3 and 7 to the third regiment and No. 4. and 8 to the fourth regiment; so that the Officers (a few unavoidable transfers excepted) stand attached to the men they have been accustomed to command, by which as little violence as possible is done to established habits.

You will perceive that by following implicitly the principle of seniority three Majors (one of which Major Peters is said to be a good Officer) will be deranged, and eight Captains. Only three Lieutenants will (without their consent) become supernumerary viz. McClean Cobb and Campbell. The first Genl Wayne says is somewhat insane; the other two should no resignations be given in previously to the arrangement taking place, may be tranferred to the Artillery.[6]

There being but three Lieutenants to the Cavalry, James V. Ball may be appointed Lieutenant, in which case it will become necessary to appoint another Cornet.[7]

While on this subject it may be observed also that the following vacancies exist in the Corps of Artillerists and Engineers. Viz. One Captain and nine Lieutenants.

You will be pleased to return the original letters. I have the honor to be with the greatest respect Your obedt servant

James McHenry

I have not heard from Capt. Lewis.[8]

LS, DLC:GW; LB, DLC:GW. For GW's reply, see his first letter to McHenry, 1 July.

1. GW had requested these items (see his letter to McHenry, 22 June, and n.3 to that document).

2. These enclosures have not been identified, but GW wrote an undated memorandum that evidently summarizes a letter from Wilkinson to McHenry of 19 May: "Again mentions the Annual present of Goods to the Indns as immediately necessary to be sent—reason.

"The British Minister shd be informed of the Conduct of McKee.

"The Contracters ought to have been the Issuers.

"Unexampled price given for Beef by [Abraham] Kirkpatrick in Kentucky.

"Order *all* Officers on Furlough to join their respective Corps.

"Wampum wanting 5,000 black & 15,000 White.

"Commissions wanting for the Indn Chiefs—Blue Jacket has the sample of one from the B[ritish]" (AD, NjMoHP).

3. These letters have not been identified, but Benjamin Hawkins had written McHenry from St. Marys, Ga., on 19 and 22 May about impending negotiations with the Creek Indians (see *ASP, Indian Affairs*, 1:588–89).

4. McHenry presumably enclosed copies of his letters to Tennessee governor John Sevier, 20 and 23 June, and his letter to Lt. Samuel R. Davidson, 21 June (all DLC:GW).

McHenry wrote Sevier on 20 June: "Within these few days past information has been received of numerous forced settlements on the Indian lands as confirmed to them by treaty, which threaten very serious consequences to the peace of that Country and the Union. These accounts which have given great uneasiness to the president, render it proper that instantaneous and effectual measures should be adopted to remove the intruders and prevent further intrusions.

"When I consider, Sir, your well founded knowledge of the Indian Character; that no one can be more sensible to the good that must result from a strict observance of our promises to or treaties with them . . . I feel relieved from much of the sensibility I should otherwise have experienced, convinced that you will sincerely employ this knowledge & the means in your power to preserve the Inhabitants of Tennessee in the full enjoyment of peace and the Indians in the occupancy of their rights.

"Thinking it probable that many intrusions on the Indian lands, and violations of their rights, may proceed from the ignorance in which some of the people are, of the laws made to protect them, it occurs that an extensive and impressive promulgation of these laws might tend to the preservation of the peace of the frontiers."

To that end, McHenry enclosed a copy of "An Act to regulate Trade and

Intercourse with the Indian Tribes, and to preserve Peace on the Frontiers," approved 19 May (1 *Stat.* 469–74), and urged its dissemination in a proclamation. "It would serve to convince the restless and rapacious adventurer, of your determination to discountenance their projects, and be a proof to the Indians that the state was sincerely disposed to protect their rights.

"I will not suppose that it can be the interest of any state to keep alive the flame of discord with it's Indian Neighbours, or have [it] surface from time to time, drenched with the blood of its innocent Citizens. If an extension of frontier should become necessary can there be a doubt entertained as to the mode in which it ought to be acquired. Is it not a matter of certainty, putting the injustice of the act of dispoiling a people of their property by force out of the question, that it is cheaper to buy than to take from the Indians. Upon what ground then can a nation presume to take land when it has it in it's power to purchase whatever it may want.

"Let me be permitted to believe that the great body of the inhabitants of Tennessee, will esteem it a moral, if not religious duty, to do justice to the Indians on their borders, and will conduct themselves under your administration, conformably to the laws of the United States which are founded on justice.

"As to those who may have settled on the Indian land in contempt of these laws or through ignorance of them, the president expects that you will bring into action all the means in your power, to dislodge them. He views their intrusion as a sure prelude to hostilities, and were they to be permitted to remain, as an express violation of treaty, and legitimate cause for recrimination and war; consequently he must resort to military force to effect this purpose, should your measures prove inadequate or ineffectual. But seeing how much the prosperity and honor of the State of Tennessee is concerned in dislodging these intruders, knowing that peace cannot long continue should they be suffered to remain, he cannot for a moment suppose, that you will employ less than the most efficacious means on so serious an occasion.

"Indeed, to compel these persons who have thus intruded, to retire, will be an act of great kindness to themselves. For if suffered to remain, the probability is, that they would be among the first victims of the Tomahawk. . . .

"Should war emerge notwithstanding such cares and endeavours on the part of the Magistracy of Tennessee, it will not be viewed as a Calamity which the State has brought upon itself, by having omitted what it ought to have done, or permitted what it ought to have prevented: the Succour of course which it may claim from the general Government in such a case will flow with good will, and without being embarrassed or with-held from an opinion, that it may have brought its sufferings upon itself.

"The president led by such considerations as these, anticipates from your administration; the Courts of Justice; and the good Citizens of the State the most happy issue as it regards the disquietudes excited among the Indians by the settlements in question.

"Such a co-operation on the part of the State and the people, with the measures of the general Government, he believes cannot fail to secure to it the continuance of peace; to augment that good will of the Indians; and dispose them to such relinquishments of Territory as the United States may at any time think it expedient should be purchased.

"It may not be improper perhaps to add a few remarks on some of these measures.

"With respect to the annuities stipulated to be paid them. Care is taken that the articles which compose these should be good and their delivery made without fraud or deception; for in all transactions with Indians, policy, as well as honesty require fairness of dealing.

"With respect to the public Agents resident with them. These hear all their complaints, administer in certain things to their comfort and convenience, make faithful representations to them of the intentions of the government; distribute its favors, and transmit to it their Complaints. As the Indians know that their grievances pass thro this medium to Government, if justice is delayed beyond a reasonable time it ought not to surprize, when they attempt, in such cases to become the avengers of their wrongs.

"As to the trading houses. These are meant to furnish them with such goods as they may stand in need of, in exchange for their Skins and peltry, without their being loaded with other or greater charges than will cover the expences attendant upon the Business.

"Among the effects expected from this institution may be reckoned the following.

"1. Its exempting the Indians from the frauds that they are subject to from itinerant Traders, and which have a tendency to sour them against the people of the United States and stimulate to retaliations and thefts.

"2. Its enabling Government to put a more effectual stop to the sale of spirituous liquors among them; a practice baneful to them, and productive of innumerable evils to our Citizens.

"3. Its rendering Indian supplies more dependent upon the nation, and consequently encreasing their motives to peace and a continued good understanding with the nation.

"Such being some of the evident results from the institution of public trading houses, whatever facility you can give to their establishment, it is taken for granted will be readily and cheerfully afforded.

"Calculating therefore upon your utmost aid whenever it can favor the execution of a law or its object, I mention without reserve and with pleasure the anxiety of the president to preserve to the State of Tennessee the Blessings of peace; and that you may assure its good Citizens of his earnest desire to extend to them every means of protection within his disposal, at the same time that he conceives it an indisputable requisite to their peace that the Indians should not be disturbed in the possession of their lands."

McHenry enclosed a duplicate of his letter dated 20 June when he wrote Sevier on 23 June. He also reminded Sevier "that no claims for militia services, which have not been authorized by the President, can be admitted or paid, agreeably to existing laws: . . .

"Should you therefore conceive the services of any part of the Militia to be requisite for the defence of the frontiers you will be pleased to mention it to me with the circumstances which induce the opinion and the number deemed necessary that it may be submitted to the President for his consideration and orders."

McHenry wrote Davidson: "The regulations for the preservation of peace with the Indians require, that they should not be furnished with spirituous liquors; and that no settlements should be permitted within their Country which are not authorized.

"With respect to the former you will be pleased to take immediate steps to prevent any person whatever from selling this destructive drink to them within their Boundaries and your controul, not specially authorized from this department."

McHenry enclosed the "Act to regulate Trade and Intercourse with the Indian Tribes" for Davidson's guidance regarding intrusions on Indian land. "It may, however, be expedient, before a resort to military force, as the law directs, to wait the issue of such measures as may be taken by Governor Sevier (who has been written to on the subject) unless it shall appear that delay would involve war or the most serious consequences."

McHenry also may have enclosed his letter to John McKee of 23 June acknowledging a report of encroachments on Cherokee lands (DLC:GW).

5. The enclosed arrangement has not been identified. The law approved on 30 May delineated "the military establishment of the United States, from and after the last day of October next" to be "the corps of artillerists and engineers . . . two companies of light dragoons, who shall do duty on horse or foot, at the discretion of the President of the United States; and four regiments of infantry, of eight companies each" (1 *Stat.* 483–86; quote on 483).

6. Lieutenants Howell Cobb and Joseph Campbell were transferred to the corps of artillery and engineers on 1 Nov.; Lt. Levi McLean was discharged on that date.

7. An undated table of officers, headed "Squadron of Light Dragoons" and filed with McHenry's letter, includes four lieutenants but notes that one, John Posey, had resigned on 19 Oct. 1795 (DLC:GW).

James V. Ball (d. 1818) of Virginia, who appears on the table as a cornet, received the available promotion to lieutenant. He rose to captain before his discharge in 1802, rejoined the army in 1812, and attained the rank of lieutenant colonel before his death.

8. Capt. Thomas Lewis had been sent to Canada to mediate the British evacuation of frontier posts and their transfer to the United States under terms of the Jay Treaty (see McHenry to GW, 9 May, and notes 1 and 2 to that letter).

McHenry wrote GW on "Tuesday morning," 28 June: "Capn Lewis says he was treated with much civility by Lord Dorchesters family—That the people seemed every where pleased at the prospect of a friendly intercourse with our citizens—Lord Dorchester was particular in his inquiries respecting your health, and seemed pleased to learn that you were well and looked well. I believe his Lordship is himself about seventy. Lewis could have dined out for a month at Quebec. The first toast the king of Great Britain, the second, invariably the President.

"He would [have] been back sooner but for a fever which laid him up six days in Quebec and arrested him only on his journey.

"The express not having appeared at 5 o'clock agreeably to orders has given me the opportunity to add these particulars and to congratulate you on an event which adds a large tract of Country and a wide source of commerce to the territory and industry of the United States" (ALS, DLC:GW; LB, DLC:GW; see also McHenry's second letter to GW, 27 June, and n.1 to that document).

From James McHenry

Sir.   Philadelphia 27 June 1796.

I have the honour to inclose you Adjutant General Beckwiths answer to my dispach to Lord Dorchester of the 10th of last month.[1]

I inclose, likewise, copy of the orders for the evacuation of the posts of Fort Miamis—Detroit and Michilimackinac the originals of which will leave this to-morrow morning at 5 o'clock by express.[2]

Capn Lewis delivered the orders requiring the evacuation of Oswego & Niagara to Capn Bruff at Albany. With the greatest respect I have the honour to be Sir your most obt Servt

James McHenry

ALS, DLC:GW; LB, DLC:GW. GW received this letter on 30 June in the late afternoon (see GW's first letter to McHenry, 1 July).

1. For McHenry's dispatch to Guy Carleton, Lord Dorchester, governor of the British provinces in North America, see McHenry to GW, 9 May, n.1. Col. George Beckwith replied to McHenry from Quebec on 3 June: "I have the honour to acquaint you that the necessary orders have been transmitted for the Evacuation of the Frontier Posts in the Upper Country, in which Officers Guards will be left for the security of the Works and Buildings, until the Troops of the United States shall be ready to take possession, Captain Lewis having represented that this measure would meet the Presidents wishes and be generally pleasing to your Government. This Gentleman has received the necessary orders to the Officers Commanding those Guards, that he may dispose of them according to his Instructions.

"As it does not appear that similar ideas of importance are attached to the small Posts held upon Lake Champlain and at Oswegatchie, our Parties will be withdrawn from those places in a few days.

"I have it in particular charge from Lord Dorchester to unite his cordial good wishes to yours, that the most solid and lasting Friendship may be perpetuated between the two Nations" (CaOOA: Archive Reports 1891; see also McHenry's first letter to GW, 27 June, n.8).

2. McHenry wrote the enclosed copy of orders provided at Quebec on 2 June over Beckwith's signature. The orders directed the officer command-

ing the British guard at each post to evacuate it "to such officer belonging to the forces of the United States of America, as shall produce this authority to you for that purpose and who will precede the troops destined to garrison it, by one day, in order that he may have time to view the nature and condition of the works and buildings, of which he is to receive a statement from you in writing. You will require this officer to sign a Duplicate of the statement which you are to forward to the Adjutant General at Quebeck" (DLC:GW).

From Thomas Mifflin

Sir   Philadelphia June 27th 1796
 I have the honor to inclose, for your Excellency's information, the copy of a Report from the Resident Physician of the Health Office of Philadelphia; and to request, that you will direct such co-operative measures, on the part of the Officers of the United States, as may effectually counteract the danger, which is apprehended from vessels holding an intercourse with the shores of New-Jersey, in evasion of the Quarantine prescribed under the authority of the laws of this State.[1] I am, with perfect respect Sir Your Excellency's Most obedient humble Servant
Tho. Mifflin

LS, MHi: Pickering Papers; copy, PHarH: Executive Correspondence, 1790–99; LB, PHarH: Executive Letterbooks; LB (marked over), PHarH: Executive Letterbooks. For GW's handling of Mifflin's communication, see his letter to Timothy Pickering, 4 July, and notes 2 and 3.
 1. Part of the enclosed letter of this date from James Mease to Mifflin reported that "some of the Masters of Vessels when I informed them, all were to remain on board, until the expiration of the quarantine, denied the authority of our State laws, in respect to preventing them from going to Jersey; and tho' it is clear to me, they are under the laws of Pennsylvania, which they [are] bound to obey, yet having no means to prevent their intercourse with that State, I can only answer for keeping them from our side" (MHi: Pickering Papers; see also Mifflin to GW, 25 June).

To Timothy Pickering

Sir,   Mount Vernon 27th June 1796.
 The Post of friday—to Alexandria—brought me your dispatches of the 22d instant.[1]
 Mr Adets answer to your communication, relatively to the Cap-

ture of the Ship Mount Vernon, leaves the matter as undecided as before; and his reserve may, it is to be feared, be considered as a collateral evidence of the truth of the information I handed to you in my last,[2] and contributes to shew the necessity of having a proper understanding of this matter. The Privateer Flying Fish, might not have *brought* orders for Capturing our Provision Vessels, bound to British Ports; but she might have *received* them thro' Mr Bournonville, who came out at the sametime the French Commissioners did, to St Domingo.[3]

My sentiments with respect to the Successor for the Office rendered vacant by the death of Mr Gorham; and the changes consequent of the removal of Mr Jonathan Jackson to it; were communicated by the last Post to the Secretary of the Treasury—who was also informed, that in case of the non-acceptance of the Office of District Attorney for Massachusetts, by Mr H. G. Otis I approved of its being given to Mr Davis the present Comptroller; provided his professional knowledge (of which I had no correct information) was deemed adequate to the discharge of the duties; and he wd place himself in a situation to render them conveniently to the Public.[4]

If Mr De Witt should decline the Office of Surveyor General, give me notice of it without delay; and you may accompany it with the names of persons (if any should occur or be brought to your view) as may be thought qualified for so important & trusty worthy an appointment.[5]

Are there any accounts yet from Captn Lewis? & what are the last Accts from the Western Posts?[6] Let the letter which goes under cover with this for Major Pinckney receive the earliest safe conveyance which may offer, since (as I find by the Papers) it has missed the hands of Mr King, by whom I intended to forward it.[7]

Go: Washington

ALS, NNPM; copy, DNA: RG 59, Miscellaneous Letters; LB, DNA: RG 59, GW's Correspondence with His Secretaries of State.

1. Friday was 24 June.

2. GW is referring to his letter to Pickering of 24 June that enclosed an undated communication from Alexander Hamilton.

3. The *Aurora General Advertiser* (Philadelphia) for 17 May reported that Charles François Bournonville was "appointed Secretary of the executive Directory, which the French Government has just sent out to superintend the affairs of their West-India Colonies." *The Argus, or Greenleaf's New Daily Advertiser* (New York) for 31 May and 1 June printed items that indicated Bournonville's

arrival at New York on 30 May after a voyage from Cap Français and his rapid departure for Philadelphia.

4. See GW to Oliver Wolcott, Jr., 24 June (first letter), found at Wolcott to GW, 20 June, n.12, and Pickering's second letter to GW, 26 July.

5. Simeon DeWitt declined his appointment as surveyor general (see Pickering to GW, this date, and n.2 to that document; see also GW to John Marshall, 15 July).

6. For Capt. Thomas Lewis and his mission regarding frontier posts, see James McHenry to GW, this date (first letter), n.8.

7. GW's letter to Thomas Pinckney, U.S. minister to Great Britain, has not been found, but Pickering wrote Pinckney on 13 July that a letter "from the President to you is now enclosed. Your letter of recall went by Mr King, your successor, who sailed from New York the 20th of June (DNA: RG 59, Diplomatic and Consular Instructions). The *Gazette of the United States* (Philadelphia) for 22 June had reported Rufus King's departure.

From Timothy Pickering

Sir,   Department of State June 27. 1796.

In my last I mentioned the arrival of Mr DeWitt.[1] On saturday afternoon he delivered me the inclosed letter, expressing his reason for not accepting the office of surveyor general.[2] The same day, in the forenoon, I received the inclosed letter from Colo. Thomas Tinsley of Virginia, desiring the appointment of Register of the Continental Land-Office; by which he doubtless means the office of surveyor general. The recommendations which accompanied his letter are also inclosed.[3] No other applications have been made.[4] I have the honor to be with the highest respect sir, your obt servant

Timothy Pickering

ALS, DNA: RG 59, Miscellaneous Letters; LB, DNA: RG 59, Domestic Letters; LB, DNA: RG 59, GW's Correspondence with His Secretaries of State.

1. No letter from Pickering to GW mentioning the arrival of Simeon DeWitt has been found. When Pickering wrote GW on 22 June, he mentioned only that DeWitt planned to travel to Philadelphia.

2. DeWitt delivered to Pickering a letter written at Philadelphia on Saturday, 25 June: "Since I received the appointment to the Office of Surveyor General of the United States, I have, after weighing all circumstances compared the prospects which that Office affords with those I have from my present establishment in the State of New York, and conclude they are not such as will Justify me in making a change. . . .

"I pray You, Sir, to express to the President how much I am impressed with a Sense of the Honor of being favored with this mark of his Confidence and to assure him that nothing but an Apprehension of making too great a sacrafice could have prevailed on me not to accept the office" (DNA: RG 59, Miscellaneous Letters).

3. Thomas Tinsley (d. 1822), a Revolutionary War veteran and militia colonel, represented Hanover County in the Virginia House of Delegates.

Tinsley wrote Pickering from Hanover, Va., on 11 June: "The Inclosed Letters, in support of the application, made in my behalf, by Mr Charles Lee, I have thought proper to forward to you; lest the appointments should come on, before I can personally attend. I meant to have delivered them myself, but my indisposition, for some short time past, has deprived me, of that pleasure" (DNA: RG 59, Miscellaneous Letters). Tinsley enclosed a recommendation from Henry Lee dated 28 May and recommendations from Robert Brooke, James Innes, and James Wood dated 10 June (all DNA: RG 59, Miscellaneous Letters). Henry Lee wrote from Richmond that Tinsley "has ever merited the best respects of his acquaintances from the undeviating propriety of his Conduct." Wood, who also wrote from Richmond, noted that Tinsley had "represented his County in the General Assembly for Several years, to the perfect Satisfaction of his Constituents" and demonstrated "in a very high Degree, Integrity, Industry, and Sobriety." Charles Lee's application, which could have been verbal, has not been identified.

4. GW replied to Pickering on 1 July.

To Oliver Wolcott, Jr.

Dear Sir,   Mount Vernon 27th June 1796

I have taken the liberty of putting two letters under cover to you; the one to Colo. Hamilton (in answer to that you forwarded to me) I pray you to put it under your cover, and send it on by the Post.[1] The other for Mr Kitt (my household Steward) I leave open for your perusal, to save a repet[it]ion of the same sentiments, with respect to the money and Wine.[2] With sincere esteem and regd I remain Your Affecte Servant

                              Go: Washington

ALS, NHC. A corresponding docket, indicating that the letter was received on 30 June, is at NN: Wolcott Papers. Wolcott replied to GW on 1 July.

1. GW's letter to Alexander Hamilton of 26 June replied to Hamilton's letter to GW, c.16 June.

2. The letter to Frederick Kitt, presumably from GW, has not been found.

From Thomas Lee, Jr.

Dear sir,   New York June 28th 1796

I have not been unmindful of the desire you expressed that I should make enquiry about your runaway Woman; From the information I have received she has certainly been here. This information has been gained from a free mulattoe Woman who is Cooke in a boarding house in this City kept by a Mr Marcelline, this Cooke acknowledges she is well acquained with Oney & that she has been here, says farther that she is gone to Boston— whether this last information is intended as a blind or not I cannot say, however I have spoken to a Constable of the City who has promised me to keep a watch & make search for her. I leave it with you, Sir, how far it may be adviseable for you to write to some person here about her, the enquiry on my part shall be continued as we proceed on & especially in Boston.[1]

We leave this in a day or two for Rhode Iland by Water, it would have given me great happiness could I inform you that Mrs Lees health was bettered since we left Philadelphia, on the contrary I think she has lost both flesh & strength, she with Mrs Washington[2] desire to be affectionately remembered to yourself and Mrs Washington. I have the honor to be Dear sir with great esteem your most Obedient Hble servant

                                                    Thos Lee Jr

ALS, DLC:GW.

1. The runaway woman was Ona (Oney) Maria Judge (Ona Judge Staines; 1774–1848), a dower slave maidservant to Martha Washington. After her successful escape from the Washingtons, Judge resided around Portsmouth, N.H., and married John "Jack" Staines. For a biography, see Dunbar, *Ona Judge.*

An advertisement over the name of GW's steward Frederick Kitt appeared in *Claypoole's American Daily Advertiser* (Philadelphia) for 24 May 1796. Headlined "Ten Dollars Reward," the advertisement reported Judge's flight "from the household of the President of the United States" on the afternoon of 21 May and described her as "a light Mulatto girl, much freckled, with very black eyes, and bushy black hair—She is of middle stature, but slender and delicately made, about 20 years of age. She has many changes of very good clothes of all sorts, but they are not sufficiently recollected to describe.

"As there was no suspicion of her going off, and it happened without the least provocation, it is not easy to conjecture whither she is gone—or fully, what her design is; but as she may attempt to escape by water, all masters of vessels and others are cautioned against receiving her on board, altho' she may, and probably will endeavour to pass for a free woman, and it is said has, wherewithal to pay her passage.

"Ten dollars will be paid to any person, (white or black) who will bring her home, if taken in the city, or on board any vessel in the harbour; and a further reasonable sum if apprehended and brought home, from a greater distance, and in proportion to the distance." A shorter advertisement ran in *The Philadelphia Gazette & Universal Daily Advertiser* for 23 and 24 May.

Late in life, Staines gave interviews to Benjamin Chase, who printed an account in *The Liberator* (Boston), 17 (1 Jan. 1847), p. 3; and to T. H. Adams, who published her remarks in *The Granite Freeman* (Concord, N.H.) for 22 May 1845. Speaking to Adams, Staines recalled taking passage on a ship bound to Portsmouth under the command of John Bolles. *The Philadelphia Gazette & Universal Daily Advertiser* for 13 May 1796 contained a notice that the sloop *Nancy*, with "John Bowles, master," was in Philadelphia intending to sail for Portsmouth. *The New Hampshire Gazette* (Portsmouth) for 4 June reported the sloop's arrival. These shipping facts and the recollection of Staines cast doubt on Lee's report of the runaway being sighted in New York. GW continued to pursue Judge (see his letter to Oliver Wolcott, Jr., 1 Sept., and n.4; see also GW to Joseph Whipple, 28 Nov., CSmH, and Whipple to GW, 22 Dec., DLC:GW).

The boardinghouse keeper may have been Anthony Marcellin (Claude Antoine Villet de Marcellin; d. 1816), a Revolutionary War officer from France who taught French at Columbia College from 1792 to 1799 (see *New-York Directory 1796*, p. 121; Thomas, *Columbia University Officers and Alumni*, 73; Kilbourne, *Society of the Cincinnati of Pennsylvania*, 1:629–32, 2:1292–93).

2. Lee probably is referring to Hannah Bushrod Washington (c.1738–c.1801), the widow of GW's brother John Augustine Washington and the mother of Lee's wife, Mildred Washington Lee. Mildred Lee died later in 1796 (see William Augustine Washington to GW, 12 Sept.).

From Oliver Wolcott, Jr.

sir,   Treasury Department June 28th 1796.

I have the honour to acknowledge your Letter of the 24th Instant.[1] the Commissions for the offices in the Revenue Department & the Marshal will be made out as directed. No inconvenience will attend a short delay in filling the vacancy in the office of District Attorney, as Mr Otis will attend to whatever is urgent. On this last point I shall consult the Secretary of State.

A novel & very perplexing question has arisen in respect to the Act of Congress of the last Session for the relief and protection of american seamen. It seems that an entire section of the bill as it passed the House of Representatives, has been omitted in the Act, although the Act has still a reference to what was struck out. by this defect the fourth section of the existing Law is deemed incapable of being executed.[2] After much consideration & different views of the subject, & pursuant to the advice & opinion of Council, the Secretary of State, the Secretary of War & myself have thought that the object of the Law can be properly attained by the interposition of the Executive. The form of an Act which is proposed to be sent to the Collectors of the Customs has been therefore prepared & is herewith submitted to the President's decision. That the President may judge of the difficulty which exists, copies of the Act & of the bill of the House, with Messrs Rawle's & Lewis's opinions will be herewith enclosed.[3]

I hope to be able by the next post to write to the President on the points which remain unanswered.[4] With perfect deference & attachment I have the honor to be &c.

Olivr Wolcott Jr

LB, DLC:GW; ADfS, CtHi: Oliver Wolcott, Jr., Papers.

1. Wolcott is referring to GW's first letter to him of 24 June, found at Wolcott to GW, 20 June, n.12.

2. The fourth section of the named act directed that each collector "keep a book or books, in which, at the request of any seaman, being a citizen of the United States of America, and producing proof of his citizenship, authenticated in the manner hereinafter directed, he shall enter the name of such seaman, and shall deliver to him a certificate." The act failed to specify the manner of authentication (1 *Stat.* 477–78).

3. The enclosures have not been identified. William Rawle, U.S. district attorney for Pennsylvania, and Philadelphia attorney William Lewis provided the opinions (see Charles Lee to GW, 4 July).

4. GW replied to Wolcott on 4 July, enclosed with GW's letter to Wolcott of 6 July.

From the Commissioners for the District of Columbia

Sir   Washington 29th June 1796

We had your favor of the 26th Inst. inclosing your approbation of the proposed alterations in the manner of improving in the City of Washington—We have given the necessary Instructions for their publication in the public prints of Boston, New York, Philadelphia, Baltimore, City, George Town, Alexandria, Richmond and Charleston;[1] if you think the publication ought to be more general, we shall readily give the necessary directions— We presume, that by the superintendant, our principal overseer and contractor, Capt. Williams, is meant; he is the only Officer of the City, residing in George Town to whom the Presidents sentiments on the subject of residence had not been made

known—He has long been in public service & has gained the entire approbation of the board and every person connected with
us—The contents of your Letter have been communicated to
him[2]—With respect to ourselves, we know not that we have any
thing new to add, being differently circumstanced, and perhaps,
entertaining different views—All hopes of Messrs Morris & Nicholson seem to be done away—No answer has yet been received
from either the Secretary of the Treasury or the President of the
Bank of Columbia; nor can we yet say what may be the success
of the applications We enclose you a Copy of our Letter to the
Bank[3]—We have been lately, a good deal surprised, by receiving
a Letter from Mr Hadfield, giving us notice, that he should at the
expiration of three months, agreeably to his Contract, quit the
public employment—We next day informed him that he was at
liberty to quit the business as soon as convenient to himself, &
that a sum equal to his passage to Europe, should be paid to him;
since the delivery of this Letter, he seems to have considered the
subject better & has applied to withdraw his notice, promising
every attention to carrying on the Capitol, as approved of by the
President—In consequence, we have consented to his continuance till the expiration of the three months, but by no means
relinquishing the advantage of the notice; on the contrary, expressly declaring the contract at an end, and only to be renewed
by consent of parties, at that time, if thought proper[4]—The
board have made the necessary arrangements for the recess of
a Week, which harvest will occasion—we hope and expect no
possible inconvenience can arise from it[5]—We have the honor
to be &c.

G. Scott
W. Thornton
A. White

LB, DNA: RG 42, Records of the Commissioners for the District of Columbia,
Letters Sent.

1. The commissioners wrote GW a second letter on this date: "To insure a
safe conveyance to the advertisements of the proposed alterations of the conditions of improvements, & to save expense; we have enclosed them to you, to
be franked, which we the more readily do, as the alteration is the Act of the
President, and not of the board" (LB, DNA: RG 42, Records of the Commissioners for the District of Columbia, Letters Sent).

The commissioners had authorized on 28 June the publication of GW's
executive order dated 25 June, and it appeared in *The Washington Gazette* for

29 June. Newspapers in other cities printed the executive order by 14 July (see also GW to Commissioners for the District of Columbia, 26 June, n.2).

2. The commissioners employed Elisha Owen Williams as overseer of the Federal City laborers from 1792 to 1799.

3. The enclosure has not been identified, but for the letter from the commissioners to the Bank of Columbia, see Commissioners for the District of Columbia to GW, 22 June, n.3.

4. George Hadfield had written the commissioners on 24 June stating his intent to resign (DNA: RG 42, Records of the Commissioners for the District of Columbia, Letters Received). The commissioners replied to Hadfield on 27 June: "The board have had your notice of the 24th Inst. under consideration, & also the conversation which past at the board; and supposing your present situation at the Capitol to be an unpleasant one, they feel every disposition to relieve you from it—As you are to quit the Capitol at the end of 3 months, & this fact is well known among the people; we Suspect it will be difficult to keep up due authority among them; and that it will be best for both the public and yourself that you should be relieved from your present situation immediately; and that the board should pay your passage to England, or thirty five Guineas, in lieu thereof, instead of paying you three months Salary" (DNA: RG 42, Records of the Commissioners for the District of Columbia, Letters Sent). No subsequent correspondence has been identified; the arrangement reported to GW presumably came about through conversation.

5. GW replied to the commissioners on 1 July.

Letter not found: to Betty Washington Lewis, 29 June 1796. Lewis wrote GW on 5 July: "I receiv'd your Letters of 26th and 29th of June."

From James McHenry

Sir.   War office 29 June 1796.

I beg you to sign the within authority to borrow for the use of the City of Washington and to have it returned to me with a power signed by the three commissioners. You may recollect that the one sent me for a duplicate contained only the names of two of them vz. Mr Scotts & Mr Thorntons. The Willinks may consider that power as imperfect as the law and your authority have reference to three.[1] With the greatest respect I have the honour to be Sir Your most obt St

James McHenry

ALS, DLC:GW; LB, DLC:GW; copy, DNA: RG 42, Records of the Commissioners for the District of Columbia, Letters Received. The copy is misfiled at 29 Nov. 1796.

1. Gustavus Scott and William Thornton, commissioners for the District of

Columbia, wrote McHenry from Washington on 12 July to inform him that his letter to GW and the enclosed document had been forwarded to them, but that Alexander White's absence prevented "remedying the defect" until his return. They inclosed a "Triplicate, with every necessary document to effect the loan" and requested McHenry "to have them put under cover for Messrs Willink & forwarded by the earliest Ship to Amsterdam, or any other convenient port."

Scott, Thornton, and White subsequently wrote McHenry on 20 July: "We do ourselves the honor of inclosing to you, a quadruplicate Copy of the power to Messrs Willink; with the Presidents assent to the intended Loan: the other necessary papers, to be had only at Philadelphia we beg the favor of you to procure and forward, together with the power, by the earliest conveyance to Holland" (both letters, DNA: RG 42, Records of the Commissioners for the District of Columbia, Letters Sent). For GW's certification, see Commissioners for the District of Columbia to GW, 13 May, n.1.

To Timothy Pickering

(Private)
Dear Sir,   Mount Vernon 29th June 1796

Did Mr Liston furnish the letter you asked of him, in favor of Cap: Talbots agency, to the West Indies?[1] Has any representation been made to him, independent of that application, consequent of the evidence you have recd of the Impressment of our Seamen?

When I left Philadelphia, it was expected, & from Mr & Mrs Liston[2] themselves, that they were to follow us in ten days; and allowing a few days between, the Chevr & Madam de Friere was to follow them: Since which I have not heard a word of either; and am held in suspence. I gave the French Minister also an Invitation; and understood from Mr la Fayette that he proposed to set out for this place in ten days after they did; which was three days later than my doing it.

As uncertainty with respect to the coming of these Gentlemen and their ladies (the French Minister's lady I have no reason to expect) and of the time they may be expected, is not very pleasant; some other arrangements being impeded thereby. I would thank you therefore or any of the other Gentlemen, if it can be accomplished indirectly—or at least without formality—to give me some items of their movements, and intentions; that I may know what to rely on, & regulate other matters accordingly.[3]

Is the Spanish Minister arrived in Philadelphia?[4] If so, what do you understand to be his Plan? If he is not, what accounts have you of him? With very great esteem & regard I am—Dear Sir Your affectionate

Go: Washington

ALS, MHi: Pickering Papers. For Pickering's reply, see his second letter to GW, 4 July.

1. GW is referring to Pickering's letter to Robert Liston of 25 June (see Pickering to GW, 12 June, n.1).

2. Henrietta Marchant Liston (1751–1828), the daughter of an Antigua planter, married Robert Liston in February 1796 after a lengthy acquaintance (see North, *Travel Journals of Henrietta Liston*, xiii–xviii). Her husband began his duties as British minister to the United States in May 1796.

3. GW had left Philadelphia on 13 June (see his letter to David Humphreys, 12 June). For reports on visitors expected at Mount Vernon, see James McHenry to GW, 5 and 7 July. The Listons reached Mount Vernon on 20 July (see GW's first letter to McHenry, 22 July, and n.2 to that document).

4. The new Spanish minister was Don Carlos Martinez de Yrujo y Tacon, later marqués de casa (Irujo; 1763–1824). He retained this post until 1807.

The *Gazette of the United States* (Philadelphia) for 11 June 1796 reported Yrujo's arrival at Norfolk, Va., on 3 June. For his stay at Mount Vernon, see GW to Pickering, 4 July.

To Bushrod Washington

Dear Bushrod,   Mount Vernon 29th June 1796.

You have not informed me what or whether any thing has been done in the Court of Chancery (in this State) for bringing the acct of my administration of Colo. Colvills Estate to a close, that my hands may be entirely clear, of it. I therefore give you the trouble of this enquiry: as I am extremely anxious to be acquitted. The balance due from me, (and at present lodged in the Bank of Alexandria) is ready to be applied in any manner and at any moment to the Chancellors order.[1]

I drew a prize in Colo. Byrds lottery, of a half acre lot—no. 265—I believe in the Town of Manchester and I have a lot in some Town that was established on James River (below Richmd) by a certain John Wood for which I have a deed (but it is in Philadelphia) if these are to be found and worth your acceptance, I will give them to you—I am entitled also in partnership with, or the Heirs of Peyton Randolph, Richard Randolph Mr Fitzhugh of Chatham, George Wythe, Richard Kidder Medde[,] Lewis Burwell, John Wales Nathaniel Harrison Junr—and Thomson Mason—to a tenth part of two or three half acre lots & 200 acre lots in the aforesaid lottery—But as Thomson Mason (with or without authority) sold this property and never to me at least accounted, for an ioto of the amount little I presume is to be expected from this concern but if you think or find it otherwise upon enquiry, I give you all the Interest I have therein & you may act accordingly.[2] With sincere friendship I remain Yr Affec. Uncle

Go: Washington

LB, DLC:GW. Bushrod Washington replied to GW on 3 July.

1. GW summarized his actions as executor of the Thomas Colvill estate when he wrote to Bushrod Washington on 10 Feb. (second letter; see also Bushrod Washington to GW, 24 Jan. and 29 Feb.).

2. William Byrd III (1728–1777) was a member of the Virginia colonial council. He served as colonel of the 2d Virginia Regiment in 1758 and subsequently succeeded GW as colonel of the 1st Virginia Regiment.

Attempting to stave off financial ruin, Byrd advertised in Purdie and Dixon's *Virginia Gazette* (Williamsburg) for 23 July 1767 a lottery of his "Land and Tenements . . . *being the entire towns of* Rocky Ridge *and* Shockoe, *lying at the Falls of* James *river, and the land thereunto adjoining.*" For GW's participation in the lottery held at Williamsburg in November 1768, see GW to Edmund Randolph, 10 July 1784, and Randolph to GW, 20 July 1784, in *Papers, Confederation Series*, 1:494–96, 2:4–5; see also Cash Accounts, May 1769, and n.10, in *Papers, Colonial Series*, 8:191–95.

The deed has not been identified. GW purchased the lot in October 1760 from John Hood (died c.1766) of Prince George County, Va. (see Cash Accounts, October 1760, and n.3, in *Papers, Colonial Series*, 6:465–66). The proposed town of Edinburgh south of the James River never came into existence. In his will, GW offered the Edinburgh lot and the Byrd lottery properties to his nephew William Augustine Washington (see *Papers, Retirement Series*, 4:485).

Peyton Randolph (c.1721–1775) was attorney general in Virginia from 1748 until 1766, when he became speaker of the House of Burgesses. He held that position until his death.

Lewis Burwell (d. 1784) lived near Williamsburg at Kingsmill in James City County.

John Wayles (d. 1773) resided in Charles City County.

Nathaniel Harrison (1703–1791), of Brandon in Prince George County, was a cousin of Benjamin Harrison.

From Alexander White

Sir　　　　　　　　　　Washington [D.C.] 29th June 1796

The Board having agreed to adjourn for a Week I shall set out for Virginia Tomorrow Morning—I shall return as soon as I see my Wheat safe—or sooner if anything occurs of sufficient importance to induce my Colleagues to give me notice[1]—I am with the highest Respect and most sincere Regard Sir your most Obt Servt

Alexr White

ALS, DLC:GW.

1. White again wrote GW from Washington on Wednesday, 20 July: "I returned to this place and took my Seat at the Board on Monday morning—Our Crops over the mountain are very fine. the Harvest being great and the labourers few rendered the securing our grain a tedious business. there was still some uncut, and much standing out, the end of last week. Mr Ames and Mr Rundle were highly pleased with that Country, they said it far exceeded their expectations; they went from Winchester to Bath where I heard they were yesterday week" (ALS, DLC:GW). Massachussetts congressman Fisher Ames wrote New Hampshire congressman Jeremiah Smith from Dedham, Mass., on 4 Sept.: "I saw Virginia, and it is not in a state to brag of; the land is good, but the inhabitants scattered, and as bad farmers as politicians. . . . A federal party is certainly rising up there, and though (as a party) it is the weaker, the citizens are now more impressible by them than by the Jacobins" (Ames, *Works*, 1:198–99).

Philadelphia merchant Richard Rundle (c.1747–1826) was a friend of Ames and may have been his travelling companion (see Ames to Richard Peters, 14 Dec. 1806, in Ames, *Works*, 1:377–78).

White next wrote GW from Washington on 29 July: "I informed you of my return to the City on the morning of Monday Se'night—Next Tuesday being Frederick Court where I expect several trials will come on at which my presence will be essential, I shall set out for Virginia this afternoon or early tomorrow morning, from whence I mean to return in time to take my Seat at the Board on Monday the 8th of August; the last week of that month it will be equally necessary for me to attend Berkeley Court, and it would be a very desirable thing to remain in that Country during the whole month, as the state of Mrs Whites health renders it necessary for her to go to Bath, I should wish to accompany her, and indeed it is not much less necessary for me than for her to spend some time there—I have been accustomed to do so at least every other year for 30 yrs. I have already omitted two successive seasons—and will omit the third rather than incur the imputation of neglect, at a time when so much is said about the non residence of the Commissioners—altho I consider those Waters as the great preservative of my health, particularly against the Rheumatism, of which I had a severe attack eleven years ago, and feel very serious symptoms of its return" (ALS, DLC:GW).

White's second wife was Sarah Cotter Hite White (c.1750–1830), widow of John Hite.

From Burgess Ball

Dear sir, Big Spring [Va.] 1st of July 96

A neighbour of mine having lately made an Excursion over the Mountains, was at the House of Mr Fairfax who formerly lived with you, and from whom the enclos'd Letters came to my Hands, requesting I wou'd forward them to you.[1]

We are now in Harvest, and hope to finish tomorrow, our wheat at least; never was there better Weather for the purpose of saving Grain, but the rains some time ago were so excessive, our latter wheat, particularly, is much injured by the Rott & Rust; 'tho upon the whole, I expect our Crops will be generally (in these parts) very good, as the Early wheat has been much dispers'd.

I receiv'd the Clover Seed you was so obliging as to procure for me,[2] and I also purchased in Alexandria two Bushells more, but, from the dry Spell in which I sow'd, I fear very little is standing. We propose staying at Home this Summer, and tryg a Cold Bath of our own, and shou'd you be making a Trip up the Potomak, we shall hope to have the pleasure of seeing you at our Cottage, and any friends you may have with you. Fanny joins in best respects to Mrs Washington & yourself, and I am Dear sir with real Esteem Yr mo. obt st

B. Ball

ALS, DLC:GW.
   1. The enclosures probably included John Fairfax's letter to GW of 10 June.
   2. About the clover seed, see Ball to GW, 29 Jan., and n.1 to that document.

From the Earl of Buchan

Sir, Kirkhill [Scotland] July 1. 1796

I had not the pleasure to receive the Letter with which your Excellency favoured me on the 20th of February until a few days ago at this place in Lothian near Edinburgh my Paternal residence[1] where I take much delight to forward the improvement of the Country and am a practical husbandman here as I am in Berwickshire at Dryburgh Abbey.

I have taken my own way of endeavoring to forward your Excellency's landable views of obtaining some spirited and intelligent farmers to settle upon your Estate of Mount-Vernon, & it would give me real satisfaction to be succesful.[2]

I apprehend however that it will not be easy to induce capitalists in the Farming business to settle, because almost all such as I have had occasion to converse with seem ambitious to be proprietors & to cultivate their own freeholds. Through the medium of an intelligent and prudent acquaintance in the rich vale of Berwickshire (Land similar to that on your Estate) I have made known the advantageous circumstances of the Mount-Vernon Farms and if fortunately any real good farmers of capital who are on the move should be induced to settle on the banks of the Potomac it might prove of the most beneficial consequence not only to the place where they shall settle but in the event to the Country at large.

It gives me much satisfaction to learn that the certificates which I endorsed after having had the good characters of the people made known to me by the Pastors of the Parishes in which they were situated have not been erroneous as may indeed frequently happen notwithstanding every precaution. There does not seem to me any thing more likely to continue peace and a good understanding between Britain and the United States than a friendly and useful interchange of people and of improvements, and having uniformly had a most sincere and ardent desire to forward this Peace and good intelligence between our respective Countrys so I have bestowed attention in giving what I knew to be a proper direction to those who were about to settle in the United States of America, and this I believe has often operated not only to their own prosperity & comfort but to the benefit of both Nations, & I exceedingly rejoice to see that the wishes I have had for paying any price for Peace & Harmony between them *Short of Honour & Safety* are likely to be accomplished. Felicia et Faustaq sint![3] Lady Buchan joins me in returning expressions of respectful regard to you & Mrs Washington and I remain with sincere Esteem & Cordial Respect Sir, yr Excellancys faithful & Obliged H. Servt

Buchan

ALS, DLC:GW.

Samuel Campbell probably enclosed this letter from Buchan when he wrote GW from New York on 14 Feb. 1797: "The inclosed letter has come to my particular care, from the Earl of Buchan, with directions to forward it in such a way that You might receive it safe, as he suspected several of his letters had been opened & detained in England when sent thro' the channel of the Mail" (ALS, DLC:GW).

1. For the forwarding of GW's letter to Buchan dated 20 Feb. 1796, see Thomas Pinckney to GW, 7 May, and n.1.

2. Buchan is referring to GW's plan to lease his Mount Vernon farms outlined in his advertisement of 1 February.

3. The Latin phrase wishes health and good luck.

To the Commissioners for the District of Columbia

Gentlemen   Mount Vernon 1st July 1796.

Your two letters, dated the 29th Ulto, have been received. The enclosures for the several Printers, to whom they are directed, are franked; and will go with this, and other letters to the Post Office this afternoon. I do not think it would be amiss to add Hartford, in Connecticut (a paper of extensive circulation altho' I do not recollect the name of the Editor of it) and some Gazette in North Carolina, to your list of publications.[1]

The decisive manner in which you treated the notification of Mr Hadfield, was, in my opinion, very proper. There ought to be no trifling in these matters. Coaxing a man to stay in Office—or to do his duty while he is in it, is not the way to accomplish the objects.

Having received (by the last Post) the certificates I wrote to Philadelphia for, I enclose them, with the Power of Attorney to Messrs Willinks, that you may forward them by the first conveyance that offers.[2] I am not in the way to hear of any.

The continual disappointments of Messrs Morris & Nicholson are really painful. One would hope that their assurances were not calculated for delay, and yet they seem to admit of hardly any other interpretation. An answer from the Secretary of the Treasury might, and I think ought to have been received by you, on Wednesday last.[3] With esteem & regard I am Gentlemen Your Obedient Servt

Go: Washington

ALS, DLC: U.S. Commissioners of the City of Washington records; copy, DLC:GW; LB, DLC:GW. The commissioners replied to GW on 12 July.

1. Hartford then had two weekly newspapers: Elisha Babcock edited the *American Mercury*, and Barzillai Hudson and George Goodwin edited *The Connecticut Courant* (see Brigham, *American Newspapers*, 1:19, 22). The commissioners apparently acted on GW's recommendations, as *The Connecticut Courant* for 15 Aug. and *The North-Carolina Journal* (Halifax) for 1 Aug. printed his executive order dated 25 June. For that order, see GW to the Commissioners for the District of Columbia, 26 June, n.2.

2. GW probably is referring to his letter to James McHenry dated 22 June (see also McHenry's reply on 29 June). GW needed to sign these certificates that authorized the commissioners to borrow money (see Commissioners for the District of Columbia to GW, 13 May, n.1).

3. The preceding Wednesday was 29 June. The commissioners had written Secretary of the Treasury Oliver Wolcott, Jr., on 20 June, and he replied on 27 June (see Commissioners for the District of Columbia to GW, 22 June, and n.3).

From Alexander Love

Sir   Norfolk [England?] July 1st 1796

Having intermarried with the only child of William Wright who fell, as I am told in Braddocks field fighting under your command, before she was born, and seeing that owing to the paternal care you were pleased to take of the Interest of his Heirs and of those who had the honor to serve under your command at that time,[1] that she is entitled to 2500 Acres of Land, part of a patent for 21,941 Acres made by your order on the Kanawha, beginning at the mouth of Pohotillico for the benefit of J. Fry, A. Stephen, Andrew Lewis, Peter Hogg, John Savage, Thomas Bullitt, her father William Wright and John D. Welper, their heirs and assigns in the several proportions mentioned in an Order of the Governor and Council bearing date the 4th November 1773 as tennants in common and not as joint tennants—the original Copy of which order of Council being lost with the Council Books of those times, I beg the favor of your Excellency when time serves, to have a Copy of the Order made, if a Copy be in your notes, and so Authenticated as to be satisfactory to our High Court of Chancery that the Lands may be divided and each Know their own.[2]

My Wife prays you Sir to accept her best thanks for this Land; saved to her by your care and at your expence and in this, I do so heartily join her as to assure your Excellency that I think more of the Act, than of the Land, altho' I am well informed by your Correspondence with our Uncle Doctor Wright of Glasgow and otherwise that the Land is of excellent Soil.[3]

The bearer my friend Mr Walker will take any trouble and defray any expence needful to accomplish this end.[4] I am with the most perfect Respect Your most Obedt Hble Servt

Alexander Love

ALS, DLC:GW. GW wrote "recd 12d Decr 1796" on the docket.

1. Born in Scotland, William Wright (1732–1755) served as a cadet in GW's Fort Necessity campaign during the French and Indian War. He became an ensign on GW's recommendation and advanced to lieutenant in October 1754. Indians killed Wright near the New River in July 1755. He was not with British general Edward Braddock's expedition (see Robert Dinwiddie to Wright, 8 July 1755, and to John Buchanan, 8 Aug. 1755, in Brock, *Dinwiddie Records*, 2:92, 154–55; see also Chalkley, *Scotch-Irish Settlement*, 2:510).

2. For the grant and order, see GW to Lord Dunmore and Council, c.3 Nov. 1773, and n.5, in *Papers, Colonial Series*, 9:358–66.

Joshua Fry (c.1700–1754), Adam Stephen (c.1718–1791), Andrew Lewis (1720–1781), Peter Hog (Hogg; 1703–1782), John Savage, Thomas Bullitt (1730–1778), and John David Woelpper (Wilper; 1709–1797) all served as Virginia officers during the French and Indian War.

3. Love presumably meant Peter Wright (1737–1819), whose career in medicine included stints as president of the Faculty of Physicians and Surgeons of Glasgow.

No correspondence between GW and Peter Wright has been found, but see a likely mistaken reference to a letter from "Dr Patrick Wright" in James Cross to GW, 15 March 1785, in *Papers, Confederation Series*, 2:434–35; see also Cash Accounts, June 1774, and n.2 to that document, in *Papers, Colonial Series*, 10:75, 78.

4. "Mr Walker" has not been identified.

To James McHenry

Sir,   Mount Vernon 1st July 1796

Your letter of the 27th Ulto by Post, with its enclosures (the originals of which, I return) came to my hands on Wednesday.[1] And your other letters of the 27th & 28th by Express, was received about five oclock yesterday afternoon.

The accounts brought in the latter, are very pleasing indeed, inasmuch as they will serve to remove the doubts of the credulous (with respect to the Western Posts); and when realized, be productive of that tranquillity, and peace with the Indians which, in itself, is so desirable; and has been so much wished and sought for, by every real friend to his Country.[2]

It is my desire that the charges exhibited against General Wayne by Brigadier Wilkenson, with the letters of crimination on both sides, should be laid before the heads of Departments; and yours and their opinions reported to me on the measures necessary to be pursued to do justice to the Public; the accused; and the accuser; As also when, and by whom, the enquiry is to be made; with the preliminary steps necessary thereto.

There are no Officers, I conceive, of sufficient rank to constitute a Court before whom the Commander in chief can be brought. Is the matter then to come before Congress? In what manner? My first impression relative to this business (though not maturely, or distinctly formed) is, that General Wayne ought, immediately, to be furnished with a copy of *all* the charges exhibited against him by the Brigadier; in order, as many of them are of old standing that he may have time allowed him to recollect circumstances; and to see what counter evidence can be produced, or what satisfactory explanations can be given; that he may not be unprepared for trial whensoever he is called upon.

It may be well if it can be accomplished, by civil expressions, to stimulate the present Governor of Tennessee to an effectual[3] repression of incroachments on Indian Territory (secured to them by Treaties): but the honor of the government, and the Peace of the Union, require, that if he is not decisive, the Laws relative thereto, be not suspended, or trifled with; but promptly, and energetically (with temper & prudence) enforced.

I will not speak upon the new model of the Army now, but will take more time to consider the scheme for resolving the Legion into four Regiments, on the plan you have suggested.

In speaking of the Generals Wayne & Wilkinson, I omitted to add, as my opinion, that the latter (if leave has not been given already) ought to obtain the furlough he has asked; and as soon as the former joins the Army; for no good will result from both being with it in the irritable temper they are in, at the sametime.[4]

Go: Washington

ALS, NhD; ADfS, DLC:GW; LB, DLC:GW.

1. McHenry's first letter to GW of 27 June arrived on Wednesday, 29 June.

2. For McHenry to GW, 28 June, see his first letter to GW, 27 June, n.8.

3. This word was underlined on the draft and the letter-book copy.

4. McHenry wrote privately to Gen. Anthony Wayne on 9 July: "Conciliate the good will and confidence of your officers of every rank; even of those who have shewn themselves your personal enemies. Gen. Wilkinson has entered upon a specification of all his charges against you both old & new, and will press for a decision inquiry or court martial. I shall, unless I should be of opinion or reflexion that it is improper, send them to you in their condensed form, that you may prepare to meet them should it become necessary" (Knopf, *Wayne*, 498). In his private reply written at Fort Greene Ville, Northwest Territory, on 28 July, Wayne thanked McHenry "for the *friendly hint*. it however does not require any great degree of penetration to discover the real Object of the Malignant and groveling charges exhibited by that worst of all bad men, to whom I feel myself as much superior in every Virtue—as Heaven is to Hell.

"The fact is, my presence with the army is very inconvenient, to the nefarious machinations of the Enemies of Government & may eventually prevent them from dissolving the Union" (Knopf, *Wayne*, 506–7). For additional actions regarding the longstanding personal dispute between Wayne and Gen. James Wilkinson, see McHenry to GW, 6 July, and n.1 to that document; see also Nelson, *Wayne*, 291–96; Jacobs, *Wilkinson*, 155–57; and Kohn, *Eagle and Sword*, 178–87.

McHenry had written Alexander Hamilton on 4 July: "Wilkinson continues to heap charges upon Wayne; is condensing them into a consistent form, and I perceive will urge them in such a manner as may oblige the Executive, to determine whether a commander of the army can be tried by a court martial, or the affair examined by a court of inquiry, or if neither can be done by what authority the case is cognizable.

"Will you take the question into your consideration and help me with your opinion." In his reply to McHenry, written at New York on 15 July, Hamilton outlined a cumbersome process that he characterized as "the best I can think of," before adding, "you must by all means avoid the imputation of evading the inquiry & protecting a favourite" (*Hamilton Papers*, 20:245, 252–53).

To James McHenry

Private   Mount Vernon 1st July 1796
Dear Sir   Friday 7 Oclock in the Morng

By the Post, rather than by the Express, you will receive my Official letter, and its Enclosures.[1] For the difference of a few hours, in a case that is not urgent, I would have you avoid sending an Express to me. The latter does not travel faster than the Mail; of course there cannot (unless Sunday intervene's) be more, in any case (supposing an occasion to arise in one hour after the Mail was closed) than the difference of 48 hours in the receipt of the dispatches; as I send regularly, every Post day, to Alexandria for my letters. Your Express came in yesterday at 5 oclock in the afternoon, and if you had sent the letters by the Mail of Wednesday, they would have been here at 9 'oclock this Afternoon; a difference of 28 hours only.[2]

The information brot by Captn Lewis is very pleasing; and I hope the orders on both sides will go smoothly into effect: but the Aurora will have doubts, that all is not well, notwithstanding. This, however, is a matter of course; for the Executive Acts *must be* arraigned.

I hope you have got perfectly recovered, and that Mrs McHenry and the rest of your family are well also.

When I left Philadelphia, it was expected that Mr & Mrs Liston (and from their own declarations) was to follow, on a visit to this place, in ten days; an interval of a few days—and then the Chevr de Freire & Lady were to follow them; and altho' Mr Adet gave *me* (tho' asked) no assurance that he would make me a visit, yet to Mr Fayette he said he should set out in ten days. Since which I have heard nothing from, or of any of them, which occasions suspence, that impede other arrangements.

If you could therefore indirectly, or at least informally, ascertain whether and when, I am to receive these visits, I should be obliged to you; as it would enable me to regulate some other matters which depend thereon. With sincere esteem & regard I am—Dear Sir Yr Affectionate

Go: Washington

Have you allotted any Infantry for the Posts of Oswego & Niagara? How many, & when will they be there?[3]

ALS, NhD.

1. GW is referring to his first letter to McHenry of this date.

2. The express carried McHenry's second letter to GW of 27 June and his letter of 28 June, found at McHenry's first letter to GW of 27 June, n.8.

3. McHenry replied to GW from Philadelphia on Sunday, 3 July, at 8:00 P.M.: "I have been honoured about an hour since with your private letter of the 1st instant by the return express.

"I had been looking very anxiously for above a week, for Captn Lewis; a circumstance that contributed to increase the pleasure I felt on learning the success of his mission, and which led me at the same time to make you the earliest communication.

"Capn Bruff marched one complete company of artillery and about twenty five infantry. There have arrived at West Point since his departure about as many infantry as he carried with him which if you think proper may be ordered to follow. I think it was about the 23 ulto that the detachment moved from Schenectady.

"I will endeavour to send you by Wendnesdays mail some information respecting what has delayed the visitors you mention; or whether all or any of them may be expected and when.

"I was very much indisposed on friday and part of yesterday but I am pretty well to-day" (ALS, DLC:GW; ADf, DLC: James McHenry Papers; GW acknowledged this letter when he wrote McHenry on 8 July). Capt. James Bruff's detachment was sent to replace the British troops evacuating forts at Niagara and Oswego, New York. McHenry wrote GW on 5 and 7 July with information on visitors expected at Mount Vernon.

To Timothy Pickering

Sir,   Mount Vernon 1st July 1796

Your letter of the 27th ulto is received. I am sorry Mr De Witt, from the competency of his abilities to discharge the duties of the Office of Surveyor General, declines accepting it.

Colo. Tinsley's recommendations, go more to the respectability of his character, than to his scientific knowledge. The first is essential, but not sufficient without the other. I will obtain the best information I can respecting the latter; but would not have you discourage any other eligable applications, on his account.

From the representation of Mr Dinsmore, it appears to be indispensable that the line between the United States and the Cherokees should be run, and distinctly marked, as soon as possible. The Indians urge this; the Law requires it; and it ought to be done; but I believe scarcely any thing short of a Chinese Wall,[1] or a line of Troops will restrain Land Jobbers, and the Incroachment of Settlers, upon the Indian Territory—I request that you, and the other two Secretaries, would take this matter into consideration, and report to me how soon and in what manner, this work should commence. Ascertaining the boundary removes the pretext of ignorance, and may with other applications *check*, if it does not effectually *cure* an evil, which is pregnant of serious consequences.[2]

G. Washington

P.S. The Spanish Minister is this moment, (as I was closing my letters) arrived here.[3]

ALS, MHi: Pickering Papers; LS (retained copy), DNA: RG 59, Miscellaneous Letters; LB, DNA: RG 59, GW's Correspondence with His Secretaries of State. Pickering acknowledged GW's letter on 8 July.

1. GW presumably is referring to the Great Wall of China, which he may have read about in a multi-volume travel work that he purchased around 1783: "The WORLD displayed; or A curious collection of voyages and travels, selected from the writers of all nations. 20 vols." (Griffin, *Catalogue of the Washington Collection*, 507; see also Hayes, *Washington*, 194–95). GW apparently owned the fourth edition, but for remarks on the Great Wall of China, see *The World Displayed* . . . (3d ed. corrected; London, 1777), 16:147–48.

2. Cherokee agent Silas Dinsmoor's representation has not been identified. Article IV of the Treaty of Holston, ratified on 2 July 1791, had described the boundary between Cherokee and U.S. lands and required its marking "to preclude forever all disputes relative to the said boundary" (Kappler, *Indian Treaties*, 2:29–30). Article II of the Treaty of Holston, ratified on 26 June 1794, indicated that the boundary remained unmarked (see Kappler, *Indian Treaties*, 2:33).

3. The postcript does not appear on the LS or the letter-book copy. For Spanish minister Yrujo, see GW to Pickering, 29 June, and n.4.

From Oliver Wolcott, Jr.

[Philadelphia, 1 July 1796]

I have had the honour to receive your Letter of June 27th and have disposed of the enclosures agreably to direction.

Last Evening I called on Mr T. W. Francis and he informed me that your Wine was in good condition & perfectly safe stored in the Compting House with two Pipes of Mr Willings: it was Mr Francis's opinion that the situation was much better for the improvement of the wine than any Cellar: I am no judge of the matter my self & can cause a removal at any time, if the President judges it adviseable.[1]

There is nothing new in town—Baches paper continues as usual to be filled with abuse against the Government & predictions of French hostility.[2] I believe however that his publications make but little impression[3]—Browns paper of last evening, stated that President was expected to return here in a few days—I have not been able to trace the origin of the report, but I presume it to be a trick of some person to incite alarm—it will be contradicted.[4]

The questions proposed by the Presidt being of great consequence we have thought it best to keep them under consideration a few days—The pressure of business with me is such that I have not been able to bestow all the attention which I wish.[5]

The new Stock will I fear remain unsold notwithstanding the long Credit which was offered—some new expedient must be adopted; what will be best I cannot yet determine.[6] I shall act with caution & pursuant to the best advice which I can obtain.[7] With perfect deference & attachment, I remain Sir, your obedt servt

                                        Oliver Wolcott Jr

ALS, DLC:GW; ADf (partial), CtHi: Oliver Wolcott, Jr., Papers. GW docketed the ALS as "without date, received the 4th July 1796." The ascribed date, which is consistent with the travel time between Philadelphia and Mount Vernon, was determined by reference to the publication in "Browns paper of last evening" (see n.4 below). The draft was dated "June [   ] 1796."

1. For GW's instructions about storage of the wine, see his private letter to Wolcott dated 24 June.

2. On the draft, Wolcott wrote "encourage the enterprises of the French" rather than the previous four words.

3. The draft ends with a closing following this word.

4. Andrew Brown's *Philadelphia Gazette & Universal Daily Advertiser* for 30 June printed an item: "We hear that the President of the United States is expected to return to this city in a few days." The *Gazette of the United States, & Philadelphia Daily Advertiser* for 1 July provided the promised contradiction: "A report was circulated last evening that the President of U.S. was arrived in town. This is not true, nor is there any foundation for the report that he is expected in a few days. And it is difficult to assign any just reason for it."

5. Wolcott pondered questions concerning French policy posed in GW's letter to Timothy Pickering of 24 June.

6. Wolcott is referring to stock certificates authorized in "An Act making provision for the payment of certain Debts of the United States," 31 May (1 *Stat.* 488–89). The *Gazette of the United States* (Philadelphia) for 16 June printed a notice from the Bank of the United States dated 14 June with conditions for the purchase of this stock.

7. GW replied to Wolcott from Mount Vernon on 6 July: "Private . . . Your private letter (without date) by the last Post, has been received.

"It is quite agreeable to me, that my Wine should remain in the Store of Messrs Willing & Francis, till I shall have occasion to remove it.

"There is little doubt, but the insertion in Browns Paper, of my sudden return, was put there to answer some insiduous purpose; for sure I am, nothing ever dropped from me to authorise such a publication. and it is to be regretted that the authors of them could not be brot to light.

"A Report has circulated here, that the William Penn has been captured by the Flying-Fish; but as it is of some days standing, & your letter is silent on the subject I hope it is void of foundation. That Mr Bache will continue his attacks on the Government, there can be no doubt—but that they will make no Impression on the public mind is not so certain, for drops of Water will Impress (in time) the hardest Marble.

"I hear with concern, that the New Stock is likely to remain unsold, notwithstanding the long credit which was offered. Let the expedient (whatever it be) be well considered.

"If any thing should occur of an interesting nature altho' it should not require official communication let me hear it" (ALS, CtHi: Oliver Wolcott, Jr., Papers). The French privateer *Flying Fish* did not capture the *William Penn,* which sailed for London on 10 June and returned to Philadelphia that fall (see *The Philadelphia Gazette & Universal Daily Advertiser,* 18 June, and *Gazette of the United States, & Philadelphia Daily Advertiser,* 13 Oct.).

From the Cabinet

To the President of the
United States.   Philadelphia July 2. 1796.

Agreeably to your directions, we have consulted together on the subject of your letter of the 24th of June;[1] and we are of opinion that a direct explanation should be asked of Mr Adet, the minister of the French Republic, in the terms of the inclosed draught of a letter to him, which, as you desired, will be sent without delay.[2] We are also of opinion that the Executive has not the power, in the recess of the Senate, to originate the appointment of a *minister extraordinary* to France; and that the recall of Mr Monroe, by creating a vacancy, can alone authorize the sending of a new minister to that country. On the expediency of this change we are agreed. We think the great interests of the United States require that they have near the French Government some faithful organ to explain their real views and to ascertain those of the French. Our duty obliges us to be explicit. Altho' the present minister plenipotentiary of the United States at Paris, has been amply furnished with documents to explain the views and conduct of the U. States, yet his own letters authorize us to say, that he omitted to use them, and thereby exposed the U. States to all the mischiefs which could flow from jealousies & erroneous conceptions of their views and conduct. Whether this dangerous omission arose from such an attachment to the cause of France as rendered him too little mindful of the interests of his own country, or from mistaken views of the latter, or from any other cause, the evil is the same. We therefore conceive it to be indispensably necessary that the present minister plenipotentiary of the United States at Paris should be recalled, and another American Citizen appointed in his stead. Such being our opinion, we beg leave to name for your consideration Patrick Henry & John Marshall of Virginia, & Charles Cottesworth Pinckney & William Smith of South Carolina, either of whom would, we believe, so explain the views and conduct of the United States as to satisfy the French Republic, and thereby remove the danger of a rupture or inconvenient controversy with that nation; or failing of this desirable effect, to satisfy the citizens of the United States that the fault was not to be imputed to their own government.

In confirmation of our opinion of the expediency of recalling Mr Monroe, we think the occasion requires that we communicate a private letter from him which came to our hands since you left Philadelphia.[3] This letter corresponds with other intelligence of his political opinions & conduct. A minister who has thus made the notorious enemies of the whole system of the government his confidential correspondents in matters which affect that government, cannot be relied on to do his duty to the latter. This private letter we received in confidence. Among other circumstances that will occur to your recollection, the anonymous letters from France to Thomas Blount and others are very noticeable.[4] We know that Montflorence was the writer, & that he was the chancellor of the Consul Skipwith; and from the connection of Mr Monroe with those persons we can entertain no doubt that the anonymous letters were written with his privity.

These anonymous communications from officers of the United States in a foreign country, on matters of a public nature, and which deeply concern the interests of the U. States, in relation to that foreign country, are proofs of sinister designs, and shew that the public interests are no longer safe in the hands of such men.

The information contained in the confidential communication you were pleased to make to us on the project of the French Government relative to the commerce of the U. States, is confirmed by the open publication of the same substantially and more minutely in the news-papers. Mr Fenno's in which it first appeared, we now inclose.[5] The execution of the project even appears to have been commenced. The following article is in Mr Fenno's paper of the 28th ulto.

"New-London June 23. Arrived Brig Aurora, S. Wadsworth of Hartford, in 14 days from port-a-paix. Left there sloop Crisis,

Cook, of Norwich, with Mules; sloop Scrub, Williams, of Middletown; and a brig from Philadelphia; all carried in by French privateers. It was not pretended to make prizes of them; but their cargoes were taken by the administration, at their own price, and due bills given therefor. Those who go there to trade and those carried in are all treated alike. Capt. Wadsworth received a due bill for 11,000 livres."[6]

The foregoing we respectfully submit to the consideration and decision of the President of the United States.[7]

> Timothy Pickering, Secy of State
> Oliver Wolcott Jr Secy of the Treasy
> James McHenry
> Secy of war

LS, enclosed with Timothy Pickering's first (secret) letter to GW, 4 July, DNA: RG 59, Miscellaneous Letters; LB, DNA: RG 59, GW's Correspondence with His Secretaries of State; Df (in Pickering's writing), MHi: Pickering Papers.

1. See GW to Pickering, 24 June.

2. The enclosure, filed with this letter, is a communication from Pickering to French minister Pierre-Auguste Adet dated 1 July: "It being the duty of the Executive of the United States to watch over their interests, I am instructed by the President to request of you an explanation on the subjects of the following questions.

"1. Whether the government of France have decreed any new regulations or orders relative to the commerce of the U. States?

"2. Whether these regulations or orders (if such exist) are confined to vessels laden wholly or in part with provisions? If not so confined, to what other articles they extend?

"3. Whether American vessels laden wholly or in part with provisions and destined to any other port than those of France or her dominions, particularly if destined to any English ports, are directed to be captured & carried into French ports, & their cargoes, entire, or such parts thereof as consist of provisions, or other specified articles, applied to the use of the French Republic or its citizens?

"[4]. If such captures are authorized by the French Republic, or by the decrees or orders of any branches of its government, on what grounds such authority, decrees or orders have been given?"

"These questions you will perceive, sir, have relation to reports of designs relative to the commerce of the U. States, which cannot fail to excite apprehensions in the minds of our merchants. The general interests of the U.S. are intimately blended with theirs. Hence the propriety of asking such explanations as may serve to tranquillize our commercial citizens, and continue the good understanding & f[r]iendship between the two nations which it has been the uniform desire of the American government to maintain.

"Permit me to request an early answer to this letter" (DNA: RG 59, Miscellaneous Letters). For Adet's reply, see Pickering to GW, 15 July.

3. A copy of the letter James Monroe, U.S. minister to France, wrote George Logan on 24 June 1795 was enclosed with Pickering's first (secret) letter to GW of 4 July.

4. The cabinet is referring to a letter from James Cole Mountflorence to Thomas Blount, 8 March, printed as an enclosure with James McHenry to GW, 10 June; and an unidentified letter from Mountflorence to William Blount dated 23 March and mentioned in the enclosure's postscript.

5. The cabinet evidently enclosed the *Gazette of the United States* (Philadelphia) for 20 June (see Alexander Hamilton to GW, c.16 June, n.3).

6. The cabinet correctly quoted from the *Gazette of the United States* for 28 June.

7. See also McHenry to GW, this date, and n.2 to that document. For GW's decision to recall Monroe as U.S. minister to France, see his letter to Pickering, 8 July.

From James McHenry

Sir   War office 2 July 1796.

I was in the Secy of States office with Mr Wolcott when he recd your letter containing queries to be submitted to the heads of departments.[1] On my return home I committed the inclosed observations to paper relative to the power of the President to remove a foreign minister.[2] Having gone so far I have determined to send it as explanatory of my reasons for signing the paper which will be forwarded to you by the Secy of State.[3] It was after I had written them down that it was proposed to me to make it a joint representation.

I have recd a letter from Mr Ross which if Mr Wolcott has time to copy will be inclosed. Otherwise it will be sent the following post, being too much indisposed to copy it, and it not being proper to be copied by a clerk.[4]

I hardly think it safe at this moment to intrust important papers to the mail. It may be robbed. It has been suggested to me, that one reason why the mount Vernon was captured, was on account of the letters which were supposed to be on board.[5] With the greatest respect I have the honour to be Sir your most ob. St

James McHenry

ALS, DLC:GW; LB, DLC:GW; ADf, DLC: James McHenry Papers. GW acknowledged this letter when he wrote McHenry on 8 July.

1. McHenry means GW's letter to Timothy Pickering of 24 June.

2. The enclosure reads: "The first point for consideration is Whether the President during the recess of the Senate has a right to send an *additional* minister to a foreign court?

"Upon this the Secry of war observes, that where there *is* a minister at a foreign court, it does not appear, that the President can *commission another to the same court*, or that he can, during the recess, appoint a minister to a court where there is none.

"To enter a little further into this subject, it will be proper, to take a short view of the executive power vested in the President as relative to the question propounded.

"The constitution declares art. II. Sect. I. That, 'the executive power shall be vested in a President of the U.S. of America.'

"This may be considered as a general grant of all executive power to the President necessary to carry into effect the objects of the constitution, subject only to such exceptions and restrictions as are found in the constitution.

"Had the constitution stopped with the general grant; had it vested no portion of executive power in any branch or department of the government other than the President; had it gone into no specifications of it; or had it imposed no restrictions upon its exercise; then and in that case, the exercise of all power strictly excutive, and necessary to carry into effect the objects of the constitution, would have belonged exclusively to the President.

"But the general grant of executive power is controuled and abridged.

"1st. By an assignment of a certain portion of it to Congress; for Congress have power 'to declare war and grant letters of marque and reprisal.'

"2. By a controuling power vested in the Senate over another portion of it: for the Senate may noncur in the appointment to offices.

"3. By a specific restriction on the same portion when exercised, as it may be, without the immediate participation of the Senate: For in appointments during the recess of the Senate, the Presidents commission's must expire at the end of their next session.

"To be more particular. The restrictions on that portion of the executive power, which relates to the appointment of ministerial characters are in the following words.

"'He (the President[)] shall nominate and by and with the advice of the Senate, shall appoint ambassadors other public ministers and consuls.'

"'The President shall have power to fill up all vacancies that may happen, during the recess of the Senate, by granting commissions which shall expire at the end of their next session.'

"The first of these rules is general. It goes to this. That no ministerial character whatever shall be appointed, without the advice and consent of the Senate.

"The second is an exception to the first as admitting of appointments in a particular case, without their consent or advice.

"That case is in *vacancies* only. Hence to enable the President to send a ministerial character to a foreign court during the recess of the Senate, it is requisite, that there should be *a minister in commission for that court*, and that he should resign die or be recalled, so that a *vacancy* may be created, and a door thereby opened to the President to appoint by granting a temporary commission.

"It is next to be considered whether the President has a right to recal officers or ministers.

"To appoint to and remove from office are equally executive powers, and equally necessary to the well being of the government. Should we confine the power to remove, to impeachment, the public safety would run the greatest danger from corrupt men.

"It is with the President, who is the eye of the constitution; the watchful guardian of the laws, and responsible for their due execution, that the *power of removal* is chiefly lodged. The Senate cannot remove from office; they have a participative influence or check only in removals; but the President may remove without consulting the Senate.

"But whence is the right derived? From its being one essential attribute of Executive power; and from its being vested by the constitution in no other body nor excerciseably by any other body, except in cases of removal by impeachment. In all other cases it belongs to the President to remove.

"Why has the constitution provided two modes of removal; vz. one by the President, and one independent of the President?

"To guard against two opposite evils. To obviate by the one, the difficulty of getting a corrupt Senate to agree to the removal of a corrupt minister or officer. In that case the President may remove during their recess. To prevent, by the other, a President from keeping corrupt men in office, by refusing to make a nomination which would remove them. In such a case they may be removed by impeachment.

"The power of removal by the President is subject to two restrictions only. 1. To the controul which the Senate has over all nominations. 2 To the limitation of all commissions granted by the President during their recess, which must expire at the end of their next session.

"It may now be asked in what cases ought this power to be exercised?

"If we are to regulate the use of it by reason, it may be lawfully exercised,

"1. When the President shall discover that his minister wants the capacity and qualifications requisite for the mission in which he has been employed.

"2. When the President shall have reason to believe, though the minister may not be deficient in capacity or resources, that he neglects the duties of his mission, to the injury or disadvantage of the U.S.

"3. When the President discovers, that tho' his minister has the requisite capacity and pays the proper attention to business, yet from his being disliked by the court, that he can render no service to his country.

"4. When the President shall be of opinion that the essential interests of the U.S. might be better promoted by a man of greater talents and capacity.

"5. When it shall appear to the President, that his minister has entered into designs of a domestic or foreign faction, hostile to the government and union.

"Either of these constitute a cause for removal from office; but when circumstances shew the existence of the last case, the necessity for a removal becomes irresistable.

"How can the President be said to see the laws, or treaties which are laws, faithfully executed, if he keeps in office a person, knowing him to be enployed in forwarding measures and projects to defeat their object or execution?

"A minister being an agent of the President is bound to execute his orders; and to obey implicitly his instructions. If he disobeys instructions; or labours to counter act them by insiduous manœuvres, he ought to be displaced.

"To apply these remarks to the minister to the French Republic.

"It appears from some of his letters which the President has been pleased to communicate; and from conversations which have passed with the heads of departments

"1. That the minister in question has been early informed of the motives and reasons which induced the U.S. to settle their differences, and enter into a commercial treaty with Great Britain, by which he was enabled to enter into explanations with the cabinet of France upon the subject.

"2. It appears by letters from the minister that the cabinet or Directory of France had taken exception to the treaty; had shewn an evident disapprobation of the U.S. for having entered into it; had it under consideration t⟨o⟩ demand, by a minister extraordinary, an eclaircissement on the subject; notwithstanding which, the minister had entered into no justification of the U.S. nor made use of any of the means with which he had been furnished to explain the motives of government.

"While these things remain unexplained, the minister must be considered as having neglected a very evident and pointed duty, and as having put in jeopardy the peace of the U.S.

"On this ground alone his removal may be considered as a proper and necessary measure.

"The next question respects a fit person to replace him, should the President determine on his recal *during the recess of the Senate.*

"In the choice of a fit person, respect is to be had to the feelings of France; to the objects connected with his recal; to the feelings of the people of the U.S. and to certain commercial arrangements with France by a new treaty.

It is of consequence that France should be convinced of the friendly intentions of this country towards her; of its earnest wish to remain connected with her; and that on no occasion where the U.S. could favour her special interest, without involving them in the war, or violating a principle of neutrality, has the opportunity been neglected: and that if a party in the U.S. have endeavoured to excite in France contrary ideas, it ought to be ascribed to the usual proceedings of party when intent upon demolishing at all risques their opponents.

"To make these and such like impressions with effect, the minister should if possible possess a character likely to smooth the way to her confidence in his representations.

"If Charles Carroll of Carrollton could be prevailed on to go, temporarily, he combined with sufficient abilities and knowledge, all the weight of an immense fortune, and the full confidence of the people of this country. Besides, as no public act of his has rendered him obnoxious to the French, he bids fair to be received by them without prepossessions or forerunning prejudices.

"Charles Cotesworth Pinckney in the latter point of view would also be a proper person. He has not, that the Secry has heard of, been branded as the enemy of France; he is besides a very respectable citisen, of independent fortune, circumstances which added to his standing in society would give dignity to the mission.

"Either of these gentlemen, would carry with them the good opinion of this country and could not be ill received by France.

"Mr Marshal of Virginia comes also into view. If he can be induced to accept he may be considered as an acquisition to the diplomatic corps.

"Mr William Smith is a man well instructed in the commercial and other interests of the U.S. of a strong understanding and ready at composition. So far therefore he is fitted for the mission. The objections to him, relate chiefly to French prejudices, which lay against every person as well as him, who has been in our public councils, and advocated measures calculated to preserve peace between the U.S. and Great Britain.

"Patrick Henry would have been earlier mentioned, had his cast of thinking at this particular moment been known. If it is not wayward, and there is a probability that he would accept, the occasion would justify sending him.

"Mr Adams, the minister to Portugal has been strongly suggested by Mr Pickering & Mr Woolcot.

"To send him would not suit the solemnity of the crises. He would not be presumed to carry with him a correct knowledge of circumstances. He might also be distrusted from the relation he stands in to the Vice President, who may be thought by France a favourer of England. He is besides (tho' a man of abilities) too young, and too little known in the U.S. for the importance of such a mission; one object of which is to dissipate a threatening storm, and restore good understanding and harmony between two nations" (DLC:GW).

3. See the Cabinet to GW, this date.

4. Secretary of the Treasury Oliver Wolcott, Jr., copied the letter from James Ross, U.S. senator from Pennsylvania, to McHenry written at Pittsburgh on 24 June. It reads: "On my way home I recd the inclosed Notes which contain much additional information & will serve as a caution against Judge T. [George Turner] who has letters of introduction to Adet & is expected to play a great part. That gentleman is yet in this place but will set out for Philadelphia in a few days.

"The writer of these & former notes has had the address to become an Agent for receiving & transmitting Letters to & from Adet; at first I doubted an imposition upon me, but I have the strongest of all proofs, the letters themselves directed to Collot, signed with a fictitious name, but evidently written by the Minister: They contain nothing material except information that the French are about to send a Commissioner who will demand a guarranty of the W. Indies & explanations of the B. Treaty, that the President has been alarmed, that Adet will not be recalled as expected & that upon the whole it is not probable that the French will break with the United States, although they will deal severely with their Ships going to English Ports—that the President will not serve again & exhorting Collot to make use of all these things as had been agreed. After examining this strange Letter I determined to send it forward as it was easy to see from the Letter itself that others of more consequence would soon follow & fall into our hands—This being settled I have thought it adviseable that our Man should go on & join Collot, that he should endeavour to see the the instructions and know where they are kept, in order that they may be seized.

"Collot opened himself pretty fully to two persons, stated that he was sent by the French Minister, was paid by him, that the French expect Louisiana & wish to have the western parts of the United States disunited from the Union; expressed hopes of Kentucky & the lower settlements, but doubted of the upper settlements in Pensylvania; he has taken plans of all the passes to the western Country through the Mountains between Potomac & the Susquehannah, dwells in every company upon the ingratitude of this Country to France & the great affection of the French for the Americans: Insinuates that most of the present administration are attached to England & some of them doubtless corrupted by it Speaks disrespectfully of the President especially for not noticing Rochambeau & himself more than he did, in their misfortunes. To a man of sense & honour he stated that there was good reason to believe that France would prevail upon Spain to refuse a final ratification of her Treaty with us, that they thought this measure in a good train for success, as pains had been taken to alarm them about the article in our Treaty with Britain respecting the Mississipi. In case of success the French would get Louisiana & establish there Ship yards & depots for Ship timber & lumber for the W. Indies; that he is to visit that Country & make report of the practicability of this project— In one word there is no doubt of the information recd in Philadelphia respecting this mission is correct, & that this man although disappointed in his hopes & expectations here, because he had no confederates in the Country, yet he will be able to do much mischief where he is going—Sebastian is gone home, he did not shew himself publickly here, but is highly praised by Collot.

"I think there is no doubt of our agents fidelity he has already gone too far to recede, but he is poor, involved in debt beyond what I expected & very importunate for money, this will be troublesome to us, but I will deal as economically as possible without loosing sight of our object—It has been sugested that *Warin* might be corrupted, but I have declined that attempt as dangerous & unecessary as things stand.

"General Wayne is arrived & I will concert the measures for seizing & securing the papers with him, before he leaves us; It is always hazardous to commit things of this description to paper, & therefore I shall never write but when there is something of consequence to communicate. It was proper to risque it now, that you might see in what shape the business stands & be ascertained of the attention & fidelity of those to whom it had been committed" (DLC:GW).

Wolcott evidently copied the notes Ross had enclosed with his letter to McHenry. The notes run from 28 May to 6 June and received Wolcott's certification: "Copied from the original paper July 3d 1796" (DLC:GW; filed under 28 May 1796). Earlier entries dated 22, 25, and 26 May, found in another version of the notes, may be the "former notes" that Ross mentions (MHi: Adams

Papers). The notes that Wolcott copied read: "May 28th Gl C. informed me that he had recd from his friend Adet the agreable news, that if a new Minister was to come over, it would be a Mr Vincent formerly a distinguished Officer in the Corps of Engineers a gentleman of great Merit and well known in this country. he knew well that this new Minister, would adopt every plan and follow every step begun or suggested by Adet, consequently things would go on smooth & easy. he added that his mind was now fully satisfied & he would continue his travels with alacrity & spirit. he also informed me, that having considered the uncertainty of my staying here or going down the River he had finally wrote to his friend Adet not to direct his dispatches to me, but forward him the same by *Express* to Kentucky or fort Washington, as soon as the new Minister was arrived and matters arranged between them, so as to establish the chain of corrospondence upon a fixed plan.

"From the different conversations I have had with him I have reason to suspect that he has powerful recommendations to Genl Wilkinson and expects a great deal of information from that quarter. he calls him the popular General & seems to entertain a very indifferent opinion of the Commander in Chief [Anthony Wayne], whom he considers as a Slave to the Executive and of course a dangerous Man.

"May 29th—I paid a morning visit to Gl C. & upon a pressing invitation I dined with him—the conversation turned upon his voyage, and a map being produced, we examined the ground he had to go through from Limestone to Lexington from thence to Fort Washington &c. &c., upon a reasonable calculation it appeared that it will require from two to three months & perhaps more, to accomplish the viewing of Kentucky, North west territory, the new State of Tennasse & Post Vincennes, before he could reach the banks of the Mississipi at Kaskakias. in the course of the conversation I intimated that in all probability I would go down the Ohio, in the course of the next month and likely would see him at Fort Washington, on his return from Lexington, he seemed highly pleased & assured me he would be very glad if I could make it convenient to accompany him for the remainder of his voyage; I told him that it would depend in a great measure upon the turn my business would take in that Country.

"June 1st. Genl C. came and spent with me two hours this morning, in this long conversation I discovered that his departure which had been postponed first by a bad state of health, and afterwards by an accident which has happened to his baggage on the road is now deferred by an intimacy which has taken place between him & Judge Turner. the latter is this moment giving copies of Notes, in the North western territory, Kentucky & he is also communicating drafts of the different Forts which he says he has taken himself on the Spot. &c. Genl C. seems to be in rapture with his new acquaintance & promises himself wonders from the information he expects; he went as far as to say, that he would not begrudge the expences of a stay of two weeks more here, if it was necessary. he is to spend this day with the Judge and will take with him his Adjutant whose name is *Warin*, this gentleman as I formerly observed, is an Engineer of great abilities & has a peculiar talent in taking drafts of any place or object. Genl C. asked me, if he might depend upon my going down the Ohio as I had hinted in our last conversation; I said I would go for certain; now said he I will write to Adet and inform him of your determinatio⟨n⟩ by the next post, he shall direct his dispatches under your Cover, by the return of the mail & that will save the expence of an Express, this will answer a good purpose for we are not rich enough *for the grand object we have in view*. I promised to wait for the dispatches a week or two longer, if it was necessary, & carry them to him at Fort Washington.

"June 2nd—Gl C. informed me that he was well satisfied with the Notes of Judge T. as also with his verbal information that his adjutant was hard at work in taking copies and that in all probability he could not leave Pittsburgh before wednesday next [8 June], in the course of this conversation he was a little more opened than before; he told me plainly that he was travelling at the expence of the French Republic that money had been advanced to him by Mr Adet for himself and his Suite; he professed a great desire to serve me, & went so far as to say, that if I would quit this Country (to which no true Frenchman ought to be attached) a proper situation would be procured for me; & in order to force conviction upon my mind, he told me *in confidence*, that part of his instructions were to prepare the way to an Exchange of the province of Louisiana for San Domingo lately ceeded to France by the Treaty of Peace with Spain; at all events he had in charge to establish or at least to ascertain the possibility of establishing in the province of Louisiana a Company to furnish the French Republic with timber & Spars for the Navy, & that I might be made the Agent of Government in that undertaking. But said he, you must shake your American prejudices, which I have often discovered in our different conversations, & of which I am well informed from other quarters; even Judge T. who has travelled with you once down the Ohio says you are the least of a Frenchman he ever saw; I have taken pains continued he, to undeceive him, because he will see Adet in Philadelphia, for whom I have given him a Letter of introduction, & he might give him an unfavourable opinion of you.

"June 4th. Genl C. came to see me this morning, informed me that he had recd no letter from Philadelphia yesterday, & that in all probability he would leave Pittsburgh to morrow or monday morning as he thought that by that time, his Adjutant would have finished his work with the Judge—he asked me again if I positively woud go the Ohio, as I had promised him & upon my answering in the Affirmative he said he would depend upon my word, as he had wrote by post yesterday to his friend Adet, who would accordingly forward me his dispatches, now said I am satisfied & shall expect you at Fort Washington by the latter end of this month, on my return from the upper settlements of Kentucky. I will then inform you of my success & prospects, & may perhaps let you more into my secret views & operations, especially if you can make it convenient to accompany me for the remainder of my voyage.

"June 6th—Genl C. came this morning to bid farewell—he informed me that he heard yesterday of Genl Wilkinson, having began his march towards the British Posts; that this intelligence, would alter his plan of voyage; that instead of taking horses at Limestone for Lexington he would proceed directly with his boat to Fort Washington & follow the Tract of the Army as expeditiously as possible to overtake Genl Wilkinson whom he must necessarily see.

on his return to Fort Washington he would order his boat to Louisville & himself with his adjutant travel by Land through Kentucky &c. Fort Washington is still our rendezvous, & the first arrived thither is to wait for the other. In the course of this conversation he informed me, that he was perfectly pleased with the communications & information he had from Judge T.; that in all probability he would be of considerable service & that he had written accordingly to Mr Adet; he blamed me for my want of attention to the Judge, strongly recommended my seeing him every day till his departure from Pittsburgh—amongst many other instructions he gave me, he particularly insisted, that I should be upon my guards in any conversation I might have with Mr James Ross Senator in Congress, who was to his certain knowledge the Champion of government & the Colleague of the infamous Bingham &c. &c. &c.—the Genl left Pittsburgh at 11 oClock."

5. For a French privateer's capture of the ship *Mount Vernon*, see Pickering to GW, 12 June, and n.2 to that document; see also Wolcott to GW, 20 June.

From Bushrod Washington

Dear Uncle   Richmond July 3d 1796

I received your favor by last post for which accept my grateful acknowledgements.[1] I shall make the necessary enquiries, and then pursue such steps as may insure to me the benefit of your bounty.

I should have written to you immediately after the end of the last Chancery Term respecting the suit agt Colvilles Legatees, but that I expected the pleasure of seeing you at Mount vernon sometime in the last month, and supposed I might as well postpone any communications respecting the business 'till I could make them in person. The enclosed order I obtained at the May Court which was as early as any thing could be done, and is what you desire.[2] this gives you the opportunity of immediately getting clear of the mony, but as your object I know is to obtain a quietus with respect to the whole business so as not to be called upon hereafter to settle accounts when vouchers &c. may be lost, I consulted with Mr Keith & finding that he could with safety go into a settlement again I shall as soon as the rules of the Court will permit obtain an order appointing Commissioners to state & settle your accounts—this may perhaps surprise you, Knowing that this has been once before done under the order of the County Court—But settlements of that kind are not obligatory at all, and are every day controverted and set aside—Knowing this & reflecting that you might hereafter be called upon when you may have lost the assistance of Mr Keith, I thought it was in every respect most consonant with your views & interest to seek a final & conclusive termination to the business.

I hope to have the pleasure of seeing you & my Aunt at Mount Vernon about the 9th Instant—Mrs Washingtons health is so bad during the summer in this lower Country, that I shall (inconvenient as it is for me to leave Town) endeavour to carry her up to the Berkley Springs.

She Joins me in love to my Aunt & yourself And believe me to be dear Uncle with sincere wishes for your hea[l]th & happiness Yr Affectionate Nephew

Bushrod Washington

P.S. you will please forward the enclosed order so as to be published at some place in England as near that where your first advertisement was published as possible—some merchant in Alexa. can no doubt have this done.[3]

ALS, ViMtvL.

1. See GW to Bushrod Washington, 29 June.

2. *The Virginia Gazette, and General Advertiser* (Richmond) for 6 July printed the chancery court order dated 4 June that noted the heirs of Thomas Colvill's mother Catharine were "not inhabitants" of the United States and directed them to appear "on the first day of the next May term" to answer GW's bill. The court also directed that "a copy of this order be forthwith inserted in some newspaper of the City of Richmond, and some public paper in the Kingdom of Great-Britain, for two months successively." Additionally, the court required GW to "deposit in the bank of Alexandria, to remain subject to the future order of the court, nine hundred and thirty-two pounds seventeen shillings and seven pence three farthings, admitted by his bill to be in his possession, of the estate of Thomas Colville." For GW's subsequent action, see his letter to James Keith dated 17 July.

3. See GW to Rufus King, 25 August.

From Alexander Addison

Sir   Philadelphia 4th July 1796

Supposing that you would be in Philadelphia when I should arrive here, Matthew Ritchie of the town of Washington in this state desired me to adjust the future payments and obtain the execution of a conveyance from you to him of the lands on Miller's

Run in Washington county in this state, sold to him by Mr Ross in your name.[1]

About two months ago a bill for 3000 dollars was sent down to Mr Ross on account of the first payment, and arrangements were made and mentioned to him for the payment of any further sum for the principal or interest, that might be due. The quantity of land was not then ascertained. A judgement bond executed by M. Ritchie & me is in my hands to be filled up with the precise sum and delivered on receiving the conveyance. A mortgage would have been executed by him at the same time but he had not then the survey of the land. The survey has been delivered to Col. Neville since I left home and while I was at Pittsburgh court. It contains 2955 acres. I presume you have received it.[2] I missed Mr Ross by the way and you were gone two weeks before I came here. I am therefore induced to write to you for information on the following points.

Where I shall pay or deposit the sum due for the interest up to the first payment and whether any interest will be required on that sum from the first of June last.

Whether a judgement bond executed by M. Ritchie and me will be satisfactory to you.

Whether M. Ritchie will be at liberty, if he should find it convenient, to anticipate any of the payments and what is the least sum that will be accepted and what notice if any must be given of the anticipation of payment, and whether any sum further than the interest will be taken now.

Whether I may expect a conveyance to Matthew Ritchie to be now executed and deposited in the hands of a third person ⟨here⟩ whom you may name to be retained if you think proper till a mortgage is executed and delivered for the remainder of the price.

I was also desired to state to you, that at the time of the sale, it was suggested to Mr Ross, as a thing to be submitted to you, that there would be a propriety in computing interest only from the 1st of April last, when possession was agreed to be given to M. Ritchie, not from the 1st of January; And it was also stated to Mr Ross that (especially if the interest should be computed from the 1st of Jany) the possession on the 1st of April would carry with it a claim to the rent not then due for the crop then in the ground.

As every thing is wished to be conducted on liberal and explicit terms, a declaration from you on this subject is requested; and, if you think proper, a direction to Charles Morgan to give up the leases with the claim of the rent for the crop in the ground on the first of April last to M. Ritchie.

If there is no certainty of your being here before the end of next week, I hope you will take the trouble of giving me the desired information by letter directed to me at Col. Gurney's Philadelphia.[3] I am with the greatest respect Your most obedt Servt

Alexr Addison

ALS, DLC:GW.

1. For the sale of GW's land on Miller's Run in Washington County, Pa., to Matthew Ritchie, see James Ross to GW, 15 April, and n.1.

2. The survey has not been identified.

3. GW replied to Addison on 8 July.

From Cyrus Griffin

Sir   Wmsburg July 4th 1796

Being engaged upon duty at the Circuit and District Courts held in the City of Richmond I had not an opportunity of sooner acknowleging the honor of your letter.[1]

I am particularly uneasy and depressed to have taken one moment from the immense labour of your public functions, or to have incured your displeasure in the remotest degree. We understood that Congress were to adjourn on the 20th of May; I thought you would do me the favor to read the letter at some more leisure period; nor had I the least claim to receive an answer but what should arise from your extreme Goodness to every description of persons.[2] Indeed Sir, I did not mean to intimate that I had been overlooked in any recent appointments, but meant to obviate some objections to me that possibly might have come to your Information, in case that another Judge of the Supreme Court should be nominated from Virginia, and upon supposition that gentlemen of better talents, from their lucrative practice at the Bar, would not think proper to accept such appointment.

I have taken the liberty to write to you three or four letters since your Benevolence was shewn to me, in one of which I expressed a wish that my destination had been fixed to a diplomatic employment[3]—the wish was a most improper one as those employments were so much better arranged, and I did wrong in fatiguing you with letters unnecessarily. repentance never reaches to restitution, but I will promise most faithfully never more to encroach upon your valuable hours, the only compensation in my power to make.

most eagerly do I thank you for those kind assurances of esteem and regard; and 'tho I am destitute of the great advantages of the mind which other gentlemen possess, yet very honestly may I take the liberty to profess the sentiments of my heart—that purest veneration, and most respectful attachment with which I shall always remain Sir Your obedient and obliged humble Servant

C. Griffin

pardon me when I take the freedom to congratulate with you upon the return of this day; and that I most fervently hope many years hence you may in health preside over the Councils of our happy Country.

ALS, DLC:GW.

1. See GW to Griffin, 8 June, found in the source note for Griffin to GW, 23 May.

2. Griffin is referring to his letter to GW of 23 May.

3. Griffin had expressed a preference for a diplomatic appointment when he wrote GW on 12 Dec. 1789, not long after GW had given him a recess appointment as the federal district judge for Virginia (see Griffin to GW, 10 July 1789, source note).

From Charles Lee

[Alexandria, Va.] 4th July 1796

The Attorney General having taken into mature consideration "the act for the relief and protection of American Seamen" which grew out of the bill "for the relief and protection of American Seamen" passed in the house of representatives of the United States on the 28th march 1796 and afterwards amended in the Senate, the opinions of William Lewis and William Rawle thereupon, the letter from the Secretary of the Treasury of the

28th of june and the proclamation proposed to be issued relative to the execution of that act of Congress, most respectfully to the President of the United States reports that[1]

1st the bill "for the relief and protection of American Seamen" passed on the 28th march 1796 in the house of representatives and went to the senate where it was long debated and where it received many alterations and from whence it was returned in its altered state and ultimately proceeded to the act approved on the 28th may 1796 as it appears in print. From this account of the passage of this act, which is believed to be correct, there is strong ground to be of opinion that the fourth section of the original bill and other parts of it were purposely omitted and did not receive the assent of the Senate. To the 4th Section of *the bill* several objections occur; for instance a man is required to swear positively to the place of his nativity; a fact that no man certainly knows, and therefore of no man ought such an oath to be exacted; again the citizens in the several states naturalized after the 26th of march 1790 according to the laws of the several states respectively are neglected & concerning them no provision has been made: But it was adjudged in a circuit court of the United States, and has been also adjudged by various *state judges* in Virginia that the act of Congress of the 26th march 1790 did not repeal the laws of the Individual states respecting naturalization and after that period many foreigners in conformity to those judgments have been admitted citizens of Virginia according to the law of the State.[2]

The act of the 26th march 1790 being affirmative only, the laws of the several states on the same subject were deemed to have concurrent force and not to be repealed; and thus they continued till the 29th of January in the year 1795 when one uniform rule of naturalization was established in exclusion of all State regulations or laws upon that subject.[3]

For these and other objections to the 4th section of the bill, it might be thought more prudent to leave the authentication of the proofs of citizenship at large and unprescribed as without any doubt the proofs themselves are left. However this may have arisen, whether from accident or design in the legislators, the act for the relief and protection of American Seamen must now be taken and if possible executed as it is found enrolled & printed.

2dly This act is capable of execution according to its true

meaning though obviously inaccurate and imperfect in this particular viz. that it does not specify or prescribe *how the proof of the citizenship of a Seaman is to be authenticated* which in the 4th Section was contemplated to be prescribed in a subsequent part of the law and which has been omitted. It is not uncommon for Legislatures to be inattentive to the rules of Syntax & even of grammar; and errors of either kind are never fatal if the real meaning of the law can be collected and ascertained and in forming an opinion upon a statute a view must be taken of all its parts as making a whole.

It is a general rule that every statute shall have its effect if it be possible by any reasonable construction and the more especially if it be of a beneficial and remedial nature. Upon this principal some words of a law may be disregarded as superfluous or as insignificant or as absurd, if otherwise the whole law or an essential part of it will be frustrated and made void—Perhaps no case can exist to which this rule would be more applicable than the present for unless it is applied, two sections, the 4th and 7th, are to be deemed null & void, and these sections form an important part of the law.

By the 4th section it is enacted "that the Collector of every district shall keep a book or books on which at the ⟨request⟩ of ⟨any⟩ seaman being a citizen of the United States of America and producing proof of his citizenship *authenticated in the manner hereinafter directed* he shall enter the name of such Seaman and shall deliver to him a certificate in the following form that is to say" &c. (here see the form).

But the act does not direct thereafter any manner of authenticating the proof of citizenship. What then is to be done? Is the whole section to be considered null & void, and the Executive authority to be called upon to supply it by an act or proclamation to that intent & purpose. The Attorney General thinks not, and is rather of opinion that the words "authenticated in the manner herein after directed" should be rejected as superfluous and inoperative. If they are so rejected, then the proof of citizenship to be produced to the Collector may be any & every kind of reasonable proof upon which in each case he is to decide according to his discretion but subject to the instructions if any are sent from the Supreme Executive prescribing the manner in which the proofs shall be authenticated.

3dly The act having stated the form of the certificate that is to be granted by the collector to the Seaman in so many words, it is thought that no other form is admissable or can be legally substituted: and such is the form of the certificate, that no alteration of it will become necessary if the above opinion be correct. These words of the certificate "produced to me proof in the manner directed in the act" appear not to create any difficulty in as much if the act leaves the manner of proof actually at large and unrestrained (which cannot be doubted) proof in any reasonable manner ought to be considered to be such *as is directed in the act.*

It is with the utmost deference that the Attorney General differs from the learned counsel, who consider the 4th and 7th sections of the act under consideration as null and void, and who recommend that the Executive authority issue instructions to supply the place of those sections consistent with the principles of the act and conducive to its object. Is it not more reasonable to consider a few words of the 4th section as redundancy, left in the law by inadvertence and therefore as idle or immaterial & by so doing to let the whole law have its operation? Is it not more safe for the Executive to give a construction to the 4th section that will leave it in force, than to supply its defect by an executive act?

Upon a subject new and general as this is, some general rules of conduct to be transmitted to the Collectors and publicly known and published, would be useful in promoting the objects of the Act—These might appear in the shape of a proclamation, or of a circular letter from the Secretary of State to the collectors: and in either mode should be universally published. Perhaps the latter would be preferable as least liable to misinterpretation and ill-natured remarks.[4] In either case if the foregoing opinions of the attorney General are approved by the President he will find occasion, to give directions materially different from those contained in the Proclamation which has been proposed by the heads of Departments & transmitted to him by the Secretary of the treasury, for all of whom the most unfeigned respect is entertained. All which is with the most profound deference & respect Submitted—

Charles Lee Attorney General

ALS, DLC:GW.

1. For the material that Lee considered, see Oliver Wolcott, Jr., to GW, 28 June, and notes 2 and 3 to that document; see also GW to Wolcott, 6 July, and n.1.

2. Lee is referring to the Pennsylvania circuit court case *Collet v. Collet*, decided in April 1792 (see *Dallas*, 2:294–96). *The Mail; or, Claypoole's Daily Advertiser* (Philadelphia) for 28 April 1792 provides additional details. For "An Act to establish an uniform Rule of Naturalization," 26 March 1790, see 1 *Stat.* 103–4.

3. See "An Act to establish an uniform rule of Naturalization; and to repeal the act heretofore passed on that subject," 29 Jan. 1795 (1 *Stat.* 414–15).

4. GW accepted Lee's recommendation (see his letter to Lee, 6 July; see also GW to Timothy Pickering, 8 July, and n.1 to that document).

To Timothy Pickering

Sir   Mount Vernon 4th July 1796

The Spanish Minister, Mr de Yrujo, spent two days with me, and is just gone.[1] I caused it to be intimated to him, that as I should be absent from the Seat of the Government until the middle, or latter end of August, that I was ready to receive his letter of credence at this place. He answered (as I understood it) that his credentials were with his Baggage, on its passage to Philadelphia; and that his reception at that place, at the time mentioned, would be perfectly convenient and agreeable to himself.[2]

He is a young man, very free and easy in his manners; professes to be well disposed towards the United States; and as far as a judgment can be formed in so short an acquaintance, appears to be well informed.

Enclosed are two letters from the Governor of Pennsylvania, applying for the Aid of the General Government to execute, effectually, the Quarantine he had Proclaimed.[3] I left Philadelphia under an impression that circular letters had been written by the Secretary of the Treasury to the Collectors of the different Ports, and by the Secretary of War to the Officers commanding the Garrisons on the Seaboard to pay proper attention to the Act of Congress relative to Quarantine.[4]

From the application of Govr Mifflin, the presumption is, there has been an omission somewhere. Let me desire that you, and the other two Gentlemen would meet, and see where it lyes;

that a remedy may be immediately applied. and I request you will acknowledge the receipt of the Governor⟨s⟩ letters, and inform him of what is, or will be, done.

I desire to be informed also, if any thing is, or can be done relatively to the appointment of an Indian agent, in place of Governor Blount? and others, for carrying on the Trade (authorised by Congress) with those People?[5]

Go: Washington

ALS, MHi: Pickering Papers; LS (retained copy), DNA: RG 59, Miscellaneous Letters; LB, DNA: RG 59, GW's Correspondence with His Secretaries of State. Pickering responded to GW on 8 July.

1. Spanish minister Carlos Martinez Yrujo wrote GW from Philadelphia on 31 July: "As during my residence at Moùnt Vérnon yoù did allow me to have the hónor to presènt yoù with ã Bóok concerning the cúlture of the Pine Apples & other different fruits on Hot-Hoùses, I do prevaìl of the opportunity of my friend Mr James Barrý going to that part of the country, to forward it to yoù. I dont doùbt that ã man, under whose direction every thing floùrish & prospèr, wìll be equally succesfùll in making those fine fruits thrive on the mild climate of virginia, & give by those means ã new reputatìon to that Book, that is already considered as ã very gòod one. On having the honòr to present it to yoù, I hope yoù wìll look at it as ã mark of my sincere consideratìon & of that attachement that only rèal merit & vertùe are able to inspire.

"Yoù will permit me to prevaìl of that opportunity to exprèss yoù my gratitude for the Kindness & hospitality I met with when at Moùnt Vernon & to remind my respècts to Mrs Washington & Miss Cùstìs" (ALS, DLC:GW). Yrujo presented John Abercrombie, *The Hot-House Gardener on the General Culture of the Pine-apple, and Methods of Forcing Early Grapes, Peaches, Nectarines, and Other Choice Fruits, in Hot-Houses, Vineries, Fruit-Houses, Hot-Walls, &c.* . . . (London, 1789), which was in GW's library at the time of his death (see Griffin, *Catalogue of the Washington Collection*, 1–2).

2. GW's official reception of Yrujo occurred on 25 Aug. (*JPP*, 341; see also GW to Pickering, 29 June).

3. GW enclosed Thomas Mifflin's letters to him of 25 and 27 June.

4. The act approved on 27 May authorized the president "to direct the revenue officers and the officers commanding forts and revenue cutters, to aid in the execution of quarantine, and also in the execution of the health laws of the states" (1 *Stat.* 474).

5. GW's concern arose from "An Act to regulate Trade and Intercourse with the Indian Tribes, and to preserve Peace on the Frontiers," 19 May (1 *Stat.* 469–74).

From Timothy Pickering

(Secret)

Sir,   Department of State July 4. 1796.

I have the honor to inclose the concurrent opinions of the heads of departments on the points stated in your letter of the 24th ulto[1] and I return the confidential copy of Colo. Hamilton's letter, agreeably to your direction. The letter to Mr Adet was sent to him on Saturday.

The paper inclosed by Mr Monroe in his letter to Dr Logan gave a very long detail about French affairs. In the last page he touched on the British treaty; concerning which he says, that the report of a new connection thereby formed between the U.S. & G. Britain, "operated like a stroke of thunder, & produced in all France amazement."[2] There was a postscript to Mr Monroes letter, but it merely referred to the project of the French constitution, which he had only heard read in the convention, & could not therefore detail.[3] I am with the highest respect sir your most obt servt

                                          Timothy Pickering

ALS, DLC:GW; ADfS, MHi: Pickering Papers. GW docketed the ALS: "From The Secrety of State 2d July 1796." The docket date matches the enclosed cabinet opinion (see n.1 below). GW replied to Pickering on 8 July.

GW acknowledged the receipt of Pickering's letter and its enclosures when he wrote Attorney General Charles Lee from Mount Vernon on 7 July: "(confidential) . . . Consider the enclosed papers, which came by the post of yesterday, as *entirely* and *absolutely* confidential. Read them attentively, & let me see & converse with you on the contents of them this evening, or very early tomorrow morning, that time may be allowed me to prepare my dispatches for the post office in the afternoon" (LB, DLC:GW).

1. See the Cabinet to GW, 2 July, and n.2 to that document.

2. James Monroe, U.S. minister to France, had written George Logan from Paris on 24 June 1795 (see *Papers of James Monroe*, 3:375–76). A copy of that letter in DLC:GW (misdated 1796) begins: "I give you within a short sketch of the actual state of things here, a copy of which I likewise send to one or two other friends of whom Mr Beckley is one. If you & Mr Beckley, if in philadelphia, deem it worthy the attention, I have no objection to your inserting it in Bache's paper, the first paragraph excepted. And if you likewise approve, I will hereafter keep you regularly apprized of the course of events, whereby the community at large may be more correctly informed of the progress of the revolution than they heretofore have been or can be from the English prints. The character will be from a gentleman in Paris to his friend in Phila-

delphia." The sketch (minus the first paragraph) subsequently appeared in Benjamin Bache's *Aurora General Advertiser* (Philadelphia) for 31 Aug. 1795, introduced as "a letter from an American gentleman in France, who possesses the best means of information." The item was touted as "a more satisfactory and interesting view of the situation of the French Republic, in relation to all its domestic and foreign concerns, and particularly with regard to its present feeling and disposition towards the United States, than any thing that has yet been published in America."

A correctly dated copy of Monroe's letter to Logan and a copy of Monroe's sketch, dated 23 June 1795, are in MHi: Pickering Papers. Writing from Paris, Monroe maintained that the revolutionary Convention remained in firm control. The strength of counterrevolutionary forces compared "like that of an infant against Hercules." Members of the Convention familiar to Monroe were "among the most enthusiastick admirers and advocates of the publick liberty. . . .

"In other respects the prospect has become more favourable to a happy termination of the revolution than was heretofore promised. The people of France may conquer their liberties and merit to be free, but without a good government it will be impossible to preserve them. This truth has latterly been more deeply impressed upon the Convention than it formerly was, and in consequence, the attention of that body seems now to be principally turned to that object, a committee consisting of Eleven members having been appointed for more than six weeks past, to report what changes it will be necessary in their judgment to make in the existing one of 1793, and whose report is dayly expected. It is believed that this committee will propose some important changes in that constitution, and that the Convention will adopt them, Such as a division of the legislature into two branches &c. after the model of the American constitutions. . . .

"The external view is still more favourable. The atchievements of the last campaign surpassed every thing that the modern world has witnessed: in every quarter their arms were triumphant, but where the greatest danger pressed there the grandeur of their exploits was most conspicuous. . . . From an enemy Holland has become a friend and ally. . . . Prussia has withdrawn from the war, and is now in the closest amity with France. Spain is negociating and will probably soon have peace: Austria is Known to wish it, and England has absolutely made overtures secretly." Monroe believed conflict would "soon be narrowed to a contest between this Republick and England. I mean such is the present prospect, and this will of course be a maritime one only" in which European powers, with the possible exception of Russia, would "wish to see the naval force of England broken or at least greatly diminished."

As for the United States and France, Monroe claimed that his arrival had reversed "unfavorable impressions" and revived "the antient and close amity which had formerly subsisted . . . Such was the actual state of things when the report of Mr Jay's treaty with the English government transpired, and by which it was circulated that a new connection was formed between the United States and that power, beneficial to the latter, and probably hurtful to France. This report operated like a stroke of Thunder, and produced upon all France amazement. What the Treaty really is, is not yet Known, but most certainly the bias in our favor has been greatly diminished, nor is it possible that the cordiality should be great under such circumstances. If the treaty is rejected, or contains in it nothing strictly objectionable, in either case we shall stand well here but if it is adopted and does contain any thing which a just criticism can censure, be assured we shall hear from this government in terms of reproach. By this time you know what the Treaty is, and therefore Know according to its fate in what light we shall be considered here. If the treaty is not precisely what we wished it to be, most certainly the most favorable opportunity that was ever offered to make a good one has been thrown away: for as France was successful, and a good understanding subsisted between us and France, it was really in our power to dictate what terms we pleased, provided we could make the English government believe that in any event we would take part against it."

Monroe concluded by noting that the French "Republick is rapidly rising to, or rather has already obtain a decided preponderance not only in the scale of Europe, but indeed in that of human affairs. . . . Upon every principle therefore it was greatly to be regretted, if America should lose in any degree the ground upon which she hath heretofore stood in the estimation of her ally."

3. The copy of Monroe's letter to Logan in MHi: Pickering Papers includes the postscript: "The plan of a constitution was reported yesterday in the Convention the outline of which according to my comprehension for 'tis not yet printed and I only heard it reported is a division of the Legislative into two branches. 1st a council of 500 and 2d one of 250. the latter to be called a council of old men—laws to originate in the first only. There is likewise a council of censors with power to remove from office and disqualify. The Executive power to be vested in five persons to be allowed each a salary equivalent to about £5000 sterg and to serve each 5 years but in such manner that one shall be annually supplied. The judicial department is also differently organized but in what form I cannot say—The Department of Paris is to be called the Department of the Seine."

From Timothy Pickering

Sir   Philadelphia July 4. 1796

I received your letter of the 29th ulto on Saturday.[1] Mr Liston has promised the necessary letters for Colo. Talbot, & to deliver them to me by the ensuing Thursday;[2] and about Friday he proposes to set out for Mount Vernon. The Chevalier de Freire told me ten days ago, that he should regulate his movements by those of Mr Liston, whose departure for Mount Vernon he waited. Mr Liston last evening mentioned as a motive for delaying his journey, the expected arrival of the British packet: but that now he should wait no longer than about Friday next.[3] Of Mr Adet's journey I have heard nothing: if I can by any means learn his intentions I will make them known to you.[4]

I have sent to Mr Jaudennes, who informs that the Spanish minister has gone from Baltimore to the city of Washington, & thence means to proceed to Mount Vernon.[5] I am most respectfully, sir, your obt servt

T. Pickering

ALS, DLC:GW; ADfS, MHi: Pickering Papers.

1. The previous Saturday was 2 July.

2. Silas Talbot was assigned to the West Indies to obtain the release of impressed Americans (see GW to the U.S. Senate, 30 May, and Pickering to GW, 12 June, and n.1 to that document). British minister Robert Liston wrote Pickering on 8 July with a circular letter to the governors and naval commanders in the West Indies dated 7 July (both DNA: RG 59: Notes from the British Legation). Writing from Philadelphia, Liston explained in the circular letter that he complied with the request because of his "principal duty . . . to cultivate a good understanding between Great Britain and America, and that the examination and removal of these grievances alluded to is essential to this important end. I am farther persuaded that the penetration of Mr Talbot will discover that the complaints which have made so unfavorable an impression in this Country have frequently been false or exaggerated." Liston further expressed a belief that Talbot's mission "will have a tendency to promote the great object of reconciliation." Liston wrote in his letter to Pickering: "My professions of a desire to effect reconciliation and to establish good humour between the two countries are thoroughly sincere. My wishes on that head are so ardent that I have complied with your request in granting Letters of recommendation to Mr Talbot, without any instructions on the subject from home; without knowing how far the establishment of a foreign agent in the West Indies (contrary to the receivd usage) may be approved of by our Government; and upon the whole with a feeling in my own breast that I have perhaps gone beyond the line of my duty. The rectitude of the motive will justify it is to be hoped the hazard I incur" (see also Pickering to GW, 27 July, postscript).

On 24 Aug., Liston advised Pickering that the British government considered "the residence of a public agent of the United States in any of the British West India Islands" as "inadmissable." Pickering then wrote: "I expressed my regret that the disposition of the British Government should be opposed to the conciliatory measure he had adopted: that if it were known, it would be ascribed to their unlawful desire still to retain a multitude of American Citizens in bondage . . . I could not but express my satisfaction that he had taken a measure so unequivo[ca]lly right. And that if the British Administration were influenced by the like maxims of sound policy, all difficulties between the two Countries would be removed" (substance of a conversation with Liston, DNA: RG 59, Domestic Letters).

3. For Liston's visit to Mount Vernon, see James McHenry to GW, 5 July,

and n.1 to that document, and GW's first letter to McHenry, 22 July, and n.2 to that document.

Portuguese minister Cipriano Ribeiro Freire subsequently postponed his visit to Mount Vernon (see McHenry to GW, 7 July).

4. At this point on the draft Pickering wrote and struck out an additional paragraph: "The news-papers of last week informed us that the Spanish minister had arrived at Baltimore, and meant to set out for Philadelphia on Thursday last. If he is charged with any business which requires the early delivery of his letters of credence, it has occurred to me that he might conveniently accompany his friend the Chevalier de Freire to Mount Vernon. In this case I would have the copy of his letters of credence previously translated & sent to you. But I shall not suggest the idea of his going to Mount Vernon without your directions."

5. For Spanish minister Carlos Martinez Yrujo's visit to Mount Vernon, see GW to Pickering, this date, and n.1 to that document.

To Gustavus Scott

Sir,   Mount Vernon 4th July 1796

If the public dispatches which I receive, & am obliged to answer by every Post, would permit; I would go more into detail, & explanation of the subject of your last (seperate) letter, than it is possible for me to do at present.[1] I will not, however, let it pass without some further expression of my ideas; & the understanding I always had of your entrance into the Office you now hold, in the Federal City.

That the Secretary of State's letter to you (which I have not by me at this place to resort to) may have been so worded as to leave the alternative of residing in the City, or in George Town;[2] is not necessary, if it was justifiable, to deny; because a change of circumstances would certainly authorise a change of measures. But independent of this, it must not be forgotten, that at the time the letter above alluded to was written, such an alternative was indispensable for as much as there were no *convenient* accommodation for the Commissioners *in the City*; and because houses could not be erected in a moment, under the circumstances which then existed. In addition to this, let it be remembered also, that the first Comrs sensible of the propriety, & advantages which would result therefrom, had resolved to build a house for their own accommodation at, or near the spot where the Hotel now stands; and were diverted from it (if my memory serves me) partly by two causes; first from a doubt of the propriety of such an application of public money; and 2dly from an opinion that they could be accommodated in the Hotel, when built; which, it was expected would have happened long since.

I mention these things to shew; that there has been no inconsistency in my sentiments, or conduct; and that, to enable the Commissioners to comply with the views of Government, and to devote their time to its service, the present Compensation was resolved on.

Your other allegation is of a more serious nature; and if deception withdrew you from what you deemed a permanent establishment, at Baltimore, it cannot be justified. But be assured, Sir, this is a new view of the subject; and that the proposal to you, to become a Commissioner, originated in assurances, confidently given to me, that you had resolved to remove to the Federal City, or to George Town; and because I knew you had a considerable interest in the vicinity of them. Was not the first application to you predicated on this information?[3]

But I must be explicit in declaring, that not only to obviate the suspicions and jealousies which proceed from a residence of the Commissioners without the City, or in a remote corner of it; not only that they may be, where the busy & important scenes are transacting, that they may judge of the conduct of others not from *Reports only*, but from occular proof, as the surest guide to Oconomy an⟨d⟩ dispatch; Independent I say of these considerations, which are momentous of themselves, I should view the Residence of the Commissioners of the City, and their Officers of different Grades, in some central part of it as a nest egg (pardon the expression) which will attract others, and prove the *surest* means of accomplishing the great object which all have in view—the removal of Congress at the appointed time—without which, every thing will become stagnant, & your sanguine hopes blasted.

To be frank, I must give it to you as *my* opinion, that in relation to the concerns of the City, the Commissioners stand precisely in the same light (if not in a stronger one) than each does to any interesting matter in a train of execution for himself. Would you then, notwithstanding you may have an Archetect to carry on your buildings on Rock Hill, and a man to superinted your attending labourers trust to their proceeding[4] without your own minute Inspection of their conduct? I think, and am sure you will answer, no. I do not mean by this question to exhibit a charge— for I do as truly tell you, that I do not know, or ever heard, how often you visit your own concerns there. It is upon general principles I argue. A man of Industry and exertion will not, on his own acct have a work of that sort on hand without giving close attention to it. And certain it is, the Obligation (because of the responsibility) is at least equally great when entrusted by the Public.

After all, as the Season is now far advanced, & houses, in the situation I have described as most eligable, may not be to be rented; I am not unwilling that the removal of the *Commissioners* if they find much inconvenience in doing it, may be suspended untill the commencement of the operations of next Spring, when it will certainly be expected; and if known, I have *no* doubt but that houses will be prepared for their accommodation by that time.

You will from the length of this letter, with difficulty give credit to my assertion in the begining of it; but as a proof; not only of its verity, but of the friendship and candour with which it is written, it shall go to you in its present rough garb; and with all its imperfections,[5] accompanied with assurances of the esteem & regard with which I am—Sir Your Obedt Hble Servt

Go: Washington

DfS, DLC:GW; LB, DLC:GW.

1. Scott's letter has not been found.

2. GW is referring to a letter from Secretary of State Edmund Randolph to Scott, then in Baltimore, written at Philadelphia on 18 Aug. 1794: "A vacancy having taken place in the Board of Commissioners for the federal City; I am instructed by the President of the United States to tender to you a seat there. The salary will be at the rate of sixteen hundred dollars per annum; and residence in the City or George Town is considered as necessary for the discharge of the duties. This latter circumstance is said to have been contemplated by you for some time; and produced a hope that the Office might not be inconvenient to you. It will give me pleasure to be able to inform the President of your acceptance" (DNA: RG 59, Domestic Letters; see also William Deakins to GW, Jr., 7 July 1794).

3. See n.2 above.

4. GW inserted the preceding three words on the draft. The last portion of the word "labourers" is also in his writing.

5. GW covered many of the same issues addressed in this letter when he wrote Scott on 25 May 1796.

From Alexander Hamilton

Sir   New York July 5. 1796

I was in due time favoured with your letter of the 26 June & consulted the Gentleman you name on the subjects of it.

We are both of opinion there is *no* power in the President to appoint an Envoy Extraordinary, without the concurrence of the senate, & that the information in question is *not* a sufficient ground for extraordinarily convening the senate—If however the President from his *information collectively* be convinced that a dangerous state of things exists between us & France and that an envoy extraordinary to avert the danger is a necessary measure, I believe this would in the sense of the constitution warrant the calling of the Senate for the purpose—But this measure may be questionable in point of expediency, as giving a stronger appearance of danger than facts warrant—If further depredations on our commerce take place, if new avowals of the principle of the last capture should appear,[1] it may alter the case—But without something more the measure would scarcely seem adviseable.

Mr Jay & Myself though somewhat out of your question talked of the expediency of removing Monroe, and though we perceive there are weighty reasons against it, we think those for it preponderate—if a proper man can be found—But here we felt both immense embarrassment, for he ought to be at the same time a friend to the Government & understood to be *not unfriendly* to the French Revolution—General Pinckney is the only man we can think of who fully satisfies the idea, & unfortunately every past experiment forbids the hope that he would accept—though but for a short time[2]—But if a character of tolerable fitness can be thought of, it would seem expedient to send him—At any rate it is to be feared, if under the symptoms of discontent which have appeared on the part of the French Government, no *actual & full* explanation takes place, it will bring serious censure upon the Executive—It will be said that it did not display as much zeal to avoid misunderstanding with France as with G. Britain—that discontents were left to rankle—that if the Agent of the Government in France was negligent or unfaithful some other mode ought to have been found &c.

As to your resignation, Sir, it is not to be regretted that the declaration of your intention should be suspended as long as

possible & suffer me to add that you should *really hold the thing
undecided to the last moment*—I do not think it is in the power of
party to throw any slur upon the lateness of your declar[a]tion.
And you have an obvious justification in the state of things—
If a storm gathers, how can you retreat? This is a most serious
question.

The proper period now for your declaration seems to be *Two
months* before the time for the Meeting of the Electors. This will
be sufficient—The parties will in the mean time electioneer con-
ditionally, that is to say, *if you decline*—for a serious opposition to
you will I think hardly be *risked.*

I have completed the full draft of a certain paper & shall
shortly transcribe correct & forward it—I will then also prepare
& send forward without delay the original paper corrected upon
the general plan of it so that you may have both before you for
a choice in full time & for alteration if necessary.[3] With true respect & Affect. Attachment I have the hon. to remain Sir Yr very
Obed. ser.

A. Hamilton

ALS, NN: Alexander Hamilton Papers.

1. Hamilton considered responses to the French seizure of the *Mount Vernon.*

2. Charles Cotesworth Pinckney previously had declined appointments as
secretary of war and secretary of state (see his letters to GW, 24 Feb. 1794 and
16 Sept. 1795). For his subsequent decision to serve as U.S. minister to France,
see GW to John Marshall, 8 July, and n.2; GW to Pinckney, same date (first letter); and Pinckney to GW, 27 July.

3. The "certain paper" was a draft of GW's farewell address. For its trans-
mittal, see Hamilton to GW, 30 July. The "original paper" was a draft of the
farewell address sent when GW wrote Hamilton on 15 May (see also "GW's
Draft for a Farewell Address" printed as an enclosure with that document).
Hamilton sent another draft more closely following that text when he wrote
GW on 10 August.

From Betty Washington Lewis

MY DEAR BROTHER   JULY 5th, 1796.

I receiv'd your Letters of 26th and 29th of June,[1] the day after I wrote to you I was attack with the ague and fever which
has lasted ever since[2] I had never been clear of a fever since,
I Expected your comeing threw Baltemore that you would ascertain Mr. Parkes fortune thoe I beleive he would not tell anything

fals on the Occation,[3] Harriot's Brother Wrote her a letter from Baltemore and likewise one to Mr. Parks congratulateing them on there Intended Union which he sayes he makes no dout will be a very happy one,[4] Lawrence was here at the time that Mr. Parks firs spoke to Harriot on the subject and I beg'd of him to make all the inquire he could but never hard from him untill the letter I have mention'd here and concluded from that he had Inquired and was well Pleas'd, when Mr. Parks ask'd my consent I told him I had nothing to say to it that you ware the Person to be appli'd to,[5] I have never concern'd myself with it I think Harriot is Old Enougf now to make choice for her self, and if they are not happy I believe it will be her one[6] falt, he bars the Best caracter of any young Person that I know,

I now my Dear Brother have to thank you for your good intention of sending me a mule if you had any to spear, but had no write to Expect you to Disfirnish your self,

I am mutch obliged to you for your invitasion to Mount Vernon but it is utterly out of my Power to get up, I believe I wrote to you last fall that I had but two old Horses and in Tenn [*word left out*] from that[7] my stable was broken open and the best of them carri'd of[8] and from that day to this I have not har'd a word of him that was the forth charriot Hors that I lost in Fredericks you may Believe I had no great Parsiallity for the Place, Harriot is Better and is gone to the forth of July in Town but I think she looks badly.

My Love to you and my Sister Washington concludes me your Affectionate sister

BETTY LEWIS.

P.S.—I fear you will hardly make out this as I have a violent Headake and a horrid caugh—I believe Harriot is distressed to know how she is to be Provided with things for a Weding Dress.[9]

Scribner's Monthly, 15 (February 1878): 510. A 1959 transcription from the manuscript described as "a rough copy" is in ViFreGWF. That transcriber improved spelling and punctuation, but the content is largely the same. For significant variations, see notes 5, 6, and 7 below.

1. These letters from GW to Lewis have not been found.

2. See Lewis to GW, 26 June.

3. For GW's concern about the financial prospects of Andrew Parks, the man engaged to marry his niece Harriot Washington, see GW to George Lewis, 7 April, and George Lewis to GW, 19 April; see also Parks to GW, 1 and 30 April, and GW to Parks, 7 April.

4. The letters from Lawrence Augustine Washington have not been identified.

5. The clause "that you ware the Person to be appli'd to" does not appear in the 1959 transcription.

6. This word is "own" in the 1959 transcription.

7. The 1959 transcription omits the previous two words as well as the preceding one mentioned in the bracketed statement.

8. No such letter from Lewis to GW has been found.

9. Entries in GW's cash accounts for 10 July show $100 "sent Harriot Washington to buy her Wedding Cloaths" and $100 to "my Sister Lewis" (Cash Memoranda, 1794–97). For Harriot Washington's wedding on 16 July, see her letter to GW, 17 July.

From James McHenry

private.

Sir　　　　　　　　　　Philadelphia 5 July 1796.

I made a visit yesterday to Chevr Freire, and to-day he called to let me know, that his secretary had seen Mr Listons Secretary, who told him that Mr & Madam Liston would set out for Mount Vernon on friday,[1] and that he and Madam Freire would follow on the 18th inst.[2]

Seeing that these ministers will avail themselves of your politeness, may it not be proper to be a little more particular with Mr Adet. Ought I to mention to him, that you had desired me to remind him of your wish to see him at Mount Vernon, and to know when you might expect that pleasure. Just now I suppose he is engaged on Mr Pickerings questions.[3] I shall therefore take no step in the affair till the result is communicated, and till I hear further from you.[4]

I inclose a letter from Major Kersey who will be deranged upon the principle of seniority.[5] If a principle applicable to the majors could be adopted which would retain him and Peters, I have no doubt, but that the army would be benefited by leaving out in their stead Cushing & Shaylor.[6] You will perceive that on the present establishment Massachusetts & Connecticut have six majors out of the 11 Infantry majors, and that following the principle of Seniority six of the 8 will belong to these two States.[7] With the most sincere respect and attachment I am Sir your most obt st

James McHenry

ALS, DLC:GW; ADf, MdAA: James McHenry Collection.

1. The following Friday was 8 July. Henrietta Marchant Liston wrote in her journal: "On the 7th of July, we determined to accept, a very kind invitation given to us, by the President & Mrs. Washington, including our Secretaries, to visit them at Mount Vernon, & in spite of the bad accounts we heard of the roads, & there being no relay of Horses (except for *Stages*), We hired four of them for the journey, & set out in a Coachee we had got made, which held six persons, the Footman sharing the Drivers Seat." Their route went through Baltimore, Annapolis, and the Federal City. They "spent two days at Washington, in which time we made an excursion to the great Falls of the Potomack . . . The day following this excursion, we pursued our journey; & reached the Town of *Alexandria* in time to dine with an old acquaintance from Scotland. . . . We had crossed the Potomack at a small Town called George Town, a mile from Washington, in a Ferryboat, on our way to Alexandria, which is situated on the Southern Bank of this River. Next day we arrived at Mount Vernon, ten miles of the worst road we had yet past" (North, *Travel Journal of Henrietta Liston*, 11–12; see also GW's first letter to McHenry, 22 July, and n.2 to that document).

2. Portuguese minister Cipriano Ribeiro Freire subsequently postponed his visit to Mount Vernon (see McHenry to GW, 7 July).

3. For the questions Secretary of State Timothy Pickering posed to French minister Pierre-Auguste Adet, see the Cabinet to GW, 2 July, n.2.

4. GW replied to McHenry from Mount Vernon on 11 July: "Private . . . Your private letter of the 5th instant, with its enclosures, has been received.

"Mr Adet was as cordially, & as repeatedly asked to visit Mount Vernon as either of the other foreign characters; but to *me*, he never said he would come. La Fayette & Mr Frestal however, the day before I left Philadelphia, understood *him* that he should set out on this visit in ten days after me; since which I have heard nothing of him.

"It was my determination, and so I acted, to place them all upon *precisely* the same ground; but as there are many who will not be *disposed* to think so. but on the contrary, will, more than probably, represent it otherwise, it will be very agreeable to me, that you should see & express to him, on my behalf, the sentiments which are mentioned in your letter: predicated on the hope, raised in me, by the Gentlemen before mentioned" (ALS, PWacD: Sol Feinstone Collection, on deposit at PPAmP). For Adet's reasons not to visit Mount Vernon, see McHenry to GW, 16–17 July.

5. Maj. William Kersey's letter, probably addressed to McHenry, has not been identified.

William Kersey (d. 1800) served in the Continental army during the Revolutionary War and rose through the ranks to brevet captain. He became a lieutenant in the new U.S. army formed in 1789 and was promoted to captain in 1791 and major in 1794. Kersey remained a major of the 3d Infantry after this reorganization and died in a duel while still in the army.

6. At this point on his draft, McHenry added a sentence that he then struck out: "The one Gen. Wayne calls a disorganiser and says the other is not fit for service."

7. "An Act to ascertain and fix the Military Establishment of the United

States," approved on 30 May 1796, reorganized the army into four regiments of infantry, each with two majors (1 *Stat.* 483–86).

William Peters (c.1754–1807), of New York, had served as an ensign in the latter stages of the Revolutionary War. Like Kersey, he was appointed a lieutenant in the U.S. army in 1789. Promoted to captain in 1791 and major in 1794, Peters remained major of the 4th Infantry and served until 1802.

Joseph Shaylor (c.1748–1816), of Connecticut, also a Revolutionary War officer, was appointed captain in the U.S. army in 1791 and then promoted to major in 1793. Assigned to the 2d Infantry during the reorganization, he resigned in May 1797.

Thomas Humphrey Cushing of Massachusetts became a major in 1793.

From Oliver Wolcott, Jr.

Sir,   Treasury Department July 5. 1796.

I have the honor to represent to the President that the preparatory arrangements for the sale of the Lands remaining unsold in the seven ranges of townships in the No. Western territory, are already compleated.[1]

George Wallace Esqr. on enquiry appears to be a suitable character for the trust of superintending the sales at Pittsburgh in conjunction with the Governor or secretary of the North Western territory;[2] and Thomas Butler or Genl John Nevill can either of them give the necessary security as receivers of money on public account—& either of them are in other respects unexceptionable, so far as has come to my knowledge. The appointment of General Nevill will perhaps be most œconomical, as he is already in the public service, & ought to be satisfyed with a slight acknowledgement for this extra service.[3]

The Secretary of State has doubtless informed the President that Mr DeWitt has declined the office of Surveyor General.[4] No information is possessed by me of any characters other than have been already mentioned to the President. I have the honor to be &c.

Oliver Wolcott Jr

LB, DLC:GW; ADf, CtHi: Oliver Wolcott, Jr., Papers.

1. "An Act providing for the Sale of the Lands of the United States, in the territory northwest of the river Ohio, and above the mouth of Kentucky river," 18 May 1796, authorized executive action (1 *Stat.* 464–69). For the seven ranges in what became east central Ohio, see *JCC*, 28:375–81.

2. McHenry probably meant George Wallace (c.1748–1812), a judge in

Allegheny County, Pa., from 1788 until his death. Wallace represented Allegheny County at the 1797–98 session of the Pennsylvania House.

3. GW replied to Wolcott from Mount Vernon on 11 July: "Your Letter of the 5th instant came duly to hand. The preparatory arrangements for the sale of the Lands, remaining unsold, in the seven ranges of townships in the No. Western territory being complete—I think from the accounts given of George Wallace, he would be a suitable character for the trust of superintending the sales at Pittsburgh in conjunction with the Governor or secretary of the North W. Territory, & desire he may be empowered accordingly. Genl John Nevill is, I conceive, a fit person to receive the money proceeding from these sales, & that from his *other* public employment he *ought* to do it upon more oeconomical terms, & if he will do it, let him be appointed thereto" (LB, DLC:GW). Wolcott wrote letters to George Wallace and John Nevill on 15 July informing them of their appointments (see Carter, *Territorial Papers*, 2:562–63).

4. See Timothy Pickering to GW, 27 June, and n.2 to that document.

To Thomas Jefferson

Dear Sir,   Mount Vernon 6th July 1796.

When I inform you, that your letter of the 19th Ulto went to Philadelphia and returned to this place, before it was received by me; it will be admitted, I am persuaded, as an apology for my not having acknowledged the receipt of it sooner.

If I had entertained any suspicions before, that the queries which have been published in Bache's Paper proceeded from you, the assurances you have given of the contrary, would have removed them; but the truth is, I harboured none. I am at no loss to *conjecture* from what source they flowed; through what channel they were conveyed; and for what purpose they, and similar publications, appear.[1] They were known to be in the hands of Mr Parker, in the early part of the last Session of Congress; They were shewn about by Mr Giles during the Cession—and they made their public exhibition about the close of it.

Perciving, and probably hearing, that no abuse in the Gazette's would induce me to take notice of anonymous publications, against me; those who were disposed to do me *such friendly Offices*, have embraced without restraint every opportunity to weaken the confidence of the People—and by having the *whole* game in their hands, they have scrupled not to publish things that do not, as well as those which do exist; and to mutilate the latter, so as to make them subserve the purposes which they have in view.

As you have mentioned the subject yourself, it would not be frank, candid, or friendly to conceal, that your conduct has been represented as derogating from that opinion *I* had conceived you entertained of me. That to your particular friends & connexions, you have described, and they have announced me, as a person under a dangerous influence; and that, if I would listen *more* to some *other* opinions all would be well. My answer invariably has been, that I had never discovered any thing in the conduct of Mr Jefferson to raise suspicions, in my mind, of his insincerity; that if he would retrace my public conduct while he was in the Administration, abundant proofs would occur to him, that truth and right decisions, were the *sole* objects of my pursuit; that there were as many instances within his *own* knowledge of my having decided *against*, as in *favor of* the opinions of the person evidently alluded to; and moreover, that I was no believer in the infallibility of the politics, or measures of *any man living*. In short, that I was no party man myself, and the first wish of my heart was, if parties did exist, to reconcile them.[2]

To this I may add, and very truly, that, until within the last year or two, I had no conception that Parties Would, or even could go, the length I have been Witness to; nor did I believe until lately, that it was within the bounds of probability—hardly within that of possibility, that while I was using my utmost exertions to establish a national character of our own, independent, as far as our obligations, and justice would permit, of every nation of the earth; and wished, by steering a steady course, to preserve this Country from the horrors of a desolating war, that I should be accused of being the enemy of one Nation, and subject to the influence of another;[3] and to prove it, that every act of my Administration would be tortured, and the grossest, & most insiduous mis-representations of them be made (by giving one side *only* of a subject, and that too in such exagerated, & indecent term⟨s⟩ as could scarcely be applied to a Nero; a notorious defaulter; or even to a common pickpocket). But enough of this; I have already gone farther in the expression of my feelings, than I intended.

The particulars of the case you mention (relative to the Little Sarah) is a good deal out of my recollection at present; and I have no public papers here to resort to. When I get back to Phila-delphia (which, unless I am called there by something new, will not be 'till towards the last of August) I will examine my files.

It must be pleasing to a Cultivator, to possess land which will yield Clover kindly; for it is certainly a great Desiderata in Hus-bandry. My Soil, without very good dressings, does not produce it well: owing, I believe, to its stiffness; hardness at bottom; and retention of Water. A farmer, in my opinion, need never dispair of raising Wheat to advantage, upon a Clover lay; with a single ploughing, agreeably to the Norfolk and Suffolk practice. By a misconception of my Manager last year, a field at one of my Farms which I intended shd have been fallowed for Wheat, went untouched. Unwilling to have my crop of Wheat at that place so much reduced, as would have been occasioned by this omis-sion, I directed, as soon as I returned from Philadelphia (about the middle of September)[4] another field, not in the usual rota-tion, which had lain out two years, and well covered with mixed grasses, principally white clover, to be turned over with a good Bar-share;[5] and the Wheat to be sown, and harrowed in at the tail of the Plough. It was done so accordingly, and was, by odds, the best wheat I made this year. It exhibits an unequivocal proof to my mind, of the great advantage of a Clover lay, for Wheat. Our Crops of this article, hereabouts, are more or less injured by what some call the Rot—others the Scab; occasioned, I believe, by high wind & beating rain when the grain is in blossom, & before the Farina has performed its duties.

Desirous of trying the field Peas of England, and the Win-ter Vetch, I sent last fall to Mr Murray of Liverpool for eigh⟨t⟩ bushels of each sort. Of the Peas he sent me two kinds (a white & dark, but not having his letter by me, I am unable to give the names). They did not arrive until the latter end of April, when they ought to have been in the ground the beginning of March. They were sown however, but will yield no Seed; of course the experiment I intended to make, is lost.[6] The Vetch is yet on hand for Autumn Seeding. That the Albany Peas will grow well with us, I know from my own experience: but they are subject to the same bug which perforates, and injures the Garden Peas, and which will do the same, I fear, to the imported Peas, of any sort, from England, in this climate, from the heat of it.

I do not know what is meant by, or to what uses the Caroline drill is applied. How does your Chicorium prosper? Four years since, I exterminated all the Plants raised from Seed sent me by Mr Young, and to get into it again, the Seed I purchased in Philadelphia last Winter, and what has been sent me by Mr Murray this Spring, has cost me upwards of twelve pounds Sterling. This, it may be observed, is a left handed way to make money; but the first was occasioned by the manager I then had, who pretended to know it well in England, and pronounced it a noxious weed;[7] the restoration of it, is indebted to Mr Strickland & othe⟨rs⟩ (besides Mr Young) who speak of it in exalted terms.[8] I sowed mine broadcast, some with, and some without grain. It has come up well, but there seems to be a serious struggle between *it* and th⟨e⟩ grass & weeds; the issue of which (as I can afford no relief to the former) is doubtful at present, & may be useful to know.

If you can bring a moveable threshing Machine, constructed upon simple principles to perfection, it will be among the most valuable institutions in this Country; for nothing is more wanting, & to be wished for on our farms. Mrs Washington begs you to accept her best wishes—and with very great esteem & regard I am—Dear Sir Your Obedient Hble Servt

Go: Washington

ALS, DLC: Jefferson Papers; LB, DLC:GW.

1. GW probably is alluding to Edmund Randolph.

2. See, for example, Henry Lee to GW, 17 Aug. 1794, and GW to Lee, 26 Aug. 1794.

3. GW is referring respectively to France and Great Britain.

4. GW had arrived at Mount Vernon on the evening of 13 Sept. 1795 (see *Diaries*, 6:211).

5. A bar-share is a type of plow in which a bar extends backward from the point of the share (blade).

6. See GW to James Maury, 20 Oct. 1795, and Maury to GW, 26 Dec. 1795. For the arrival of the peas and GW's instructions for sowing, see GW to Tobias Lear, 29 April 1796, and to William Pearce, 1 May 1796.

7. For Arthur Young's shipment of *Cichorium intybus* (chicory, succory), see his letter to GW, 25 Jan. 1791, and GW to Young, 15 Aug. 1791. For its extermination as a noxious weed, see GW to Anthony Whitting, 3 and 24 Feb. 1793. GW sent chicory seed from Philadelphia to Mount Vernon in November 1795 (see GW to Pearce, 22 Nov. 1795).

8. While visiting the United States in 1795, William Strickland gave GW some chicory seeds (see GW to Pearce, 15 and 29 March 1795).

To Charles Lee

Sir,   Mount Vernon 6th July 1796.

Having shewn you the answr of the French Minister, to the communication of the Secretary of State, relatively to the Capture of the Ship Mount Vernon, by the French Privateer Flying Fish.[1] Having read you also, the contents of a Letter from —— respecting information from St Domingo, of the intended measures of the French government, to Harrass our commerce with Great Britain; and also my letter to the Secretary of State on that Subject; to which I have, by the last Mail, received the enclosed acknowledgment: Let me now ask what you think of the opinion therein given, respecting the recall of our Minister at Paris?[2] Whether *that* act will authorise the appointment of an Envoy Extraordinary, or Minister Plenipotentiary? Whether it is, in that case, expedient to do it under *present* circumstances, as far as they are known—or await a further developement of his conduct & the views of the Directory of France? And in case it is judged expedient to send a Person to Paris, to explain the motives for the conduct of this government, and to ascertain the views of that, Whether you think either of the Characters mentioned in the Secretary of State's letter would go? and whether there be any other occurring to you as eligable? Would Doctr McClerg go? & does he possess fit abilities if he would accept?

Answer all these queries as soon as you conveniently can.[3] And let me have the draught you promised (on Monday last) for the purpose of supplying the deficiency in the Act for the relief of Seamen.[4]

Make frequent inquiries for a fit character to fill the Office of Surveyor General—I wish much to have it ably executed.

Go: Washington

ADfS, DLC:GW; LB, DLC:GW.

1. For Secretary of State Timothy Pickering's communication to French minister Pierre-Auguste Adet about the seizure of the *Mount Vernon*, dated 13 June, see Pickering to GW, 12 June, n.2. Adet replied on 14 June (see Pickering to GW, 22 June, n.1).

2. See Alexander Hamilton to GW, c.16 June, and GW to Pickering, 24 June, and n.4 to that document.

3. For Lee's reply, see his letter to GW on 7 July.

4. See Lee to GW, 4 July.

From James McHenry

Sir,   War Office 6. July 1796.
    In conformity with your Commands of the 1st instant, I have transmitted to the Secretary of State and the Secretary of the Treasury, letters of which the inclosed is a Copy.[1]
    In the mean while I shall turn my attention to the subjects on which you have desired my report, which I shall make as soon as the unavoidable duties of the Office will permit.[2] With the greatest respect I am Sir Your most obedt humble servt

James McHenry
Secy of war

LS, DLC:GW; LB, DLC:GW; ADfS: DLC: James McHenry Papers.
    1. McHenry enclosed a copy of his letter dated 5 July to Secretary of State Timothy Pickering, in which he presented GW's request for opinions about the course to pursue with regard to Gen. James Wilkinson's charges against Gen. Anthony Wayne. McHenry's letter continued: "I submit to you in conformity with this order the letters and papers it refers to and request to be favoured as soon as convenient with your opinion.
    "When you have read the documents I beg they may be given to the Secretary of the Treasury for his perusal; my Clerks being too much engaged to make copies" (DLC:GW; see also GW's first letter to McHenry, 1 July).
    GW wrote McHenry from Mount Vernon on 11 July: "Your letter of the 6th instant, with copies of other letters to the Secretaries of State, and Treasury; respecting the charges exhibited by Brigadier Wilkinson against General Wayne, has been received; and when an opinion is formed thereon, I shall expect to receive it.
    "I know of nothing, at present, that will prevent my being in Philadelphia between the 15th of August and first of September: As then, there will be abundant time between that period and the 31st of October (when the new Military Establishment is to take place) to arrange the Officers to the several Corps; and as much information may be obtained, & many things cast up between this and then to lessen the difficulty, and obtain relief from the disagreeable task of *deranging* Officers I am induced to postpone a final decision in this case 'till I return to the Seat of Government, unless there are causes which do not occur to me, to require it sooner; of which you will not fail to inform me" (LS [retained copy], DLC:GW; LB, DLC:GW; see also McHenry to GW, 18 July and 10 Oct., the last in DLC:GW). GW's second paragraph responds to an issue McHenry raised when he wrote GW on 5 July.
    2. McHenry evidently is referring to subjects raised in GW's second letter of 1 July.

To Oliver Wolcott, Jr.

Sir,   Mount Vernon 6th July 1796.

When the letter herewith enclosed, dated the 4th instant was written in answer to yours of the 28th Ulto, part of it, as you will perceive, was dictated under the impression of much hesitation & doubt; for I am not fond of rectifying Legislative mistakes by Executive Acts. I determined however to take the Attorney Generals opinion on the case: resolving, if it accorded with those which had been sent me, to give the Act you forwarded, my signature.[1]

For this purpose I requested that his opinion might be *fully* stated to me in *writing* and delivered at Alexandria on the 4th where I had promised to be at the celebration of the Anniversary of Independance;[2] that I might, by the Post of next day, or rather the Mail of that evening, if his opinion had not a tendency to increase my own doubts, forward the Act to you.

Knowing, that neither time nor opportunity would be allowed at a crowded meeting, to write, I prepared my letter in the morning, before I left home, on the supposition of a concurrence; & in that case, that I might have nothing to do but to sign & enclose the Act; but his opinion being adverse to this (as you will see by the enclosure, which I request may be returned to me) I declined doing it; and have desired him to draught something anew.

This, when it comes to hand, (wch I expected would have been in time for this days Post) shall be sent.[3]

                                        Go: Washington

ALS, CtHi: Oliver Wolcott, Jr., Papers.

1. GW had written Wolcott from Mount Vernon on 4 July: "Your letter of the 28th Ulto with its enclosures, was received by the Mail on friday.

"I wanted no delay in the Commissioning of Mr Jno. Davis, to be Attorney for the District of Massachusetts; if to you, or those who were better acquainted with his professional knowledge (before he embarked in the Comptrollership) than I am, thought them competent to the duties thereof.

"That an entire Section of a Bill which had passed both Houses of Congress should be omitted in copying of it; and that such omission should have escaped the Committee of Inrolment; is a circumstance so singular in its nature as scarcely to have a parallel. Being desirous, however, of carrying the *intentions* of the Legislature into effect—I have, though I confess not willingly, endeavoured to supply the defect by the Executive Act which is herewith enclosed. The consequences that might result from delay, have produced this Act on my part; otherwise, as its operation is to be Exterior I should have hesitated longer, before the signature was given; if at all.

"By the last Mail, I received a Letter from the Governor of Pennsylvania, requesting 'that I would direct such co-operative measures, on the part of the Officers of the United States, as may effectually counteract the danger, wch is apprehended from Vessels holding an intercourse with the shores of New Jersey, in evasion of the Quarantine prescribed under the authority of the Laws of this State.' I expected, from what passed previous to my leaving Philadelphia, that circular orders had issued, long since, to the Collectors of the different Ports; and to the Officers commanding the fortifications of our Harbours, to afford *such* aid, agreably to the Act of Congress relative to Quarantine. As there are two letters from the Governor on the same subject, I shall send both of them by this days Post, to the Secretary of State; & desire that if any thing needful, remains to be done, that orders to that end may issue immediately" (ALS, CtHi: Oliver Wolcott, Jr., Papers; LB, DLC:GW). For the quarantine issue, see Thomas Mifflin to GW, 25 and 27 June; see also Timothy Pickering to GW, 8 July.

2. GW's attendance at the celebration in Alexandria, Va., was reported in *The Centinel of Liberty and George-Town Advertiser* for 12 July: "The President came to town about 12 o'clock, under escort of the troop of Light Dragoons, at three sat down to an elegant dinner which had been prepared for the occasion; after spending a cheerful day with a numerous company of his fellow-Citizens, he retired in the evening amidst their reiterated acclamations." GW withdrew after fifteen toasts, and a sixteenth—"The President of the United States—May he ever enjoy the patriot's best reward—The confidence, affection and gratitude of his Fellow-citizens"—received nine cheers after his departure.

3. See Charles Lee to GW, 4 July, and GW to Lee, this date.

From Oliver Wolcott, Jr.

Treasury Department July 6. 1796.

The Secretary of the Treasury respectfully transmits to the President of the United States a Letter from the Commissioner of the Revenue dated the 5th instant, covering a provisional contract entered into by William Allibone superintendent of the Light house establishment for the Bay of Delaware, with Garret Hulsecamp for placing & manageing the floating Beacons & Buoys in the said bay of Delaware.

Proposals for executing the business in question were received from several other persons; but as the one made by Hulsecamp was the lowest & perhaps not unreasonable considering the advanced price of living, the Secretary is of opinion that it will be for the interest of the U. States if the President should think proper to approve of the said provisional contract between the Superintendent & Garret Hulsecamp.[1] All which is most repect-fully submitted to the consideration of the President U.S.[2]

Olivr Wolcott Jr
Secy of the Treasury

LB, DLC:GW.

1. Garret Hulsekamp (died c.1812) was a pilot for the Delaware bay and river.

Commissioner of the Revenue Tench Coxe wrote Wolcott on 5 July 1796 that Hulsekamp was "an old pilot of Philadelphia" and had provided "satisfactory Sureties. . . . The former contract was at two hundred pounds, & many efforts have been made by the late contractor to procure an advance. He has lately resigned and made an Oral offer at 934 Dollars" (DNA: RG 29, Lighthouse Letters). Hulsekamp's contract, dated 4 July, offered him $750 per year for tending the beacons and buoys; it received GW's approval on 12 July (DNA: RG 29, Lighthouse Deeds and Contracts).

2. GW replied to Wolcott from Mount Vernon on 13 July: "The contract entered into between William Allibone, Superintendent of the Light House establishment for the Bay of Delaware, and Garret Hulsecamp, for placing and managing the floating Beacons & Buoys in the said Bay, of Delaware, is returned approved.

"It is to be presumed that these contracts are not more frequent than necessary; yet, as they are so often repeated; and are heavy in the aggregate, for the above mentioned Bay; it may not be inexpedient to make indirect enquiries whether these frequent renewals is the result of *real* necessity. And to what account the old materials are carried" (ALS, CtHi: Oliver Wolcott, Jr., Papers; LB, DLC:GW). Wolcott acknowledged this letter when he wrote GW on 23 July.

From Charles Lee

Sir   Alexandria [Va.] 7th July 1796

After bestowing the best consideration upon the several matters mentioned in your letter of the 6th I had formed an opinion that our minister plenipotentiary at Paris, ought not to be permitted to continue there, any longer than until the arrival of his Successor; and that it was not only expedient but absolutely necessary that he should be immediately recalled and another minister appointed. Upon this subject I concur in Sentiment with the heads of departments as expressed in their letter of the 4th instant.[1]

As well during the session of the Senate as during its recess, the President alone has power to remove from Office; and the Senate is not authorised to give, nor he to demand their advice & Consent relative to a removal or dismission from office. Whenever a vacancy occurs during the *recess* of the senate, whether produced by death, inability resignation, *dismission* or other just cause, it may be filled by the President until the end of the next session after the appointment.

If the present minister be recalled, his place may and I think ought to be supplied by a Minister Plenipotentiary.

I am inclined to the opinion that an Envoy Extraordinary to the French Republic cannot be sent by the President without the advice of the Senate: for without their advice he cannot make a new Office and fill it, though he may alone fill for a limited time an old office become vacant during its recess. Whether such envoyship ought to be considered as a new office or not, would be made a question, and therefore on that account even if the President could send an Envoy Extraordinary without the advice of the Senate, it is expedient that he should not; for his conduct should be as unquestionable as possible. Besides at this time I do not think a necessity exists for such an appointment; and as much good may be reasonably expected from the services of a new minister Plenipotentiary, as from an Envoy Extraordinary.

My reasons for holding the opinion that the present minister should be recalled are

1. From his letters in the office of department of State it appears he has neglected or failed to justify or truely represent to the Republic of France, the conduct & motives of his own country relative to the treaty with Great Britain. This was a most important duty of his Station to which, he was fully and pointedly instructed: and though he may have proposed at various times verbal communications on the subject which were slighted, yet knowing as he must or ought to have known the sentiments of that government, and that no verbal communications were in fact received from him but only proposed by him to be made, it became his indispensable duty to present in writing that view of his country's conduct which he was directed and enabled by our secretary of State to present.

2. His correspondence with the Executive of the United States has been and is unfrequent, unsatisfactory, reserved & without cordiality or confidence on his part.

I might add other reasons if they were necessary for instance, that he corresponds less confidentially with the Executive of the United States, than with the opposers and libellers of his administration, & that there is too much reason to believe he is furthering the views of a faction in America more than the peace and happiness of the United States &c. &c.

As to the capture of the Mount Vernon, the answer of Mr Adet was so evasive, as in my mind to confirm the truth of those things that had been heard from other quarters respecting to the designs of france against our trade; and therefore the second letter written by the Secretary of state to him, became proper & necessary.[2] Of itself the capture of that vessel would not be much regarded as declaratory of the disposition of the french nation, but connected with other things, it deserves some attention, and the more so, if the privateer accompanied the ship down the river or laid in wait for her and so soon as they were out of *territorial* jurisdiction made prize of her.

No person would be fitter than John Marshall to go to France for supplying the place of our minister but it is scarcely short of absolute certainty that he would not accept any such office. The same may be said of Mr Henry.

I am a stranger to C. C. Pinkney; If he has fitness & will take the charge, I should prefer him to Mr William Smith, because the latter is a member of Congress and because he is by general reputation disagreable to the french people in America, and rather more than some others who go with him in Politicks—Mr Carroll is too rich, & leads now too retired a life, to be acceptable in any public character, to very many persons.

After all objections that are to be made, to any individual to fill the vacancy that is contemplated, I feel no hesitation in declaring that some person ought to be appointed to fill the office occupied by our minister at Paris, and I have no doubt that your acquaintance with men in America, will enable you to supply his place with advantage to the community.[3] I have the honor to be sir with the most perfect respect your obed. servant

Charles Lee Attorney General

ALS, DLC:GW.

1. The cabinet had written GW on 2 July to advise the removal of James Monroe as U.S. minister to France. In his first (secret) communication to GW dated 4 July, Secretary of State Timothy Pickering enclosed the cabinet's letter.

2. See Pickering to French minister Pierre-Auguste Adet, 1 July, found at Cabinet to GW, 2 July, n.2.

3. Charles Cotesworth Pinckney replaced Monroe as U.S. minister to France (see GW to John Marshall, 8 July; GW's first letter to Pinckney, same date; and Pinckney to GW, 27 July).

From James McHenry

private.

Sir   Philadelphia 7 July 1796.

Since I had the honour of writing you, the Chevalier Freire's Secry has called to inform me, that the extreme heat of the weather had induced Madam Freire, to induce Chevalier Friere to postpone the projected visit to Mount Vernon till September.[1] You will not therefore I presume have the pleasure of seeing them.

Mr Pickering has mentioned to me, that such of the materials as are not wanted for the three frigates now building, may be employed in the construction of the frigate promised to the Dey of Algiers.[2] If it should be determined so to use the materials, and to commence the building before the meeting of Congress, will it belong to the department of war or department of State to have her built and equipped? From the laws instituting the two departments it would seem to fall under the duties specified as appertaining to the former, so far at least as respects building and equippment.[3]

I do not wish to have new duties assigned to me; but if matters relative to vessels of war belongs to the department of war, (of which you will judge in looking over the laws instituting the several departments) it might possibly give rise to remarks, were it to be assigned to a different one. Should you think however that it comes more properly within the duties of the department of State, than that of war I shall be perfectly satisfied.

I do not know that Mr Pickering has formed any opinion on this question, or that it has even occured to him; and I do not wish it to pass beyond yourself that I have suggested any doubt on the subject; because, it would look (which is very remote from the truth) as if I was either desirous to have the management of the building, or was jealous of encroachments on the department.[4]

You have no doubt read the accounts of the success of the

French arms in Sardinia.[5] I am disposed to think that what has happened there will produce a peace with the Emperor. With the sinceresent respect and attachment, I have the honour to be Sir Your ob. st

James McHenry

ALS, DLC:GW; ADfS, MiU-C: James McHenry Papers.

1. McHenry previously wrote GW on 6 July, but he last mentioned Portuguese minister Cipriano Ribeiro Freire's plans to visit Mount Vernon in a letter dated 5 July.

2. For this frigate, see GW to the Dey of Algiers, 13 June.

3. "An Act to establish an Executive Department, to be denominated the Department of War," approved 7 Aug. 1789, entrusted the secretary of war with duties relative "to the land or naval forces, ships, or warlike stores of the United States, or to such other matters respecting military or naval affairs, as the President of the United States shall assign to the said department (1 *Stat.* 49–50). For the laws structuring the State Department, see "An Act for establishing an Executive Department, to be denominated the Department of Foreign Affairs," 27 July 1789; and "An Act to provide for the safe-keeping of the Acts, Records and Seal of the United States, and for other purposes," 15 Sept. 1789 (1 *Stat.* 28–29, 68–69).

4. McHenry again wrote GW on 8 July: "private. . . . Mr Pickering has called upon me this morning and mentioned, that he thought the building of the proposed frigate for Algiers lay more particularly with the war department; of course the question I suggested, so far as respects the Secry of State is answered.

"I shall proceed to take preparatory measures to ascertain what timber and materials can be spared for this frigate from the others, and whether it will be cheaper for the public to have her built by contract (furnishing certain materials) or in the way the other frigates are built.

"It will be proper that I should receive particular orders and instructions from the President before taking any ultimate step as it is a case not expresly contemplated or enjoined by any law or treaty" (ALS, DLC:GW; ADf, MiU-C: James McHenry Papers; LB, DLC:GW). GW replied to McHenry on 13 July.

5. The kingdom of Sardinia then included Savoy and the Piedmont region of Italy as well as the islands of Sardinia and Corsica. Reports about French victories and heavy casualties among the Sardinian and Austrian forces in the spring appeared in the *Independent Gazetteer* (Philadelphia) for 25 and 29 June. The *Gazette of the United States, & Philadelphia Daily Advertiser* for 6 July included a report that the king of Sardinia had sued for peace and sought an alliance with France against Austria. *The Philadelphia Gazette & Universal Daily Advertiser* for 7 July printed the terms of a suspension of arms between the Sardinian and French armies to allow for negotiations.

To Alexander Addison

Sir,   Mount Vernon 8th July 1796

Your favor of the 4th Instant came to my hands by the last Post.

When I inform you that Mr Ross (who on my behalf, disposed of the Land I held on Millers run, to Mr Ritchie) is authorised to do all that is necessary on my part, towards carrying the bargain into complete effect; it almost supercedes the necessity of giving answers, in detail, to the queries you have propounded. I shall however, inform you—

That three thousand dollars has been received, by me, on that account.[1]

That I executed a deed, conveying the Estate in fee Simple, with a relinquishment of Dower, to Mr Ritchie; and left it in trust with Mr Ross, to be delivered when the requisites on the part of Mr Ritchie were complied with.[2]

That if Mr Ritchie should be disposed to pay a greater sum— not less than a third *more* than the Instalment becoming due—it shall be received, provided notice thereof is given on, or before the first day of April in each year. and

That, a decisive answer has already been given (through Mr Ross) of my expectation of Interest from the first of January.

With respect to the Rents of the Land on Millers run, not knowing when, by agreement, they become due; and in truth, being very little acquainted with the circumstances attending them, it would be imprudent in me to say any thing, definitively, concerning them: whatever, therefore, Mr Ross may do in this regard, I will abide by; as I seek justice only, on liberal principles.

The money due on account of interest, to the first of June, may be deposited with the Secretary of the Treasury— Mr Wolcott—&, as it was in Philadelphia soon after that period, I require no interest thereon subsequent thereto. I believe it would be best also, at this time, not to receive money on any other account; lest it should militate with arrangements under a power given to Mr Ross. I have no doubt but that a judgment Bond executed by Mr Ritchie and yourself will be perfectly satisfactory; but every thing of this sort is already in the hands of Mr Ross to arrange.[3]

The Survey has been returned to me—and the quantity I be-

lieve (not having it at hand) is, as you say, 2955 Acres.[4] I am—Sir
Your most Obedt Hble Servt

G.W.

Copy (docketed by GW), CSmH; LB, DLC:GW.

1. GW recorded this payment, "through the Hands of the Honble James
Ross," at 1 June in his cash accounts (Cash Memoranda, 1794–97).

2. See Indenture with Matthew Ritchie, 1 June.

3. For GW's power of attorney to James Ross for the sale of GW's lands in
Washington County, Pa., see GW to Ross, 29 Aug. 1795, n.3.

4. The survey has not been identified.

Addison replied to GW from Philadelphia on 13 July 1796: "I was yesterday
honoured with yours of 8th current; and regret, that, having taken the proper
measures for settling the business, which was the subject of it, you had the additional trouble of detailing them to me.

"I have this day paid to Mr Wolcott (as you directed) two hundred and
ninety five dollars and a half; which I compute to be the interest on the whole
money due you by Matthew Ritchie, on the first of June, from the first of
January last" (ALS, DLC:GW). GW recorded the $295.50 payment in his cash
accounts for 18 July (Cash Memoranda, 1794–97).

GW then wrote Secretary of the Treasury Oliver Wolcott, Jr., from Mount
Vernon, on 20 July: "By letter from Judge Addison of Pennsylvania, I am informed, that in behalf of Mr Ritchie, he has deposited in your hands on my
account—two hundred and ninety five dollars and a half.

"Let them remain there, if you please, until I arrive in Philadelphia; or may
find occasion to call for them" (ALS [facsimile], Paul C. Richard Autographs,
Catalog #148 [1981], p. 11; copy, CtHi: Oliver Wolcott, Jr., Papers). Wolcott
acknowledged this letter when he wrote GW on 23 July.

Letter not found: to the Commissioners for the District of Columbia,
8 July 1796. The commissioners wrote GW on 12 July: "We had the
honor of your two Letters, first and eighth Inst."

To John Marshall

Private
Dear Sir,   Mount Vernon 8th July 1796

In confidence I inform you, that it has become indispensably
necessary to recall our Minister at Paris; and to send one in his
place who will explain, faithfully, the views of this government,
and ascertain those of France.

Nothing would be more pleasing to me, than that you should
be this Organ; if it were only for a temporary absence of a few

months. But it being feared that even this could not be made to comport with your present pursuits, I have, in order that as little delay as possible may be incurred, put the enclosed letter under cover to be forwarded to its address, if you decline the present offer; or to be returned to me, if you accept it.[1]

Your own correct knowledge of circumstances render details unnecessary, I shall only add therefore that I am—Dear Sir Your Obedt

Go: Washington

P.S. Hearing that you propose to attend the next meeting of the Supreme Court at Philadelphia I should be glad to see you at this place in your way.[2]

ALS, NNGL; LB, DLC:GW. The postscript only appears on the ALS.

1. GW enclosed his first letter to Charles Cotesworth Pinckney of this date.

2. Marshall replied to GW from Richmond on 11 July: "I will not attempt to express those sensations which your letter of the 8th instant has increasd.

"Was it possible for me in the present crisis of my affairs to leave the United States, such is my conviction of the importance of that duty which you woud confide to me, & (pardon me if I add) of the fidelity with which I shoud attempt to perform it, that I woud certainly forego any consideration not decisive with respect to my future fortunes, & woud surmount that just diffidence I have ever entertaind of myself, to make one effort to convey truely & faithfully to the government of France those sentiments which I have ever beleivd to be entertaind by that of the United States.

"I have forwarded your letter to Mr Pinkney.

"The recall of our minister at Paris has been conjecturd while its probable necessity has been regretted by those who love more than all others our own country.

"I will certainly do myself the honor of waiting on you at Mount Vernon" (ALS, DLC:GW). GW replied to Marshall on 15 July.

GW subsequently wrote Marshall from Mount Vernon on 10 Aug.: "If you can recollect by whom, or in what manner the letter for General Pinckney, which went under cover to you, was sent to the Post Office in Richmond, I would thank you for information respecting it.

"That letter, with a note enclosed therein, containing three bank bills for one hundred dollars each, for the sufferers by fire in Charleston, had not on the 26th of July been received by that Gentleman; although duplicates, written *after* I had been favoured with your answer has been acknowledged by him.

"In confidence, I inform you that General Pinckney accepts his appointment to France, and will soon be in Phila. to prepare for the Mission" (ALS [facsimile], in Sotheby's, *Fine Printed and Manuscript Americana* . . . sale 5837 [25 April 1989], item 89; ALS [retained copy], Germany: Kunstammlungen der Veste Coburg; LB, DLC:GW). For the safe arrival of GW's original letters to Pinckney dated 8 July, see Pinckney to GW, 2–5 Aug., postscript. Pinckney had commented on duplicates reaching him before the originals when he wrote GW on 27 July.

Marshall replied to GW from Richmond on 12 Aug.: "Your letter to General Pinckney was deliverd by myself to the postmaster, the night on which I receivd it, & was, as he says, immediately forwarded by him. Its loss is the more remarkable as it coud not have been opend from a hope that it containd bank notes.

"Permit me Sir to express my gratification as a citizen of the United States, that a gentleman of General Pinckneys character will represent our government at the court of France" (ALS, DLC:GW). Marshall again wrote GW on 14 Aug.: "I take the liberty to inform you that the delay experienced by your letter to Genl Pinckney is probably producd by its having been inattentively forwarded by the post-master to Pinckney court house instead of Charlestown. This mistake, if it has been committed, will, I trust, produce no other inconvenience than delay. An enquiry into it has been directed" (ALS, RuSpRNB).

Pinckneyville, also known as Pinckney Court House, was located on the southwest side of Broad River in current Union County, S.C., roughly 150 miles from Charleston.

To James McHenry

Dear Sir: Mount Vernon 8th July 1796.

Having written a great many letters for this day's Post, and being a good deal fatigued thereby and with the heat of the weather, I shall do no more, at present, than to inform you that your letters of the 2d and 3d instant[1] with the enclosures of the first came perfectly safe, and that my letter to the Secretary of State, of this date, will inform you confidentially of my decision with respect to the recall of Col. M—— and the measures which I am pursuing to provide a Successor.

I am sorry to hear you have been [un]well, and glad to hear you are better—Keep so—one well day is worth a dozen sick ones. I am Yours always

Go. Washington

Transcript (photostat), DLC: James McHenry Papers. Notes on the document indicate that Richard Bassett Bayard made this transcript in 1871 to replace the original letter received from James Howard McHenry.

McHenry replied to GW on 13 July 1796: "I was truely gladdened by your letter of the 8th. The Jacobins gave out that you were to be here on the 4th inst., after which they circulated a report that you had been thrown from your Phaeton, in consequence of which your life was despaired of. I did not beleive a word of all this, and yet I was uneasy till I received your letter. you are in good health and good spirits and god send that both may continue. I know not what new sacrifices we may yet have to require of you. The world grows older, and republicans occupy more and more of its surface, but I do not find that it becomes better.

"I shall endeavour to keep well according to your kind wish" (ALS, DLC:GW).

GW replied to McHenry on 18 July: "Private . . . I have not segacity enough to discover what end was to be answered by reporting—first, that I was to be in Philadelphia on the 4th July—and secondly, when that report was contradicted by my non-appearance, then to account for it by a fall from my Phæton.

"If any scheme could have originated, or been facilitated by these, or any other reports, however unfounded, I should not have been surprised at the propagation of them; for evidence enough has been given that Mith or falsehood is equally used, and indifferent to that class of men if their object can be obtained" (ALS [facsimile], DLC: James McHenry Papers).

1. For McHenry to GW, 3 July, see GW's second letter to McHenry, 1 July, n.3.

To Timothy Pickering

(Confidential)

Sir,   Mount Vernon 8th July 1796

My letters to the Secretary of the Treasury of the 4th & 6th Instant, with the present enclosure, conveys fully the sentiments of the Attorney General with respect to the best mode of executing the Act "For the relief and Protection of American Seamen." He has, since his opinion was transmitted in the above letter of the 6th, consulted two of our most eminent Lawyers, in these parts, and finds an entire accordance of opinion. I request, therefore, that the measure recommended may be pursued.[1]

Your letters of the 1st and 2d instant, with several enclosures in the latter, came safe, and duly to hand.[2] After that serious consideration which the subject deserved,[3] I have determined to recall the American Minister at Paris; and am taking measures to supply his place; but the more the latter is revolved, greater the difficulties appear, to do it ably, & unexceptionably. By this, I mean one, who will promote, not thwart the Neutral policy of the government, & at the same time will not be obnoxious to the People among whom he is sent.

Proofs, little short of positive, are already in my possession, that neither Mr Henry, nor Mr Marshall wd accept of such an appointment. The chances against General Pinckney's doing it are strong, tho' not quite so great; and with respect to Mr Smith, altho' it would be a very agreeable choice to me, I am sure it would not concenter those opinions which policy would require. Mr Carroll of Carrolton, tho' sensible, and attached to Federal measures, would find himself on quite new ground; and besides he has such large concerns of his own to attend to, & is so tenacious of them, that it is morally certain he could not be prevailed on to go.

Having taken this view of the subject, I am, by this days Post, writing to General Pinckney. This letter I shall enclose to Mr Marshall (as he is in the line, Mr Henry being much out of it) to be forwarded—or returned—as he shall decide with respect to himself[4]—In the meantime, as the offer ends with General Pinckney, other characters should be held in contemplation, in case of his refusal.

The letter to the Minister Plenipotentiary of France, in Philadelphia, appears to be well conceived, and is accordingly approved.[5] The transmitted copy of Mr Monroes letter to [   ][6] must be erroneously dated—"Paris June 24th *1796*"—I presume it is in the year, and should be *1795*.

Go: Washington

Copy (docketed by GW), DNA: RG 59, Miscellaneous Letters; LB, DNA: RG 59, GW's Correspondence with His Secretaries of State. Pickering received GW's letter on 11 July (see his letter to GW, 12 July, found at Pickering to GW, this date, n.1). A transcript made in 1866 by Octavius Pickering, evidently from the letter received, is in MHi: Pickering Papers. Other than punctuation and the use of ampersands, it has only two differences from GW's retained copy (see notes 3 and 6 below).

1. GW evidently enclosed Attorney General Charles Lee's letter to him of 4 July. The eminent lawyers have not been identified. For the circular instructing collectors, see Pickering's third letter to GW, 21 July, n.3.

2. GW had docketed Pickering's first (secret) letter of 4 July with a date of 2 July and evidently is referring to that letter.

3. This word is "required" in the transcript.

4. For GW's determination on how to proceed with replacing James Monroe as U.S. minister to France, see his letter to John Marshall, this date.

5. For Pickering's letter of 1 July to French minister Pierre-Auguste Adet, see the Cabinet to GW, 2 July, n.2.

6. The transcript gives "Doctr Logan" as the name. For this letter from Monroe to George Logan, see Pickering's first letter to GW, 4 July, n.2.

From Timothy Pickering

Sir,   Department of State July 8. 1796.
I have the honor to acknowledge the receipt of your letters of the 1st and 4th instant. On the appointment of a superintendant of Indian Affairs in the room of Governor Blount—and on the running & marking the Cherokee boundary, I expect to be able to report to you on Monday next the opinion of the Heads of Departments.[1]

The Secretary of the treasury informs me that he directed the Comptroller to transmit to the Collectors of the Customs the act of Congress requiring their aid in the execution of the health laws of states relative to quarantine, with an injunction to render all the aid in their power to the State-Officers.[2]

The Secretary of War has furnished me with a copy of the orders issued from his office, on the subject of quarantine, which I have the honor to inclose.[3] The date, I observe, is three days earlier than Governor Mifflin's first letter requesting the aid which had been ordered.[4] To prevent the crews or passengers of vessels from landing on the Jersey shore is impossible, unless the garrison of Mud Island were so numerous as to admit of placing a guard in each vessel. I am with the highest respect, sir, your most obt servant

                                               Timothy Pickering

ALS, DNA: RG 59, Miscellaneous Letters; LB, DNA: RG 59, Domestic Letters; LB, DNA: RG 59, GW's Correspondence with His Secretaries of State. GW received this letter on 13 July (see his letter to Pickering, 18 July).

1. Pickering subsequently wrote GW on Tuesday, 12 July: "I have consulted the Secretaries of the Treasury & of War on the subject of running the Cherokee boundary, and the appointment of a Superintendant of Indian affairs for the southern department, and of agents for conducting a trade with the Indians; & now respectfully submit to you our joint opinions.

"The Secretary of War having informed us that some of the principal Cherokee Chiefs are to visit philadelphia the ensuing autumn, we think it will be best to postpone any decision until their arrival. The measure may then be taken up; and the time & place for commencing the running of the line be agreed on. We are the more inclined to advise this course, because the Cherokees are extremely desirous, according to Mr Dinsmoor's information, that General Pickens, who is now engaged in the Georgia treaty, should be one of the Commissioners on the part of the United States; and because the winter would arrest the progress of the business soon after it should be commenced, seeing the distance of the parties & persons to be appointed is so great and that some months must be occupied in the previous arrangements. Mr Dinsmoor thinks also that a military guard must accompany the Commissioners.

"We are all of opinion that the appointment of agents for conducting a trade with the Indians, under the last act of Congress, should also be postponed: seeing there are no funds with which the goods necessary for that trade can at present be procured.

"With respect to a superintendant of Indian Affairs, in the room of Governor Blount, it would seem that no appointment can be made. By the act of Congress for the government of the territory south of the river Ohio, passed the 26th of May 1790, the office of superintendant was united with that of *governor* of the *territory*: but the *territory* being merged in the *new state* of *Tennessee*, and the *territorial governor* extinct, there remains no official character to which by law the office of superintendant can be annexed. It appears however that such an appointment is not of immediate necessity. Mr Dinsmoor, the Agent appointed to reside in the Cherokee nation, has manifested a judgement and discretion which will enable him very well to perform any services which may be required relative to the Cherokees; and Colo. Henley may be instructed as to the general conduct to be observed towards them and the Chickasaws & Choctaws; until Congress shall make provision for the office of superintendant—if such an office should by them be deemed necessary.

"Your letter of the 8th of July was received yesterday: I have communicated the same to the Secretaries of the Treasury and of War" (ALS, DNA: RG 59, Miscellaneous Letters; LB, DNA: RG 59, Domestic Letters; LB, DNA: RG 59, GW's Correspondence with His Secretaries of State). In this letter, Pickering referenced "An Act to regulate Trade and Intercourse with the Indian Tribes, and to preserve Peace on the Frontiers," 19 May 1796, and "An Act for the Government of the Territory of the United States, south of the river Ohio," 26 May 1790 (1 *Stat.* 469–74, 123). GW replied to Pickering on 20 July.

2. Secretary of the Treasury Oliver Wolcott, Jr., wrote Pickering to this effect on this date (CtHi: Oliver Wolcott, Jr., Papers). The letter of instruction to the collectors has not been identified.

3. Secretary of War James McHenry sent a circular letter dated 22 June to officers at Governors Island, N.Y.; Mud Island, Pa.; Baltimore; Charleston, S.C.; and Norfolk, Va.: "I am directed by the president in conformity with a law of the United States to instruct you to aid and assist, as far as may comport with the nature of your Command 'in the execution of Quarantine and also in the execution of the health laws' of the State in which you are stationed" (DNA: RG 59, Miscellaneous Letters).

4. Pickering is referring to Thomas Mifflin to GW, 25 June (see also Wolcott to GW, 11 July, and n.4 to that document).

To Charles Cotesworth Pinckney

Private & confidential
My dear Sir,   Mount Vernon 8th July 1796
 The situation of Affairs, and the interests of this Country as they relate to France, render it indispensably necessary that a faithful organ near that government—able & willing to explain its views, and to ascertain those of France, should immediately fill the place of our present Minister Plenipotentiary at Paris.[1]
 Policy requires that this character should be well attached to the government of his own Country; and not be obnoxious to the one to which he is sent; to be essentially serviceable.
 Where then can a man be found that would answer this description better than yourself?
 It is a fact too notorious to be denied, that the greatest embarrassments under which the Administration of this government labours, proceed from the counteraction of people among ourselves, who are more disposed to promote the views of another Nation than to establish National character of their own; and that, unless the virtuous, and independent men of this Country will step forward, it is not difficult to predict the consequences.
 Such is my decided opinion. After what has passed between us, on former occasions (respecting your filling some of the important Offices in our government)[2] I must confess that I hesitated before I resolved on this Address, lest you might think I was too importunate; & that your former answers ought to have outweighed the desire of making it. Had not the case been important & urgent, I might have hesitated longer; but in finding a character of the description I have mentioned, you will be at no loss to percieve the difficulty which occurs. He must be a man whose abilities, & celebrity of character are well known to the People of this Country; whose honor & integrity are unimpeached;[3] and who ought, as far as the nature of the thing will admit, be acceptable to all parties. Doubtless many such there are, but those who have been, either in the Executive or Legislative departments of the General government, and are best known to me, have been so decisive in their politics, and possibly so frank & public in their declarations, as to render it very difficult to chuse from among them, one in whom the confidence

of this country could be placed, and the prejudices of the other not excited.

Thus, my good Sir, you have a candid exposition of my sentiments & wishes. I have only to add to them, a request, that you would be so obliging as to give me a prompt answer; and, if in the affirmative, that you would repair to Philadelphia, prepared to proceed on the Mission, with as little delay as can be avoided. Possibly you might have less objection to the excursion, if it would occasion a few months absence only, than to a permanent residence; but the Power of the Executive (in the recess of the Senate) extends only to the filling of vacancies; and one will be occasioned by the recall of the present incumbent; a measure resolved on.[4] It is unnecessary to add how much, and how sincerely I am—Dear Sir Your obedt & Affecte Servt

Go: Washington

ALS, ScC; ALS (duplicate), PWacD; LB, DLC:GW. The ALS was posted from Richmond on 11 July (see also GW to John Marshall, 10 Aug., found at GW to Marshall, 8 July, n.2).

1. For the decision to remove James Monroe as U.S. minister to France, see GW to Timothy Pickering, this date.

2. Pinckney previously had declined appointments as secretary of war and secretary of state (see his letters to GW, 24 Feb. 1794 and 16 Sept. 1795).

3. The preceding clause is omitted on the duplicate.

4. Pinckney replied to GW on 27 July.

To Charles Cotesworth Pinckney

Duplicate

My dear Sir,   Mount Vernon 8th July 1796

Sincerely commisserating the distresses of the Citizens of Charleston, occasioned by the late unfortunate fires—I take the liberty of offering, through you, my mite toward their relief; without any desire of having my name mentioned.[1] With affectionate regard I am always Yours

Go: Washington

ALS (duplicate), ScC; ADfS, DLC:GW; LB, DLC:GW. The duplicate was posted from Alexandria, Va., on 15 July. The original letter was enclosed with GW's first letter to Pinckney of this date (see GW to John Marshall, 10 Aug., found at GW to Marshall, 8 July, n.2). Pinckney acknowledged receipt of the duplicate when he wrote GW on 27 July.

1. A footnote on the draft and letter-book copy states that "$300 were enclosed." The entry for this date in GW's cash accounts identifies the money as "Columbia Bank Notes" (Cash Memoranda, 1794–97).

The Philadelphia Gazette & Universal Daily Advertiser for 23 May 1796 printed an extract from a letter written at Charleston, S.C., on Monday, 16 May: "A little after 2 o'clock on Saturday morning last, a fire broke out in this city . . . Nothwithstanding the exertions of the citizens, the progress of the fire was not arrested till 6 o'clock in the morning, during which short space of time, sixty-five dwelling houses were destroyed in King Street, Clifford Street and Beresford Street. Property to a very considerable amount was consumed, and upwards of seventy industrious families were driven from their dwellings."

The same paper for 24 and 29 June printed accounts of a second fire in Charleston that began during the afternoon of 13 June and continued until the following morning. This fire burned some 500 buildings and left "upwards of two hundred families" in distress.

From Isaac Heard

London, 10 July 1796. Heard reports his latest genealogical findings on GW's ancestry.

ALS, DLC:GW. For a partial transcription, see William Augustine Washington to GW, 23 March 1798, n.2, in *Papers, Retirement Series,* 2:154; see also Heard to GW, 9 Aug. 1793.

From James McHenry

Sir.   War Office 10 July 1796.

With the view of keeping you informed of the course of the most important business of the war department I here inclose, packets

No. 1. which contains the last letters I have received from Gen. Wayne. vz. one private of the 27 June and one of the 28,[1] with copies of two letters to the general[2] and one to the Quarter master general.[3]

No. 2. Contains the last communications from the commissioners to the Creeks, by which you will perceive, that (after a few embarrasements[)] the treaty had commenced.[4]

I shall mention to you in my next the inquiries which I have made relative to running the Cherokee boundary line.

With respect to agents for the trading houses to be erected, you will see by the inclosed letter from the Secry of the treasury, that he does not think money can be furnished in all this year for the purchase of goods.[5] It will of course be unnecessary at this time to make appointments.

Mr Dinsmore who is agent to the Cherokees, and a sensible and judicious man, and who receives one thousand dollars salary, may perhaps be considered as adequate to all the duties of superintendant required to be performed under the existing state of things.[6]

I shall as the mail is about closing take the next oppertunity to be more full on both these subjects.[7] With the greatest respect I have the honour to be Sir Your most ob. st

James McHenry
Secy of war

ALS, DLC:GW; LB, DLC:GW. GW received this letter on 16 July (see his letter to McHenry, 18 July).

1. Gen. Anthony Wayne's letter to McHenry dated 27 June, written at Pittsburgh and given an official number, reports information that Wayne—responding to a private letter from McHenry on 25 May—had collected about Victor Collot's mission. Wayne wrote that Collot had "freely" expressed French resentment over "the Treaty with Great Britain" and claimed that orders were issued "to Capture every American Vessel bound to or from a British port" if the United States did not uphold "the Guarantee of the French Island in the West Indies . . . agreeably to a former treaty with France." Collot claimed that the treaty with Spain was achieved through the influence of the French Directory, who would stall it and disrupt Missisippi River navigation. Furthermore, "a secret Article in the treaty of peace between the French Republic & Spain" restored Louisiana to France, and "it was the true Interest of the American Citizens west of the Allegany Mountains to seperate from the Union & become free & independent—under the protection of & in alliance with France." Collot planned to meet Gen. James Wilkinson, explore the country, and proceed down the river to New Orleans. Wayne reported Collot as "busy in Electioneering for Mr. J–n," presumably Thomas Jefferson, "& advises a *proper* choice of Electors for that purpose." Wayne also identified Benjamin Sebastian and Thomas Power as "incendiaries" whom he would watch, confident that he would make "the necessary discoveries in due season & without Alarm" (Knopf, *Wayne*, 489–92; see also McHenry to GW, 2 July, n.4).

Wayne wrote McHenry from Pittsburgh on 28 June regarding arrangements related to ordnance and supplies. He also requested that some officers be ordered to join the army (Knopf, *Wayne*, 492–93).

2. McHenry had written Wayne on 25 June with directions to appoint qualified subaltern officers "at each post to receive the rations and issue them to the Troops." The letter also covered accounting procedures (DLC:GW).

McHenry also wrote Wayne on 8 July to acknowledge his letters of 27 and

28 June and approve his arrangements with the exception that the barracks be built separately from the storehouse at Fort Le Boeuf, Pa., to reduce fire or water damage risks (DLC:GW).

3. McHenry had written John Wilkins, Jr., from Philadelphia on 8 July: "I have received your letter of the 10th ultimo signifying your acceptance of the Commission of Quarter Master General.

"It may be proper for the present that you should appoint an Agent in this City to accept your Bills and receive the money from the Treasury which you may be authorized to draw for.

"I shall expect to be furnished with a quarterly Estimate of the sum of Money and the Items for which it may be wanted, in your department, that I may take measures with the Treasury to meet your demands." The letter concluded with instructions on how to proceed "should any pressing occasion arise" before regular procedures could be implemented (DLC:GW).

4. George Clymer, Benjamin Hawkins, and Andrew Pickens served as commissioners to the Creek Indians. McHenry's specific enclosures in this letter to GW have not been identified, but they likely included a letter from the commissioners to McHenry written at Colerain, Ga., on 16 June that reported the start of negotiations with 22 kings, 75 principal chiefs, and 152 warriors in attendance. "The chiefs appear to be well disposed, and to have a well grounded confidence in the justice of our Government" (*ASP, Indian Affairs*, 1:597).

5. Secretary of the Treasury Oliver Wolcott, Jr., had written McHenry on 8 July "that the measures proposed by the Commissioners of the sinking fund for the sale of Stock, from the proceeds of which new loans in aid of the revenue were expected, have failed of success—As no substitute has yet been devised, that can be relied upon, I cannot promise that the sum appropriated for the Indian trade can be furnished this year" (DLC:GW).

6. See Timothy Pickering to GW, 12 July, found at Pickering to GW, 8 July, n.1.

7. See McHenry to GW, 12 July.

To John Dandridge

Dear Sir,   Mount Vernon 11th July 1796.

I have received, at this plac⟨e,⟩ your letter of the 23d Ulto; but long after the date of it. whether occasioned by neglect in the Post Offices, or by its having made a journey to Philadelphia & back, I know not.

With respect to the Negroes—Frederick, George, Burwell & Pleasant—I have no objection to your taking them with you to your new habitation; Provided you can arrange matters with your Mother to her ⟨en⟩tire satisfaction. I shall set no Price on them, because it is not probable I shall ever avail myself, or heirs, of that property in your Mothers possession.

Your brother Bat's conduct is too Enigmatical for me to develope. I have conjecture only to resort to, for a solution of it: and as that might prove erroneous I shall say nothing concerning the causes, further than that I have no charge to make against his honesty or fidelity—and that his sudden and abrupt departure was not occasioned by any difference between us— and further that I had no more suspicion of his intention to leave me (until he was gone & left a line informing me thereof) than you had. His first letter to me (four days after he had left the family) requested I would harbour no unfavorable opinion of him; intimating, that when he was more composed, he wd write me more fully and give some explanation of his conduct. A second, & a third letter has been received from him since (dated at Greenbrier Court House) without doing this, but expressing an inclination to return to his former station[1]—which cannot be—as another Gentleman has taken his place.[2] If, however, I can render him any service I shall do it chearfully as I always entertained and continue to entertain a favorable opinion of his integrity and abilities. With best regards to your Mother & other friends I am—Dear Sir Your Obedt Servant

Go: Washington

P.S. Since closing this letter your Brother Bat has arrived here— and as he is writing to you, or some other of his friends—I shall refer you to his own explanations which ought to be the most accurate.

ADfS, NjMoHP; LB, DLC:GW.
    1. The note and the first letter from Bartholomew Dandridge, Jr., to GW have not been found, but see GW to Bartholomew Dandridge, 5 June. For the second and third letters, see Bartholomew Dandridge to GW, 10 May, and the source note to that document.
    2. George Washington Craik had become GW's private secretary (see Richard Graham to GW, 12 April, source note).

From Timothy Pickering

Sir,   Department of State July 11. 1796.
    Agreeably to the intimation in your letter respecting a surveyor general,[1] I take the liberty to inclose the application of Israel Ludlow, with the certificates of recommendation which he

has this morning delivered to me. He is about twenty nine years of age, of a good person and agreeable manners.[2]

I have thought it proper on this occasion to inclose the applications of Mr John Hall & Joseph Ellicott,[3] whose names were formerly mentioned as applicants. Mr Hall, I understand, is of a respectable family in Maryland; which I suppose has led Mr Murray to urge his appointment. He married a daughter of Dr Ewing, is upwards of thirty years old, and now I take it resides in Pennsylvania. His politics, I am assured, are perfectly correct. Personally I know nothing of him.[4]

I have yet heard nothing from Mr Adet.[5] With the highest respect, I am, sir, your most obt servant

Timothy Pickering

ALS, DNA: RG 59, Miscellaneous Letters; LB, DNA: RG 59, Domestic Letters; LB, DNA: RG 59, GW's Correspondence with His Secretaries of State. GW received this letter on 15 July (see his letter to Pickering, 18 July).

1. See GW to Pickering, 1 July.

2. Israel Ludlow had written Pickering from Philadelphia on 9 July seeking appointment as surveyor general. He based his qualifications on having "been employed by the General Gove[r]nment for a number of years to conduct and compleat certain surveys and to ascertain the exterior lines or boundaries of the purchases made of the United States by the Ohio, the Scioto, & the Miami Company." Ludlow enclosed recommendations from Oliver Wolcott, Jr., Robert Patterson, and Elias Boudinot and noted that Alexander Hamilton "was good enough to give me a certificate of my services with his opinion concerning my abilities which was handed the President by Mr Wolcott."

Wolcott's certificate, dated 9 July, listed Ludlow's various public employments and stated "that all these services so far as I know or am able to judge have been performed to public satisfaction & with fidelity industry and ability—Of his skill in the business of Surveying lands, I am no personal judge, but in this and other respects he has been well recommended to me, by persons in whom I place confidence."

The certificate from Patterson, a professor at the University of Pennsylvania, also dated 9 July, stated that Ludlow had studied mathematics and "practical astronomy" under him "and that from the abilities which he then discovered, as well as his subsequent application, and experience in the business of Surveying, I have no doubt of his being well acquainted with whatever relates to that branch of practical science."

Boudinot's certificate, dated 11 July, stated "that I have been acquainted with Mr Israel Ludlow from his childhood—He is the Son of a worthy Citizen of New Jersey and has been well educated in the principles of the Mathematics as a Science, particularly in that part of it, relative to Surveying & Mensuration—That he has been engaged for several Years in practical Surveying & plotting of Lands in the Western Country, on behalf of the Government as well as for Individuals, and from my knowledge of his Conduct, he has given general Satisfaction to his employers" (all DNA: RG 59, Miscellaneous Papers; see also Wolcott to GW, this date, and Pickering's second letter to GW, 19 July).

3. Joseph Ellicott had written Pickering from Philadelphia on 25 May: "I am Embold[e]ned to make this Application, from a persuasion that my Knowledge of the Science of Surveying, is Commensurate to the Object, Both as to ascertaining Astronomically the Latitudes of places, and Running the true instead of the Magnetic Courses." He mentioned David Rittenhouse among witnesses to his abilities (DNA: RG 59, Miscellaneous Letters; see also Pickering's second letter to GW, 19 July, and GW's first letter to Pickering, 25 July).

4. John Hall (1760–1826) was the son of Elihu Hall, a Cecil County planter who served in the Maryland House, 1779–80. In 1783 he married Sarah Ewing (1761–1830), daughter of John Ewing, a clergyman and provost of the University of Pennsylvania. Sarah Ewing Hall later gained recognition as an author, perhaps most notably for *Conversations on the Bible* (Philadelphia, 1818). John Hall was secretary of the Pennsylvania land office and remained in that position until President John Adams appointed him federal marshal for Pennsylvania in 1799.

Hall's letter of application has not been identified, but Pennsylvania congressman John W. Kittera and Maryland congressman William Vans Murray had written Pickering on 23 May to recommend Hall. Kittera "always entertained a very favorable opinion both of his integrity & his abilities." Murray recommended Hall as "a sensible and worthy man, & one who has been a good deal engaged in that sort of business—I believe him to be well qualify'd in all respects to serve the public in that character & should be gratify'd if this application should meet with your approbation" (both DNA: RG 59, Miscellaneous Letters).

5. Pickering probably is referring to French minister Pierre-Auguste Adet's response to questions regarding French interruption of U.S. commercial shipping (see Cabinet to GW, 2 July, n.2; see also Pickering to GW, 15 July, and his third letter to GW, 19 July). Pickering also sought to learn Adet's intentions with regard to visiting Mount Vernon (see Pickering's second letter to GW, 4 July, and his first letter to GW, 13 July; see also James McHenry to GW, 16–17 July).

From David Stuart

Dear Sir,   Hope Park [Va.] July 11th 1796

I am informed by Mr Lyon whom I found at my house on my return home on Saturday,[1] that Mr Dawson[2] passed through Ge: town on friday, on his way to Philadelphia—This is the second visit he has made there in the space of three months. Mr Lyon further says, from the extraordinary speech[3] Dawson made last fall, which you have heard, no doubt is entertained by people in general that a correspondence is carried on by his means with the French Court. My motive in informing you of Dawson's jaunt is, that you may judge of the propriety of writing to some persons in Philadelphia, to watch his conduct, and those with whom he associates. Perhaps it might be usefull that the Post Master, or his Clerks should attend to the direction of his letters; tho' it is probable that those intended for France will be entrusted to the French Minister alone[4]—Governor Brooke I learn from Mr Lyon, was allso to have gone to Philadelphia about the close of the Session of Congress; but could not get accomodated with money for his journey, tho' he was bold enough to try the unjustifyable expedient with which you was charged by the calm Observer of raising it by an anticipation of his salary, which he says has been severely noticed in some of the Richmond papers.[5] I am with great respect Your Affecte Servt

Dd Stuart.

P:S: If there be any reality in the opinion, that a correspondence is held by any party in this country with France, I think it probable at this time, that their dispatches will contain the result of their deliberations, and their future plan of operations—It is allso I think not improbable that Dawson may visit his friend Mr Burr.[6]

D:S:

ALS, DLC:GW; extract (in GW's writing), MHi: Pickering Papers. GW enclosed the extract when he wrote Secretary of State Timothy Pickering on 13 July. It suppressed Mr. Lyon's name and omitted a portion of the last paragraph (see n.4 below).

1. The previous Saturday was 9 July.

2. GW inserted an asterisk on the extract at this point to identify John Dawson in a marginal note as "one of the Executive Council of Virginia."

3. GW inserted a symbol here on the extract to reference an explanatory note: "This speech was in the Council chamber (Virga), but in private conversation (overheard by a third person). It was supposed by Mr Dawson's friend, in this conversation, that Mr R——ph would *now* become a very useful man to them—He answered No! they had a much better channel thro' which to carry on their *foreign Correspondence*." The note probably is referring to former Secretary of State Edmund Randolph.

4. GW omitted the remainder of this paragraph from the extract.

5. A letter from "A Calm Observer" that appeared in the *Aurora General Advertiser* (Philadelphia) for 23 Oct. 1795 charged GW with submitting warrants for illegal extra compensation (see Alexander Hamilton to GW, 26 Oct. 1795, n.1).

6. For an earlier political exchange between Dawson and Aaron Burr, see Burr to Henry Tazewell, 11 Oct. 1795, in Kline, *Burr Papers*, 1:229.

From Collen Williamson

Honourable Sir   City of Washington July 11th 1796

I should not have given you the Trouble of writing you, hade it not been to shew how far Ignorance hase got the better of knowledge and experence, in this city as to the public business your Excelency will see by my contract with the commissioners that I was In general to conduct the work, and when it was proposd to build the inside of the extereor walls with bricks I was deciddly against, that method of building, and told the commissioners that was never done but in countrays where stone could not be got, and that bricks hade not the weight and solidaty of stone for the out side walls, besides it would run them into some thousand pounds of expences extra, and for my good advice in comming from the commissioners out of georgeton Hoben told me if the commissioners or me should contradict him in the least he should not serve, and Encedently he established one of my Journaymen in my place at the presedents House, when I told the commissioners they sent me to superentend the capatol, where I continued till the 27th of aprile last year, beeing working by the parch it was hard for me to get the work properly don,[1] I compleand to the commissioners of the trouble I hade with those workmen they employed mr Scott told me at their first meating I should have a letter empowring me to discharge such of them as did not attend to my orders, but instade of this power at their first meeting I got a letter of Dismission, and the work Intrusted to those very vegbons that hade nather honour or honesty to lose,[2] two of the commissioners beeing strangers Carral and Hoben got the better of their Judgment in order to gett placess for those of their own way of thinking as they call themselves Catholeeks—I have been at some pains investegating the difference of expence between brick and stone work by the parch, in the capatol the insid of the outer walls amounts to 3408 parches at 500 bricks for each parch, the present price of 500 bricks 26 sh. 3d or 7 dollars pr 1000 the
price of 3408 parches at 26 sh. pr parch   £4430.8 sh

the price of the parch of stone of the above
number of parches as the bricks Laid down on
the pleace at 9 sh. pr parch   £1533.12 sh
                                    in favour of the stone   £2896.16
there would £1000 saved by the lime for laying the said stone
that would be too tedeous to give the reasons the above work is
suposd to be 40 feet in hight and 3 feet thick a third deduc[t]ed
for the spans of doors and windows—the presedents house suposd to be 30 feet high above the first storry and 3 feet thick the
third of the solid measure deducted for doors and windows as
to ma[t]ereals
the measurement Remaining as to the number of
parches at 26 sh.   1248
at 26 sh. pr parch of brick work   £1[6]22.8³
the same number of parches of stone laid down
on the spot at 9 sh. pr parch   561.
In favour of stone at the presedents House   £[10]61.0
The ballance one the above two buildings besids
at least £1000 extra for lime   £3[9]57.16
When this is considred with 8 or 10 thousand pounds thron away
at the Capatol by my dismision it will be thought, no winder that
the money should be short, besides all that I have said I would
have saved mor then my sellary to the Intrest of the city by tem-
pering of the morter amongst the multitude of my operations
in Scotland I repaired four old castels that was liker to pleaces of
defence then Dwelings for great men I got more knowledge by
their long standing as to morter then otherwayes I should ever
hade, the morter that was blak as earth with sand was hard as
stone, the fat morter soft as chalk which taught me that lime is
only cement to sand, I send this merly for your excelencys privet
infore mation as I have not the least Doubts but the laws of the
state will give me the sellary contracted for. I am Honourable Sir
with great Respect your exelency obedent servnt
                                                Collen Williamson

Copy of the contract dated Agust 29th 1792
    It is agreed between Collen Williamson and the commission-
ers of the Federal Buildings That the said collen Williamson will
superentend the stone cutting in the city of washington for the
public Buildings and other matters that he may from Time to

Time be Desired by the commissioners and the laying the same stone and such parts of the masonry as his attention and skill may be thought necessary or useful in and will afford his assistance in the hiring stone cutters and adjusting their accounts and in general in promoting and conducting the work for which services the said Williamson is to be paid four Houndred pounds Maryland money that is in Dollars at 7/6 each by the year and if any travling expence should be incurred by Jurnes to the stone quarres or other of the public Business such expences are Also to be paid beyond the yearly compensation the year to begin the first Day of this Instant the said Williamson having incurrd expences in attending for some time past

Witness presant   signed Thomas Johnston
John M. Gant   David Stuart
                                                             Danl Carrell
                                                    Collen Williamson

The Copy of a letter addressed to me in New york dated the 12th aprile 1792.

Sir your Kinsman John Suter has communicated to us your letter to him of the 18th of last october we want to employ twenty stone cutters perhaps more in preparing stone for the public Buildings in the new city some of them at least most be very good workmen the public buildings alon will requier a great deal of work and we hope and expect before that can be done privete Buildings will mak Avrie consideral Demand settled as you ar at the Distance of only afew days stage travle we think it will be best for you to come & have a conversation with us we ar inclined to employ you and those you get to work under you Things may be adjusted probaly to your intire satesfaction if not it will be better to have no begining to a connection under which you might probely be Dissatisfied.

                              signd the three commissioners

The copy of a se[c]ond letter when with the commissioners dated 10th may 1792.

The intercourse the commissioners have hade with mr Williamson has given them hopes that they will not be obliged to go farther but that they may have the stone cutting under his direction and that they may probaly derive further assistance from him in the present state of things the commissioners request mr Williamson not to enter into any extensive or lasting engagement they propose to give him information of the expected Resolution as soon as it is taken that he may be able to calculate the number of hands nec[e]ssary and be in the way of providing them the forgoing communication is made at the request of the commissioners I being sent to the quarres to see them and to have my opinion of the stone this letter was delivered by mr Carral the other two hade gon off before my Return from the quarres.

Signes Danl Corral

Whether true or false, it hath been reported thy told your excelency that there was no Contract Subsisting between the commessioners and me, lett the letters and contract speak for them selves as I have faithfully performd the deutys on my part, hade I been guilty of any fault or breach of contract, an inv[e]stigation should have taken place and if found falty Dismissed me acording to law, but as they could advance nothing against me they would dow it by arbetary power, somthing lik a court of inqueisision and when they found that I was to sew for my wages they began to strik hard at the Root of my abletys, but these second causes will not serve their purpose, I could mak it apear by the first storry of the presadents House that there is not apiec of better work any where acording to the stile of it, and as I was not p[e]rmited to derect it farther, no bleam can be laid to my Charge, the first or second day of agust I will demand my sellary and if not complyd with I am desird to send a copy of the contract and letters to anoplas wher I expect Justice.

I have said before that this is merly for your excelencys privet information as I dow not chous to commit to writing what I know how the public hath been served.

Collen Williamson

I intended to have built all the walls with stone both extereor and intereor which at least would savd twenty thousand pounds and the work much better but I was oblidged to yeald to ignorance.[4]

C.W.

ALS, DLC:GW.

1. A perch or rod is a unit of length that measures 16½ feet in standard usage.

2. D.C. commissioners Daniel Carroll, Gustavus Scott, and William Thornton had written Williamson on 27 April 1795: "The Arrangements made this Day for carrying on the Capitol render it unnecessary for us to engage you

longer in the public employment. We do not wish you however to be immediately thrown out of employment, We therefore do not mean to withdraw your Salary until six weeks from this Day, and in the mean time we neither ask nor expect any Services from you in behalf of the public" (DNA: RG 42, Records of the Commissioners for the District of Columbia, Letters Sent).

3. The figures in square brackets correct Williamson's calculations, which he had underestimated by £100.

4. Williamson pursued his grievance after GW left the presidency (see Williamson to John Adams, 9 June 1797, in MHi: Adams Papers).

From Oliver Wolcott, Jr.

sir,   Philadelphia July 11th 1796.

I have had the honor to receive your letters dated the 4th[1] and 6th instant addressed to me as Secretary of the Treasury, & the private letter of the 6th[2]—The question arising under the act concerning seamen is a perplexing one. My original impressions were not unlike those of the Attorney General—namely, that the defect in the Law ought to be supplied by construction, & as no proof was specified in the Law, *reasonable* proof was to be presumed as intended.[3] a draft of instructions to the Collectors was framed upon this idea; but there being some diversity of opinion, the point being novel & difficult & the opinion of counsel decided, I renounced my project of executing the law as erroneous. Either of the proposed modes would accomplish the views of the Legislature, but that ought to be preferred which would furnish the least ground for captious criticism.

The suspension of the appointment of Mister Davis will be attended with no kind of inconvenience, what I wrote in his favor was not owing to any intimation from him. Since the president's letter was received I have had some general conversation with him; when he arrives at Boston he will inform whether the appointment would be acceptable under all circumstances. In the mean time enquiries will be made of his qualifications comparatively with those of others; at present I have no doubt that the appointment would be proper.

As soon as the act concerning quarantine was printed, copies, with an instruction to the Collectors were transmitted, requesting them "to cooperate with the State authorities in giving effect to any regulations established by State laws, applying to the objects mentioned in the act." Governor Mifflin has only to signify his wishes in respect to the mode in which the aid of the Revenue Officers is to be given, & they will be fulfilled. Of this he has been informed by the Secretary of State.[4]

The measures for selling the new stock failed of success. I am now endeavouring to obtain a Loan of the Bank of New York, in which I have some reasons to expect a favorable result.[5] Though my situation is very unpleasant & very different from what it ought to be, yet I feel a confidence that I shall preserve the public credit until an appeal can be made to Congress, who are alone responsible for these embarrassments. I feel a consciousness that all was done by me, at the last session, that could have been done with propriety by any person, & that in any event this can be made incontrovertibly evident.

If the President has not already decided on the appointment of a surveyor general, the name of Israel Ludlow will doubtless be presented to him. I have given Mister Ludlow a Certificate of what I know respecting him at his request.[6] I believe him to be a man of sense & industry, & on enquiry of several persons I am informed that he possesses a good character. He would be an acquisition as a Deputy surveyor, but as he is a young man, & not much known, he appears to be hardly fit for the charge of a Department of such consequence. If a character of some celebrity & general estimation cannot be obtained, Mister Ludlow may be considered as an eligible candidate.

There is no intelligence that the Flying Fish has made any capture since the Mount Vernon. the alarm of French resentments is, however, still circulated: all the malcontents are uttering predictions of something terrible from France. A French emissary is said to have appeared at Portsmouth in New Hampshire, & his conversations as stated in the newspapers, concur with other accounts of the project already known to the President.[7] The Secy of State tells me that Mister Adet remains silent on the subject of the explanation requested last week.[8] As so much is threatened & so little done, there is room to hope that the mischief will end in a paltry intreague to excite discontent: the evidence of unfriendly intentions is however so strong, as to justify precautions on the part of the Government. If Mister Adet does not reply in a few days, it may be well to enquire whether an answer is to be expected; but this will deserve consideration. In haste, I remain with perfect deference &c.

Olivr Wolcott jr

LB, DLC:GW.

1. For this letter, see GW's second letter to Wolcott, 6 July, n.1.

2. For this letter, see Wolcott to GW, 1 July, n.7.

3. See Charles Lee to GW, 4 July.

4. Wolcott is referring to "An Act relative to Quarantine" approved on 27 May (1 *Stat.* 474). Secretary of State Timothy Pickering wrote Pennsylvania governor Thomas Mifflin on 8 July to acknowledge Mifflin's letters to GW of 25 and 27 June. He also enclosed Secretary of War James McHenry's circular letter about the quarantine law and Wolcott to Pickering, 8 July, which repeats the information Wolcott gave in this paragraph (all PHarH: Executive Correspondence, 1790–99; see also Pickering to GW, 8 July, n.3).

5. For the stock, see Wolcott to GW, 1 July, and n.6 to that document. The Bank of New York agreed to advance to the United States about $120,000 and to postpone the receipt of another $200,000 payable in October (see Wolcott to the president and directors of the Bank of New York, 11 Aug., in CtHi: Oliver Wolcott, Jr., Papers).

6. For the certificate, see Pickering to GW, this date, n.2.

7. *The Oracle of the Day* (Portsmouth, N.H.) for 30 June noted the arrival of a "gentleman from France" who "reports that the whole Republic of France resents the conduct of the American Congress in making a shameful and derogatory treaty with Britain, which so interfered with the existing Treaty between France and America, that the alliance, which was founded in torrents of blood, and for the preservation of the liberties of the U. States procured and defended by the aid of French armies and navies, would (it was feared) soon be at an end. An American in France is treated with enmity & contempt, as inimical to the rights of man, and all familiarity with them had ceased. Our national faith is despised, and the whole people are united in a full belief that the greater part of the American government are under British influence, or they never could have refused the *proffered* terms of a most honourable commercial connection with France, to a treaty with England, which appears with every humiliating circumstance of abject petitioners and adulating sycophants." The gentleman believed "our peace and neutrality will soon be interrupted by the present vigilant *Directory*, which may too suddenly adopt some decisive measures to punish America for her ingratitude." *The Philadelphia Gazette & Universal Daily Advertiser* for 8 July reprinted the report.

8. Pickering had written French minister Pierre-Auguste Adet on 1 July (see Cabinet to GW, 2 July, n.2; see also Pickering to GW, this date, n.5).

From the Commissioners for the District of Columbia

Sir.   Washington, 12th July 1796

We had the honor of your two Letters, first and eighth Inst., covering a letter from the Secretary of War (which is returned) and also the several papers to be forwarded to Messrs Willink of Amsterdam[1]—One complete set of those papers, with a [   ] of the power, signed by all of the Commissioners, will be forwarded to the Secretary at War by him, to be transmitted to Holland by fridays Mail—We shall transmit a [   ] to Baltimore to be forwarded thence[2]—Since our last to you, we have had a Letter from the Secretary of the Treasury—He gives no hopes of aid from the Bank of the United States,[3] and Mr Clement Biddell, in a Letter of the 6th Inst., says, that no sales have been made of the new-Created Stock; and that there is no appearance of a Sale being effected, without a loss of 8 or 10 ℔ cent[4]—Such being the case, there can be no just expectation of receiving a supply through the Bank of the United States—The bank of Columbia have agreed to lend us $40,000 for 6 months; to be advanced in 4 Installments of 10,000 Doll[ar]s ℔ month; the first payment to commence in Augt: the whole sum loaned, with 42,000 Dolls. heretofore loaned, to bear an Interest of 6 ℔ cent, & to be secured by our note, indorsed by at least, two unquestionable securities[5]—It remains for us yet to obtain them—Some who have been applied to, have appeared rather backward—We think, however, we shall be able to obtain the money: and that with rigid œconomy, it will carry us to the first of December—Morris & Nicholson have not yet appeared—We expect Mr White down tomorrow, and in the course of the present Week, shall take some decisive measures respecting these gentlemen. We have the honor to be &c.

G. Scott
W. Thornton

LB, DNA: RG 42, Records of the Commissioners for the District of Columbia, Letters Sent.

1. GW's letter to the commissioners dated 8 July has not been found. The returned letter almost certainly was James McHenry to GW, 29 June.

2. The commissioners wrote McHenry on this date (see McHenry to GW, 29 June, n.1). The following Friday was 15 July.

3. The commissioners most recently wrote GW on 29 June. Secretary of the Treasury Oliver Wolcott, Jr., had written the commissioners on 27 June (see Commissioners for the District of Columbia to GW, 22 June, n.3).

4. The letter from Clement Biddle to the commisioners dated 6 July has not been identified.

5. The D.C. commissioners had written the president and directors of the Bank of Columbia on 21 June to request a loan (DNA: RG 42, Records of the

Commissioners for the District of Columbia, Letters Sent). For its tentative approval and terms, see Benjamin Stoddert to the commissioners, 30 June (DNA: RG 42, Records of the Commissioners for the District of Columbia, Letters Received).

From James McHenry

Sir   War office 12 July 1796.

In addition to the suggestions in my letter of monday[1] I would beg leave to submit the following considerations.

With respect to the running of the Cherokee line.

On Mr Dinsmore's arrival from that nation I questioned him concerning the fittest persons to be employed on the part of the U.S. He said, that Gen. Pickens would be more agreeable to the Cherokees than any other person: that he knew them; and that they had great confidence in him. He gave it also as his opinion, that a military guard would be necessary for the security of the commissioners. I inquired then if any inconvenience would result from delaying to run the line till after the visit which the Cherokees were permitted to make to the President in the autumn, when that and other matters relative to their concerns might be talked over and finally adjusted. He thought not.

You will recollect that it is stipulated in the treaty of 1791, that the boundary line is to be run and plainly marked by three persons appointed on the part of the U.S. and three Cherokees on the part of their nation: and that by the supplementary treaty of 1794 it is further stipulated, that "the Cherokee nation shall have ninety days notice of the time and place at which the commissioners of the U.S. intend to commence their operations."[2]

Should the rule which is here laid down be followed, it would be late in November before the work of marking could even be commenced, which would necessarily throw its completion into the winter.

This appeared to me an objection to entering upon it during the present year; and with other circumstances induced me to think that it might be undertaken with more propriety during the next.

In the interval, the character of the administration of Tenessee will be more developed, and the disposition of its inhabitants better known to government. Peace may also take place in Europe and the minds of the frontier people, be more inclined to concur in measures calculated to preserve the tranquility of the union; for tho' the war is so distant from the U.S. it acts nevertheless to indispose those characters which naturally tend to the frontiers to acts of insubordination and disobedience. It affords besides the oppertunity to know whether General Pickens will serve as commissioner,[3] and to fix a precise time with the Indians for commencing the work without risk of disappointment.

If you should conclude upon such considerations as these, to suspend the business till next year, it may be proper that I should desire McKee or Dinsmore to inform the Cherokees, that the President wishes those of their chiefs who have been permitted to visit him in autumn to come prepared with the names of the three persons which their nation may appoint to attend the commissioners on the part of the U.S.; that the President will then communicate to them the time when and place where his commissioners will be ready to commence running the line, in order that they may make it known to their nation on their return.

With respect to superintendant of Indian affairs.

The late act of Congress which admitted Tenessee into the union as a State has virtually repealed so much of the ordinance of Congress as vested its governor whilst a territory with the office of superintendant of Indian affairs.[4]

So far that act divested its governor of the office. Does any other act authorise the President to appoint a superintendant or agent of Indian affairs?

I think the act "to regulate trade and intercourse with the Indian tribes, and to preserve peace on the frontiers" passed the 19th of May ulto may be construed as having vested this power in the President.[5]

Granting licences to trade with the Indians or purchase articles from them are among the duties assigned to a superintendant.

Sect. 3. of the act just quoted tho' it contemplates two territorial districts provides nevertheless that no person shall go into any country allotted or secured by treaty to any of the Indian tribes South of the river Ohio, without a passport from the governor of some one of the U.S. or the officer of the troops of the U.S., commanding at the nearest post on the frontiers, or *such other person*, as the President of the U.S. may from *time to time* authorise to grant the same.

Sect. 7. enacts that no person shall be permitted to reside at any of the towns, or hunting camps, of any of the Indian tribes as a trader, without a licence under the hand and seal of the superintendant of the department, or of *such other person* as the President of the U.S. shall authorise to grant licences for that purpose.

Sect. 14. enacts, that if any Indian belonging to any tribe in amity with the U.S. shall come over or across the boundary line into any State or territory inhabited by citizens of the U.S. and there take steal or destroy any horse, horses, or other property, belonging to any citizen or inhabitant of the U.S., or of either of the territorial districts of the U.S. or shall commit any murder, violence, or outrage, upon such citizen, or inhabitant, it shall be the duty of such citizen or inhabitant, his representative attorney or agent to make application to the superintendant, or *such other person* as the President of the U.S. shall authorise for that purpose.[6]

From these and other parts of this act it appears that the President may authorise a person to reside within any of the States bordering upon Indian tribes, in amity with the U.S. and vest them with the powers and functions of superintendant of Indian affairs.

Tenessee having become a State, and being organised, and admitted into the union as a State, the President has the same power to appoint an agent of Indian affairs to reside within it, as he has to appoint an agent to reside within the State of Georgia.

Under the impression that this construction ought to be given to the act in question, I wrote to Col. Henly agent of the war department June 23d to govern himself on applications from the Inhabitants of Tenessee for indemnification for waste or injury done their property by friendly Indians, by the 14th section of the said act.[7]

Should this construction of the intercourse act strike you as a justifiable one, Mr Henley and Mr Dinsmore may be authorised to perform such duties as the present State of things may require without the formality of a new appointment or any additional salary.

With respect to the appointments of agents for trading houses. I do not know that I can add any thing to what I have said in my last on this subject. To the Southward, the scites are yet to be determined by treaty; and till the treasury can furnish the means to purchase the goods I do not perceive any apparent advantage from the appointment of factors. With the greatest respect I have the honour to be Sir your most ob. st

James McHenry
Secy of war

ALS, DLC:GW; LB, DLC:GW. GW received this letter on 16 July (see his letter to McHenry, 18 July).

1. McHenry is referring to his letter to GW written on 10 July, which was a Sunday.

2. See Article IV of the Treaty of Holston, 2 July 1791, and Article II of the Treaty of Holston, 26 June 1794 (Kappler, *Indian Treaties*, 2:29–34; see also GW to Timothy Pickering, 1 July, and n.2).

3. GW eventually nominated Andrew Pickens as one of three commissioners "for ascertaining and marking the Boundary lines, agreeably to Treaties, between the United States and the Indian Nations" (GW to the U.S. Senate, 19 Jan. 1797, in DNA: RG 46, entry 52).

4. See "An Act for the Government of the Territory of the United States, south of the river Ohio," 26 May 1790, and "An Act for the admission of the State of Tennessee into the Union," 1 June 1796 (1 *Stat.* 123, 491–92).

5. For this act, see 1 *Stat.* 469–74; see also Pickering to GW, 12 July, found at Pickering to GW, 8 July, n.1.

6. McHenry added emphasis to selected words in the preceding three paragraphs.

7. A copy of the relevant extract from McHenry's letter to David Henley written on 23 June is in DLC:GW.

From Oliver Wolcott, Jr.

sir, Treasury Department July 12th 1796.

I have the honour to transmit to the President two Letters from the Commissioner of the Revenue, dated the 8th & 11th Instant.[1]

It appears to be expedient to entrust the inspection of the Lighthouse at Seguin to David Coney who is recommended by Genl Lincoln. Both Jonathan Coffin and Saml Coffin are well recommended for the appointment of Lighthouse keeper at Nantucket. The experience of Jonathan Coffin in this business is however a circumstance which may determine the preference in his favor.[2] I have the honor to be &c.

Olivr Wolcott jr

LB, DLC:GW.

1. Commissioner of the Revenue Tench Coxe wrote Wolcott on 8 July that the lighthouse being constructed at Seguin, Maine, required inspection and that Boston collector Benjamin Lincoln had recommended Daniel Coney (DNA: RG 26, Lighthouse Letters). For authorization to build a lighthouse near the mouth of the Kennebunk River, see 1 *Stat.* 368–69.

Writing to Wolcott on 11 July, Coxe reported the death of Tristram Coffin, who had kept the lighthouse at Nantucket, Mass., and listed recommendations in favor of Coffin's son Jonathan, the acting keeper. Coxe also noted that Samuel Coffin, a former keeper, had applied for the vacancy (DNA: RG 26, Lighthouse Letters).

2. GW replied to Wolcott from Mount Vernon on 20 July: "From your Letter & the evidence exhibited in those which it enclosed, it would seem that Daniel Coney is a fit character to entrust the inspection of the Lighthouse at Seguin to; & Jonan Coffin a proper person for Keeper of the Lighthouse at Nantucket. Let them be appointed accordingly" (LB, DLC:GW). Coxe announced the appointments of Daniel Cony and Jonathan Coffin in separate letters to Lincoln dated 23 July (both DNA: RG 26, Lighthouse Letters).

Trained as a doctor, Daniel Cony (Coney; 1752–1842), of Hallowell, Maine, served as a militia lieutenant during the Revolutionary War and subsequently spent many years as a state legislator and judge.

Jonathan Coffin (1757–1831) was appointed lighthouse keeper at Nantucket and served until at least 1816.

To James McHenry

Private

Dear Sir   Mount Vernon 13th July 1796

The purport of your private letter, of the 7th instant (that part of it I mean, which relates to the Frigate for the Regency of Algiers) has surprised me exceedingly.

That no step yet, should have been taken to carry this measure into vigorous execution; and that it should be asked, near six weeks after it had been resolved to comply with the Deys request, and an actual stipulation of our Agent, or Agents there; by what Department it is to be carried into effect? is, on account of the delay which has been occasioned (if contrary to the Ideas which have been communicated to the Dey, & Colo. Humphreys) extremely unpleast.

Disagreeable as this requisition was found in its reception, and more so in the compliance with it; yet, as there appeared no other alternative but to comply, or submit to the depredations of the Barbary Corsairs on our Citizens, and Commerce, the former was preferred: & I had no doubt (after pressing as often, and as earnestly as I did before I left Philadelphia, that all matters requiring my opinions, or Acts, might be laid before me) that every thing relative to this Frigate was in a perfect train of Execution, agreeably to whatever assurances had been given, by Captain OBrian.

If the Laws establishing the different Departments (I have them not by me) does not expressly, or by analogy, designate the one to which the care of such business is entrusted, I must, no doubt, assign it; but where these speak, it is best for me to be silent.

If the building of this Vessel could have been suspended until the meeting of Congress, for the Agency of the Senate, the answer to the Dey might have been suspended also.[1] But to avert, if possible, the disagreeable consequences of delay, a prompt decision was come to; and Captn OBrian hurried off with the result. This decision, and the letters which he carried, ought to be resorted to; and the measures accorded thereto, strictly. Whether it will be best to purchase a Ship ready built, if one fit for the purpose can be had (and such an one on the Stocks at Philadelphia was talked of); Whether to contract for the building & equipping of one (some of the materials being found) if entire confidence can be placed in the Undertaker; or whether to furnish the materials (in which case all that can be spared from our own Frigates ought, unquestionably, to be applied) and pay for the building; depends upon enquiries not within my power at this time, and place to make; & must, therefore, be a matter of investigation, & consultation among yourselves; especially with the Secretary of the Treasury, on the means.

Before I conclude, let me, in a friendly way, impress the following maxims upon the Executive Officers. In all important matters, to deliberate maturely, but to execute promptly & vigorously. And not to put things off until the morrow which can be done, and require to be done, to day. Without an adherence to these rules, business never will be *well* done, or done in an easy manner; but will always be in arrear, with one thing treading upon the heels of another.[2] With very great esteem and regard I am—Dear Sir Your Affecte friend &ca

Go: Washington

ALS, CSmvRRL; LB, DLC:GW.
 1. See GW to the Dey of Algiers, 13 June.
 2. McHenry replied to GW on 16–17 July.

From James McHenry

Sir.   War office 13th July 1796.

I do myself the honour to inclose you the directions given to Mr Fox one of the clerks of the department of war, and well skilled in the quality of ship timber and construction of vessels of war relative to an examination of the materials on hand and such a disposition of them as may comport with the safe keeping of such as may be useful in future, and such as may be fit for the vessel contemplated for the mediteranean service. They have been approved of by the Secy of State and Secry of the treasury.[1] With the greatest respect, I have the honour to be Sir Your most ob. st

James McHenry
Secy of war

ALS, DLC:GW; LB, DLC:GW. GW received this letter on 16 July (see his letter to McHenry, 18 July).

 1. In the enclosed instructions to Josiah Fox, dated 12 July, McHenry directed him "to proceed to New York, Portsmouth in New Hampshire, and Boston.

"The general objects of your Journey to these Towns are:

"1st To examine, assort and arrange into distinct parcels the Shiptimbers and Planks, the property of the U.S. in the different yards in New York, Portsmouth and Boston.

"2nd To examine into the State of the Naval Stores at those places, and procure for them greater protection and security where wanted.

"3rd To obtain from the principal Ship builders of New York, Portsmouth and Boston, upon what terms, and within what time they will agree to build a 36 Gun Frigate of the dimensions described in sketch A."

Fox then received detailed instructions for sorting the timber and was told to obtain written estimates from the shipbuilders based on different ways to procure or value timber and plank (DLC:GW).

To Timothy Pickering

(Private & confidential)

Sir,   Mount Vernon 13th July 1796.

Yesterday, I was informed by a Gentleman from Richmond, that Mr Dawson was gone on to Philadelphia in order to embark for France; and about an hour ago, I received a letter of which the enclosed is an extract from a well informed acquaintance, & a stanch frd to his country.[1]

What, or whether any thing can with propriety be done in consequence of this information, must be left to yourself and the two other Secretaries to decide, from circumstances, & appearances on the Spot.

It may not be amiss to observe further, that Mr Dawson is the Son in law of Mr Jones—one of the Circuit Judges of this state,[2] and, as I am informed, unfriendly to the Genl Government—and that Mr Monroe is the Nephew of Mr Jones, & has his son with him in France.[3] As every day brings fresh matter to view—Vigilence, with caution becomes more & more necessary.[4]

Go: Washington

ALS, MHi: Pickering Papers; LB, DLC:GW.

1. GW enclosed an extract from David Stuart's letter to him dated 11 July. The gentleman from Richmond has not been identified.

2. John Dawson was the son of Joseph Jones's second wife, Mary Waugh Dawson Jones.

3. Joseph Jones, Jr. (c.1780–1808) travelled with James Monroe to be educated in France (see Journal, 19 June 1794, in *Papers of James Monroe*, 3:18; see also Monroe to his uncle Joseph Jones, 9 June 1796, in *Papers of James Monroe*, 4:32–33).

4. For Pickering's reply, see his first letter to GW, 19 July.

From Timothy Pickering

(Private)

Sir,   Philaa July 13. 1796

I saw Mr Vaughan last evening, whom I had desired to ascertain Mr Adet's intentions relative to a journey to Mount Vernon. He had made some indirect enquiries, & is inclined to think the journey will be made, but suspended for four or five weeks. He will endeavour to reduce the matter to a certainty, & give me the earliest information.[1]

Last evening a Mr Bird, a London merchant, gave me a letter from Mr Pinckney, in which he expresses his regret at Mr Livingstons motion which induced your answer of the 30th of March, on which he adds "This answer appears to me to have been dictated by a just sense of propriety, and in the true spirit of the constitution." There is nothing beside in the letter to require its being forwarded to you.[2] The inclosed letter addressed to you came with it.[3]

No answer has yet been received from Mr Adet.[4] I have the honor to be most respectfully sir your obt servant

Timothy Pickering

ALS, DLC:GW.

1. Pickering's informant probably was Philadelphia merchant John Vaughan. French minister Pierre-Auguste Adet did not visit Mount Vernon that summer (see James McHenry to GW, 16–17 July).

2. Pickering quoted from Thomas Pinckney's letter to him written at London on 5 May (DNA: RG 59, Despatches from U.S. Ministers to Great Britain). Robert Bird, junior partner in the London firm Bird, Savage & Bird, carried Pinckney's letter (see Bird to Pinckney, 7 May, in DLC: Pinckney Family Papers).

3. For the probable enclosure, see Pinckney to GW, 7 May.

4. Pickering waited for Adet's reply to questions posed on 1 July (see Cabinet to GW, 2 July, n.2; see also Pickering to GW, 11 July, n.5).

From Timothy Pickering

Sir,   Department of State July 13. 1796.

In your last dispatches were received two patents passed by the Attorney General for your signature, which I now return for that purpose.[1] I have also the honor to inclose a duplicate commission for John Trumbull Esqr.[2] The original went by Mr King; and to be with perfect respect, sir, your most obt servant

Timothy Pickering

ALS, DLC:GW; LB, DNA: RG 59, Domestic Letters; LB, DNA: RG 59, GW's Correspondence with His Secretaries of State. GW replied to Pickering on 20 July.

1. Only two patents received approval during the time of GW's visit to Mount Vernon: one on 1 July issued to Luden McKechnie of Pennsylvania

for stays to support the spine of the back, and another dated 2 July issued to James F. Mangin of New York for a machine to saw marble (see *List of Patents*, 464, 257).

2. John Trumbull eventually declined his appointment as an agent to aid American seaman (see GW to the U.S. Senate, 30 May, and n.1 to that document).

To John Marshall

Dear Sir,   Mount Vernon 15th July 1796

I have received your letter of the 11th instant, and regret that present circumstances should deprive our Country of the services which I am confident your going to France, at this time, would have rendered it.[1]

It is difficult to fill some offices with characters which would fit them in *all* respects. Another case of this sort is now before me—namely—that of Surveyor General. A gentleman well qualified to discharge the duties of this Office was appointed, but has declined accepting it.[2] Several others have been mentioned, but the recommendations of them have gone more to the general respectability of their characters, than to their Scientific knowledge; whilst both are equally essential. For it is a trust, which in the execution, requires skill to arrange, instruct, Inspect, and report correctly, the conduct of others; and integrity to resist the temptation which opportunities, and an overweening fondness for speculating in Lands, may throw in his way.

Among the characters from the State of Virginia who have been presented to my view on this occasion—are Generals Wood & Posey[3]—and Colonels Tinsley and Anderson;[4] the last of whom is, I believe, an Inhabitant of Kentucky; and having been in that line, the presumption ought to be, that his Mathematical knowledge (which should extend beyond common Surveying) is adequate to the duties which would be required; but how he is in other respects, and what may be the course of his Politics, I know *nothing*; and but *little* of those of the other three—particularly of Tinsley's.

The object therefore of writing this letter to you is, to ask confidentially, such information as you possess—can acquire—and give me, respecting the qualifications of these Gentlemen; or of any other fit character that may occur to you for Surveyor General; accordant with the ideas I have expressed above. The Office is important & respectable; of cour⟨se⟩ the Incumbent, besides his Scientific abilities, should possess a celebrity of character that would justify the appointment.

To learn your sentiments of the characters, and on the points I have mentioned, will be in time when I shall have the pleasure of seeing you, on your way to Philadelphia[5]—With very great esteem & regard, I am—Dear Sir Your Obedient Servant

Go: Washington

ALS, NNGL; ADfS, DLC:GW; LB, DLC:GW. "Private" is written on the cover of the ALS and also appears on the two other variants.

1. For the letter dated 11 July that conveyed Marshall's decision to decline appointment as U.S. minister to France, see GW to Marshall, 8 July, n.2.

2. Simeon DeWitt had declined his nomination as surveyor general (see Timothy Pickering to GW, 27 June, and n.2 to that document).

3. Thomas Posey, Revolutionary War officer and a brigadier general in the 1793 campaign against the Northwest Indians, settled in Kentucky in 1794. He later served as lieutenant governor of that state, U.S. senator from Louisiana, and governor of the Indiana Territory. For Posey's interest in a federal appointment, see James Madison to GW, 25 May 1796, and n.3 to that document.

4. Richard Clough Anderson (1750–1826), a lieutenant colonel in the Virginia line during the Revolutionary War, had served as the surveyor general to divide western lands reserved for Continental army veterans from Virginia. He settled near Louisville, Ky., in 1784.

5. For another failed attempt to find a surveyor general and the subsequent selection of Rufus Putnam, see GW to James Wood, 12 Sept., and n.3 to that document; see also Pickering to GW, 29 Sept. (DNA: RG 59, Miscellaneous Letters).

Marshall believed William Heth to be a suitable nominee for surveyor general (see Edward Carrington to GW, 10 Oct., in DLC:GW).

From Timothy Pickering

Sir,   Department of State July 15. 1796.

Yesterday I received from the Minister of the French Republic an answer to my letter of the 1st instant, and have now the honor to inclose a translation of it.[1] His entire ignorance of any new orders from his government relative to neutral vessels trading with the enemies of the French Republic, may authorize a conclusion, that none have been issued: and that the captures & appropriations (not condemnations) of the cargoes of American vessels carried into French ports in the West Indians, are the result of orders given by the Colonial administrations. This may be only a *variation* of the practice in use a year or two past, during which time they have actually compelled the delivery of cargoes for the use of government, with promises of payments within certain periods, which very often were so procrastinated as to induce the return of American vessels unpaid, after waiting six months or more for the performance of those promises. From the instances referred to in my former letter it seems probable that the administrations give *due-bills* without fixing definitively the times of payment.[2]

Mr Adet asks whether the President has caused orders to be given to prevent the sale of prizes conducted into the ports of the United States by vessels of the Republic or privateers armed under its authority. On this I have the honor to inform you, That the 24th article of the British treaty having explicitly forbidden the arming of privateers and the selling of their prizes in the ports of the United States, the Secretary of the Treasury prepared, as a matter of course, circular letters to the Collectors to conform to the restrictions contained in that article, as the law of the land. This was the more necessary as formerly the Collectors had been instructed to admit to an entry and sale the prizes brought into our ports.[3] On the 30th of June I received from Mr Liston, the British Minister, a Note mentioning the prizes which had been recently carried into Boston by a French privateer, and desiring that the sale of those prizes, which were British property, might be prevented.[4] In consequence, I wrote the same day to Judge Lowell, Genl Lincoln, & to Mr Otis who had manifested a disposition to do the business of District Attorney until one should be appointed, desiring them to take such measures as were practicable to prevent an infraction of the above cited article of the British treaty. At the same time I wrote to the Chief Justice, Mr Elsworth, who had the same question discussed before him at his circuit court in So. Carolina, praying him to write to Judge Lowell immediately, to inform him of the determination in that case, presuming it to be the result of a full consideration of the subject. Thus the matter rests. I requested from the Chief Justice the like information; but have not yet received his answer.[5] The circular letter from the Secretary of the Treasury was confined, agreeably to the article of the British treaty, to the prizes brought in by *privateers*. With the highest respect I am, sir, your obt servant

Timothy Pickering

P.S. Since writing the above, the Secretary of the Treasury has given me a copy of his circular letter, which is inclosed.[6]

ALS, DNA: RG 59, Miscellaneous Letters; LB, DNA: RG 59, Domestic Letters; LB, DNA: RG 59, GW's Correspondence with His Secretaries of State.

GW replied to Pickering from Mount Vernon on 22 July: "Your letter of the 15th Inst., enclosing a copy of Mr Adets answer to your requisition of the first; and the circular of the Secretary of the Treasury, to the Collectors, has been received; but did not get to my hands until the 20th.

"There is a studied delay in the answer of the first, and a misteriousness in his conduct, not easy to be accounted for. It did not, surely, if he had received no information from his Government, and was ignorant of its intentions relatively to the points on which explanations were asked, require (be the pressure of his business what it might) fifteen days to make that declaration; nor will candour & good disposition, justify the measure.

"Not having Papers here of a public nature to resort to, I shall hope that the circular letter of the Secretary of the Treasury, to the Collectors; and all the Orders respecting French Prizes, have, in time & manner, been the result of necessity; and not the exercise of discretion; for the restriction *now*, after a contrary practice has been *allowed*, will be a source of much discontent; and of course calls for very correct proceedings in the execution of the Treaties, and Laws respecting the case" (ALS, NjP: De Coppet Collection; LS [retained copy], DNA: RG 59, Miscellaneous Letters; LB, DNA: RG 59, GW's Correspondence with His Secretaries of State).

1. For Pickering's letter to French minister Pierre-Auguste Adet written on 1 July, see Cabinet to GW, 2 July, n.2. The enclosed translation of Adet's reply, dated 14 July, reads: "The business with which I have been burthened has prevented me from answering sooner. . . .

"I am sorry, Sir, to be obliged to leave you in an uncertainty, in which I myself participate. I do not know the nature of the orders which may have been given by my Government to the Officers of war vessels of the Republic, or what conduct it has prescribed to them to hold with regard to neutral vessels trading with our enemies. I am not informed whether the ancient arrets of the Committee of public safety relative to the Commerce of the United States, are or are not still in force; some considerable time having elapsed since I have received news from France, I cannot have recourse to them to resolve your doubts. I can only refer to the answer which I had the honor of giving to your letter relative to the mount vernon.

"The Consul at Boston has just informed me that the Collector of the Customs of that place has prevented the unlading and sale of the prizes carried into that port by two french privateers. The Consul has ineffectually complained to him. The Collector founds his refusal upon a letter which he says he received from you.

"I request you, sir, to inform me whether the President has caused orders to be given for preventing the sale of prizes conducted into the ports of the United States by vessels of the Republic or privateers armed under its authority and if so, upon what foundation this prohibition rests" (DNA: RG 59, Miscellaneous Letters; see also Pickering's third letter to GW on 19 July).

2. Pickering may be referring to discussion of American vessels held at Port au Paix, Saint Domingue, related in the Cabinet's letter to GW dated 2 July.

3. For Article XXIV of the Jay Treaty, see Miller, *Treaties*, 262.

The circular from Secretary of the Treasury Oliver Wolcott, Jr., to the collectors, dated 30 June, quoted instructions issued on 30 May 1793 that had extended special entry rights to French warships and privateers. The circular continued: "The *entry* and *sale* in our ports, of prizes to privateers commissioned by France, not being stipulated in our treaty as a right, to be enjoyed by that nation" while the new treaty with Great Britain contained "an express stipulation" against allowing any foreign privateers to arm their ships or sell their prizes in the ports of either nation. Wolcott instructed "that hereafter vessels and property captured from the subjects of Great-Britain by privateers commissioned against that nation, are not to be admitted to an entry in the ports of the United States; of course any goods or property landed therefrom will be subject to seizure as being imported contrary to law" (DNA: RG 59, Miscellaneous Letters).

4. British minister Robert Liston wrote Pickering on 29 June to ask that customs officials be instructed "to prohibit the entry of British prize goods into the territories of the Union" and that "particular attention" be directed to "two captures" brought into Boston by the French privateer *Eagle* (DNA: RG 59, Notes from the British Legation).

5. Pickering's separate letters dated 30 June to Massachusetts District Judge John Lowell, Boston collector Benjamin Lincoln, and Harrison Gray Otis directed their attention to Article XXIV of the Jay Treaty and asked them to consult on measures to prevent treaty infractions. Pickering elaborated to Otis: "All that the French nation are entitled to by our treaty with them, is an *asylum* for their privateers and their prizes. The privilege hitherto enjoyed by them of *selling* their prizes in our ports was a mere *indulgence* and not a *right*." He then referred to Chief Justice Oliver Ellsworth's decision to stay the sale of a prize at Charleston, S.C. (all DNA: RG 59, Domestic Letters).

The Charleston case involved the *Amity*, prize to the French privateer *Leo* (see *Documentary History of the Supreme Court*, 3:89–90). William Rawle's opinion for the secretary of state, dated 30 June, about how to prevent a sale of the prize at Boston brought the *Amity* case to Pickering's attention (PHi: William Rawle Papers). Pickering then wrote Ellsworth on the same date seeking details regarding his decision to stay the sales and asking his opinion if judges in Massachusetts could issue a similar injunction. Pickering requested Ellsworth's immediate communication "to Judge Lowell at Boston, to whom I have written on this occasion, and at your leisure to indulge me with an answer; particularly as circular instructions may be proper to be transmitted to all the District

Judges and Attornies, as well as to the collectors of the Customs" (DNA: RG 59, Domestic Letters).

6. See n.3 above.

From John Lathrop, Jr.

Sir,   Boston July 16 1796

The enclosed oration solicits your acceptance.[1] The manner in which it was received by an assembly of more than 2000 free-men, is a fresh instance of the warm federalism of the inhabitants of Boston, their unabated attachment to your person, their decided approbation of your administration and their firm confidence in your wisdom and integrity. At the close of that part, which contains a faint tribute to your services, your patriotism and virtues, every voice and every hand united in the loudest acclamations and testimonials of applause. The partizans of faction are silent—they hang their heads, overwhelmed with shame and confusion. The triumph of Merit is the severest punishment of Vice, and thus, it was reserved for you, Sir, to inflict the vengeance of heaven, upon the sons of lawless Anarchy. The very arrows, which they had aimed at you, have recoiled upon their own bosoms and become the instruments of their destruction. With sentiments of respect, gratitude and affection, as lasting and ardent, as they are inexpressible, I am, Your most humble, obliged and devoted Servant

John Lathrop, junr

ALS, DLC:GW.

1. Lathrop enclosed his *An Oration, Pronounced July 4, 1796, at the Request of the Inhabitants of the Town of Boston, in Commemoration of the Anniversary of American Independence* (Boston, 1796). A portion celebrated GW's presidency: "AMERICANS could not hesitate in their choice of a chief magistrate. From the calm shades of Mount Vernon, called by the voice of his country, he, who was our cloud and pillar, during our pilgrimage and warfare, arose to govern and guard us in peace. Every heart beat with transports—every tongue hailed him welcome, thrice welcome!—Under his wise and unequalled administration, all ranks and degrees of our fellow citizens have been happy and prosperous. The lofty pyramid of American glory has been compleated. . . . And though ingratitude has dared to impeach the most inflexible integrity;—though disappointed ambition has emitted all its venom to blacken the fair reputation of unsullied virtue; though the best intentions have been misrepresented and the noblest motives ascribed to viler purposes than ever were conceived by a

Clodius or a Cataline, the confidence of the AMERICAN PEOPLE can never be removed, nor their affections diverted from their long tried, their long loved WASHINGTON" (pp. 15–16).

GW replied to Lathrop from Mount Vernon on 8 Aug.: "I have received, & pray you to accept my thanks, for your Oration delivered the 4th of July, which you so obliging as to send" (ALS, DLC:GW, ser. 9).

The *Oration* remained in GW's library at his death (see Griffin, *Catalogue of the Washington Collection*, 120).

From James McHenry

private.

Sir.   Philad. 16[–17] July 1796.

I have just reced your private letter of the 13th inst.

I am sorry and vexed, that what I said in my letter of the 7th should have conveyed an idea that the least avoidable delay had taken place in the arrangements for the Algiers frigate; nothing like which was intended.[1]

But the inclosed papers will shew you that every thing has been done which the case required.

You will see by Mr Pickerings letter to me, July 8th, No. 3, in answer to my note of the same date No. 2, which was written immediately after the receipt of letter No. 1. that the draught of the vessel was begun on the 29th Ulto. And you will perceive, by sketch A, digested by Mr Fox (the only clerk I have, who knows any thing of naval matters) that it required both thought and time to prepare it. The Sketch was not, consequently finished till the 8th inst., the day Mr Pickering mentioned to me (letter No. 1.) the necessity of sending Mr Fox on monday.[2]

So far the business had been conducted by the Secry of State, to whom it belonged to furnish the dimensions of the frigate &c., agreeably to stipulations with the Dey; without which nothing could be by the department of war relative to her construction.

It now came before me on the 8th (letter No. 1). Accordingly, I framed instructions for Mr Fox (the same which I have transmitted you)[3] and sent them the day following to Mr Wolcott for his perusal and correction, with a request to him to send them to Mr Pickering for the same purpose. Mr Pickering returned them to me on tuesday the 12, and on the 13th Mr Fox left this on his mission. I could have wished to have employed another person, and had requested Mr Pickering to look out for a substitute, which he informed me in his letter of the 8th No. 1. was not to be obtained.

This detail will shew you, that the object has met with due attention from all parties, and, that what depended particularly on the department of war, was promptly attended to and executed.

Mr Fox's absence is a real loss to me. I have naval questions frequently to consider. I cannot draw Mr Humphreys from his duties to aid me. I work also with two clerks less than any of my predecessors, and am besides without the assistance of my chief Clerk, Mr Stagg, who is on a tour for the recovery of his health.

Notwithstanding this, I hope the business will not suffer. I mention too, because, as a child of your own, you must feel an interest in the course of my conduct, that I have endeavoured to follow the maxim you have laid down, which you have always, and so successfully practiced upon yourself; and that in consequence thereof I have subdued the business of the office; and am now able to meet the daily calls, and spare a little time occasionally to an examination of the permanent objects of the department.

I find the Indian department wants revisal; that new regulations in it are become necessary for the agents; and that the department of military stores, as it regards their safe keeping and distribution, has never been arranged or subjected to the rules which were devised when Mr Hamilton was in office, the principal of which appear to me extremely important.[4] I am engaged in these considerations and inquiries, and as I complete the system for each shall lay it before you.

Sunday 17.

I called on Mr Adet yesterday. He had intended to have made you a visit, as he said, and is very much disappointed at not being able to accomplish it. He will have to go to New-London respecting masts for the West Indies, and has besides such an increase of West India business on hand as to shut out the hope of seeing you at Mount Vernon. I expressed to him; what I was sure would be your regret, on hearing that you could not see him with the other ministers; and added such other things as comported with your ideas on the subject.[5]

I understand that Mr Adets reply to the Secy of States letter is evasive. I do not think however that the republic means to quarrel with the U.S.; or that she has issued orders to capture their merchantmen.[6]

The case of the mount vernon is at least equivocal,[7] and by very recent arrivals from the west Indies it would appear, that our trade there remained on the same footing as heretofore.

Had positive orders to capture or carry in for examination issued from the Directory, they would before this time have been in operation in the west Indies and upon this coast. You would moreover have been favoured with information from Mr Monroe, because to have given secrets would have quadrated with the system of opposition.

I consider, consequently, the information to Mr Hamilton, by a french client of his, which he communicated to you, as another Gallic trick, played upon him, that it might reach you, under the impression of his having credited it.[8]

I have had nothing since my last communication to you from the West-ward. Volney it se[e]ms, is gone to watch the course of the winds. I hope we shall be able to know the result of his discoveries, before their transmission to the national institution. With the sincerest respect & attachment I am Sir your most obt hble

James McHenry

ALS, DLC:GW; ADfS, MiU-C: James McHenry Papers. GW acknowledged this letter when he first wrote McHenry on 22 July.

1. At this point on the draft, McHenry wrote and struck out: "Till the Secry of State determined upon and furnished me with the dimensions &c. I could do nothing."

2. McHenry's draft continues with text that he struck out: "before which no person could have been sent. You will observe also that it was necessary to have the Sketch to be able to take."

Versions of the enclosures numbered 1, 2, and 3, all dated 8 July (Friday), have been identified. The draft (sketch A) has not been identified.

In letter number 1, Secretary of State Timothy Pickering informed McHenry that he and Secretary of the Treasury Oliver Wolcott, Jr., agreed "that the first step towards building *the frigate* is to send Mr Fox to the different Navy yards, to take an account of the timber, and to converse with the principal builders, to see on what terms & within what time they will, any of them, undertake to have her completed" (DLC: James McHenry Papers). McHenry replied to Pickering in letter number 2 by asking for the frigate's dimensions, proposed armament, and "any other particulars of the engagement with the Dey" that might assist in framing instructions (MiU-C: James McHenry Papers). Pickering responded to McHenry in letter 3 that the frigate was to carry thirty-six guns and that he had asked Joshua Humphreys to calculate the dimensions and prepare a draught of the ship, presumably now completed by Josiah Fox (DLC: James McHenry Papers).

3. For the instructions given Fox, see McHenry's second letter to GW, 13 July, n.1.

4. McHenry is referring to the "Regulations for the receiving distributing and accounting for all public property designed for the Army of the United States," issued by the War Department in August 1792 (DNA: RG 217, Money Receipts [Advances]; see also Alexander Hamilton to GW, 10 Aug. 1792). Wolcott had drawn McHenry's attention to the regulations in a letter written on 1 July 1796 (CtHi: Oliver Wolcott, Jr., Papers).

5. For GW's concern over French minister Pierre-Auguste Adet's plans to visit Mount Vernon, see his first letter to McHenry, 11 July, found at McHenry to GW, 5 July, n.4.

6. Pickering had written Adet on 1 July about French interruption of U.S. commercial shipping (see Cabinet to GW, 2 July, n.2). Adet replied to Pickering on 14 July (see Pickering to GW, 15 July, n.1).

7. For a French privateer's capture of the ship *Mount Vernon*, see Pickering to GW, 12 June, and n.2 to that document; see also Wolcott to GW, 20 June.

8. See Alexander Hamilton to GW, c.16 June.

To James Keith

Dear Sir,   Mount Vernon 17th July 1796

You will perceive by the enclosed letter from Mr Bushrod Washington to me, what is enjoined by the High Court of Chancery of this Commonwealth.[1]

By Mr George W. Craik, I send in Bank Notes of the United States—the Sum required to be deposited in the Bank of Alexandria, by the decree. Had I known of this decree before I left Philadelphia I could, & would have drawn the Specie for this purpose; and I think to avoid any caval hereafter, the receipt from the Bank of Alexandria ought to be expressed in such a manner as to imply this—or rather not to imply the contrary; and this it may well do, for the presumption is, that this Sum will remain there *long* before the proper claimants are ascertained.

As Mr Craik is young in business, you would do me a favor by accompanying him to the Bank (in Alexandria) for the purpose of arranging this matter properly, at that place; thereby placing me on secure ground. I have directed Mr Craik to take a copy of the Decree; on the back of which it may be best, perhaps, to take the receipt from the Bank.

Not having the Will of Colo. Thos Colville by me; nor recollecting distinctly where the relations of his Mother were said to reside; and being unacquainted with characters in Alexandria who would have it most in their power to cause the notification required by the Decree, to be inserted in "Some public paper in the Kingdom of Great Britain for two Months" thereby serving the parties, and fulfilling the intention of the Court; let me ask the favor of you to ingage, if you can hit upon a suitable person for this purpose, the doing it. Mr Hodgden[2] some years ago, presented claims in behalf of *some* who conceived themselves *entitled* under the Will of Colo. Thos Colvill:[3] and if in Alexandria, may be as eligible a character to apply to as any.[4] With very great esteem and regard I am Dear Sir Your most Obedt and obliged Servant.

Go: Washington

LS, (retained copy), DLC:GW; LB, DLC:GW.

1. See Bushrod Washington to GW, 3 July, and n.2 to that document.

2. For William Hodgson, see n.4 below.

3. These claims have not been identified.

4. Keith replied to GW from Alexandria, Va., on 18 July: "Mr Craik has deposited in the Bank the money your Excellency directed, and procured a Receipt from the Cashier which I hope will be conformable to your Expectations: The Deposit is entered on the Bank Books in the Stile of the Receipt There is no Vessell bound from this place to Europe in any short time. The Executors of Colo. Colville inserted their Advertisement notifying his Death and Residuary Legacy of Colo. Colville in one of the Newcastle papers, in that place it may best answer to publish the decree of the High Court of Chancery and the deposit made by you in the Bank of Alexandria in pursuance of it. Mr Hodgson went to England last Spring with an Intention to return this Fall, if he does, he will leave England before a Letter can reach that Country. If I Remember right Mr Rumney of that house had powers of Attorney from some of the Claimants of Colo. Colville's Legacy to state their Claims and receive payments of their dividends—if it be so, he appears the most proper person to apply to on this Occasion. A short Advertisement in your Name explanatory of the Decree may not be improper. If your Excellency approves of an Advertisment, shall I draw it up and write to Mr Rumney on that Subject, or woud your Excellency prefer doing it yourself?" (ALS, DLC:GW). GW recorded on this date a payment of $3,110 "into the Bank of Alexandria, Agreeably to a Decree of the High Court of Chancery of Virginia; being the Balance due from me as Surviving Exr of the Will of Thos Colvil decd to that Estate as pr Settlement with the court of Fairfax Cty—and which is in full" (Cash Memoranda, 1794–97).

John Rumney, Jr. (1746–1808), was a partner in the mercantile firm Robinson, Sanderson, & Rumney of Whitehaven, England, that operated a store in Alexandria.

For his involvement with claimants to the Colvill estate, see GW to Rumney,

6 April 1787 and 24 Jan. 1788, and Rumney to GW, 22 Jan. 1788 in *Papers, Confederation Series*, 5:125–26; 6:58–59, 53–54.

William Hodgson, associated with Robinson, Sanderson, & Rumney, held a power of attorney (see Munson, *Alexandria Hustings Court Deeds, 1783–1797*, 55, 204).

From Harriot Washington Parks

Mill-Brook [Va.] July 17 [17]96

Aunt Lewis received a letter from my dear & Honor'd Uncle a few days ago wherein he was pleas'd to send me thirty pound also a great deal of good advice which I am extremely obleiged to you for and intend adhereing most strictly to it.[1]

Beleive me my dear Uncle my heart will ever with the liveliest gratitude most gratefully acknowledge and remember your's & Aunt Washington's great goodness and attention to me and if my Uncle will only answer my letter and say he is not offend'd at my Union (which took place yesterday Aunt Lewis's going immediately to Berkley to stay untill the fall & finding it not convenient to carry me with her wish'd us married before she went) I shall be happy for after my dear Uncle's protection and kindness toward's me I should be a most miserable being to reflect that I had displeas'd my greatest freind.

I shall take the liberty of troubleing my Uncle to return my thank's to Aunt Washington for the earings she sent me from Philadelphia which I received but a week ago from Berkley— Aunt Lewis is much mend'd & intend's answering your letter by the next post Aunt Lewis join's me in love to you and Aunt Washington.[2] I am my dear @ Honor'd Uncle your affectionate Neice

Harriot Parks

ALS, DLC:GW.

1. GW's letter has not been found. For his wedding gifts, see Betty Washington Lewis to GW, 5 July, n.9.

2. GW replied to Parks from Mount Vernon on 22 July: "The last Post brought me your letter of the 17th instant informing me of your Marriage the preceeding day with Mr Parks.

"Far from being displeased at the event, I offer you my congratulations thereon; and sincerely wish it may prove the source of continual happiness to you. Much of this depends on your own disposition; on a prudent deportment towards your husband; and on the accomodation of *your* views to *his* circumstances. If the first are more extensive than the latter, it will involve both of you

in difficulties; perhaps in ruin. always keep the old adage in remembrance—
'Take your measure according to your cloth' and do not, because you see
others do so, (some because their fortunes enable them, and others because
they are excited to it by vanity) endulge yourself either in dress, or a mode of
living that will be productive of embarrassmt.

"Having much company in the house, at prest I have time only to add,
that your Aunt, & Nelly Custis unite with me in best wishes for the happiness
& prosperity of your self & Mr Parks; and that if it shd suit his business at
any time, to make a visit here, while we are at home we should be glad to see
you both at Mount Vernon. With great regard I remain—Your affecte Uncle"
(ADfS, NNGL).

Parks replied to GW from Fredericksburg, Va., on 9 Sept.: "I need not repeat to my dear & Honord Uncle, the infinite pleasure I experienced on reading his kind, & affectionate letter, the 22d of July, which I only received a few
day's ago, being in Berkley at the time it reached Fredericksburg and no safe
conveyance offering for it to me. Mr Parks and myself return our most grateful
thank's, to you and Aunt Washington for your congratulation's and also polite
invitation, to visit you which no circumstance whatever could afford us more
satisfaction. & if his business will permit this fall I flatter myself, with the pleasing idea of seeing my dear Uncle and Aunt at Mt Vernon.

"Aunt Lewis has been to Berkley for a month past & is very much mend'd
in her health I have not seen her look so well for a great while cousin Robert
Lewis has had the misfortune to loose his youngest child[.] My love to Aunt
Washington & Nelly Custis. I am my dear & Honord Uncle Your ever affectionate Neice" (ALS, MH: Jared Sparks Collection). For the infant Betty Washington Lewis, see Robert Lewis to GW, 26 July, and n.2 to that document.

To James McHenry

Sir,   Mount Vernon 18th July 1796
Your letters of the 10th, 12th and 13th instant, with their enclosures, came all by the last Mail to Alexandria; and were received by me on Saturday morning.[1] The contents of such parts
as require it, shall be noticed.

The greatest, and what appears to me to be an insuperable
difficulty in the way of running and marking the boundary line
between the United States and the Cherokee tribe of Indians,
the ensuing Autumn (which is certainly the most agreeable season for a work of this sort) is, that no Commissioners are, or
can be appointed to superintend the same, in the recess of the
Senate; which, unless extra: causes should render it expedient,
will not happen before the first Monday in December. This circumstance, in addition to the reasons assigned in your letters,

renders a postponement of this measure until next year, unavoidable. But that it may not be delayed beyond a convenient time in the Spring, the Indians may be requested to come instructed to arrange matters for carrying the measure into effect *at that period. Their* interest, & the tranquillity of *our* frontier, requires that this line should not only be run (with as little loss of time as can possibly be avoided) but be very distinctly marked also; that ignorance may no longer be offered as a plea for transgressions on either side. and to ascertain in the interem, whether Genl Pickens will serve as a Commissioner.

I hope, & expect that the proposed visit from the Cherokee Chiefs, will be managed so, as not to take place before the Month of Novembr. I have already, been incommoded, at this place, by a visit of several days, from a party of a dozen Cuttawbas;[2] & should wish while I am in this retreat, to avoid a repetition of such guests. The reason why I name November, is, that between the middle & latter end of August, I shall repair to the Seat of the government; remain there until between the middle and last of September; and then return to this place again for my family.[3]

The extract which you enclosed in your letter of the 10th, from the Secretary of the Treasury, declaring his inability to furnish money for carrying on Commerce with the Indian Tribes, renders the appointment of Agents for that purpose, *at present*, altogether improper—and whether the Act "to regulate Trade and intercourse with the Indian Tribes, and to preserve Peace on the Frontiers" does, or does not go fully to the points which are enumerated in your letter of the 12th, there seems, under existing circumstances, no expedient so proper to execute the requisites of the above Act—and the duties enjoined on the late Superintendent of Indian Affairs in the Southwestern Territory, which have become stagnant by the admission of it as a State into the Union, as by applying the Services (under temporary regulations, & proper Instructions) of Colo. Henley or Mr Dinsmore, or both, as the case shall, after duly considering it, appear to require. But if this expedient is resorted to, Mr Dinsmore ought to return *immediately*.

My ideas with respect to the most eligable mode of procuring the 36 Gun Frigate, have, already (in a former letter) been conveyed to you; and your Instructions to Mr Fox does, I perceive, accord therewith;[4] but lest I may not perfectly understand another part of them, which relates to Timber & Plank—which certainly come under the description of "Perishable articles"— in the Act discontinuing three of the Frigates, and directing such of the Materials as are perishable to be sold; I shall give it as my decisive opinion, that *all Wood*, not necessary for the retained Frigates; and the one wanted for Algiers; except the large pieces which have been obtained with difficulty & at a heavy expence, & which would not answer for ordinary Vessels & would sell for little; ought to be sold, agreeably to the directions of the afore-said Act.[5] If they are reserved; Secured from the weather; and persons employed to take care of them; the expence & impo-sition will exceed all calculation: and be wasted, or embezzled notwithstanding.

Go: Washington

ALS, NhD; ADfS, DLC:GW; LB, DLC:GW.

McHenry replied to GW on 22 July: "I have received your letter of the 18th instant and its inclosures.

In the letter to Mr Blount of the 27th of Febry ulto he was authorised to communicate to the Cherokees that a visit from their influential chiefs would be permitted in autumn. I shall write to Col. Henley or McKee to inform them that their arrival in this City must be in November, as it will not be conve-nient for the President to see them earlier" (ALS, DLC:GW; LB, DLC:GW). For McHenry's letter to William Blount dated 27 Feb., see Bartholomew Dan-dridge, Jr., to McHenry, 28 Feb., n.2.

1. The previous Saturday was 16 July.

2. *Claypoole's American Daily Advertiser* (Philadelphia) for 11 July reported that on 29 June "seven men, two squaws, and a boy, belonging to the Ca-taw[b]a nation of Indians" passed through Winchester, Va., "on their way to visit [t]he President of the United States." They likely left Mount Vernon on 6 July because on that date GW recorded in his cash accounts that he gave them $40, "which is to be charged to the Public." McHenry repaid the money that GW "advanced to the Cattawba Indians" on 3 Sept. (Cash Memoranda, 1794–97).

3. For the Cherokee delegation visit, see GW to the Cherokee Nation, 29 Aug.; see also McHenry to GW, 24 Aug., and n.1 to that document.

4. The former letter was GW to McHenry, 13 July. For the instructions to Josiah Fox, see McHenry's second letter to GW, 13 July, n.1.

5. See "An Act supplementary to an act entitled 'An act to provide a Naval Armament,'" approved 20 April (1 *Stat.* 453–54).

From James McHenry

Sir.   War office 18 July 1796.

The annexed packets contain the most essential letters received since my last.[1]

No. 1. Gen. Wilkinsons letters of the 11th, 16, 17th ulto. I have not thought it necessary to send the continuation of his charges which came by the same mail.[2]

No. 2. Is copy of a letter to Major Gen. Wayne resulting from Gen. Wilkinsons information relative to Fort Miamis.[3]

No. 3. A dispatch from Mr Seagrove and extracts of letters to Mr Habersham.[4]

No. 4. A letter from Capn Bruff.[5]

With the greatest respect, I have the honour to be, Sir your most ob. st

James McHenry

ALS, DLC:GW; LB, DLC:GW. GW acknowledged this letter when he wrote McHenry on 22 July (second letter).

1. See McHenry to GW, 16–17 July.

2. These documents from Gen. James Wilkinson have not been identified but probably related to his dispute with Gen. Anthony Wayne (see McHenry to GW, 6 July, and n.1 to that document).

3. McHenry wrote Wayne on 16 July: "It has been stated to me that Fort Miamis has proved fatal to a majority of the British stationed there, that the sickly season is at hand—and that wine, bark, and Brandy have proved ineffectual to the prevention or cure of intermittents and bilious fevers, which has prevailed at that post.

"Assuming this state of facts, it may be proper, if Miamis is not absolutely essential as a place of depot, and link in the chain of communication and defence, that it should be left ungarrisoned. If necessary only as a place of depot, a subalterns command, may be sufficient; if as a link in the chain of defence, still the troops to be subjected to its climate ought to be as few as possible" (Knopf, *Wayne*, 499–500).

4. The dispatch from Creek agent James Seagrove, and the extracts (probably of letters to John Habersham, collector at Savannah), have not been identified.

5. The letter from James Bruff has not been identified, but see GW's second letter to McHenry, 1 July, n.3.

To Timothy Pickering

Private

Dear Sir,   Mount Vernon 18th July 1796.

If there be any thing *yet to do,* which can with *propriety* be done, towards fulfilling the several Treaties which the United States have entered into (without specifically naming them) it is my desire that there may be no delay in the execution: and if upon examining of them carefully, any matters should be found therein requiring the attention of either of the other Departments, that these sentiments may be conveyed to the Secretaries thereof, as proceeding immediately from myself.

The new requisition of the Dey of Algiers, which has been yielded, will require to be laid before the Senate for its ratification; together with such Papers as are necessary to explain, and account for the measure.[1] It might be well therefore to revise, and to prepare them accordingly, in time.

The continual attacks which have been, and are still making on the Administration in Bache's, and other Papers of that complexion (indecent as they are void of truth and fairness) under different signatures, and at present exhibited under that of Paulding; charging it not only with *unfriendly,* but even with *unjust* views towards France; and to prove it, resort to misrepresentation & mutilated authorities; and oftentimes to unfounded, but round assertions; or to assertions founded on principles which apply *to all* the Belligerent Powers, but which, *by them* are represented as aimed at France *alone.* Under these circumstances, it were to be wished that the enlightened public could have a clear & comprehensive view of facts[2]—But how to give it, lies the difficulty; and I see no method at present, however desirable the measure, that is not liable to objections; unless the predicted, & threatned conduct of France towds this country (under the pretext of our Treaty with G: Britain)—or its demand, that the Guarantee of their West India Islands, agreeably to the Treaty of Paris, should be fulfilled, presents the occasion.[3]

Whether either of these will, or will not happen; or whether any other mode may occur which, after mature consideration shall appear expedient or not, I wish that in your moments of leisure (if such you have) you would go most carefully & *critically* over the whole of the correspondence between the different

Secretaries of State & the French Minister in this Country; & with our own Minister at Paris, from the Period matters began to change from the antient habits, & to assume their new form, in that country. If circumstances should render explanations of this sort expedient & necessary for Congress, a previous examination of the Papers with notes & remarks, will be essential. If they should not, the measure nevertheless will be satisfactory & useful. I would have the *whole* of the transactions, in all its direct, & collateral relations, examined with as critical an eye as Mr Bache, or any of his numerous correspondents or communicants would do; that if there is any thing in them (not recollected by me) that can be tortured into an unfriendly disposition towds France, & not required by the Neutral policy adopted by the Executive; approved by the People; and sanctioned by the Legislature: or which the Peace, honor & safety of this Country did not require, that I may be apprised of it, as my conviction of the contrary is strong.

I request also, that you would begin to note down all the subjects as they may occur, which may be proper to communicate to Congress at their next meeting; either at the opening of the Session, or by seperate messages in the course of it. Many things are forgot when the recollection of them are postponed until the period at which they are wanting. Minute details will not be amiss, because a selection will, at any time, be easier than a collection to make.

Your letter of the 8th instt did not reach my hands until the 13th—nor did that of the 11th until the 15th. I mention these facts that you may know whether the delay has been occasioned by their not getting to the Post Office in time, or were detained at it. Other letters from Philadelphia of the same dates, came to hand two days sooner in both instances. With very great esteem & regard—I am—Dear Sir Yours—always

                                        Go: Washington

P.S. I am frequently receiving letters from Philp Wilson, similar to the one I now enclose. Let me request therefore, if his case admits of redress, that an attempt may be made to obtain it. If it does not, that he may be so informed, in explicit terms.[4]

ALS, MHi: Pickering Papers; LB, DLC:GW. For Pickering's acknowledgement of this letter, see his first letter to GW dated 21 July.

1. GW is referring to the agreement to furnish the Dey of Algiers with a frigate (see GW to the Dey of Algiers, 13 June; see also James McHenry to GW, 7 July, and GW to McHenry, 13 July).

2. Between 21 May and 11 Aug., "PAULDING" addressed fourteen letters critical of GW's administration to the printer of *The Independent Gazetteer* (Philadelphia) and to the editor of the *Aurora General Advertiser* (Philadelphia). Both papers printed the letters, which appeared in the *Aurora* on 24 and 30 May; 9, 13, 15, 18, 22, and 30 June; 4, 11, 22, and 25 July; and 2 and 11 Aug. (two additional letters appeared in the *Aurora* for 24 Aug. and 2 Sept.).

PAULDING argued in "Letter I" that GW had "interpre[t]ed the *same* parts of the Constitution variously at different times, and that he has thereby converted the great charter of our country into a thing of chance, liable to the direction of whim, caprice or design."

PAULDING argued in "Letter II" that GW had favored Great Britain over France: "We have heard much lately about public faith; but what kind of faith is it, which impelled the first Executive Magistrate to declare to the French Minister that the forms of the Constitution prohibited treating with him, and yet under the same forms negociated a Treaty with a British Commissioner?" (referring to the negotiation of the explanatory article to the Jay Treaty during a recess of Congress).

Usurpation of power and subservience to Great Britain dominated PAULDING's critique throughout his letters. PAULDING's effort printed in the *Aurora* for 11 July (his tenth, although misnumbered as "Letter IX") continued his analysis (begun in "LETTER III") of queries that GW submitted to the cabinet in April 1793 (see GW to David Humphreys, 12 June, n.3). PAULDING quoted from a GW letter written on 18 April 1793 (misdated in the *Aurora* as 8 April) and claimed that it showed GW's determination "that his fiat should be supreme, and that his own omniscience was commensurate to every object." Not convening Congress "exhibited in the Chief Magistrate of a free people, an usurper, whose arrogance was not to be restrained by an overweening fondness for fame, or by the limits of our Constitution." The opinions of the cabinet (which PAULDING argued in "Letter XI" was an unconstitutional body) "were the stepping stone to future measures which were to throw our country into the arms of Great Britain . . . and to alienate the freemen of America from *their* best friend, the Republic of France. The assumption of power in the Executive to act independently of Congress in things in which their decision was constitutionally essential, was the key stone in the arch, and bound together the system manifested in the queries." GW apparently "imagined Congress" like the French parliament under the ancien regime, with "no right to deliberate but to act, and that according to the information *he* should think proper to give, and the promptitude *he* should conceive fit to direct." Evidence of GW's sense of "Royal as well as Papal importance" could be found in his many proclamations: "We have had a Proclamation of Neutrality, a Proclamation for a day of thanksgiving (as if we had a *Vatican* and a *Tiara*) and a Proclamation declaring a supreme law of the United States before it had passed through all the necessary forms!" PAULDING concluded that GW wanted "to assimilate our government to a Monarchy. Every measure seems to squint towards this darling object, and hence *irredeemable debt, excise systems, National Banks, loans, federal cities, reports for raising revenue by an Officer unknown to the Constitution, and dependant upon the Executive—hence the plan to excite Western Insurrection, to increase the national debt, to furnish a pretext for a standing army, and to supply arguments against the cause of Republicanism—hence the pious wish of the most pious Secretary, in the presence of 'the Benefactor of Mankind!' that the Insurgents would burn Pittsburgh!"*

3. GW is referring to Article XI of the 1778 Treaty of Alliance with France in which "from the present time and forever" the United States guaranteed "to his most Christian Majesty the present Possessions of the Crown of france in America as well as those which it may acquire by the future Treaty of peace" (Miller, *Treaties*, 39–40).

4. No letters from Philip Wilson to GW have been found, but Pickering wrote Rufus King, U.S. minister to Great Britain, on 20 Aug.: "I inclose a petition from Philip Wilson now living in Westminster Great Britain, to the President of the United States, exhibiting a statement of his losses while a merchant in Philadelphia, by Captures of his property by the British, particularly of the ship Mentor and Cargo captured and destroyed in time of peace, meaning after the close of the late American war. . . .

"Mr Wilson is frequently teasing the President with his claims, intimating that failing of obtaining indemnification from the British Government, it is due to him from that of the United States. You will see that he has consulted Sir William Scott, who can give you probably a history of the business. If Wilson has any just claims against either Government, he is entitled to the attention and patronage of his own. You will therefore render an acceptable service to the President by inquiring into this case and putting it in train for settlement or stopping Wilson's claims and complaints if they are unfounded" (DNA: RG 59, Diplomatic and Consular Instructions).

King replied to Pickering from London on 10 Nov. that Wilson had accepted a "£2000 Sterling" settlement from the British government in 1793 and executed a release from further claims, "making at the same time a Protest before a Notary, in which he declares himself dissatisfied with the Terms, and that he had from his necessitous situation alone been induced to accede to them—Since that time to the present he has been making applications without Effect to obtain a revision of his Case—This Short view of it, will shew the answer that I should receive, should I make a formal Application on the Subject—I will however in an informal manner and as a case of extreme hardship, represent the situation of Mr Wilson and his Family to Lord Grenville, and request his interference to obtain something more for this unfortunate & helpless family" (DNA: RG 59, Despatches from U.S. Ministers to Great Britain).

Wilson subsequently wrote GW. In a postscript to a petition dated 14 Nov. and addressed "To the Honourable the President and Senate of the United States of America," Wilson referenced three documents he had sent to GW (DNA: RG 46, Sen. 4A-G1). When Pickering wrote Wilson on 13 March 1797, he mentioned that Wilson's petition dated 3 Dec. 1796 "addressed to the President, Senate and Representatives of the United States of America in Congress Assembled, was delivered to me, by the late President Washington, with a direction to inform you, that after what has actually taken place between you and the British Government respecting your claim for an indemnification for your Ship and cargo destroyed by her forces, the American Government cannot formally and officially interfere in your behalf" (MHi: Pickering Papers).

From Timothy Pickering

Sir,   Department of State July 18. 1796.

As soon as you had decided on the expediency of substituting a consul in the place of Mr Parrish at Hamburg,[1] I requested Mr FitzSimons at Philadelphia, and Mr King at New-York, to enquire for a suitable person to succeed him. I also wrote to Mr Cabot at Boston making the same request.[2] The two former gentlemen informed me that they found no fit character in Philadelphia or New-York. Last Friday I received the inclosed letter from Mr Cabot, strongly recommending Samuel Williams of Salem.[3] His name did not occur to me, and if it had occurred, I should have hesitated to have *originally* presented it to you; tho' merely because Mr Williams is my nephew; for a man more trust-worthy or more able to execute the office of consul will not often be found. He is about six & thirty years old, was liberally educated, as soon as he left college engaged in mercantile business with his father, and ever since has pursued that course of life. He has been in Europe about three years, in France, in England, & I think at Hamburg.[4] It seemed to me so very desirable to substitute an American Citizen to Mr Parrish, under the circumstances of his removal, that I feel myself happy in recommending a successor for the propriety of whose conduct I can undertake to be responsible. With the highest respect I am, sir, your most obt servant

Timothy Pickering

ALS, DNA: RG 59, Miscellaneous Letters; LB, DNA: RG 59, Domestic Letters; LB, DNA: RG 59, GW's Correspondence with His Secretaries of State. For GW's reply, see his second letter to Pickering on 25 July.

1. See Pickering to GW, 24 May, and n.4.

2. Pickering wrote George Cabot from Philadelphia on 11 June: "(*Private.*) . . . The President has determined to make a change in the consulate at Hamburg. Do you know of any respectable American citizen, of a mercantile character, who would be willing to accept the appointment? It has, I take it, been a lucrative place, even by the fees of office; although these could be of

little consequence to a merchant of Mr. Parish's great wealth and extensive dealings. Yet there have been repeated complaints against him for taking exorbitant fees (as seven dollars instead of two for every certificate), which, considering his established reputation and riches, appears unaccountable. Of this, however, an explanation would have been asked, if other causes of a political nature had not influenced the decision. The change will be softened to Mr. Parish, if a worthy American succeeds him; and in this light I have placed the matter in my letter, advising him of the President's determination.

"Pray inquire among your friends, and favor me with an answer" (Lodge, *George Cabot*, 107–8). Pickering's letters to Thomas FitzSimons and Rufus King have not been identified.

3. The previous Friday was 15 July. The enclosure was a letter from Cabot to Pickering written at Brookline, Mass., on 8 July: "I have enquired diligently for a character to supply the vacancy at Hamburg, & all my friends unite in the belief that Mr Samuel Williams of Salem is a very suitable man—his reputation for integrity & good sense is thoroughly established & I fully believe his appointment wou'd be thought a wise one by those who know him—he has been for some time past in France & is now in England where his Brother Timothy . . . thinks it in the highest degree probable that he woud readily accept the trust" (DNA: RG 59, Miscellaneous Letters).

4. Samuel Williams (c.1760–1841) served as the U.S. consul at Hamburg, 1797–98, and U.S. consul at London, 1798–1801. He later became a London banker. His parents were Pickering's sister, Lydia Pickering Williams (1736–1824), and George Williams (c.1731–1797), a merchant sometimes elected to the Massachusetts legislature.

From John William Bronaugh

Sir   Aquia [Va.] 19th July 1796.

I am anxious to make sale of some Lands given me by my Father on the great Kanhawa River, and having understood that you have lately had an offer of five dollars ⅌ Acre for all your Lands in that country, have taken the liberty to enquire of you from whom this offer was made, I trust and hope if you have it in your power to give me any information by which I can effect a sale at the price above mentioned you will do it.

My Father wishes very much to take in his bond given you some years ago, he mentioned this to you in a letter last Fall, but as you were then at Philadelphia you mentioned you cou'd not send it unless you were at Mount Vernon[1] if it is not too much trouble, to come at this bond, will thank you to enclose it by the bearer.[2] I am Sir, Yr mo. obt hume Servt

John W. Bronaugh

ALS, DLC:GW.

1. For William Bronaugh's letter to GW dated 17 Oct. 1795, see John William Bronaugh to GW, 18 Oct. 1795, n.1. GW replied to John William Bronaugh on 26 Oct. 1795. William Bronaugh's bond had been given for the delivery to George Muse of the 2,000 acres of Kanhawa River bounty lands that GW had purchased to exchange with Muse (see GW to Battaile Muse, 6 April 1789).

2. John William Bronaugh again wrote GW from Aquia on 9 Aug. 1796: "Yours of the 21st July I have received and am greatly obliged to you for your information respecting the Kanhawa Land—You will please direct your letter with my Father's bond to the Dumf[rie]s post office" (ALS, DLC:GW). GW's letter to Bronaugh dated 21 July has not been found.

GW replied to John William Bronaugh from Philadelphia on 28 Aug.: "Among the first things I did after my arrival in this City, was to look for the Bond given to me by your father, for conveyance of the land he sold me on the Great Kenhawa; ⟨a⟩nd among my Papers *for those Lands* I found the Bond; but could find no Deed conveying the said Land, although in the same bundle I perceived conveyances from others, from whom I had made similar purchases. I have, notwithstanding, some recollection that your father has made, or did propose to make me, a Deed for the 2000 acres of land that is mentioned in the Bond; but as there is no such Deed among those Papers which contain my title to the Lands on the Kenhawa, as the recollection of what I have mentioned above (from the deversified scenes I have passed through since) is more like a dream than reality—and as the Bond is of no importance to him—if he has complied with the Conditions of it—but *all important* to me if he has not—I shall postpone the surrender of it until the fact respecting this matter can be explained.

"Let me pray you therefore to learn from your father when, and where the conveyance was made—and if he is enabled so to do—to info⟨rm⟩ me in what Court it was recorded—for if the event did happen (as I presume it did) the Deed as it is not among my Land Papers must be in the Clerks Office where it was deposited for the purpose of recording" (ADfS, NNPM). John William Bronaugh replied to GW on 7 Oct. (DLC:GW).

From Timothy Pickering

(private)

Sir,   Department of State July 19. 1796.

I was honored with your confidential letter of the 13th and showed it to the other two secretaries. Last Friday[1] Mr Dawson called on the Secretary of War, and mentioned his being on a journey to the eastward, to contract for the manufacturing of five thousand stand of arms for the State of Virginia; and requested his information where he might apply without interfering with any contracts or operations of the U. States. The Secretary of War answered, that his acquaintance at the eastward was too imperfect to give him the information requested; but referred him to Mr Hodgdon (giving a note where to find him) who could amply satisfy him on that subject. Yesterday I asked Mr Hodgdon if any gentleman had been with him to get the information referred to: he answered, that no person had called upon him for such a purpose: but that a Mr Annely, a gunsmith of Philadelphia, had for three months past been making guns of a particular kind (smaller than the common musket) for the state of Virginia.[2]

For the manufacture of arms, Pennsylvania has long been more celebrated than any state in the Union; & since the peace I have heard of no manufactory of arms in New-England, except at the public works at Springfield; and there, I recollect, the superintendant had to instruct the workmen, at the outset. The journey eastward (if Mr D. is gone eastward) is for some other purpose than that mentioned to the Secretary of war. I should not suppose Mr Dawson was going to France; at least not immediately: for the same day on which I received your letter, I received one from Joseph Jones Esqr. covering one for Mr Monroe, to be forwarded agreeably to a former request; it having been the practice in this office so to transmit Mr Jones's letters to Mr Monroe.[3]

The Secretary of War told me that he wrote you yesterday, that he had seen the French minister, who said his business was so increased by the operations in the West Indies, that he should not have it in his power to visit you at Mount Vernon.[4] With the highest respect, I am sir, your obt servant

Timothy Pickering

P.S. To-day I received a letter from Mr Monroe dated the 8th of April. He has obtained from the Directory permission for a Mr La-Motte, a Cannon Founder selected last autumn by Colo. Vincent, to come to the United-States. Mr Lamotte is making arrangements with Mr Monroe to come to the United States with his family. I shall hand the letter to the Secretary of War. The letter also informs that Colo. Vincent suggested that Engineers would be wanted, to construct works and to instruct our officers; "if such are wanted, two of the first eminence may now be had: one called [   ] has long been at the head of the French Academy for that science, in this city, and by his lectures laid the foundation of the education of many of those who are now distinguished in the field." These are Mr Monroe's words. The other gentleman is a Mr Sonolet, represented as a man of superior merit in that branch.[5] Different views may be entertained of this very ready compliance on the part of the French government to furnish a cannon-founder agreeably to our request—with the addition of two of their ablest engineers. In one, it may be considered as extremely friendly—In the other as designed "to draw closer the ties of fraternity" between the two Republics, in the modern and democratic sense of the phrase; & particularly to promote the French interest on the secret plan of Mr ——.

ALS, DLC:GW; ALS (letterpress copy), MHi: Pickering Papers. For GW's reply, see his first letter to Pickering on 25 July.

1. The previous Friday was 15 July.

2. Thomas Annely (d. 1804), a gunsmith, had worked as a foreman in the shops at West Point, N.Y., before moving to Philadelphia around December 1793. The War Department employed him as an inspector of arms, and he became master armorer at Harper's Ferry, Va., in 1798.

3. The letter to Pickering from Joseph Jones, James Monroe's uncle, has not been identified.

4. See James McHenry to GW, 16–17 July.

5. No letter from Monroe to Pickering dated 8 April has been identified, but a draft of a letter from Monroe to the secretary of war dated 7 April is in NN: James Monroe Papers. The summarized information and passage Pickering quotes appear in that letter, indicating that it is the draft for the letter discussed in the postscript (see also Pickering to Monroe, 7 Nov. 1795, in *Papers of James Monroe*, 3:509–10).

Delamotte's contract with Monroe, written in French, is dated 8 April 1796 (NN: James Monroe Papers). Monroe wrote the secretary of war from Paris on 11 April that Delamotte "happens to be a brother of our consul at Havre" (*Papers of James Monroe*, 4:5–6). For Delamottes's arrival in New York and an explanation that James McHenry now served as secretary of war, see Pickering to Delamotte, 16 Aug., in DNA: RG 59, Domestic Letters; see also Delamotte to Monroe, 27 May, in *Papers of James Monroe*, 4:29–30.

Jacques Sonolet (1740–1799) was a non-resident associate member of the Institut de France.

The unnamed engineer has not been identified.

From Timothy Pickering

(private)

Sir,   Department of State July 19. 1796.

This morning I received the inclosed letter from Mr Dayton, expressing fully his opinion of Mr Israel Ludlow,[1] whose application for the office of Surveyor General I had the honor lately to transmit to you.[2] While it must be acknowledged that Mr Dayton is perfectly competent to pronounce accurately on the character of a man so well known to him as Mr Ludlow must be, it is proper for me to mention, that I have understood that he & Mr Ludlow have been closely connected in land affairs in the northwestern territory, where I believe Mr Dayton has speculated largely. In this very service Mr Dayton may have experienced Mr Ludlow's skill & fidelity to their common interest. This common interest may be further extensively promoted by the appointment of Mr Ludlow to the office of Surveyor General. This suggestion I respectfully submit to your consideration. At the same it may be doubted whether any very competent person for surveyor general can be found, who will not improve the opportunity presented by his station, of making or advancing his fortune in lands over the Ohio. If Congress intended to exclude the Surveyor General from any land ⟨*illegible*⟩, his pay should have been so increased as to induce a proper character to submit to the restriction.[3] The defect of compensation was a principal reason of Mr DeWitt's declining the office.[4] I also recd to-day the inclosed letter from Robert Morris Esqr. the Judge of the District Court of New-Jersey, on the same subject.[5] With the highest respect, I am, sir, Your obt servant

                                                            T. Pickering.

ALS, DNA: RG 59, Miscellaneous Letters; ALS (letterpress copy), MHi: Pickering Papers. For GW's reply, see his first letter to Pickering on 25 July.

1. Pickering enclosed Jonathan Dayton's letter to him written at Elizabeth, N.J., on 18 July: "A letter received this morning from Mr Israel Ludlow informs me that his name is placed upon the list of Candidates for the appointment of Surveyor General. He requests me to inform you what I know of him and his family, & I undertake it with pleasure, because my acquaintance with them has been long, and is such, as to enable me to speak of them very satisfactorily.

"His father, a colonel of the Militia, was very active in the course of our War with Great Britain, a good Whig, a decided federalist, and is highly respected.

"As to the gentleman in question, he is much esteemed by all whom I have heard to mention him—He is truly exemplary in his general deportment & moral character; temperate, diligent, enterprizing & faithful, he joins to a thorough knowledge of the duties of a practical Surveyor, that of portraying or drafting neatly and correctly.

"This recommendation is not, I assure you sir (as too many are) a thing of course a mere act of friendship without any idea of responsibility, but such is my knowledge of, & confidence in, Mr Ludlow, that I should not hesitate to become responsible for his discharging the duties of this office, with ability, fidelity & general satisfaction" (DNA: RG 59, Miscellaneous Letters).

2. See Pickering to GW, 11 July, and n.2 to that document.

3. Congress had set the surveyor general's compensation at \$2,000 per year (see 1 *Stat.* 468).

4. See Timothy Pickering to GW, 27 June, n.2.

5. In the enclosed letter from Robert Morris to Pickering written at New Brunswick, N.J., on 18 July, he described Ludlow's father as "a very respectable citizen of this State.

"Mr Ludlow early in life went into the North Western Territory in the capacity of a surveyor, & Settler, where he has pri[n]cipally resided. Little of his conduct therefore has fallen within my personal observation: But every account I have heard of him bespeaks him a Young Gentn of good character & understanding and of great activity & enterprise, and I am happy in adding that as far as I have known him he has verified this description.

"I am intirely unacquainted with, and uninformed of his professional ability" (DNA: RG 59, Miscellaneous Letters).

From Timothy Pickering

Sir,   Department of State July 19. 1796.

I have the honor to inclose for your information a copy of the letter I sent this day to the Minister of the French Republic, in answer to his enquiry relative to the prohibition of the sale of prizes brought by French armed vessels into the ports of the United States.[1] I presume the answer will preclude any reply; the rather because similar ideas have been formally reported to the council of ancients at Paris, and will probably be adopted. The rights of neutral nations, and particularly of the United States, as they have been maintained by the Executive from the commencement of the war between France and Britain, are recognized in the report. The reporter, Mr Marbois, is supposed to be the same who was in America with the Chevalier de la Luzerne.[2] With the highest respect I am, sir, your most obt servant

                                            Timothy Pickering.

ALS, DNA: RG 59, Miscellaneous Letters; LB, DNA: RG 59, Domestic Letters; LB, DNA: RG 59, GW's Correspondence with His Secretaries of State. For GW's reply, see his second letter to Pickering on 25 July.

1. For French minister Pierre-Auguste Adet's inquiry about the sale of prizes in his letter to Pickering of 14 July, see Pickering to GW, 15 July, n.1. Pickering replied to Adet on this date: "I have to acknowledge the receipt of your letter of the 14th instant in answer to mine of the 1st. . . . And you enquire whether the President has given orders to prevent the sale of prizes carried into the ports of the United States by vessels of the Republic, or privateers armed under its authority? and on what foundation this prohibition rests? I will be very frank, sir, in answering these questions, after making some preliminary observations.

"The question about the sale of prizes is not a new one. It was agitated, and the point of right settled, in the year 1793. Among the State papers communicated to Congress at the close of that year, and which have been published, is a letter from Mr Jefferson to Mr Morris dated the 16th of August, in which is the following passage: 'The 17th article of our treaty (meaning with France) leaves armed vessels free to *conduct* whithersoever they please, the ships & goods taken from their enemies, without paying any duty, and to depart and be conducted freely to the places expressed in their commissions, which the captain shall be obliged to shew. It is evident that this article does not contemplate a freedom *to sell their prizes here*; but, on the contrary, *a departure* to some other place, always to be expressed in their commission, where their validity is to be finally adjudged. In such case, it would be as unreasonable to demand duties on the goods they had taken from an enemy, as it would be on the cargo of a merchant vessel touching in our ports for refreshment or advices. And against this the article provides. But the armed vessels of France have been also admitted to land & sell their prize goods here for consumption; in which case it is as reasonable they should pay duties as the goods of a merchantman landed and sold for consumption. They have, however, demanded, and as a matter of right; to sell them free of duty; a right, they say, given by this article of the treaty, *though the article does not give the right to sell at all.*'

"It is plain that France understood this 17th article in the same sense. And accordingly, in her treaty of commerce with Great Britain, in 1786, she entered into a stipulation which in case of a war between the U. States & Great Britain, would have prevented the vessels of the U. States from arming as privateers or selling their prizes, in the ports of France. In like manner the United States, in their commercial treaty with Great-Britain, agreed on a similar prohibition. Indeed the 24th article of the latter treaty is but a translation of the 16th between France & Great-Britain.

"Under this view of the case, sir, as soon as provision was made on both sides to carry into effect the treaty between the U. States & Great Britain, it behoved the Government of the former to countermand the *permission* formerly given to French Privateers to sell their prizes in our ports. Such sales, you have seen, the U. States had always a *right* to prohibit; and by the abovementioned stipulation this right became a *duty*. These, sir, are the foundations of the orders which have been given to prevent the sale of the prizes lately carried into Boston by French privateers, to which you refer; it being understood that the prizes were British property. Those orders have since been made general, and communicated to the Collectors in all the ports of the United States. But at present, those orders are confined to prizes brought into our ports by *privateers*" (DNA: RG 59, Miscellaneous Letters).

2. The *Gazette of the United States, & Philadelphia Daily Advertiser* for 18 July reprinted from the *Columbian Centinel* (Boston) for 13 July news of "a resolution on the subject of the sale of prizes, presented by Barbe de Marbois, to the Council of Ancients" on 20 April "in which he informs, that the Committee had carefully analysed the various treaties subsisting between France and other nations; among other things it declares, that the treaty of commerce, made in 1778, between France and the United States, forbids the admiralty officers of American ports, into which the French may conduct their prizes, cognizance of the validity of said prizes, and so reciprocally: but this same article adds, that they may freely depart from the port where the captors were fitted out—And the spirit of the treaty is, that judgment upon the prizes belongs to the tribunals of the nation to which the captors belong, *but not to the Consuls.*" The item continued: "Speaking of prizes carried into neutral ports, Barbe Marbois proceeds, '*The captors and the captured, after a stay longer or shorter according to the spirit of existing treaties, must again proceed to sea; and the prizes must be conducted to the ports of the nation of the captor, and it is there they ought to be tried.* This, Colleagues, is the reciprocity which we demand; and it is thus we will fulfil the duties of friendship and benevolence towards our allies, and even towards nations with which we are only at peace.'" The *Columbian Centinel* for 20 July 1796 printed more extensive excerpts from the speech of François de Barbé-Marbois, who had come to the United States in 1779 as secretary of the legation with French minister La Luzerne (see GW to Lafayette, 30 Sept. 1779, in *Papers, Revolutionary War Series,* 22:557–63; see also Chase, *Letters of Barbé-Marbois*).

From the Commissioners
for the District of Columbia

sir, Washington, 20th July 1796

Since our last to you,[1] we have been obliged to abandon all hopes of seeing Mr Morris here; in consequence of which, we forwarded to him, on the 15th a Letter of which, the enclosed is a Copy—We certainly mean to pursue the measures intimated in our Letter.[2]

A second Letter from Mr Wolcott of the 13th Inst. gives us no hopes of any aid from the Bank of the United States—We are proceeding to carry into effect our intended Loan with the Bank of Columbia, which, we expect, will be compleated tomorrow.[3] With sentiments of perfect respect &c.

G. Scott

W. Thornton

A. White

LB, DNA: RG 42, Records of the Commissioners for the District of Columbia, Letters Sent.

1. The commissioners last wrote GW on 12 July.

2. The commissioners wrote Robert Morris on 15 July: "The time which has elapsed since we have been led to expect you and Mr Nicholson in the City, leaves us no hope of an adjustment of our affairs, by your presence here—We cannot, therefore, in justice to our public situation, longer delay addressing you on a subject highly interesting to the City and not less so to you—There is a certain point beyond which forebearance becomes folly and a total dereliction of public Trust . . .

"When the loan Bill received the Sanction of Congress, we were taught to believe, that if every other expedient to raise money failed, you would, without delay, expose to Sale, as much of the property bought of the late Commissioners as would raise a sufficient fund to pay off the Instalments due on the purchase—We too easily gave into a belief of a measure so just, and one which at all hazards promised to clear you from any loss; as the Lots would probably sell for considerably more than the original purchase money—Much time has past, many hopes have been held out, great preparations have been made for the divisions and Selections, and we still find ourselves in the same distressed situation as in the Autumn of 1795—The whole payments made since that period are not nearly sufficient to cover the arrears of that Year, and no step has been taken toward erecting a single house stipulated by the Contract to be built in 1795 and 1796—Whatever may be our Inclinations, your own good sense and experience in public Office, must tell you, that it is impossible for us, as Commissioners of the Federal Buildings patiently to bear, forever with this line of Conduct; and to use no exertions to obtain that redress for which the repeated breaches of your Contract so loudly call.

"We once more beg leave to repeat, that we will still receive the debt due from you—and Mr Nicholson, in monthly Instalments of 12,000 Dolls. the first payment to commence on the first monday of August, and to be paid on the first Monday of each succeeding month; until the debt shall be discharged. Or, if you can not make payments, as proposed, authorize us to sell at a Credit of 60 & 90 days, for good negotiable paper, indorsed to our satisfaction; as much of your City property as will discharge the debt due: or, if neither of these propositions are admissible, at least give us judgment Bonds at 60 and 90 days, for the debt, that we may avoid the necessity, of either in advertizement of your property, or a Law suit.

"These propositions appear, themselves, so just and shew so strong an Inclination to fall on any expedient, rather than carry things to extremity; that we know not how they can be refused by a Gentleman of Character, once celebrated for his punctuality throughout all Europe and America.

"You will no doubt remark that no proposition is made respecting that part of the Contract which relates to the Buildings. We think it best not to entangle the subject at present, with any thing relating to that part of the case, however important to the City. . . .

"We are highly sensible it cannot be pleasant to a gentleman of Reputation and feeling to be called on so repeatedly for a debt, the detention of which evidently Injures the Creditor to double the amount of the claim; and to the Contracting of which Debt, the creditor yielded his assent from a firm persuasion of its being discharged with the most pointed punctuality—Permit us to assure you that nothing can be more disagreeable to us, than to be compelled to address you on this occasion and in this urgent manner; but if some decisive measure for payment, be not adopted in 15 days from this date, we must proceed to such compulsory measures as may bring our transactions to an end" (DNA: RG 42, Records of the Commissioners for the District of Columbia, Letters Sent). For further troubling developments regarding Morris and John Nicholson, see Commissioners for the District of Columbia to GW, 12 August.

3. The commissioners had written Secretary of the Treasury Oliver Wolcott, Jr., on 7 July with a proposition: "Could the stock belonging to the Bank be borrowed and sold at par, at One, two & three months credit, it appears to be our best means of obtaining money, until the fate of the application at Amsterdam can be known" (DNA: RG 42, Records of the Commissioners for the District of Columbia, Letters Sent). Wolcott replied to the commissioners on 13 July: "Various causes have recently operated to render the proposals lately published for the sale of Stock uninviting to monied people—of course no applications were made.

"It is impossible for me therefore to express a satisfactory opinion of the price which the new Stock would bear, if put in circulation; when I can possess myself of information which can be useful to you it shall be communicated" (DNA: RG 42, Records of the Commissioners for the District of Columbia, Letters Received). For Wolcott's first letter to the commissioners on this topic, dated 27 June, see Commissioners for the District of Columbia to GW, 22 June, n.3.

To Timothy Pickering

Sir,   Mount Vernon 20th July 1796.

Your letters of the 12th & 13th instant, with their enclosures, were received by Mondays Mail, the 18th.

The duplicate Commission for John Trumbull; the blank Commissions for the Revenue Officers; and the Patents passed by the Attorney General; are all signed & returned under cover with this letter.

The want of funds to carry on Commerce with the Indian

Tribes (agreeably to a late Act of Congress) is an unanswerable objection to the appointment of Agents, *at this time,* for that purpose. And in addition to the reasons you have assigned for not appointing a Superintendent of Indian Affairs, in place of Governor Blount; and for Postponing running & marking the line between the United States and the Cherokee Nation of Indians, the want of Power—in the President—to appoint Commissioners to attend the Survey; and a successor to the other, would, I conceive, appear upon investigation; as the first would be an original appointment—and the latter, did not take place in the recess of the Senate. It follows then of course, that these measures must stand suspended, and the best temporary uses made of the present situations, and Services of Colo. Henly and Mr Dinsmore that the nature of things will admit.[1]

Not knowing myself, the purport of the German letter herewith enclosed, and having no body about me that can translate it, I send it to you for this purpose; in order that I may know what attention to give it.[2]

Go: Washington

ALS, MHi: Pickering Papers; LS (retained copy), DNA: RG 59, Miscellaneous Letters; LB, DNA: RG 59, GW's Correspondence with His Secretaries of State.

1. See Pickering to GW, 12 July, found at Pickering to GW, 8 July, n.1.

2. Pickering subsequently wrote GW from Philadelphia on Tuesday, 26 July: "I have the honor to send you a translation of the German letter received from you last Saturday with a pamphlet in the same language by Joachim Detler Wittmack. My clerk who made the translation says he could not find in the English language words to convey the sentiments of extreme humility expressed in the original, and which are familiar in the German: So debasing to the human mind are the absolute, hereditary governments of monarchs & nobles!

"Judge Peters understanding both the language and the subject of Mynheer Wittmack's pamphlet, I will place it in his hands, to be disposed of afterwards as you shall be pleased to direct. But however considerable may be Mr Wittmack's practical knowledge of husbandry, he could not have written the pamphlet in its present style; his manuscript letter being (the Clerk says) extremely incorrect" (ALS, DLC:GW; ALS [letterpress copy], MHi: Pickering Papers). GW received this letter on 29 July (see GW to Pickering, 1 Aug.).

The enclosed translation of Jochim Detlev Wittmack's letter to GW dated 7 March reads: "From my youth I have devoted myself to husbandry and every sort of oeconomy; and by long experience and much practice I have attained a considerable knowledge of this so noble employment. I therefore undertook to publish books upon this subject, in which I demonstrate briefly but comprehensively, that the earth does not produce by far as much as it is capable of. And as the world knows, that Your Excellency's true object is to promote the best welfare of your subjects, I have ventured to take the humble liberty to send you herewith one of my small books; and as I hope and wish, that it may obtain your most gracious Excellency's most gracious approbation, I humbly pray that I may have the happiness of an answer from your Excellency, informing me that my small work has been well received; and, as myself and my family are in distress, accompanied with such a present, as your Excellency shall think I deserve: which shall for ever be thankfully acknowledged" (DLC:GW). Pickering probably enclosed Wittmack's *Allgemein nützliches Handbuch von der Landwirthschaft: samt verschiedenen dahin einschlagenden Materien* (Odense, Denmark, 1796).

From Timothy Pickering

(private)

Sir,   Department of State July 20. 1796.

Last evening, about nine o'clock, when sitting in my office, the Messenger brought me a letter from Mr Monroe. When going to open it, I found it had already been broken open, but the broken edges of the paper had been slightly fastened again by introducing some pieces of wafer. The original sealing, as usual with Colo. Monroe's letters, was with wax. The wife of the Messenger went to the door and received the letter. The bearer of it asked if I lived here; she answered that I did not, but was then in the office, and asked if he wished to see me. He said it was no matter, if the letter was safely delivered to me. She took the letter, returned to her room, gave it to her husband who immediately brought it to me.

Upon my enquiries she informs me that the man who brought the letter was 30 or 40 years old, appeared sun-burnt as if he had just come off a journey, and his cloaths, particularly his linen, looked dirty, as seemed common in such case. His speech was plainly English, like that of a Virginian, philadelphian or New Englandman, without any semblance of French or any other foreign language. She had a light in her hand, and saw nothing in the man's countenance or deportment that indicated any concern, like what might be imagined to result from a consciousness of guilt or impropriety of conduct.

The letter is dated the 2d of May, and the cover had on it, in the usual place of franking, the name of Mr Monroe, written with his own hand. The superscription was in the same handwriting with the letter of the 8th of April, mentioned in the postscript to one of my letters accompanying this. That letter of April 8th has on it the post office mark of Alexandria—thus "Alex. 15 July."[1]

No part of the letter of May 2d is in cypher. It is on the subject of the explanation which was to take place between Mr Monroe and the Minister of foreign affairs, agreeably to the orders of the directory; and is accompanied by the complaints of the latter (in French) & Mr Monroe's answer.[2] The French shall be translated, and I will do myself the honor to transmit the packet by the next post.[3] The complaints are not of the formidable nature to have been expected after all the solemn advices concerning them which have been received from Mr Monroe. In short, I should be disposed to apply to this affair the trite fable of the mountains being in labour and bringing forth a mouse. Most respectfully your obt servt

Timothy Pickering

ALS, DNA: RG 59, Miscellaneous Letters; ALS (letterpress copy). MHi: Pickering Papers. For GW's reply, see his first letter to Pickering on 25 July.

1. For Monroe's letter to Pickering dated 8 April, see Pickering's first letter to GW on 19 July.

2. Only a copy apparently survives of James Monroe's letter to Pickering dated 2 May. For this document and the other enclosures, see Pickering's second letter to GW, 21 July, n.1, and Statement from the French Republic, 9 March, printed as an enclosure with Pickering's second letter to GW on 21 July; see also Pickering's first letter to GW on 29 July.

3. Pickering enclosed a translation of the French complaints with his second letter to GW on 21 July.

Letter not found: to John William Bronaugh, 21 July 1796. Bronaugh wrote GW on 9 Aug.: "Yours of the 21st July I have received" (see Bronaugh to GW, 19 July, n.2).

From Timothy Pickering

(Private)

Sir   Department of State July 21. 1796.

I received this morning your favour of the 18th. The subjects of it shall have all the attention of which I am capable. De la Croix exhibition of the causes of complaint from the French

Republic against the *"government"* of the U. States (which you will receive with Colo. Monroe's answer in my public letter of this date) will place you at ease with respect to that country. The statement is as feeble as could have been desired; and serves to confirm the suspicions some months since entertained, that the ominous letters of Mr Monroe composed a part of a solemn farce to answer certain party purposes in the U. States. The fifteen sail of the line (as announced in the anonymous letters) and an envoy extraordinary, just to shew himself, make a declaration and return, were to begin the second act.[1] The defeat of the British treaty, and perhaps a change in our own administration, & possibly a war, were to make up the catastrophe.[2]

The delay of the letters you refer to I suppose to be in getting to the post office, owing probably to a difference in the clocks. A letter which I wrote on Monday last, & sent off a quarter before ten, will also be delayed.[3] In future I will (as I do now) take the precaution of writing the day preceeding, when it shall be practicable. I am most respectfully sir your obt servt

Timothy Pickering.

ALS, DLC:GW; ALS (letterpress copy), MHi: Pickering Papers.

1. The letters Pickering termed "ominous" were likely those from James Monroe to him dated 16 and 20 Feb. detailing French government dissatisfaction with U.S. ratification of the Jay Treaty (see *Papers of James Monroe*, 3:590–91, 594–95). For the anonymous letters, see Cabinet to GW, 2 July, and n.4, and James McHenry to GW, 10 June, and enclosure).

2. For GW's reply, see his second letter to Pickering on 27 July.

3. The previous Monday was 18 July.

From Timothy Pickering

Sir,   Department of State, July 21. 1796.

I have the honor to inclose a letter from Colo. Monroe, dated the 2d of May (and which was received late in the evening of last Tuesday)[1] with the papers accompanying it, containing the complaints of the French Republic against the Government of the United States, and Mr Monroe's answer to those complaints. I have only substituted a translation of the statement of M. De la Croix, the French minister for foreign affairs, for the French copy, which I retain in the office.[2]

After the multiplied rumours of serious uneasiness, & even

of resentment, on the part of the French Republic, towards the U. States, it will afford you great satisfaction to find their complaints to be such only as the statement of M. de la Croix exhibits: all being either wholly unfounded, or resting on erroneous representations or misconceptions of facts, or misconstructions of treaties and the law of nations. Mr Monroe's answer to these complaints is sufficient to obviate them; altho' the facts and arguments with which he had been furnished authorized, on some points, a more forceable explanation.

Yesterday I received a letter from Mr Polanen, in New-York, announcing his appointment to be the minister Resident of the United Netherlands to the United States; of which I have the honor to inclose a translation, & to request your instruction thereon. To-day I acknowledged the receipt of his letter, and promised to communicate to him your determination as soon as made known to me.[3]

Connected with this subject are the advices from the Hague. On the 13th instant I received a letter from Mr T. B. Adams, dated the 28th of February last, relative to the change of government in that country, and his virtual acknowledgement of the new order of things, on the part of the U. States. I have since received a duplicate, and now do myself the honor to send you the original.[4]

Mr Adams grounds his proceeding on a letter to his brother from the department of State, dated the 27th of February 1795, in which I find the following passage. "The maxim of the President towards France has been to follow the government of the people. Whatsoever regimen a majority of *them* shall establish, is both de facto and de jure that to which our minister there addresses himself. If therefore the *Independency* of the United Netherlands continues, it is wished that you make no difficulty in passing from the old to any new constitution of the people. If the new rulers will accept your old powers & credentials, offer them. If they require others, adapted to the new order of things, assure the proper bodies or individuals that you will write for them, and doubt not that they will be expedited."[5]

Mr Adams's conduct appears to be perfectly conformable to this instruction, which I perceive was given in answer to a question on the subject proposed by his brother in his letter of November 2. 1794.[6] I am, sir, with the highest respect, your most obt servant

> Timothy Pickering.

ALS, DNA: RG 59, Miscellaneous Letters; LB, DNA: RG 59, Domestic Letters; LB, DNA: RG 59, GW's Correspondence with His Secretaries of State. For GW's reply, see his first letter to Pickering on 27 July.

1. The previous Tuesday was 19 July. James Monroe, U.S. minister to France, had written Pickering from Paris on 2 May: "I informed you in my last of the 25. of March that I was promised by the Directoire in an audience I had obtained of that body that the minister of foreign affairs should state to me such objections as were entertained by this government to certain measures of our own, and in the interim that no step should be taken under the existing impression, nor until my reply was received, and fully weighed, and I now have the pleasure to transmit the result of the communication which afterwards took place between the minister and myself on that subject.

"I do not know what effect my reply has had upon the mind of the Directoire because it was only sent in a few days since. . . .

"I think proper to communicate to you an incident which took place between the minister and myself, after I had obtained from the Directoire a promise that he should state the objections above referred to and discuss their merits with me. . . . Soon after that period I received from the minister the communication promised in a note of the same date but differing in some other respects from the present one, and particularly in the number of complaints, two of the catalogue being now given up by him, and to which I replied as soon as I could prepare my reply, in a note bearing likewise the same date with that which I now inclose you. After he had perused my reply he was sensible he had insisted on some points that were not tenable, and in consequence asked that I would permit him to retake his note, returning mine, that he might correct himself, and of course that I would consider the discussion as yet to be commenced. I told him immediately that I would do so with pleasure, because I did not consider myself in the light of a sollicitor bound to catch at and take advantage of little errors: that I wished upon all occasions, and with every one, and especially upon the present occasion with him to act with candour, and in consequence I soon afterwards restored him his note and took back my own. . . .

"The minister thought proper to give his second communication the same date with the former one, although more than a fortnight had intervened between the one and the other: and in consequence I followed his example giving my latter reply the same date with the former one. His motive I did not enquire into: mine was that the Directoire might see that the delay which took place did not proceed from me" (*Papers of James Monroe*, 4:14–15; see also Pickering to GW, 20 July). For French foreign minister Charles Delacroix's initial communication to Monroe dated 9 March, and Monroe's reply dated 15 March, see *Papers of James Monroe*, 3:612–14, 621–26; see also Comments on Monroe's *A View of the Conduct of the Executive of the United States*, circa March

1798, in *Papers, Retirement Series,* 2:169–70, 209–13, 217; *Autobiography of Monroe,* 112–29, 133–36; and DeConde, *Entangling Alliance,* 374–78. For the two versions of Monroe's letter to Pickering dated 25 March, see *Papers of James Monroe,* 3:631–34.

2. The translation of Delacroix's summary of French complaints is printed as an enclosure with this letter.

3. A translation of the letter from Roger Gerard Van Polanen to Pickering written at New York on 18 July reads: "I have just received from the National Convention of the Republic of the United Provinces of the Netherlands, my letters of Credence, as minister Resident to the United States of America.

"His Excellency the President not being now at Philadelphia, and being myself attacked by a slight indisposition, I have the honor of transmitting them to you, requesting you to inform him thereof, and to communicate to me the intentions of his Excellency, on the subject of my admission and reception in that character" (DNA: RG 59, Miscellaneous Letters). In his reply written at Philadelphia on this date, Pickering informed Van Polanen that GW "is at Mount Vernon, his seat in Virginia, whence he will probably return to this City in about five weeks" (DNA: RG 59, Domestic Letters). For Van Polanen's official reception, see Pickering to GW, 29 Aug.; see also Batavian Republic to GW, 3 May.

4. Thomas Boylston Adams (1772–1832), a brother of John Quincy Adams, was secretary of legation at The Hague.

The letter from Adams to Pickering dated 28 Feb. 1796 has not been identified, but it presumably covered the opening of the first national assembly under the Batavian Republic.

5. Pickering quoted from Edmund Randolph to John Quincy Adams, 27 Feb. 1795 (DNA: RG 59, Diplomatic and Consular Instructions).

6. When John Quincy Adams wrote the secretary of state on 2 Nov. 1794, he asked about the status of his diplomatic mission following the French invasion of the Netherlands and that country's possible loss of sovereignty or change in government (DNA: RG 59, Despatches from U.S. Ministers to the Netherlands).

Enclosure
Statement from the French Republic

Paris the 19th ventose 4th year of the french Republic; one and indivisible (=9 march 1796) Summary statement of the complaints of the French Republic, against the Government of the United States. 1st Complaint.
The inexecution of the Treaties.

1. The courts of Justice of the United States have taken cognisance and still take cognisance of the prizes which our privateers conduct into their ports, notwithstanding the express

clause of the Treaty against it. Our ministers have proposed various arrangements for limiting these usurpations. The federal
Government had itself proposed measures on this subject—the
first propositions were not accepted, and the latter measures fell
into disuse. The disgusts, the delays, the losses resulting to our
seamen from such a State of things, are palpable. They almost
entirely deprive the Republic of the advantages which it should
expect from this article of the Treaty.[1]

2. The admission of English ships of war, even in cases where
they are excluded by the 17th article of the Treaty, that is, when
they have made prizes on the Republic or on its citizens. The
weakness with which the federal Government conceded this
point in the first instance has increased the pretentions of Great
Britain, and now the ports of the United States have become a
station for the squadron of Admiral Murray, who for two years
past has there victualled his Ships, in order to cruize on the
american Commerce, and to pillage our property. This division
carries its audacity even to the conducting thither its prizes.[2]

3. The Consular Convention, forming a part of our treaties,
is equally unexecuted in its two most important clauses. The
first granting to our Consuls the right of judging exclusively in
disputes arising between frenchmen, is become illusory, for the
want of laws giving to the Consuls the means of having their decisions executed. The consequence of this inability tends to an-
nihilate the prerogative of our Consuls, and materially to injure
the interest of our merchants. The second gives to our consuls
the right of causing our mariners who desert to be arrested. The
inexecution of this part of the Convention affects beyond all
expression, our maritime service, during the stay of our vessels
in the american ports. The Judges charged by the laws with issuing the mandates of arrest, have lately required the presentation
of the *original* Roll of the Crew, in contempt of the 5th article,
admitting in the Tribunals of both powers copies certified by the
Consul. Local circumstances in a thousand instances oppose the
production of the original Roll—and then the seamen are not
liable to be apprehended.[3]

4th The arrestation in the port of Philadelphia, in the month
of August 1795, of the Captain of the Corvette the Cassius, for
acts committed by him on the high Seas. This is contrary to the
19. article of the treaty of commerce, which stipulates "That the

Commanders of public, and of private vessels shall not be detained in any manner." Besides it violates the most obvious law of nations, which places the Officers of public vessels under the safeguard of their Flag. The United States have had sufficient proofs of deference on the part of the Republic, to count upon its Justice in this instance. The Captain was imprisoned, notwithstanding the Consul of the Republic produced bail. Scarcely was he set at liberty, when the Corvette, altho' very regularly armed at the Cape, by General Lavaux, was arrested (and it appears she is still so) under pretext, that, eight months before, she sailed from Philadelphia, suspected of having armed in that port.[4]

2d Complaint. The impunity of the outrage committed on the Republic in the person of its minister, the Citizen Fauchet by the English ship (Africa) in concert with the vice Consul of that nation.

The arrestation in the waters of the United States of the Packet boat having Citizen Fauchet on board, the search made in the Trunks of that minister, with the avowed object of seizing his person and papers, merited an example. The insult was committed on the first of august 1795 (old style) the Ship all the rest of the month blocked up the medusa frigate belonging to the Republic at newport, and did not receive orders to depart till after the sailing of that vessel. For a new outrage on the United States by a menacing letter, the Exequatur was withdrawn from the Consul merely for having taken a part in the *latter* insult.[5]

3rd Complaint—The Treaty concluded in November 1794 between the United States and Great Britain. It will be easy to prove that the United States in this treaty have knowingly and evidently sacrificed their Connections with the Republic and the most essential and least contested prerogatives of neutrality.

1st The United States, besides having departed from the principles established by the armed neutrality during the war for their independence, have given to England, to the detriment of their first allies, the most stirling mark of an unbounded condescension, by abandoning the limit given to contraband by the law of nations, by their treaties with all other nations, and even by those of England with the greater part of the maritime powers.[6] Is it not evidently straying from the principles of neutrality to sacrifice exclusively to that power, the objects proper for the equipment and construction of vessels?

2. They have gone still further. They have consented to extend the denomination of contraband even to Provisions. Instead of pointing out particularly, as all treaties do, the cases of the effective blockade of a place, as alone forming an exception to the freedom of this article—they have tacitly acknowledged the pretentions raised by England to create blockades in our Colonies and even in france by the force of a bare proclamation.[7]

This abandonment of the independence of their commerce, is incompatible with their neutrality. Mr Jefferson has himself acknowledged it in his letter of 7th September to the minister plenipotentiary of the United States at London, on the subject of the order of the 8th of June 1793.[8] From this confession— especially from all the tyranical Edicts of the King of Great Britain, from which the commerce of the United States as well as their national honor have suffered so much, a result quite different was hoped from Mr Jay's negotiation. It is evident by the clause of the treaty limiting the existence of this desertion from neutrality to the duration of the present war, that Mr Jay did not hesitate to sacrifice our Colonies to Great Britain, during the remaining hostilities which should decide their fate.[9] Mr Monroe is left to judge how far these concessions accord with the obligation contracted by the United States to defend our Colonial possessions,[10] and with the no less sacred duties imposed on them by the immense and invaluable benefits, which they draw from their commerce with them.

The minister for foreign affairs
Ch. De la Croix
Faithfully translated from the original by
Geo: Taylor Jr

Translation, DNA: RG 59, Miscellaneous Letters; copy, in French, DNA: RG 59, Despatches from U.S. Ministers to France; copy, in French, FrPMAE.

James Monroe, U.S. minister to France, had responded initially to French foreign minister Charles Delacroix in a letter dated 15 March (*Papers of James Monroe*, 3:621–26). Specific comments from Monroe's letter can be found in the notes below.

1. Delacroix is referring to Article XVII of 1778 Treaty of Amity and Commerce with France (Article XIX before the suppression of original articles XI and XII; Miller, *Treaties*, 16–17). Monroe wrote Delacroix that "exceptions to the general principle" outlined in the complaint made it "unfounded, and that we have only done our duty; a duty we were bound to perform as well from a respect to our rights as a sovereign and free people, as to the integrity of our

character being a neutral party in the present war" (*Papers of James Monroe*, 3:622). For a more detailed summary of previous French complaints and U.S. responses, see Pierre-Auguste Adet to Timothy Pickering, 15 Nov. 1796, in *ASP: Foreign Relations*, 1:579–88; see also Thomas Jefferson to Edmond Charles Genet, 25 June 1793, in *Jefferson Papers*, 26:358, and Jean Antoine Joseph Fauchet to Edmund Randolph, 17 Oct. 1794, in *ASP: Foreign Relations*, 1:589.

2. Monroe wrote Delacroix that the French treaty did "not stipulate that the vessels of war belonging to your Enemies shall not enter but simply that they shall not enter with their prizes." If violations occurred, Monroe continued, "I will venture to affirm that no countenance was given by our government to those vessels whilst they were there, and that all suitable means were taken to compel them to retire, and without delay. You know we have no fleet and how difficult it is without one to execute a stipulation of this kind with that promptitude which your agents in our Country ardent in your cause and faithful to your interest, might expect" (*Papers of James Monroe*, 3:622).

3. For the consular convention with France signed on 14 Nov. 1788, see Miller, *Treaties*, 228–44 (Delacroix mentions articles IX and XII on 237–40). Monroe replied to Delacroix that Article IX did require original rolls and that the United States had enacted legislation to enforce the convention (*Papers of James Monroe*, 3:623–24; see also "An Act concerning Consuls and Vice-Consuls," approved 14 April 1792, in 1 *Stat.* 254–57).

4. For the case of *Le Cassius*, see Alexander Hamilton to GW, 31 Jan. 1795 (third letter), and n.2 to that document. For Article XIX (originally XXI) of the 1778 Treaty of Amity and Commerce with France, see Miller, *Treaties*, 17–18. Monroe wrote Delacroix that the article "was intended to establish a general principle in the intercourse between the two nations, to give a priviledge to the ships of war of each to enter and retire from the ports of the other, and not to secure in favor of any particular delinquent an immunity from crimes: nor in my opinion does the law of nations admit of a different construction or give any other protection. . . .

"With respect to the seizure of the corvette upon the pretext that she was armed in Philadelphia, I have only to say that if she was armed there, it was the duty of our government to seize her, the right to arm not being stipulated by treaty. And if that was alledged upon sufficient testimony as I presume was the case, there was no other way of determininig the question, than by an examination into it, and in the interim preventing her sailing. It would be no satisfaction to the other party to the war, for us to examine into the case after she was gone" (*Papers of James Monroe*, 3:624).

5. For the earlier French complaint about the actions of the British ship *Africa*, see Pickering to GW, 26 Aug. 1795, n.1. For the revocation of the exequatur of British vice-consul Thomas William Moore, see Pickering to GW, 4 Sept. 1795, and notes 1 and 2 to that document. As the letter of revocation cited Moore's transmission of an insulting letter to Rhode Island governor Arthur Fenner, Delacroix contended that the revocation was in consequence of that letter and not the original offence. In his reply, Monroe denied that the two were separable and contended that the revocation of the consul's exequatur and the denial of supplies to the ship formed an "adequate" response.

He continued: "I think proper here to add, as a farther proof that the President was neither inattentive to what was due to your rights upon that occasion nor to the character of the United States, that he gave orders to our Minister at London to complain formally to that government of that outrage and to demand of it such satisfaction upon the parties as the nature of the insult required" (*Papers of James Monroe*, 3:624–25).

6. The Jay Treaty defined contraband in Article XVIII (Miller, *Treaties*, 258–59). Monroe wrote Delacroix that Great Britain had refused to accept a more restrictive definition of contraband even "when the combination against England was most formidable, all the maritime powers being arranged against her. . . . How compel her then upon the present occasion, when that combination was not only broken, but many of the powers then parties to it, and against England, were now enlisted on her side in support of her principles." Monroe added: "Is it urged that we have made any article contraband that was not so before by the known and well established law of nations? which England had not a right to seize by that law, and did not daily seize when they fell in her way? This cannot be urged because the fact is otherwise: for although we have not ameliorated the law of nations in that respect, yet certainly we have not changed it for the worse, and which alone could give you just cause of complaint" (*Papers of James Monroe*, 3:625).

7. In his reply to Delacroix, Monroe denied that any treaty stipulation prohibited bringing provisions from the United States to France and that "in no respect is the law of nations changed, or any right given to the british to seize other than they had before." For Monroe, "the article in question" probably encouraged trade with France (*Papers of James Monroe*, 3:626).

8. For the British orders dated 8 June 1793 that authorized the detention of ships carrying grain to France, see Jefferson to GW, 30 Aug. 1793, n.1. For directions to protest those orders, see Jefferson to Thomas Pinckney, 7 Sept., in *Jefferson Papers*, 27:55–59.

9. Delacroix is referring to Article XXVIII of the Jay Treaty (Miller, *Treaties*, 264).

10. See Article XI of the 1778 Treaty of Alliance with France (Miller, *Treaties*, 39–40).

From Timothy Pickering

Sir,   Department of State July 21. 1796.

On the receipt of your letter directing the mode suggested by the attorney general, of obtaining passports by American seamen, to be carried into effect, I communicated the same to the Secretary of the Treasury.[1] We were both of opinion that the circular letter of instructions to the Collectors of the Customs would more properly be signed & transmitted by him than by me; the collectors being officers under the immediate superintendance of the Secretary of the Treasury; who was moreover required, by the act for the relief & protection of American seamen, to transmit it to the collectors.[2] We believed the attorney general did not advert to this established arrangement; and persuaded that the adoption of the prescribed mode of executing the law, and not the medium of conveying your directions to the collectors, was the object of your solicitude, it was concluded that the signing & transmitting of the circular letter, containing those directions, should devolve on the Secretary of the Treasury.[3] Were this to be done by the department of State, much inconvenience would result: for doubts will arise, in the progress of the business, & explanations be sought for: which will require an extended correspondence with a numerous set of officers between whom & the Secretary of State there is no relation. For these reasons we trust the course we have pursued will meet your approbation.[4] With the highest respect I am, sir, your obt servt

Timothy Pickering

ALS, DNA: RG 59, Miscellaneous Letters; LB, DNA: RG 59, Domestic Letters; LB, DNA: RG 59, GW's Correspondence with His Secretaries of State.

1. See GW to Pickering, 8 July.

2. Section 6 of the cited act required the secretary of state to transmit copies to foreign ministers and consuls and the secretary of the treasury to transmit copies to the collectors (1 *Stat.* 478).

3. The printed circular letter dated 19 July from Secretary of the Treasury Oliver Wolcott, Jr., directed that those eligible "to be registered and furnished with certificates of citizenship" included "Free white persons born within the limits of the United States, or of any of them, and free white persons born in any foreign country but actually settled within the limits of the United States on" 3 Sept. 1783; "Persons naturalized pursuant to the laws of any of the United States prior to" 29 Jan. 1795; "Persons naturalized pursuant to the law of the United States passed on" 26 March 1790, "while it was in force." Also eligible were "Persons naturalized pursuant to the law of the United States passed on" 29 Jan. 1795; "Children of citizens of the United States or any one of them, born at any place out of the limits of the United States;" and "Children of naturalized citizens, dwelling in the United States and under twenty one years of age at the time of such naturalization." The circular then listed five methods to prove citizenship, including birth, baptismal, or naturalization certificates and affidavits from credible witnesses.

Wolcott continued: "In addition to the foregoing instructions, I think proper to recommend, that the Collectors cause the proofs of citizenship to be progressively numbered, as also the certificates which may be issued thereon. The books containing the Registry of the Certificates are to be kept alphabetically. . . .

"The Collectors will observe that they are to make known the provisions of the law to all masters of American vessels, entering and clearing in their offices, this may be done by affixing a copy of the Act in some conspicuous place in the several Custom Houses; all masters of American vessels are also before entry, to be required to declare on oath or affirmation, how far they have complied with the provisions of the law, and particularly whether any of their crews have been impressed or detained. In cases where impressment or detentions shall be disclosed by the oaths or affirmations of the masters; information of such impressments or detentions is to be transmitted to the Secretary of State" (CtHi: Oliver Wolcott, Jr., Papers).

4. For GW's reply, see his first letter to Pickering on 27 July.

To James McHenry

(private)
Dr Sir,   Mount Vernon 22d July 1796.

Your private letter of the 16 came to my hands at the same time that your official one did of the 18th.

From what is there said it appears by the enclosures, I am satisfied no unnecessary delay respecting the Algierine frigate has taken place. From a former one, & perhaps from a solicitude to execute promptly whatever is entrusted to me, I had conceived otherwise.[1]

As I have Mr Liston here, & the house full of other company,[2] I shall only add that I am, what you will always find, Yr &c.

G. Washington

LB, DLC:GW. A purported ALS of this letter was offered for sale in *The Collector*, July-Sept. 1955, n. 640. A transcript made in 1855, probably from the ALS, is at NhD; it shows no significant variation from the letter-book copy. McHenry acknowledged this letter when he wrote GW on 26 July.

1. See McHenry to GW, 7 July.

2. British minister Robert Liston, accompanied by his wife Henrietta Marchant Liston, his secretary Edward Thornton, and Henry Stuart (1777–1809), arrived at Mount Vernon on 20 July. For their trip from Philadelphia, see McHenry to GW, 5 July, n.1.

Henrietta Liston wrote in her journal that the mansion at Mount Vernon was "a respectable old House, the beauty of which consists in a very large Piazza opening *nobly* on the Potomack, which is here two miles broad. We were kindly received, & sumptuously entertained by the President & Mrs. Washington, & spent some days most agreeably. But our visit was shortened by a wish to make a *tour* in Virginia by the Vale of Winchester, which we were told would afford us a view of the best land, & most picturesque view we had yet seen."

The party stopped at Harpers Ferry and Winchester, Va., and Lancaster, Pa., on their return to Philadelphia (North, *Travel Journals of Henrietta Liston*, 12–13).

Henrietta Liston provided other observations on the visit to Mount Vernon when she wrote her uncle James Jackson from Germantown, Pa., on 6 Sept.: "We reached Mount-Vernon next day [20 July] to dinner & were received with the utmost kindness by the President & Mrs Washington, his Family consists of the Marquis la Fayettes Son, & his Tutor [Felix Frestel], the former a gentle, melancholy, interesting youth, the latter clever & accomplished, but apparently proud & Sullen—the Presidents Secretary, a Modest young Man [George Washington Craik], & a Miss Custis, the Grand Daughter of Mrs Washington by a former Marriage, one of the prettiest Girls I have seen—as Mr Liston was anxious to reach home by the arrival of the packet, & desireous of extending his journey to the *Vale of Winchester*, We departed, after three days stay, in spight of all entreaties: the President was at great pains to show Us eve[r]y part of his Farm, He is, indeed, one of the best Farmers in America, & it seems to be his favourite occupation" (StEdNL: Liston Papers).

To James McHenry

Sir,　　　　　　　　　　　　　　　　　　Mount Vernon 22d July 1796

Your letter of the 18th instant with its enclosures, came to hand by the last Mail. Such of the latter, as are original, I herewith return to your Office.

It would appear from the extract of Mr Habersham's letter, that the Treaty (or rather meeting) between the Georgians and Creek Indians, has terminated unfavourably; and will tend, it is to be feared, to hostilities.[1] A favorable result could not have been predicted from the Speech of the Georgia Commissioners, at their commencement of the business with the Indian Chiefs; and it having ended without a Cession of Land, I shall be agreeably disappointed if there are not other means, soon used, to get possession of them.[2]

By the letters from General Wilkinson and Captn Bruff, I expect the Western Posts will soon be in our possession;[3] and I hope proper measures will be adopted to keep the Garrisons well supplied with Provisions and Military Stores.

Go: Washington

ALS, NhD; DfS, DLC:GW; LB, DLC:GW. McHenry acknowledged this letter when he wrote GW on 26 July.

1. The extract has not been identified. John Habersham, collector at Savannah, probably authored the letter.

2. The Georgia commissioners spoke to the Creeks at Colerain on 18 June:

"The hatchet has been frequently lifted, as well by your mad people, as by the mad people of Georgia. We are now met, under the eye of the great beloved man, General Washington, who has sent his beloved men, the commissioners of the United States, here, to settle all disputes between us and you.

"It is true, that many of our people have been killed by your mad people, and it is also true, that many of your people have been killed by our mad people. We are sorry for it, because we were all formed by the same Great Spirit, and ought to live as bethren of the same great family. Yet, when we recollect that we have mad people on each side, we should make allowances for each other; and when we are assured that the conduct of those mad men has not been countenanced by the beloved men, we ought to forget and forgive the blood which has been spilled.

"As to the murders on the Oconee . . . the good citizens of Georgia were as much displeased at them as you were. It gave the beloved men of Georgia, when they met in council, much pain, and they told the great beloved man, General Washington so." Creek retaliation prior to trials of all the perpetrators caused "sorrow" as did the failure to return "prisoners, and property, such as negroes, horses, cattle" as promised in three prior treaties. The commissioners wanted the Creeks to turn over "a slip of land" between the Ocmulgee and Oconee rivers. "We wish to pay you for it, and are desirous of obtaining it, because it will heal all old differences, and rivet the chain of friendship between us so firmly, that it will last for ages, and prevent the spilling of our and your blood, and the blood of our and your children after us. . . . Now, when one nation has fewer people and more land than another nation, which has a great many people, and not land enough for them to live on, the earth being the nursing mother for all, white men or red men, the nation which has fewest people, and most land, ought to part with a little of it to the other nation, at a reasonable price." The commissioners also stated dissatisfaction with a boundary line negotiated in the Treaty of New York that omitted their claim to land left to the Indians and asserted that unless the Creeks fulfilled obligations under that treaty "to restore all our negroes and property, with the prisoners you had taken, belonging to our people . . . this land must be considered as ours" (*ASP, Indian Affairs*, 1:614–16).

3. These letters have not been identified.

From William Washington

Sir   Charleston [S.C.] July 23d 1796

Before the arrival of Mr Purviance's Vessel last Fall, on board of which it was intended that Royal-Gift should have been shipped for Baltimore, that most inveterate disorder called the Farcy, which I believe to be incurable in a warm climate, plainly manifested itself on him. The effects of that disorder had debilitated him to such a degree that he could not be travell'd to Charleston.

He lingered with it all last winter & part of the Spring and finally fell a victim to it. I can only regret that Royal-Gift was brought hither by my instrumentality, being urged by several Gentlemen of this Country to make the application.[1] I have, now, no doubt that he was affected with that disorder at a very early period after his arrival in this Country because it was found impracticable to fatten him and because running ulcers about the legs the usual symptoms of the Farcy always attended him.

Notwithstanding the repeated applications made to Mr Fraser I have not been able to prevail on him to render an account of the second years covering, of Royal-Gift, at his house, but as he was only to charge for the Mares or Asses actually in foal, I don't believe that more money will be recovered than will pay for the hire of the groom.[2] I am Sir with the greatest Respect yr very H. Servt

W. Washington

ALS, PHi: Gratz Collection.

1. For the initial decision to send Royal Gift to South Carolina, see Tobias Lear to GW, 15 May 1791, n.6. For GW's directions regarding the animal's return, see his letter to William Washington, 14 July 1795.

2. Royal Gift stood two seasons at John Freazer's place on the Ashley River in St. Andrew's Parish, S.C. (see William Washington to GW, 6 Jan. 1794). Poor results from Royal Gift's first season persuaded GW to charge covering fees during the second season only when foals were produced (see GW to William Washington, 9 Feb. 1794).

From Oliver Wolcott, Jr.

Sir. Phila. July 23d 1796

I have had the honour to receive your favours dated July 13th[1] 18th[2] & 20th and shall punctually obey your directions.

The money mentioned by Judge Addison was paid to me;[3] in addition to the advances requested by Mr Kitt I have paid Captain Tingey for freight of Wine £66.13.4 Currency or Dolls. 177 77/100—the duties have not yet been demanded[4]—I shall pay Mr McEuen as soon as I can see him.

I know of nothing to communicate to the President which he will not receive from other quarters. the public mind appears to be generally tranquil & satisfied.

I wrote a private Letter dated about the 9th or 11th instant, but as I kept no copy, I may be mistaken—the Letter was on two sheets of paper & contained an acknow[ledgement] of your Letters of the 4th & 6th instant—I mention this merely that it may be known whether it went safely.[5] I have the honour to be with perfect respect Sir, your most obedt servant

Oliver Wolcott Jr

ALS, DLC:GW; copy, CtHi: Oliver Wolcott, Jr., Papers.

1. See Wolcott to GW, 6 July, n.2.

2. See Jeremiah Wadsworth to GW, 12 June, n.2.

3. See Alexander Addison to GW, 13 July, found at GW to Addison, 8 July, n.4.

4. For this wine shipment, see GW's first letter to Wolcott, 13 June, and n.1 to that document; see also n.5 below.

5. GW replied to Wolcott from Mount Vernon on 29 July: "Your letter of the 23d instant came to me by the last Post; and the letter therein alluded to, dated the 11th, was received in due course. The receipt of which I as certainly acknowledged, whatever may have become of it; but having kept no copy thereof, I am unable to repeat the contents. Sure I am, because I remember well, that an acknowledgment was given by the Post after it was received.

"I am glad the freight of my Wine to, and from India has been paid to Captn Tingey; and whenever the duties are demanded I pray they may be paid also, if you have means of mine in your hands sufficient thereto" (ALS, CtHi: Oliver Wolcott, Jr., Papers; no prior acknowledgment of Wolcott's letter to GW dated 11 July has been found). Wolcott acknowledged GW's letter dated 29 July when he wrote GW on 3 August.

Letter not found: from Betty Washington Lewis, 24 July 1796. The letter was offered for sale in Parke Bernet Galleries, Inc., Catalog 1663 (27 March 1956), item 160. That publication printed a partial text: "My dear brother, it is with infinite pleasure I here (sic) you intend to retire to your owne (sic) home, there I hope you will enjoy more satisfaction than you possibly can do in public life . . . Howell joines (sic) in love to you and my sister Washington" (see also *ABPC*, 4:473).

From Wilhelm Louis Wernecke

at Mrs Hickingbottom

No. 116. North front Street[1]

Sir   Philadelphia July 24th 1796

I take the Liberty to Address your Excelence Concerning the affair that I waited on your Excelence four weeks ago with Mr Graff as my Nominated Gaurdian, and Mr Erdman as Interpreter,[2] at which time your Excelence was pleased to promise

Asistance in geting the Estate of my Uncle Col. Wernecke, deceased in Posession according to your Excelence Direction.[3]

I waited on Mr Nottnagle in order that he might Assist me, but during your Excelence absence Mr Nottnagle turned his Back on me and even left the Sity, it is said he is gone to Long-Island for his Health,[4] I am at present in A very poor Situation I have neither Money nor friends, Mr Graff holds the Writings Still, I cannot get them, He lives high upon my Property in German Town, while I am in want of Bread And have been Obliged to serve A Farmer on the Ridge road for Subsistance, I should be very happy if I could have an Oppertunity once more of Speaking to your Excelence, as I am of Opinion that Mr Graff & Mr Nottnagle are United in keeping me out of my right, I have here Inclosed the Copy of A Letter from Ebenezer Stott, to Mr Nottnagle as A clearer Explanation of the Affairs,[5] upon which I Ernest Intreat your Excelence advice how to proceed in the Affair,[6] Which shall be greatfully Acknowledged by Your Excelence most Humble servant

Wilhelm Louis Wernecke

ALS, DLC:GW.

1. Elizabeth Hickenbottom kept a boarding house at this address. She was probably the widow of William Hickenbottom, an innkeeper who died in 1793.

2. Charles Erdman (c.1744–1813) worked as an interpreter until his death. An advertisement in *Finlay's American Naval and Commercial Register* (Philadelphia) for 1 July 1796 began "Charles Erdman, *Sworn interpreter of the English, French, German and Low-Dutch Languages.*"

3. For the estate of Frederick Christian Wernecke, see Officers of the Grand Bailiwick of Nassau to GW, 10 March 1794.

4. Leopold Nottnagel (Notnagel; c.1757–1813) was at this time a partner in the firm Nottnagel, Montmollin & Co., sellers of dry goods and other imported products at Philadelphia.

5. Ebenezer Stott, a merchant in Petersburg, Va., wrote Nottnagel, Montmollin & Co. on 11 July that he had "applyed Unceasenly to Mr Mark, by letter as well as Verbaly for A Settlement of the Affairs of the late Col. Wernecke . . . I am now perfectly Perswaded that he never will render any Account or give up any part of the Effects untill Compelled by due Course of Law, and I think the sooner you Adopt that Measure the better—He says there are Considerable Claims against the Estate, and that after paying them there will be little left to the Heirs, How far this is true I cannot pretend to say" (DLC:GW).

6. GW's secretary George Washington Craik replied to Wernecke from Mount Vernon on 3 Aug.: "I am directed by the President of the United States to acknowledge the receipt of your letter to him, dated the 24th of July. To express his concern that your prospect of recovering the Estate, which you are

in pursuit of, is so unpromising; and to add, that Mr Erdman who Interpreted between you, either greatly misunderstood *him*, or *you* have greatly misunderstood Mr Erdman; for that so far from promising to have any Agency in the business, he requested that Gentleman to inform you, in explicit terms, that he could not meddle in the affair at all. That the Courts of Justice (over whom he had no controul) were alone competent to decide on the justice and equity of your claim. . . . This he directs me to repeat to you again. and to assure you that it is Law alone not men that govern in this Country.

"His advice to you however, is, to lay all your title papers before some eminent Lawyer in Richmond, (of whom there are many)—and as you are not in Cash to fee him well (which in this, as in most other Countries is essential) to inform the Gentleman you employ (if he thinks your title good, & worth prosecuting) that he shall receive a certain sum—or a certain proportion of whatsoever he shall recover if he succeeds—but that you are unable to pay any thing if he does not" (Df, in GW's writing, DLC:GW; LB, DLC:GW). This letter may not have been delivered (see GW to Bartholomew Dandridge, Jr., 5 Aug., and Dandridge to GW, 10 Aug., both found at GW to George Lewis, 28 April, n.2).

From de Beaulieu

My General   July 25th 1796

As I know your kind heart, I put myself into your hands, I like better to address myself to God than to his Saints. My Wife is taken away from me as a second Penelope indeed with some modifications, for it is because we have been under an obligation all last Winter till now, that She is tore from my Arms: great Gods![1] Such are the virtuous men of our age! If I was born of low conditioned Parents, I would be used to hard labors and I could make out for myself or at least I should know a trade which I would make use of. but having been only a Cultivator in the Colonies, and deprived of every thing which I possessed, I am in extreme want, and I address myself to your good heart. I cannot go back to my home, because the flag Vessels carry over only Women and old Men.[2] perhaps some new sacrifice will be made of them: as it happened at the last disturbances of the Cape.[3] I was not here when you had shared the World: and in consequence I have not an Inch of ground. if some pieces of land were remaining uncultivated near some City I should bless you all the moments of my life if you would do me the honor of admitting me amongst those who have the happiness to live under Your laws: for I possess nothing at all but tenderness for my Wife, who expresses to me her satisfaction of joining again with me, if I could procure her an easy existence.

I make vows for the conservation of Your precious days and I am—very great and mighty General, president & Dictator with very great respect Your very humble obedient Servant

(signed) debeaulieu

living at Baltimore on the road of the point in a Wooden house.

Translation, DLC:GW; ALS, in French, DLC:GW.

1. In Greek mythology, Penelope remained faithful to her husband Odysseus while he was away despite the advances of several suitors.

2. From late 1795 into 1797 French consuls advertised the departures of flag of truce vessels (Parlementaires) to carry French citizens to France or to Saint Domingue. Vessels for Saint Domingue only carried women, children, the aged, and the infirm. For an example, see the notice printed in French in *The Centinel of Liberty and George-town Advertiser*, 17 June 1796.

3. De Beaulieu is referring to the burning of Cap Français in June 1793 (see Thomas Millet to GW, 20 Aug. 1793, and n.8).

From La Rochefoucauld-Liancourt

Sir   Phil. 25 July 1796

I should ought apologise for my Liberty in writing to you, when I am deprived from the advantage to be known of you, and when political considerations have made you thinking, I should not to be introduced to you, at my arrival in this country. but my apology for that liberty, shall be found in the motive of this Letter.

Unfortunate La fayette's friends & relations send to me those two enclosed Letters, which he wished should be Communicated to me, & which I receive only now at my returning from the Southern States.[1] those friends are wishing, I should present them to you; they wish I could converse with you about the ways to make end to the long and cruel captivity of that honest man. I know some persons, & namely generous dr Bolman, have discoursed with you on that subject.[2] I know also, that, should La fayette's name have not been pronounced to you by any, invariable constanc⟨y⟩ of your friendship to him, should never Let you forgetting his dreadful situation, and without thinking for the most proper way of being serviceable to the friend, whose you appreciate the merits, & whose you know the misery. However, so superflous it may be, I call your attention upon him, you will judge, that dut⟨y⟩ being prescribed to be, it should be a fault to me if I was to not acquit my self of it. and if my particular affection to La fayette, makes me looking at that duty as a more imperious one, you'll excuse me for it. besides my Letter to you being yet unknown at every one, its inconveniency is limitated to the trouble youll have in reading of it. by Mrs Lafayettes Letter to gnl *ferrary*, youll see how barbarous is the rigor of the treatement she receives, ⟨*mutilated*⟩ treatement she received in robespierres prisons, during sixteen months, seems mild to her remembrance.[3] you are, certainly acquainted, with the audience granted by the Emperor to Mrs de lafayette on her passage in Vienna. & you know, when she implored of him her husbands liberation Emperor answered to her, *his own hands were tied up on that subject, and Mr De Lafs. liberation being out of his own power.* you know Emperors ministers, less reserved a little, than their master had been, did pronounce to her that *if His Imp. Maj. should be to grant Mr delaf.' liberation even if the watch upon him to prevent his escape were Less rigourous, Emperor should then became object of diffidence to his own ally, the King of England*: and you have, Sir, unquestionably concluded, with all of those who are acquainted with those authentical answers, that, the part of Lafy. conduct by which, his fetters have been forged, & are now daily rivetted, is not his participation to the french revolution, but only his participation to the American revolution, his unbounded devotion to the Cause of Liberty & independency of the United States. that is the very real *crime* never to be forgotten, by the King of England, and on account of which only la fayette is plunged in a dungeon.

youll read, sir in Laf.' Letter to Mr bolman & huger how, Confident as he is in your friendship and in the kindness of american nation, he relys upon his title of *american Citizen*. youll read how, being by the circumstances deprived as he is from the ⟨*illegible*⟩ country, he depends firmly upon his right to be claimed by that to the Cause of which he ⟨had de⟩voted his youth, and which he has served with all his heart & means, and youll observe, Sir Laf. being ignorant, when he wrote that Letter, that a so honorable employment of his first years, is the ⟨*unic*⟩ motive of his actual Captivity, by which; if longer, his Life even shall be Lost. youll find, also, by that Letter how Confident he is in dr bolman's active mind, & courageous generosity, proper, as he thinks, to help ⟨usefully⟩ your good ⟨sensations⟩ to him, and the interest of his fellow citizens.[4]

I should look at myself, as acting improperly, ⟨*mutilated*⟩ even hurting your feellings, if I was to urge you, Sir, either in the name of Lafes friends & relations, even as in his own to employ all the means you can, for ⟨*mutilated*⟩ his liberty and Life. the man, whom you have seen, embracing with a so compleat devotion, as your⟨self⟩, the Cause which places you among the greatest men, the man who should have expose his life, to make your safe, & to contribute to your glory, the man, whom you have judged deserving the title of *your friends* and to whom that honorable title seems the more precious ornament; the man whose the Son receives from you the proofs of a paternal affection, such man can not be unfortunate and you without employing youself very ⟨*mutilated*⟩ for making his misery to be terminated. and if political considerations, (which deepness I can not be judge of,) are to stop you, in the ⟨public⟩ proceedings, you & american nation who has adopted La fayette, could do with a so great ability in his favor, you are ⟨*mutilated*⟩ so miserable, as he is himself. I will per⟨mit myself⟩ only to repeat once more, that Lafes life, shall not resist to his captivity, if it is to be Longer and also that, if his cherissed wife, & childrens' Company, are of great comfort to him in his gaol, the wiew of inhum⟨ane⟩ treatement they received for their devotion to him, is a continual subject of sorrow and despair to your frien⟨d⟩ Some words I have exchanged with Mr bolman on the berckley County's road, Let me suspecting, those two Lett⟨ers⟩ could have been presented to you already: but I am n⟨ot⟩ sure enough of it, to ⟨*illegible*⟩ not risk to send you them on⟨ce⟩ more.

you should have yet read in the public papers, Mrs Laf. Letter printed. I should blame ⟨dissimulation⟩ by which I should ⟨*illegible*⟩ be prevented to ⟨Confess⟩ you, I did myself make that Letter published. in all parts of america, where I have travelled and I have been almost in all State of the Union, I heard Mr de Laf. name pronounced every where almost with so much of ⟨*mutilated*⟩ friendship & interest, as I heard your own pronounced with respect, admiration confidence & affection. that Letter's publication seemed to me proper to keep alive the deserved disposition. and I did not see any inconveniency in it.[5] very strange

⟨*illegible*⟩ both by my situation and mental disposition, from any political Circumstance, I am & never shall be so, stra nge to the duties of friendship. and should I be Less friend of Laf. than I am, I should look at me as obliged only by the duties of Humanity to ressemble all means in my power to alleviate his misery.

Sollicited to ⟨*mutilated*⟩ those Letters, I send them to his direction, without Letting him know I have the honor to write to you.[6] I am Sir with the greatest respect for your eminent qualities your most humble & most obt ⟨servant⟩

La Roche⟨foucauld⟩ Liancourt

ALS, DLC:GW. A French text of this letter, drawn from a copy, was printed in Jean Marchand, ed., "Trois Lettres Inédites du Duc de Liancourt," *D'Histoire Diplomatique* 44 (1930): 390–95. Where the ALS was illegible or mutilated, Marchand's text guided the selection of words in angle brackets.

1. La Rochefoucauld-Liancourt left Philadelphia for South Carolina on 24 March and returned on 20 July after travels in the southern states (see La Rochefoucauld, *Voyage*, 4:2 and 5:123).

2. See Justus Erick Bollmann to GW, 1 April.

3. Joseph Johann Graf Ferraris (1726–1814) served in the Austrian military and was vice president of the Aulic War Council, 1793–96.

An extract of Madame Lafayette's letter to Ferraris, undated but probably written around January 1796, reads: "I am particularly greatful, for the regret you express at the impossibility of granting my requests. I made them in the first instance to the commanding officer of Olmuts, because his Imperial Majesty had told me to address myself to him—I made them in writing because I had no means of Seeing him.

"I Ask'd 1st permission to go to mass, because I ought to do everything in my power to go to it, on sundays and hollidays.

"2d To Be attended occasionally by a servant, because having learnt When at Vienna, that . . . Conventional prisoners, Who had servants, enjoyed here the Liberty of seeing them all the day long, I flattered myself that the same favor might be granted to me for some moments.

"I have also asked that Mr. de [Latour-]Maubourg and [Bureax] Depuzy might pass some hours With us, because in the different prisons of France, In Robespiere's time (Where as you know, I have passed sixteen months) I was in the habit of Seeing the prisoners Communicate with each Others.

"I beg pardon, for having in this respect allowed my Confidence to carry me to far.

"I Confess with great pleasure that we agreed to participate all the rigours of Mr de La fayette's prison, and that this was the only favor we applied for, Our sentiments are still the same, and we repeat With all our Hearts, that we are happier with Mr de la fayette, even in this prison, than we Should be any Where else Without him.

"To Justify, however, the liberty I have taken With you, I will remind you,

Sir, that his Imperial Majesty in the Audience he was pleas'd to grant me, had the goodness to Say to me that 'I should find Mr de la fayette very well treated, and that if I had any request to make, I should be well satisfied with the Commanding Officer.'

"I have also the honor of reminding you Sir, that his Imperial Majesty permitted me to write directly to himself and to Address my Letters to the prince of Rosemberg [Orsini-Rosenberg], and, as since we have been shut up I have been utterly deprive'd of the means of Writing to the Emperor, or even to Mr Rosemberg, I conceiv'd it my duty to address my requests to you, and beg you will excuse me, if they have appeared somewhat exaggerated to you" (DLC:GW).

4. La Rochefoucauld-Liancourt sent GW a translation of Lafayette's letter to Justus Erick Bollman and Francis Kinloch Huger written "with his own blood" in June 1795. Lafayette expressed "unbounded gratitude" at the men's efforts on his behalf and his "distress" at their capture. He begged for news about his family, reported improved health, and asked that GW be informed of his situation. When interrogators asked his title, he answered "*Citysen of america where my intention was to settle.* When Called, upon my motives in my attempt for escaping, my answer was *because my detention is injure,* & my *situation dreadful.*" Lafayette fully supported Bollman. "I beg of all my friends to have a full confidence in him." In a note at the end, La Rochefoucald-Liancourt begged GW's pardon "for so incorrect a translation, but, if I should have made done by some more clever person I should not been so sure of the secrecy" (DLC:GW).

5. The extract from Madame Lafayette's letter to Ferraris was printed in *The Philadelphia Gazette & Universal Daily Advertiser* for 21 July and reprinted widely (see n.3 above).

6. A translation, dated 27 July at Philadelphia, of La Rochefoucauld-Liancourt's letter to George Washington Motier Lafayette reads: "your father's friends send me from London two letters, inclosed here, which they ask me to forward to you, and of which they assure me that your mother desired communication should be made to me. . . .

"It is now unquestionably ascertained that your father is held in chains by the despotick will of the King of England: for you know that the Emperor's Ministers have avowed it plainly to your Mother. . . .

"You are near the President: and your solicitation and tears, must have upon him, even upon his policy, a more influential effect, than any other application. A Son speaking for his father in the very country, which he has defended, which he has covered with his blood, and where he is beloved, can by no means be troublesome: and should his repeated entreaties be So, it would not be, in my opinion, a sufficient reason to discontinue them. On an interference of this country depends your father's liberation.

"the case is no more now Lafayette victim of arbitrary powers and of the hatred which they bear to every friend of liberty: it is Lafayette in dungeon for his exertion in the cause of the American Independance: it is your respectable Mother and your unfortunate Sisters victims of their devotion to their father and treated with more indignity than they were in Robespierre's prisons. or the Americans have strong reasons to remain unactive, or you may move their heart. Let it to be permitted to me to advise you to get in that respect over the extreme diffidence and modesty which Suit So well your age; to your incessant importunity your family may perhaps be indebted for its liberation: and who knows whether it is not now the only way from which it can be expected?" (DLC:GW).

GW replied to La Rochefoucauld-Liancourt on 8 August.

To James McHenry

Sir,   Mount Vernon 25th July 1796

The enclosed letter from Mr Landais, transmitting one from you to him, was received by the last Post.[1]

Filling the vacancies in the Corps of Artillery, before the adjournment of the Senate, was suggested; but why, as it was not proposed by the military Act,[2] that it should undergo any diminution, it was not done, my memory does not serve me.

If there are more Cadets in that Regiment than Mr Landais, and there are not some distinguishing circumstances between his case & theirs, no discrimination, even if the authority in the recess of the Senate was competent, can be made in his favor notwithstanding his desires and the peculiarities which are detailed in his letter. I send it however that you may consider the case & report thereon.[3]

Go: Washington

LS (retained copy), DLC:GW; LB, DLC:GW.

1. French native Philip Landais was appointed a cadet in the corps of artillery and engineers in March 1795, became a lieutenant in December 1796, and served until 1802.

Neither the letter from Landais, presumably to GW, nor McHenry's letter to Landais has been identified.

2. GW is referring to "An Act to ascertain and fix the Military Establishment of the United States," approved on 30 May 1796 (1 *Stat.* 483–86). Congress had adjourned on 1 June.

3. McHenry replied to GW on 29 July: "I have received your letter of the 25th with that of Mr Landais.

"There are three cadets only in the corps of artillerists and Engineers viz. Philip Landais and Philip Rodrigue, both appointed the 16 of March 1795, and James Triplet appointed the 14th of April following.

"In the entry of their names Landais stands first. He may therefore be considered as senior cadet, and so far (were there but one vacancy) as having a claim to be first noticed.

"I do not recollect any other circumstance intitling Landais to preference over Rodrigue and Triplet; and you know how incessantly importunate foreigners usually have been, when promotion was the object.

"Why were not the vacancies in the corps of artillerists filled up during the late session of Congress, when the cadets might have been appointed?

"It was then thought that the bill for new arranging the legion, which did not become a law till a day before Congress adjourned, would throw out of the legion several Captns and Lieutts some of whom might, wouthout wounding the rights of others be appointed into the artillery corps.

"Had a nomination in favour of the cadets taken place before or immediately after the passage of the law, the other vacancies then existing must have been provided for at the same time; consequently as the supernumeraries could not have been ascertained, they would have lost the chance of being continued in the service. Besides, had the cadets been appointed they would rank before any deranged officer of the same grade who might be subsequently appointed; an advantage to which their services have not intitled them.

"As therefore no special reason occured during the session, for pressing the promotion of the cadets; and as it was more natural and proper, that attention should be paid to natives who had gone through some campaigns and seen service, than to a foreigner, however well recommended, it was not conceived, that the interests of the former ought to have been neglected to further the wishes of the latter.

"But independent of considerations of this kind, it was known, in case it should appear, after digesting the new plan, that the supernumeraries were unfit for or would not serve in the corps of artillerists, that it would be in the power of the President to fill up all the vacancies except one, which he did not intend for the cadets; as all but one had happened in the recess.

"upon the whole, and to apply the matter in question to Mr Landais it may be observed. That as there are more vacancies open than three; (as you will see by the inclosed paper) and as each of the cadets have nearly equal pretensions from standing and service in the corps, one could not be appointed (were it even constitutional) without at the same time promoting the others" (ALS, DLC:GW; LB, DLC:GW). McHenry enclosed a list of "Vacancies in the Corps of Artillerists and Engineers" that reported the names of ten officers—two deceased, seven resigned, and one who had not accepted his appointment (DLC:GW).

French native Philip Rodrigue (Rodrique; d. 1802) and James Triplett, a Virginian, were commissioned as lieutenants, like Landais, in the corps of artillery in December 1796. Rodrigue served until shortly before his death; Triplett until 1800.

GW responded to McHenry from Mount Vernon on 3 Aug.: "In reply to your statement of the case of the Cadets, in the Corps of Artillerists and Engineers; I give it as my opinion that no promotion of them should take place at present, under the circumstances you have related.

"When I return to Philadelphia, it will be expected that you will bring forward the general plan for new modeling the Army agreeably to the late Act of Congress, at which time it may be exp⟨e⟩dient to take into consideration the case of Landais, & other Cadets in the above Corps" (LS [retained copy], DLC:GW; LB, DLC:GW; see also n.2 above).

From James McHenry

Sir.   War office 25 July 1796
   I here inclose a dispatch received on saturday[1] from the South-ward, containing a letter of the 27th ulto from James Seagrove; one of the 30th from Benjn Hawkins;[2] and one of the 1st instant from the commissioners for treating with the Creeks, with a copy of the treaty concluded at Coleraine on the 29th of June ulto and a protest by the Georgia commissioners.[3]
   I shall on the papers being returned give them due consider-ation, and report to you such measures as may appear necessary to be taken relative to their objects.[4] With the greatest respect, I have the honour to be Sir your most ob. st
                                    James McHenry

ALS, DLC:GW; LB, DLC:GW.
   1. The previous Saturday was 23 July.
   2. The letters from James Seagrove and Benjamin Hawkins have not been identified.
   3. The commissioners wrote McHenry from Colerain, Ga., on 1 July that the Creek Indians had come to the treaty determined "not to part with any of their lands" because they viewed the conduct of Georgia officials "as inimical to them; they complain of unfairness in all their intercourse with them; of the recent murders and promise to punish the murderers, as being of a piece with former conduct. . . .
   "Finding that the expectations of the commissioners of Georgia were at an end, we entered on the other objects of our mission. . . .
   "We find, in the present temper of the citizens of this country, that it is indispensably necessary, that the posts and garrisons should be out of the ju-risdiction of the State, and solely under that of the United States. Without obtaining this, we saw no prospect of peace on the frontiers; and the jealousy of the Creeks, is all alive on the least mention of an acquisition of land from them. . . . Since the signing of the treaty, several of the chiefs have urged that the President should cause the line to be run, as soon as possible, and make choice of the places for the posts." The commissioners promised a response "from the President in four months."
   The Indians also wanted "the advice of the President" on punishment for those who had murdered Indians.
   "The line with Spain, we explained fully, and they acquiesced; yet some fur-ther explanations will be necessary, to remove the jealousy attached to every act, relative to their boundary. They have asked that this explanation may be

sent from the President, with the plan of trade; and that, after he has seen what is done here, that he will have the whole explained in their land.

"We have preferred, instead of an increase of the annuity, as contemplated in our instructions, to give the sum mentioned in the treaty. The situation of the chiefs required some attention in this way; yet they were desireous, that we, during the negotiation, should keep every thing of this sort out of view, until they had fully comprehended us. . . .

"When we mentioned the sum, the chiefs expressed themselves satisfied. We had another motive in this business for satisfying the Indians with the small sum contemplated in the treaty. We were not certain that the chiefs can restore all the property taken from the citizens, according to the stipulations in the treaty, and eventually it may be deemed advisable, in the General Government, to pay up the deficiency, rather than incur the resentment of the Creeks, which they would do, by insisting on a cession of lands" (*ASP, Indian Affairs,* 1:610–11). For the treaty, see *ASP, Indian Affairs,* 1:586–87; see also Pound, *Benjamin Hawkins,* 81–98.

The protest of the Georgia commissioners, dated 28 June at Colerain, specified seven complaints, primarily onerous rules for the conduct of treaty negotiations and procedures that infringed "civil and actual jurisdictional rights of the State." The fifth item protested "any cession of land within the territorial limits of the State of Georgia, by the Creek Indians, to the United States, whether for the purposes of posts, trading houses, or otherwise, without the consent of the State of Georgia, as contrary to the eighth section of the first article of the United States' constitution. . . ." The final item protested "the payment, or liability of payment, of any share of the enormous and unnecessary expense attending the present treaty, by the State of Georgia; which, so far from being conducted in a fair, open, and honorable manner, the answer of the Indians, one party thereunto, if so it can be called, has been dictated to them in secret council, by undue influence, and cannot be considered their answer; and for that the State of Georgia has not had a fair and open opportunity to contract for the lands." If reports were true that the Indians had come with instructions not to cede land, then the treaty "is a fraud on the State, and a trick, unworthy the dignity and honor of the United States, transacted through their Superintendent, to fling one-half of the expense of a treaty, to serve their own purposes, on an individual State, which would possibly reap no benefit thereby" (*ASP, Indian Affairs,* 1:613–14).

4. GW replied to McHenry from Mount Vernon on 29 July: "Your letter of the 25th instant, enclosing the Treaty with the Creek Indians, and other Papers relative thereto, has been received.

"The Papers are returned, & due consideration, it is expected, will be given them; and a report thereof made.

Four months (the time allowed by the above Treaty; for running the boundary line between that Nation and the United States) seems, under any circumstances, to be hardly sufficient to arrange matters for such a Work; but if it is to be done under the Authority of the Treaty newly entered into, and the Senate are to have an Agency in the appointment of the Surveyor &ca—The Commissioners (on the part of the United States) have agreed to a measure, the execution of which is impracticable; as there is an interval of more than five Months between the date of the Treaty and meeting of the Senate; consequently, no ratification of it in that period; nor appointments, if the advice & consent of the Senate to them, be necesary, can be obtained without convening that body.

"Conformably to the Treaty of New York, with the Creeks, a Mr Ellicot was empowered to run the line; but whether any person on behalf of the United States was commissioned to see it done, or whether the appointment of Mr Ellicott was made with, or without the participation of the Senate, my memory does not enable me to pronounce. Be this however as it may, the Constitution & Laws must govern in this case" (LS [retained copy], DLC:GW; LB, DLC:GW). GW confused time allowed in the treaty for running a boundary line with the promise given the chiefs to hear a response on the subject in four months (see n.3 above). For the appointment of Joseph and Andrew Ellicott to run the boundary line described in Article IV of the 1790 Treaty of New York, see Tobias Lear to Henry Knox, 1 Sept. 1791, and n.2; see also Kappler, *Indian Treaties*, 2:25–29. For McHenry's reply, see his first letter to GW on 3 Aug.; see also McHenry's second letter to GW on that date.

To Timothy Pickering

Private
Dear Sir,   Mount Vernon 25th July 1796
Your private letters of the 19th 19th, and 20th instant[1] have been duly received.

The request of Mr J. Jones, to forward his letter to Colo. Monroe, is opposed to the speedy departure of Mr D—— for France; and yet the Gentleman who gave me the information spoke of it as a matter not doubtful: but added indeed (a circumstance I did not mention in my former letter) that it was on Mr Swan he leaned for money; and possibly, if that Gentleman is at Boston, this may be the occasion of Mr D——'s journey to that place; under the pretext of contracting for Arms.

Was Colo. Monroe requested to engage a Cannon founder on behalf of the United States? If so, on what terms? To remove a Person with his family, will be attended with considerable expence; and unless with condition to *secure* his services, it will be done under great uncertainty. With respect to the Engineers, policy requires a further developement of the unfavorable disposition with which we are threatned, before any encouragement ought to be given to the measure. But even if *that* objection was fully removed, there are no funds (within my recollection) that would enable the Executive to incur the Expence. therefore, as a Law must precede, in this case, any Executive Act, the answer to the quere is quite easy & plain.[2]

I am continuing, and extending my enquiries for a fit character to fill the Office of Surveyor General, without any great prospect of doing it to my satisfaction. Mr Ludlow, besides what is mentioned in your letter (which requires attention) has not, according to my ideas of him, celebrity of character; and is of too short standing in the Community to fill an Office of so much importance from its trusts, and the abilities and integrity which is required, tho' deficient in compensation; unless by means which ought to be prevented.[3]

It is much to be regretted that you did not discover the broken seal of Mr Monroe's letter, to you, before the departure of the bearer of it; that an attempt—at least—might have been made to trace the channel thro' which it had passed; and thereby (if proofs could not have been obtained) to have found ground for just suspicion. You confine the Post mark of Alexandria to his letter of the 8th of April; had you included that also of the 2d of May, I would have caused enquiry to have been made at that Office with respect to the appearance of the letters when they went from thence.

I am glad to find that more smoke than fire is likely to result from the representation of French discontents, on account of our Treaty with Great Britain. Had the case been otherwise, there would have been no difficulty in tracing the effect to the cause. And it is far from being impossible, that the whole may have originated in a contrivance of the opposers of the Government, to see what effect such threats would Work; and finding none that would answer their purpose, and no safe ground to stand on, if they pushed matters to extremity, the matter may terminate in gasconade. Be this as it may, the Executive have a plain road to pursue; namely, to fulfil all the engagements which *his* duty requires. Be influenced, beyond this, by none of the contending Parties; maintain a strict neutrality, unless obliged by imperious circumstances to depart from it; Do justice to all; and never forget that we are Americans; the remembrance of which will convince us, that we ought not to be French or English. With great esteem & regard, I am always and Sincerely Yours

Go: Washington

ALS, MHi: Pickering Papers; LB, DLC:GW.

1. See Pickering's first and second letters to GW on 19 July, and Pickering's letter to GW on 20 July.

2. See Pickering's second letter to GW on 29 July.

3. For Israel Ludlow's application to become surveyor general, see Pickering to GW, 11 July, and n.2.

To Timothy Pickering

Sir,   Mount Vernon 25th July 1796

Your letters of the 18th and 19th instant were received by fridays Post the 22d.[1]

If the answer which you returned to the Minister of the French Republic, to his enquiry relative to the prohibition of the sale of Prizes, brought by French armed Vessels into the Ports of the United States; should, as it ought, preclude any reply, it would be very agreeable: but it has not been found, that where the interest, or convenience of that Nation is at stake, that the Minister thereof can be satisfied with reasons—however cogent—which are opposed to their views. But in this case, as in all others, the Executive must be governed by the Constitution & Laws. and preserving good faith, & an unbiassed conduct—leave the rest to the good sense of our own Citizens, and the justice of the Nations with whom we have intercourse.

As it has been resolved for political considerations—to put an American Citizen as Consul at Hamburgh in place of Mr Parish, it is fortunate that so eligible a character as Mr Samuel Williams of Salem presents itself; and I desire he may be commissioned accordingly; and advice thereof (as *mere* matter of information) given, among othe[r] communications which may be made, to Mr Monroe.[2]

Copy (docketed by GW), DNA: RG 59, Miscellaneous Letters; LB, DNA: RG 59, GW's Correspondence with His Secretaries of State. A transcript made in 1866, presumably from the now-unlocated letter received, is in MHi: Pickering Papers. It does not vary significantly from the copy.

1. GW was responding to Pickering's third letter on 19 July.

2. For Pickering's reply, see his second letter to GW on 29 July.

From Robert Lewis

Hond Uncle,   Spring Hill [Va.] July 26th 1796

Your favor dated the 24th ultimo came duly to hand, altho' it remained a fortnight in Fredericksburg before an opportunity offered to this place.[1]

I am felicitated with the idea of your becoming a private Citizen once more. Indeed I might venture to affirm that it is the ardent wish of every friend and relative you have in this world.

I shall leave home in a few days for Frederick and Berkley where I should have been long ere this, but the sudden and unexpected death of my youngest daughter has prevented me.[2] The tenants, I expect, are prepared to pay up all arrearages, and witho⟨ut⟩ fail (barring accidents) I shall be at Mt Vernon before the middle of August wit⟨h⟩ all the money which I may collect in that time.[3]

Previous to receiving your letter I had consented to Sally Hanies going over the ridge to widow of Colo. Calme⟨s[4] who has pressingly invited her to come and live with her—As she had formerly lived with the old lady who seems attached to her, and has no children of her own—besides being a notable discreet matron, I thought the opportunity too favorable to let it escape fixing her in so eligible a situation—As we have had some little experience of the conduct of Sally Haynie, I conceive myself at liberty to give some hints that wou'd set aside the idea of carrying her to Mt Vernon, for I am well convinced she would not suit my Aunt at any rate—In the first place she is extremely deficient in household Economy—Her situation has always been obscure and retired, and it cannot be supposed that she could have gained any knowledge in Housekeeping so circumstanced; therefore in place of being useful in relieving my Aunt from some of the cares of a family, she would in fact become her pupil. Mrs Lewis has, and would still have taken pains to instruct her in the various avocations of a housekeeper had she continued with us but her temper was of a kind not easily to be controlled, and she appeared anxious to leave us, before she had been with us three weeks—In short she possessed a degree of pride very unbecoming and which I did not conceive belonged to her composition. I shall insist upon Mrs Calmes's taking some authority, as she is too young and giddy to have her way.

I have always impressed her with an idea that an independant state was preferable to all others, and moreover, that you cou'd never think of supporting a person who was so healthy, and with a little pains so capable of furnishing herself with every thing which she might want necessarily. She has not wanted for anything that is decent or proper, and shall have (as you directed) whatever her necessities may require; although what she has hitherto had, has always been given by way of a present ordered by you, so that she might not expect any further supplies, unless her conduct was deserving of them.

The crops of wheat in this part of the country are remarkably fine and exceed the warmest expectations of the Farmer. As to corn I do not believe their ever was such prospects before, where there has been early planting and proper tillage. The meadows are equally fine in richness and great abundance of grass.

Mrs. Lewis unites with me in affectionate regards to you—my Aunt & family. In the interim I remain Your much obliged & dutifull Nephew—

Robt Lewis⟩

AL (incomplete; photocopy of first page) and typescript, supplied (1973) by Mrs. Simon Bolivar Buckner, Sausalito, California. The name "Calmes" has been corrected from inaccurate renderings in the typescript; two obvious typographical errors also have been corrected silently.

1. Lewis is referring to GW's letter to him of 26 June.

2. The infant Betty Washington Lewis was born in June and died on 17 July.

3. For a facsimile of the receipt GW gave Lewis at Mount Vernon on 13 Aug. for £54.16.10 "on account of his Collection of my Rents," see Charles Hamilton, Auction 41 (23 April 1970), item 278.

4. The remaining text is taken from the typescript.

Lewis probably meant Elizabeth (Betty) Combs Calmes (d. 1804), widow of Marquis Calmes (1726–1794) of Calmes Neck in Frederick (now Clarke) County, Virginia.

From James McHenry

Sir.   War office 26 July 1796.

The agent of the department of war in Tenessee having requested that the vacant office of deputy paymaster and store keeper might be filled up; and it appearing, that Mr Henley the agent cannot go through the business himself; and if he could, that it would be improper, inasmuch as it would center in one person, 1st. the *keeping* and *distribution* of stores, and 2dly the power to *determine the sum due* upon a claim, and *to pay it.*

I inclose you therefore a rough draught of instructions for the deputy pay master and store keeper; a draught of a letter to the agent of the department of war; and copy of the instructions of 1793 to the deputy pay master and store keeper when the office was instituted.[1]

You will perceive wherein these instructions vary from those of 93; and the reasons (without my suggesting them) which have induced to the creation of further checks upon both the Principal & Deputy.

I have thought of a Mr Hillis for Deputy who writes in the accountants office. As he has been employed there in the settlement of Col. Henley's accounts, he understands of course the train of business in that quarter and the general objects of expence; and besides is very well recommended. If you should approve of him to fill the office (on looking over his recommendations) you will be pleased to mention it; and to return the draught of instructions, and letter designed for the agent, with such alterations as you may think proper.[2]

I have this moment received your letters of the 22d inst.

Mondays mail carried you the result of the meeting of the Creeks at Coleraine.[3] Considering the aspect of things in that quarter, perhaps you may conceive it expedient that one of the companies of dragoons should be directed to join Col. Gaither. In the mean while, and that no time may be lost, should you so determine, I shall write to Gen. Wayne to hold one of the companies in readiness to march thither at the shortest notice.[4]

I should expect, that the presence of this company on the frontiers of Georgia would render it unnecessary to employ the one hundred militia dragoons which are kept up at the Expence of the U.S.

I have also received this morning the inclosed letter, and representation from the officers at West-point, praying that Lt Geddis may be released from his arrest.[5]

On this subject I would observe, That the act passed last session of Congress fixing the military establishment of the U.S. contains the following section.

Sect. 18. "And be it further enacted that the sentences of

general courts-martial, in time of peace, extending to the loss of life, the dismission of a commissioned officer; or which shall, either in time of peace or war, respect a general officer, shall with the whole of the proceedings in such cases, respectively, be laid before the President of the U.S.; who is hereby authorised to direct the same to be carried into execution or otherwise as he shall judge proper."[6]

This clause was incorporated into the act in order to remove some doubts heretofore started respecting the power of the President to pardon certain military offences in time of peace.

For my own part, I have no doubt, that independent of this act, the President possesses the power to remit sentences of courts martial extending to the loss of life or dismission of a commissioned officer I consider that part of the act therefore as surplusage.

If however it was to serve as authority it would not apply to the present case; inasmuch as it has had no retroactive effect given to it. The sentence on Geddis was pronounced on the 16th of May; and the act in question passed on the 30th.

I look to a higher authority for the power of the President to remit sentences of courts-martial.

The constitution art. II. sect. 2. constitutes the President ["]commander in chief of the army and navy of the U.S." and vests him with "power to grant reprieves and pardons for offences against the U.S., except in cases of impeachment."

Congress cannot pass any regulations for the government of the land and naval forces which may intrench upon, invalidate or nullify this power to pardon offences against the United States.

If this is a true exposition of the constitution, the President may if he should think proper comply with the request in favour of Lt Geddis.[7] With the greatest respect, I have the honour to be Sir Your most ob. st

James McHenry

ALS, DLC:GW; LB, DLC:GW. For GW's reply, see his second letter to McHenry on 1 August.

1. The rough drafts have not been identified. For the appointment of Stephen Hillis as "deputy pay Master and Storekeeper of the public property in Tennessee," see McHenry to David Henley, 13 Aug. (MHi: Adams Papers). A copy of the instructions for Hillis, also dated 13 Aug., is in DNA: RG 94, Post Revolutionary War Papers.

2. Levi Hollingsworth had written McHenry from Philadelphia on 6 July that "Mr Stephen Hillis, of Christiana Bridge, New Castle County, applies to me for a recommendation as a Clerk in your office. I knew the young man's family for many years past, they were respectable & worthy of confidence nor have I ever heard any thing to the disadvantage of Mr Hillis, his abilities as a Clerk I am ignorant of, but have heard him Spoken of as a person of application" (MiU-C: James McHenry Papers). Thomas and Samuel Hollingsworth wrote McHenry from Baltimore on 10 July that despite a relationship to Hillis through marriage "our personal knowledge of him is so slight, that our regard for him proceeds more from the pleasing reports we have heard of him . . . We have ever heard him spoken of as Youth of good morals, decent deportment attentive and industrious in the service of his Employers" (MiU-C: James McHenry Papers). Hillis received the appointment (see n.1 above).

3. See McHenry to GW, 25 July.

4. McHenry wrote Gen. Anthony Wayne on 30 July: "The Creek Indians having refused to sell any of their land to the State of Georgia, it cannot yet be ascertained whether the frontier people will confine themselves within the bounds of the treaty of New York, which the Indians have confirmed. It may therefore become expedient in order to obviate intrusions upon their lands and preserve the peace, to augment the military force in that quarter.

"It may also be proper, in an oeconomical point of view, to employ there, one of the troops of Cavalry as patroles between the posts, to announce to the inhabitants the approach of hostile marauders, and to give greater security to the garrisons. Besides their presence may relieve the public from an expensive militia establishment, which has been kept up on Georgia, for some years past.

"I mention these circumstances that you may have time to consider of the best route, and to take the preparatory steps for their march, in case the President should determine upon sending them" (Knopf, *Wayne*, 507–8).

5. The enclosed letter has not been identified.

6. For the act under consideration, see 1 *Stat.* 483–86; quote on 485.

7. For GW's pardon of Lt. Simon Geddis, see his letter to McHenry on 12 Aug.; see also McHenry to GW, 14 June.

From Timothy Pickering

Sir,   Department of State July 26. 1796

In the letter with which you honored me, bearing date the 27th of June, your expressed your approbation of John Davis, the late Comptroller, to be appointed to the office of District Attorney of Massachusetts, provided his professional knowledge (of which you had no correct information) should be deemed adequate to the discharge of its duties, and he would place himself in a situation to render them conveniently to the public.

I was hence induced to write to Stephen Higginson, Esqr. of

Boston, a private letter, requesting him, by enquiring among gentlemen of law-knowledge, to ascertain Mr Davis's professional talents. Mr Higginson's answer I received yesterday, and have now the honor to inclose.[1] I also wrote to a nephew of mine in Boston for the same information; and his answer corresponds with Mr Higginson's.[2] Both being so decidedly in favour of Mr Davis, I have this day transmitted to him his commission; it appearing to the Secretary of the Treasury & to me, upon comparing your letters to us, that you desired no delay in the commissioning of Mr Davis, when we should be satisfied of his professional abilities.[3] With the highest respect I am, sir, your most obt servant

Timothy Pickering

ALS, DNA: RG 59, Miscellaneous Letters; LB, DNA: RG 59, Domestic Letters; LB, DNA: RG 59, GW's Correspondence with His Secretaries of State.

1. Stephen Higginson had written Pickering from Boston on 20 July that Judge John Lowell "& all whom I consider as the best Judges, think very handsomely of mr Davis in his profession; &, taking his whole character into view, They think him the best man in the District for the Office. . . . he has qualities important in that Office, beside professional Talents." Higginson added that Davis had contemplated "the Subject, he has decided upon moving here, & will take the office" (DNA: RG 59, Miscellaneous Letters).

2. Timothy Williams (1765–1846), a merchant, was the son of Pickering's sister Lydia Pickering Williams.

Williams had written Pickering from Boston on 13 July 1796 that he knew John Davis better "from others—that he is a man of genius as well as talents, that he is well-bred to his profession; his private character perhaps irreproachable" (MHi: Pickering Papers).

3. GW discussed Davis in his letters to Secretary of the Treasury Oliver Wolcott, Jr., dated 24 June, found at Wolcott to GW, 20 June, n.12, and 4 July, found at GW to Wolcott, 6 July, n.1.

GW replied to Pickering on 1 August.

To Timothy Pickering

Sir,   Mount Vernon 27th July 1796

Your two letters—both bearing date the 21st instant—with their enclosures, were received by the last Mail to Alexandria.[1]

It would have been unfortunate, and much indeed to have been regretted, if the French government had had as great cause of complaint against the conduct of the United States, as they have shewn a disposition to complain. It was natural to expect, tho' it was not easy to conceive on what ground, the French discontents, which had been so often announced—accompanied with such terrific threatnings—chiefly by anonymous writers, that the formal exhibition of them under the authority of the Directory, by their Minister of Foreign Affairs, would have had something serious, formidable, and embarrassing in their appearance; instead of which, most, if not all the charges seem to have originated either in a misinterpretation, or from want of attention, to Treaties and the Law of Nations; or to the want of a just, and timely representation of facts, with accompanying explanations; which our Minister near the French government had it in his power, and was directed to make.[2]

Presuming that Mr Polanen is regularly accredited by the proper authority of the existing government of the United Netherlands, I see no cause—accordant with the principles which have actuated the government of the United States—why, when I return to Philadelphia he should not be received as the Minister Resident of that Country. And if no objection (unknown to me) should occur to you, Mr Polanen may be so informed.[3] My arrival there will be by the first of September.

Instructions from the Treasury department to the Collectors, relative to the mode of obtaining Passports by American Seamen, will certainly be as effectual, and probably is as proper, as if they had issued from the Department of State; and this was my opinion to the Attorney-General: But he observed, first, that it was not in any respect connected with the Revenue of the Country. And 2dly that there were some other Provisions in the Law (I do not now recollect of what nature) that required the Agency of the Department of State.[4] I am satisfied, however, with the Circular which has been adopted; as the design will be equally well answered by it.[5]

The original papers, forwarded with your last dispatches, are herewith returned.[6]

Go: Washington

ALS, NjP: De Coppet Collection; LS (retained copy), DNA: RG 59, Miscellaneous Letters; LB, DNA: RG 59, GW's Correspondence with His Secretaries of State.

1. GW acknowledged Pickering's official letters, his second and third dated 21 July.

2. See Statement from the French Republic, 9 March, printed as an enclosure with Pickering's second letter to GW on 21 July.

3. GW is referring to Roger Gerard Van Polanen.

4. "An Act for the relief and protection of American Seamen," approved 28 May, gave duties to the secretary of state and secretary of the treasury (1 *Stat.* 477–78). Section 5 required shipmasters to protest immediately any impressment or detention of seamen from their vessels and to send a duplicate of the protest to the secretary of state. Section 7 directed that every three months the collectors "send a list of the seamen registered under this act . . . to the Secretary of State, together with an account of such impressments or detentions, as shall appear, by the protests of the masters, to have taken place." Section 6 ordered that the secretary of the treasury send a copy of the law "to the several collectors of the districts of the United States."

5. See Pickering's third letter to GW on 21 July, n.3.

6. Pickering acknowledged this letter when he wrote GW on 30 July, found at GW's second letter to Pickering, this date, n.5.

To Timothy Pickering

Private

Dear Sir,   Mount Vernon 27th July 1796

Your private letter of the 21st instant has been received.[1]

Mr Monroe, in every letter he writes, relative to the discontents of the French government at the conduct of our own, always concludes without finishing his story, leaving great scope to the imagination to divine what the ulterior measures of it will be.

There are some things in his correspondence, & your letters, which I am unable to reconcile. In one of your last to me, you acknowledge the receipt of one from him of the 8th of April (which I have not seen) and in his letter of the 2d of May, he refers to one of the 25th of March as the last he had written. This letter of the 25th of March (if I recollect dates rightly) was received before I left Phila.; and related his *demand* of an Audience of the French Directory and his having had it; but, that the conference which was promised him with the Minister of Foreign Affairs, had not taken place; nor had he heard any thing from him; altho' the catalogue of complaints exhibited by *that* Minister, is dated the 9th of March, & his reply thereto the 15th of the same month. If these recitals are founded in fact, they form an enigma wch requires explanation.[2]

Has the letter, said to be dispatched by a Doctr Brokenbrough got to your hands? I hope it will, if it has not done so already.[3]

Mr De la Croix alludes, I perceive, in the close of his third, and last head of complaints, to our guarantee of their West India Islands:[4] but whether to bring the subject to recollection *only*, or to touch upon it more largely thereafter, is problematical.[5] I am always—& sincerely Your Affectionate

Go: Washington

ALS, Pickering Foundation, Salem, Mass.; LB, DLC:GW.

1. See Pickering's first letter to GW on 21 July.

2. For Pickering's explanation of this correspondence involving James Monroe, U.S. minister to France, see n.5 below; see also Pickering's second letter to GW on 21 July, and n.1 to that document.

3. When Monroe wrote Pickering from Paris on 2 May, he mentioned that John Brockenbrough, Jr., carried a letter for Pickering with the initial complaints of French foreign minister Charles Delacroix and Monroe's response (see *Papers of James Monroe*, 4:14–15, and n.5 below).

4. See Statement from the French Republic, 9 March, printed as an enclosure with Pickering's second letter to GW on 21 July.

5. Pickering replied to GW in a first letter written on 30 July: "(private) . . . I have to-day been honored with your public & private letter of the 27th. The letter which Mr Monroe delivered to Dr Brockenbrough has not come to hand. The one dated the 8th of April, merely respected the cannon-founder & engineers, as I had the honor to inform you in the postscript of my letter of the 19th instant. I received no other letter from Mr Monroe than that dated May 2d, since that of the 25th of March, in which he speaks of the discussion promised by the Directory between him & Mr Delacroix *as then pending*: altho' the complaint of the latter bears the date of March 9th, & Mr Monroe's answer, of March 15th. What effect his answer had upon the mind of the Directory, he knew not, 'because it was only sent in a few days since'; says Mr M. in his letter of May 2d.

"It was on the 8th of March he had his audience of the Directory; and in his letter of May 2d he says 'soon after that period I received from the minister the communication promised, *in a note of the same date*'; that is, of March 8th; (it should be March 9th) to which Mr Monroe replied in a note dated the 15th. But these two notes were mutually returned; or rather so intended to be, if Dr Brockenbrough had not departed with them for London, on his way to America; and the discussion considered on both sides in suspense.

"Mr Delacroix then presented a new note, and Mr Monroe a new answer, the same he has now transmitted in his letter of May 2d. But M. Delacroix thought proper to give to his new note the date of the old one, altho' more than a fortnight had intervened between the two; and in consequence, Mr Monroe gave the date of his first answer to his second; that the Directory might see the delay had not proceeded from him. From this detail (which is collected from Mr Monroe's letter of May 2d) it appears that when he wrote on the 25th of March, the discussion had not been closed" (ALS, DLC:GW;

ADfS, MHi: Pickering Papers). For GW's acknowledgement of this letter, see his second letter to Pickering on 5 August.

From Timothy Pickering

Sir,   Department of State July 27. 1796.

On the 25th I received letters from Colo. Humphreys dated April 30. May 30. & June 1. accompanied by a large packet from Mr Barlow at Algiers.[1] The substance of the information respecting the pending treaty with Algiers is, That Mr Donaldson had gone to Leghorn, with orders from Mr Barlow to transmit two hundred thousand dollars to Algiers, which would procure the redemption of our captive citizens—That Mr Humphreys had sent to Mr Donaldson at Leghorn a letter of credit for 400,000 dollars; and in case he failed of obtaining the half of that sum, Colo. Humphreys authorized Mr Barlow to draw on Bulkeley & Son at Lisbon for 200,000 dollars payable at sight, so as to ensure the liberation of our prisoners within the three months allowed by the Dey; but with his explicit opinion that no part of it should be paid unless the captives were released. From these arrangements, it seems to me highly probable that our fellow citizens will now recover their liberty; & that the payment of the gross sum of 200,000 dollars will so far soothe the Dey as to prolong his patience until the original stipulations and the new one for the frigate can be accomplished.[2]

Altho' the Dey's disappointment in not receiving the stipulated sums, on Mr Barlow's arrival, put him into so violent a rage as to render all applications fruitless, yet after some days he sent notice to Mr Barlow that he was willing to receive him as the Consul of the U. States, & desired him to bring his Consular presents. Mr Barlow readily complied. The presents were distributed to the Dey & his grandees. The Dey in return presented Mr Barlow with a fine Barbary stallion. Cathcart writes that Mr Barlow gives great satisfaction, & is respected by every one who knows him.[3] This admission of Mr Barlow as Consul, with the distribution of the Consular presents, cannot fail to have a favourable influence on the affairs of the United States at Algiers. And from his information of the customary and periodical delivery of Consular presents, it does not appear that it will occasion any material extra expence to the U.S.

Mr Barlow's packet contains long and interesting details of the nature of the algerine government, whence results the fickleness of its measures, and its frequent breaches of peace with the Christian states, on the most trifling and unreasonable pretexts. Because the armed vessels of the King of Naples carried into his port a Danish vessel having on board 320 Turkish soldiers bound from the Levant to Algiers, the Dey ordered his cruisers immediately to bring in all the Danish vessels they could meet with. In a few days about a dozen were captured & brought in; and their fate remained undecided. Mr Barlow details divers instances of breaches with other powers: whence he concludes that on an average we might count on a renewal of hostilities with ourselves once in six years. But the expences of renewing thus after our treaties with that regency, may be willingly incurred, when the commercial profits of the Mediterranean trade are taken into view. Of one and the other Mr Barlow has given estimates, which, with his observations on the commerce of that part of the world, manifest much information and that good sense for which he is distinguished.[4]

Mr Barlow describes the policy and utility of forming commercial & friendly relations with the Italian States, with Austria on account of her great trading port of Trieste, and with the Grand Seignior.[5] Colo. Humphreys concurring in these ideas (so far as respects the Grand Seignior he has formerly expressed the same)[6] strongly recommends Mr Barlow as the fittest person for the negociator; particularly with the Turk, under the countenance of France; Mr B. being a French as well as American Citizen. Mr Barlow would cheerfully engage in these enterprizes; and I am now inclined to think it would not be easy to find another person equally qualified for these negociations.

As these matters do not demand an immediate decision, I imagined it would be acceptable to you to receive this general account of the contents of the dispatches from Colo. Humphreys, & that the perusal of these would be more agreeable to you on your return to philadelphia.[7] I have the honor to be, with the highest respect sir, your most obt servant

Timothy Pickering.

P.S. Colo. Talbot expected to sail yesterday or the day before for the West Indies.[8]

ALS, DNA: RG 59, Miscellaneous Letters; LB, DNA: RG 59, Domestic Letters; LB, DNA: RG 59, GW's Correspondence with His Secretaries of State.

1. David Humphreys, U.S. minister to Portugal and chargé d'affaires to the Barbary States (but nominated as U.S. minister to Spain on 19 May), wrote Pickering from Lisbon on 30 April–3 May and 1 June (DNA: RG 59, Despatches from U.S. Ministers to Spain; see also GW's first message to the U.S. Senate, 19 May, and n.2 to that document). His letter to Pickering dated 30 May has not been identified. The packet from Joel Barlow, acting consul at Algiers, included his letters to Pickering dated 18 March and 8 and 17 April as well as enclosures (DNA: RG 59, Despatches from U.S. Consuls in Algiers). Pickering based his subsequent remarks to GW on items in Barlow's packet and possibly the missing letter from Humphreys.

When Humphreys wrote Pickering on 30 April–3 May, he highlighted the need for a U.S. consul at Lisbon and recommended Jacob Dohrman as a candidate. Humphreys also suggested men for diplomatic posts in the Barbary States. When he wrote Pickering on 1 June, Humphreys conveyed European news largely related to French military and diplomatic developments. He also reported the response in Great Britain to news that the U.S. House of Representatives had voted to implement the Jay Treaty.

2. For the impatience of the Dey of Algiers and the promised frigate, see GW to the Dey of Algiers, 13 June.

3. James Leander Cathcart (1767–1843) had been captured by an Algerian vessel in 1785. While a prisoner, he became the chief Christian secretary to the Dey of Algiers. Cathcart later received several U.S. consular appointments.

Cathcart wrote Humphreys from Algiers on 6 April 1796 that Barlow "is a Gentleman I much esteem and who I make no doubt will in a great measure contribute to the happy completion of our affairs in this Infernal Regency" ("Diplomatic Journal and Letter Book of Cathcart," 388–91; quote on 389). For overviews of Barlow's diplomatic service at Algiers, see Todd, *Life and Letters of Barlow*, 115–50, and Buel, *Barlow*, 196–214.

4. In a document dated 20 April and headed "Estimate of advantages & expences of maintaining a peace with Barbary," Barlow believed that over five years the "freights in and for the Mediterranean" and the "Augmentation of our commerce arising from the circumstance of our being our own carriers" would generate $1,050,000, while the expenses of peace would amount to $60,000, leaving a "Clear advantage" of $990,000. Alternatively, the loss of one ship in the absence of peace would involve with ransom and other outlays an expenditure of $60,000, or a sum equal to the cost of peace for five years (DNA: RG 59, Despatches from U.S. Consuls in Algiers).

5. Barlow alluded to Ottoman emperor Selim III (1761–1808), who ruled from 1789 until 1807.

6. Humphreys had written a "Secret & Confidential" memorandum delivered on 28 Aug. 1795 to James Monroe, U.S. minister to France, that he also

enclosed with his letter to State Department dated 11 Sept. 1795. In his memorandum, Humphreys suggested enlisting French aid to ask whether "the Grand
Seignior would issue an Order or Regulation for giving within his Territories
ample protection & such commercial privileges as he may think proper, to the
Citizens of the United States." Such an action "might have considerable influence in inducing the Barbary Powers to enter into Treaties of Peace with us
& to adhere to them" (DNA: RG 59, Despatches from U.S. Ministers to Spain).

    7. GW replied to Pickering on 1 August.

    8. For complications related to Silas Talbot's assignment to obtain the re-
lease of impressed Americans, see Pickering to GW, 4 July (second letter), and
n.2 to that document; see also GW to the U.S. Senate, 30 May, and Pickering
to GW, 12 June, and n.1 to that document.

From Charles Cotesworth Pinckney

Dear Sr   Charleston [S.C.] July 27th 1796

    Duplicates of your two favours of the 8th of July I received this
morning; the originals are not yet arrived. Tho' my affairs have
not hitherto been arranged as I could wish them, the manner
in which you state our political situation, & the Interests of this
Country as they relate to France, obliges me to accept your appointment without hesitation. I am only apprehensive that your
friendship has been too partial to the little merit I may possess,
& that the matters intrusted to me may fail through my want of
ability. You may however depend that what talent I have, shall be
diligently exercised in performing the objects of my mission, &
promoting, as far as I can, the honour & interest of our Country. I will endeavour to arrange my affairs in a fortnight or three
weeks, & shall then proceed with Mrs Pinckney by the first Vessel
for Philadelphia, where I hope to return you thanks in person
for all your kindness to me, & to assure you that I always am with
the sincerest regard & the highest veneration, Esteem, & attachment Your affectionate & obliged Sevt

Charles Cotesworth Pinckney

ALS, MHi: Pickering Papers; ALS (duplicate), DLC:GW; ALS (triplicate),
DLC:GW.

    GW replied to Pinckney from Mount Vernon on 10 Aug.: "With sincere
pleasure I acknowledge the receipt of your letter of the 26th ulto—learning
by it that you may be so soon expected with your lady in Phila. to proceed on
the Mission to Fr.

    "If this letter should find you in Charleston, it is intended to express a regret, that my original letters had not been received by you; and to ask, if there has been any miscarriage of a Mail in the Southern quarter—aiming thereby to come at some clue to the discovery of this accident. The Sum sent was three hundred dollars in 3 Bank notes of Columbia. My best respects attend Mrs Pinckney" (ADfS, DLC:GW; LB, DLC:GW). GW mistakenly wrote "26th" for Pinckney's letter to him accepting appointment as U.S. minister to France. For Pinckney's decision and eventual departure for Paris in late September, see Zahniser, *Pinckney*, 133–39; see also Pinckney to GW, 2–5 and 12 August. GW had sent Pinckney money for the relief of fire victims in Charleston (see GW's second letter to Pinckney, 8 July).

From John Churchman

Union Street Philadelphia
No. 31[1] July 29th 1796

With pleasure do I acknowledge to have received from the President of the United States the honour of a Letter dated 10th September 1792. enclosing two other introductory ones to the American Ministers at the courts of Paris & London.[2]

I take the Liberty to say that my new universal work on the Variation of the Compass being presented to the National Convention in France, they sent the same to the committee of public Instruction, who referred it to the Bureau des Longitudes, & altho both of these Bodies have made flattering reports on the project,[3] I hardly expect the Nation will explore the places of the two magnetic points untill the conclusion of peace, & I have to lament that the war which broke out between two great maritime powers soon after my departure from my native country has continued ever since. Nevertheless I rejoice to have had an opportunity to make a multitude of observations, at Sea & Land, & I hope these will serve to prove how near the principles may be reduced to practice.

Having spent some time & money in an affair which I still suppose will be highly useful to mankind, I now apprehend it may not be amiss to apply myself to some kind of Business, & I must confess that Business connected with my favourite pursuits would be the most agreeable.

Understanding that an Act has passed providing for the sale of Lands of the United States in the Territory North West of the River Ohio, & above the mouth of Kentucky River, & several other laws that may require actual surveys,[4] It would give me pleasure to render some service to my country & myself in some way or other, & I hope to be excused when I hint at the diffidence which I can not help feeling when I introduce this subject. this is a task I could not have attempted at present had I not yesterday understood that the Surveyor general had resigned.[5] With the greatest sentiments of respect, I hope to be permitted to make an offering of my service & esteem

J. Churchman

ALS, MHi: Pickering Papers.

Churchman again wrote GW from Philadelphia on 22 Aug.: "J. Churchman offers his respectful compliments to the President of the United States, & sends enclosed a Letter from Baron Vall-travers, this Letter Churchman has lately received from his friend William Barton Esqr. in a parcel containing thirteen other articles, including Letters, Memoirs, &ca from some of the principal Learned societes in Europe, all of which to himself are highly interesting. As the said parcel is said to have come through the hands of the President, soon after he left America, Churchman considers himself under many obligations to the President for his kindness & care, but partly on account of the good old Baron (who called upon him in London) Churchman is very sorry not to have had it in his power, to send the said Letter until the present late period" (AL, DLC:GW). For the parcel, see Rodolph Valltravers to GW, 6 June 1792, and n.2 to that document.

1. Churchman's brother Mordecai Churchman, a shipmaster, resided at this address (*Philadelphia Directory, 1797*, 43). For Churchman's arrival in Philadelphia, see Timothy Pickering's first letter to GW on this date.

2. For these letters, see John Churchman to GW, 5 Sept. 1792, and n.4 to that document.

3. Churchman apparently is referring to a new version of his book first published as *An Explanation of the Magnetic Atlas, or Variation Chart . . . By which the Magnetic Variation on any Part of the Globe may be Precisely Determined. . . .* (Philadelphia, 1790). The Committee of Public Instruction in France sent Churchman's work to the Bureau of Longitudes on 18 Oct. 1795. The bureau's report praised the effort as worthy of attention but requested more observations. The committee subsequently conveyed this report to Churchman (see Guillaume, *Comité d'Instruction Publique*, 6:803, 856; see also Churchman, *The Magnetic Atlas, or Variation Charts of the Whole Terraqueous Globe . . .* [3d ed., New York, 1800]).

4. Churchman named an act approved on 18 May 1796 (1 *Stat.* 464–69). Two other laws enacted during the recent congressional session called for surveys: "An Act to regulate Trade and Intercourse with the Indian Tribes, and to preserve Peace on the Frontiers" and "An Act regulating the grants of land appropriated for Military services, and for the Society of the United Brethren, for propagating the Gospel among the Heathen" (1 *Stat.* 469–74, 490–91).

5. For consideration of Churchman as surveyor general, see GW to Timothy

Pickering, 5 Aug. (second letter); see also GW to John Marshall, 15 July, and the notes to that document.

From Timothy Pickering

(private)

Sir,   Department of State July 29. 1796.

About noon to-day Mr John Churchman, who has been these two or three years in Europe, on account of his supposed discoveries relative to the variation of the Magnetic Needle, called at the office.[1] He came last from Bourdeaux, and was the bearer of Mr Monroe's letter of the 2d of May.[2] I told him it had been broken open; & after a few questions, asked him to give me a certificate of the circumstances which attended his receipt of it; and offered him pen, ink & paper to write it; unless he chose to do it at home. He said he would go home, and call himself at five in the afternoon (if that hour was convenient to me) as the matter required some consideration. He called at five accordingly; and then told me (with some emotion) that he thought it best to be candid; for he could not think of giving a certificate that might excite suspicions of innocent people—He had himself broken the seal, tho' by mere accident; and as soon as he discovered his mistake, closed the letter again without reading it. He handed me a letter from his friend in London (a quaker) inclosing the copy of a diploma, in Latin, given him by order of the Empress of Russia, declaring him a member of the Russian Academy of Sciences. This letter he recd thro' Mr Monroe; and by the same channel expected to receive the diploma itself. When therefore, at the point of his embarkation at Bourdeaux for America, he received a letter from Mr Monroe addressed to him, and within the cover, another of a size likely to contain the diploma, without looking at the superscription, he broke the seal. He hoped this inadvertence would be excused; and especially as he was careful to deliver the letter with his own hand: it was he who called & delivered it in the evening, as mentioned in my former letter.[3] This account having all the marks of truth & candour, I begged him to give himself no further uneasiness about it; promising to communicate the explanation to you.

I then entered into conversation with him about his travels in

France, and the sentiments of the French people towards America, & particularly the *government*; and as he had been so long in France, whether he had observed any material change of sentiment, especially on account of the treaty with Great-Britain. He answered, That he had observed no material change; that very little was said by *Frenchmen* about the treaty—tho' much was said against it by the *American Citizens* in Paris.[4] With the highest respect I am sir, your most obt servt

Timothy Pickering

ALS, DLC:GW; ALS (letterpress copy), MHi: Pickering Papers. The docket on the letterpress copy states that this letter was "sent Augt 1."

1. See John Churchman to GW, this date.
2. The reference is to a letter from James Monroe, U.S. minister to France, to Pickering (see Pickering's second letter to GW on 21 July, and n.1).
3. See Pickering to GW, 20 July.
4. For GW's reply, see his second letter to Pickering on 5 August.

From Timothy Pickering

Sir,   Department of State July 29 1796.

I was yesterday honoured with your letter of the 25th and agreeably to your directions have had a commission made out for Samuel Williams to be Consul of the U. States at Hamburg, & now inclose it for your signature. I will take care to advise Mr Monroe of the appointment.

The untoward situation of the Cannon foundaries last year, excited apprehensions that the Contractors might fail of furnishing such as were fit for our frigates. Numerous essays had been made at both furnaces, and with little success.[1] On my representing this to you, and the probability of obtaining a capital founder from France, you gave your approbation of the measure.[2] It will certainly be the interest of this country to secure by liberal pay the services of such a man as Mr La Motte is represented to be; and his intention to come with his family I think a favourable circumstance, as it looks towards a permanent residence here as his future country. I supposed that a cannon foundary would compose an important part of our arsenal establishment; and that the presence of an accomplished founder would be essential to its most perfect construction.

I will inform Mr Monroe, that already possessing some engineers which are competent to our present undertakings, and there being no legal provision for others, we cannot invite any gentlemen of that profession from France.[3] With the highest respect I am sir your most obt servt

Timothy Pickering

ALS, DNA: RG 59, Miscellaneous Letters; LB, DNA: RG 59, Domestic Letters; LB, DNA: RG 59, GW's Correspondence with His Secretaries of State.

1. The government had contracted in 1794 with the Hope Furnace in Rhode Island and another furnace in Cecil County, Maryland. Problems arose with Hope Furnace (see Jabez Bowen to GW, 20 Feb. 1796, and n.1). For cannons delivered under these contracts, see James McHenry to the U.S. House of Representatives, 12 April 1798, in *ASP, Military Affairs*, 1:123.

2. Pickering had written James Monroe, U.S. minister to France, on 7 Nov. 1795 that GW had approved the procurement of a cannon founder from France (*Papers of James Monroe*, 3:509–10).

3. GW replied to Pickering from Mount Vernon on 3 Aug.: "Herewith you will receive my signature to the Commission appointing Samuel Williams of Massachusetts, Consul for the United States at the Port of Hamburgh &ca—transmitted to me in your letter of the 29th Ulto.

"If Mr La Motte possesses much experimental as well as theoretical knowledge in the casting of Cannon &ca there can be no doubt of the utility of his Services—and coming with his family will be an evidence of his intention to remain—but the latter ought not to be accomplished at the expence of the United States unless his Services are secured. But Mr Monroe it is to be presumed will take care that one does not happen without the other" (LS [retained copy], DNA: RG 59, Miscellaneous Letters; copy, MHi: Pickering Papers; LB, DNA: RG 59, GW's Correspondence with His Secretaries of State).

From Alexander Hamilton

Sir   New York July 30. 1796

I have the pleasure to send you herewith a certan draft which I have endeavoured to make as perfect as my time and engagements would permit—It has been my object to render this act *importantly* and *lastingly* useful, and avoiding all just cause of present exception, to embrace such reflections and sentiments as will wear well, progress in approbation with time, & redound to future reputation—How far I have succeeded you will judge.[1]

I have begun the second part of the task—the digesting the supplementary remarks to the first address which in a fortnight I hope also to send you—yet I confess the more I have considered the matter the less eligible this plan has appeared to me—There seems to me to be a certain awkwardness in the thing—and it seems to imply that there is a doubt whether the assurance without the evidence would be believed—Besides that I think that there are some ideas which will not wear well in the former address, & I do not see how any part can be omitted, if it is to be given as the thing formerly prepared. Neverthe[le]ss when you have both before you you can better judge.

If you should incline to take the draft now sent—and after perusing and noting any thing that you wish changed & will send it to me I will with pleasure shape it as you desire. This may also put it in my power to improve the expression & perhaps in some instances condense.

I rejoice that certain clouds have not lately thickened & that there is a prospect of a brighter horison.[2] With affectionate & respectful attachment I have the honor to be Sir Yr very Obed. Serv.

A. Hamilton

ALS, NN: Alexander Hamilton Papers.

1. Hamilton enclosed a draft for GW's farewell address that reorganized GW's initial version and omitted material James Madison had written in 1792 (see *Hamilton Papers*, 20:265–88, 293–303, or Paltsits, *Farewell Address*, 179–99; see also GW to Hamilton, 15 May 1796, and the enclosure—"GW's Draft for a Farewell Address"—printed with that document). Hamilton docketed the draft "Original Draft Copy considerably amended," and it contains many small textual adjustments. Most likely, Hamilton's docket did not refer to the alterations on this draft, but instead conveyed that this draft was a more extensive alteration of GW's original version than another draft that Hamilton eventually submitted on 10 Aug. (see the editorial note to Farewell Address, 19 Sept.).

2. GW replied to Hamilton from Mount Vernon on 10 Aug.: "The principal design of this letter, is to inform you, that your favor of the 30th ulto, with its enclosure, got safe to my hands by the last Post, and that the latter shall have the most attentive consideration I am able to give it.

"A cursory reading it has had, and the Sentiments therein contained are extremely just, & such as ought to be inculcated. The doubt that occurs at first view, is the length of it for a News Paper publication; and how far the occasion would countenance its appearing in any other form, without dilating *more* on the present state of matters, is questionable. All the columns of a large Gazette would scarcely, I conceive, contain the present draught. But having made no accurate calculation of this matter, I may be much mistaken.

"If any matters should occur to you as fit subjects of communication at the opening of the next Session of Congress I would thank you for noting and furnishing me with them. It is my wish, and my custom to provide all the materials for the Speech in time that it may be formed at leizure" (ALS, DLC: Hamilton Papers).

From Thomas Paine

Paris, July 30th, 1796,

As censure is but awkwardly softened by apology, I shall offer you no apology for this letter. The eventful crisis to which your double politics have conducted the affairs of your country requires an investigation uncramped by ceremony.

There was a time when the fame of America, moral and political, stood fair and high in the world. The lustre of her revolution extended itself to every individual; and to be a citizen of America gave a title to respect in Europe. Neither meanness nor ingratitude had then mingled itself into the composition of her character. Her resistance to the attempted tyranny of England left her unsuspected of the one, and her open acknowledgment of the aid she received from France precluded all suspicion of the other. The Washington of politics had not then appeared.

At the time I left America (April 1787) the continental convention that formed the federal constitution was on the point of meeting. Since that time new schemes of politics and new distinctions of parties, have arisen. The term *Antifederalist* has been applied to all those who combated the defects of that constitution, or opposed the measures of your administration. It was only to the absolute necessity of establishing some federal authority, extending equally over all the States, that an instrument, so inconsisent as the present federal constitution is, obtained a suffrage. I would have voted for it myself, had I been in America, or even for a worse rather than have had none; provided it contained the means of remedying its defects by the same appeal to the people by which it was to be established. It is always better policy to leave removeable errors to expose themselves, than to hazard too much in contending against them theoretically.

I have introduced those observations, not only to mark the general difference between antifederalist and anti-constitutionalist, but to preclude the effect, and even the application, of the former of those terms to myself. I declare myself opposed to several matters in the constitution, particularly to the manner in which,

what is called the Executive, is formed, and to the long duration of the Senate; and if I live to return to America I will use all
my endeavours to have them altered.[1] I also declare myself opposed to almost the whole of your administration; for I know it
to have been deceitful, if not even perfidious, as I shall shew in
the course of this letter. But as to the point of consolidating the
States into a federal government, it so happens, that the proposition for that purpose came originally from myself. I proposed
it in a letter to Chancellor Livingston in the spring of the year
1782, whilst that gentleman was minister for foreign affairs. The
five per cent. duty recommended by Congress had then fallen
through, having been adopted by some of the States, altered by
others, rejected by Rhode Island, and repealed by Virginia after
it had been consented to. The proposal in the letter I allude to
was to get over the whole difficulty at once, by annexing a continental legislative body to Congress; for, in order to have any
law of the Union uniform, the case could only be, that either
Congress, as it then stood, must frame the law, and the States
severally adopt it without alteration, or, the States must elect a
Continental Legislature for the purpose. Chancellor Livingston,
Robert Morris, Governeur Morris and myself had a meeting at
the house of Robert Morris on the subject of that letter. There
was no diversity of opinion on the proposition for a Continental
Legislature. The only difficulty was on the manner of bringing
the proposition forward. For my own part, as I considered it as
a remedy in reserve, that could be applied at any time, *when the
States saw themselves wrong enough to be put right* (which did not appear to me to be the case at that time) I did not see the propriety
of urging it precipitately, and declined being the publisher of
it myself. After this account of a fact, the leaders of your party
will scarcely have the hardiness to apply to me the term of antifederalist. But I can go to a date and to a fact beyond this; for
the proposition for electing a Continental Convention to form
the Continental Government is one of the subjects treated of
in the pamphlet *Common Sense.*

Having thus cleared away a little of the rubbish that might
otherwise have lain in my way, I return to the point of time at
which the present Federal Constitution and your administration
began. It was very well said by an anonymous writer in Philadelphia, about a year before that period, that *"thirteen staves and ne'er*

a hoop will not make a barrel," and as any kind of hooping the barrel, however, defectively executed, would be better than none, it was scarcely possible but that considerable advantages must arise from the federal hooping of the States. It was with pleasure that every sincere friend to America beheld, as the natural effect of union, her rising prosperity; and it was with grief they saw that prosperity mixed, even in the blossom, with the germ of corruption. Monopolies of every kind marked your administration almost in the moment of its commencement. The lands obtained by the revolution were lavished upon partizans; the interest of the disbanded soldier was sold to the speculator; injustice was acted under the pretence of faith; and the chief of the army became the patron of the fraud. From such a beginning what could be expected, but what has happened? A mean and servile submission to the insults of one nation, treachery and ingratitude to another.

Some vices make their approach with such a splendid appearance, that we scarcely know to what class of moral distinctions they belong. They are rather virtues corrupted, than vices originally. But meanness and ingratitude have nothing equivocal in their character. There is not a trait in them that renders them doubtful. They are so originally vice, that they are generated in the dung of other vices, and crawl into existence with the filth upon their back. The fugitives have found protection in you, and the levee-room is their place of rendezvous.

As the Federal Constitution is a copy, not quite so base as the original, of the form of the British government, an imitation of its vices was naturally to be expected. So intimate is the connection between *form* and *practice*, that to adopt the one is to invite the other. Imitation is naturally progressive, and is rapidly so in matters that are vicious.

Soon after the Federal Constitution arrived in England, I received a letter from a female literary correspondent (a native of New York) very well mixed with friendship, sentiment and politics. In my answer to that letter I permitted myself to ramble into the wilderness of imagination, and to anticipate what might hereafter be the condition of America. I had no idea that the picture I then drew was realizing so fast, and still less that, Mr. Washington was hurrying it on. As the extract I allude to is congenial and with the subject I am upon, I here transcribe it.[2]

Impressed, as I was, with apprehensions of this kind, I had America constantly in mind in all the publications I afterwards made. The first, and still more, the second part of Rights of Man bear evident marks of this watchfulness; and the Dissertation on First Principles of Government goes more directly to the point than either of the former. I now pass on to other subjects.

It will be supposed by those into whose hands this letter may fall, that I have some personal resentment against you; I will therefore settle this point before I proceed farther.

If I have any resentment, you must acknowledge that I have not been hasty in declaring it; neither would it be now declared (for what are private resentments to the public) if the cause of it did not unite itself as well with your public as your private character, and with the motives of your political conduct.

The part I acted in the American revolution is well known; I shall not here repeat it. I know also that had it not been for the aid received from France in men, money and ships, that your cold and unmilitary conduct (as I shall shew in the course of this letter) would, in all probability, have lost America; at least she would not have been the independent nation she now is. You slept away your time in the field till the finances of the country were completely exhausted, and you have but little share in the glory of the final event. It is time, sir, to speak the undisguised language of historical truth.

Elevated to the chair of the Presidency you assumed the merit of every thing to yourself, and the natural ingratitude of your constitution began to appear. You commenced your Presidential carreer by encouraging and swallowing the grossest adulation, and you travelled America from one end—to the other, to put yourself in the way of receiving it. You have as many addresses in your chest as James the II. As to what were your views, for if you are not great enough to have ambition you are little enough to have vanity, they cannot be directly inferred from expressions of your own; but the partizans of your politics have divulged the secret.

John Adams has said (and John, it is known, was always a speller after places and offices, and never thought his little services were highly enough paid) John has said, that as Mr. Washington had no child, that the Presidency should be made hereditary in the family of Lund Washington. John might then have

counted upon some fine-cure for himself and a provision for
his descendants. He did not go so far as to say also, that the Vice
Presidency should be hereditary in the family of John Adams.
He prudently left that to stand upon the ground, that one good
turn deserves another.[3]

John Adams is one of those men who never contemplated
the origin of government, or comprehended any thing of first
principles. If he had, he must have seen that the right to set
up and establish hereditary government never did, and never
can, exist in any generation, at any time whatever; that it is of
the nature of treason; because it is an attempt to take away the
rights of all the minors living at that time, and of all succeeding
generations. It is of a degree beyond common treason. It is a sin
against nature. The equal right of generations is a right fixed
in the nature of things. It belongs to the son when of age, as it
belonged to the father before him. John Adams would himself
deny the right that any former deceased generation could have
to decree authoritatively a succession of Governors over him,
or over his children; and yet he assumes the pretended right,
treasonable as it is, of acting it himself. His ignorance is his best
excuse.

John Jay has said (and this John was always the sycophant of
every thing in power, from Mr. Girard in America to Grenville
in England) John Jay has said, that the Senate should have been
appointed for life. He would then have been sure of never wanting a lucrative appointment for himself, or have had any fears
about impeachments. These are the disguised traitors that call
themselves federalists.[4]

Could I have known to what degree of corruption & perfidy
the administrative part of the government in America had de-
scended, I could have been at no loss to have understood the
reservedness of Mr. Washington towards me, during my imprisonment in this Luxembourg. There are cases in which silence is
a loud language.

I will here explain the cause of my imprisonment, and return
to Mr. Washington afterwards.[5]

As my citizenship in America was not altered or diminished,
by any thing I had done in Europe (on the contrary it ought to
have been considered as strengthened, for it was the American
principle of government that I was endeavouring to spread in

Europe) and as it is the duty of every government to charge itself with the care of any of its citizens who may happen to fall under an arbitrary persecution abroad, and is also one of the reasons for which Ambassadors or Ministers are appointed,—it was the duty of the executive department in America to have made (at least) some enquiries about me, as soon as it heard of my imprisonment. But if this had not been the case, that government owed it to me on every ground and principle of honor and gratitude. Mr. Washington owed it to me on every score of private acquaintance, I will not now say, friendship; for it has for some time been known, by those who know him, that he has no friendships; that he is incapable of forming any; he can serve or desert a man or a cause with constitutional indifference; and it is this cold hermophrodite faculty that imposed itself upon the world, and was credited for a while by enemies as by friends, for prudence, moderation and impartiality.[6]

I had then been imprisoned seven months, and the silence of the executive government of America, Mr. Washington, upon the case and upon every thing respecting me, was explanation enough to Robespierre that he might proceed to extremities.

A violent fever which had nearly terminated my existence, was, I believe, the circumstance that preserved it. I was not in a condition to be removed, or to know of what was passing, or of what had passed for more than a month. It makes a blank in my remembrance of life. The first thing I was informed of was the fall of Robespierre.

About a week after this Mr. Monroe arrived to supercede Gouverneur Morris, and as soon as I was able to write a note legible enough to be read, I found a way to convey one to him, by means of the man who lighted the lamps in the prison; and whose unabated friendship to me, from whom he had never received any service, and with difficulty accepted any recompence, puts the character of Mr. Washington to shame.

In a few days I received a message from Mr. Monroe, conveyed to me in a note from an intermediate person, with assurance of his friendship, and expressing a desire that I would rest the case in his hands. After a fortnight or more had passed and hearing nothing further, I wrote to a friend who was then in Paris, a citizen of Philadelphia, requesting him to inform me what was the true situation of things with respect to me. I was sure that something was the matter. I began to have hard thoughts of Mr. Washington; but I was unwilling to encourage them.

In about then days I received an answer to my letter in which the writer says:[7]

I was now at no loss to understand Mr. Washington and his new fangled faction, and that their policy, was silently to leave me to fall in France. They were rushing as fast as they could venture, without awakening the jealousy of America, into all the vices and corruptions of the British government; and it was no more consistent with the policy of Mr. Washington, and those who immediately surrounded him, than it was with that of Robespierre or of Pitt, that I should survive. They have however, missed the mark and the reaction is up themselves.

Upon the receipt of the letter just alluded to, I sent a memorial to Mr. Monroe which the reader will find in the appendix,[8] and I received from him the following answer. It is dated the 18th of September, but did not come to hand till about the 10th of October. I was then falling into a relapse, the weather was becoming damp and cold, fuel was not to be had, and the abscess in my side, the consequence of these things, and of the want of air and exercise, was beginning to form and which has continued immoveable ever since. Here follows Mr. Monroe's letter.[9]

The part in Mr. Monroe's letter in which he speaks of the President (Mr. Washington) is put in soft language. Mr. Monroe knew what Mr. Washington had said formerly, and he was willing to keep that in view. But the fact is, not only that Mr. Washington had given no orders to Mr. Monroe, as the letter stated; but he did not so much as say to him, enquire if Mr. Paine be dead or alive, in prison or out, or see if there is any assistance we can give[10] him.

While these matters were passing the liberations from the prisons were numerous; from twenty to forty in the course of almost every twenty four hours[.] The continuance of my imprisonment, after a new minister had arrived immediately from America, which was now more than two months, was a matter so obviously strange, that I found the character of the American government spoken of in very unqualified terms of reproach; not only by those who still remained in prison, but by those who were liberated, and by persons who had access to the prison from without. Under these circumstances I wrote again to Mr. Monroe, and found occasion, among other things to say:[11]

The case, so far as it respected Mr. Monroe was, that having to get over the difficulties which the strange conduct of Gouverneur Morris had thrown in the way of a successor, and having no authority from the American government to speak officially upon any thing relating to me, he found himself obliged to proceed by unofficial means with individual members; for though Robespierre was overthrown, the Robespierrian members of the Committee of Public Safety still remained in considerable force, and had they found out that Mr. Monroe had no official authority upon the case, they would have paid little or no regard to his reclamation of me. In the mean time my health was suffering exceedingly, the dreary prospect of winter was coming on, and imprisonment was still a thing of danger.

After the Robespierrian members of the Committee were removed by the expiration of their time of serving, Mr. Monroe reclaimed me, and I was liberated the 4th of November [1794]. Mr. Monroe arrived in Paris the beginning of August before. All that period of my imprisonment, at least, I owe not to Robespierre, but to his colleague in projects, George Washington. Immediately upon my liberation Mr. Monroe invited me to his house, where I remained more than a year and an half; and I speak of his aid and his friendship, as an open hearted man will always do in such a case, with respect and gratitude.

Soon after my liberation the Convention passed an unanimous vote to invite me to return to my seat among them. The times were still unsettled and dangerous, as well from without as from within, for the coalition was unbroken, and the constitution not settled. I chose, however, to accept the invitation; for as I undertake nothing but what I believe to be right, I abandon nothing that I undertake; and I was willing also to shew, that, as I was not of a cast of mind to be deterred by prospects or retro-prospects of danger, so neither were my principles to be weakened by misfortune, or perverted by disgust.

Being now once more abroad in the world I began to find that I was not the only one who had conceived an unfavourable opinion of Mr. Washington. It was evident that his character was on the decline as well among Americans as among foreigners of different nations. From being the chief of a government, he had made himself the chief of a party; and his integrity was questioned, for his politics had a doubtful appearance. The mission of Mr. Jay to London, notwithstanding there was an American minister there already, had then taken place, and was beginning to be talked of. It appeared to others, as it did to me, to be enveloped in mystery, which every day served either to encrease or to explain into matter of suspicion.

In the year 1790, or about that time, Mr. Washington as President had sent Gouverneur Morris to London as his secret agent to have some communication with the British ministry. To cover the agency of Morris it was given out, I know not by whom, that he went as an agent from Robert Morris to borrow money in Europe, and the report was permitted to pass uncontradicted. The event of Morris's negociation was, that Mr. Hammond was sent minister from England to America, and Pinckney from America to England, and himself minister to France. If while Morris was minister in France he was not an emissary of the British ministry and the coalesced powers, he gave strong reasons to suspect him of it. No one who saw his conduct, and heard his conversation, could doubt his being in their interest; and had he not got off at the time he did, after his recall, he would have been in arrestation. Some letters of his had fallen into the hands of the Committee of Public Safety, and enquiry was making after him.

A great bustle has been made by Mr. Washington about the conduct of Genet in America; while that of his own minister, Morris, in France was infinitely more reproachable. If Genet was imprudent or rash, he was not treacherous; but Morris was all three. He was the enemy of the French revolution in every stage of it. But, notwithstanding this conduct on the part of Morris, and the known profligacy of his character, Mr. Washington, in a letter he wrote to him at the time of recalling him on the complaint and request of the Committee of Public Safety, assures him, that though he had complied with that request, he still retained the same esteem and friendship for him as before.[12] This letter Morris was foolish enough to tell of; and, as his own character and conduct were notorious, the telling of it could have but one effect, which was that of implicating the character of the writer. Morris still loiters in Europe, chiefly in England; and Mr. Washington is still in correspondence with him; Mr. Washington ought therefore to expect, especially since his conduct in the affair of Jay's treaty, that France must consider Morris and Washington as men of the same description. The chief difference, however, between the two is (for in politics there is none) that the one is profligate enough to profess an indifference about *moral* principles, and the other is prudent enough to conceal the want of them.

About three months after I was at liberty, the official note of Jay to Grenville on the subject of the capture of American vessels by British cruisers appeared in the American papers that arrived at Paris. Every thing was of a-piece. Every thing was mean. The same kind of character went to all circumstances public or private. Disgusted at this national degradation, as well as at the particular conduct of Mr. Washington to me, I wrote to him (Mr. Washington) on the 22d of February (1795) under cover to the then Secretary of State (Mr. Randolph) and entrusted the letter to Mr. Letombe, who was appointed French consul to Philadelphia, and was on the point of taking his departure. When I supposed Mr. Letombe had sailed, I mentioned the letter to Mr. Monroe, and as I was then in his house, I shewed it to him. He expressed a wish that I would recall it, which he supposed might be done, as he had learned that Mr. Letombe had not then sailed. I agreed to do so, and it was returned by Mr. Letombe under cover to Mr. Monroe.

The letter, however, will now reach Mr. Washington publicly, in the course of this work.[13]

About the month of September following, I had a severe relapse, which gave occasion to the report of my death. I had felt it coming on a considerable time before, which occasioned me to hasten the work I had then in hand, the *Second part of the Age of Reason.* When I had finished that work, I bestowed another letter on Mr. Washington, which I sent under cover to Mr. Benj. Franklin Bache of Philadelphia. The letter is as follows.[14]

Here follows the letter above alluded to, which I had stopped in complaisance to Mr. Monroe.[15]

That this letter was not written in very good temper is very evident; but it was just such a letter as his conduct appeared to me to merit, and every thing on his part since has served to confirm that opinion. Had I wanted a commentary on his silence with respect to my imprisonment in France, some of his faction has furnished me with it. What I here allude to is a publication in a Philadelphia paper, copied afterwards into a New York paper, both under the patronage of the Washington faction, in which the writer, still supposing me in prison in France, wonders at my lengthy respite from the scaffold; and he marks his politics still further by saying:[16]

I am not refuting or contradicting the fals[e]hood of this publication, for it is sufficiently notorious; neither am I censuring the writer; on the contrary I thank him for the explanation he has incautiously given of the principles of the Washington faction. Insignificant, however, as the piece is, it was capable of having had some ill effect, had it arrived in France during my imprisonment and in the time of Robespierre; and I am not uncharitable in supposing that this was the intention of the writer.[17]

I have now done with Mr. Washington on the score of private affairs. It would have been far more agreeable to me, had his conduct been such as not to have merited these reproaches. Errors or caprices of the temper can be pardoned and forgotten; but a cold deliberate crime of the heart, such as Mr. Washington is capable of acting, is not to be washed away. I now proceed to other matter.

After Jay's note to Grenville arrived in Paris from America, the character of every thing that was to follow might be easily foreseen; and it was upon this anticipation that my letter of February 22d was founded.[18] The event has proved, that I was not mistaken, except that it has been much worse than I expected.

It would naturally occur to Mr. Washington, that the secrecy of Jay's mission to England, where there was already an American minister, could not but create some suspicion in the French government; especially as the conduct of Morris had been notorious, and the intimacy of Mr. Washington with Morris was known.

The character, which Mr. Washington has attempted to act in the world, is a sort of non-describable, cameleon-coloured thing, called *prudence*. It is, in many cases, a substitute for principle, and is so nearly allied to hypocrisy, that it easily slides into it. His genius for prudence furnished him in this instance with an expedient, that served, as is the natural and general character of all expedients, to diminish the embarrassments of the moment and multiply them afterwards; for he authorised it to be made known to the French government, as a confidential matter

(Mr. Washington should recollect that I was a member of the Convention, & had the means of knowing what I here state) he authorized it, I say, to be made known, and that for the purpose of preventing any uneasiness to France on the score of Mr. Jay's mission to England, that the object of that mission, and of Mr. Jay's authority, was restricted to that of demanding the surrender of the western posts and indemnification for the cargoes captured in American vessels. Mr. Washington knows that this was untrue; and knowing this, he had good reason to himself for refusing to furnish the House of Representatives with copies of the instructions given to Jay; as he might suspect, among other things, that he should also be called upon for copies of instructions given to other ministers, and that in the contradiction of instructions his want of integrity would be detected. Mr. Washington may now, perhaps, learn, when it is too late, to be of any use to him, that a man will pass better through the world with a thousand open errors upon his back, than in being detected in ONE sly fals[e]hood. When one is detected, a thousand are suspected.

The first account that arrived in Paris of a treaty being negociated by Mr. Jay (for nobody suspected any) came in an English newspaper, which announced that a treaty *offensive* and *defensive* had been concluded between the United States of America and England. This was immediately denied by every American in Paris, as an impossible thing; and though it was disbelieved by the French, it imprinted a suspicion that some underhand business was going forward.[19] At length the treaty itself arrived, and every well-affected American blushed with shame.

It is curious to observe how the appearances of character will change, whilst the root that produces them remains the same. The Washington administration having waded through the slough of negociation, and whilst it amused France with professions of friendship contrived to injure her, immediately throws off the hypocrite, and assumes the swaggering air of a bravado. The party papers of that imbecile administration were on this occasion filled with paragraphs about *Sovereignty*. A paltroon may boast of his sovereign right to let another kick him, and this is the only kind of sovereignty shewn in the treaty with England. But these dashing paragraphs, as Timothy Pickering well knows, were intended for France; without whose assistance in men, money and ships, Mr. Washington would have cut but a poor figure in the American war. But of his military talents I shall speak hereafter.

I mean not to enter into any discussion of any article of Jay's treaty: I shall speak only upon the whole of it. It is attempted to be justified on the ground of its not being a violation of any article or articles of the treaty pre-existing with France. But the sovereign right of explanation does not lie with George Washington and his man Timothy; France, on her part, has, at least, an equal right; and when nations dispute, it is not so much about words as about things.

A man, such as the world calls, a sharper, and versed, as Jay must be supposed to be, in the quibbles of the law, may find a way to enter into engagements, and make bargains in such a manner as to cheat some other party, without that party being able, as the phrase is, *to take the law of him.* This often happens in the cabalistical circle of what is called law. But when this is attempted to be acted on the national scale of treaties, it is too despicable to be defended, or to be permitted to exist. Yet this is the trick upon which Jay's treaty is founded, so far as it has relation to the treaty pre-existing with France. It is a counter-treaty to that treaty, and perverts all the great articles of that treaty to the injury of France, and makes them operate as a bounty to England with whom France is at war.

The Washington administration shews great desire, that the treaty between France and the United States be preserved. Nobody can doubt their sincerity upon this matter. There is not a British minister, a British merchant, or a British agent or sailor in America, that does not anxiously wish the same thing. The treaty with France serves now as a passport to supply England with naval stores and other articles of American produce, whilst the same articles, when coming to France, are made contraband or seizable by Jay's treaty with England. The treaty with France says, that neutral ships make neutral property, and thereby gives protection to English property on board American ships; and Jay's treaty delivers up French property on board American ships to be seized by the English. It is too paltry to talk of faith, of national honour, and of the preservation of treaties, whilst such a bare-faced treachery as this stares the world in the face.

The Washington administration may save itself the trouble of proving to the French government its *most faithful* intentions of preserving the treaty with France; for France has now no desire that it should be preserved. She had nominated an Envoy extraordinary to America, to make Mr. Washington and his government a present of the treaty, and to have no more to do with *that* or with *him.* It was, at the same time, officially declared to the American minister at Paris, *that the French Republic had rather have the American government for an open enemy than a treacherous friend.* This, sir, together with the internal distractions caused in America, and the loss of character in the world, is the *eventful crisis,* alluded to in the beginning of this letter, to which your double politics have brought the affairs of your country. It is time that the eyes of America be opened upon you.

How France would have conducted herself towards America and American commerce after all treaty stipulations had ceased, and under the sense of services rendered and injuries received, I know not. It is, however, an unpleasant reflection, that in all national quarrels, the innocent, and even the friendly, part of the community, become involved with the culpable and the unfriendly; and as the accounts that arrived from America continued to manifest an invariable attachment in the general mass of the people to their original ally, in opposition to the new-fangled Washington faction,—the resolutions that had been taken were suspended. It happened also fortunately enough, that Gouverneur Morris was not minister at this time.

There is, however, one point that yet remains in embryo, and which, among other things, serves to shew the ignorance of the Washington treaty-makers, and their inattention to pre-existing treaties when they were employing themselves in framing or ratifying the new treaty with England.

The second article of the treaty of commerce between the United States and France says:[20]

All the concessions therefore made to England by Jay's treaty are, through the medium of this second article in the pre-existing treaty, made to France, and become engrafted into the treaty with France, and can be exercised by her as a matter of right, the same as by England.[21]

In what a fraudulent light must Mr. Washington's character appear in the world, when his declarations and his conduct are compared together! Here follows the letter he wrote to the Committee of Public Safety whilst Jay was negociating in profound secrecy this treacherous treaty.[22]

Was it by entering into a treaty with England, to surrender French property on board American ships to be seized by the English, whilst English property on board American ships was declared by the French treaty not to be seizable, *that the bonds of friendship between America and France were to be drawn the closer?* Was it by declaring naval stores contraband when coming to France, when by the French treaty they were not contraband when going to England, that the *connection between France and America was to be advanced?* Was it by opening the American ports to the British navy in the present war, from which ports that same navy had been expelled by the aid solicited from France in the American war (and that aid gratuitously given) that the gratitude of America was to be shewn, and the *solicitude* spoken of in the letter demonstrated?

As the letter was addressed to the Committee of Public Safety, Mr Washington did not expect it would get abroad in the world, or be seen by any other eye than that of Robespierre, or be heard by any other ear than that of the Committee; that it would pass as a whisper across the Atlantic, from one dark chamber to the other, and there terminate. It was calculated to remove from the mind of the Committee all suspicion upon Jay's mission to England, and, in this point of view, it was suited to the circumstances of the moment then passing; but as the event of that mission has proved the letter to be hypocritical, it serves no other purpose of the present moment than to shew that the writer is not to be credited. Two circumstances served to make the reading of the letter necessary in the Convention. The one was, that those who succeeded on the fall of Robespierre, found it most proper to act with publicity; the other, to extinguish the suspicions which the strange conduct of Morris had occasioned in France.

When the British treaty, and the ratification of it by Mr. Washington, was known in France, all furthur declarations from him of his good disposition, as an ally and a friend, passed for so many cyphers; but still it appeared necessary to him to keep up the farce of declarations. It is stipulated in the British treaty, that commissioners are to report at the end of two years on the case of *neutral ships making neutral property.* In the mean time neutral ships do *not* make neutral property, according to the British treaty, and they *do*, according to the French treaty. The preservation, therefore, of the French treaty became of great importance to England, as by that means she can employ American ships as carriers, whilst the same advantage is denied to France. Whether the French treaty could exist as a matter of right after this clandestine perversion of it, could not but give some apprehensions to the partizans of the British treaty, and it became necessary to them to make up, by fine words, what was wanting in good actions.

An opportunity offered to that purpose. The Convention, on the public reception of Mr. Monroe, ordered the American flag and the French flag to be displayed unitedly in the hall of the Convention. Mr. Monroe made a present of an American flag for the purpose. The Convention returned this compliment by sending a French flag to America, to be presented by their minister, Mr. Adet, to the American government. This resolution passed long before Jay's treaty was known or suspected; it passed in the days of confidence; but the flag was not presented by Mr. Adet till several months after the treaty had been ratified. Mr. Washington made this the occasion of saying some fine things to the French Minister, and the better to get himself into tune to do this, he began by saying the finest things of himself.[23]

Mr. Washington having expended so many fine phrases upon himself, was obliged to invent a new one for the French, and he calls them "wonderful people!" The coalesced powers acknowledge as much.

It is laughable to hear Mr. Washington talk of his *sympathetic feelings*, who has always been remarked, even among his friends, for not having any. He has, however, given no proof of any to me. As to the pompous encomiums he so liberally pays to himself, on the score of the American revolution, the reality of them may be questioned; and since he has forced them so much into notice, it is fair to examine his pretentions.

A stranger might be led to suppose from the egotism with which Mr. Washington speaks, that himself, and himself only, had generated, conducted, compleated, and established the revolution: In fine, that it was all his own doing.

In the first place, as to the political part, he had no share in it; and therefore the whole of *that* is out of the question with respect to him. There remains then only the military part, and it would

have been prudent in Mr. Washington not to have awakened
enquiry upon that subject. Fame then was cheap; he enjoyed it
cheaply; and nobody was disposed to take away the laurels, that,
whether they were *acquired* or not, had been *given*.

Mr. Washington's merit consisted in constancy. But constancy
was the common virtue of the revolution. Who was there that
was inconstant? I know of but one military defection, that of
Arnold; and I know of no political defection, among those who
made themselves eminent, when the revolution was formed by
the declaration of independence. Even Silas Deane, though he
attempted to defraud, did not betray.

But when we speak of military character, something more is to
be understood than constancy; and something more *ought* to be
understood than the Fabian system of *doing nothing*. The *nothing*
part can be done by any body. Old Mrs. Thompson, the housekeeper of head-quarters (who threatened to make the sun and
the *wind* shine through Rivington of New-York) could have done
it as well as Mr. Washington.[24] Deborah would have been as good
as Barak.

Mr. Washington had the nominal rank of Commander in
Chief; but he was not so in fact. He had in reality only a separate
command. He had no controul over, or direction of, the army to
the northward, under Gates, that captured Burgoyne; nor of that
to the south, under Green, that recovered the southern States.
The nominal rank, however, of Commander in chief, served to
throw upon him the lustre of those actions, and to make him
appear as the soul and centre of all the military operations in
America.[25]

Nothing was done in the campaigns of 1778, 1779, 1780, in
the part where Gen. Washington commanded, except the taking
Stony Point by Gen. Wayne. The Southern States in the mean
time were over-run by the enemy. They were afterwards recovered by Gen. Greene, who had in a very great measure created
the army that accomplished that recovery. In all this Gen. Washington had no share. The Fabian system of war, followed by him,
began now to unfold itself with all its evils, for what is Fabian war
without Fabian means to support it.

The finances of Congress, depending wholly on emissions of
paper money, were exhausted. Its credit was gone. The continental treasury was not able to pay the expence of a brigade of

waggons to transport the necessary stores to the army, and yet
the sole object, the establishment of the revolution, was a thing
of remote distance. The time I am now speaking of is the latter
end of the year 1780.

In this situation of things it was found not only expedient but
absolutely necessary for Congress to state the whole case to its
ally. I knew more of this matter (before it came into Congress or
was known to General Washington) of its progress, and its issue,
than I chuse to state in this letter. Col. John Laurens was sent to
France as Envoy Extraordinary on this occasion, and by a private
agreement between him and me I accompanied him. We sailed
from Boston in the Alliance frigate, Feb. 11th, 1781. France had
already done much in accepting and paying bills drawn by Congress. She was now called upon to do more. The event of Col.
Lauren's mission, with the aid of the venerable minister, Franklin, was, that France gave in money, as a present, six millions of
livres, and ten millions more as a loan, and agreed to send a fleet
of not less than thirty sail of the line, at her own expence, as an
aid to America. Col. Laurens and myself returned from Brest the
1st of June following, taking with us two millions and an half of
livres (upwards of one hundred thousand pounds sterling) of
the money given, and convoying two ships with stores.[26]

We arrived at Boston the 25th August following. De Grasse
arrived with the French fleet in the Chesapeak at the same time,
and was afterwards joined by that of Barras, making 31 sail of
the line. The money was transported in waggons from Boston to
the Bank at Philadelphia, of which Mr. Thomas Willing, who has
since put himself at the head of the list of petitioners in favour
of the British treaty, was then President, and it was by the aid of
this money, and of this fleet, and of Rochambeau's army, that
Cornwallis was taken; the lawrels of which have been unjustly
given to Mr. Washington. His merit in that affair was no more
than that of any other American officer.

I have had, and still have, as much pride in the American revolution as any man, or as Mr. Washington has a right to have;
but that pride has never made me forgetful from whence the
great aid came that compleated the business. Foreign aid (that
of France) was calculated upon at the commencement of the
revolution. It is one of the subjects treated of in the pamphlet
Common Sense, but as a matter that could not be hoped for, unless
Independence was declared.

It is as well the ingratitude as the pusillanimity of Mr. Washington and the Washington faction, that has brought upon America the loss of character she now suffers in the world, and the numerous evils her commerce has undergone, and to which it is yet exposed. The British ministry soon found out what sort of men they had to deal with, and they dealt with them accordingly; and if further explanation was wanting, it has been fully given since in the snivelling address of the New-York Chamber of Commerce to the President,[27] and in that of sundry merchants of Philadelphia, which was not much better.[28]

When the revolution of America was finally established by the termination of the war, the world gave her credit for great character; and she had nothing to do but to stand firm upon that ground. The British ministry had their hands too full of trouble to have provoked unnecessarily a rupture with her, had she shewn a proper resolution to defend her rights. But encouraged as they were by the submissive character of her executive administration, they proceeded from insult to insult till none more were left to be offered. The proposals made by Sweden and Denmark to the American administration were disregarded. I know not if so much as an answer has been returned to them. The minister *penitentiary* (as some of the British prints called him) Mr. Jay, was sent on a pilgrimage to London, to make all up by penance and petition. In the mean time the lengthy and drowsy writer of the pieces signed *Camillus* held himself in reserve to vindicate every thing; and to sound, in America, the tocsin of terror upon the inexhaustible resources of England. Her resources, says he, are greater than those of all the other powers. This man is so intoxicated with fear and finance that he knows not the difference between *plus* and *minus*—between an hundred pounds in hand, and an hundred pounds worse than nothing.[29]

The commerce of America, so far as it had been established by all the treaties that had been formed prior to that by Jay, was free, and the principles upon which it was established were good. That ground ought never to have been departed from. It was the justifiable ground of right, and no temporary difficulties ought to have induced an abandonment of it. The case now is otherwise. The ground, the scene, the pretensions, the every thing, are changed. The commerce of America is, by Jay's treaty, put under foreign dominion. The sea is not free for her. Her right to navigate it is reduced to the right of escaping; that is, until some ship of England or France, stops her vessels and carries them into port. Every article of American produce, whether from the sea or the land, fish, flesh, vegetable, or manufacture, is, by Jay's treaty, made either contraband or seizable. Nothing is exempt. In all other treaties of commerce the article which enumerates the contraband articles, such as fire arms, gun powder, &c. is followed by another article which enumerates the articles not contraband: but it is not so in Jay's treaty. There is no exempting article. Its place is supplied by the article for seizing and carrying into port; and the sweeping phrase of "provisions and *other articles*," includes every thing.[30] There never was such a base and servile treaty of surrender since treaties began to exist.

This is the ground upon which America now stands. All her rights of commerce and navigation have to commence anew, and that with loss of character to begin with. If there is sense enough left in the heart to call a blush into the cheek, the Washington administration must be ashamed to appear.————And as to you, sir, treacherous in private friendship (for so you have been to me, and that in the day of danger) and a hypocrite in public life, the world will be puzzled to decide, whether you are an apostate or an impostor; whether you have abandoned good principles, or whether you ever had any?[31]

THOMAS PAINE.

Thomas Paine, *Letter to General Washington, President of the United States of America. On Affairs Public and Private* (Philadelphia, 1796).

James Monroe, U.S. minister to France, wrote Virginia congressman James Madison from Paris on 5–31 July: "*From what I learn from the bearer of this and notwithstanding my efforts to prevent it Paine will probably compromit me by publishing some things which he picked up while in my house.* It was natural unaided as *I have been here or rather harassed from every quarter that I talked with this man but it was not so to expect that he would commit such a breach of confidence as well as of ingratitude—perhaps it may appear to proceed from other sources if so my name will not be involved* and that is greatly to be wished: *but otherwise the above is the state of facts*" (*Papers of James Monroe*, 4:38–42; quote on 41; italics represent Madison's decipherment of material written in code). For Monroe's relationship with Paine while minister to France, see Ammon, *James Monroe*, 135–37; see also Monroe to Enoch Edwards, 12 Feb. 1798, and Edwards to Monroe, 20 April 1798, in *Papers of James Monroe*, 4:247, 267–68.

Paine's pamphlet drew interest from Federalists. Vice President John Adams wrote his wife Abigail from Philadelphia on 4 Dec. 1796: "Mr Paines long threatned Pamphlet against the President it is Supposed is Arrived and Mr Bache is to publish it, in the form of a Letter to George Washington. It is even

Said that a Patent is to be obtained for the exclusive Priviledge of publishing it" (*Adams Family Correspondence*, 11:430–32; quote on 431).

John Adams wrote more colorfully to Abigail on 8 Dec.: "They kept back Paines Letter Several Weeks, presuming no doubt that it would not promote their Election. It appeared for the first, this morning.

"I think, of all Paines Productions it is the weakest and at the Sametime the most malicious.—The Man appears to me to be mad—not drunk—He has the Vanity of the Lunatick who believed himself to be Jupiter the Father of Gods & Men" (*Adams Family Correspondence*, 11:440–41; see also Charles Adams to John Adams, 28 Dec., in *Adams Family Correspondence*, 11:463–65).

Abigail Adams commented on Paine's effort when she wrote her son John Quincy Adams from Quincy, Mass., on 3 March 1797: "Tom Paynes Letter to the President has greatly Served the cause of Liberty and Religion. even the Jacobins are ashamed of him. he is considerd as an apostate an out cast. like Cain there is a Mark sit upon him. he is accursed on the Earth" (*Adams Family Correspondence*, 12:4–7; quote on 6).

The *Massachusetts Mercury* (Boston) for 13 Jan. 1797 printed a lengthy commentary under the heading "*OF PAINE'S LETTER to WASHINGTON.* THOMAS PAINE, has written a letter to the President of the U.S. dated Paris, July 30, 1796, which his correspondent Benjamin Franklin Bache, has published and *secured the copy right according to law.* It might admit of some doubt, whether the entry of this letter according to law would secure the exclusive right of publication, either to the writer or printer—one would think the President at least might dispute the point, tho it is certain that the good and great man will care as little about the copy right of the calumny, as about the calumny itself.

"This letter however is the most extraordinary composition of abuse, petulance, falsehood and boyish vanity that ever came from Grub-street, a prison or a garret. . . .

"Such a mixture of meanness, ignorance and vanity, is a rare thing even in the history of 'Republican ingratitude.'" For Benjamin Franklin Bache's involvement with Paine's pamphlet, see Tagg, *Benjamin Franklin Bache,* 282–83.

William Cobbett published a refutation of Paine's pamphlet in his production titled *Porcupine's Political Censor, For December, 1796. Containing, Remarks on the Debates in Congress, Particularly on the Timidity of the Language Held Towards France. Also, A Letter to the Infamous Tom Paine, In answer to his brutal attack on the Federal Constitution, and on the conduct and character of General Washington* (Philadelphia, [1796]). GW took cognizance of Paine's pamphlet and Cobbett's response (see GW to David Stuart, 8 Jan. 1797, DLC:GW).

For an exchange centered on Charles Lucas Pinckney Horry's anonymously published *A Five Minutes Answer to Paine's Letter to Genl Washington* (London, 1797), see Horry to GW, 23 April 1798, and GW to Horry, 6 May 1798, in *Papers, Retirement Series,* 2:245–46.

1. Paine supplied a footnote at this place: "I have always been opposed to the mode of refining Government up to an individual, or what is called a single Executive. Such a man will always be the chief of a party. A plurality is far better: It combines the mass of a nation better together: And besides this,

it is necessary to the manly mind of a republic, that it loses the debasing idea of obeying an individual" (p. 5).

2. The extract appears here in Paine's pamphlet: "You touch me on a very tender point when you say, *that my friends on your side the water cannot be reconciled to the idea of my abandoning America, even for my native England.* They are right. I had rather see my horse Button eating the grass of Bordentown or Morrisenia, than see all the pomp and shew of Europe.

"A thousand years hence, for I must indulge a few thoughts, perhaps in less, America may be what England now is. The innocence of her character, that won the hearts of all nations in her favour, may sound like a romance, and her inimitable virtue as if it had never been. The ruins of that liberty, which thousands bled to obtain, may just furnish materials for a village tale, or extort a sigh from rustic sensibility; whilst the fashionable of that day, enveloped in dissipation, shall deride the principle and deny the fact.

"When we contemplate the fall of empires & the extinction of the nations of the ancient world, we see but little more to excite our regret than the mouldering ruins of pompous palaces, magnificent monuments, lofty pyramids, and walls and towers of the most costly workmanship: But when the empire of America shall fall, the subject for contemplative sorrow will be infinitely greater than crumbling brass or marble can inspire. It will not then be said, here stood a temple of vast antiquity, here rose a babel of invisible height, or there a palace of sumptuous extravagance; but here, ah painful thought! the noblest work of human wisdom, the grandest scene of human glory, the fair cause of freedom rose and fell. Read this, and then ask, if I forget America?" (pp. 8–9).

3. Paine supplied a footnote at this place: "Two persons to whom John Adams said this, told me of it. The secretary of Mr. Jay was present when it was told to me" (p. 11).

4. Paine supplied a footnote at this place: "If Mr. Jay desires to know on what authority I say this, I will give that authority publicly when he chuses to call for it" (p. 12).

5. Paine explained over the next three paragraphs how his imprisonment in France related to his birth in England (see pp. 13–15).

6. Paine presented over the next three paragraphs circumstances of his imprisonment (see pp. 16–17).

7. A portion of the letter completes this paragraph in Paine's pamphlet: "Mr. Monroe has told me that he has no orders (meaning from the President, Mr. Washington) respecting you, but that he (Mr. Monroe) will do every thing in his power to liberate you; but from what I learn from the Americans lately arrived in Paris, you are not considered, either by the American government or by the individuals, as an American citizen" (p. 19).

8. Paine's memorial to Monroe, dated 14 Sept. 1794 at "Prison of the Luxembourg," detailed his views on why members of the U.S. government should seek his release from imprisonment on the basis of his being an American citizen (*Papers of James Monroe*, 3:67–73; Paine's pamphlet misdates an abridged version of this memorial as 10 Sept. 1796 [65–76]; see also Paine's two letters to Monroe, dated 13 Oct. 1794, in *Papers of James Monroe*, 3:104–9).

9. The letter from Monroe to Paine written at Paris on 18 Sept. 1794 refuted Paine's position that members of the U.S. government took no interest in his release from prison and declared that he considered Paine "an American citizen, and that you are considered universally in that character by the people of America." Monroe also ventured: "Of the sense which the President has always entertained of your merits, and of his friendly disposition towards you, you are too well assured to require any declaration of it from me. That I forward his wishes in seeking your safety is what I well know, and this will form an additional obligation on me to perform what I should otherwise consider as a duty" (pp. 20–23; see also *Papers of James Monroe*, 3:81–82). For Paine's reply to Monroe dated 4 Oct. 1794, see *Papers of James Monroe*, 3:97–98.

10. This word is misprinted as "given" in Paine's pamphlet (p. 23).

11. A portion of a letter from Paine to Monroe completes this paragraph in Paine's pamphlet: "It will not add to the popularity of Mr. Washington to have it believed in America, as it is believed here, that he connives at my imprisonment" (p. 24). Similar language appears in Paine's letter to Monroe written on 21 Oct. 1794 (see *Papers of James Monroe*, 3:128–34, especially 131).

12. See GW to Gouverneur Morris, 19 and 25 June 1794.

13. See n.15 below.

14. Paine's pamphlet presents his letter to GW written at Paris on 20 Sept. 1795. The letter questioned the president's lack of interest in freeing him from prison (see pp. 29–31; for an edited version of the ALS, see *Papers, Presidential Series*).

15. A letter from Paine to GW written at Paris on 22 Feb. 1795 appears here in Paine's pamphlet: "As it is always painful to reproach those one would wish to respect, it is not without some difficulty that I have taken the resolution to write to you. The dangers to which I have been exposed cannot have been unknown to you, and the guarded silence you have observed upon that circumstance is what I ought not to have expected from you, either as a friend or as President of the United States.

"You know enough of my character to be assured, that I could not have deserved imprisonment in France, and without knowing any thing more than this, you had sufficient ground to have taken some interest for my safety. Every motive arising from recollection of times past, ought to have suggested to you the propriety of such a measure. But I cannot find that you have so much as directed any enquiry to be made, whether I was in prison or at liberty, dead or alive; what the cause of that imprisonment was, or whether there was any service or assistance you could render. Is this what I ought to have expected from America after the part I have acted towards her, or will it redound to her honour or to yours, that I tell the story. I do not hesitate to say, that you have not served America with more disinterestedness or greater zeal, or more fidelity, than myself, and I know not if with better effect. After the revolution of America was established I ventured into new scenes of difficulties to extend the principles which that revolution had produced, and you rested at home to partake of the advantages. In the progress of events you beheld yourself a President in America and me a prisoner in France. You folded your arms, forgot your friend, and became silent.

"As every thing I have been doing in Europe was connected with my wishes for the prosperity of America, I ought to be the more surprised at this conduct on the part of her government. It leaves me but one mode of explanation, which is, *that every thing is not as it ought to be amongst you*, and that the presence of a man who might disapprove, and who had credit enough with the Country to be heard and believed, was not wished for. This was the operating motive with the despotic faction that imprisoned me in France (tho' the pretence was, that I was a foreigner) and those that have been silent and inactive towards me in America, appear to me to have acted from the same motive, of wishing me out of the way. It is impossible for me to discover any other.

"Considering the part I have acted in the revolution of America it is natural that I feel interested in whatever relates to her character and prosperity. Though I am not on the spot, to see what is immediately acting there, I see some part of what she is acting in Europe. For your own sake, as well as for that of America, I was both surprised and concerned at the appointment of Gouverneur Morris to be minister to France. His conduct has proved that the opinion I had formed of that appointment was well founded. I wrote that opinion to Mr. Jefferson at the time, and I was frank enough to say the same thing to Morris—*that it was an unfortunate appointment.* His prating, insignificant pomposity, rendered him at once offensive, suspected, and ridiculous; and his total neglect of all business had so disgusted the Americans, that they proposed entering a protest against him. He carried this neglect to such an extreme, that it was necessary to inform him of it, and I asked him one day if he did not feel himself ashamed to take the money of the country and do nothing for it. But Morris is so fond of profit and voluptuousness that he cares nothing about character. Had he not been removed at the time he was, I think his conduct would have precipitated the two countries into a rupture; and in this case, hated *systematically*, as America is and ever will be by the British government, and suspected by France, the commerce of America would have fallen a prey to both countries.

"If the inconsistent conduct of Morris exposed the interest of America to some hazard in France, the pusillanimous conduct of Mr. Jay in England has rendered the character of the American government contemptible in Europe. Is it possible that any man who has contributed to the independence of America, and to free her from the tyranny and injustice of the British government, can read, without shame and indignation, the note of Jay to Grenville? It is a satire upon the declaration of Independence, and an encouragement to the British government to treat America with contempt. At the time this minister of petitions was acting this miserable part, he had every means in his hands to enable him to have done his business as he ought. The success or failure of his mission depended upon the success or failure of the French arms. Had France failed, Mr. Jay might have put his humble petition in his pocket and gone home. The case happened to be otherwise, and he has sacrificed the honour and perhaps all the advantages of it, by turning petitioner. I take it for granted, that he was sent to demand indemnification for the captured property; and in this case, if he thought he wanted a preamble to his demand, he might have said: 'That tho' the government of England might suppose itself under the necessity of seizing American property bound to France, yet that supposed necessity could not preclude indemnification to the proprietors, who, acting under the authority of their own government, were not accountable to any other.'— But Mr. Jay sets out with an implied recognition of the right of the British government to seize and condemn; for he enters his complaint against the *irregularity* of the seizures and the condemnation, as if they were reprehensible only by not being *conformable* to the *terms* of the proclamation under which they were seized. Instead of being the Envoy of a government he goes over like a lawyer to demand a new trial. I can hardly help believing, that Grenville wrote the note himself and Jay signed it, for the stile of it is domestic and not diplomatic. The term, *His* Majesty, used without any descriptive epithet, always signifies the king whom the Minister that speaks represents. If this sinking of the demand into a petition was a juggle between Grenville and Jay, to cover the indemnification, I think it will end in another juggle, that of never paying the money, and be made use of afterwards to preclude the right of demanding it; for Mr. Jay has virtually disowned the right, *by appealing to the magnanimity of his Majesty against the capturers.* He has appointed this magnanimous Majesty to be umpire in the case, and the government of the United States must abide by the decision. If, Sir, I turn some part of this affair into ridicule, it is to avoid the unpleasant sensation of serious indignation.

"Among other things, which I confess I do not understand, is the proclamation of neutrality. This has always appeared to me as an assumption on the part of the executive not warranted by the constitution. But passing this over, as a disputable case, and considering it only as political, the consequence has been that of sustaining the losses of war without the balance of reprisals. When the profession of neutrality on the part of America was answered by hostilities on the part of Britain, the object and intention of that neutrality existed no longer, and to maintain it after this was not only to encourage further insults and depredations, but was an informal breach of neutrality towards France, by passively contributing to the aid of her enemy. That the government of England considered the American government as pusillanimous is evident from the encreasing insolence of the former towards the latter, till the affair of General Wayne. She then saw it might be possible to kick a government into some degree of spirit. So far as the proclamation of neutrality was intended to prevent a dissolute spirit of privateering in America under foreign colours, it was undoubtedly laudable; but to continue it as a government neutrality, after the commerce of the country was made war upon, was submission and not neutrality. I have heard so much about this thing called neutrality, that I know not if the ungenerous and dishonorable silence (for I must call it such) that has been observed by your part of the government towards me, during my imprisonment, has not in some measure arisen from that policy.

"Tho' I have written you this letter, you ought not to suppose it has been an agreeable undertaking to me. On the contrary, I assure you, it has cost me some disquietude. I am sorry you have given me cause to do it; for as I have always remembered your former friendship with pleasure, I suffer a loss by your depriving me of that sentiment" (pp. 31–38; this letter does not appear elsewhere in *Papers, Presidential Series*). For correspondence referenced in

Paine's letter, see Paine to Thomas Jefferson, 13 Feb. 1792, in *Jefferson Papers*, 23:115, and John Jay to Lord Grenville, 30 July 1794, in Johnston, *Jay Papers*, 4:38–41.

16. An extract from the newspaper publication completes this paragraph in Paine's pamphlet: "It appears moreover, that the people of England did not relish his (Thomas Paine's) opinions quite so well as he expected, and that for one of his last pieces, as destructive to the peace and happiness of their country, (meaning, I suppose, the *Rights of Man*[)] they threatened our knight-errant with such serious vengeance, that, to avoid a trip to Botany-bay, he fled over to France, as a less dangerous voyage" (p. 38).

17. Paine supplied a footnote at this place: "I know not who the writer of the piece is; but some late Americans say it is Phineas Bond, an American refugee, and now a British Consul; and that he writes under the signature of Peter Skunk, or Peter Porcupine, or some such signature" (p. 39).

18. See n.15 above.

19. Paine supplied a footnote at this place: "It was the embarrassment into which the affairs and credit of America were thrown at this instant by the report above alluded to, that made it necessary to contradict it, and that by every means arising from opinion or founded upon authority. The Committee of Public Safety, existing at that time, had agreed to the full execution, on their part, of the treaty between America and France, notwithstanding some equivocal conduct on the part of the American government, not very consistent with the good faith of an ally; but they were not in a disposition to be imposed upon by a counter-treaty. That Jay had no instructions beyond the points above stated, or none that could possibly be construed to extend to the length the British treaty goes, was a matter believed in America, in England and in France; and without going to any other source it followed naturally from the message of the President to Congress, when he nominated Jay upon that mission. The secretary of Mr. Jay came to Paris soon after the treaty with England had been concluded, and brought with him a copy of Mr. Jay's instructions, which he offered to shew to me as a *justification of Jay*. I advised him, as a friend, not to shew them to any body, and did not permit him to shew them to me. Who is it, said I to him, that you intend to implicate as censureable by shewing those instructions? Perhaps that implication may fall upon your own government. Though I did not see the instructions I could not be at a loss to understand, that the American administration had been playing a double game" (pp. 41–42).

20. The article completes this paragraph in Paine's pamphlet: "The most christian king and the United States engage mutually, not to grant any particular favour to other nations in respect of commerce and navigation that shall not immediately become common to the other party, who shall enjoy the same favour freely, if the concession was freely made, or on allowing the same compensation if the concession was conditional" (p. 46; see also Miller, *Treaties*, 5).

21. An analysis of the Jay Treaty and its impact on relations between the United States and France continues for three paragraphs in Paine's pamphlet (see pp. 46–49).

22. Paine presents GW's letter introducing Monroe as the new U.S. minister

to France charged with "*drawing closer the bonds of our friendship*" (pp. 49–50; see also GW to the Committee of Public Safety of the French Republic, 28 May 1794, second letter).

23. Paine quotes the opening of GW's remarks to French minister Pierre-Auguste Adet dated 1 Jan. 1796: "Born, sir (said he) in a land of liberty; *having* early learned its value; *having* engaged in a perilous conflict to defend it; *having*, in a word, devoted the best years of my life to secure its permanent establishment in my own country; *my* anxious recollections, *my* sympathetic feelings, and *my* best wishes are irresistibly excited, whenever, in any country, I see an oppressed people unfurl the banners of freedom" (p. 53; see also GW to the U.S. Senate and House of Representatives, 4 Jan. 1796, and GW to the President of the French Directory, 7 Jan. 1796).

24. For Elizabeth Thompson (born c.1703) and her services as GW's housekeeper during the Revolutionary War, see GW to Caleb Gibbs, 1 May 1777, and n.4 to that document, in *Papers, Revolutionary War Series*, 9:320–23, and Thompson to GW, 10 Oct. 1783 (DLC:GW).

25. Paine reviewed the course of the Revolutionary War starting in June 1775 over the next four paragraphs (see pp. 55–58).

26. For correspondence on this mission to France, see Samuel Huntington to Benjamin Franklin, 27 Dec. 1780 and 1 Jan. 1781; Samuel Cooper to Franklin, 1 Feb. 1781; and John Laurens to Franklin, 9 March 1781, in *Franklin Papers*, 34:212–13, 243–45, 334–38, 433–34; see also GW to Franklin, 15 Jan. 1781 (DLC:GW).

27. Paine apparently alludes to a letter dated 14 Dec. 1795 only known from other correspondence (see Bartholomew Dandridge, Jr., to Timothy Pickering, 23 Dec. 1795, and n.1 to that document).

28. Paine probably refers to Philadelphia Subscribers, Merchants, and Traders to GW, 20 Aug. 1795.

29. Camillus served as a pseudonym for Alexander Hamilton and Rufus King. For GW's approval of Camillus, see his letter to Hamilton, 29 July 1795.

30. Paine refers to Article XVIII in the Jay Treaty (see Miller, *Treaties*, 258–59).

31. For an example of Paine's disparagement of GW in private correspondence, see his letter to Madison, 24 Sept. 1795, in *Madison Papers*, 16:89–93.

From Nathaniel Pendleton

Sir   Savannah. July 30th 1796.

It is with reluctance I find myself Obliged to resign the appointment I hold in the judicial department as judge of the district of Georgia—The duty I owe to my children compels me to quit an office, the compensation for which will not afford me the means of giving them an education suitable to their condition.

I have therefore determined to resign on the first day of September next, which compleats the seventh year since I had the honor to be appointed to this office.

I have thought it most proper thus early to inform you of this determination, from an idea that it would be agreeable to you to have some time to think of the most proper person to fill the vacancy. I have the honor to be with sentiments of the most respectful Attachment, Sir, Your most obedient Humble Servant

Nathl Pendleton

ALS, DNA: RG 59, Letters of Resignation and Declination from Federal Office.

Pendleton again wrote GW on 31 Aug.: "I had the Honor some time since, of apprising you of my intention of resigning my commission as District judge of Georgia, and of the motive that induced it. I do now accordingly resign the said Commission" (ALS, NN: Emmet Collection). Joseph Clay, Jr., replaced Pendleton (see Joseph Habersham to GW, 10 Aug.).

From Timothy Pickering

Sir,   Department of State July 30. 1796.

With very sincere pleasure I announce to you the ratification of the treaty with Spain. I received the ratified copy this day by the mail from New-York, with a certificate signed by the Prince of Peace and Mr Rutledge of the exchange of the ratifications, as on the 25th of April. I do not know why the certificate and the ratification on the part of Spain bear that date; for the treaty ratified by the Executive of the U. States did not get to Mr Rutledge's hands until the third of May; unless it was to bring the transaction within the six months allowed by the treaty for the exchange of the ratifications: the treaty having been signed on the 27th of October.[1]

A letter, also recd to-day, from Mr Simpson, our Consul at Gibraltar, dated the 18th of June, mentions that he had been alongside a Swedish brig from Algiers, which she left on the 7th and tells the unwelcome news that the plague had broken out in that city; 15 to 20 dying in a day, agreeably to the bill of health from Consul Skjoldebrand:[2] but the master of the brig assured Mr Simpson that no American or other captive had then fallen a victim to it. The Swedish Captain said also that Mr Donaldson had not returned from Leghorn when he left Algiers—June 7th.[3] I am most respectfully sir, yr obt servt

Timothy Pickering

ALS, DNA: RG 59, Miscellaneous Letters; LB, DNA: RG 59, Domestic Letters; LB, DNA: RG 59, GW's Correspondence with His Secretaries of State.

1. Article XXIII of the 27 Oct. 1795 treaty of friendship and navigation with Spain specified that ratifications should be exchanged within six months "or sooner if possible" (Miller, *Treaties*, 338; see also GW's Notes on the Treaty with Spain, 22–26 Feb. 1796; GW to the U.S. Senate, 26 Feb., and n.1 to that document; and GW to Pickering, 6 March, and n.4).

Charles Rutledge (1773–1821) was the U.S. chargé d'affaires at Madrid.

2. Simpson is referring to the Swedish consul at Algiers, Mathias (Mattias) Arkimboldus Skjöldebrand (1765–1813), rather than his brother Pierre Eric (Per Erik) Skjöldebrand (1769–1826), who had declined an offer to become U.S. consul at that place.

3. James Simpson's letter to Pickering dated 18 June 1796 is in DNA: RG 59, Consular Despatches, Gibraltar. For the reason Joseph Donaldson, Jr., traveled to Leghorn, see Pickering to GW, 27 July.

GW replied to Pickering from Mount Vernon on 5 Aug.: "With much pleasure did I receive the information, contained in your letter of the 30th Ulto, of the ratification of the Treaty with Spain, by the Government of that Country. The unwelcome news of the Plague being at Algiers, is an Alloy thereto; but we must trust that Providence will prevent our unhappy fellow-citizens at that place from suffering by that malady.

"Much is it to be regretted that so many untoward accidents should have prevented the redemption money from getting to that Regency before this event took place; but as there has been no want of exertion in the government to accomplish this; no *blame* attaches itself, whatever may happen" (ALS, MHi: Pickering Papers; copy, DNA: RG 59, Miscellaneous Letters; LB, DNA: RG 59, GW's Correspondence with His Secretaries of State).

From Thomas Pinckney

Dear Sir   London 31st July 1796

In my letter of the 7th of May I took the liberty of assigning my reasons for postponing for the present to make the overtures, authorized by your favor of the 5th of March, to the imperial Minister as I then entertained some hope that this Government might be induced to interfere in behalf of M. La Fayette. this hope was not quite extinguished till the begining of this month, and I was prepared to open the business to Count Stahremberg the Imperial Minister here, when I received your letter of the 22d May with its inclosures.

As I was apprised of no former attempts which I considered of equal weight to influence the Emperor to liberate our friend & as I conceived it to be possible that in the present uncertain & fluctuating state to which late events must have reduced the politics of the Court of Vienna with respect to french Affairs,[1] that the Emperor might not be displeased at having so fit an opportunity of freeing himself at the same time from the Odium of this imprisonment & of avoiding any embarrassment which might eventually arise on this account in negociating with the Government of France, I took an early opportunity of conferring with Count Stahremberg & of committing your letter to his charge, urging him at the same time to support the request therein contained with his interest: this he promised to do & if he acts in conformity to his declarations the influence of his friends at Vienna may be advantageous.[2]

I was happy, Sir, to find you had an opportunity of making so unexceptionable an appointment to this Mission as occurred by Mr Kings resolution, to quit his Seat in the Senate:[3] this Gentleman arrived just in time to be presented to their Majesties previous to their setting out for Weymouth & he accordingly had his introductory audiences on the 27th & 28th of this month: the necessary papers shall be immediately transferred, & every information in my power to impart shall be cheerfully communicated to him.

Lord Grenville shall be informed of the sense you entertain of his politeness in directing the permit to be sent to Liverpool for the embarkation of the seed peas & vetches which your agent there had purchased for your use.

As my departure has been unavoidably postponed to this period I do not now purpose to embark 'till after the Autumnal Equinox when it is my intention to sail direct for Charleston.

At this close of my diplomatic career permit me, Sir, to express my unfeigned thanks for the confidence with which you first appointed[4] & have since continued to support me in the execution of the duties of my Mission, & to assure you of the continued attachment and affectionate respect of Dear Sir Your faithful & most obedt Servant

Thomas Pinckney

ALS, PHi: Gratz Collection.

1. Pinckney presumably referenced French military successes in Italy and Germany. *The Times* (London) for 24 June 1796 printed a summary: "The reverses which have happened to the Imperial armies in Italy, as well as on the Rhine, have prepared the Public to expect that the EMPEROR must be forced into a Peace, in order to save those dominions still in his possession. The with-

drawing of the Neapolitan troops, who form a considerable part of General BEAULIEU's army, and the discouragement of the Austrian troops, who are forced to retreat in every direction, may at length have disposed the Cabinet of VIENNA to accede to the propositions of the DIRECTORY for a Peace.— However disadvantageous such a Peace may be, it appears to be the only means of extricating the EMPEROR from his difficulties."

2. For other efforts to free Lafayette from prison, see Justus Erick Bollman to GW, 1 April; GW to Francis II (Holy Roman Emperor), 15 May; and La Rochefoucauld-Liancourt to GW, 25 July.

3. GW had nominated Rufus King to replace Pinckney as U.S. minister to Great Britain (see GW's first message to the U.S. Senate, 19 May, and n.1 to that document).

4. For Pinckney's nomination as U.S. minister to Great Britain, see GW to the U.S. Senate, 22 Dec. 1791; see also Thomas Jefferson to GW, 6 Nov. 1791, and n.2 to that document.

From Solomon Cotton, Jr.

Sir   Boston Augt 1 1796

In confidence of your indulgence towards whatever is conducive to the public good, you are now addressed by a young man, with all that respect and veneration, due to your revered character; who intreats your acceptance of the Volume accompanying this letter.[1]

That you may enjoy all the happiness this life will admit of, & be received hereafter into the immortal temple of the most High is the ardent wish of Sir Your Most Obedient & very Humble Servant

Solomon Cotton Junr

ALS, DLC:GW.

Solomon Cotton, Jr. (1775–1806), a Boston bookseller, shifted his business to Baltimore in 1797.

1. Cotton presented GW with *A Collection of the Speeches of the President of the United States to Both Houses of Congress, At the opening of every Session, with their Answers. Also, the Addresses to the President, with his Answers, from the Time of his Election: With an Appendix, Containing The Circular Letter of General Washington to the Governors of the several States, and his Farewell Orders, to the Armies of America, and the Answer* (Boston, 1796). The likely presentation volume with GW's signature on the title page was in his library at his death (see Griffin, *Catalogue of the Washington Collection*, 219).

To James McHenry

Sir,   Mount Vernon 1st August 1796

The Post of Friday last brought me your dispatches of the 26th Ulto, with the Papers therein enclosed.[1]

The draught of a letter to the Agent of the Department of War, and the Instructions for the person proposed as Deputy paymaster and Storekeeper in the State of Tennessee, are guarded, and proper. The only doubt remaining with me, is whether so many Officers, in that quarter, are realy necessary; and whether some of them may not, in the public estimation, be considered (after the Indian Agent for that Department is appointed) in the light of sinecures. If, however, upon a thorough investigation of the duties of their several Offices, it shall be found that the service would be too hard upon a less number, or that they are necessary as checks, I consent to the appointment of Mr Hillis as Deputy Paymaster and Store keeper—provided his conduct in the Accomptants Office has afforded sufficient evidence of his fitness to discharge the duties required by your Instructions: to do which, properly, he ought to be a person of some experience in business; to be able to execute it with judgment; to possess firmness; and great integrity.

What will be the occupations of Mr Dinsmore? and what is become of a Mr Shaw (this was, if I recollect rightly the name of a person) who was sent some time ago by Genl Knox (while Secretary of War) into that quarter? There certainly can be no occasion for continuing the latter, if the former is retained.[2]

A Troop of Horse, in my opinion, may, for the reasons you have assigned, be necessary on the frontiers of Georgia, and I desire they may join Conolel Gaither accordingly.[3]

I have no objection to the releasement of Lieutt Geddis from his present arrest, at the request of those Officers who have asked it; But as the Attorney General will be at Philadelphia, I would have his opinion taken on the *power* of granting a pardon for the Offence of which he has been found guilty, and Cashiered; and the mode by which it may, with propriety, be accomplished: for it may be questioned, whether a remital of the Sentence of the Court, ought not to be preceeded by an act of approval, or rejection, as the foundation. At any rate some attention to the form (which I request may be given) will be necessary.

I am glad to find by Mr Byers letter to Colo. Henley, that Spiritous liquor is not necessary to carry on trade with the Indians.[4] I have always been of opinion that it was productive of more discontent & mischief than good, and therefore hope it will cease to be an article of Traffic on public Account.[5]

Go: Washington

LS (retained copy), DLC:GW; LB, DLC:GW.

1. The previous Friday was 29 July.

2. Leonard D. Shaw had served as an agent to the Cherokee Indians between January 1792 and his dismissal in 1793 (see Henry Knox to Tobias Lear, 16 Feb. 1792, and the source note to that document; Knox to GW, 8 April 1793, and n.4 to that document; and Lear to Knox, 20 April 1793).

3. McHenry wrote Gen. Anthony Wayne on 5 Aug. that GW had directed a company of cavalry "to join Lt. Colonel Gaither, who will be either at Coleraine on the St. Mary's or Fort Fidius. You will therefore be pleased to carry into immediate execution the President's commands" (Knopf, *Wayne*, 508).

4. James Byers, Jr. (1771–1854) of Springfield, Mass., became U.S. factor at the Tellico blockhouse in 1795. He subsequently acted as an army contractor during the War of 1812.

The letter from Byers to David Henley has not been identified.

5. McHenry replied to GW on 8 August.

To Timothy Pickering

Sir,   Mount Vernon August 1st 1796

Your letters of the 26th[1] and 27th Ulto were received by the Post on friday last.[2]

Forwarding without further direction, the Commission appointing Mr Davis Attorney for the District of Massachusetts in place of Mr Otis, after satisfactorily ascertaining those points which had occasioned the hesitation, was perfectly conformable to my intention.

I rejoice to find by the account you have given of the contents of the dispatches from Colo. Humphreys, that there is a probability of the speedy release of our captives in Algiers; that the Dey had recovered his temper; and that Mr Barlow had been received as our Consul at that place.

The suggestions of that Gentlem[an] relatively to the policy and utility of forming commercial, and friendly relations with the Italian States; with Austria; and with the Grand Seignior; deserves serious attention; & I not only request you to bestow it, but to ascertain in the best manner you can against my arrival in Philadelphia, the principles on which such connexions could be advantageously formed. Good measures should always be executed as soon as they are conceived—and circumstances will permit.

It has ever been my opinion from the little I have seen, and from what I have heard of Mr Barlow, that his abilities are adequate to any employment; & improved as they must have been by travel, & the political career he has run, there can be little doubt of his fitness, as a Negociator, for some of the countries abovementioned—with proper Instructions.

Go: Washington

ALS (duplicate), MHi: Pickering Papers; copy, in the writing of Bartholomew Dandridge, Jr., DNA: RG 59, Miscellaneous Letters; LB, DNA: RG 59, GW's Correspondence with His Secretaries of State.

1. For one of the letters that Pickering wrote GW on 26 July, see GW to Pickering, 20 July, n.2.

2. The previous Friday was 29 July.

To Oliver Wolcott, Jr.

Private

Dear Sir,   Mount Vernon 1st Augt 1796

Mr Dandridge having rejoined my family again, preceeds me to Philadelphia,[1] in order to bring up, & facilitate my Recording.[2]

He will ease you of the trouble of supplying Mr Kitts weekly calls, by placing the money you have receivd on my private account, in his hands, & furnishing him with more, if necessary, on account of my compensation as formerly.[3] With very great esteem & regard I am Dear Sir Your Affecte Servt

Go: Washington

ALS, CtHi: Oliver Wolcott, Jr., Papers.

1. For the resumption of Bartholomew Dandridge, Jr., as GW's private secretary, see GW to James McHenry, 1 Aug., found at GW to Dandridge, 5 June, n.4; see also GW to John Dandridge, 11 July.

2. Bartholomew Dandridge resumed entries in the account book on 8 Aug. after they had ceased on 14 June with GW's departure from Philadelphia. Among the entries recorded under 8 Aug. was one for $20 to cover "Dandridge's expenses from Mount Vernon" (Household Accounts; see also GW's first letter to Wolcott on 13 June, and Dandridge to GW, 7 Aug.).

3. Wolcott replied to GW from Philadelphia on 12 Aug.: "I have had the honour to receive your Letter of the first instant by Mr Dandridge & have paid to him the balance of the monies placed in my hands, & a sum of Five hundred Dollars on account of your compensation.

"There is nothing new here; the enclosed came under cover to me this morning" (ALS, DLC:GW; copy, CtHi: Oliver Wolcott, Jr., Papers). The enclosure has not been identified, but it may have been Alexander Hamilton's letter to GW dated 10 August.

From Charles Cotesworth Pinckney

(Duplicate)

Dear Sr   Charleston [S.C.] August 2d[–5] 1796

You will find from my letter of the 27th ultimo that I have accepted the very important mission you have confided to me. I shall be prepared to sail for Philadelphia this day week if any Vessel is ready, but we have none of the usual Traders now in the Harbour, and whether any will arrive and be ready to sail by that time depends on the Wind which has for some time past been adverse. Should a good opportunity offer for New York & none for Philadelphia, I shall take my passage for the former port, & proceed from thence by Land to the latter. The intense heat of the weather, & the sickliness of our lower Country at this Season prevent my attempting the Journey from this City by Land. As I wish to be detained at Philadelphia as short a time as you may think consistent with the public service, I should be very glad if all the necessary papers & instructions were prepared before my arrival.[1] If not improper I should request copies of all the letters & memorials that have passed both recently, & formerly from such a period as you may think necessary between the Gentlemen abroad & the Ministry there, and the Secretary of State at home, and also such as have passed between the Secretary of State & Minister at Philadelphia. As I do not know that I have any authority to entrust any person at Philadelphia with my appointment; I am obliged to request you to have the goodness to direct some proper person to engage a Passage in a good & safe Vessel for Mrs Pinckney, one of my Daughters & myself,[2] in such time that we may arrive at the destined port if possible before the Equinox; & if that is improbable, that then the time of departure may be so contrived, that we may be on neither

Coast but upon the open Sea at that season—I have desired my friend Mr Burrows by this opportunity to take lodgings for us, as I intended to spend a short time at Philadelphia in my way to the Eastern States.[3]

I received yesterday a Letter from my Brother dated London the 8th of June mentioning that the non arrival of his Letters of recall & the reasons urged by me against his arrival in this Climate in the Autumn, would probably induce him to remain there till after the Equinox. He says they were in an unpleasant state of suspence in that Country with regard to the passing of Laws in this to give effect to the provisions of the Treaty. He adds that if the Emperor should follow the King of Sardinia's example in making Peace,[4] he does not see any probability that France and England will soon agree upon terms, as the French seem determined not to cede any of their own or the Dutch possessions conquered by the English, & none of the parties in England appear to be disposed to relinquish the whole of their conquests as the price of Peace.[5] The original of your Letters have not yet arrived. With the sincerest veneration, esteem & attachment, I ever am your affectionate & obliged Sert

Charles Cotesworth Pinckney

August 5th 1796.
P.S. The originals of your letters arrived to day the postmark is Richmd July 11. 1796—I shall appropriate the Three hundred Dollars as you designed them[6]—There is no vessel in this Port bound for Philadelphia, but the Wind is Easterly & one is hourly expected, it is the Anne Capt: Switzer.[7]

ALS, MHi: Pickering Papers and DLC:GW. The body of the letter is in MHi; the postscript and cover are in DLC:GW.

1. For the instructions given Pinckney as the new U.S. minister to France, see Timothy Pickering's first letter to GW on 15 Sept., n.2; see also GW to Pickering, 10 August.

2. Eliza Lucas Pinckney, Pinckney's youngest daughter from his first marriage, accompanied Pinckney and his second wife, Mary Stead Pinckney, to France.

3. Originally from Charleston, S.C., William Ward Burrows (1758–1805) subsequently resided in the Northern Liberties about four miles from Philadelphia. President John Adams appointed him commandant of the newly created United States Marine Corps in 1798.

4. Sardinia and France signed an armistice on 28 April 1796 (see Parry, *Consolidated Treaty Series*, 53:81–85).

5. This letter from Thomas Pinckney, former U.S. minister to Great Britain, has not been identified.

6. See GW's two letters to Pinckney dated 8 July. The shorter communication contained $300 that GW had sent to relieve fire victims in Charleston.

7. Benjamin Sweetser commanded the brig *Ann.*

From James McHenry

Sir.   War office 3 August 1796.

I have received your letter of the 29th ulto with the treaty and papers relative to the Creeks.[1]

On looking over the treaty I find that it leaves to the President to mark the boundary line at such time and in such manner as he may direct. It is however mentioned by the commissioners, that since signing the treaty "several of the chiefs have urged that the President should cause the line to be run as soon as possible and make choice of the places for the posts," to which they add "we have promised them they shall hear from the President in four months."

I shall consider the whole and report upon it as soon as possible.

Captn Bruff received possession of Oswego on the 14th ulto. I transmit his letters announcing the event which came to hand yesterday.[2] That part of letter, July the 15, included in brackets, I have thought would be agreeable to you should be published. I shall therefore send it to one of the printers.[3]

I presume it will be proper to provide for supplying the garrisons of Oswego and Niagara with wood in the manner suggested by Cap. Bruff and at the same time to allow each post a siene.

From the arrangements relative to provisions I expect that the troops will be well and regularly supplied. I have also been collecting to West point the recruits within a certain circle to form another small detachment for Niagara.[4] I have the honour to be with the greatest respect Sir your most ob. st

James McHenry

ALS, DLC:GW; LB, DLC:GW.

1. For GW's letter to McHenry dated 29 July, see McHenry to GW, 25 July, n.4.

2. The enclosed letters from Capt. James Bruff have not been identified.

3. The *Gazette of the United States, & Philadelphia Daily Advertiser* for 3 Aug. printed an extract from Bruff's letter to McHenry "dated Fort Oswego or On-

tario, July 15 . . . I have the pleasure to announce that the British commandant at Fort Ontario wrote to me on the 13th instant that the king's stores were embarked and sent off; that he wished to get away with the detachment next morning at day light, and requested me to send an officer *that day* as early as possible.

"In consequence of this information and request, I instantly dispatched an officer; and next day (being the 14th) followed with the troops and two field pieces. On my arrival found the British garrison gone and Lieut. Elmer in possession of the fort. Immediately I landed the detachment and artillery and marched in, the music playing the President's march; and under a federal salute, displayed the flag of the United States from the citadel.

"With pleasure I mention that the British commandant left the barracks and every other building clean, and in the best order they would admit of." The British also "left their gardens filled with vegetables and fruit."

4. For GW's reply, see his second letter to McHenry on 8 August.

From James McHenry

Private.

Sir.   War office 3 August 1796.

It strikes me, as among the first measures arising out of the proceedings of the Creek commissioners,[1] that of a letter to the Governor of Georgia, somewhat in the stile of the inclosed.[2] It would prove a considerable saving to the U.S. could the defence of the frontiers be carried on by regular troops without the aid of militia. It would give more consistency to military operations there, and more certainty to their effects. It would besides lessen that thirst for Indian land & plunder which is kept up by militia incursions into their country.

I have thought also, that it might be proper to take off the edge from Mr Jacksons representations, by a letter that would hold up the prospect of obtaining through the means which he censures, the object which his party has seemingly at heart:[3] whilst, in another point of view, it is right, that militia which were expresly called into service on the ground that the frontiers were in danger should be dismissed when that danger is over.[4]

If you should approve of the draught with such amendments as may occur, you will be pleased, as I have no copy of it, to return it by next mail.[5] With the greatest and most sincere respect and attachment, I have the honour to be Sir your most ob. st

James McHenry

ALS, DLC:GW; ADf, MiU-C: James McHenry Papers.

1. McHenry had communicated the proceedings of the commissioners assigned to negotiate with the Creek Indians when he wrote GW on 25 July.

2. The enclosed draft has not been identified, but it presumably was an early version of the letter McHenry sent Georgia governor Jared Irwin on 23 Aug.: "The Agents appointed by the State of Georgia, to attend the meeting of the Representatives of the Creek Nation at Coleraine, have no doubt informed you of their refusal to sell any part of their lands.

"I am directed by the President to express on the occasion, his sincere regret, that a conference which he had flattered himself would have obtained the object for which it was principally projected, has failed of success.

"As he felt in this manner, he could not but receive with surprize, the protest of the Agents against the proceedings of the Commissioners of the United States, and lament that regulations calculated to inspire the Indians with confidence in the fairness of the intended negociation, should have worn to these Gentlemen a different aspect. . . .

"The Creeks . . . have among other things agreed, that Military and Trading posts may be erected within their boundary line, and that all animosities for past aggressions, shall henceforth cease, with an exception to the violaters of the Treaty of New York, now under arrest, who are to abide the decision of the law.

"These circumstances which evidence the sincerity of the Indians, and their disposition to peace, offer as you must perceive, the fairest opportunity of leading them by degrees to grant whatever is reasonable, and does not involve their ruin. It is therefore to be presumed, that the Citizens of Georgia will patiently wait their operation, and avoid whatever might disturb the tranquillity thus re-established. You no doubt in particular will duly appreciate the blessings of peace, and heartily co-operate with the President in every measure calculated to perpetuate its continuance.

"With this view, the President has directed such an arrangement, and use of the Troops of the United States, as ought to satisfy the Indians that their rights will be protected, and the Inhabitants of the frontiers, that they have nothing to apprehend from the Indians.

"These arrangements rendering it unnecessary to keep up the Militia Corps of Infantry and Cavalry; the Agent of the Department of War in Georgia, will be directed to settle their Muster and pay rolls up to the 15th September ensuing, after which time they will be considered as discharged" (GU-HR: Telamon Cuyler Collection; see also n.5 below).

3. McHenry was referring to James Jackson, one of the commissioners from Georgia that had protested the conduct of the U.S. commissioners sent to negotiate with the Creeks. Jackson's representations have not been identified.

4. For the authorization to use militia in Georgia's frontier defense, see Cabinet Opinion on Georgia and the Creek Indians, 29 May 1793, and n.1 to that document.

5. GW replied to McHenry from Mount Vernon on 8 Aug.: "Private . . . Your private letter of the 3d instant, accompanying the official one of the same date, came to hand by the last Post. The draught of the letter to the Governor

of Georgia is approved. I have added a word or two to the last paragraph but one—by way of *hint*, where we shall look for the cause, if Peace is not preserved on the frontier of that State.

"I request that you would *begin* to note the occurrences that have happened in the War Department (since the Adjournment of Congress) which will require to be communicated to that body in the Speech, or by messages, at the next Session. It is from the materials furnished by each Department, and the Memorandums taken by myself, that the first is framed; and it will be an omission, not to commit these to writing in the moment they occur; it being much easier to select, than to collect matter, for these purposes, when the hour arrives for digesting them into form. If other things (although they may be extraneous to your department) should occur, let them be noted also. It is better to have them *in all* than to *escape all* the Memorandums I shall be furnished with" (ALS, NhD; copy, DLC:GW; LB, DLC:GW). McHenry acknowledged this letter when he wrote GW on 11–12 August. For McHenry's revised letter to the Georgia governor, see n.2 above.

From Timothy Pickering

Sir,   Department of State August 3. 1796

In my letter of the 30th ulto which was forwarded by post the first instant, I had the pleasure to mention the arrival of the Spanish treaty, ratified by His Catholic Majesty.[1] I now do myself the honor to transmit the treaty itself (being a duplicate original) with a proclamation, for your signature, in order to promulgate the same to the citizens of the U. States.[2] I also inclose for your information, a translation of the form in which the treaty was ratified by his Catholic Majesty;[3] and am, with the highest respect, sir, your most obt servant

Timothy Pickering.

ALS, DNA: RG 59, Miscellaneous Letters; LB, DNA: RG 59, Domestic Letters; LB, DNA: RG 59, GW's Correspondence with His Secretaries of State.

1. See Pickering's second letter to GW dated 30 July.

2. GW replied to Pickering from Mount Vernon on 8 Aug.: "Your letter of the 3d instant, accompanying the ratified copy of the Spanish Treaty, by His Catholic Majesty, came to my hands by the last Post.

"The Proclamation annexed thereto, has received my Signature, and is herewith returned" (ALS, NjP: De Coppet Collection; LS [retained copy], DNA: RG 59, Miscellaneous Letters; LB, DNA: RG 59, GW's Correspondence with His Secretaries of State). The signed proclamation, dated 2 Aug., with a duplicate original of the treaty, is in DNA: RG 11, Treaty Series 325.

The treaty appears in *The Philadelphia Gazette & Universal Daily Advertiser* for 12 Aug. 1796.

3. The translation, filed with Pickering's letter to GW, reads: "Don Carlos, by the Grace of God . . . having seen and examined the said twenty three Articles, have approved and ratified, the contents thereof . . . wholly, in the most ample and best possible form, promising on the Word and Faith of King to fulfil and observe them, and to cause the same to be completely fulfilled and observed, as if I myself had signed them" (DNA: RG 59, Miscellaneous Letters).

From Oliver Wolcott, Jr.

Sir   Philadelphia Augt 3. 1796
    I have recd your favour of July 29th—the one refered to in answer of mine dated the 11th never came to hand: to what cause the accident is to be attributed I cannot conjecture.[1]
    We have no news more than appears in the papers; our Country was never more tranquil than at present: so far as I know the public business is in a good train, except that the Treasury is in want of Loans. I shall be able to prevent injury to the public credit, but the building of Frigates, will proceed more slowly than I could wish, & some arrears in the War Department will accumulate.
    There will be a meeting of the Commissioners of the Sinking Fund to consider whether circumstances do not require Sales of the Bank Stock held by the United States.[2] nothing will be done without the most mature consideration, in which I shall be assisted by the advice & opinion of the Chief Justice & Attorney General.[3]
    I take the liberty to enclose a Copy of an Oration delivered by Mr Smith at Charleston which I understand was well received by a numerous audience of all descriptions of people.[4] This I consider as a proof that the prejudices which lately existed in that City have greatly moderated.[5] I have the honour to be with perfect respect Sir, your most obedt servt

                                                Oliver Wolcott Jr

ALS, DLC:GW; copy, CtHi: Oliver Wolcott, Jr., Papers. GW replied to Wolcott on 10 August.
    1. For GW's letter to Wolcott dated 29 July, see Wolcott to GW, 23 July, n.5.
    2. See Proceedings of the Sinking Fund Commissioners, 1 June.
    3. Charles Lee was then-U.S. attorney general, and Oliver Ellsworth presided as chief justice of the U.S. Supreme Court.
    4. Wolcott enclosed William [Loughton] Smith, *An Oration, Delivered in St.*

Philip's Church, Before the Inhabitants of Charleston, South-Carolina, on the Fourth of July, 1796, in Commemoration of American Independence. By Appointment of the American Revolution Society, and Published at the Request of that Society, and also of the South-Carolina State Society of Cincinnati (Charleston, 1796), held in GW's library at his death (see Griffin, *Catalogue of the Washington Collection*, 189). In his oration, Smith praised Revolutionary War veterans and American women but primarily defended GW and his policies. He declaimed in a characteristic passage: "To reconcile a prudent temporizing with the rapidity of ever shifting events, and with the considerations justly due to our foreign relations, to resist the shocks continually produced by the exaggerated insinuations of intrigue and malevolence, or of an inconsiderate patriotism, to calm resentments, explain and remove difficulties, and draw a reflecting and judicious people around a single rallying point, the scrupulous observance of a fair neutrality; this was the arduous and sublime conduct which our federal executive has displayed; the maintenance of peace has been the grand pivot on which all his actions have turned, and on which he was content to hazard that, which, after his love for his country, holds the first place in his breast, its affection. Illustrious citizen! will posterity believe, that while you were thus struggling with difficulties before unknown, in a situation before untried, and straining all the vigorous faculties of your energetic mind, to shield the happiness of your country from impending danger, some of your very countrymen, with base ingratitude, and shameless indecency, not only reviled your judgment, but dared to impeach your purity.

"You once astonished the world by your military fame; you have since astonished it by your civil virtues; what will the astonished world exclaim at ingratitude like this?" (pp. 36–37).

5. Wolcott likely recalled opposition to the Jay Treaty (see Charleston, S.C., Citizens to GW, 22 July 1795, and Edmund Randolph to GW, 29 July 1795, n.1).

From Ségur

Paris August the 4th. Thermidor the 17th
Sir the 4th year of the Republic [1796]

I hope that your excellency will permit me to remember myself to you.[1] you have so much accustomed my relations and myself to your kindnesses that I don't fear to be troublesome in begging of you to be so kind as to forward the inclosed letter to Mr Lafayette my nephew. you are his second father, and I hope this motive will make you forgive the liberty which I take to put under your direction the letter which I write to him.[2]

I have received by an undirect way some news of his unfortunate father, his health is better, but his captivity does not soften at all, and his wife cannot obtain any thing from the Emperor. the passions which weaken and wear themselves out here, begin to let more than one influential person feel that it should be shameful to make peace without obtaining from the court of Vienna the liberation of the french men arrested for the cause of Liberty but this happy disposition is not as yet sufficiently general or pronounced. all what I desire is that it would be the wisdom and interest of the American government which would determine the french government to that measure. I know that my friend would doubly enjoy his liberty if he owed it to you. and it appears to me that the moment is arrived when the advice that I speak of, could be given to the directory without compromising the minister who would be entrusted with the commission.[3] I beg you would permit me with your usual Kindness to assure you of the tender attachement and of the profound respect with which I have the honour to be Sir of your excellency the most humble and most obedient Servant

signed L. P. segur

Translation, DLC:GW; ALS, in French, PHi: Gratz Collection.

1. GW had written Ségur on 1 July 1790; see also Ségur to GW, 24 Aug. 1789, 30 Sept. 1791, and 8 Feb. 1795.

2. Ségur's letter to George Washington Motier Lafayette has not been identified, but see n.3 below. Ségur had married Antoinette Daguesseau, Marquise de Lafayette's aunt, making him a great-uncle to young Lafayette.

3. For other efforts to assist Lafayette, see Justus Erick Bollman to GW, 1 April; GW to Francis II (Holy Roman Emperor), 15 May; and La Rochefoucauld-Liancourt to GW, 25 July; see also Thomas Pinckney to GW, 31 July.

In his reply to Ségur written at Mount Vernon on 24 June 1797, GW apologized for his tardy response occasioned by the letter's arrival "at a time when my official duties engrossed all my attention, to prepare for the Session of Congress which was then about to be held; and which, as was intended, closed the scene of my political career." GW also related that Ségur's letter for "Young La Fayette . . . was delivered immediately upon the receipt of it" and that he hoped "the joint efforts of Mr La Fayettes friends will be able to accomplish what neither my wishes, nor exertions have been able to do" (*Papers, Retirement Series*, 1:209–10).

To Timothy Pickering

Private

Dear Sir   Mount Vernon 5th Augt 1796.

Your private letters of the 29th & 30th have been received.[1]

If Mr Churchmans account respecting the broken seal of Mr Monroes letter, to the Department of State be true, it bespeaks the man of candour, and does him credit; but I do not see why, when called upon, he should require time to consider whether he should relate the truth—or "give a certificate that might excite suspicions of innocent people" the impropriety of the latter, would strike a man of honor the moment the thought arose.

He has written to me the enclosed letter (which may be returned); but I know too little of his *real* character; the respectability of his family & connexions; or his former pursuits; to form any opinion of his fitness to fill an Office of such importance & respectibility, to public acceptance.[2] As a Mathematician I should suppose him competent; but there are other qualifications equally necessary in a Surveyor General. I wish you would make all the enquiries respecting these matters, your opportunities will permit.

And, if Mr Hawkins should be in Philadelphia, as he wrote the Secretary of War he should be,[3] let me desire also, that you would indirectly, & without any commitment, ascertain 1st whether he possesses such Mathematical knowledge as would qualify him for the above Office; and in that case, 2dly find out whether he would accept it.

I have not yet, been able to hear of a character that combines the requisite qualifications for this trust, nor is it likely I shall do so before my return to Philadelphia.[4] I am always & sincerely Your Affectionate

Go: Washington

ALS, owned (1984) by Mary A. Benjamin of Walter R. Benjamin Autographs, Inc.; LB, DLC:GW.

1. See Pickering's first letter to GW on 29 July, and his first letter to GW on 30 July, found at GW's second letter to Pickering, 27 July, n.5.

2. See John Churchman to GW, 29 July.

3. GW probably is referring to a letter from Benjamin Hawkins enclosed when James McHenry wrote GW on 25 July; see also GW to McHenry, 10 August.

4. For GW's exasperation finding a surveyor general, see his letter to John Marshall, 15 July, and the notes to that document.

From Bartholomew Dandridge, Jr.

Dear Sir,   Philada August 7 1796.

I reached this place on the thursday morning after I left you,[1] & found Mr Kitt & the family well, & every thing as far as I have yet seen in good order. He has not finished his accounts for my examination; I presume however I shall have them today.[2] I fear they will be high, as the sum remaining in Mr Wolcotts hands (with whom I settled yesterday) amounted only to about 26$. The Letters wch you were so good as to give me for the heads of Depts have been severally delivered, and I offer my sincere thanks for them. The gentlemen & their families are well. As far as my enquiries have extended I find nothing of a domestic nature wch is worth mentioning to you, unless it be that there is no appearance of yellow fever in the City—so far from it the inhabitants I am told are remarkably healthy, the summer having been one of the coolest ever known here. It is now raining, & the mercury at 66. For foreign news I refer you to the daily papers which will be forwarded to you with this.[3] I find the books papers &c. much in the same order I left them—& you may depend I shall diligently apply myself to the recording such as require it. Be pleased Dr Sir, to offer my affectionate regards to my Aunt, & be assured that your reiterated kindnesses are recollected by me with the most sincere gratitude. With the greatest respect & attachment I am Dr Sir, Yr obliged Servt

B. Dandridge

P.S. Be pleased to inform Mr Frestel, that the packet with wch he entrusted me was delivered into the hands of Mr La Colombe.

Mr Kitt desires me to remind Mrs W. of a bbl. of Shad wch she promised to send by water.

ALS, DLC:GW.

1. Dandridge left Mount Vernon around 1 Aug. and arrived at Philadelphia on Thursday, 4 Aug. (see GW to Oliver Wolcott, Jr., 1 Aug.).

2. In the account book under 8 Aug., Dandridge recorded a payment of $82.73, representing household steward Frederick Kitt's "bal[an]ce of his accots from 13 June" (Household Accounts).

3. The enclosed newspapers have not been identified.

To Henry Glen

Sir   Mount Vernon 8th Augt 1796

As it appears by the Secretary of Wars letter to me, that you have lately been to the Forts of Oswego and Niagara[1] and must have a competent knowledge of the time and manner of making a tour to the latter, I request the favor of you, as well for my own satisfaction, as to enable me to answer the enquiries of others, to solve the following question, in detail—viz.

How long would it take a *small* party, unincumbered with heavy baggage—who should not, on the journey, waste time unnecessarily—nor proceed so as to fatiegue themselves—to perform this Tour from the *City* of New York?

To explain what I mean, by desiring that the above question may be answered in detail permit me to propound the following queries.

1st What is the usual time in going from New York to Albany by Water conveyance? the same by land?

2d Is a passage in the Packets, or Stages, always to be had from N. York?

3d What time does it require to go from Albany to Fort Schuyler (or Stanwix)[2] by Water? the same by land?

4th Could a light Boat, or two, according to circumstances, with Batteau Men *always* be had at Schenectady? On what terms?

5th If Boats are not to be had, could Horses be hired at Schenectady to go to Fort Schuyler?

6th How long in getting from Fort Schuyler to Fort Oswego? Would there be any certain dependence of procuring Craft at the former, to descend by the Wood Creek, &ca &ca to the latter?[3] And whether with the assistance of a Cloak, & a little roughing, one could pass through that Country without carrying tents or bedding? and could moreover be supplied with Provisions, if not taken along?

7th What is the usual passage from Oswego to Niagara? Could there be any dependance on a vessel at the former (as we have none of our own) without risking an uncertain—perhaps tedious delay? And is there any way, in case this should be likely to happen, of going by land? What is the distance, and are there any settlements, and a Road between those places?

Answers as full & precise, as the nature of the case, & your knowledge of circumstances will enable you to give, would go near to ascertain the time required to perform this rout in, and the provision, necessary to be made for it. After requesting these, as soon as you can conveniently give them, and apologizing for the trouble you will have in complying with this request, I have only to add that with very great esteem, I am—Sir Your Obedt Hble Servt

Go: Washington

P.S. Would such Batteaux as could be obtained at Schenectady be fit to perform the *whole* voyage to Niagara? and in that case could they be engaged for it with *proper* hands?[4]

LS (retained copy), DLC:GW; LB, DLC:GW. GW wrote the postscript on the LS.

Henry Glen (1739–1814), from Schenectady, N.Y., served as a deputy quartermaster general during the Revolutionary War. He entered the U.S. House of Representatives in 1793 and remained until 1801.

1. A letter from Glen to an unknown recipient, dated 17 July, apparently was among the enclosures with James McHenry's first letter to GW on 3 Aug., found at GW to McHenry, 25 July, n.3. (see also GW to McHenry, 8 Aug.). Glen had acted as a military agent with the U.S. troops that went to Fort Oswego, N.Y., and then chartered a vessel to accompany the departing British garrison to Fort Niagara, N.Y. (see *Albany Gazette*, 24 June 1796, and *Albany Register*, 1 Aug. 1796).

2. Fort Schuyler (previously called Fort Stanwix) stood at what is now Rome, New York.

3. Wood Creek proceeded from Fort Schuyler to Oneida Lake, where the Oswego River flowed into Lake Ontario near Fort Oswego.

4. Glen replied to GW on 2 September.

To Joseph Habersham

Sir   Mount Vernon 8th Augt 1796

You were obliging enough a few Posts ago, to send young Mr Lafayette a dead letter, which had been deposited in your Office (from his friends in Europe).

As his anxiety to hear from, or of his Parents, can only be exceeded by his uneasiness at their unhappy situation;[1] I pray you to direct the deputy Post masters in the Sea Port Towns, if any letters with his Superscription thereon, or that of Mr Frestal (to whose care he is committed) should get to their Offices, to put them under a cover to me.

This would avoid delay—insure their safe delivery—and might be a source of consolation to the young Gentleman. With esteem I am Sir Your very Hble Servt

Copy (docketed by GW), DLC:GW; LB, DLC:GW.

Habersham replied to GW from Philadelphia on 11 Aug.: "I am just honoured with your Letter of the 8th Instant, and I shall give the necessary directions to the Deputy Post Masters of the Sea Port Towns to forward all Letters that may be deposited in their Offices for Mr La Fayette or Mr Frestal, in the manner you have desired.

"If I am not much mistaken the dead Letter I sent the young Gentleman was directed to Mr Motier; it may be proper for him to inform me if it was, and whether Letters from Europe are usually directed to him by that name?

"It will afford me great pleasure to be in the least instrumental in securing the safe delivery of Mr La Fayettes Letters; and I have given particular instructions to the Clerk in this Office, who examines the dead Letters to be careful in preserving any that may be for him, or his friend Mr Frestal. Whenever any such Letters are found here, they shall be immediately forwarded to them" (ALS, DLC:GW; LB [dated 10 Aug.], DNA: RG 28, Letters Sent by the Postmaster General, 1789–1836).

1. Lafayette remained in prison (see Justus Erick Bollman to GW, 1 April; GW to Francis II [Holy Roman Emperor], 15 May; La Rochefoucauld-Liancourt to GW, 25 July; see also Thomas Pinckney to GW, 31 July, and Ségur to GW, 4 August.

To La Rochefoucauld-Liancourt

Sir,　　　　　　　　　　　　　　　Mount Vernon 8 Aug: 1796

The Letter which you did me the honor of writing to me the 25th of last month, came duly to hand; & the enclosure for Mr George Fayette was immediately presented to him.

The name & character of the duke de Liancourt were not unknown to me, before his arrival in this Country; and the respect which I entertained for the Latter (although political considerations have deprived me of the honor of a personal acquaintance with him) was, & is as great as he or his warmest friends could desire.

Mr de Liancourt must be too well acquainted with the history of governments; with the insidious ways of the world; & with the suspicions and jealousies of its rulers; not to acknowledge that men in responsible situations cannot, like those in private life, be governed *solely* by the dictates of their own inclinations, or by such motives as can only affect themselves.

To dilate upon this observation, or to attempt to point at the distinction between the conduct of a man in public office who is accountable for the consequences of his measures to others; and one in private life, who has no other check than the rectitude of his own actions, would be superfluous to a man of information: but if exemplification of these facts was necessary, it might be added with truth, that in spite of all the circumspection with which my conduct has been marked towards the gentlemen of your nation, who have left France under circumstances which have rendered them obnoxious to the governing power of it, the countenance said to be given to them, is alledged as a cause of discontent in the Directory of France against the government of the U. States. But it is not my intention to dwell on this subject: how far the charge is merited no one better than yourself can judge; & your candour & penetration will, I am persuaded, appreciate my motives for the reverse of the charge, however contrary the operation of them may have been to your expectation or to my wishes.

With respect to Mr La Fayette I may, without troubling you with the details, venture to affirm that whatever private friendship could require, or public duty would allow, has been, & will continue to be essayed by me to effect his liberation. the difficulty in accomplishing of which has, no doubt, proceeded in a great measure from the cause you have mentioned, & will probably exist while the war between the belligerent powers continues to rage.

No man regrets this, & the present unhappy situation of this amiable family more than I do; but it is an ascertained fact, that altho' Fayette is an *adopted* citizen of this Country, the Government of it, nor the people themselves, notwithstanding their attachment to his person & the recollection of his services, have any right to demand him as *their* citizen by the law of nations. consequently, an expression of their earnest wishes that liberty may be restored to him, is all they can do towards accomplishing it. to attempt more, would avail *him* nothing, & might involve the *U. States* in difficulties of great magnitude.

This letter, sir, you will consider as a private one; originating from yours to me, relatively to Mr La Fayette. In replying to the sentiments contained in it, I could not, from respect to your character, & the indulgence of my own feelings, miss the occasion of giving you this explanation of matters, which otherwise might have the appearance of mystery. It affords an occasion also of assuring you that with sentiments of the highest esteem & greatest respect I have the honor to be &c.

G: Washington

LB, DLC:GW.

To James McHenry

Sir,   Mount Vernon 8th Augt 1796

Your letter of the 3d instant, with the information of our possession of Fort Ontario (lately occupied by the Troops of Great Britain) and the correspondence between Captn Bruff of the United States Troops, and Captn Clarke of the British was brought to me by the last Post.[1]

Several matters are submitted by the former for consideration; among them, the mode of supplying the Garrison with fire Wood, and furnishing it with a Sein. With respect to the first of these, providing it with a Horse, or pair of Horses, and a Batteau (as the fuel is to be transported so far) seems to be matters of necessity; but the practice of the American Army should be consulted for precedents, before the British allowance or indeed any allowance, is made to the Soldiers for cutting and transporting of it to the Fort, when the means by which it is done are furnished by the public. If no allowance of this sort has been made heretofore—except in Towns where the Wood was to be bought—which, if I remember rightly, was the case invariably while I commanded the Army; it would be a dangerous innovation to begin it now; for it would instantly pervade *all the Garrisons* and the whole Army; be their situation what it may. In time of peace, where no danger is to be apprehended, and where the duty is light, I see no hardship in the Soldiers providing fuel for their *own* use, and comfort. With regard to a Sein, as the expence will be small, (if it is taken care of) and the convenience great, I think the Garrision should be indulged with one.

There is another part of Captn Bruffs letter which I do not perfectly understand, where he says, "he is at a loss what orders to give Lieutt Rowen respecting the continuance of his command," &ca &ca "or whether to join me, or stay, on the arrival of a reinforcement, or detachment."[2] Doubts of this sort should be removed as soon as possible.

There is a suggestion in Mr Glens letter of the 17th of July which merits consideration—I mean the purchase of a Vessel (now in use) on Lake Ontario.[3] The Utility of this measure depends very much, if not altogether, upon the cheapest & best channel through which to supply the Garrison at Niagara, with Provisions & Stores. If by the rout of the Mohawk & Oswego, a *proper* Vessel on Lake Ontario would certainly be useful; If by the way of Presque-Isle & Lake Erie, it would be unnecessary; and if by a middle communication suggested (I think by Mr Weston) to the Canal Company in the State of New York, in some report which has been published,[4] it would depend much upon the place of its entrance into the above mentioned lake for its utility.

Go: Washington

Copy (docketed by GW), DLC:GW; LB, DLC:GW. McHenry acknowledged this letter when he wrote GW on 11–12 August.

1. Thomas Clarke, a captain in the 60th (Royal American) Regiment of Foot, commanded the British detachment at Fort Oswego. He had entered the regiment as an ensign in 1779 and left as a major in 1807.

The correspondence between Clarke and James Bruff has not been identified.

2. Bruff's letter has not been identified.

Robert Rowan (d. 1800) of North Carolina was a lieutenant in the corps of artillerists and engineers. He remained in the U.S. army until his death.

3. New York congressman Henry Glen's letter has not been identified, but see GW to Glen, this date.

4. GW is referring to a publication titled *Report of the Directors of the Western and Northern Inland Lock Navigation Companies, in the State of New-York, to the Legislature: Together with the Report of Mr. William Weston, Engineer* (New York, 1796). William Weston had written in his report that "it will be adviseable to examine, attentively, every other line of communication with lake Ontario, that has the least appearance of practicability. For this purpose, I shall suggest to the board, the propriety of exploring the intermediate country, between Rotterdam and Salmon creek." (p. 18).

From James McHenry

Sir.   War office 8 Augt 1796.

I have received your letters of the 1st and 3d instant.[1]

The inclosed packet No. 1. contains the opinion of the Attorney General on the power of the President to pardon military offences previous to the late act of Congress; and the form of a pardon for Lt Geddis for your signature.[2]

No. 2. contains the last dispatches from General Wayne, and copy of a letter which I have sent to General Wilkinson relative to his correspondence with Col. England, which as appeared to me, I could not with propriety have omitted to write.[3]

No. 3. Is the draught of a letter to Lt Col. Gaither, which if approved of you will be pleased to transmit as soon as convenient.[4]

No. 4. Is a letter from Gen. Pickens respecting the agent of Indian affairs in Georgia.[5] With the greatest respect, I have the honour to be Sir your most obt St

James McHenry

ALS, DLC:GW; LB, DLC:GW. GW replied to McHenry on 12 August.

1. See GW's second letter to McHenry on 1 August. For GW's letter to McHenry dated 3 Aug., see his letter to McHenry on 25 July, n.3.

2. For an examination of the legalities complicating the case of Lt. Simon Geddes, see McHenry to GW, 26 July, and notes 6 and 7. Charles Lee had written McHenry on 4 Aug.: "The Attorney General is of opinion that the President of the United States has power to Pardon Lieutenant Geddes for the offence of which he has been found guilty, though the sentence of the court martial has neither been rejected or approved. The enclosed form may be used" (DLC:GW).

GW's pardon for Geddis, dated 12 Aug. at Mount Vernon with McHenry's countersignature, overturned the sentence of dismissal from the service given at a court-martial held on 12 May "in consideration of the youth and inexperience of Lieutenant Geddes and for divers other good causes" and directed that he "be reinstated in his command in the Corps of Artillerists and Engineers" (DS, PHi: Dreer Collection; GW filled in blanks for day, month, and year on an otherwise prepared document).

3. McHenry presumably enclosed copies of Gen. Anthony Wayne's letters to him dated 8 and 11 July, which he acknowledged when he wrote Wayne on 5 Aug. (see Knopf, *Wayne*, 495–99, 508). In his letter written on 8 July, Wayne reported the activities of Victor Collot and indicated a possible connection with Gen. James Wilkinson. He also related his inquiries into the Spanish complaint about Capt. Zebulon Pike's insult to their flag (see GW to Timothy Pickering, 10 June, and n.3 to that document). Wayne wrote on 11 July "that the Troops of the United States are by this period in peaceable possession of the posts of Detroit & Miamis, & that the polite & friendly manner, in which the Evacuation has taken place . . . is truly worthy of British Officers & does honor to them & the Nation to which they belong."

McHenry's letter to Wilkinson has not been identified, but it evidently concerned the publication of Wilkinson's letter written on 27 May to Richard G. England, the British officer commanding at Detroit, and England's reply dated 10 June (see *The Philadelphia Gazette & Universal Daily Advertiser*, 30 July).

4. The draft for McHenry's letter to Lt. Col. Henry Gaither has not been identified. In the final version dated 23 Aug., McHenry warned about a possible increase in hostilities between settlers and Creek Indians in Georgia arising from the recently negotiated treaty at Colerain. He directed in GW's name that Gaither "give such an arrangement to the military force within the Indian line, as may on the one hand, prevent the Indians from carrying into effect thieving or hostile incursions on the frontier Inhabitants of Georgia, and on the other hand the Citizens of the United States from intruding on the Indian land contrary to treaty and law." (DLC: James McHenry Papers).

5. The letter from Andrew Pickens about Creek agent James Seagrove has not been identified.

From William Stephens

Sir   Savannah—Georgia 8th Aug: 1796

Mr Pendleton, district Judge of this State, having removed with his Family, to reside in New York, of Consequence intends resigning his office.

Amongst the applications, that may be made for the appointment, It is with great deference; Sir, that I am enboldened to add to the number, that may Solicit you on this occasion. If my Situation and Character be such, as to warrant me in the application, I flatter myself, that although not having the Honour, probably of being much known to, or heard of, by you, Yet, the result of your enquiries, I trust, cannot but terminate in my Favor.

As a native of this State, whose Grand Father and Family, were amongst the first to Migrate and Settle in Georgia—I cannot but feel, for its Welfare and Dignity.

Being early Brought up in the Study of the Law, in this Country, I had the good Fortune, previous to the Revolution, to profit myself, by obtaining a more General Knowledge of the profession, by Study in the Inns of Court, Attached to Westminster Hall, and returning, entered into a Liberal practice, Shared the Vicissitudes of Fortune, with my Country, during its Greatest Troubles, and have now the happiness to see it Flourish.

If the Enjoyment of Legislative, and other Appointments by the people, and that too, unsolicited, are marks of Confidence, it is with flattering truth, I can assert, I have a full share, as well of the public, as private Testimony of my Fellow citizens. Under the protection of Providence, my circumstances are tolerably easy, but feeling, a strong desire, to be of Service to my common

Country, I have not hesitated, to trespass on your time, by craving the Appointment now about to be vacant.

If then, Sir, in the exercise of your correct Judgment, in the appointment of a Judge of this District, it shall occur to you, that my Services may be adequate, it will not only be considered by me, amongst the first of Honors—and that very much heigthened, by receiving it from your hands. with sentiments, of very high Respect, I am sir yr very obt sert

Wm Stephens

ALS, DLC:GW.

William Stephens (1752–1819) was a judge on the Georgia Supreme Court. Joseph Clay, Jr., received the appointment from GW as district judge for Georgia, but President Thomas Jefferson appointed Stephens after Clay's resignation. Stephens then served from 1801 to 1818.

Jacob Read, U.S. senator from South Carolina, wrote GW from Philadelphia on 6 Sept.: "Mr Nathaniel Pendleton late District Judge of Georgia having quitted that State and as it is Understood resigned his Commission at the request of Mr William Stephens of Savannah I pray leave to mention him to your Excellency as a Candidate for the Vacant Seat on the District Bench.

"I have known Mr Stephens intimately from my early youth and with pleasure offer You assurances of his great Probity and respectability—I am Certain he is as well informed and as Sound a Lawyer as any at Present in the State of Georgia altho' he is not perhaps so emminent as a Speaking Counsel at the Bar.

"Mr Stephens Studied with a Gentleman of great Ability and afterwards had the advantage of three or four Years Attendance at Westminster Hall—From his length of practice at the Georgia Bar he has had an opportunity of Maturing opinions and is not likely to be on every occasion pursuing the Uncertain guide of Individual Immagination—and rejecting precedents and long established and approved Law, to be taking up new and Undigested Opinions Call them Principles & fly in the face of all Authority and received Law which I Can Assure you is not unfrequent in this day of Innovation.

"Mr Stephens has heretofore filled the Offices of Attorney General and of Chief Judge of the State of Georgia and is at this time a Judge of the Supreme Court of that State and no man in Georgia has a greater Weight of character.

"I take leave further to Mention that Mr Stephens is a native of Georgia Son of one of the original Setlers under the Trustees of the Province of Georgia and a descendant of a very respectable English family—At the Commencement of the Revolution he Chose to relinquish forever Very flattering offers & prospects in England and under that Government—(when from his near relationship to an English Baronet of a Very wealthy & Antient family with Considerable parliamentary Interest his Success was Considered as Certain) to take part with his Countrymen—I also knew Mr stephens to be a real friend to order & good Gouvernment in the United States.

"I hope I Shall be pardoned for the length of this Letter but in Obeying the request of Mr Stephens to Present him to the Notice of the President I felt it a duty to my friend to State fully his Pretensions to the Office he Sollicits and My own knowledge of his Character & ability to fulfill the duties of the apppointment Shou'd he be so fortunate as to obtain it" (ALS, DLC:GW; see also Nathaniel Pendleton to GW, 30 July, and Joseph Habersham to GW, 10 Aug.).

Stephens was the son of Newdigate Stephens (d. 1757), who was the son of William Stephens (1671–1753), clerk to the Georgia trustees and later president of the colony. Read also probably referred to Roger Newdigate (1719–1806), fifth baronet of Harefield, a member of Parliament for many years. Newdigate was a grandson of the second baronet, Richard Newdigate (d. 1709), and the younger William Stephens was a great-grandson.

From Nathan Crocker

Wilmington N:C. August 9th 1796.
The Petition of Nathan Crocker of the Town of Wilmington in the State aforesaid Mariner.

Respectfully Sheweth

That Your Petitioner is a natural born Citizen of the United States, that he has been a Sailor upwards of thirty Years, twenty of which he has been a Master; that he serv'd his Country through the whole of the American War, and mostly on board United States Ships of War—that since the War, he has commanded various Vessels from the Port of Wilmington, and that he is now acting Lieutenant for the Cutter Diligence on the N. Carolina Station.

Your Petitioner (first premising that the late Commander of the Cutter Diligence is dead)[1] respectfully solicits your Excellency's attention to his past services—his knowledge of the Coasts of America—and the good Character he has uniformly supported among his fellow Citizens—and relying on his merit alone he Petitions Your Excellency for the vacant place of Commander of the Cutter Diligence[2]—And Your Petitioner shall &c.

Nathan Crocker

DS, DLC:GW. Bartholomew Dandridge, Jr., incorrectly docketed the letter as dated 6 August.

1. William Cooke, commander of the *Diligence*, disappeared earlier in 1796, thought to be the victim of smugglers.

2. John Brown became the new commander.

From Joseph Habersham

Sir.   Philadelphia 10th August 1796.

I take the Liberty to enclose you a Letter from Mr Clay, who is a Candidate for the appointment of District Judge of the State of Georgia, which he has been informed is vacant by the resignation of Judge Pendleton.

Mr Clay is a Man of Honour and Virtue, and I have reason to think that he is well qualified for the appointment for which he is a Candidate, but as he is a distant connection of mine it is probable that I may overrate his Merit on this occasion. I have the Honour to be, with great respect, Sir, Your most obedient humble servant

Jos. Habersham

ALS, DLC:GW.

Habersham enclosed a letter from Joseph Clay, Jr. to GW dated 25 July: "Having been informed that Judge Pendleton has forwarded to you the resignation of his office as Judge of the district of Georgia I take the liberty of proposing myself to your Excellency as a candidate for that office" (ALS, DLC:GW; see also Nathaniel Pendleton to GW, 30 July).

Joseph Clay, Jr. (1764–1811) graduated from the College of New Jersey (now Princeton University) in 1784 and practiced law in Savannah. His father, a prominent Georgia planter and merchant, was Habersham's cousin.

Henry William DeSaussure wrote GW from Charleston, S.C., on 6 Aug.: "The kindness which I experienced at Your hands in calling me unsolicited to an office of Trust, and in bestowing a liberal approbation of my conduct in that office, emboldens me to make application to you on the behalf of a friend and a man of worth, who is desirous to be honored with your Confidence. It is understood that Mr Justice Pendleton is about to resign the office of District Judge of the state of Georgia—Mr Joseph Clay Junr of Georgia, is disposed to be a Candidate for that Office, and he is desirous that this inclination should be made known to you. He is not willing to obtain that by solicitation, to wch his general character may not be deemed to entitle him. Yet he apprehends that the privacy which he has heretofore cultivated, may have prevented your attaining much knowledge of his Character—Under these Circumstances I venture to assure you from long & Intimate acquaintance with him, that he is distinguished for uniting a sound Judgment with firm Integrity and mild amiable manners. He is also eminent in his profession.

"Thus much I have said, because to have said less would have been less than the truth—to say more might be deemed to proceed from my friendship.

"I am fearful that I owe an apology for Interfering in relation to an appointment in another state—Should it be deemed Improper, I hope I may find Shelter in the purity of my motive. Perhaps too afflicted as that state is by violent parties, the estimation in which a Gentleman is held in a neighbouring state may be deemed valuable Information, in forming a Judgment of Character. In this respect the testimony of Carolina would be favorable to Mr Clay: He is greatly respected by all the Carolinians who have had opportunities of knowing him" (ALS, DLC:GW). DeSaussure had served as director of the U.S. Mint. For approbation of his official conduct, see GW to DeSaussure, 1 Nov. 1795.

Secretary of State Timothy Pickering wrote GW on 24 Aug.: "Yesterday I received a letter from Mr Desaussure, late Director of the Mint, in answer to one I had written to him about some law business, in the close of which is the following paragraph.

"'Permit me, sir, to say one word to you on the behalf of a friend who would accept the office of District Judge of Georgia, which Judge Pendleton has communicated his intention to resign. Mr Joseph Clay junior will be a candidate for that office. I know him perfectly well, and I know him to be a man of fine talents & sound integrity. He is attached to the General Government, & has not meddled in the party disputes in Georgia. My attachment to him impels me to state his character to you.'

"I beg leave to add, that yesterday Mr Habersham, the postmaster general, called on me, and upon being pressed, was more explicit than I understood him to have been in his letter to you. His answers correspond exactly with the character given of Mr Clay by Mr DeSaussure, and with what I understood from Mr Wolcott was expressed to him by the Chief Justice, Mr Elsworth" (ALS, DLC:GW; LB, DNA: RG 59, GW's Correspondence with His Secretaries of State).

Georgia congressman Abraham Baldwin wrote GW from Long Branch, probably Monmouth County, N.J., in August: "I am just informed that the office of District Judge in the State of Georgia is become vacant by the resignation of Judge Pendleton.

"It is a trust on which the good order of the government, as well as the satisfaction of the people so much depends, that I cannot forbear to express my opinion and wishes on the subject of filling that vacancy. The State is at this time unhappily in a situation to make it more than commonly difficult to collect that satisfactory information which is desirable in making such appointments. I submit my opinion with the expectation that it may be compared and crossed by the information and opinions received from others that a proper result may more readily be seen. Since the death of the late Judge Houstoun, of which I am just informed, who had very respectable recommendations to that office when the first appointment was made, my opinion is that Joseph Clay Jr Esqr. is the person most proper to be appointed to the office. His name has been before brought into the view of the President, if I mistake not, by a unanimous recommendation from the Senators and Representatives of that State, for the appointment of attorney General of the United States at the time when the late Mr Bradford was appointed. Their unanimous opinion at that time is perhaps a stronger testimony in his favor, than can at this time be obtained for any one.

"I have intimately known him for many years, and have known few persons, who have possessed so great a share of my respect. He is a native of Savannah, of the most respectable connexions. He received a regular education at

Princeton College, I have often heard Dr Witherspoon and Dr Smith observe that they had known few superior to him at that College. He received his law education under Dr Wythe at Williamsburgh in Virginia. His natural talents are very distinguishing. His virtues and moral character have been uncommonly respected from his childhood. He has been a steady friend to the present form of the constitution of the United States; and I have no doubt will discharge the duties of a Judge in a manner to reflect dignity on the government and to procure the respect and confidence of the people" (ALS, DLC:GW). Regular wagons ran between Philadelphia and the beachside resort called Long Branch during the summer season (see *Philadelphia Gazette and Universal Daily Advertiser,* 10 July 1794, 17 June 1795). John Houstoun had died on 20 July 1796. No recommendations have been identified for his appointment as district judge in 1789, but he received recommendations for appointment to the U.S. Supreme Court (see James Gunn to GW, 7 March 1791, found at John Rutledge to GW, 5 March 1791, n.1; see also Gunn to GW, 11 Feb. 1793). No recommendation from the Georgia delegation to Congress to appoint Clay as attorney general, probably dated early 1794, has been identified.

Samuel Stanhope Smith (1751–1819), a professor at Princeton while Clay was a student, succeeded his father-in-law John Witherspoon as president of the college in 1795 and served until 1812.

A letter from Pickering to Clay written on 16 Sept. announced his appointment as district judge for Georgia and enclosed his commission (DNA: RG 59, Domestic Letters). For unsuccessful aspirants, see George Walton to GW, 1 April, n.4; Matthew McAllister to GW, 10 June; and William Stephens to GW, 8 August.

From Alexander Hamilton

Sir   [New York] Aug. 10th 1796
About a fortnight since, I sent you a certain draft.[1] I now send you another on the plan of incorporating.[2] Whichever you may prefer, if there be any part you wish to transfer from one to another any part to be changed—or if there be any material idea in your own draft which has happened to be omitted and which you wish introduced—in short if there be any thing further in the matter in which I can be of any, I will with great pleasure obey your commands. Very respectfully & Affecty I have the honor to be Sir Yr Obed. Ser.

                                                A. Hamilton

ALS, NN: Alexander Hamilton Papers.
    1. See Hamilton to GW, 30 July.
    2. The enclosed draft followed the organization of an earlier one that GW had sent Hamilton on 15 May: a brief introduction, quotation of the draft ad-

dress written by James Madison in 1792, and a lengthy final section described as GW's "further reflections and sentiments dictated by an ardent concern for your welfare" (*Hamilton Papers*, 20:294–303; quote on 295; see also Paltsits, *Farewell Address*, 200–208).

To James McHenry

Private
Dear Sir,   Mount Vernon, 10th Augt—96
    Colo. Hawkins is now here, on his way to Philadelphia, & proposes to proceed in the S⟨ta⟩ge of tomorrow.
    He has related many matters, and read many papers relative to the Treaty with the Creek Indians; the conduct of the State Commissioners of ⟨Georgia; &ca &ca.⟩[1] But as this is not the regular way of bringing business, of this sort, before me; I have requested that he and Mr Clymer (who he supposes will be in Philadelphia before him⟨)⟩ will report to ⟨you,⟩ not only what appertains to ⟨the⟩ Commission, but ⟨their⟩ observations and remarks *generally* as may be interesting ⟨for⟩ the government ⟨to⟩ be in⟨formed of for⟩ the regulation of its con⟨duct in that quarter. I wis⟩h you, therefore to be minute in your enquiries ⟨&⟩ entries.
    My present intention is to leave this about the middle of next week for Philadelphia, but as I shall spend a day in the Federal City, and on account of the weather, propose to travel slow, it will, probably, be t⟨he⟩ middle of the week after, before I sh⟨all⟩ arrive there. With very great esteem & regard I am—Dear Sir Your Affecte Servt

                                                    Go: Washing⟨ton⟩

ALS, NBuHi; LS (retained copy), DLC:GW; LB, DLC:GW. Damaged portions of the ALS are supplied in angle brackets from the LS.
    McHenry replied to GW from Philadelphia on 15 Aug.: "This is merely to acknowlege the receipt of your letter of the 10th and to inform you that Mr Clymer and Mr Hawkins are both in Town and that I shall receive their official communications to-day" (ALS, DLC:GW).
    1. See McHenry to GW, 25 July, and his second letter to GW on 3 Aug.; see also McHenry to GW, 11–12 August.

To Timothy Pickering

Private

Sir.   Mount Vernon 10th Augt 1796

The last Post brought me the enclosed letter from General Pinckney.[1] It becomes necessary *now* to prepare Instructions for him without delay. To bring him fully and perfectly acquainted with the conduct and policy of this government towards France &c. and the motives which have induced the recall of Mr Monroe.

As this measure will excite, when known, much speculation; and set all the envenomed pens to work; it is worthy of consideration what part, and how much, of the causes which have produced this event, should be spoken of *unofficially* by the Officers of government.[2]

It Will be candid, proper and necessary, to apprise Mr Monroe (as the measure, and his successor are decided on) of his recal; and in proper terms, of the motives which have impelled it.[3]

In the course of next week (probably about the middle of it) I expect to commence my journey for Philadelphia; but as I shall be obliged to halt a day at the Federal City, and from the heat of the season, and other circumstances, must travel slow, it is not likely I shall arrive there before the middle of the following week.

Go: Washington

ALS, MHi: Pickering Papers; LS (retained copy), DNA: RG 59, Miscellaneous Letters; LB, DNA: RG 59, GW's Correspondence with His Secretaries of State.

1. See Charles Cotesworth Pinckney to GW, 27 July.

2. GW expressed this same sentiment when he wrote Secretary of the Treasury Oliver Wolcott, Jr., on this date.

3. Pickering wrote James Monroe on 22 Aug. that GW believed "it necessary to send a new minister to represent the United States at Paris, and had made a tender of the appointment to General Charles Cotesworth Pinckney." GW based his decision on "feeling forcibly the obligations of his office to maintain the honor and interests of the U. States in relation to foreign nations; and our connections with France in particular demanding, from various causes, the most constant & pointed attentions, to prevent or remove jealousies & complaints" (*Papers of James Monroe*, 4:81; see also Cabinet to GW, 2 July, and GW to Pickering, 8 July).

Monroe shared thoughts on his recall as U.S. minister to France when he wrote Virginia congressman James Madison from Paris on 1 Jan. 1797: "My recall is an aff[ron]t upon w[hic]h I presume the adm[inistratio]n has given some expl[anatio]n to the Senate if not to the publick. I sho[ul]d be glad to know what reason they have given for it. I rejoice they have given me that testimony that I had no share in their councils nor portion of their confidence" (*Papers of James Monroe*, 4:139–40; see also Monroe to Madison, 8 Jan., *Papers of James Monroe*, 4:141, and *Autobiography of Monroe*, 139–41).

To Oliver Wolcott, Jr.

Private
Dear Sir   Mount Vernon 10th Augt 96

Your letter of the 3d Instant did not get to my hands until the 8th. I most assuredly wrote the letter mentioned in my last;[1] but I find it is no uncommon thing for my letters to miscarry. The originals to Genl Pi[n]ckney, of the —— Ulto (one of which containing 300 dollrs. in Bank notes for the Sufferers by fire in Charleston) had not been received by that Gentleman on the 26th of that Month, altho' duplicates dispatched eight days afterwards, had.[2] I have heard of no miscarriage of a Mail, and I have evidence that the above letters (under one cover) proceeded *safely*, as far as Richmond.[3]

General Pinckney accepts the appointment to France, and will, very shortly, with his lady, be in Philadelphia to embark. As this circumstance will furnish a new Subject for envenomed Pens, it merits consideration how far the causes which have occasioned it, should, *unofficially*, be spoken of by the Officers of Government.[4]

Let me desire that you would *begin* to note such occurrences (not only those in your own Department, but all others which may occasionally present themselves) as may be fit and proper to communicate to Congress at their next Session. It is from these materials, and such Memorandums as I take myself, my speech is composed. It is better to note down *every* thing which *may* be requisite on this occasion, than to omit *any* thing; because it is easier to select, than to collect matter, at the moment I am going to compose it.

I am sorry the Treasury is unable to answer all the appropriated calls upon it. My present intention is to leave this for Philadelphia in the course of next Week, but as I shall travel slow, and have to halt a day or two on the Road, my arrival there is a little uncertain. With very great esteem & regard I am Dear Sir Your affectionate

Go: Washington

ALS, CtHi, Oliver Wolcott, Jr., Papers; copy, DLC:GW; LB, DLC:GW.

1. GW is referring to his letter to Wolcott dated 29 July, found at Wolcott to GW, 23 July, n.5, and not his brief letter to Wolcott on 1 August.

2. For this information, see Charles Cotesworth Pinckney to GW, 27 July. GW's miscarried letters to Pinckney were dated 8 July.

3. See John Marshall to GW, 11 July, found at GW to Marshall, 8 July, n.2.

4. GW expressed this same sentiment when he wrote Secretary of State Timothy Pickering on this date.

From James McHenry

Sir. War office 11 [–12] Augt 1796.

I received the inclosed letter from Mr Hendricks on the 9th and that from Mr Clymer the 6th inst.[1]

One of these gentlemen you will perceive thinks another negotiation indispensible to prevent war; the other, that an augmentation of the regular force is absolutely necessary to the preservation of peace. Both, of course, meet in the opinion, that there is serious ground to apprehend hostility on the frontiers of Georgia unless measures are adopted to prevent it.

Such being the aspect of things in that quarter, I would submit for consideration; whether it might not be expedient, in aid of the military dispositions contemplated, to incorporate in the letter proposed to be written to the governor of Georgia, sentiments to the following import.[2]

"That the President has read the protest of the commissioners on the part of Georgia against the proceedings of the commissioners of the U.S.;[3] that he laments, that regulations calculated to preserve confidence in the Indians, in the fairness of the intentions of government, should have worn a different aspect to these gentlemen; that from the sincerity which he used in communicating to the Indians the desire of the State of Georgia to make a purchase from them of certain described land, and the instructions which he gave to the commissioners of the U.S. to facilitate and obtain it, and from the view which he has taken of the transactions at the meeting, as connected with that object, he cannot ascribe the refusal of the Indians to sell to those regulations or the conduct of the commissioners, but to a predetermination of the Creek nation not to dispose of their land: That as a further proof of the Presidents intentions, and in order to remove every doubt on this subject he will, as soon as possible, have ascertained in the most unequivocal manner, whether a change of mind has taken place in the nation respecting the land and the terms upon which they will sell; that should the inquiry turn out favourably he will cheerfully consent to the opening of another negotiation."

I would hope from such a communication 1st. That it would have a tendency to allay the agitation which the representations of the State commissioners may have excited and perhaps arrest violent proceedings. 2. That it would afford time to government (should it suspend dangerous projects only) to arrange the military force in such a manner as to render all attempts at settlement nugatory. & 3d. That it would shew, that the Executive is disposed to obtain the land in question for the State, and preserve peace to the frontiers. With the greatest respect I have the honour to be Sir your most obt & hble st

James McHenry

August 12th.
P.S. Since writing the foregoing I have received your two letters of the 8th inst.[4] I shall pay particular attention to their contents.

I now inclose you the draught of the letter to the governor of Georgia modelled agreeably to the preceding suggestions. If it is approved of I should be glad to have it returned by the next post for immediate transmission.[5] It is understood that the instructions to Lt Col. Gaither will accord with it.[6]

With respect to the inquiry it proposes. That can be made by the person who shall be appointed to explain certain things to the Creeks in their nation, which they required and which the Commissioners have consented should be given.[7]

I have this moment received the inclosed letters & from Gen. Wilkinson & Cap. De Butts,[8] as also one from Governor Sevier. I shall as the post goes tomorrow acknowlege it, and express the satisfaction which I expect it will give to the President.[9]

ALS, DLC:GW; LB, DLC:GW; copy, MHi: Adams Papers; copy (letterpress), DLC: James McHenry Papers.

GW replied to McHenry from Mount Vernon on 16 Aug.: "As I propose to enter upon my journey to Philadelphia to morrow; this letter only serves to cover the Papers which I received from you by the last Post; and to inform you that the draught of the Letter to the Governor of Georgia meets my approbation, under the general lights I have of the subject; but before you part with it, I again desire that you would learn the Sentiments of Colo. Hawkins & Mr Clymer on that part of it which holds up the idea of again negociating with the Creeks for a Sale of Land to that State. I shall add no more" (ALS, PHi: Washington MSS).

1. The letters from George Clymer, one of three U.S. commissioners who negotiated the Treaty of Colerain with the Creek Indians in spring 1796, dated 6 July, and James Hendricks, who served as chairman for the three Georgia commissioners at that treaty, dated 9 July, have not been identified.

James Hendricks (died c.1804), Revolutionary War officer and merchant in Alexandria, Va., moved to Georgia around 1789 and became a justice of the peace in Wilkes County.

2. See n.5 below.

3. For the protest from the Georgia commissioners, see McHenry to GW, 25 July, n.3.

4. For GW's first letter to McHenry dated 8 Aug., see McHenry's second letter to GW, 3 Aug., n.5.

5. This draft has not been identified, and the letter McHenry eventually sent Georgia governor Jared Irwin did not include the suggested sentiments (see McHenry's second letter to GW on 3 Aug., and notes 2 and 5 to that document).

6. For McHenry's letter to Lt. Col. Henry Gaither, see his letter to GW on 8 Aug., n.4.

7. Creek Indian chiefs had requested further explanations regarding compensation for murders of their men and the boundary line negotiated in the U.S. treaty with Spain (see Timothy Pickering to GW, November 1795, and n.3 to that document, and U.S. commissioners to McHenry, 1 July 1796, in *ASP, Indian Affairs*, 1:610–11).

8. The enclosed letters from Gen. James Wilkinson and Capt. Henry De Butts have not been identified, but *Claypoole's American Daily Advertiser* for 13 Aug. 1786 printed extracts. Wilkinson wrote McHenry from Greenville, Tenn., on 16 July "that in consequence of my orders and arrangements Lieut. Col. Hamtramck on the 11th inst. actually displayed the American stripes from Fort Miami, and embarked the same day, with about 400 men for Detroit, of which place I have no doubt he is now in possession." De Butts wrote McHenry from Detroit on 14 July "that on the 11th inst. about noon, the flag of the United States was displayed on the ramparts of Detroit, a few minutes after the works were evacuated by Col. England and the British troops under his command, and with additional satisfaction I inform you that the exchange was effected with much propriety and harmony by both parties."

9. Tennessee governor John Sevier had written McHenry from Knoxville on 20 July: "Yours of the 20th Ultimo I had the honor to receive. Am extremely sorry any uneasiness should be occasioned by any of the citizens of the South Western Territory, now the state of Tennessee.

"You are pleased to mention, you have been informed that numerous forced settlements are made on Indian lands, as confirmed to them by treaty, but have not informed me, where, or by whom the same have been made.

"It is not unknown to the executive that I have but recently come into the administration, and that Indian affairs at best are generally managed with much difficulty and trouble. . . .

"I have had an extensive acquaintance with several Indian tribes upwards of thirty years and I can with great propriety say that the more my knowledge is of those people, more difficult it is to find a person calculated with address to transact the business of a savage nation. . . .

"I do not mean to excuse the people of this country and say that none of them are not guilty of encroachments and often times doing injustice to their neighboring tribes, neither is it to be expected when we find that the laws of the original states at various times have been insufficient to restrain the unruly from various and innumerable disorders of this kind. And when we consider the many unprovoked and wanton barbarities so often and recently exercised by the savage on the frontier citizens, might we not wonder that the spirit of discord and irreconciliation does not in a much greater degree prevail.

"Permit me to assure you, that I am authorized to say that our Legislature together with myself, are sincerely disposed to regard and observe all the treaties that are, or may be, sanctioned and ratified by the Federal Government, so far as they are not pernicious, odious nor in[i]quitous. . . .

"Beg leave to observe that the Cherokee settlements are in our vacinity, and a great part of that nation is within our territorial limits, of course they frequently resort among our inhabitants and particularly at this place. And notwithstanding the agents resident among them, we are constantly engaged, and much time taken up in the transaction of Indian business. In order to prevent any misunderstanding, and a wish that we might mutually cultivate friendship and tranquility with those people, I shall have no objection to lending my assistance in any thing that may not be incompatible with the dignity and duties of my station" (T: Governor John Sevier Papers; see also McHenry's first letter to GW, 27 June, and n.4 to that document).

McHenry replied to Sevier on 13 August. His letter began: "I had the satisfaction of receiving your letter of the 20th of July ulto by yesterdays Mail. As the president was at Mount Vernon I immediately transmitted it to him. Your readiness to co-operate with him in preserving peace to the frontier Inhabitants and in those measures which Congress have thought proper to adopt in the same view will I am persuaded give him sincere pleasure" (MH: Frederick M. Dearborn Collection).

Richard Bowen to Bartholomew Dandridge, Jr.

Sir   [c.12 Aug. 1796]
    As above is the acct for advertising the President's farms. your remitting the amount per post will much oblige.[1] If you have op-

portunities to Alexandria, it may be lodged in the hands of Mr McRea, post master, who will send it on by the rider to this place (Anthony Moore) whose receipt in my behalf shall be sufficient.[2] Am, Sir, your hble Sert

Richd Bowen

ALS, DLC:GW. This letter has "Martinsburg Augt 12th" written on its cover, which was initially addressed to Dandridge at Mount Vernon before those words were struck out and "Philadelphia" written instead. Dandridge wrote "Septr 1796" on the docket.

Richard Bowen (d. 1808) established *The Virginia Centinel; or, the Winchester Mercury* at Winchester, Va., in 1788 and published the newspaper under various titles until his death.

1. Bowen's tabular account written above the letter showed that GW owed $12 for three printings of his advertisement to lease his Mount Vernon farms that began on 26 Feb. (see also Advertisement, 1 Feb.). The advertisment appeared in Bowen's *Virginia Gazette: and the Winchester Centinel* for 26 Feb. and 25 March. A third printing, probably on 11 March, has not been verified.

2. Dandridge wrote at the bottom of this letter: "Sent to Mr McRea by Mr Craik, for Mr Bowen." He recorded payment directed to Bowen on 19 Sept. (Household Accounts).

From the Commissioners for the District of Columbia

sir, Washington, 12th August 1796

Our affairs with Messrs Morris & Nicholson bearing something like an appearance of drawing to a crisis; we beg leave to enclose you our two last letters to those gentlemen, with their Answers[1]—We hope and believe that things are now in a train to raise some money from that unfortunate Contract, and we think it not prudent to let the breaches of Contract respecting the buildings until after the next Instalment shall become due, which will be on the first of May next. We are &c.

G. Scott
W. Thornton
A. White

LB, DNA: RG 42, Records of the Commissioners for the District of Columbia, Letters Sent.

1. The commissioners evidently enclosed their letters to Robert Morris dated 15 July and 3 Aug. and the answers from Morris written on 25 July and

8 August. For their letter of 15 July, see Commissioners for the District of Columbia to GW, 20 July, n.2.

Morris wrote the commissioners from Philadelphia on 25 July that he had expected to be at the Federal City, but "Mr Nicholson & myself have so many things to adjust before we can leave home, that more time is required for the purposes than ever ourselves had any Idea of—I must pray you to extend your patience a little longer, for we shall certainly be with you soon & we have serious expectations of adjusting every thing to mutual satisfaction" (DLC: Robert Morris Papers).

The commissioners wrote Morris on 3 Aug. that "a personal interview might greatly facilitate an adjustment of all our differences—It is quite agreeable to us to give every Indulgence which can be done with justice to the public—Should however, any unforeseen event intervene to prevent your acceptance of any of the Propositions mentioned in our last Letter to you, we think it highly just, that no delay should arise on account of the Indulgence, granted, at your Instance—And we can consent to it, on no other Terms, except that you and Mr Nicholson will enter voluntary appearances and Special Bail to such Suit or Suits as it may be thought proper to institute against you, in the Supreme Court of Pensylvania, at September Term, next, should no Settlement take place—We will Wait for your answer until the 15th Inst., & if not, by that time received, we shall consider the proposition as not accepted" (DNA: RG 42, Records of the Commissioners for the District of Columbia, Letters Sent)

Morris replied to the commissioners from Philadelphia on 8 Aug. that he and John Nicholson agreed to the "Proposition of entering if it becomes necessary, voluntary appearances in the September Term at our Supreme Court & giving Special Bail in the usual time & manner to the Suits you may think proper or necessary to institute—we expect however to render any Such Proceedings unnecessary" (DLC: Robert Morris Papers).

The commissioners wrote Morris on 11 Aug.: "We received your favor of the 8th Inst. We will forward the Documents of your debt and the statement of your account to Mr Edward Tilghman, & shall be much pleased, should it prove unnecessary to use them in a legal course, of which necessity, Mr Tilghman will judge" (DNA: RG 42, Records of the Commissioners for the District of Columbia, Letters Sent). Morris and Nicholson never met their obligations to the commissioners, and their failed speculation in Federal City property contributed to their eventual imprisonment in Philadelphia for debt (see Arbuckle, *Pennsylvania Speculator and Patriot*, 114–38, and Rappleye, *Robert Morris*, 498–508).

From Bartholomew Dandridge, Jr.

Dear Sir,   Philada August 12. 1796.

I received your letter covering one for the Duke de Liancourt yesterday.[1] I enquired agreeably to your direction, of Mr Lacolombe concerning the residence of the duke, & find he is either at New York or Boston—most probably the latter. Mr Lacolombe advises me to put the letter for him under cover to Mr Casenove at Nw York, which I intend doing by this days post, with a request to Mr Casenove that if the duke is not in Nw York he will give it a safe conveyance.[2]

The other directions contained in your letter shall receive due attention. I have conversed with Mr Sheaffe, who owns half the garden, about putting it in order; & he assures me it is not his wish that anything should be done to it, as he means to begin his preparations for building on it this fall. That part which joins Mr Kennedy's belongs to a brother of Dr Kuhn. he is not in town at present; but Mr Sheaffe tells me it is his intention to build on it the next spring, & does not believe that he wishes any expense to be incurred on account of it.[3] I will see him about it, however, as soon as he returns to the City. At any rate it would not do to disturb the grape vines at this time: they are laden with fine fruit which I presume would be lost if the vines were disturbed at this stage of their growth.

Altho' Mr Kitt never mentioned to you that he had discharged Peter, yet he tells me it was done soon after you left the City. I have directed him to look out for a servant such as you describe; & shall myself make the same enquiry. I fear the getting a *good* one will be found difficult, as there appears to be a great demand for them. Several gentlemen have been here to know of Mr Kitt if he could recommend one to them. Major Jackson called on me the day before yesterday to get Peter's character, whom I believe he means to employ, tho' I could not say much to his advantage.[4] The office and the two bed rooms adjoining were white washed before I arrived here. the white washing those below will be postponed 'till the fly-season is over. Be pleased to present my affection to my Aunt, and accept Dr Sir, the sincere esteem & attachmt of Yr obliged Servt

B. Dandridge

ALS, DLC:GW.

1. GW's letter to Dandridge has not been found.

2. Dandridge forwarded GW's letter to La Rochefoucauld-Liancourt dated 8 August. He recorded under 12 Aug. a "Cont[in]g[en]t Expenc[e]" of sixty cents for its "postage" to New York (Household Accounts).

3. Henry Sheaff (c.1750–1820), a Philadelphia wine merchant, and Peter Kuhn (1751–1826), a Philadelphia merchant and the brother of Dr. Adam Kuhn, purchased the garden lots from Robert Morris in 1795.

Andrew Kennedy (d. 1800) was a Philadelphia merchant who purchased the Morris house and lot in 1795.

4. The discharged servant may have been Peter Helm, who subsequently worked as steward at the Philadelphia City Hospital in 1799.

To James McHenry

Sir   Mount Vernon 12th Augt 1796

The originals and drafts of letters enclosed in yours of the 8th instt are herewith returned.

The publication of the letters to and from Lieutt Colo. England was certainly improper: and the reprehension of Genl Wilkinson for *doing it,* or suffering it *to be done,* is just; and the manner in which it has been conveyed to him is delicate.

The draught of the letter to Colo. Gaither, predicated on the information you *had* received, is very proper: But as Colo. Hawkins is on his way to Philadelphia, & Mr Clymer probably arrived there, I would not have it dispatched until you communicate fully & freely with them on all matters & things relative to that frontier; the establishment of Posts—&ca &ca. Many things in oral conversations often cast up that never can be well explained, and understood by written transmissions from so distant a part of the Union. It is better to encounter a little delay in acquiring perfect information (as much so I mean, as the nature of the case will admit) than to have a second letter to write on the same subject: corrective perhaps, in some instances, of the first. This appears the more necessary in the present case, for as much as Colo. Hawkins is furnished with suggestions from the Indians themselves relative to proper sites for the establishment of Military & trading Posts.

General Pickens's sentimts respecting the conduct of the

Indian Agent to the Southward, accords precisely with the ideas I have entertained of that person, sometime past. It is necessary therefore that every information, derivable from the Commissioners, and other sources should be obtained that the government may take its measures accordingly.

As I expect to be in Philadelphia about the 22d instant, I shall not enlarge on these, or touch any other subject, except informing you that the Pardon for Lieutt Geddis is returned with my signature.

Go: Washington

LS (retained copy), DLC:GW; LB, DLC:GW.

From Timothy Pickering

Sir,   Department of State Augt 12. 1796.

This week I received letters from Colo. Humphreys dated the 4th and 8th of June. The latter covered an edict of the government of Portugal for opening a *free port* at Junguara, just at the Entrance of the harbour of Lisbon. Colo. Humphreys embraced this occasion to compliment the Minister on the liberal policy of the government, and to express his hopes that the subject of the free admission of flour from America, would not escape its attention.[1] But it is so apparently for the interest of the Portuguese to refuse it, I entertain but the slightest expectation of the indulgence. From the information given me by the Chevalier Freire, there is a vast number of mills in the environs of Lisbon, abundantly sufficient to supply every part of the kingdom depending on that port with fresh flour, of which the proprietors would be injured in proportion to the quantity of American flour admitted. They receive great quantities of wheat from Morocco, and generally cheaper than from America. It is in this trade that some American Vessels have probably been taken by the Moors: for at the present time they have gone to the ports in possession of Muley Isham, the rival prince to the reigning emperor, who considering the former as a rebel, has doubtless ordered his cruisers to take any vessels trading to the rebel ports.[2] Colo. Humphreys long ago warned the Americans of the danger: but tempted by the high freights they were willing to run the risque.

And by the news paper accounts it seems that some have been captured.[3]

Colo. Humphreys' letter of the 4th of June covered the copy of a letter from the Dey of Algiers to the President of the United States, of which I have now the honor to inclose a copy.[4] By this it seems clear that the Dey has at length divested himself of his extreme impatience; and that we may entertain, on good grounds, hopes of a happy termination of the Algerine affairs. The letter was brought to Alicant by Mr Cathcart, who was there performing quarantine. Cathcart was one of the American Captives, and the Dey's head Christian Clerk. He had the Dey's orders to come to America in a vessel obtained at Algiers, & was furnished with a passport for one year, commencing the first of May, within which time, the Dey told him the terms of the treaty could certainly be fulfilled. The Dey expects the frigate destined for him should be coppered. This I had always contemplated. Indeed it has seemed to me that good policy required that she should be a very complete vessel, to ensure a *permanent* as well as present satisfaction: for if the one furnished should become shortly defective, we should undoubtedly be obliged to give him a second.[5]

Yesterday I received some packets from Mr Monroe but they were only duplicates of those of the 25th of March and 2d of May.[6] I have the honor to be with the highest respect, Sir, your most obt servt

Timothy Pickering.

ALS, DNA: RG 59, Miscellaneous Letters; LB, DNA: RG 59, Domestic Letters; LB, DNA: RG 59, GW's Correspondence with His Secretaries of State.

1. Pickering described a letter from David Humphreys, U.S. minister to Portugal and chargé d'affaires to the Barbary States (but nominated as U.S. minister to Spain on 19 May), that is dated 7 June. Humphreys wrote Pickering on 8 June about military operations in Europe (both DNA: RG 59, Despatches from U.S. Ministers to Spain). The letter from Humphreys dated 4 June has not been identified.

2. Mawlay Sulayman Ibn Muhammed then reigned as sultan of Morocco (see James Simpson to GW, 24 Sept. 1795, and notes 1 and 3 to that document). For the civil war in Morocco, see Giuseppe Chiappe to GW, 12 Dec. 1794; see also Humphreys to GW, 3 Feb. 1795, n.1.

3. *Claypoole's American Daily Advertiser* (Philadelphia) for 9 Aug. reported that "a Moorish cruizer" had detained the *General Washington*, taken "a few small articles," and allowed the ship to proceed only after the captain signed "a declaration of having received no injury." The captain's mate learned that the cruiser previously had captured "the brig Emmeline, of Boston" and "that

two frigates were cruizing to the westward, and had taken 14 American and British vessels. It appeared . . . that they took none but such as were loaded with grain."

4. Pickering enclosed Hassan Bashaw, Dey of Algiers, to GW, dated 5 May: "Whereas Peace and harmony has been settled between our two Nations through the medium of the two Agents of the United States, Joseph Donaldson and Joel Barlow, and as eight months have elapsed without one article of their agreement being complied with, we have thought it expedient to dispatch James Lea[nde]r Cathcart, formerly our christian Secretary, with a note of such articles as is required in this Regency; likewise with a form of a mediterranean passport in order that you may furnish your Consul here with such as fast as possible; for further intelligence I refer you to your Consul resident here and to the said James Lea[nde]r Cathcart, and I pray whatever they may inform you of to forward our negotiation may be fully credited and that said Cathcart may be dispatched with such part of the articles specified in our negotiation, as are ready with all possible expedition, for which purpose we have granted said Cathcart a mediterranean passport for one year, commencing the date thereof from the first of may in the year of your Lord 1796" (copy, DNA: RG 59, Miscellaneous Letters; the original document is in DNA: RG 59, Consular Despatches, Algiers).

5. For the promised frigate, see GW to the Dey of Algiers, 13 June; see also James McHenry to GW, 7 July, and GW to McHenry, 13 July.

6. For this correspondence from James Monroe, U.S. minister to France, see Pickering's second letter to GW on 21 July, and n.1 to that document, and GW's second letter to Pickering, 27 July, and n.5 to that document.

GW replied to Pickering from Mount Vernon on Tuesday, 16 Aug.: "As I propose to commence my journey to Philadelphia tomorrow, the intention of this letter is only to acknowledge the Receipt of yours of the 12th instant, enclosing a translation of that from the Dey of Algiers to the President of the United States.

Although I begin my journey to morrow, I am unable to say when I shall conclude it. So constant, & excessive have the Rains been in this quarter, that, according to my information, the Roads in many places are almost impassible; but patience & perseverence will, I expect take me to Philadelphia by Monday or Tuesday next. . . P.S. Be so good as to have the enclosed letter decyphered against my arrival" (ALS, MWiW-C: Gates W. McGarrah Collection of Presidential Autographs). For the enclosure mentioned in the postscript, see James Monroe to GW, 24 March; see also GW to Monroe, 25 August.

From Charles Cotesworth Pinckney

Dear Sr   Charleston [S.C.] August 12th 1796

I am prepared to sail for New York or Philadelphia as soon as a good opportunity offers. None of the Philadelphia pacquets are now in our harbour. There is one for New York called the

John; and I went this morning to take my passage in her, when I was credibly informed that she was a very bad sailer, did not obey her helm, always made tedious voyages, & therefore her last Commander (a very good one) left her, & that she has now a new one.[1] This account has deterred me from going in her. Capn Garman is hourly expected from Philadelphia, and I will sail with him on his return, should not a speedier opportunity offer.[2] I am sorry for the delay, but your Letters by the post were very long in coming;[3] and when we depend on ships & winds, a rigid punctuality is out of the question. This City is at present sickly, but no contagious or malignant disorder rages here; for your satisfaction I enclose you a certificate of the medical society to this purpose.[4] With the highest veneration, esteem & attachment, and the sincerest wishes for your happiness, I always am your affectionate & obliged Sert

Charles Cotesworth Pinckney

ALS, DLC:GW.

1. The *City Gazette & Daily Advertiser* (Charleston) for 14 March 1796 advertised John Webb as captain of the brig *John*, "a constant trader" between New York and Charleston. The *Columbian Herald or, the New Daily Advertiser* (Charleston) for 23 Aug. 1796 gave Bent as the name of her captain.

2. The *Columbian Herald or, the New Daily Advertiser* for 23 Aug. reported the arrival at Charleston from Philadelphia of the ship *South-Carolina* under the command of John Garman.

Pinckney wrote GW from Charleston on Friday, 26 Aug.: "I shall embark for Philadelphia on Wednesday next in the Ship south Carolina Captn Garman" (ALS, MHi: Pickering Papers). The *City Gazette and Daily Advertiser* for 3 Sept. reported Pinckney's departure on Friday, 2 September.

3. See GW's two letters to Pinckney on 8 July, and Pinckney to GW, 27 July.

4. Pinckney probably enclosed a medical society resolution dated 10 Aug. that appeared in the *City Gazette and Daily Advertiser* for 12 Aug.: "That in the opinion of the members of the society, the diseases usual in the present season of the year are neither more common, nor more mortal, than they have been for several of the preceding years: that, on the strictest investigation, there does not at present exist in Charleston any contagious malignant fever, known to them; in proof of which they observe, that no medical person, or other attendant on the sick, has caught any disease in the discharge of their respective functions: nor do they know of any case in which there is ground to believe, or even to suspect, that a fever has been communicated from one person to another."

From Lamelin

General, New York August 13th 179[6][1]

Common report has made me acquainted with the pleasure you take to oblige—with whom better than a soul of sensibi[li]ty should I participate the sad situation of an ancient defender of the Continent, if it is not to the military Cheif who has made the happiness, & insured the tranquility of it.

unfortunate by the misfortunes which have overwhelmed us until this, & deprived of the means of existence, to support me & many honest persons, worthy of general commiseration.

I dare to intercede with your good Heart to send me some assistance under the title of a loan, to share with these unhappy victims, they have been already sustained by many compassionate souls who are in the Continent who moved by my solicitations, have softened the fate of those for whom I intercede.

I do not doubt of suceeding with you, be persuaded beforehand of our gratitude, & of the exactness with which we shall return that which we shall receive so Obligingly.

I do not name to you the persons for whom I intercede, I am tender of their delicacy, but I engage my word of honour for them for the quick restitution of the said loan.

they inhabit the City of New York, & have no one but me for a protector & for consolation.

The persuasion they have of your benevolence, has engaged them to charge me to assure you of their respects. I have the honour to be in the same sentiments, General Your very humble & obedient servant

Lamelin

Translation, DLC:GW; ALS, in French, DLC:GW.

1. The translation is dated 1797, but the ALS is dated 1796. Although the ALS is docketed 1797, that letter was addressed to GW at Philadelphia, where he would have been in August 1796. Additionally, the cover of the ALS does not show it being forwarded from Philadelphia as would have been the case in 1797.

Deed to Robert Lewis

[Mount Vernon, 13 Aug. 1796]

I do by these presents give, and (if Deeds of Conveyance should not have been made before) hereby oblige my heirs, Executors and Administrators to fulfil, all the Lands which I hold on Deep run, or its branches in the County of Fauquier[1] unto my Nephew Robert Lewis and to his heirs or Assigns forever. Given under my hand and Seal this 13th day of August 1796

Go: Washington

ADS (facsimile), *Scribner's Monthly*, 14 (May 1877): 75.

1. These lands formed part of GW's inheritance from his father (see GW to Charles Washington, 25 Jan. 1771, n.2, in *Papers, Colonial Series*, 8:430–31).

From Timothy Pickering

Sir,   Department of State Augt 16. 1796.

Expecting from Mr Blodget an improved design for a mediterranean passport, I delayed putting the one he sent me, & which I had the honor to lay before you,[1] into the hands of the engraver. But receiving nothing more from him, I shewed his original design to Mr Wolcott & Mr McHenry who both approved of it, with some little alterations. The engraving has proved a more tedious work than I had imagined, so that I have obtained the first impressions not till to-day. There will be no difficulty in transmitting the passports to reach the remotest ports by the first of September (from which day the law requires their being issued)[2] except those of Charleston and Savannah. And to gain time with respect to these, I shall dispatch a person in the stage to-morrow, to meet you with a few passports, to be completed by your signature; after which the Bearer will forward them in the mail for Charleston and Savannah—that mail which is but the continuation of the one which will leave Philadelphia to-morrow-morning. I shall prepare others to be sent by water to those ports. The whole number of passports committed to the Bearer is twenty four. They are necessary only for those vessels which go to Europe or elsewhere in the other hemisphere. I am most respectfully, sir, your obt servt

Timothy Pickering.

ALS, DNA: RG 59, Miscellaneous Letters; LB, DNA: RG 59, Domestic Letters;
LB, DNA: RG 59, GW's Correspondence with His Secretaries of State. For
GW's probable receipt of this letter, see his letter to John Fitzgerald, 19 August.
    1. See Pickering to GW, 10 June, and n.2 to that document.
    2. See "An Act providing Passports for the ships and vessels of the United
States," approved 1 June (1 *Stat.* 489–90).

To James Anderson

Mr Anderson   City of Washington[1] 18th Augt 1796
    In Passing through Alexandria yesterday, on my way to Phila-
delphia, I saw Colo. Fitzgerald, who informed me of a letter he
had received from you in consequence of one which Doctr Stuart had written to his relation, Mr Fitzhugh of Stafford.[2] It might
have promoted both our views, if you had come immediately to
my house upon the receipt of that letter, as more satisfaction
would have resulted from the conversation of an hour or two,
than from all the letters that can be written on the subject.
    As this however was not the case, and as I shall not be at Mount
Vernon again until the latter end of next month, and consequently cannot see you sooner; I will be candid, & explicit in
what I am going to say to you; from whence, and your answer,
some opinion may be formed of the probability of our mutual
expectations being answered.
    Mr Pearce who at present looks after my business is a person
with whose management I am very well pleased. He is a man of
property; of great integrity; very great industry; and much experience in the superintendence of a large concern; having been
the manager of one for a Gentn on the E.⟨S.⟩ fifteen or 18 years,
before he came to me. In consideration of these qualifications,
& on acct of my being absent from home, when a confidential
character was peculiarly necessary for my concerns I agreed to
give him as an inducement to remove from the Eastern Shore
& on acct of his established character as an expd Manag⟨er⟩
One hundred Guineas a year—although a hundred pounds
(Virga money curr[enc]y) was the most I had ever given before.
He superintends *all* my concerns, which appertain to the Estate
of Mount Vernon; consisting besides Tradesmen of four large
Farms, and the Mansion house farm, the last of which (though
not much is raised at it) is not the least troublesome part of his

duty in ⟨*illegible*⟩—At and over each of these seperate farms & workmen there is as good an Overseer as has been in the power of the superintended to procure, to reside *constantly* on their respective farms &ca & to obey his orders.

This, in general, is the outline of the business—to detail the particular parts, would be tedious, & to a man of experience would be unnecessary. I am altogether in the farming & meadowing line; the last of which I have much grds propr for & want to encreas them considerably.

I will now tell you frankly what kind of a person I must engage to conduct my business *well*. Besides being sober, & a man of integrity, he must possess a great deal of activity and firmness, to make the under Overseers do their duty strictly. He must be a man of foresight & arrangement; to combine & carry matters on to advantage; & he must not have these things to learn after he comes to me. He must be a farmer bred—and understand it in all its parts. I would wish him too to understand grazing— & particularly the care & management of Stock. How to Ditch— Hedge &ca—and how to conduct a Dairy.

Now let me request you to declare truly, whether from practice the matters here detailed are, or could soon be made familiar to you—designating those which you have a competent practical knowledge of, from those which you may be less perfect in. A letter put into the Post office at Fredericksburgh—directed to me in Philadelphia, will be certain of arriving safe, and may enable me to say something more decisive to you in my next, by way of reply to your answer to this letter.

I ought to have added, that the only cause of Mr Pearce's leaving my business is, an increasing Rheumatic affection which he says will not allow him to discharge his duty as he conceives he ought; for which reason, and thinking it the part of an honest man to retire. He has, at one of my farms a good dwelling house pleasantly situated; & every thing comfortably about him.[3] I am—Your Hble Servt

G. Washington

ADfS, DLC:GW.

James Anderson (1745–1807), a native of Scotland, emigrated to Virginia in late 1790 or early 1791. He contracted in October 1796 to serve as GW's farm manager, commencing January 1797 (see Anderson to GW, 8 March 1797, source note, in *Papers, Retirement Series*, 1:21–22). Anderson remained at

Mount Vernon until Martha Washington's death in 1802. He later worked for George Washington Parke Custis.

Richard Kidder Meade wrote GW from Alexandria, Va., on 18 Aug. 1796: "Last evening I met with Mr Fitzhugh, & made inquiry of him about the character of Mr Anderson, of which he is himself totally unacquainted; but from report inform'd me, that he was well spoken of as a Man of industry & very clever at accots but rather advanc'd in years.

"I have as you desir'd requested Mr Fitzhugh to get the best information he could respecting him, & to communicate it to you by letter.

"I hope you compleated your journey to Philadelphia with comfort to yourself" (ALS, ViMtvL; see also John Fitzgerald to GW, 29 Aug., found at GW to Fitzgerald, 19 Aug., n.5).

1. *The Washington Gazette* for 17 Aug. printed an item: "Three o'clock P.M.— The PRESIDENT OF THE UNITED STATES has just arrived from Mount Vernon. Whether on a visit to this City, or on his way to the northward, we cannot tell."

2. These letters have not been identified.

3. Anderson replied to GW on 28 Aug. (see also GW to Anderson, 5 Sept., and Anderson to GW, 11 Sept.).

From Joseph Buell

Sir   Marietta [Northwest Territory] 18th Augt 1796

Agreable to your Advertisement[1] I have Explored your tract of land lying on the bank of the Ohio five or six Miles below the little Kenhaway the situation of which pleases me. I will Give you five dollars pr Acre for the tract and make the payment agreable to the mode prescribed in your advertisemt.[2] I am Sir your Excelences Most Obedient humble Servt

Joseph Buell

ALS, DLC:GW.

Joseph Buell (1763–1812), born in Killingworth, Conn., served as a U.S. army sergeant in the Ohio country between 1786 and 1788 and was an early settler at Marietta, where he kept a tavern. Buell later held local and state offices.

1. See Advertisement, 1 Feb. 1796.

2. GW received other communications regarding his western lands over the next weeks. Jalcott Camp wrote GW from Philadelphia on 1 Sept., 8:00 P.M.: "Having but just arivd at this place I trouble you—to inform myself If I come too late to make proposals for 4395 acres of Land described in your Advertisement of the 1st of Feby as situate a little above the great bend on the River Ohio—If proposals can yet be receivd—would call on you or Mr Dandridge at any hour you will be pleased to name for the purpose of seeing the survey &c.

Having lately visited the several tracts of Land referd to in your Advertisement down to the big Kanaway (except round bottom) any circumstances respecting the present situation of the Lands, in my power to comunicate for your information shall be given with the greatest chearfullness" (ALS, DLC:GW).

O. Fuqua also wrote GW from Philadelphia on 1 Sept.: "Observing the period is Expired, by Your Advertisements to receive proposals for your Western *Lands*, and that Others may be Offered; provided you have, or may Not, incline to Accept Such as have been made; from the Circumstance of my being Engaged to Explore them And for the purposes I had the honor Of Communicating to your Excellency, I feel unwilling to See the Gentlemen, without having it in my power to Satisfy them, So far at least, As may Enable them to make up their Minds, from my description And your price—should they Enter immediately into Contract with you Or Not, I am too Much Effected with the Importance of it, to do any thing in the Matter on my part to show Any precipitancy, As they have promised to Make it Interesting to me should they purchase, this Circumstance will Apprise your Excellency, that my Situation is delicately fixed—Your price And Terms, with the description I Shall hand them will doubtless Incline them to Accede to your Terms or decline the purchase—For this I Should be Thankful, Giving As Lengthy payments As may be Convenient, to Enable the purchasers to be punctual" (ALS, DLC:GW). GW's advertisement for his western lands indicated that he would receive proposals until 1 Sept. and then give preference to the highest sufficient offer on that date.

The correspondent may have been Obadiah Fuqua (d. 1804), who lived in Kanawha County, Va., at the time of his death.

Edward Graham wrote GW from Lewisburg, Va., on 3 Sept.: "It is supposed by many that your lands on the Kenhawa & Ohio rivers will not be sold advantageously untill some person is invested with authority to retail them out in small tracts—You know before this Date how far the plan contained in your Advertisements has succeeded—If any considerable quantity of the aformentioned lands yet remain unsold & you still wish to dispose of them by sale, I am willing to undertake the business if you should think me a proper person to entrust with it.

"My character & connections you may learn from the Honbl. Andrew Moore who has been acquainted with me many years—The Honbl. Messrs Hancock & Preston also know something of me.

"I went through the course of study usual at public Seminaries, under the care of my Brother the Rev: William Graham at Liberty Hall Accademy—From there I went to New London in Campbell County & the Accademy at present established at that place took its rise under my immediate tuition—From New london I was called to Liberty Hall to assist as tutor under my Brother—Last Spring I resigned my place at the Academy & removed to Kenhawa which is my present place of residence & I practice law there & in this County.

"I have given you these outlines of my history that you may the better judge how far I might suit the business for which I offer myself & that you may the better know what enquiries to make respecting me if you should think my proposals worthy your attention.

"My proposals you will readily perceive are very indefinite; the reason is, I do not know in what manner you might wish your lands disposed of—However I would expect to attend to the division of the land agreeably to the directions that might be given, pay all expences of Surveying &c., transmit to you the monies arising from the sales, give security for the due performance of my part of the contract & as a compensation for my trouble & expence receive a certain proportion of the land.

"You will please to transmit me an answer as soon as convenient—It may be sent to the post office in Lewisburgh" (ALS, DLC:GW; the cover indicates that the letter was posted at "Greenbrier Ct House" on 8 Sept.). Andrew Moore, George Hancock, and Francis Preston were Virginia congressmen.

Edward Graham (d. 1840) represented Kanawha County in the Virginia House of Delegates for the 1797–98 session. His affiliation with Washington College (formerly Liberty Hall Academy) included service as a trustee from 1807 until his death.

From James Ross

Sir   Pittsburgh 18. august 1796.

Since my return home I have delivered your conveyance to Colo. Ritchie & received the enclosed bond together with a Mortgage upon the land sold which I have lodged with the recorder of washington County, in whose hands it will remain to be proceeded upon if necessary. The quantity fell short of what we expected as you will see by the enclosed draft of a survey made by Charles Morgan.[1] All expences of Surveying this land will be charged to you, the deeds & different writings are paid by the purchasors. Colo. Ritchie sent forward the interest due upon the whole purchase money up to the first of June last which upon your order has been paid to Mr Wolcott. The Bond & Mortgage are dated on the first of June that being the date of your deed.[2]

I have not seen Colo. Shreve since my return, but I well recollect that when his brother paid me the 1160 Dollars last winter I gave a receipt on account of the second installment *Not* to be credited untill the ballance and all the interest was produced to you, so that Colo. Shreve is altogether without excuse for his delinquency. at all events he should have sent forward my receipt which would have constituted with you a part of the payment.[3]

I wrote to Charles Morgan as you requested respecting the rents due from Shreve & the accounts of Colo. Canon together with Some business of my own, you will learn his answer from his letter of the 26th July which I enclose.[4] Since that time I have not heard from him, nor has he sent me the bonds upon Colo. Shreve as he propos⟨ed⟩.

In my mind Colo. Shreve has acted very improperly he has made a good bargain & has it in his power to fulfill it without difficulty the rents ought long since to have been paid, And he can at any time procure bills of ex[c]hange in this town upon Philadelphia for cash, so that the remittance would occasion no expence to him.

The ratification of the Spanish treaty,[5] & the possession of the Western Posts have completed the measure of our political happiness,[6] The angry discontented politicians of this country are Silenced, Honest men who doubted are satisfied, & all good men feel the liveliest emotions of Joy in contemplating our situation. With most sincere respect I have the Honour to be Sir your most Obedient Humble Servant

James Ross

ALS, DLC:GW.

1. This survey has not been identified, but Charles Morgan had written Ross from Raccoon Creek, Pa., on 26 July: "Inclosed I send you the draught of the presidents land on Millers Run, I survey'd it in April last and Sent Colonel Ritchie a plot. and another to Colonel Nevill Who Informd me the President had desir'd him to get the land Surveyd and Send him a plot &c. Colonel Nevill has Since Informd me he has Sent it— I was with Colonel S[h]reve about Six weeks ago. and had no do[u]bt of Receiving the Rents he was due to the President, but he Informd me he had directed a Gentleman Who had purchas'd land from him, to pay the Sum due for Rent into the Bank of pennsylvania together with a gale for the land he purchas'd of the President, and that he had no do[u]bt but the money was deposited before that time, which he Expected you Could Inform him of on your Return from Philadelphia—as this is not done I Shall (if you think it advisable) put the bonds into your hands in order to Recover the money—In Regard to the millers Run business I have Collected the Chi[e]f part that Colonel Cannon put into my hands Which was but a Small Sum, he having previous to giving up the papers to me Collected all he possibly could.

"I Sent the Statement I Receivd from Cannon last fall, to the president, and the Rents for which I Rented the land does not become due till November next—I have not got the ballance from Flannagin yet, as I have not Seen him Since I came home from Kentuckey." The letter concludes with a few lines on business involving only Ross (DLC:GW).

2. For items related to Matthew Ritchie's purchase of GW's land on Miller's

Run in Washington County, Pa., see Ross to GW, 15 April; Indenture with Matthew Ritchie, 1 June; Alexander Addison to GW, 4 July; and GW to Addison, 8 July.

3. For GW's receipt of this payment, see Ross to GW, 15 April, and n.3 to that document.

4. See GW to Ross, 11 June, and n.1 above.

5. For the ratification of the treaty with Spain, see Timothy Pickering's second letter to GW, 30 July, and n.1 to that document.

6. Ross is referring to the transfer of western posts from the British to the United States under terms of the Jay Treaty.

To John Fitzgerald

Dear Sir,   Baltimore 19th Augt 1796.

I intended to have written to you on the subject of the enclosed letter, from the Federal City,[1] but by dining in a large company at Mr Laws (the day I parted with you) and examining the public buildings afterwards, I was prevented:[2] and letters from the Secretary of State which I met on the Road, and which required my attention yesterday afternoon[3] I was again prevented from doing it in time for the Mail of this morning.

After giving this information (wch is designed principally for Mr Gill) let me request the favor of you to inform, that I am willing to accomodate his wishes for a Deed in Fee, for the land he leased of me, upon the Security of Bank-stock (agreeably to the proposal in his letter) Provided the said Stock is transferred, or so secured to me at *his* expence, in such a manner as the Attorney-General shall deem proper and adequate; and provided also, I receive my proportion of the Dividends when paid, or they become due, in proportion to the quantum of Rent which may be due at the time—for instance, my Rent being £130 pr annum—if the dividends are paid half yearly, I shall expect to receive £65 at each of those times—and if quarter yearly £32.10. This it may be said will amount (calculating interest thereon) to more than the simple Rent; I acknowledge it; but as no security in my estimation is to be compared with that of Land, the difference and advantage of these payments are not an equivolent.[4]

I have mentioned the Attorney General (Mr Lee) because he drew the former writings, and is better acquainted with the principles by which I was governed than any other: but it is not my intention to incur any expence in effecting this change—nor shall I make any apology for the trouble I am giving you in doing it[5]—being with great esteem & regard Dear Sir Your Affecte Servant

Go: Washington

ALS, PPRF; ADfS, PPRF.

1. The enclosure has not been found, but it evidently was a letter from GW to John Gill (see n.5 below).

2. GW left Mount Vernon on 17 Aug., passed through Alexandria, Va., and apparently spent the night at Thomas Law's residence in the Federal District before continuing his trip on 18 Aug. (see Cash Memoranda, 1794–97).

3. GW presumably received Timothy Pickering's letter to him dated 16 August.

4. For John Gill's agreement to lease and ultimately purchase GW's land along Difficult Run, Va., see GW to Gill, 17 May 1795, and n.1 to that document, and Charles Lee to GW, 18 July 1795.

5. Fitzgerald replied to GW from Alexandria on 29 Aug. 1796: "On Monday the 22d Inst. I was honor'd with your letter of the 19th. Mr Gill set out for Baltimore on Monday & did not return 'till friday night, I waited on him on Saturday & now take the first opportunity of forwarding his answer.

"The Bank Shares which he proposes to put you in possession of as a security for your land are not yet in his power, nor will they perhaps for some time— Upon the Sale of this Land & what he purchased from Doctr Dick, which he thinks can be readily effected, when he can give assurance that a deed in Fee simple will be given, he entertains no doubt but the security offer'd to you can be immediately obtained but could not make this promise untill your consent was first had[.] Mr Gill does not seem to have the most distant Idea of getting a deed from you untill he fully complies with his proposal untill which time the Property of course is security to you.

"The day after I had the pleasure of seeing you I had an opportunity of writing to Mr Anderson by a Mr Garnet (the present proprietor of traveller's rest) he assured me that it should be deliver'd in a short time after he got home, & same time spoke much in Anderson's favor[.] I mention'd to him that it was your desire he should be informed that you would be at Mount Vernon about the first of Octor when he might have an opportunity of an interview & you might form a more just opinion of his pretensions & expectations[.] It will always afford me the greatest pleasure to have an opportunity of being the least serviceable to you here" (ALS, DLC:GW; see also GW to James Anderson, 18 Aug.).

Thomas Garnett (d. 1798), formerly a merchant in Fredericksburg, Va., later owned Traveller's Rest, an estate off the King's Highway in Stafford County, Virginia.

To William Pearce

Mr Pearce,   Baltimore 19th Augt 1796.

At this place I have seen Mr Thos Ringgold, who is very desirous of availing himself of your testimony in his pending suit.[1] I have told him, that my consent to this measure has been freely given—and that it depended entirely upon yourself, and the state of your health, whether you attended or not.

Mentioning to him the probability of your quitting the Superintendance of my business, he said it was reported, that a person of the name of Cannon, who Manages for Saml Chew Esqr. was about to leave that employ; and that in his opinion, he was most excellently qualified for such a trust as mine.[2]

You know that it is not my inclination to part with you; but if you are decided on doing it, it will be better for both you & me (if I can get a suitable person for a successor) that it should take place at the usual time (the first of Jany) than in March or April; when, it is not probable, I should be able to find a competent character unengaged to Superintend my concerns for the remainder of that yea⟨r.⟩

From these considerations, and understanding further, from Mr Ringgold, that you are well acquainted with the person & character of Mr Cannon, I am lead to request, if you should go to the Eastern shore; that you would ascertain with precision whether he means to quit Mr Chew'⟨s⟩ Service or not. and if he does, and you (who know the nature of my concerns so well) should be *clearly* of opinion that he is competent to the judicious management of them, that you would know whether he would undertake the trust, and on what terms; for I never gave more than a hundred pounds Virga currency to any, except yourself; nor do I think I shall ever do it again to any one, whose character in this line, is not perfectly established.

It is not my wish to entice Mr Cannon (however deserving he may be) from Mr Chew; but if he has thoughts of leaving that Gentleman, I may as well apply to him—if you do not continue another year—as any one Else. and it is necessary for me to hear from you as soon as possible on this subject; as some persons have, and others may, offer as Managers.

If you have not re-engaged Violet and Cash, fail not to use your utmost exertions to supply their places, especially from the best farming parts of the Eastern Shore, if it can be accomplished.[3] A letter from you to me, written on the Eastern shore will certainly get to my hands if it is put into the line of Any Post Rider.[4] I wish you well and am Your friend

Go: Washington

ALS, owned (1969) by H. Bartholomew Cox, Oxon Hill, Md.; ADfS, NjMoHP: Lloyd W. Smith Collection.

1. Thomas Ringgold was probably the man who previously employed Pearce (see GW to William Tilghman, 21 July 1793).

2. James Cannon had received consideration as GW's farm manager before he hired Pearce. Cannon may have worked for Samuel Chew (1737–1809), who resided in Cecil County, Maryland.

3. GW names his overseers, John Violet (Union farm) and Joseph Cash (Dogue Run farm). Both remained for 1797. For GW's thoughts on these men, see his letter to Pearce written on 5 September.

4. Pearce's reply to GW has not been found, but see GW to Pearce, 28 Aug. 1796.

From "A Friend to the People"

Sir   Baltimore August 21st 1796

I took the liberty of writing you from Richmond about the time the Virginia assembly met;[1] and the tempers of men were so variously agitated at that period, induced a belief that I might have made some observations more important than the event produced. I promised to Communicate some information of characters, which I imagined would have useful effects; but the *ayes* and *noes* being published, on every question of moment, and the *Counties* which the different *members* represented being also *published* rendered this intention unnecessary.

There were few of the Counties of any notice, which I did not visit, and tho many skilful attempts were practised, to produce every species of hostility, against the meas⟨ures⟩ of Government, yet the Counteracting influence predominate⟨d⟩ with visible triumph. It appeared certain to demonstration, from all I could see or find out, that the strength of understanding, in Virginia, even among the people, favoured with the busiest exertions what government had done, and which every good man, regarding the present and future welfare of his Country, must Conscientiously approve. In the course of my Journey, I generally was informed of every corrupt influence sowing sedition, and as generally laid down a rule to be the last visitant, and the most recent impression seemed not to be without a portion of utility. Many of the County Courts where the people were collected, was found experimentally, to be a good scene for exertion.

Whenever I met a town, where there was a newspaper, I published what appeared, to my understanding, right and applied it in other places. This appeared both just and necessary, on a Consideration of the studied artifices employed to corrupt the public mind. Upon the whole there is one truth certain, to my humble judgment, that the voice of the virginia people is not to be ascertained by the voice of their Constituents. This I could prove by a variety, nay innumerable instances, which Came within my observation, but it might be too tedious, as well as an unnecesary recital, for your perusal.

When the Commissioners come to act, on the spoliations Committed on our trade, a question may probably be made on the part of England unproductive of amicable adjustment. You know, Sir, it has been a rule of the English Law, that a Subject cannot forfeit his allegiance, nor Consequently claim expatriation. A large majority who have suffered by the depredations, of the English, on our trade may be included in this description. However the law made by a particular nation, cannot by any Construction, operate so as to affect another nation, in Cases where the Laws of nations have an uncontrouled right to determine. This then, being one of the Cases, embraced by the Laws of nations, and every authority having acquesced, that subjects or citizens may surrender their allegiance, and become citizens of another nation, on the usual Conditions establis⟨hed⟩ by such nation, it becomes conclusive that England must give up this principle, which possibly will be contend⟨ed⟩ for. But you are the best authority to determine, if any remedy should be wanting. I mention this with submission and diffidence.

There were several papers through the virginia Counties, in the form of petitions before last Congress met, remotely disapproving of what government had done. The principles in drawing these documents, were not positively know⟨n⟩ but strong presumptive circumstances unfolded well grounded suspicions of the source from whence they flowed. One of these papers, was handed through Frederick County, by Mr Hite who married a

Sister of Mr Madison, which (as was generally the Case) proved unsucessful.[2]

I hope you will excuse this intrusion, on your more important avocations. The object is well intended, and tho no important benefit may result from the Communicati⟨on⟩ yet it is the duty of every good citizen to disclose to the executive any matter which occurs, particularly as you are in a great degree sequestered from the Common wal⟨ks⟩ of busy life, and immediate intercourse with the people.

I fervently wish you, a long and happy life, as it ha⟨s⟩ been glorious and virtuous, which I am assured, is most sincerely wished by the *People* of our happy Country, and by not one man than

A Friend to the People

AL, DLC:GW.
    1. See "A Friend to the People" to GW, 8 Nov. 1795.
    2. Isaac Hite, Jr. (1758–1836), of Frederick County, Va., married James Madison's sister Nelly Conway Madison (1760–1802) in 1783 (see Rutland, *James Madison Encyclopedia*, 191).
    For petitions against the Jay Treaty sent to Congress from Virginia, see Edward Carrington to GW, 6 Dec. 1795, and n.3.

From Benjamin Henry Latrobe

Sir,   Richmond Augt 22d 1796.
    The plough which you did me the favor to say you would try, is now ready, and I shall send it, directed to the care of Mr Porter, merchant, Alexandria, by the first vessel that is bound from hence to that port. Its merits in working you will easily ascertain upon trial, and should you be satisfied on that head, you will, I believe, find, that with very little care and precission your own people may repair or copy it. I am sorry I could not procure for you in time a castiron Mould-board. I shall be able to send you one soon. The *turn* of the board appears to me to be the most perfect possible, and applicable to any plough whatever.

Mr Gilbert Richardson under whose direction this plough has been made, has been in the habit of using the heavy Rotheram plough in England, and perfectly understands its construction. I should conceive myself particularly favored by your sending me the stock of your plough, which the loss of your ironwork has rendered useless to you; as I think I can get it perfectly reinstated here. Should your engagements permit your attention to these lesser objects, I should be extremely flattered by your suffering me to show my sense of the very polite reception with which you honored me at Mt Vernon in endeavoring to be of the slightest assistance to your agricultural views.

We have had such constant rains *here,* and lower down upon James river, that almost all the lowland corn is much injured, and a great quantity totally destroyed. The highland crop looks and promises well should the weather become more favorable. There has been no fresh, nor even a considerable rise in James river notwithstanding the daily rains of the two months past. I have the honor to be Sir Your most obedient hble Servt

Benjn Henry Latrobe.

ALS, DLC:GW. GW wrote "recd 17th Septr 1796" on the docket.

Latrobe had visited Mount Vernon in July and stayed overnight. Latrobe wrote about his visit in his journal: "Having alighted at Mount Vernon, I sent in my letter of introduction, and walked into the portico next to the river. In about ten minutes the President came to me. He was attired in a plain blue coat, his hair dressed and powdered. There was a reserve but no hauteur in his manner. He shook me by the hand, said he was glad to see a friend of his nephew's, drew a chair, and desired me to sit down." Latrobe and GW then discussed Bath, Virginia.

"The conversation then turned upon the rivers of Virginia. He gave me a very minute account of all their directions, their natural advantages, and what he conceived might be done for their improvement by art. He then inquired whether I had seen the Dismal Swamp, and seemed particularly desirous of being informed upon the subject of the canal going forward there. He gave me a detailed account of the old Dismal Swamp Company and of their operations, of the injury they had received by the effects of the war, and still greater, which their inattention to their own concerns had done them. After many attempts on his part to procure a meeting of directors, the number of which the law provided should be six in order to do business, all of which proved fruitless, he gave up all further hopes of anything effectual being done for their interests, and sold out his shares in the proprietary at a price very inadequate to their real value. . . .

"This conversation lasted above one hour, and, as he had at first told me that he was endeavoring to finish some letters to go by the post upon a variety of business 'which notwithstanding his distance from the seat of Government still pressed upon him in his retirement,' I got up to take my leave." GW prevailed upon Latrobe to remain, and they proceeded to discuss mining.

"After conversing with me more than two hours he got up and said that 'we should meet again at dinner.'" Latrobe then met Martha Washington and Eleanor Parke Custis. "I introduced myself to Mrs. Washington as a friend of her nephew, and she immediately entered into conversation upon the prospect from the lawn, and presently gave me an account of her family in a good-humored free manner that was extremely pleasant and flattering. She retains strong remains of considerable beauty, seems to enjoy very good health, and to have a good humor. She has no affectation of superiority in the slightest degree, but acts completely in the character of the mistress of the house of a respectable and opulent country gentleman. Her granddaughter, Miss Eleanor Custis, the only one of four who is unmarried, has more perfection of form, of expression, of color, of softness, and of firmness of mind than I have ever seen before or conceived consistent with mortality. . . .

"Young La Fayette with his tutor came down some time before dinner. He is a young man about seventeen, of a mild, pleasant countenance, favorably impressing one at first sight. . . .

"Dinner was served about half after three. It had been postponed about a half-hour in hopes of Mr. Lear's arrival from Alexandria. The President came into the portico about half an hour before three, and talked freely upon common topics with the family. . . . There was very little conversation at dinner. A few jokes passed between the President and young La Fayette, whom he treats more as his child than as a guest. I felt a little embarrassed at the silent, reserved air that prevailed. . . .

"Coffee was brought about six o'clock. When it was removed the President, addressing himself to me, inquired after the state of the crops about Richmond. I told him all I had heard. A long conversation upon farming ensued, during which it grew dark, and he then proposed going into the hall. He made me sit down by him and continued the conversation for above an hour. During that time he gave me a very minute account of the Hessian fly and its progress from Long Island, where it first appeared. . . . It has not yet appeared in Virginia, but is daily dreaded. The cultivation of Indian corn next came up. He dwelt upon the advantages attending this most useful crop, and then said that the manner in which the land was exhausted by it, the constant attendance it required during the whole year, and the superior value of the produce of land in other crops would induce him to leave off entirely the cultivation of it, provided he could depend upon any market for a supply elsewhere. As food for the negroes, it was his opinion that it was infinitely preferable to wheat bread in point of nourishment. He had made the experiment upon his own land and had found that though the negroes, while the novelty lasted, seemed to prefer wheat bread as being the food of their masters, soon grew tired of it. He conceived that should the negroes be fed upon wheat or rye bread, they would, in order to be fit for the same labor, be obliged to have a considerable addition to their allowance of meat. But notwithstanding all this, he thought the balance of advantage to be against the Indian corn.

"He then entered into the different merits of a variety of plows which he had tried, and gave the preference to the heavy Rotheram plow from a full experience of its merits. The Berkshire iron plow he held next in estimation. He had found it impossible to get the iron work of his Rotheram plow replaced in a proper manner, otherwise he should never have discontinued its use. I promised to send him one of Mr. Richardson's plows of Tuckahoe, which he accepted with pleasure.

"Mrs. Washington and Miss Custis had retired early, and the President left the company about eight o'clock. We soon after retired to bed. There was no hint of supper.

"I rose with the sun and walked in the grounds near the house. The President came to the company in the sitting room about one-half hour past seven, where all the latest newspapers were laid out. He talked with Mr. Lear about the progress of the work at the great falls and in the City of Washington. Breakfast was served up in the usual Virginia style. Tea, coffee, and cold broiled meat. It was very soon over, and for an hour afterwards he stood upon the steps of the west door talking to the company who were collected round him. The subject was chiefly the establishment of the University at the federal city. He mentioned the offer he had made of giving to it all the interests he had in the city on condition that it should go on in a given time, and complained that, though magnificent offers had been made by many speculators for the same purpose, there seemed to be no inclination to carry them into reality. He spoke as if he felt a little hurt upon the subject." Latrobe described his departure from Mount Vernon: GW "shook me by the hand, desired me to call if I came again into the neighborhood, and wished me a good morning.

"Washington has something uncommonly majestic and commanding in his walk, his address, his figure, and his countenance. His face is characterized, however, more by intense and powerful thought than by quick and fiery conception. There is a mildness about its expression, and an air of reserve in his manner lowers its tone still more. He is sixty-four, but appears some years younger, and has sufficient apparent vigor to last many years yet. He was frequently entirely silent for many minutes, during which time an awkwardness seemed to prevail in everyone present. His answers were often short and sometimes approached to moroseness. He did not at any time speak with very remarkable fluency; perhaps the extreme correctness of his language, which almost seemed studied, prevented that effect. He appeared to enjoy a humorous observation, and made several himself. He laughed heartily several times in a very good-humored manner. On the morning of my departure he treated me as if I had lived for years in his house, with ease and attention, but in general I thought there was a slight air of moroseness about him as if something had vexed him" (Latrobe, *Journal,* 54–63).

From Timothy Pickering

Sir   Department of State Augt 22. 1796.

The inclosed letter came under cover to me from Wm Lithgow Attorney for the district of Maine, which he says contains his resignation.[1] Daniel Davis Esquire of Portland is a lawyer well recommended by the Members of Congress to suceed Mr Lithgow, & I think has been doing the business of the office since Mr

Lithgow's indisposition prevented his attending the courts. The enquiries concerning a successor were made by me before the rising of Congress, in expectation of Mr Lithgow's resignation.[2] I am with the highest respect sir your most obt servt

T. Pickering

ALS, DNA: RG 59, Miscellaneous Letters; LB, DNA: RG 59, GW's Correspondence with His Secretaries of State.

1. Pickering enclosed a letter from William Lithgow, Jr., to GW dated 20 July: "I have the honour to sustain by your appointment, the Office of District Attorney for Maine, and a very melancholy chronic Disease, which is thought permanent, having rendered me incompetent to the discharge of the more active duties of that station; I find myself compelled, in justice to the public, to solicit your permission to resign the same.

"It seems peculiarly unfortunate, & hard Sir, that this, should be the second resignation, with which I have had occasion to trouble you; and both arising from mere adventicious inability, to execute the duties of the Offices relinquished—The first, was, of a military Command; and the inevitable consequence of a desperate wound received in Action; and this last, is, the unhappy result, of a still more dreadful Malady.

"That the United States, may long be aided by your tried Patriotism, & distinguished Abilities at the head of her affairs: and that you, Sir; for many, very many happy years to come, may enjoy in tranquil Dignity, the just reward of all your toils & labours, so nobly exerted in the Cause of Liberty and your Country" (ALS, DNA: RG 59, Miscellaneous Letters; see also William Heath to GW, 25 July 1778, in *Papers, Revolutionary War Series*, 16:165–66).

2. For the nomination of Daniel Davis as U.S. attorney for the District of Maine, see GW to the U.S. Senate, 21 Dec. 1796 (DNA: RG 46, entry 52).

From Thomas Smith

Sir,   South 12th Street [Philadelphia] 22d August 1796.

William Alexander of Carlisle Esquire, by a Note which he left for me when he left the City last Week, informs me that application has been made on his behalf, for the Office of Surveyor, in the room of Mr Dewit, & requests that I would inform you what Character he has supported in civil life since the conclusion of the War. I comply with his request with pleasure, because, from a particular acquaintance with him during this period, I can say that his moral & political deportment, has been, not only unexceptionable, but such as to secure the esteem of every upright man—of every friend to good order & government, to whom he is known.

As a Justice of the Peace, & as Lt Colonel Commandant of the Carlisle Regiment of Militia, he has given general satisfaction.

That he was an active & useful Officer on the late expedition against the Western insurgents, you have probably been informed by the Commander in Chief on that expedition.

He was in the occasional practice of Surveying while I resided in Carlisle. I have the honour to be, with profound respect, Sir, Your most obedient humble servant

Thomas Smith

ALS, DLC:GW.

Finding a surveyor general had vexed GW (see his letter to John Marshall, 15 July, and the notes to that document).

Letter not found: from William Pearce, 23 Aug. 1796. GW wrote Pearce on 28 Aug.: "Your letter of the 23d instt . . . came to my hands yesterday."

From the French Directory

Monsieur le Président, [c.24 Aug. 1796]

Le Directoire Exécutif informé que le Congrès des Etats-unis, vient de passer le bill nécéssaire à l'exécution du traité de Londres du mois de 9bre 1794,[1] a cru qu'il étoit de son devoir, dans ces circonstances, de rappeller la Légation française de Philadelphie.

La retraite de cette Légation ne doit point être considerée par vous, et par le peuple américain, comme une rupture, mais seulement comme une marque d'un mécontentement légitime. Le Citoyen Adet, Ministre plenipotentiaire est chargé, avant de prendre congé de vous, de vous faire, au nom du Gouvernement français, une déclaration que le Directoire Exécutif vous prie de regarder comme l'expression formelle de ses justes plaintes et de ses vœux. Puissent le Congrès et le Président des Etats-Unis, par un prompt retour à des principes plus conformes aux vrais intérests de ⟨la⟩ nation Américaine, hâter l'heureuse époque où il Sera permis au Directoire Exécutif de rétablir entre le Gouvernement fédéral, et lui, tous les anciens rapports d'amitié d'harmonie et de bonne intelligence!

Ce Sont là, Monsieur Le Président, les vœux du Directoire Exécutif. Ils sont tous pour la gloire et la prospérité des Etats-Unis.

Donné au Palais national du Directoire Exécutif, muni du sceau de la République à Paris le [7] fructidor[2] l'an 4e de la République française une et i⟨ndivisible⟩

Les membres composant le Directoire Exécutif

Copy, FrPMAE: Correspondence Politique, États Unis, vol. 46.

1. See "An Act making an Appropriation towards defraying the Expenses which may arise in carrying into effect the Treaty of Amity, Commerce and Navigation, made between the United States and the King of Great Britain," approved 6 May (1 *Stat.* 459).

2. The day was left blank on the copy, but the letter sent French minister Pierre-Auguste Adet with instructions to deliver this protest was dated 7 Fructidor (FrPMAE: Correspondence Politique, États Unis, vol. 46).

From James McHenry

private.

Sir.   War office 24 Augt 1796

I inclose you a rough draught of a talk to the Cherokees and instructions to agent Dinsmore, containing a plan for promoting their civilization and rendering the management of them easier and more œconomical. If you think favourably of it I will revise and correct it and have Mr Dinsmore dispatched to his station. You will find it to contain little more than a mode for executing the laws respecting the Indians which contemplate approximating them nearer to the civilized State, and the law passed at the late session of Congress.[1] Dinsmore seems a prudent man. I have consulted him upon the practicableness of teaching the women to spin and weave, and he thinks it may be accomplished. With the most sincere respect I have the honor to be Sir your ob. st

James McHenry

ALS, DLC:GW; copy, MHi: Adams Papers. A letterpress of the copy is in DLC: James McHenry Papers.

1. McHenry's rough drafts have not been identified, but see GW to the Cherokee Nation, 29 August.

McHenry's penned instructions to Silas Dinsmoor, temporary Cherokee agent, dated 29 Aug.: "You will be pleased to have the annexed talk to the Cherokee Nation from the President carefully distributed, translated and explained in their respective Towns and Tribes; you will also consider it as forming a part of your standing instructions, at least, so far as you may have it in your power to facilitate the accomplishment of the objects to which it has relation.

"It is to be lamented, that the experiments, heretofore made, with a view to civilize the Indians, have issued so unsuccessfully. Notwithstanding the pains that have been taken on this subject, the Indian differs but little at this day from what he was when first known to the Europeans. Neither the time which has since elapsed; nor our intercourse with them; nor our establishments among them, seem to have rendered them more civilized or less savage. We still find them characterized by the same habits and manners; the same pursuits and pleasures, varied only by certain incidental vices derived from the outcasts of Society.

"What is it that can have perpetuated such an uniformity of character, and acted as a barrier against the different attempts that have been made to civilize them?

"Is not the cause to be found in their mode of life? Is it not hunting and trapping which continues them indolent, savage and warlike, and must not this practice be broke in upon before they can be made to approach civilization? To trap and hunt for subsistence amidst immense deserts and wilderness would gradually approximate civilized Man to the Savage. How unreasonable then is it to expect that the Indian who does nothing else, and who spends so large a portion of his time in such situations should yet be civilized. I can entertain no such expectation.

"To civilize him he must be weaned from hunting and trapping, by having set before his eyes other pursuits by which he may obtain a less precarious and more comfortable subsistence; and by rendering hunting and trapping by indirect means, disreputable as a mode of livelihood.

"The Indian will have advanced one step towards this point, when he shall discover, that he has it in his power to provide better for his wants, by raising Cattle and Grain than by hunting and trapping. He will moreover be stimulated by strong motives to avail himself of the discovery, when he shall find that he can get more money or gratifications for his redundant Cattle, Grain or Tobacco, than he can for his Skins or Peltry.

"To aid his sensations on this subject, it would seem expedient, that what he raised in the one way should meet a ready market and as much encouragement as possible; and what he got in the other be at least negatively discouraged. For in proportion as the Indian will perceive and experience this distinction or preference between Skins and Cattle or Grain, he will gradually and involuntarily desert hunting and trapping or practice it only as an occasional amusement.

"I have made these observations with a view to illustrate the basis upon which the talk of the President is founded, and to direct your attention and efforts to the execution of the civilizing system which it contemplates. After the talk has been sufficiently explained to the Indians, you will communicate their understanding of it, and how far they appear to relish it or disposed to concur in its objects.

"I conceive it will be no difficult thing to satisfy them of the utility of a general Council, as suggested in the talk, to be composed of two wise men from each town or tribe and held annually at Oostinahli, at which all affairs respecting their nation may be settled and plans for bettering their situation proposed & considered.

"Complaints against those Cherokees who may violate the treaty may be made to this Council and modes of restitution or punishment devised and agreed to by the wise men. Here also the principal and you as resident agent will hear their Grievances and inform them, when founded, how and in what way they are to receive redress.

"Such an institution as this it is conceived, will render the conducting of business with the nation easier and more œconomical than heretofore.

"Should the Nation agree that an attempt should be made to introduce into it the art of spinning and weaving, you will give information of their Consent, and take immediate measures in conjunction with the Agent for the department of War to have the necessary apparatus and instructors provided and sent you.

"It occurs that it may be advisable to commence the experiment under your own eyes and to have a kind of School opened at Oostinahli for teaching to spin and weave.

"Women being every where more docile and disposed to sedentary employments than Men, excites a hope that the manufacture of coarse Cotton and linen may, through their means, be introduced into the nation; and that it will be considerably quickened and extended as soon as they shall experience that a few yards of their manufacture will bring them more money, or exchange for articles of greater Value than a Bear Skin.

"With respect to *Stock* raising. As this is an employment more congenial to the habits of the Men, than agriculture, it is likely to be more immediately relished by them. It will be relished upon another account. Persons will come into their Nation to buy Cattle as soon as it is known they have them to sell; a circumstance which may be converted into a powerful stimulus by proper management. Besides giving the Indians such instructions as may help them to increase their flocks, it will be permitted you upon a representation of its being necessary, to add such domestic animals as may serve to improve the breed of each kind.

"It may also be an eligible measure, when the experiment has taken effect to concert with the wise men in Council upon the times and places proper to hold a fair for the sale of their superfluous stock, of which the Whites should have due information and at which you should always attend. Perhaps too, it would be a good regulation for the wise men in Council to establish, that no Indian should sell either a horse or any kind of stock to a White Man at any other time or place. Were such a regulation adopted it would be a check upon frauds to which they will be otherwise exposed, and to thefts that may be practiced under cover of licences. If no horses or Cattle were to be sold but at fixed times; horses or Cattle brought out of their Country at other times would necessarily be considered as having been stolen.

"But these ideas are offered, rather for consideration, than as rules for your government.

"With respect to agriculture. You will use your best endeavours to encourage it among them; and from time to time, help them to such implements for tillage as they may actually stand in need of, and as you have reason to believe will be usefully employed.

"You will perceive by all this how essential it is to success that you should understand their language and be able to converse fluently in it[.] The President expects therefore, that you will apply yourself diligently to acquire it, as without it your power of being useful will be greatly abridged."

McHenry continued his instructions to Dinsmoor with specific items intended to assist "in the execution of this act. . . .

"1. You will require from every person who comes into the Cherokee Country where you reside or of whom you have knowledge to exhibit his pass and you will keep a book in which you will record their names and by whom their pass is signed. If the person has no pass or refuses to produce it, you will forthwith report his or their names to the Governor of the State of Tennessee, and the Agent for the department of War and signify to the Indians that such person having violated the law may be expelled by them from their Nation; but that in driving him out they must do him no injury or violence.

"2d. Should any white Citizen of or resident in the United States offend against the second section of the aforesaid act, his or their property may be drove off, and he or they apprehended by the Indians and delivered to the Officer commanding at Tellico Block house or to any Magistrate in Tennessee: but no injury must be offered to their persons. The name of every Offender is also to be reported to the Agent for the department of war; and for every person delivered and for which the Indian shall produce you a receipt from the commanding Officer or a Magistrate as aforesaid, you may pay him Ten dollars.

"3d. In cases of property taken or destroyed belonging to an Indian or other offence committed within the purview of the fourth section aforesaid, you will as soon as possible ascertain with precision and have authenticated by the best evidence in your power the value of the property taken or destroyed and the nature of the offence committed and make report of the case to the Governor of the State of Tennessee and the Agent for the department of War that means may be taken to obtain restitution.

"4. Should it come to your knowledge that any Citizen of, or other person resident in the United States, has made a settlement on any lands belonging or secured or granted by treaty to the Cherokees, you will give immediate notice of the name of the person so offending and the place where he has settled to the Officer of the Troops of the United States commanding at the post nearest to the said Intruder and the Governor of the State of Tennessee. And should any Citizen or resident of the United States survey or attempt to survey any of their land or designate it by marking Trees or otherwise, you will report them in like manner and as aforesaid.

"5. You will require of every person acting as a Trader among the Cherokees and who comes within your knowledge or that of your Assistants, a sight of his licence, which you will make a record of and report to the Agent[for the department of War. And if any person is found without a licence you will report his name also and at the same time give information to the Indians that he has forfeited all the goods in his possession to the nation. You will in like manner inform the Agent of the names of such persons as may violate the ninth and tenth sections of the law aforesaid.

"6. Till such time as the Cherokees shall meet in Council agreeably to the plan of civilization, you will make application for compensation or satisfaction for offences described by the fourteenth section of the aforesaid act, to the tribe of the Indian committing the Offence, if known, or to the nation generally if not known, and should satisfaction be refused or neglected to be made in the time prescribed by law you will inform the Agent for the department of War of the said neglect or refusal."

McHenry required Dinsmoor to submit semi-annual reports to the War Department, manage interpreters in the Cherokee nation, move his residence or the place of Cherokee meetings as necessary, and "agree with the Cherokee Indians upon a more equitable plan than has been heretofore adopted for the apportionment among them of their annual stipend." McHenry also covered basic administrative items (MHi: Adams Papers; see also "An Act to regulate Trade and Intercourse with the Indian Tribes, and to preserve Peace on the Frontiers," approved 19 May, in 1 *Stat.* 469–74).

From William Brunner

State of South Carolina
Honourable Sir   Orangebourgh District[1] August the 25th 1796
Since your Excellence President of the united States, ev'ry Subject ought to gratify with Submissive Thankfullness this great blessing to your Honour. I take the Liberty in these Lines, to reveal, that (while Science, Art, and Agriculture &c: most florishing) some usefull Instruments to the ease of the Labourers of Oeconomie very beneficial, having Studied many years to find out Machines for that purpose, finding a possibility of a Machine for a Saw-Mill without Wind, Water and Horse, that one Man can Saw more planks with great ease, than Two Men of hand with hard Labour; this Saw-Mill may be erected at any place, at the River bank, Swamps, Shipyards to Saw great and Small Timber; to any desire and pleasure. Secondly a Machine, that one Man can easely drive four great Water-pumps, to be used in cities, Salt Works, and might be fitted to Ships or Vessels to have them in Time of need these Same Machine may be used if 2. or 4. Mortars is made instead of pumps, to Stamp Rice, peal Barley, and for the Western parts, where Mills is Scarce, to crake Corn with great ease, further for the cultivators of Hemp to apply 4. Breaks with once to clean it, if their was only tenders to each, and to Soften it in the afore Said Mortars; it may be applied to

make Gun powder with Sifters to it, the Man driving the Work may Stand a distance of it. hoping to grant! I am Born in Germany learning no trade, but from my Infancy tried to Work in Wood advanced with Such genuity, that I have Build Gear Mills and Saw-Mills; joiner and Cooper Work done. Missfortune fell upon me for about 30 Years getting Sore leggs, now a cripple these many Years, maintaining myself and family under great difficulty and misery honestly; tho not to be a burden to any person. I had Studied as a fore Said many Years upon those Machines, but never brought it to a perfect idea, till now. Time and Season produces its own! now am poor, 66. Years old, Scarce able to Work upon account the afore Said Misery, had in mind that the Mistery of those Machines should die with me; revealing to a friend the project of these Machines with my intention, this friend Sayd: he had no doubt, if I make it known to your Excellency, Such a valuable Mistery would be greatly rewarded, to comfort me, in my circumstance miserys because it was an Oeconomical, very valuable one, for public Trade and Agriculture. am informed, that ancient customary the inventors being greatly rewarded, for Such advantageous, usefull Project for all the united States. Supposing, it may be Said: that these Machines was Costly and Expensive? Answer: No. the first Machine, the Saw-Mill, can be made of Wood, it takes but little Iron (except the pushing Wheel and Saw) a Workman may finish the hohl in about Two Week's, if their is found an attendance. The second, is but Simple, and easy to be made, if required without any Iron. Therefore beeing afraid I am a poor Man, my invention might be rejected and despised as that poor Man's Written Ecclesiastes 9 vers 15. 16.[2] Nevertheless, having Confidence unto your Excellency to make me a most generous promise of Reward, and after receiving your Excellency's promise and Answer, I Shall make the afore Said Machines in Small, put them in a Chest carefully and Send over at your pleasure and View⟨,⟩ than afterwards, if desired, to make it at large, to the perfect Use, to give a full complete Mansion and description of every piece belonging to it, and how to place it, to every Persons Satisfaction who is intented to enjoy the benefit of it. I have the Honour to Remain with a Submissive devotion; to be Your Excellence most humble Servant

William Brunner

N.B. the Saw-Mill can be taken depart an[d] moved at any place.

Address: To William Brunner the Dutch Cooper living 7 miles from Orangeburgh To the care of Mr Abraham Marckley King Street Charleston South Carolina.[3]

ALS, DLC:GW.

1. The Orangeburgh District in South Carolina, established with seven others in 1769, eventually included parts or all of seven counties in the southwestern portion of the state.

2. "Now there was found in it a poor wise man, and he by his wisdom delivered the city; yet no man remembered that same poor man.

"Then said I, Wisdom *is* better than strength: nevertheless the poor man's wisdom *is* despised, and his words are not heard" (Eccles. 9:15–16).

3. Abraham Markley (1745–1824), a merchant in Charleston, S.C., had kept a store at 125 King Street.

To Alexander Hamilton

Private
My dear Sir,   Philadelphia 25th Augt 1796
    I have given the Paper herewith enclosed, several serious & attentive readings; and prefer it greatly to the other draughts, being more copious on material points; more dignified on the whole; and with less egotism.[1] Of course less exposed to criticism, & better calculated to meet the eye of discerning readers (foreigners particularly, whose curiosity I have little doubt will lead them to inspect it attentively & to pronounce their opinions on the performance).

    When the first draught was made, besides having an eye to the consideration above mentioned, I thought the occasion was fair (as I had latterly been the subject of considerable invective) to say what is there contained of myself—and as the Address was designed in a more especiall manner for the Yeomanry of this Country I conceived it was proper they should be informed of the object of that abuse; the silence with which it had been treated—and the consequences which would naturally flow from such unceasing & virule⟨nt⟩ attempts to destroy all confidence in the Executive part of the Government; and that it was best to do it in language tha⟨t⟩ was plain & intelligable to their understand⟨ing.⟩[2]

    The draught now sent, compr⟨e⟩hends the most, if not all

these matters; is better expressed; and I am persuade⟨d⟩ goes as far as it ought with respect to any personal mention of myself.

I should have seen no occasi⟨on⟩ myself, for its undergoing a revision—But as your letter of the 30th Ulto whi⟨ch⟩ accompanied it, intimates a wish to do this—and knowing that it can be more correctly done after a writing has been out of sight for sometime than while it is in hand, I send it in conformity there⟨to⟩—with a request, however, that you w⟨d⟩ return it as soon as you have carefully reexamined it;[3] for it is my intention to hand it to the Public before I leave this City, to which I came for the purpose of meeting General Pinckney—receiving the Minesters from Spain & Holland[4]—and for the dispatch of other business which could not be so well executed by written communications between the heads of Departments & myself as by oral conferences. So soon as these are accomplished I shall return; at any rate I expect to do so by, or before the tenth of next month for the purpose of bringing up my family for the Winter.

I shall expunge all that is marked in the paper as unimportant &ca &ca and as you perceive some marginal notes, written with a pencil, I pray you to give the sentiments so noticed mature consideration. After which, and in every other part, if change or alteration takes place in the draught, let them be so clearly interlined—erazed—or referred to in the Margin as that no mistake may happen in copying it for the Press.

To what Editor in *this* City do you think it had best be sent for Publication? Will it be proper to accompany it with a note to him, expressing (as the principal design of it is to remove doubts at the next Election) that it is hoped, or expected, that the State Printers will give it a place in their Gazettes—or preferable to let it be carried by my private Secretary to that Press which is destined to usher it to the World & suffer it to work its way afterwards? If you think the first most eligable, let me ask you to sketch such a note as you may judge applicable to the occasion.[5] With affectionate regard I am always Yours

Go: Washington

ALS, DLC: Hamilton Papers; copy, DLC: Hamilton Papers. The characters in angle brackets have been supplied from a tracing of the ALS in DLC: Hamilton Papers.

1. GW enclosed what was probably a fair copy of the draft for his farewell

address that Hamilton had sent to him on 30 July (see headnote to Farewell Address, 19 Sept.).

2. GW is referring to the draft enclosed when he wrote Hamilton on 15 May.

3. GW subsequently asked Hamilton to prepare new material (see his letter to Hamilton, 1 Sept.).

4. GW alludes to Spanish minister Carlos Martinez Yrujo and Dutch minister Robert Gerard Van Polanen.

5. Hamilton replied to GW on 5 Sept.; see also Hamilton to GW, 4 September.

To Rufus King

Private

Dear Sir   Philadelphia 25th Augt 1796

Will you do me the favor to cause the enclosed notification to be inserted in some public Paper, agreeably to the Decree of the High Court of Chancery in Virginia—annexed thereto.[1]

It has been a long, troublesome and vexatious business to me; and I wish to close it *finally* and *effectually* in the manner designated. One part of which (depositing of the money) I have already complied with—and wish to do the same by the other part— namely, the Publication in England.

The persons interested (if any of them are in existence) lives, most probably, at or near Newcastle in Northumberland County England. Whether it would be best therefore to send it there in the first instance for publication, or to publish it in the Metropolis (London) with a request that it may be re-published there, I leave to your better judgment in these matters.

Whatever expence is incurred, be pleased either to charge in your public account, or send me a note of it, and the amount shall in either case be paid to the Secretary of State here.[2]

I am sorry and almost ashamed to give you trouble in so trifling (though to me, interesting a business) but as I conceived it would be the most effectual mode of executing it, I rely on your goodness to excuse it—and to send me one of the Papers containing the publication of the notice.

I hope you and family had a short and pleasant passage— Present me if you please to Mrs King,[3] and be assured of the esteem & regard with which I am—Dear Sir Your most Obedt Servt

Go: Washington

ALS, NHi: Rufus King Papers; ADfS, DLC:GW; LB, DLC:GW. The word "Copy" has been written near the top of the ALS in an unknown handwriting.

1. GW enclosed a notice dated 25 July: "The Administration of the Estate of Colo. Thomas Colville late of Fairfax County in Virginia being now closed, it appears by the Settlement that there is a Ballance in my Hands of Nine hundred and Thirty two Pounds Seventeen Shillings and Seven pence three Farthings Current Money of Virginia (Dollars at Six Shillings) which by the Will of Colo. Colville is to be divided among the nearest Relations of his Mother Catherine Colville of the name of Stott, Wills, Richards and Smith. Not chusing to take upon myself a decision of the various Claims to this Legacy I have filed a Bill in the High Court of Chancery to bring the several Claimants into that Court for a discussion of their Claims. In this Suit the customary Order has been made where the parties or any of them reside out of the State which by the Laws of the State is equivalent to the Service of the Subpœna. Those who are interested will pay attention to this Order, as a neglect may bar their Claims. The Money is deposited in the Bank of Alexandria and the Order of Court hereto subjoined" (NHi: Rufus King Papers). For the chancery decree, see Bushrod Washington to GW, 3 July, n.2. The notice and decree appeared in *The London Gazette* several times between the issues dated 29 Nov. 1796 and 21–24 Jan. 1797.

2. King enclosed this paragraph of the ALS in square brackets. He also marked an open bracket before the first sentence of the letter and at the end of the first sentence of the second paragraph. King then wrote in the left margin of the first page: "N. Yk Ap. 28. 1804. the sentences included in Brackets sent to the treasury as a voucher for the charge of advertising &c."

3. Mary Alsop King (1769–1819) had married Rufus King in 1786.

To James Monroe

Duplicate
Dear Sir,   Philadelphia 25th Augt 1796

Your favor of the 24th of March written in Cypher, never got to my hands until the 10th instant at Mount Vernon; nor were the contents of it known to me until my arrival in this City on the 21st. For the information contained in it, and your attention thereto; I offer you my best thanks.

Having no clue by which to discover the fact, I am very much at a loss to conjecture by what means a private letter of mine, written to a friend—and sent by an American Vessel should have got into the hands of the French Directory. I shall readily acknowledge however, that the one you allude to, directed to Mr Gouvr Morris was a long & confidential one; but I deny that there is any thing contained in it that the French Government could take exception to, unless the expression of an ardent wish that the United States might remain in Peace with *all the World*—taking no part in the disputes of *any* part of it, should have produced this effect. Giving it as my further opinion that the sentiments of the mass of the Citizens in this country were in unison with mine.[1]

Confidential as this letter was expected to be, I have no objection to its being seen by *any body*; and there is certainly some mistake in saying I had no copy thereof when there is a *press* one now before me, in which I discover no expression that in the eye of liberality & candour would be deemed objectionable.

To understand the scope & design of *my* letter properly, and to give it a fair interpretation, it is necessary to observe (as will appear by the contents of it) that it was written in answer to very long ones from the Gentleman to whom it was Addressed; which contained much political information of the state of things in different parts of Europe; and related among others, the substance of a conversation in which he, and Lord Grenville, as private Gentlemen had just been engaged, and in which it was observed by the latter, that if they were to judge from the publications in this country, the disposition of it was unfriendly to Great Britain; but in free countries he could readily account for such publications: However, that there was *one* which wore a more serious aspect, as indicative of the sense of the government; and alluded to Colo. Innes's report of his proceedings in Kentucky.[2]

In my noticing this part of Mr Morris's communication I tell him, that with respect to the Publication of that report it was an unauthorised act, and declared by that Gentleman as soon as he saw it in the Gazettes to have been done incorrectly; and that, with respect to the temper of the People of the United States, as it respected Great Britain, his Lordship ought not to be surprized, if it appeared disturbed & irritated, after the sense of the government had been so often expressed in strong remonstrances against the conduct of their Indian Agents—Privateersmen—Impressment of our Seamen—Insults of their Ships of War &ca &ca.—Adding, that it afforded us very litle satisfaction, their disclaiming these as unauthorised Acts (which the British Administration had done in some instances) while the actors were suffered to go unpunished. I dwell chiefly, and fully on this part of his letter; and reminded him of the indifference with which the advances of the United States, to form a Commercial Treaty with Great Britain, as well since as before the establishment of their present government had been received—and concluded by saying that a liberal policy towards us (though I did not Suppose sentiments of that sort from me to a member of the British Administration would have much weight) was the only road to a perfect reconciliation—and that, if he should again converse with Lord Grenville on this Subject he was at liberty unofficially to express these as my sentiments.

Thus, Sir, you have the substance, candidly related, of a letter which you say, you have been told by a person "who has read it, has produced an ill effect" when, in my opinion, the contrary (viewing it in the light of an unreserved and confidential communication) ought to have been produced. For I repeat it again, that unless my pacific disposition was displeasing, nothing else could have given umbrage by the most rigid construction of the letter; or that will shew in the remotest degree any disposition on my part to favor the British interest in their dispute with France.

My conduct in public and private life, as it relates to the important struggle in which the latter Nation is engaged has been uniform from the commencement of it, and may be summed up in a few words. That I have always wished well to the French Revolution. That I have always given it as my decided opinion that no Nation had a right to intermeddle in the internal concerns of another—That every one had a right to form, and adopt whatever Government they liked best to live under themselves—and that if this country could consistently with its engagements, maintain a strict Neutrality and thereby preserve Peace, it was bound so to do, by motives of Policy—Interest—and every other consideration that ought to actuate a People situated and circumstanced as we are; already deeply in Debt, and in a convalescent state from the struggle we have been engaged in ourselves.

On these principles I have uniformly and steadily proceeded—bidding defiance to calumnies calculated to sow the Seeds of distrust in the French Nation, and to excite their belief of an influence possessed by Great Britain in the Councils of this country—than which nothing is more unfounded or injurious; the object of its pacific conduct being truly deliniated above.[3]
I am—Dear Sir Your Obedient and Very Humble Servt

Go: Washington

ALS (duplicate), PP; LB, DLC:GW; copy, MHi: Washburn Autograph Collection.

1. See GW to Gouverneur Morris, 22 Dec. 1795.

2. For Lord Grenville's complaint about James Innes, see Morris to GW, 3 July 1795, and n.2.

3. For GW's continued concern over this diplomatic correspondence, see his letter to Charles Cotesworth Pinckney, 12 Sept. 1796.

From Robert Morris

Sir.   Philada August 25th 1796

In the year 1791—I purchased of the State of Massachusetts a Tract of Country lying within the boundaries of the State of Newyork which had been Ceded by the latter to the former State under the Sanction & with the Concurrence of the Congress of the United States, This Tract of Land is bounded to the East by the Genesee River, to the North by Lake Ontario, to the West partly by Lake Erie & partly by the Boundary Line of the Pensylvania Triangle & to the South by the North Boundary Line of the State of Pensylvania, A Printed Brief of my Title I take the liberty to transmit Herewith,[1] To perfect this Title it is necessary to purchase of the Seneca Nation of Indians their Native right, which I should have done soon after the purchase was made of the State of Massachusetts, but that I felt myself restrained, from doing so by Motives of Public consideration. The War between the Western Indian Nations & the United States did not extend to the Six Nations of which the Seneca's Nation is one, and as I apprehended that if this Nation should sell its right during the existance of that War, they might the more readily be induced to join the Enemies of my Country I determ⟨ined⟩ not to make the purchase whilst that War lasted. When peace was made with the Indian Nations[2] I turned my thoughts towards the purchase which is to me an object very interesting, but upon its being represented that a little longer patience untill the Western Posts should be delivered up by the British Government might still be of public utility I concluded to wait for that event also which is now happily accomplished,[3] and there seems no obstacle remaining to restrain me from making the purchase, especially as I have reason to believe the Indians are desirous to make the Sale[.] the delays which have already taken place & which arose solely from the considerations above mentioned have been *extremely detrimental to my private affairs,* but still being desirous to comply with Formalities prescribed by Certain Laws of the United States, altho' those Laws probably do not reach my Case, I now make application to the President of the United States and request that He will Nominate and appoint a Commissioner to be present and Preside at a Treaty which He will be pleased to Authorize to be held with the Seneca Nation for the purpose of enabling me to make a purchase in Conformity with the Formalities required by sd Laws of the Tract of Country for which I have already paid a very large Sum of Money.[4] My right to the preemption is unequivocal, and the Land is become so necessary to the growing Population and surrounding Settlements that it is with difficulty that the white People can be restrained from Squatting or setting down upon these Lands, which if they should do, it may probably bring on Contentions with the Six Nations. This will be prevented by a timely fair & honorable purchase[.] This proposed Treaty ought to be held immediately before the Hunting Season, or another year will be lost, as the Indians Cannot be Collected during that Season, The loss of another year under the payments I have made for these Lands, would be ruinous to my affairs, and as I have paid so great deferrence to Public considerations whilst they did exist, I expect & hope that my request will be readily granted now when there can be no cause for delay, especially If the Indians are willing to sell, which will be tested by the offer to buy.[5] With the most perfect Esteem & respect I am Sir Your most Obedt & most hble Servt

R.M.

ADfS, NHi: Henry O'Reilly Collection; copy, Gemeente-Archief van Amsterdam, Netherlands.

1. Morris enclosed *Brief of the Titles of Robert Morris, Esquire, to a Tract of Country in the county of Ontario, in the State of New-York.* . . . (Philadelphia, [1791)]). See also Seneca Chiefs to GW, 10 Jan. 1791, n.3, and Tobias Lear to GW, 8 May 1791, and n.5.

Both Massachusetts and New York had claimed the land in western New York. An agreement reached at Hartford on 16 Dec. 1786 gave New York sovereignty and jurisdiction over the land, but Massachusetts gained the right to quiet the Indian title and sell the land. Congress had encouraged a compromise between the two states and sanctioned the agreement in October 1787 (see *JCC,* 33:617–29).

2. Morris alludes to the Treaty of Greenville, 3 Aug. 1795 (see GW's first message to the U.S. Senate, 9 Dec. 1795).

3. Morris is referring to the transfer of western posts from the British to the United States under terms of the Jay Treaty.

4. Section 4 of "An Act to regulate trade and intercourse with the Indian tribes," approved 22 July 1790, provided that no sale of Indian lands would be valid "unless the same shall be made and duly executed at some public treaty, held under the authority of the United States" (1 *Stat.* 137–38). Subsequent laws reaffirmed the principle (see 1 *Stat.* 330–31, 472).

5. Secretary of State Timothy Pickering wrote GW on Saturday, 27 Aug. 1796: "I have conversed with Mr Morris on the subject of his letter of the 25th requesting you to appoint a Commissioner to hold a treaty with the Seneka Nation of Indians, to give him an opportunity to purchase their title to a portion of their territory, of which he has the right of pre-emption. I showed him the written opinion of the Attorney General, that the President had not power by the Constitution to appoint a Commissioner without the advice and consent of the Senate, and that the appointment must unavoidably be postponed. In the conversation, I remarked, that the two great objections having been removed, by the peace with the Western Indians, & getting possession of the posts, the way was open for holding the treaty requested; and especially, if, as he suggested, the Senekas themselves desired to sell any portion of their lands. I also expressed my opinion, that the hunt of the Senekas was not so remote or of so much consequence, as to prevent their meeting in January next for the purpose requested.

"He desired a copy of the Attorney General's opinion, which I shall send him this afternoon. Mr Morris thought a written answer would be necessary for him, to satisfy those persons who were depending on his purchase, that the delay was unavoidable: but he suspends his request on this point till Monday. That reverence for the laws & government of his country which has hitherto influenced his conduct, will prevent his pressing for any measure incompatible therewith; altho' the situation of his affairs is singularly urgent" (ALS, DNA: RG 59, Miscellaneous Letters; LB, DNA: RG 59, Domestic Letters; LB, DNA: RG 59, GW's Correspondence with His Secretaries of State). Pickering enclosed the opinion of Attorney General Charles Lee, dated 26 May 1796, when he wrote Morris on this date (see DNA: RG 59, Domestic Letters; see also *House Exec. Doc.* 55, 31st Cong., 2d sess., 3 March 1851, p. 36). For GW's eventual nomination of a treaty commissioner, see Morris to GW, 23 Dec. 1796 (NHi: Henry O'Reilly Collection), and GW to the U.S. Senate, 2 March 1797 (DNA: RG 46, entry 52).

From William Persse

Roxburrow Near Loughrea
Sr   Ireland August 27th 1796
    Mr Abraham Bradly of the Town of Loughrea, Informs me that a Mr Abraham Bradly of Carolina, has Lodged in your Hands a sum of Money, amounting to four Hundred and fifty pounds, to

be paid to any of his Brors if Liveing, if not to his next Heirs— I request the Favor of you to Inform me, if such Sum has been left with you for the above purposes—& what Steps will be Necessary for obtaining it[1] please to Excuse the Trouble I give you & believe me Sr your Faithfull Huml. Servt

Wm Persse

P:S: Mr Wallace Desires his best respects to you & Mrs Washington.[2]

ALS, DLC:GW.

1. No reply has been found, and no evidence of the reported deposit of money has been identified.

An Abraham (Abram) Bradley appears in the 1790 and 1800 U.S. censuses for Greenville County, South Carolina.

2. Persse probably is referring to John Wallace, a minister who was Edward Newenham's son-in-law. Newenham had introduced "a Mr. Wallace," who visited Mount Vernon in 1786 (see *Diaries*, 4:301–3, 344; see also GW to Newenham, 10 June 1786, and Alexander McCabe to GW, 26 June 1786, in *Papers, Confederation Series*, 4:105–6, 129–30). Persse's daughter had married one of Newenham's sons.

From Daniel Stevens

Supervisor's Office Dist. so. Carolina
Sir   Charleston 27th August 1796

This will be handed you by Benjamin Cudworth Esqr. Inspector of the Revenue for Survey No. 2. in my District, the ill State of health of this Gentleman, for some months past has induced me to give him permission to go to Philadelphia to see if the change of Climate for a few Weeks may not contribute towards a restoration thereof, my personal esteem for Mr Cudworth as an upright valuable Citizen, and a steady supporter of the Federal Government and an Officer of the Revenue, in whom may be placed the most unbounded confidence, for integrity abilities, attention and vigilance in his official duties, and whose conduct has justly merited my warmest approbation, induces me to take the liberty of introducing him to your kind attention. with great regard and esteem I am sir Your most Obt sevt

Danl Stevens

ALS, DNA: RG 59, Miscellaneous Letters.

From James Anderson

Sir   Salvington[1] [Va.] 28 August *1796*

Only Yesterday I had the honor to receive Your favor of 18th And in Answer, am well satisfied of Mr Pearce being a Man of Character, and of Abilitys. And circumstanced as You are, must be of great value to You—You are pleased to say that from this and other reasons You advanced the Salary from £100 to 100 Gu[inea]s.

I have to beg leave to observe that if You, & me come on Terms the lowest I will accept is 100 Gu[inea]s a House, Garden &c. &ca and every suitable provisions.

I am well informed that Your superintendant has as much to do as any one Man can execute. And in my Opinion He ought to have an Assistant in the writing part—That the business out doors, And that within may both be regularly attended to.

I Observe You are entirely in the Farming and wish to connect that & grazing—This I always conceive to be two branches of the same business, and never should be separated. And as to Your Query's on that subject, can say, Farming, as Practised in Scotland and some County's in England, is what I was bred to from my Youth the management of Stock We say is an Essential part of the Farmers business, the knowledge of a Dairy, Ditching, & Hedging with Thorns are I think things Familiar to me, as well as the practical parts of Farming in Britain, conjoined with six Years experience in this Country, where Soil, & Climate make some alterations necessary—But whether my knowledge in these, my Sobriety, Integrity, Industry, Foresight in Arrangements, And Firmness are such as will Answer Your expectations, I will not pretend to say to draw my own Character is what I would rather decline, I shall leave this part to them who know me, And who I hope will be impartial.

As soon as You find it convenient, will expect the favor of Your reply.[2] And I have the honor to be with great respect Sir Your most Obedt Humble Servt

Jas Anderson

ALS, ViMtvL.

1. Salvington was a Selden family plantation south of Potomac Creek in Stafford County.

2. GW replied to Anderson on 5 September.

To William Pearce

Mr Pearce, Philadelphia 28th Augt 1796
Your letter of the 23d instt with the Reports, came to my hands yesterday;[1] and this will be put into the Post office tomorrow for Chester Town.

From what you have said of the person I wa⟨s⟩ enquiring after, I am well Satisfied h⟨e⟩ would not answer my purposes, as a Manager.[2] Propensity to gaming, & running about, are such disqualifications in ⟨m⟩y estimation, as scarcely to find a coun⟨te⟩rpoise in all the good properties (h⟨owev⟩er numerous they may be) he can po⟨ssess.⟩ No further thought therefore ne⟨ed⟩ ⟨*mutilated*⟩ed on him.

⟨*mutilated*⟩ person, I hav⟨*mutilated*⟩ as yo⟨*mutilated*⟩ a very good ⟨*mutilated*⟩—but ⟨*mutilated*⟩er acted u⟨*mutilated*⟩ Scale ⟨*mutilated*⟩ ever had hi⟨s⟩ ⟨*mutilated*⟩riety of objects ⟨*mutilated*⟩e (to use a c⟨*mutilated*⟩ of Water. I⟨*mutilated*⟩d of any, as yo⟨*mutilated*⟩ stand upon better g⟨ro⟩und than he does; being bred a Farm⟨er⟩ and understanding, as I am told he ⟨d⟩oes, Stock and Meadowing well. I shall continue my enquiries, more ⟨mi⟩nutely, into his qualifications;[3] Bu⟨t⟩ as it is a matter interesting to me, t⟨o o⟩btain a person of experience, & es⟨ta⟩blished character, I wish you would m⟨a⟩ke my wants known, and if yo⟨u s⟩hould find a person whom you judge ⟨fr⟩om your own knowledge, or such inform⟨a⟩tion as you can entirely rely on; You ⟨w⟩ould mention him to me, and ascertai⟨n⟩ whether he is to b⟨e⟩ had, and on wha⟨t⟩ terms.

At any ra⟨te en⟩deavor to get ⟨*mutilated*⟩ good Oversee⟨rs⟩ ⟨*mutilated*⟩ ⟨t⟩he places of Vi⟨o⟩let & Cash. ⟨*mutilated*⟩uld be had from ⟨*mutilated*⟩est farm ⟨*mutilated*⟩ ⟨t⟩he East⟨ern⟩ ⟨*mutilated*⟩e, I should ⟨*mutilated*⟩ ⟨be⟩cause they ⟨*mutilated*⟩ more in ⟨*mutilated*⟩ ⟨fa⟩rming than ⟨*mutilated*⟩e in Virg⟨inia⟩ ⟨*mutilated*⟩ but Much ⟨*mutilated*⟩s at it, mergin⟨g⟩ ⟨*mutilated*⟩ cultivation ⟨*mutilated*⟩ ⟨com⟩patible with ⟨*mutilated*⟩ & Graising.

⟨You⟩ have not said whether Neal conti⟨nues⟩ or not, on his present lay; nor n⟨ot⟩hing concerning Allison.[4] The latter ⟨*mutilated*⟩eed, as he has a wife, I am myself in d⟨ou⟩bt about; even if he was disposed to stay, ⟨& I⟩ would not agree to it at any rate, u⟨n⟩less his wife will undertake the ca⟨re⟩ & management of the Spinners & knit⟨te⟩rs, under his Inspection, & authority to make them do their duty properly; without suffering such imposions in the yarn, and idle doings as the Garde⟨n⟩ers wife submitted to.

If you get this l⟨etter⟩ on the Eastern s⟨hore⟩, answer it by ⟨the fi⟩rst Post, th⟨at I m⟩ay know it ha⟨s bee⟩n received, ⟨mutilated⟩ t my repea⟨mutilated⟩ sam⟨mutilated⟩ts in a Seco⟨mutilated⟩ to ⟨mutilated⟩ ⟨t⟩he receipt ⟨mutilated⟩ it ma⟨mutilated⟩cur powe⟨r⟩ ⟨mutilated⟩swer ⟨mutilated⟩ parts of ⟨mutilated⟩, & presu⟨me⟩ ⟨mutilated⟩ will send the Se⟨mutilated⟩ particular attent⟨mutilated⟩ ⟨yo⟩ur friend & h⟨mutilated⟩

Go: W⟨ashington⟩

P.S.

I sent last We⟨ek⟩, in a letter to Mrs Washington,[5] but if y⟨o⟩u left Mount Vernon on friday,[6] it coul⟨d⟩ not have got to hand before—Doctr P⟨er⟩kins's Patent Instrument, with directions for curing Pains & Inflamations of all sorts—particularly such as af⟨f⟩ect you. He himself speaks confidently of his Success; and there are many respectable certificates in confirmation of what he asserts—Be these as they may, there is one thing in it we are sure of—and ⟨tha⟩t is, if it does no ⟨g⟩ood, it will do ⟨no⟩ harm—conseque⟨nt⟩ly the applica⟨tion⟩ may be made ⟨with⟩out apprehen⟨sion⟩ of bad ⟨or⟩ da⟨ngerou⟩s consequences ⟨mutilated⟩ ⟨illegible⟩ tried ⟨mutilated⟩.[7]

ALS (fragmentary), CSmH.

1. Neither Pearce's letter to GW dated 23 Aug. nor the reports have been found.

2. GW presumably is referring to James Cannon (see his letter to Pearce, 19 Aug., and n.2).

3. GW probably means James Anderson.

4. John Neale, who supervised GW's carpenters, and John Allison, overseer at Mansion House farm, remained employed at Mount Vernon during 1797.

5. GW's letter to Martha Washington has not been found.

6. Pearce apparently left Mount Vernon on 26 August.

7. Elisha Perkins (1741–1799), a Connecticut doctor, obtained a patent in February 1796 "for an improvement in the method of removing pains & inflamations from the human Body by the application of Metallic Substances" (*JPP*, 333).

An advertisement in the *Aurora General Advertiser* (Philadelphia) for 3 March 1796 announced that Perkins proposed "selling the privilege of practising agreeable to his discovery, by Towns, Districts, or States, as shall be most agreeable to the purchasers." An advertisement in *The Philadelphia Gazette & Universal Daily Advertiser* for 1 June claimed that the treatment was "particularly useful in relieving pains in the head, face, teeth, breast, side, stomach, back, rheumatisms, recent gouts, &c. &c. Nothwithstanding the utility of this practice, it is not presumed, but there are cases in which this and every other remedy may sometimes fail."

An entry on 27 Aug. showed that GW paid $20 "for a transfer of Dr Perkins's Metallic instruments to Send to Mount V——n" (Household Accounts). Benjamin Douglas Perkins, "son to the Discoverer," referenced GW's purchase in *The Influence of Metallic Tractors on the Human Body, In removing various painful Inflammatory Diseases . . . And demonstrated in a Series of Experiments and Observations . . . By which the Importance of the Discovery Is fully ascertained, and a new Field of Enquiry opened in the Modern Science of Galvanism, or, Animal Electricity* (London, 1798), 9. See also Benjamin Douglas Perkins, *Directions for Performing the Metallic Operation with Perkins's Patent Tractors* [London, 1799].

To the Cherokee Nation

BELOVED CHEROKEES,   [Philadelphia, 29 Aug. 1796]

MANY years have passed since the White people first came to America. In that long space of time many good men have considered how the condition of the Indian natives of the country might be improved; and many attempts have been made to effect it. But, as we see at this day, all these attempts have been nearly fruitless. I also have thought much on this subject, and anxiously wished that the various Indian tribes, as well as their neighbours, the White people, might enjoy in abundance all the good things which make life comfortable and happy. I have considered how this could be done; and have discovered but one path that could lead them to that desirable situation. In this path I wish all the Indian nations to walk. From the information received concerning you, my beloved Cherokees, I am inclined to hope that you are prepared to take this path and disposed to pursue it. It may seem a little difficult to enter; but if you make the attempt, you will find every obstacle easy to be removed. Mr. DINSMOOR, my beloved agent to your nation, being here, I send to you this talk by him. He will have it interpreted to you, and particularly explain my meaning.[1]

Beloved Cherokees,

You now find that the game with which your woods once abounded, are growing scarce; and you know when you cannot meet a deer or other game to kill, that you must remain hungry; you know also when you can get no skins by hunting, that the traders will give you neither powder nor cloathing; and you know that without other implements for tilling the ground than the hoe, you will continue to raise only scanty crops of corn. Hence you are sometimes exposed to suffer much from hunger and cold; and as the game are lessening in numbers more and more, these sufferings will increase. And how are you to provide against them? Listen to my words and you will know.

My beloved Cherokees,

Some among you already experience the advantage of keeping cattle and hogs: let all keep them and increase their numbers, and you will ever have a plenty of meat. To these add sheep, and they will give you cloathing as well as food. Your lands are good and of great extent. By proper management you can raise live stock not only for your own wants, but to sell to the White people. By using the plow you can vastly increase your crops of corn. You can also grow Wheat, (which makes the best bread) as well as other useful grain. To these you will easily add flax and cotton, which you may dispose of to the White people, or have it made up by your own women into cloathing for yourselves. Your wives and daughters can soon learn to spin and weave; and to make this certain, I have directed Mr. DINSMOOR to procure all the necessary apparatus for spinning and weaving, and to hire a woman to teach the use of them. He will also procure some plows and other implements of husbandry, with which to begin the improved cultivation of the ground which I recommend, and employ a fit person to shew you how they are to be used. I have further directed him to procure some cattle and sheep for the most prudent and industrious men, who shall be willing to exert themselves in tilling the ground and raising those useful animals. He is often to talk with you on these subjects, and give you all necessary information to promote your success. I must therefore desire you to listen to him; and to follow his advice. I appointed him to dwell among you as the Agent of the United States, because I judged him to be a faithful man, ready to obey my instructions and to do you good.

But the cares of the United States are not confined to your single nation. They extend to all the Indians dwelling on their borders. For which reason other agents are appointed; and for the four southern nations there will be a general or principal agent who will visit all of them, for the purpose of maintaining peace and friendship among them and with the United States;

to superintend all their affairs; and to assist the particular agents with each nation in doing the business assigned them. To such general or principal agent I must desire your careful attention. He will be one of our greatly beloved men. His whole time will be employed in contriving how to do you good, and you will therefore act wisely to follow his advice. The first general or principle agent will be Colonel Benjamin Hawkins, a man already known and respected by you. I have chosen him for this office because he is esteemed for a good man; has a knowledge of Indian customs, and a particular love and friendship for all the Southern tribes.[2]

Beloved Cherokees,

What I have recommended to you I am myself going to do. After a few moons are passed I shall leave the great town and retire to my farm. There I shall attend to the means of increasing my cattle, sheep and other useful animals; to the growing of corn, wheat, and other grain, and to the employing of women in spinning and weaving; all which I have recommended to you, that you may be as comfortable and happy as plenty of food, clothing and other good things can make you.

Beloved Cherokees,

When I have retired to my farm I shall hear of you; and it will give me great pleasure to know that you have taken my advice, and are walking in the path which I have described. But before I retire, I shall speak to my beloved man, the Secretary of War, to get prepared some medals, to be given to such Cherokees as by following my advice shall best deserve them. For this purpose Mr. DINSMOOR is from time to time to visit every town in your nation. He will give instructions to those who desire to learn what I have recommended. He will see what improvements are made; who are most industrious in raising cattle; in growing corn, wheat, cotton and flax; and in spinning and weaving; and on those who excel these rewards are to be bestowed.

Beloved Cherokees,

The advice I here give you is important as it regards your nation; but still more important as the event of the experiment made with you may determine the lot of many nations. If it succeeds, the beloved men of the United States will be encouraged to give the same assistance to all the Indian tribes within their boundaries. But if it should fail, they may think it vain to make any further attempts to better the condition of any Indian tribe; for the richness of the soil and mildness of the air render your country highly favorable for the practice of what I have recommended.

Beloved Cherokees,

The wise men of the United States meet together once a year, to consider what will be for the good of all their people. The wise men of each separate state also meet together once or twice every year, to consult and do what is good for the people of their respective states. I have thought that a meeting of your wise men once or twice a year would be alike useful to you. Every town might send one or two of its wisest counsellors to talk together on the affairs of your nation, and to recommend to your people whatever they should think would be serviceable. The beloved agent of the United States would meet with them. He would give them information of those things which are found good by the white people, and which your situation will enable you to adopt. He would explain to them the laws made by the great council of the United States, for the preservation of peace; for the protection of your lands; for the security of your persons; for your improvement in the arts of living, and for promoting your general welfare. If it should be agreeable to you that your wise men should hold such meetings, you will speak your mind to my beloved man, Mr. DINSMOOR, to be communicated to the President of the United States, who will then give such directions as shall be proper.

Beloved Cherokees,

That this talk may be known to all your nation, and not forgotten, I have caused it to be printed, and directed one, signed by my own hand, to be lodged in each of your towns. The Interpreters will, on proper occasions, read and interpret the same to all your people.

Beloved Cherokees,

Having been informed that some of your chiefs wished to see me in Philadelphia, I have sent them word that I would receive a few of the most esteemed. I now repeat that I shall be glad to see a small number of your wisest chiefs; but I shall not expect them 'till November.[3] I shall take occasion to agree with them on the running of the boundary line between your lands and ours, agreeably to the treaty of Holston. I shall expect them to inform me what chiefs are to attend the running of this line, and I shall tell them whom I appoint to run it; and the time and place of beginning may then be fixed.[4]

I now send my best wishes to the Cherokees, and pray the Great Spirit to preserve them.

GIVEN at the City of Philadelphia, the twenty-ninth day of August, in the year one thousand seven hundred and ninety-six, and in the twenty-first year of the Independence of the United States of America

Go: Washington

By Command of the President of the United States,

[James McHenry
Secy of War][5]

DS (printed broadside), DLC:GW; Df (in Timothy Pickering's writing), in private hands; Df (revisions in Pickering's writing to a printed text), MHi: Pickering Papers. The top of the DS reads: "Talk of the President of the United States, to his Beloved Men of the Cherokee Nation." Although the DS is dated 29 Aug. and docketed by GW as "Sent to the Cherokee Nation of Indians" on that date, this version of the speech arose from Secretary of State Timothy Pickering's drafts not written until 2 Sept. (see Pickering's first letter to GW on that date and notes 1 and 2 below; see also James McHenry to GW, 24 Aug., and GW to Pickering, 2 Sept.).

1. At this point on Pickering's draft, he continued with a paragraph that was deleted from the final text: "Beloved Cherokees, Instead of beginning with books, I wish you first to learn those things which will make books useful to you. When you shall have learned to till the ground, to build good houses, & to fill them with good things, as the white people do, then, like them, you will find the knowledge of books to be pleasant & useful. But first you must learn how to obtain the necessaries of life in plenty. The most essential are food and cloathing. Tolerable houses you can build already: but you may learn from the white people to make them better & more lasting."

2. Pickering inserted this paragraph in the margins of both drafts—evidently a late thought.

3. For previous discussion about a Cherokee visit, see Bartholomew Dandridge, Jr., to James McHenry, 28 Feb., and note 2 to that document.

4. The fourth article of the 1791 Treaty of Holston defined the boundary between the United States and the Cherokee nation and called for three persons from each nation to form a commission for its delineation. A subsequent treaty at Philadelphia in 1794 promised the Cherokees ninety days' notice before the arrival of the U.S. commissioners (see Kappler, *Indian Treaties*, 2:29–34).

5. McHenry's signature is absent from the DS in DLC:GW, but it appears on the broadsides issued to the public.

From William Gordon

My dear Sir   St Neots Hunts [England] Augt 29. 1796.

The most cordial congratulations attend your Excellency on your firm & successful conduct during the last Session. The United States are as much indebted to you for the same, as for procuring them a treaty with Great Britain; truly & greatly advantageous, though it may not equal the sanguine wishes of many; still infinitely preferable to a rupture, which would have ruined multitudes, benefited but very few comparatively, & might have endangered your national existence.[1] Under God, you have been the happy instrument of saving your country twice; first in a time of war, & now in a time of peace.

I contemplate your retirement from the Presidency at the close of your second tour of service, with no small pleasure; under the persuasion, that it will not only redound to your credit, equally with your quitting the military command after you had seen the war brought to an honorable conclusion; but put you in possession of that retired private life, of which you are so desirous. Yours will be in truth Otium cum Dignitate.[2] May you long find the sweets of it; & while you are enjoying earthly comforts, experience the pleasures of religion; & by meditation & the various acts of devotion prescribed in the sacred Oracles, be preparing for the eternal glories & joys of heaven, which every real christian is promised by his divine Leader, the Captain of his salvation, the King of kings & the Lord of lords!

This will be accompanied with a small miniature coloured print of me. I sat for the original painting, before Mr Jay had his first audience, & in the adjoining street, which gave me the opportunity of seeing him oftener than I should otherwise have done. You will be pleased to accept of it & Wyvill's Correspondence with Pitt, as a small token of that sincere affection which I bear towards you.[3] Mrs Gordon & Self enjoy, through the goodness of our heavenly Father, no small share of health, considering that we are in the sixty eighth year of our pilgrimage. It is our wish & prayer, that you & your Lady may be equally favored, & if it pleases God even more so.

We are much obliged to your Excellency for the kind notice you took of our nephew Oliver Field. His father died the last friday in his 78th year.[4]

In Great Britain our gathering storm seems to be thickening apace over the heads of the inhabitants. And, old as I am, were my circumstances sufficient for my living in a state of independence, I should be strongly inclined to prepare for a removal next spring, if spared, & should we not have a peace, of which I have no idea; for I suppose the French terms will be—The restoration of all taken from France & her ally the Dutch—& that these we shall not consent to, while we can continue the war which our rulers may attempt doing, till a national convulsion exists & hazards every thing.

Your Excellency & Lady will be pleased to accept of our most affectionate regards. I remain Dear Sir, Your sincere friend & humble servant

William Gordon

ALS, DLC:GW.

1. Gordon praised GW for the Jay Treaty.

2. The Latin phrase, which might translate literally as "leisure with honor" (or with reputation), probably references Cicero's use of those words to describe a goal of the political life.

3. Ebenezer Hazard wrote GW on Monday, 7 Nov.: "On Saturday Evening I received a Package from London, containing among other Things some Pictures of our Friend Doctor Gordon, and the Correspondence between Messrs Wyvill and Pitt, one of each of which the Dr directs me to hand to your Excellency" (ALS, DLC:GW).

Thomas Conder of Bucklersbury, London, had published Gordon's engraved portrait on 1 August. One copy of the engraving, apparently taken from Charles Hayter's original painting, is in UkLoBM.

A copy of the second edition of *The Correspondence of the Rev. C. Wyvill with the Right Honourable William Pitt. Part I* (Newcastle, Eng., 1796) was in GW's library at the time of his death (see Griffin, *Catalogue of the Washington Collection*, 230).

Christopher Wyvill (1740–1822) advocated for Parliamentary reform, which led to correspondence and conversations with William Pitt in the 1780s.

4. Oliver Field apparently had emigrated to the United States and reported to Gordon on meeting GW (see Gordon to GW, 16 Jan. 1796). Field's father was John Field (1719–1796), a noted London apothecary.

From James McHenry

Sir.　　　　　　　　　　　　　　　　　　War office 29 Augt 1796

It appears from the conferences between the representatives of the Creek nation at Coleraine, and Commissioners of the U.S. that the former have required and the latter promised, that the

President would send into their country, within four months from the date of the treaty, a person instructed upon the following points.[1]

1. To fix upon proper scites for trading houses & posts, and explain to the nation by towns or tribes, the reasons for having them established within their boundary line.

2. To explain the plan of trade to the different Towns or tribes.

3 To confer with and advise the nation, how it ought to conduct itself in case the murderers of the Indians by Harrison & others should escape without being punished.[2]

4. To explain the object for running the boundary line between Spain and the United States.

5. To notify the nation of the time when the President will be pleased to run the boundary line between the Creeks and the U.S. and the place where the running is to commence, in order that persons may be appointed to attend on the part of the nation.

As these explanations have been promised and have been deemed necessary by the Indians who convened at Coleraine and the commissioners, it might not be proper to with hold them upon a mere point of œconomony, especially as there are other objects of importance that may be accomplished by the person whom the President be pleased to employ on this occasion.

One of the points I allude to is; to ascertain, in execution of the intimation given by the President to the State of Georgia, whether the Creek nation are disposed to sell their land laying between the Oconee and Oakmulgee; and if they are the terms upon which they will part with it.[3]

Another point, is to ascertain, whether the state of things in the Creek nation, be favourable to the introduction of a system of civilization, such as has been adopted for trial for the Cherokees.[4]

It strikes me, that several circumstances conspire, which would render such an experiment more likely to succeed now than at any former period.

The Creeks are strongly impressed with the opinion, that the U.S. mean to conduct towards them with candor and justice; to protect all their rights; to perform the promises which have been made them; and besides, are become sensible that the arm of the U.S. is too powerful to be resisted.

Whatever therefore may be proposed by the President, (so long as they find themselves & their land protected by the U.S.) will it is probable be well received by them, and submitted to or adopted if not too repugnant to their habits or established prejudices.

This idea cherishes the hope that something effectual may be done towards their civilization. That what has been long contemplated is not far distant. That the seed which has been sown is not all destroyed. And that the time is arrived, to benefit the poor Indian by the same means which will preserve them in a state of peace and attract to the U.S. the most honourable fame.

The States which are anxious to get the Indian land will see large portions of it, by the operation of these causes become useless to them, and consequently placed in a situation to be easily obtained. Besides. If they can be brought to support themselves on a smaller circumference of land, they will have fewer points from which to attack the frontier inhabitants, and will be more in the power of the U.S. than when spread over an immense tract of country.

To render the system from which those effects are expected, operative, requires no more than a certain degree of patience on the part of the States which covet their land; and a due application of the means which the laws have placed within the reach of the executive.

If you should approve of sending a person into their country to execute any or all of these purposes I shall turn my attention to frame the proper instructions and lay them before you as soon as possible for consideration.

Mr Hawkins appears to me to possess the necessary feelings and character for such a mission, if he will undertake it; and should you approve may be spoken to on the subject.[5] With the greatest respect I have the Honour to be Sir your most ob. & hble st

James McHenry

ALS, DLC:GW; LB, DLC:GW; copy, MHi: Adams Papers. A letterpress of the copy is in DLC: James McHenry Papers.

1. For the proceedings of the treaty at Colerain, see *ASP: Indian Affairs*, 1:586–616; see also McHenry to GW, 3 (second letter) and 11–12 August. The commissioners reported their promise to the Creek Indians when they wrote McHenry on 1 July (see McHenry to GW, 25 July, and n.3 to that document).

2. The *Gazette of the United States* (Philadelphia) for 17 Feb. 1796 printed an address from George Mathews to the Georgia Senate dated 12 Jan. with information on murders that occurred in September 1795: "Capt. Benjamin Harrison and one Vessels, aided by some others, committed a wanton and barbarous murder on ten Indians of the Uchee towns, and that Harrison, still actuated by the same cruel motives, was the inviter of eight Indians more over the river Oconee, and by false and delusive colorings induced several peaceable and well disposed citizens of this state to aid and abet him in killing seven of them. Shortly after this horrid deed, a man by the name of Tarvin barbarously killed two other Indians at the high shoals of the Appalachees, one a Creek, the other a Cherokee."

Benjamin Harrison (1755–1811), a Revolutionary War veteran from North Carolina, who settled in Montgomery County, Ga., appears to have escaped a trial despite a report in the *Columbian Herald; or, the New Daily Advertiser* (Charleston, S.C.) for 3 March 1796 that the Georgia House had resolved on 15 Feb. "that Harrison and the others charged may be brought to a fair and speedy trial agreeably to the existing laws."

3. McHenry's letter to Georgia governor Jared Irwin written on 23 Aug. covered this point: "To remove however every cause for doubt on this subject, the President has determined to have ascertained in the most unequivocal mode, whether the mind of the Nation has undergone any change relative to the land in question, and if it has, the terms upon which they will sell it" (GU-HR: Telamon Cuyler Collection).

4. See McHenry to GW, 24 Aug., and n.1 to that document.

5. For the instructions given Benjamin Hawkins, see GW to McHenry, 7 Sept., and n.1 to that document; see also GW's second letter to McHenry on 22 July, and n.2 to that document, and McHenry to GW, 10 July, and n.4 to that document.

From Timothy Pickering

Sir   [Philadelphia] Monday Evening, 9 o'clock [29 Aug. 1796]

I have this moment left Colo. Hawkins—I called twice in the course of the day without finding him at his lodgings. His ideas & wishes correspond with what I mentioned to-day—to be the superintendant of the four southern nations—Chickasaws, Cherokees, Choctaws & Creeks—the latter requiring at present peculiar attention.[1] He would prefer the Indian Department to that of the Surveyor. Two thousand dollars a year he thinks enough.

Mr Van Polanen called upon me to-day. I informed him that probably it would be convenient for you to receive him to-morrow noon as the Minister Resident of the U. Netherlands. If I am honoured with your orders on this subject in the morning, I will advise him thereof.[2] I am most respectfully, sir, your obt servant

T. Pickering

ALS, DNA: RG 59, Miscellaneous Letters; LB, DNA: RG 59, GW's Correspondence with His Secretaries of State. The date is taken from the docket on the ALS.

1. See James McHenry to GW, this date.

2. Roger Gerard Van Polanen was received as minister from the Batavian Republic at the specified time (see *JPP*, 341; see also Batavian Republic to GW, 3 May, and Pickering's second letter to GW on 21 July, and n.3).

From James McHenry

Sir.   War office 31 Augt 1796.

I inclose you a draught of a letter to Colonel Stevenson which if approved of may be sent to him to-day.[1]

If you are not using the plans of the Forts Detroit and drawings of the lakes &c. in that quarter which Gen. Wayne left with you I will be much obliged to you for them to correct and complete a map which is in hand for the war office.[2] With the greatest respect I have the honour to be Sir your most ob. St

James McHenry

ALS, DLC:GW; LB, DLC:GW.

1. Neither the draft nor the addressee has been identified, but a possibility is Stephen Stevenson, who served as a lieutenant colonel in the Pennsylvania militia. For Stevenson, see *The Herald; A Gazette for the Country* (New York), 12 Nov. 1796; see also William Irvine to GW, 12 Jan. 1780, in *Papers, Revolutionary War Series*, 24:100–101.

2. The drawings have not been identified.

Letter not found: from William Pearce, 31 Aug. 1796. GW wrote Pearce on 5 Sept.: "Your letter of the 31st of Augt . . . came duly to hand."

To Alexander Hamilton

Private

My dear Sir,   Philadelphia 1st Septr 1796

About the middle of last Week I wrote to you; and that it might escape the eye of the Inquisitive (for some of my letters have lately been pried into) I took the liberty of putting it under a cover to Mr Jay.[1]

Since then, revolving on the Paper that was enclosed therein; on the various matters it contained; and on the just expression of the advice or recommendation which was given in it, I have regretted that another subject (which in my estimation is of interesting concern to the well-being of this country) was not touched upon also: I mean Education *generally* as one of the surest means of enlightening & givg just ways of thinkg to our Citizens, but particularly the establishment of a University; where the Youth from *all parts* of the United States might receive the polish of Erudition in the Arts, Sciences & Belle Letters; and where those who were disposed to run a political course, might not only be instructed in the theory & principles, but (this Seminary being at the Seat of the General Government) where the Legislature wd be in Session half the year, and the Interests & politics of the Nation of course would be discussed, they would lay the surest foundation for the practical part also.

But that which would render it of the highest importance, in my opinion, is, that the Juvenal-period of life, when friendships are formed, & habits established that will stick by one; the Youth, or young men from different parts of the United States would be assembled together, & would by degrees discover that there was not that cause for those jealousies & prejudices which one part of the Union had imbibed agains[t] another part: of course, sentiments of more liberality in the general policy of the country would result from it. What, but the mixing of people from different parts of the United States during the War rubbed off these impressions? A century in the ordinary intercourse, would not have accomplished what the Seven years association in arms did: but that ceasing, prejudices are beginning to revive again, and never will be eradicated so effectually by any other means as the intimate intercourse of characters in early life who, in all probability, will be at the head of the councils of this country in a more advanced stage of it.

To shew that this is no *new* idea of mine, I may appeal to my early communications to Congress;[2] and to prove how seriously I have reflected on it since, & how well disposed I have been, & still am, to contribute my aid towards carrying the measure into effect, I enclose you the extract of a letter from me to the Governor of Virginia on this Subject, and a copy of the resolves of the Legislature of that State in consequence thereof.[3]

I have not the smallest doubt that this donation (when the Navigation is in complete operation, which it certainly will be in less than two years,[)] will amount to twelve or £1500 Sterlg a year, and become a rapidly increasing fund. The Proprietors of the Federal City have talked of doing something handsome towards it likewise and if Congress would appropriate so⟨me of⟩ the Western lands to the same uses, funds sufficient, and of the most permanent and increasing sort might be so established as to envite the ablest Professors in Europe, to conduct it.

Let me pray you, therefore, to introduce a Section in the Address expressive of these sentiments, & recommendatory of the measure—without any mention, however, of my proposed personal contribution to the plan.

Such a Section would come in very properly after the one which relates to our religious obligations, or in a preceeding part, as one of the recommendatory measures to counteract the evils arising from Geographical discriminations.[4] With Affecte regard I am always Yours

Go: Washington

ALS, DLC: Hamilton Papers; copy, DLC: Hamilton Papers.

1. See GW to Hamilton, 25 August. No cover letter from GW to John Jay has been found.

2. For example, see GW to the U.S. Senate and House of Representatives, 8 Jan. 1790.

3. The enclosed extract from GW's letter to Robert Brooke dated 16 March 1795 has not been found. The full letter explained GW's intention to use Potomac Company shares put at his disposal by the Virginia legislature for a national university and his desire that James River Company shares at his disposal be applied to education in Virginia. The Virginia legislature approved GW's ideas on 1 Dec. 1795 (see Brooke to GW, 9 Jan. 1796, n.2).

4. Hamilton replied to GW on 4 Sept.; see also Hamilton to GW, 5 September.

From Thomas G. Johnston

Sir   [Philadelphia] Septr 1st 1796

I have been Informed this day Since I came to this Citty, that you have been receiving proposals for Some time past, for the Sale of Some Lands, which Lay on the Western Waters, which if you have not Disposed of, I wish to know the Lowest price that will be taken for the *first*, Called round bottom, about fifteen miles below Wheeling also of the three Other tracts Which Lay Lower Down in the Ohio, an Ansr to this letter Sent to my Lodgings at Mr Thompson Sine of the Indian Queen fourth Street[1] this Evening or tomorrow will be Immedy Attended to[2] by Sir Your Most Obedient Humble Servant

Thos G. Johnston

The Conditions of Sale I have been Informed of.

ALS, DLC:GW.

The correspondent may have been the Thomas G. Johnston who practiced law in western Pennsylvania during the late 1790s and early 1800s.

1. James Thompson (d. 1800) moved from Wilmington, Del., to Philadelphia in 1777. He operated several taverns before acquiring the Indian Queen (on S. Fourth Street between Chesnut and Market) in 1783. Thompson kept that tavern until his death.

2. No reply to Johnston has been found. For others interested in purchasing the Round Bottom tract, see Jeremiah Claypole to GW, 3 June, and Robert McLean to GW, 7 June.

From Joseph Vanmeter

1 Sept. 1796. Writing from Fort Pleasant (Van Meter's Fort) on the North Branch of the Potomac River, Vanmeter explains how he procured a sword presented to GW.

ALS, DLC:GW. For a full transcription and other information related to the sword, see GW to John Quincy Adams, 25 June 1797, in *Papers, Retirement Series*, 1:210–14.

To Oliver Wolcott, Jr.

Dear Sir,   Thursday Morning 1st Sep. [1796]

Enclosed is the name, and description of the Girl I mentioned to you last night. She has been the particular attendent on Mrs Washington since she was ten years old; and was handy & useful to her, being a perfect Mistress of her needle.[1]

We have heard that she was seen in New York by some one who knew her, directly after she went off. And since by Miss Langden, in Portsmouth; who meeting her one day in the Street, & knowing her, was about to stop and speak to her, but she brushed quickly by, to avoid it.[2]

By her being seen in New York (if the fact be so) it is not probable she went immediately to Portsmouth by Water from this City; but whether she travelled by land, or Water to the latter, it is certain the escape has been planned by some one who knew what he was about, & had the means to defray the expence of it & to entice her off; for not the least suspicion was entertained of her going, or having formed a connexion with any one who could induce her to such an Act.

Whether she is Stationary at Portsmouth, or was there *en passant* only, is uncertain; but as it is the last we have heard of her, I would thank you for writing to the Collector of that Port, & him for his endeavours to recover, & send her back: What will be the best method to effect it, is difficult for m⟨e⟩ to say. If enquiries are made openly, her Seducer (for she is simple and inoffensive herself) would take the alarm, & adopt instant measures (if he is not tired of her) to secrete or remove her. To sieze, and put her on board a Vessel bound immediately to this place, or to Alexandria which I should like better, seems at first view, to be the safest & least expensive. But if she is discovered, the Collector, I am persuaded, will pursue such measures as to him shall appear best, to effect those ends; and the cost shall be re-embursed & with thanks.

If positive proof is required, of the identity of the person, Miss Langden who must have seen her often in the Chamber of Miss Custis—and I dare say Mrs Langden,[3] on the occasional calls on the girl by Mrs Washington, when she has been here, would be able to do this.

I am sorry to give you, or any one else trouble on such a trifling occasion—but the ingratitude of the girl, who was brought up & treated more like a child than a Servant (& Mrs Washington's desire to recover her) ought not to escape with impunity if it can be avoided.[4] With great esteem & regard I am always Yours

Go: Washington

ALS, CtHi: Oliver Wolcott, Jr., Papers. For an analysis of this letter, see Dunbar, *Ona Judge*, 137–40.

1. GW was referring to Ona (Oney) Judge, who had left the presidential household in May. GW may have enclosed the description of her published in a newspaper advertisement (see Thomas Lee, Jr., to GW, 28 June, and n.1).

2. Elizabeth Langdon (1777–1860), the only daughter of U.S. senator John Langdon, married Thomas Elwyn in July 1797.

3. Elizabeth Sherburne Langdon (c.1761–1813), daughter of John Sherburne of Portsmouth, N.H., had married John Langdon in 1777.

4. Wolcott wrote GW from Philadelphia on 21 Sept.: "I have the honour to put under cover a Letter from Mr Whipple in answer to one I wrote respecting the Servant Girl" (ALS, NHi: Vail Collection). The enclosure was a letter from Joseph Whipple, collector of customs at Portsmouth, who wrote Wolcott from that place on 10 Sept.: "I have to acknowledge the receipt of your letter of the 1st instant and to Assure you that I shall with great pleasure execute the Presidents wishes in the matter to which it relates. I have just asscertained the fact that the person mentioned is in this Town" (DLC:GW).

From Henry Glen

Sir   Schenectady [N.Y.] 2d Septr 1796.

Your letter of the 8th Ulto from Mount Vernon was handed to me last evening, on my return from Niagara—It did not reach my Family 'till the 24th, and as I was then momently expected home, my son thought it most Safe to retain it till my arrival.

I now take the earliest opportunity of answering the several questions therein contained: permit me however previously to congratulate you on the peaceable delivery, by the British, of the Garrisons of Oswego and Niagara to the Commissioners of the United States, and on the display of our Colours at those places—The behaviour of the British commandants at both Garrisons on our arrival was extremely polite and friendly, and during my stay at Niagara, which was a week, for the purpose of discharging the vessels, which I had chartered from the British; to carry our Troops, cannon &c. from Oswego to Niagara, I had the pleasure of witnessing the good understanding which prevails on both sides.[1] The British Troops having crossed the river at Niagara, are waiting the arrival of vessels, to carry them to Kingston, from which place they are to embark in boats for Montreal. Govr Simcoe had sailed previous to the arrival of our Troops. The command of the Civil Government is left by the King's orders in the absence of Govr Simcoe to Peter Russel the oldest King's counsel, to collect in that quarter, by the title of Lieut. Govr of Upper Canada.[2] The British Troops from Detroit had previous to my departure, gone on to Kingston, from which place they are to proceed to Quebec. I left Niagara on the 20th

Ulto. our Troops were in good spirits and much pleased with their situation. The Garrison is large and in good order.

In answer to the 1st question proposed in your letter, to wit how long it will take a person to go from New York to Albany by land, and how long by water; I beg leave to observe, that as we have a good deal of Southerly wind generally at this season, until about the 20th of this month passages by water are from two, to four days, & sometimes indeed vessels come up from New York in twenty four hours, this however, is not common; after the 20th generally from four, to eight days—By land Stages, similar to those which run from New York to Philadelphia, ply between the former place and Albany—there are two lines; the one runs thro' in forty eight hours, the other in seventy two.

2d—A passage cannot at all times be had in packets, but always by land.

3d—The distance from Albany to Fort Schuyler or Stanwix is 110 miles. agreeable to an admeasurement, which I had made during the late war, the distance from my house in Schenectady to Fort Schuyler, is 93 miles. A line of Stages runs thro' from Albany to Fort Schuyler, in three days. The upper part of the road, altho' better than when the President Saw it, in Augt '83, is still not very good. By water, with three good Batteaumen, in what is called a three handed boat, of about 800 lb. burthen, the passage, from this place to Fort Schuyler, is five days. The distance by water is at least 20 miles farther, than by land, as the President experienced, when I had the honor to come down with him from that place to Schenectady in '83.[3]

4th—Hands and Boats can always be had at Schenectady— The most convenient ones are the three handed boats, which with the implements for working them costs 40 dolls. The wages of hands to Oswego 30 dolls. each, to Niagara 50 dolls. each— the men finding themselves in provisions and liquor, and the employer paying the toll through the lock at the Little falls,[4] and the carriage at Fort Schuyler—Toll at the Lock, one dollar, for the Boat & load—Carriage at Fort Schuyler one dollar for each load.

5th—Stages and horses can always be had from Schenectady to Fort Schuyler.

6th—Three men in a three handed boat, with about 800 lb. of baggage, can get to Oswego, from Fort Schuyler, in three days, with ease, unless the wood creek, which is 24 miles in length, should be very low, and the wind against you on the Oneida lake, which is 26 miles in length.

7th—The usual passage from Oswego to Niagara is from 4 days, if the lake is calm to 8 days—high winds are very frequent. No dependence can be made on a vessel at Oswego, as those of the British are all employed by their own merchants and Government. There is no way by land, from Oswego to Niagara, the only road there is, strikes off eastward at a place called whitestown about ten miles below Fort Schuyler—On this road there are settlements till within about 80 miles on this side of Niagara. The roads to the westward are in general rough, and in Spring and fall extremely bad. The distance from Schenectady, to Niagara, is better than 400 miles.

8th Batteaux, of the Size which I have before mentioned, are fit to perform the whole voyage, to Niagara, and can at all times be procured, with proper hands.

The rout from Schenectady to Niagara is generally, as follows, vizt.

1st Days journey, as far as a place called Fort hunter—about 20 miles.[5]

2d To Fort Plain or Canajoharie—about 25 miles.[6]

3d Through the lock at the little falls, & as far as Fort Herkemer, or perhaps a little above it—25 miles.[7]

4th To old Fort Schuyler, or possibly a little above it—25 miles.[8]

5th Over the Carrying place, at Fort Schuyler (or Stanwix) into wood creek.

6th Down wood creek, and a few miles on the Oneida Lake.

7th To the 3 river point.[9]

8th To Oswego—In the whole about two hundred and twenty miles. From Oswego to Niagara, the distance is One hundred and Sixty miles.

As boats in crossing the lake, always keep along shore the passage from Oswego to Niagara is generally from three and an half to four days—There are however instances of boats lying by, for ten days, in consequence of the high winds, which generally begin in October; so that the passage, after that time is somewhat uncertain. The harbours, between those two places, one of which should always be made towards evening, [(]as it is dangerous to proceed on the lake in the night) are as follows,

1st Little Sodus, 14 miles from Oswego.[10]

2d Big Sodus, 14 miles farther.

3d Yerondequet—36 miles farther, and 4 miles from the Genesee river; all which are Safe harbours.[11]

4th At a place called Braddocks bay.[12]

5th At the oak orchard.[13]

6th At the 18 mile Creek.[14]

7th At the 12 mile Creek.[15]

8th At Johnsons Landing. In all one hundred and Sixty miles from Oswego.[16]

I would observe further that provisions, tents &c. &c., would be indispensably necessary, in performing the Tour. I am Sir with Sentiments of regard and esteem Your most obedt hume servt

Henry Glen

ALS, DLC:GW.

1. Glen reported on the transfer of western posts from the British to the United States under terms of the Jay Treaty.

2. Peter Russell (1733–1808), a British army veteran, came to Canada in 1792 to serve as receiver and auditor general. He was appointed temporary administrator on 20 July 1796, the day before Gov. John Graves Simcoe's departure. Russell served as administrator until a new governor for Upper Canada arrived in 1799.

3. For the observations of another traveler who accompanied GW on his tour through western New York, 17 July–4 Aug. 1783, see Cometti, *Verme Journal*, 12–19.

4. The Little Falls canal on the Mohawk River, completed in 1795, was located at the current town of Little Falls, New York.

5. Fort Hunter established 1711–12, was located at the confluence of the Mohawk River and Schoharie Creek in modern Montgomery County, New York.

6. Fort Plain (officially Fort Rensselaer) was a Revolutionary War fort situated at the present-day town of Fort Plain in Montgomery County.

7. Fort Herkimer was rebuilt in 1756 around the Herkimer Dutch Reformed Church, on the south side of the Mohawk River near the present-day town of Herkimer, New York.

8. Old Fort Schuyler, erected in 1758, was located at modern Utica, New York.

9. Three River Point named the location where the Seneca and Oneida rivers meet to form the Oswego River.

10. Little Sodus Bay on Lake Ontario is the inlet on which Fair Haven, N.Y., is located.

11. Irondequoit Bay is the eastern boundary of the town of Irondequoit, N.Y., near Rochester.

12. Braddock Bay is at Braddock Heights in Monroe County, New York.

13. Oak Orchard Creek enters Lake Ontario in what is now Oak Orchard State Marine Park in Orleans County, New York.

14. Eighteenmile Creek enters Lake Ontario at Olcott, N.Y., in Niagara County.

15. Twelvemile Creek enters Lake Ontario about one mile west of Wilson, N.Y., in Niagara County.

16. Johnsons Landing was at the mouth of Fourmile Creek on Lake Ontario, about four miles east of the Niagara River.

From Timothy Pickering

(Private)

Sir,   Philadelphia Septr 2. 1796.

The day before yesterday, Mr McHenry put into my hands a printed Talk of the President of the United States to the Cherokee Nation. I had not an opportunity of examining it till to-day. You will permit me, sir, to say, that it appears to me in many parts exceptionable. As it was handed to me not for advice, but merely for information of a thing done, I think it most proper to communicate my ideas directly to you. The alterations & omissions which appear to me expedient, are marked on the printed Talk itself, which I inclose.[1] Mr McHenry has aimed at a familiarity of style as the most likely to make an impression on Indian minds: but there are bounds in all things which mark the extent of propriety and decorum. The dignity of the President of the United States is not to be sacrificed for any consideration: nor is it necessary to expose it to the least diminution to attain the object in view. The Talk may be in such plain language as to be perfectly intelligible to the interpreters who are to translate it, and yet not expose it to the Animadversion of well informed men. This Talk being printed, will soon get into the news-papers, and be read by other nations as well as our own. Pardon me if I think it open to much censure. It is expressed to be among the last acts of your administration, and ought to command respect from the civilized world. I cannot but express my fears that in its present form the reverse would be its fate. It abounds in tautologies and other faults, arising, I suppose, from a mistaken idea of the manner in which the untutored Indians should be addressed. But their own Chiefs speak in a manner incomparably more dignified. It would mortify me to see it, in its present form, exhibited to the world. I am strangely mistaken in my conceptions of it, if all your friends would not be extremely mortified. The alterations I have taken the liberty to note, are not all which a more attentive examination might suggest.

I have marked this letter *private*, because intended only for your eye. Both the letter and the notes on the talk are most respectfully submitted to your consideration.[2]

T. Pickering.

ALS, DLC:GW; ADfS, MHi: Pickering Papers.

1. Pickering enclosed an undated printed talk: [1] "BELOVED CHEROKEES, I HAVE been long thinking how I could better your condition, and enable you to procure more good things for yourselves; and now, I believe, I have discovered the right way, and that it may be done by degrees, if you will follow my advice.

[2] "Don't you know, that when you are hungry and cannot find a Deer to kill, that you must fast. Don't you know, that when you can get no skins by hunting and trapping, that the traders will neither give you powder nor cloth. And don't you know, also, that corn will not grow, wherewith to make you bread, unless it has been first planted.

[3] "If then every beloved Cherokee chief, and father of children, had plenty of sheep, and hogs, and cows, of which he could kill at any time, and a net to catch fish with, he would always have plenty of meat, for himself and his wife and children, whenever he disliked to hunt, or could find nothing to kill. If, besides, his wife and daughters could raise cotton, or flax; and spin and weave it, which they might soon learn to do, he would always have wherewithal to make nets, to catch fish, and to clothe himself and them, though there were no traders in the world. And, lastly, if he should plant corn and wheat, he would always have plenty of bread to eat, and grain to sell to the whites, as often as they should want it.

[4] "To better your condition, then, you see, is no very difficult matter; no more being necessary, than that each of you should get as large a flock of sheep, hogs, and cattle as possible; that you should raise cotton and flax, and have your wives and daughters taught to spin it up into thread, and weave it into cloth; and that you should plant more corn, and learn to grow wheat, which makes excellent bread.

[5] "BELOVED CHEROKEES, When you do these things, you will no longer have to depend upon hunting and trapping for your subsistence; nor upon the sale of skins, to procure you a little clothing; because you will have plenty of provisions, in your sheep, hogs and cattle; plenty of bread from your corn and wheat; and plenty of cloth from your cotton and flax; and may either hunt or let it alone as you think proper.

[6] "But can you have all these things without help? No, you cannot. You must have help to make you strong, and I will give it. You will remember, however, that I can only assist you; that I can only shew you the right way; which it rests with you to follow. The trees, you know, would never form dams for the

beaver, if he did not cut them into pieces, and fix them in the ground; nor would the flowers furnish honey to eat, unless it was collected by the bees. I will therefore give you certain thing, necessary to increase your stock of cattle; to raise corn; and make cloth; but when you get them, you must do like the bee and beaver, otherwise you can neither expect to have cattle, cloth nor corn.

[7] "How are you to obtain these things in abundance? Listen to me and I will tell you. In the first place, I shall give orders to have you supplied with such kinds of stock, as you are without; or with a better breed than what you may have. In the mean while, I desire that such of you as have sheep, hogs, or cows, should endeavor to increase them. To accomplish this you should keep them near your towns, or in places where the wolves cannot get at them to kill them, and where they will find plenty of food. I desire next, that you may lend to your brothers, who may have no flocks or cattle, some young ones of each kind, as you can spare them; for your brothers, if they are good men, will soon repay you with an equal number. By these means, my beloved Cherokees, your flocks will multiply exceedingly 'till your country be covered with them.

[8] "Well, my beloved Cherokees, when you have large flocks of cattle, and sheep, and hogs, how will it be with you? Will not these furnish you with plenty of meat, at all seasons of the year, and with plenty besides to sell to the white people, for which you may get money or goods, as you please, in exchange.

[9] "In the second place, my beloved Cherokees, to enable your women to make cloth, I have directed my beloved agent, Mr. Dinsmoor, to procure for them cotton seed and flax seed; cards to card the cotton and flax with; wheels to spin it; reels to wind it; and looms to weave it into cloth. But this is not all. I have directed him to hire a woman to teach your women to raise the flax and cotton, and to card, spin and weave it.

[10] "Among the whites a woman will lean to spin and weave in less than six months; I hope my beloved Cherokee women will learn quite as soon; and that my beloved Cherokee men will, like good white men of the United States, encourage their women to spin and weave to clothe their families.

[11] "In the third place, my beloved Cherokees, I have directed my beloved agent, Mr. Dinsmoor, to provide for your use, some plows and hoes, and other implements for working your fields, so as to raise you large crops of corn, wheat and grass. I have also commanded him to talk with you often on these subjects; and to instruct you in whatever you ought to know, with respect to your flocks, corn-fields, or making cloth. You will therefore listen to him seriously, and remember what he says; for unless you would incur my displeasure, and the displeasure of all the beloved men of the United States, you must follow in all these things his advice, because he knows how such things are to be managed, and, as yet, you do not.

[12] "MY BELOVED CHEROKEES, I am grown old, and will soon retire to my farm, where I shall employ part of my time in attending to the means of increasing my sheep, hogs and cattle; in raising of corn and wheat; and rewarding the women who spin and weave best for my family. This is just what I want you to do, and then you will be as happy as I am going to be.

[13] "I say that I have grown old, my beloved Cherokees, and am desirous to spend the remainder of my life on my own farm, free from the cares of

government; but nothwithstanding this, I shall be glad to learn that you have taken my advice, and covered your whole country with cattle, and corn, and filled your houses with cloth.

[14] "I shall know from the great man who is to succeed me, whether you have followed this advice. I shall also, before I go, speak to my beloved man, the Secretary of War, to have a set of medals prepared, to be in readiness to bestow upon such of my beloved Cherokees as shall follow it, and best deserve them.

[15] "I shall direct him to give the largest of these medals, to those who shall raise the largest flocks of cattle; the largest crops of grain; and whose wives shall spin and weave the largest quantities of cloth. As to those who will do nothing for themselves, they cannot expect any. I do not love Idlers. The beloved men of the United States do not love Idlers; the Great Spirit does not love them; because idlers are generally bad and mischievous men; thieves, or promoters of war. Such men therefore can get no medals.

[16] "But further, that you may go on right, and always keep right, I shall order my beloved man Mr. Dinsmoor, to visit every town in the nation from time to time; to give instructions and advice to those who do not like to be idlers; to see how the flocks and grain fields look; to examine the plows and implements of husbandry; to mark the advances which the women make in spinning and weaving; and to report thereof to the President of the United States; that, should any thing be wanted to render my beloved Cherokees happier, it may be done for them, by the beloved men of the United States.

[17] "Besides this, my beloved Cherokees, it will be necessary and useful, that every town should choose two of its wisest men, to meet my beloved agent, Mr. Dinsmoor, at Oostinahli, where he resides, once every year, at such time as he and you may fix upon; there to hold a council, and talk over with him the state of things in the whole nation, that whatever is wrong may be known, and as far as possible righted.

[18] "At these meetings, the representatives of the town will have explained to them, which they will explain to their tribes when they return, what laws of the United States have been made to keep bad white people from doing them harm; and how these bad people are to be punished; and the means which are to be used by the Cherokees, to preserve a perpetual peace with the United States.

[19] "BELOVED CHEROKEES, I recommend it to you to send wise men only to those meetings, where so many things may be talked over which concern the nation, and where you will always hear from the President and wise men of the United States.

[20] "And now, that this talk may be known to all the nation, and never forgotten by it; I have had it printed, and directed one to be lodged in every town, which I have signed with my own hand.

[21] "BELOVED CHEROKEES, I have but one thing more to say to you. I have sent into your nation in consequence of having been informed that some of your chiefs wished to see me in Philadelphia, that I consented to be visited by a few of those whom the nation most esteemed; and that I would not expect to see them before November. I now repeat, that I shall be glad to see in Philadelphia, at that time, a few of your chiefs or wise men.

[22] "But I must mention one thing which must be attended to in fixing on the chiefs who shall visit me.

[23] "Send me no Cherokee who has killed a white person on the frontiers, by way of revenge, in time of peace; or who lives by plunder or pillage. I will only receive Chiefs or Warriors who fight bravely after an open declaration of war; not those who creep to the frontiers to kill or rob in time of peace, under pretext of revenge or retaliation. My beloved warriors of the United States never kill an Indian but in open war, nor destroy his property in time of peace. If Indians are murdered by bad whites, in time of peace, or their property stolen by such men, the United States disowns them, and will, whenever they can catch them, and prove the fact upon them, punish them; and where they cannot make them restore what they have stolen, they will pay for it, if the Indian does not attempt retaliation. Send to me, therefore, only good Cherokees, for I will take such only by the hand.

[24] "Lastly, beloved Cherokees, you will let me know by these good men, the names of the persons whom you wish to attend the running of the boundary line agreeably to the treaty of Holston. I shall let them know which of my beloved men are to run it, and the time and place where the running is to commence, that so the persons appointed by you may know when and where to attend.

[25] "I now send my best wishes to my beloved Cherokees, and pray the Great Spirit to have you in his keeping" (MHi: Pickering Papers; the numbers in square brackets represent editorial delineation of the paragraph sequence).

In addition to many smaller alterations, Pickering rewrote the last sentence of the second paragraph to read: "And you know, that without other instruments of tilling the ground than the hoe, you will continue to raise only scanty crops of corn."

He commented in the margin to the left of the fifth paragraph: "This clause might be wholly omitted: it being but the repetition of the ideas expressed in the two preceeding clauses."

He substituted for the first three sentences of the sixth paragraph "But how are you to get & to do these things? I will show you the way & give you such aid as I can. Thus assisted, you must exert yourselves." Pickering also deleted the first part of the last sentence in the sixth paragraph and began that sentence: "Now you must do like the bees."

He made several changes in the seventh paragraph, most notably replacing the sentence that began "I desire next" with the following text: "Those among you who have more stock than are neces⟨sar⟩y for their comfort, can ⟨*mutilated*⟩ to others who have none, until the borrowers can pay for or return them. You will know among your brothers who have industry & honesty to deserve such assistance & to make the payment sure."

He deleted the first sentence of the eighth paragraph and revised the start of the next sentence: "Then you will have plenty of meat."

In the eleventh paragraph, he replaced the text following "what he says" with "& follow his advice; for in so doing you will greatly benefit yourselves, & give much pleasure to me & to all the beloved men of the U.S."

He suggested altering the twelfth and thirteen paragraphs to read: "I shall myself soon retire to my farm, where I shall attend to the means of increasing my sheep, hogs and cattle; to raising of corn and wheat; and employing the women at spinning & weaving. This is just what I wish you to do, that you may be as comfortable and happy as a plenty of these things can make you. I shall be glad to learn that you have taken my advice, and that all your families abound in cattle, corn & cloathing."

He reduced the fifteenth paragraph to a single sentence: "I shall direct him to give the largest of these medals, to those who shall be most industrious & deserving in doing what I have recommended."

Pickering commented in the margin to the right of the seventeenth paragraph: "Mr Dinsmoor must for this purpose be enabled to feed them & give them some drink: they will probably require both."

In the twenty-third paragraph Pickering underlined the reference to any Cherokee "who lives by plunder or pillage" and wrote in the margin "are there any of this description?" He then added in the margin to the right of this paragraph: "I doubt the expediency of every part of this clause. To take *revenge* is the known *law* of the Indian Nations. To refuse to see those who have taken revenge, will go to the exclusion of perh⟨aps⟩ most of the Chiefs."

2. For the final version of this talk, see GW to the Cherokee Nation, 29 Aug.; see also GW to Pickering, this date.

To Timothy Pickering

Private

Dear Sir,   Friday Evening 2d Sep. [1796]

I thank you for your private letter of this date, & will arrest the talk intended for the Cherokee Indns until it can be further considered. For this purpose I send the one I have just received from you, back again; with a request that you would pursue the remarks you have begun; and let me have them as soon as you can, conveniently, in the morning; that I may be possessed of them before I see the Secretary of War.[1] Yours sincerely, & always

                                       Go: Washington

I did not admire the draught when it was presented to me & told the Secretary so; but I am so pressed, & allowed so little time to consider matters that my signature, or approbation is, I am persuaded given, sometimes, rather too hastily.

Transcript, MHi: Pickering Papers. Octavius Pickering certified this transcript as "A true copy" in 1866.

1. In response to GW's request, Pickering submitted a fully revised draft of the talk with a cover letter dated 2 Sept.: "The day before yesterday the Secretary of War put into my hands a printed Talk to the Cherokees. I have not found time to consider it till now. It does not accord with my ideas or my expe-

rience in Indian affairs. I attempted to make alterations: but my train of thinking was so different from that of the Secretary of war—not in the Substance, but in the manner, that I found it necessary to leave the subject, or make a new draught: and deeming it a matter of consequence, seeing it is to proceed from the supreme executive of the U. States, I could not withhold the draught from you. It is now respectfully submitted to your consideration" (ALS, DNA: RG 59, Miscellaneous Letters; ALS [letterpress], MHi: Pickering Papers; LB, DNA: RG 59, GW's Correspondence with His Secretaries of State). For the final version of GW's talk, which followed Pickering's draft with few variations, see GW to the Cherokee Nation, 29 Aug., and notes 1 and 2 to that document.

From Timothy Pickering

Department of State Septr 2d 1796.

The Secretary of State respectfully lays before the President of the United States, the draught of a letter to lieutenant governor Wood of Virginia, concerning the ship Eliza, Captain Hussey, captured by the Thetis British frigate, and carried into Hampton-road. It was intended to send the letter by this day's post: but the absence of the Clerk who had locked up the inclosed papers, prevented a timely submission of the whole to the President.[1]

It appears to be an established rule in the British Courts, that a capture, *without a sentence of condemnation,* in due form of law, does *not* change the property so as to entitle a purchaser to hold the captured vessel against the original owner, or a recapture.

T. Pickering.

ALS, DNA: RG 59, Miscellaneous Letters; LB, DNA: RG 59, Domestic Letters; LB, DNA: RG 59, GW's Correspondence with His Secretaries of State.

1. The enclosure was a draft of Pickering's eventual letter to Virginia lieutenant governor James Wood with this date: "I received your letter of the 23d Ulto covering a copy of one from the Collector of Norfolk and the deposition of George G. Hussey, master of the ship Eliza, which had been taken by the British frigate Thetis and carried into Hampton Road.

"The object of the communication to the Executive of Virginia is not expressed; but I presume it was made in the expectation of its interference to demand of the commander of the Thetis a restitution of the captured Ship: and the insufficiency of the facts stated, to enable the Executive to decide whether it would or would not be proper to interfere probably occasioned the transmission of the papers to the Executive of the United States.

"The two questions arising on the case are first, Whether the capture was made within the jurisdiction of the united States? secondly, whether the legal situation of the Eliza in Holland where it is supposed Captain Hussey purchased her, admitted of his acquiring her in full property?

"As to the first question, the distance of the place of capture from the shore of the united States is mentioned only by the Captain himself, who claims the vessel and Cargo as his own; and he States it to be *about* three miles. If his mate and crew and especially if his pilot, had formed and sworn to the same estimate of the distance, a presumption would arise, that the capture was made within our jurisdiction; which has been fixed (at least for the purpose of regulating the conduct of the Government in regard to any events arising out of the present European war) to extend three geographical miles (or nearly three and a half English miles) from our Shores; with the exception of any waters or bays which are so land locked as to be unquestionably within the jurisdiction of the United States, be their extent what they may. Now from the difficulty of judging precisely of such a distance on the water, it is probable there will in the present case be a diversity of opinion; and perhaps no man can pronounce decisively upon it: but beyond a doubt what Captain Hussey estimates to be *about* three miles Captain Cochran and his officers will estimate at *about* four miles. On this ground then the Executive of the United States cannot authoritatively interfere, without further evidence of the fact.

"The defect of information on the Second question must also forbid such interposition on the part of the Executive. Captain Hussey does not say how he acquired the property of the Eliza, and we can only gather from his recital of Captain Cochran's observations that she was originally an English vessel, had been captured by the French, carried into Holland and there not regularly condemned. But, if, on the contrary, a trial and sentence of condemnation were had and passed in the Admiralty of Holland, doubtless the recapture by Captain Cochran is unlawful; and it will be immaterial in what place the recapture was made: or if the recapture were clearly within the jurisdiction of the United States, then it will be immaterial whether the Eliza was or was not regularly tried and condemned before she was purchased by Captain Hussey.

"In this state of uncertainty about the facts, the President does not deem it proper to interfere farther than to cause the papers to be exhibited to the British Minister Mr Liston. This has been done; and he will write to Captain Cochran on the subject. But for the same reason that the President can take no decided steps in the case, the British minister can only suppose facts on which to express his opinion; and add those cautionary observations which may influence a prudent commander to abstain from proceedings the legality of which may be questionable, and which excite much irritation on the part of the United States: and on every occasion mr Liston has manifested a disposition both friendly and just" (DNA: RG 59, Domestic Letters).

Wood had written Pickering from Richmond on 23 Aug., enclosing a letter from Norfolk collector William Lindsay to Virginia governor Robert Brooke, dated 20 Aug., and a deposition of George G. Hussey, dated 18 Aug. (all DNA: RG 59, Miscellaneous Letters). The substance of Hussey's deposition reads: "That he is a native of the State of Massachussetts and a Citizen of the United States of America; that he took in a Cargo of salt at the Isle of May with which he was bound for Norfolk, the said Ship and Cargo being bona fide his property, that on the 16th of August when about three miles distant from Cape

Henry several Guns were fired at him by the British frigate Thetis, He short-ened Sail, the frigate came up, he was hailed, when it was said on board the Frigate that a boat should be Sent along side the Eliza; that a boat was accord-ingly sent when the deponent was desired to go to the Frigate with his papers. He did so. After Captain Cochrane had examined the papers, he observed that he found the deponent had bought her in Holland, that She had been a prize Ship illegally taken, and that as Great Britain did not acknowledge the French Republic he should consider her a prize to him; that he accordingly ordered the Crew from the Eliza to be brought to the Frigate and sent a Crew with a prize Master on board the Eliza permitting the deponent to remain on board; that the Said frigate Thetis and the Ship Eliza are now in Hampton Road. He having been thus deprived of his property."

From Alexander Hamilton

Sir   New York Sep. 4. 1796
   I have received your two late letters, the last but one transmit-ting me a certain draft.[1] It will be corrected & altered with atten-tion to your suggestions & returned by Monday's or Tuesday's post[2]—The idea of the university is one of those which I think will be most properly reserved for your speech at the opening of the session. A general suggestion respecting education will very fitly come into the address[3]—With respectful & affect. attach: I have the honor to remain Sir Yr very obedt Serv.
                                          A. Hamilton

ALS, NN: Alexander Hamilton Papers.
   1. See GW to Hamilton, 25 Aug. and 1 September.
   2. Hamilton returned the draft when he wrote GW on Monday, 5 September.
   3. GW replied to Hamilton on 6 September.

Letter not found: from William Pearce, 4 Sept. 1796. GW wrote Pearce on 11 Sept.: "Your letter of the 4th instt came to my hands yesterday."

To James Anderson

Mr Anderson   Philada 5 Septr 1796.
   Your Letter of the 28 ulto has been received; but leaves the matter we have been treatg of, pretty much as it stood before I wrote to you,[1] except that certain stipulations on your part are made while you refer me for a solution of the queries I pro-

pounded (important to me) to others for information, when the means of obtaing it is not within my reach.

I can only say therefore, that it will not be in my power to decide anything finally without seeing & conversing fully with you on many points essential to this business, which may certainly take place at Mount Vernon (if you chuse it) by the last of this month—probably by the 22d—but of the last I cannot speak positively; tho' I can promise to give you notice so soon as a day can be fixed for my leavg this City.

I am sensible it is not a pleasant thing for any man to speak of himself; but not knowing the extent of the concerns you superintend at present, & having heard that, they were upon a small scale before, I knew that none could be more competent than yourself to give the information asked. I should have expected it would have been given with candour; because deceiving of me wou'd ultimately, have been deceivg yourself.

Mr Pearce as I mentioned to you in my former Letter, had superintended a very large Estate for 15 or 18 years for one gentleman on the Eastern Shore of Maryland & had acquired an established character & fitness for the purpose I wanted—& this too at a time when my public duties rarely permitted me to visit my Estate more than once a year—a thing which will never happen again, for assuredly if I am alive, I shall be a resident on it myself in March next; which will ease the future Manager of much trouble & a great deal of perplexity.

I am at a loss to conjecture what is meant by an Assistant to do the writing business within doors. It was always a custom when I lived at home, & it has been continued since, for each overlooker or sub-intendent of an individual farm &c. at the end of the week to give an account in writing how his people have been employed—what they have done—what increase or decrease the Stock has sustained &c. &c. for which purpose each is supplied with pen, ink & paper.

These *particular* returns form a *general* Report, & are handed to me once a week. If I am at home they are given in naked; if I am from home, they are enclosed in a Letter with other occurrences if worthy of notice. All of which I could do myself without devoting more than two hours in the week to the accomplishment. Beyond this, even in my absence, there is nothing that

I am apprised of further than the common entries of debit & credit for things bought and sold—& these in a great measure will be done away when I am fixed at home.

If after this explanation of my ideas, you shall deem it expedient to meet me at Mount Vernon, having notice given you of the time I shall be there, or whether you judge it worth while to come there or not, I request in either case to be informed, that I may be placed on a certainty & govern myself accordingly. I am Yr hble Servt

Go. W.

P.S. I presume you know that the Fredericksburgh Mails are made up every Sunday, Tuesday, & Thursday Evenings—and proceed the next Morning.

Copy, ViMtvL. The postscript is in GW's writing. Although Anderson acknowledged receiving GW's "favors" of 5 Sept., only this one letter on that date has been found (see Anderson to GW, 11 Sept.).

1. See GW to Anderson, 18 August.

From Alexander Hamilton

Sir   New York Sep. 5. 1796.

I return the draft corrected agreeably to your intimations.[1] You will observe a short paragraph added respecting *Education.* As to the establishment of a University, it is a point which in connection with military schools, & some other things, I meant, agreeably to your desire to suggest to you, as parts of your Speech at the opening of the session. There will several things come there much better than in a general address to The People which likewise would swell the address too much—Had I had *health* enough, it was my intention to have written it over, in which case I could both have improved & abriged. But this is not the case. I seem now to have regularly a period of ill health every summer.

I think it will be adviseable *simply* to send the address by your Secretary to *Dunlap.*[2] It will of course find its way into all the other papers. Some person on the spot ought to be charged with a careful examination of the impression by the proof sheet.[3] very respectfully & Affect. I have the honor to be Sr Yr very obed. serv.

A. Hamilton

ALS, NN: Alexander Hamilton Papers.

1. Hamilton is referring to the draft for GW's farewell address enclosed with GW's letter to Hamilton dated 25 August.

2. Hamilton presumably had forgotten or did not know that John Dunlap's partnership in the Philadelphia newspaper known in 1796 as *Claypoole's American Daily Advertiser* had ceased at the end of 1795 (see Brigham, *American Newspapers*, 2:896, 903).

3. GW replied to Hamilton on 6 September.

To William Pearce

Mr Pearce   Philadelphia 5th Septr 1796

Your letter of the 31st of Augt from Chester Town, came duly to hand;[1] but as you did not acknowledge the receipt of the one I wrote you from hence, this day week, I presume it had not got to hand;[2] Owing, I conceive to a misapprehension of mine as to the time of closing the Mail for the Eastern shore which I find is an hour and an half earlier than those which go Southerly or Easterly. I put my letter under cover to the Postmaster in Chester Town with a request to forward it to Mount Vernon if you should have left that place.

As you appear (by your letter abovementioned) to have attended to most of the matters which were recommended in mine, your not receiving it at Chester Town was not very material.

By my letters from Mount Vernon I find the weather up to the date of them has continued extremely wet[3]—of course Seeding must have gone on slowly, if not badly.

Washington Custis writes me that Mr Stuart, at the River farm was very ill of a fever, on thursday last.[4] I hope it will not prove a fatal one, & thereby add to your present difficulties in providing *good* Overseers. If Scoon is a *first rate* Overseer, I had rather give him £75 Maryland curr[enc]y than run the risk of getting an indifferent one; especially if he can bring another whom *you know* to be a good one, along with him; although the wages of that other should exceed 133⅓ dollars. I do not know what Violet's & Cash's present wages are, I did not care to increase it with them (although they may be industrious men) as *they* cd have no plea to ask higher wages for the year to come, than for the year past. Men who are old, experienced, and of established reputation & skill, have better ground to stand upon, than they.

Washington in his letter mentioned further that the weavil was very much in Stuarts Wheat. If this is really the case, it is much to be regretted, but there is no other remedy but to get it out as quick as possible; and as he has no place to keep it securely in the Chaff, to grind it up with all the dispatch the Mill is capable. He said something also about one of the Bolting cloths being out of order, or unfit for use—this will require attention.

Write me by the first Post (fridays) after you get this letter, how every thing is, and going on; for if I can accomplish the business which ⟨brot⟩ me here, I hope by Wednesday, or thursda⟨y⟩ in next week, to leave this, on my return to Mount Vernon.[5] I wish you well & am Your friend

Go: Washington

ALS, ViMtvL.
1. Pearce's letter to GW dated 31 Aug. has not been found.
2. See GW to Pearce, 28 August.
3. These letters from Mount Vernon have not been found.
4. The previous Thursday was 1 September.
5. GW is referring to Wednesday, 14 Sept., or the following day.

Letter not found: from William Strickland, 5 Sept. 1796. GW wrote Strickland on 15 July 1797: "I have been honored with Yours of the 30th of May and 5th of Septr of last Year" (see *Papers, Retirement Series*, 1:253–59).

From Oliver Wolcott, Jr.

Treasury Department [Philadelphia]
September 5th 1796

The Secretary of the Treasury has the honor most respectfully to report to the President of the United States.

That by an Act of Congress passed on the sixth day of May 1796, the President of the United States is authorised to cause other Revenue Cutters to be built or purchased in lieu of such as are or shall from time to time become unfit for further service and to cause such Revenue Cutters as shall so become unfit for service to be sold at public Auction.[1]

The Secretary as soon after the passing of said Act as his other engagements would permit, caused reports to be made to him of the state of the Revenue Cutters,[2] and he now submits the result of the information which has been obtained, so far as any immediate Act of the President appears to be necessary thereon.

1st The Cutter on the Pennsylvania station was sold in December last by direction of the Secretary, she being found utterly unfit for service and in a state which rendered an expensive repair necessary to prevent an absolute loss to the Public—of this transaction a report was made to Congress, who have tacitly approved thereof;[3] it is therefor now necessary to take measures for building a new Cutter and by the communications herewith transmitted from Sharp Delany it appears that one in every way adequate may be obtained for four thousand and seventy four Dollars.[4]

2d The letter from Robert Purviance dated August 13th herewith transmitted, States, that a repair will be necessary upon the Maryland Cutter, which will cost about five hundred and fifty Dollars—but as the Vessel is not well adapted for the Revenue Service, it appears expedient to direct a Sale and to purchase a smaller Vessel which will draw less Water and be navigated at a less expence.[5]

3d The Cutter on the Virginia station is a heavy Sailor, her hull is decayed and her rigging worn out—as appears from the communications from William Lindsay, Capt. Francis Bright and others. the purchase of a new Vessel is decidedly recommended.

4th The Cutter on the South Carolina station is represented as originally too small and as being now utterly unfit for service. The Collector Isaac Holmes Esqr. and the Capt. Robert Cochran both concur in recommending the purchase of a new Vessel.

The Secretary has not received definitive information respecting the State of the Cutters on the New York North Carolina and Georgia stations; in respect to the others not before mentioned, no immediate measures by the President appear to be necessary.

The Secretary deems it proper to state that the present derangement of the Cutter system appears to have arisen in the first instance from the inadequacy of the fund originally allotted for the purchase of Vessels,[6] which rendered it impossible to commence the establishment on a proper scale, and latterly to the incompetency of the compensation which prevented the inlistment of skilful and industrious mariners; this last evil is now obviated by an authority to allow adequate wages.[7]

The Secretary in consequence of the premises, respectfully

requests the Presidents permission to procure by Contract or otherwise suitable Vessels to be employed as Cutters on the Pennsylvania, Maryland, Virginia and South Carolina Stations, and to sell those on the said Stations, now belonging to the United States at public Auction upon condition that the proceeds of such Sales shall be paid into the Treasury of the United States.[8] All which is most respectfully submitted by

Oliv. Wolcott
Secy of the Treasury

LB, DLC:GW.

1. Wolcott alluded to section 3 of "An Act making further provision relative to the Revenue Cutters" (1 *Stat.* 461–62).

2. Wolcott had written Robert Purviance confidentially on 14 July seeking specifics about the Baltimore revenue cutter (CtHi: Oliver Wolcott, Jr., Papers). In that communication, Wolcott mentioned a letter he wrote on the same date making "certain general inquiries," probably referencing a circular letter to collectors at ports with cutters.

3. Writing the U.S. House of Representatives on 15 March, Wolcott reported the sale of the Pennsylvania cutter and considered petitions from revenue cutter officers for increased compensation (CtHi: Oliver Wolcott, Jr., Papers).

4. The documents transmitted from Sharp Delany, collector at Philadelphia, to Wolcott have not been identified.

5. The letter from Purviance has not been identified.

6. An act approved on 4 Aug. 1790 had limited expenditures to build and equip up to ten revenue cutters to no more than $10,000 (see 1 *Stat.* 145, 175).

7. The act approved on 6 May 1796 had increased the pay of mariners to as much as $20 per month from no more than $10 per month in an act approved on 2 March 1793 (see n.1 above and 1 *Stat.* 336–38).

8. GW replied to Wolcott on 6 Sept.: "Having considered your Report of the fifth instant, I do hereby authorize you to take suitable and legal measures for procuring by contract or otherwise as shall appear to be most for the public Interest, four Revenue Cutters, to be employed on the Pennsylvania, Maryland, Virginia and South Carolina Stations. And I do hereby direct you to cause the Revenue Cutters belonging to the United States on the Maryland, Virginia and South Carolina Stations to be sold at public Auction, and to cause the proceeds of such Sales to be paid into the Treasury of the United States; and for so doing this shall be your Warrant" (LB, DLC:GW).

To Alexander Hamilton

Dear Sir, Philadelphia 6th Septr 1796.

I received yesterday, your letter of the 4th instant. If the promised paper has not been sent before this reaches you, Mr Kitt the bearer of it, who goes to New York partly on mine, and partly on his own business, will bring it safely. I only await here, now, and shall in a few days do it impatiently, for the arrival of General Pinckney.[1]

If you think the idea of a University had better be reserved for the Speech at the opening of the Session, I am content to defer the communication of it until that period. But even in *that* case, I would pray you (as soon as convenient) to make a draught for the occasion; predicated on the ideas with which you have been furnished—looking at the sametime into what was said on this head in my *second* Speech to the *first* Congress—merely with a view to see what was said on the subject at that time—and this you will perceive was not so much to the point as I want to express now—though it may, if proper, be glanced at, to shew that the subject had caught my attention early.[2]

But to be candid, I much question whether a recommendation of this measure to the Legislature will have a better effect *now* than *formerly*. It may shew indeed my sense of its importance, and that is a sufficient inducement with *me* to bring the matter before the public in some shape or another, at the closing Scenes of my political exit. My object for proposing to insirt it where I did (if not improper) was to set the People to ruminating on the importance of the measure as the most likely means of bringing it to pass.[3] With much truth I am Your Affectionate

Go: Washington

ALS, DLC: Hamilton Papers; copy, DLC: Hamilton Papers.

1. Charles Cotesworth Pinckney, new U.S. minister to France, was en route from Charleston, S.C., to Philadelphia to receive instructions prior to his departure overseas (see Pinckney to GW, 12 Aug.).

2. In his message to the U.S. Senate and House of Representatives dated 8 Jan. 1790, GW extolled "the promotion of Science and Literature" and hinted that Congress might consider "the institution of a national University."

3. Hamilton replied to GW from New York on Thursday, 8 Sept.: "I have received your letter of the 6th by the bearer. The draft was sent forward by Post on Tuesday.

"I shall prepare a paragraph with respect to the University & some others for consideration respecting other points which have occured" (ALS, NN: Alexander Hamilton Papers).

From Oliver Wolcott, Jr.

Treasury Department September the 6th 1796.
The Secretary of the Treasury respectfully transmits to the President of the United States, a letter from the Commissioner of the Revenue dated the 11th of August last, covering one to him from the Collector of Washington, on the subject of sundry Contracts made by the said Collector for placing and keeping up the Stakes under his superintendence and shifting and clearing the Buoys at the South West Straddle for the year 1797.[1]

It is the opinion of the Secretary that it is adviseable to authorise Contracts on the terms proposed. All which is respectfully Submitted

Oliv: Wolcott
Secy of the Treasury

LB, DLC:GW.

1. Tench Coxe, commissioner of the revenue, had written Wolcott on 11 Aug. that contracts in the enclosed statement were "more favorable than could have been expected in the present expensive times." He asked Wolcott to transmit the statement to GW "for his Decision" (DNA: RG 26, Lighthouse Letters). For a letter-book copy of the enclosed letter from William Keais, collector and inspector for the port of Washington, N.C., to Coxe dated 25 July, see DNA: RG 26, Lighthouse Deeds and Contracts. It indicates GW's approval of the contracts on 7 Sept. (see also *JPP*, 342).

"An Act supplementary to the act for the establishment and support of lighthouses, beacons, buoys, and public piers," approved 2 March 1793, had authorized "a beacon or floating buoy at the southwest straddle on the Royal shoal, near Ocracoke inlet, in North Carolina" (1 *Stat.* 339).

From "A feeling Sufferer"

Much respected Sir, New-England, Sept. 7, 1796
Pardon the seeming Indecency of an anonymous Epistle, for which the *Occasion* may be some Apology.

The Growth of the City of Washington was supposed an Object near your Heart. On this Presumption, great Numbers of Tickets in the present Lottery were purchased in New-England, which the Adventurers have long since had Cause to regret. Do not suffer that unblushing, Bottle-conjuring Villain (Blodget) any longer to gull and bubble us. A bare Recommendation from you, Sir, to proceed in the Drawing with Celerity, he would not dare to disrespect.[1] Yours most devotedly,

A feeling Sufferer

P.S. At a late Meeting, a Collection of the Tickets was Proposed, in order to a personal Demand being made of the Money paid for them, with Interest. This was over-ruled, in the Hope that the triple-bronzed Manager would draw more than 150 Numbers per Week. What an Insult on the People of the United States!

ALS, DLC:GW. The cover is dated 10 Sept. and bears a Providence postal stamp.

1. For the Federal City lotteries, see Commissioners for the District of Columbia to GW, 9 April 1793 (second letter), n.1. "A feeling Sufferer" is referring to the second lottery, which the commissioners had disavowed (see Commissioners to GW, 23 Dec. 1793, n.7). In the *Gazette of the United States and Daily Evening Advertiser* (Philadelphia) for 30 Aug. 1794, Samuel Blodget, Jr., advertised that the drawing would begin no later than December 1794. He offered 50,000 tickets for sale: 16,739 winners and 33,261 "Blanks" that would receive no prize.

Drawings did not commence until 4 July 1796, and results published for the second and third drawings (9 and 11 July) showed 150 numbers drawn and 44 prizes awarded (see *Centinel of Liberty and George-town Advertiser*, 8 July 1796; *Gazette of the United States, & Philadelphia Daily Advertiser*, 16 July 1796).

To James McHenry

Private

Dear Sir   Wednesday morning [7 Sept. 1796]

The principles of the Enclosed Instructions I approve; and since they are drawn, I shall not object to the Phraseology; tho' considering that it is Addressed to *our* agent, for *his* government part of them, I think is too much in the stile of a talk to the Indians. And I think too, as he is intended for the *general* Superintendent his attentions seems to be too much confined to the Creek Nation.[1] Yours always—& sincerely

Go: Washington

ALS, NhD. The date comes from the docket.

1. The enclosure has not been identified, but McHenry issued instructions dated 8 Sept. to Benjamin Hawkins as "principal temporary Agent for Indian Affairs, South of the Ohio." McHenry first repeated the five subjects for discussion with the Creek Indians outlined in his letter to GW dated 29 Aug. and directed that Hawkins "give all possible satisfaction" on those items. Ad-

ditional instructions echoed those already given Cherokee agent Silas Dins-moor (see McHenry to GW, 24 Aug., and n.1). The long middle portion of the instructions covered administrative and financial records that needed to be sent to the War Department. With legislation providing only $15,000 per year to furnish "the Indian Nations with domestic animals, implements of Hus-bandry, and with Agents to reside among them," McHenry explained in the closing paragraph that it was "necessary to confine the chief experiments to the Creeks and Cherokees for the present and to require regular estimates as a guide for its distribution. It is not however to be understood from your prin-cipal care being directed to the Creeks, that you are not to extend such help to the Choctaws and Chickasaws of the means put in your power, as in your judgment may be of service either to the preservation of their friendship or their advancement in Civilization. You will therefore as a matter of course and appertaining to the nature of your appointment give these nations as much of your attention as on a general view of things may seem proper or necessary" (MHi: Adams Papers).

From John Carey

Sir, London Septemb. 8. 1796.

when you consider the serious nature of the business, on which I have the honor to address you, I trust your good sense will induce you to overlook & excuse any impropriety or indeli-cacy which there may be in my writing to you on the subject. A few days since, I, for the first time, saw a book entitled "*Epistles Domestic, &c. from General Washington.*"[1] As you also have prob-ably seen it, I need not describe its contents. On reading it, I felt, what every honest man must feel, indignation & contempt for the anonymous editor. Happening luckily to be acquainted with some of the gentlemen who write for the Critical Review, I requested an indulgence which I scorned to ask last year when my own interests were concerned (i.e. on the publication of the two vols. of your "Official Letters")[2]—I requested & obtained permission to write a critique of the volume in question. I have the honor of inclosing it—for *your own private inspection only*, un-til it appear in print, which will be on the first of October with perhaps some alterations or amendments, if any occur in the interim between this first half execution of my thoughts, & my seeing the proof sheet.[3] As soon as published, I shall do myself the honor of transmitting a printed copy of the Review that con-tains it.

I regret extremely that I cannot (without openly avowing my-self the author) point out to the public the prodigious incor-rectness of Mr Duché's letter.[4] Having compared it with a cor-rect copy which I have taken from the files, I find no less than *one hundred and forty* deviations from the genuine text; in which number I do not at all count orthography or punctuation.

Permit me, Sir, to add, that I am much at a loss to know whether I ought openly to take any notice of this affair in case I should publish a continuation of your "Official Letters"; which I wish to do as soon as I can make it convenient. Perhaps some means may be found to guide my feeble & fallible judgment. I wish to act for the best: & if I err, the uprightness of my intention will, I trust, excuse me. I take it for granted that Mr Randolph has informed Your excellency of my intention respecting the whole letters, & passages of letters which I have omitted in my former publication—which is (as I informed him in 2 letters written in November last) not to publish them during your excellency's lifetime, not even afterwards if deemed unadvisable by persons on whose judgment & integrity I can rely.

I shall shortly take the liberty of waiting on Mr King, who may perhaps be able to furnish me with some useful advice—though I do not mean to inform him of my being the writer of the critique.

I hope sir, you will excuse this incorrect & hasty scrawl—The vessel by which I mean to send it, is already down at Gravesend, & the captain just going—The same apology will serve for the critique.[5] I have the honor to be, with very sincere respect, & warm wishes for your Excellency's welfare & that of the U.S., Sir, your most obedt humble servant,

John Carey.

ALS, DLC:GW. The enclosure filed with this letter (see n.3 below) is followed by a "Nota Bene" in Carey's writing, probably used as a cover: "This letter not relating to public affairs, and not being written to the President, *as* President of the U.S., but intended for General Washington in his private capacity, is not to be opened by his Secretary, or by any other person than himself."

1. *Epistles Domestic, Confidential, and Official, from General Washington, written about the Commencement of the American Contest, when he entered on the Command of the Army of the United States. With an Interesting Series of his Letters, particularly to the British Admirals, Arbuthnot and Digby, to Gen. Sir Henry Clinton, Lord Cornwallis, Sir Guy Carleton, Marquis de la Fayette, &c. &c. To Benjamin Harrison, Esq. Speaker of*

the House of Delegates in Virginia, to Admiral the Count de Grasse, General Sullivan, respecting an attack of New-York; including many applications and addresses presented to him with his answers: Orders and Instructions, on important occasions, to his Aids de Camp, &c. &c. &c. None of which have been printed in the two Volumes published a few months ago was first sold by James Rivington at New York in 1796 and was reprinted in London the same year.

The volume consisted of the seven forged letters designed to discredit GW that had appeared in a 1777 London pamphlet, buttressed by a much longer appendix of genuine documents. For the spurious letters, see Richard Henry Lee to GW, 2 Jan. 1778, and n.3, in *Papers, Revolutionary War Series*, 13:120–22; see also Ford, *Spurious Letters.*

2. Carey had published a two-volume edition of *Official Letters to the Honorable American Congress, Written, during the War between the United Colonies and Great Britain, by His Excellency, George Washington, Commander in Chief of the Continental Forces, Now President of the United States. Copied, by Special Permission, from the Original Papers preserved in the Office of the Secretary of State, Philadelphia* (London, 1795).

3. The assertion that GW's slave William "Billy" Lee provided the first seven letters prompted Carey to begin his undated six-page manuscript review with great skepticism. On reading the letters, Carey suspected "that the design of the anonymous fabricator was no very laudable one." The seven letters, "chiefly filled up with the doubts, anxieties, & vague apprehensions of the supposed writer, intermingled with some private matter of an uninteresting nature," merely serve "as a convenient vehicle for a few remarkable passages" that "are the marrow & quintessence of the whole."

Before looking at those passages, Carey turned to the appendix. More than 100 pages of the *Epistles* concern the American reluctance to exchange prisoners, a position that GW "ever reprobated . . . In the publication before us, however, the unwary reader is taught to impute the whole blame to him alone, since a resolution of Congress is produced (p. 104) *Seemingly* giving him full power to treat for a general exchange. But, in comparing the resolution with the printed Journals of Congress, we find that the anonymous editor has falsified it, to answer his own purposes." Another 27 pages of documents concern the grievances of the Continental army in 1783. Carey identified many revisions to actual texts that tend to portray GW as "a favourer, at least, if not the prime instigator, of the mutiny."

Having established the editor's ill will toward GW, Carey returned to the seven letters that form the main text. Carey quoted numerous passages in which GW claimed an aversion to American independence meant to make supporters of independence "hostile to the supposed writer, & to excite a thousand injurious surmises in the bosoms of those who are dissatisfied with the late commercial treaty, & who accuse the president of having sacrificed the interests of the U.S. to those of G. Britain."

Carey concluded that the *Epistles* were "a performance which can, to no impartial considerate man, appear in any other light than that of an arrant forgery, trumped up for the purpose of rendering the President of the U.S.

unpopular, & thus, probably, either compelling him to resign his high office in disgust, or, at least, preventing his re-appointment, in short, an *electioneering manœuvre* altogether" (DLC:GW).

For the printed review, significantly revised, see *The Critical Review; or, Annals of Literature*, 2d. ser., 18 (Sept.–Dec. 1796): 81–88. Carey sent this publication when he wrote GW on 1 Oct. 1796 (DLC:GW).

4. Carey was referring to Jacob Duché's letter to GW dated 8 Oct. 1777, in which Duché urged GW to negotiate peace with the British (see *Papers, Revolutionary War Series*, 11:430–37). This letter began the appendix of the *Epistles*.

5. GW expressed appreciation when he replied to Carey on 30 Dec. 1796: "I am much indebted to you for the interest you feel, to have the imposition that has been attempted upon the public, detected" (DLC:GW).

Letter not found: from John Carey, 9 Sept. 1796. GW wrote Carey on 30 Dec.: "I have received your letters of the 8th and 9th of September" (DLC:GW).

From Timothy Pickering

Sir,   Department of State Septr 9. 1796.
In draughting the letter of credence for Mr Pinckney, the motives for his appointment, arising out of the present state of things between the U. States & France, pressed me to depart from the usual *formalities* of this diplomatic instrument: it is therefore respectfully submitted to your consideration, for any alterations you may deem proper previous to its being transcribed. I also submit the draught of a letter to Mr Monroe, and of his letter of recall.[1] With the highest respect I am, sir, your obt servt
                                                    T. Pickering.

ALS, DNA: RG 59, Miscellaneous Letters; LB, DNA: RG 59, GW's Correspondence with His Secretaries of State.

1. The drafts have not been identified, but GW replied to Pickering on the same morning: "The enclosed draughts appear to me to be pertinent to the occasions which have given rise to them; and of course, in my judgment, are to be preferred to *general* forms. I would have you, however, look to the letter of credence from the French government to Mr *Fauchet* as somewhat analogous to the recall of Mr Monroe & also to the one given Mr Jay" (Transcript, MHi: Pickering Papers; Octavius Pickering certified this transcript as "A true copy" in 1866). For the letters of credence for Jean Antoine Joseph Fauchet and John Jay, see the Provisional Executive Council of France to GW, 15 Nov. 1793, and Notice of John Jay's Powers as Envoy Extraordinary to Great Britain, 6 May 1794, source note.

GW signed a letter of credence to the Directory of the French Republic on this date: "Very, Dear Great Friends and Allies, Sincerely desirous to maintain that good understanding which from the commencement of their alliance, has subsisted between our two Nations; and to efface unfavourable impressions, banish suspicions and restore that cordiality, which was at once the evidence and pledge of a friendly Union; I have judged it expedient to appoint Charles Cotesworth Pinckney, one of our distinguished citizens, to reside near you, in the quality of Minister Plenipotentiary of the United States of America. He knows the friendship our Republic bears to yours, and our desire to strengthen and confirm it. From my knowledge of his abilities, prudence and integrity, I have entire confidence that he will be diligent and faithful to accomplish the objects of his mission, and render himself acceptable to you. I beseech you, therefore, to give full credence to whatever he shall say to you on the part of the United States, and especially when he shall assure you of their Friendship and Wishes for the Prosperity of the French Republic, which may God preserve" (ADS, ScC; copy, FrPMAE: Correspondence Politique, États Unis, vol. 46; copy, DNA: RG 59, entry 33). A letter addressed to Charles Cotesworth Pinckney on this date commissioned him as U.S. minister to France "to the end of the next session of the Senate and no longer" (LB, DNA: RG 59, entry 33).

In the letter of recall addressed to the Directory of the French Republic on this date, GW advised that it "appeared to me expedient to grant to James Monroe, our Minister Plenipotentiary with the French Republic, permission to return to the United States. He is accordingly charged to take his leave of You in a manner most suitable to the respect and friendship which the United States bear to your Nation" (LS, FrPMAE: Correspondence Politique, États Unis, vol. 46; LB, DNA: RG 59, entry 33).

Pickering also wrote Monroe on this date and enclosed a triplicate of his letter to Monroe written on 22 Aug. that explained the recall decision. Pickering additionally asked Monroe to give information to Pinckney on the claims of American merchants against France (see *Papers of James Monroe*, 4:88–89; see also GW to Pickering, 10 Aug., and n.3).

From Samuel Benjamin Morse

Billerica (Massachusetts)

Most excellent Sir,   Septr 10, 1796.

As you are the universal friend of mankind, and to numerous individuals in particular have manifested your bounty and generosity in divers ways and manners, I take the liberty relying on the great and noble disposition of your mind for an assurance of not giving offence, to request the favor of your smiles of beneficence in some way which it may be in your power or pleasure to grant. For to whom can I look with more propriety for assistance, than to the great and good Father of his country; whose wish is, that al⟨l⟩ may be assisted, as far as the extensive sphere of his influence and ability can effect it.

The favor I have to request, Sir, is the privelege of being employed as a Clerk in the Secretary of State's Office; or in some other Office of profit and advantage of the like kind. As to my character, Sir, I believe I can obtain sufficient recommendation from General Lincoln; with whom indeed I cannot claim the honor of much personal acquaintance; but I am well known to, and acquainted with the Clergyman of the Parish, who can claim the honor of intimate friendship with the General.[1] I further give you the trouble, great and good Sir, first to inform you that I have been regularly educated at Harvard University, and have received the honor of two degrees there.[2] From the Government of the College I can produce the most honorable testimonials of my character and scholarship.

If, Sir, it should at any time be consistent with your power and will, to bestow on me the Office above mentioned, or any other Clerkship, your granting me that favor would heighten, if possible, the love and admiration with which myself and millions of others are already filled at your unrivalled Greatness and Goodness. I am, Illustrious Sir, With the Profoundest Esteem and Respect Your devoted Servant

Saml B. Morse

ALS, DLC:GW.

Samuel Benjamin Morse (c.1774–1798) graduated from Harvard in 1791 and later practiced law.

1. Henry Cumings (1739–1823), a Harvard graduate, was ordained as pastor at Billerica in 1763 and remained until his death. He represented Billerica at the Massachusetts constitutional convention of 1779 and 1780.

2. Morse received the degrees of bachelor of arts and master of arts.

From Timothy Pickering

Department of State Sept. 10. 1796.

The Secretary of State respectfully submits to the President of the U. States a letter intended for Mr King, the occasion of which is exhibited in the accompanying letter from the deputy collector of Norfolk.[1]

T. Pickering

ALS, DNA: RG 59, Miscellaneous Letters; LB, DNA: RG 59, GW's Correspondence with His Secretaries of State. GW replied to Pickering on this date.

1. The deputy collector at Norfolk, Va., was Francis Stubbs Taylor, a distant relation of James Madison. His letter has not been identified, but it probably reported that the captain of the British navy frigate *Prevoyante* had refused to cooperate with an inquiry about impressed seamen aboard his ship. According to a newspaper account of the incident, the inquiry was initiated after receipt of a letter asserting that there were "upwards of" twenty impressed men aboard the vessel. The captain responded to the man sent to investigate "that he would not suffer any man to come on board his ship to make enquiries" and "that *he had Americans on board, and in irons; and that he should keep them until they agreed to serve his majesty, in defiance of the president of the United States, or any authority!*" (*Greenleaf's New York Journal, & Patriotic Register,* 20 Sept. 1796).

Pickering's first letter to Rufus King, U.S. minister to Great Britain, written on this date expostulates that if "the *dignity* of the British Government will not permit an inquiry on board their Ships for American seamen, their doom is fixed for the war: and thus the rights of an independent neutral nation are to be sacrificed to *British dignity*! Justice requires that such inquiries and examinations should be made, because the liberation of our seamen will otherwise be impossible. For the British Government then to make professions of respect to the rights of our Citizens, and willingness to release them, and yet deny the only means of ascertaining those rights, is an insulting tantalism. If such orders have been given to the British Commanders," then sending U.S. agents to discuss impressment "will be fruitless; and the sooner we know it the better. But I would fain hope other things; and if the British Government have any regard to our rights, any respect for our nation, and place any value on our friendship, they will even facilitate to us the means of releiving our oppressed citizens. The subject of our impressed seamen makes a part of your instructions: but the President now renews his desire that their relief may engage your special attention" (DNA: RG 59, Diplomatic and Consular Instructions; see also Pickering to GW, 10 June, and n.1).

To Timothy Pickering

Saturday 10th Sep. 1796

The enclosed is approved,[1] and if there is any Authentic ground to go upon, it ought to be extended to the case of Captn Jessup by strong & solemn expostulation or remonstrance. This conduct of G. Britain cannot, must not be suffered with impunity.[2]

G. Washington

ALS, ViMtvL.

1. See Pickering to GW, this date.

2. After receiving GW's reply, Pickering wrote a second letter to Rufus King, U.S. minister to Great Britain, on this date. Pickering explained GW's desire

"that the case of Captain Jessup may be noticed: We waited only for the original documents to arrive, to make to the British Government a solemn remonstrance on the tyrannical and inhuman conduct of Captain Pigot: but those documents having not yet arrived, I must content myself for the present, with transmitting to you the newspaper account of the transaction. Nobody doubts but that it is substantially exact. I am only astonished at the quiet submission of Captn Jessup, and other american Citizens, victims of the frequent tyranny and cruelty of British officers; and that some of them do not take instant vengeance on the Ruffians who thus put them to the torture. The affair is left, in its present form, to your discretion. When the original documents come to hand, I shall hasten to forward them to you; in the mean time the transaction seems to merit some attention" (DNA: RG 59, Diplomatic and Consular Instructions).

According to an account in *The Argus, or Greenleaf's New Daily Advertiser* (New York) for 25 July, and widely reprinted, Hugh Pigot, in command of the British frigate *Success*, boarded the ship *Mercury*, of New York, and ordered his men "to cut and bring on board every thing that they could lay their hands on." As the men cut away yards, stays, and sails, Capt. William Jesup of the *Mercury* requested "that they would cut as little as they could help." Pigot ordered Jesup taken to the *Success*, where he was flogged until "he fainted under the blows." Regaining his senses, Jesup asked Pigot to return a sail. Pigot replied: "*You damned rascal, if you say one word more, I will have you to the gang-way and flog you to death!*" Surgeons who later examined Jesup at Port-au-Prince "all expressed their surprize and indignation on seeing his bruised body" and eventually stopped his "vomiting of blood."

The Daily Advertiser (New York) for 3 Aug. printed Jesup's petition dated 4 July to Richard Rich Wilford, British commander at Port-au-Prince. Jesup described his ordeal and asked that "the proper authority" act to give him "that justice and satisfaction which the nature of an offense so glaring and unprecedented loudly calls for."

King wrote Pickering on 9 Dec. to report his protest and the British reply (see DNA: RG 59, Despatches from U.S. Ministers to Great Britain).

From John Sinclair

sir   Whitehall [London] Sepr 10th 1796.

I had yesterday the pleasure of receiving your's of the 12th of June, which Mr King had the goodness to take Charge of, & which he delayed delivering until my return from Scotland. The information which it contains regarding the Use of Gypsum, seems to be extremely important, and throws much Light upon a very curious & interesting branch of Husbandry. The difficulties you have found in collecting additional information respecting manures, convince me more and more, that the Farmers of

America want *some Spur* to acquire agricultural information, as well as a Spirit to communicate to others, what they have already acquired: In short, that they should *read, speak, and write more,* upon that Subject, than they are accustomed to at present. It is not yet Six Years since I began the Statistical & Agricultural Surveys,[1] at which period, there were very few in the Island thought capable of giving a proper account either of a County or even a Parish, & now there are above a thousand, who have been so trained and educated to those investigations, that they are equal to any task of the sort. But that is in Consequence of a great deal of practice, & of those subjects having been so frequently discussed. For the common conversation of male Society, there are but three General Topics, namely Politics, Subjects of an amorous nature, & farming. Sir Robert Walpole, who was shy of speaking Politics, and knew nothing of farming, used to say that *bawdy,* to make use of his own vulgar expression, was the only conversation for a general company.[2] But I happened to dine the other Day at Mr Secretary Dundas's, where Mr Pitt was, and I was glad to find that our present Minister agreed with me in thinking that farming was a much better one.

I am wandering however, from the Point to which I wish to call your Excellency's attention. The People of this Country, as well as of America, learn with infinite regret, that you propose resigning your situation as President of the United States. I shall not enter into the Discussion of a Subject, of which I am so incompetent to judge; but if it is so, I hope that you will recommend some Agricultural Establishment, on a great Scale, before you quit the Reins of Government. By that, I mean, *A Board of Agriculture,* or some such Establishment at Philadelphia, with Societies of Agriculture in the Capital of each State to correspond with it. Such an Establishment would soon enable the farmers of America to acquire Agricultural Knowledge, and what is of equal importance, the ability of communicating what they have learnt, to their Countrymen.

I scarcely think that any Government can be properly constituted, without such an Establishment. As mere individuals, 4 things are necessary; 1. food. 2. Clothing. 3. Shelter. 4. Mental Improvement. As Members of a large Community, 4 other points seem to be essential, namely, 1. Property. 2. Marriage. 3. Laws for our Direction in this world, and 4. Religion to prepare us for another. But the foundation of the whole is *food*, and that Country must be the happiest, where that *sine qua non* can be most easily obtained. The first means of securing abundance of food, however, is by ascertaining the best mode of raising it, & rouzing a Spirit of industry for that purpose, for both of which, the countenance, & Protection of the Government of a Country, through the Medium of some Public Establishment, are absolutely essential. The trifling expence for which such an Institution might be kept up, is another argument in its favor.

I am induced more particularly to dwell upon this Circumstance, as it might be in my power on various occasions to give useful hints to America, were I satisfied that they would be duly weighed, &, *if approved of, acted upon*. For instance you will herewith receive some Egyptian Wheat, which produces at the rate of 180 Bushels per English Acre. Indeed without such a Grain, so narrow a Country as Egypt could never have fed such Multitudes of People. I have no Doubt of its thriving in America equally well. It occurred to me also the other Day, that in the Southern States, both the Tea Plant, & the New Zealand kind of hemp might be raised in great perfection, and we could send over both these plants from this Country. Indeed I propose giving some of them in charge to Mr Pinckney.[3] But to introduce any new article of produce, the countenance, & in some Cases, the assistance of the Government of a State is necessary. When once however the Practicability of cultivating any article is ascertained, unless it can stand upon its own bottom, it cannot be of any real advantage to a Nation.

But I have already tired your Excellency with too long a Dissertation, which I am persuaded you will attribute to its real Cause, enthusiasm in favor of Agriculture, and respect for so valuable a friend to it, as General Washington. For other Particulars, I must refer to our intelligent friend Dr Edwards, to whose charge I take the Liberty of delivering a parcel, with some papers we have lately printed, and a Sandwich Box with the Egyptian Wheat, and some Straw Rings, of which I request your acceptance. Is there no chance of seeing General Washington in England? I should be proud of his accepting an apartment in this House, and I am sure that he would meet with the most flattering Reception in every part of the Island, but from none with more real attachment & regard, than from Your Excellency's Faithful & Obedient Servant

John Sinclair

N.B. Excuse my taking the liberty of using a borrowed hand. Dr Edwards will inform you, that I have of late been much troubled with an inflammation in my eyes, which I trust will be a sufficient apology. It will give me much pleasure to be of any use to Mr King, Mr Gore, or Mr Pinckney, during their residence in this Country.[4] Indeed I have always felt a strong Desire of shewing every attention in my power to any American Gentleman who may have visited this Country; for though our Governments are now distinct, the People are in fact the same, without any possible inducement to quarrel, if they knew their respective interests, and with every reason to wish each other well, and to promote their mutual Prosperity.

LS, DLC:GW. GW acknowledged this letter when he wrote Sinclair on 10 Dec. (DLC:GW).

1. Sinclair was referring to the county surveys published by the Board of Agriculture (see Sinclair to GW, 30 May, n.7).

2. Sir Robert Walpole (1676–1745) was a Whig leader in the British House of Commons during the reigns of George I and II. His preference for "bawdy" conversation is reported in James Boswell, *The Life of Samuel Johnson, LL.D.* . . . (2 vols., London, 1791), 2:73.

3. Thomas Pinckney, former U.S. minister to Great Britain, planned to sail to Charleston, S.C., in the fall (see Pinckney to GW, 31 July).

4. Christopher Gore and William Pinkney had been appointed to the commission to adjust the claims of American merchants against Great Britain under Article VII of the Jay Treaty (see GW to the U.S. Senate, 31 March).

From James Anderson

Sir   Salvington [Va.] 11 Septr *1796*

I have the Honor of receiving Your favors of 5th Yesterday And am sorry You think me not so explicit as I should have been, I will say my intention in it is remote from deceit, that sort of conduct I think myself a stranger to. And the respectability of Your Character has a different claim from all who know it.

I now beg leave more fully to explain myself And give an Account of my manner of life My Father was a Farmer in Scotland on the River Forth nearly 40 miles above Edinh And at the Age of 21 thinking the business more fully understood upon the English border I agreed with a Gentleman, Famous in Farming, Feeding Horned Cattle & Sheep, in Summer on Grass, and in Winter on Potatoes, Turnip & Hay, Had a good Dairy, properly managed. with Him I was an apprentice 2 Years at the expiry of which I took the management of a large Estate possest by His uncle an Old Gentn which I conducted for 3 Years. And I beleive with approbation. For 19 Years after I farmed on my own account, 18 of which I was also largely in the Grain line, And had several manufactering Mills, But by the failure of a Sett of Distillers in 1788 I nearly lost all, And many more were ruined.

In begining of 1791 I came to this Country. and during a few weeks stay in Alex[and]ria was once on Your Estate at Mount Vernon in Company with Messrs Prescott & Hannah,[1] this was in Feby 1791 when You was in Philadelphia I then formed some Opinion of Your business, and was led to think from the regularity You might require in keeping Your Books, much time would be spent in that way, And of course prevent that strict Attention, Absolutely necessary, to all the parts of the Estate, and the Stock thereon, this induced me to make the former remark, this You have fully explained—In the spring 1791 I rented a Farm of poor Land on the upper part of Fairfax County in which I did not find my expectations Answered—In the begining of 1793 I took the Management of Mr Prescotts Estate in Prince William 1100 Acres Land on which there was 14 or 15 Slaves employed—The narrowness of that Gentlemans circumstances, prevented the neccessary improvements being made, And induced me to relinquish the business—In 1795 I came here, the Estate is 1700 Acres of Land, one part on the Creek fine meadow, the other part Hilly & poor, last Year I had no Assistant. this I have one. We employ about 25 hands, We have a Distillery which I also Conduct. And turns to good Account, my Incomes besides Board &c. are upward this Year of £100 I take some share in this Distillery—And beg leave to Observe that I do think one properly conducted is one of the best means for the improving of a Farm, As by feeding, so much manure is procured which otherwise could not be obtained. And if properly compounded & applyed will not fail in Answering the Farmers expectations.

I beg leave here to appeal to Your knowledge, & experience,

that tho, dividing the Soil by proper ploughings & Harrowings, laying down & Following proper Schemes for the Rotation of Crops, Intermixing pasture therein will do much. Yet without the assistance of manure will never Fully improve the Land.

I should have added in the Accot of myself that I still have a small Farm in Loudon, But if You are pleased to employ me I will give up—I now have no Fortune, but cannot say I am poor And I am contented. And my present situation is agreable. My employer a Young unmarried man, Mr Cary Selden, His Mother a Lady advanced in life and sister of John F. Mercer of Marborough, with whom I suppose You are accquainted[2]—And I am I think in good Company. But permit me to say I would prefer Your employ to any I know of, provided I could render it profitable to You—& worth my while. And if this reciprocity of Interests are not Answered I would never wish to be employed.

I shall be very ready to wait on You whenever You do incline. And have ventured this to Philadelphia not doubting of its arrival in time And with much respect I have the Honor to be Sir Your most Obedt Humble servt

Jas Anderson

ALS, ViMtvL.

Anderson again wrote GW from Salvington on 18 Sept.: "I had the honor to receive Your favors of 5th And replyed thereto on the 11th Addressed to You at Philadelphia And beg leave to refer You to the contents.

"But as You was uncertain of the time that You would leave that City, In Obedience to Your Orders have Adressed this to You as desired (not doubting of the other being in Your hands before now) informing that I will wait on You at Mount Vernon when You please to Advise, And hope You will think well of doing this by the first Opportunity, being now time that I might know, how to conduct myself, in case You should not employ me" (ALS, ViMtvL). Anderson became GW's farm manager in accordance with an agreement the two men signed on 5 Oct. (ViHi: Custis Papers).

1. Anderson may have referred to Roger Prescott (d. 1795) of Enfield plantation in Prince William County, Va., and Nicholas Hannah (d. 1794) of Alexandria, Virginia. Hannah had been a merchant, but he was appointed a captain of the first regiment of levies in April 1791 and later became a captain in the regular army.

2. Wilson Cary Selden (1772–1822) was the son of Sarah Ann Mason Mercer Selden (1738–1806) and Samuel Selden (1725–1791).

To William Pearce

Mr Pearce,   Philadelphia 11th Sep. 1796

Your letter of the 4th instt came to my hands yesterday, and the one you wrote me from Chester Town has also been received.[1] My last would have informed you of the reason, which, probably, prevented your receiving a former one at that place, but which I expect has got to hand 'ere this; as the Postmaster was requested, in case you had left it to send it by the Mail to Alexandria.[2]

As your letter says very little with respect to the Situation of matters on the Farms, I have the less to say in answer to it. But wish that the Wheat may be sown as soon as possible; but not faster than the ground can be put in good Order for its reception; especially for that which was sent by Mr Lewis.

Having made no mention of Stuart, I hope he has got well again; from the Tenor of Washington's letter, I began to apprehend he was in danger.[3] As you have said nothing concerning the Fly, in your stacks, I hope his account in this respect also was more the effect of his fears than of accurate examination; but let it be closely attended to; for neither interest nor policy will Suffer a Crop *made*, to be lost, in order to prepare for another which a thousand accidents may destroy before it gets into the Barn: and when, possibly, and even probably, the price may be lower than it is at present by 50 pr Ct. This, supposing no danger from the fly, is a strong reason for grinding up & selling the flour before the Market is glutted with this article, from Wheat of this years growth.

Do not let the proper Season escape you, for sowing the Winter Vetch—I should conceive it ought not to be much longer delayed. But among the Books you have, of mine, it is probable the precise time, & quantity of Seed to the Acre, may be mentioned. Let these be attended to; and unless the directions are given in some authors of modern date, be more sparing of your seed than is mentioned by them. I recollect a year or two ago to have sent some rape Seed to Mount Vernon, but do not recollect what has been the result of it: but particular care ought always to be paid to these kind of Seeds, as they are, generally, given to me, because they are valuable—rare—or curious.

I hope you have received favorable answers from the persons you were in treaty with on the Eastern Shore. It is very interesting to me, at all times, to have good Overseers; but may be particular so next year. Did you receive any benefit from Doctr Perkins's Metallic application. which, possibly ought to be repeated & continued for sometime. I wish you well & am Your friend

Go: Washington

ALS, ViMtvL.
1. Pearce's letters dated 4 Sept. and 31 Aug. have not been found.
2. GW's last wrote Pearce on 5 Sept.; he previously had written on 28 August.
3. The letter from George Washington Parke Custis to GW has not been found, but GW mentioned its contents when he wrote Pearce on 5 September.

To John Quincy Adams

Philadelphia, 12 September 1796. In a letter marked private, GW asked Adams to look into the history of a sword that had come into his possession in an enigmatic manner.

ALS, MHi: Adams Papers. For a full transcription and other information related to the sword, see GW to Adams, 25 June 1797, in *Papers, Retirement Series,* 1:210–14.

From Robert Fulton

Sir   London September 12th 1796

By my Friend Dr Edwards I beg leave to present you with this publication; which I hope will be honoured with your Perusal at a Leisure hour; The object of which is to Exhibit the Certain mode of Giving Agriculture to every Acre of the immense Continent of America; By means of A Creative System of Canals.

When this Subject first entered my thoughts, I had no Idea of its Consequence: But the scene Gradually opened and at Length exhibited the most extensive and pleasing prospect of Improvements; hence, I now Consider it of much national Importan[c]e; And View it Like the application of those particuler principles which produce certain effects.

Thus the discovery of the Mariners Compass Gave Commerce to the World.

The Invention of printing is dissipating darkness and giving a Polish to the Mass of Men.

And the Introduction of the Creative System of Canals as certain in their Effects: will Give an Agricultural Polish To every Acre of America.

I Therefore Beg Leave to Submit to your Contemplation the Last Chapter with the Supplement; which exhibits the Specific System for America:[1] And hoping that your Excellencies Sanction will awaken the Public attention to the Subject:[2] I Remain with all possible Respect your Excellencies most Obedient And Very humble Servant—

Robert Fulton

ALS, PPL. The letter is tipped into a copy of Fulton's *A Treatise on the Improvement of Canal Navigation; Exhibiting the Numerous Advantages to be Derived from Small Canals. . . .* (London, 1796) that GW signed on the title page.

Robert Fulton (1765–1815), artist, civil engineer, and inventor, most famously promoted steamboat transportation.

1. The "Last Chapter" appears to refer to Fulton's letter to Pennsylvania governor Thomas Mifflin that concludes the printed text but is not numbered as a chapter.

In the copy of his *Treatise on the Improvement of Canal Navigation* sent to GW, Fulton signed an eight-page "Supplement" that is handwritten on the first four of the eight leaves bound at the end of the book. It reads: "I am aware that the freezing of Canals may be stated As an argument against their universal Construction: But it must be Considered that we Cannot Calculate on more then six weeks Ice in twelve months: *on an average*, Which Interruption is Similar on the navigable Rivers; And on the Canals of Russia and Holland, hence the great Carriage of the Country is performed in those Seasons when the Canals are open to which Custome fits the other operations of society.

"But as I have Recommended Canals Instead of turnpike Roads: It may be a Question how is the traveler to be Accommodated? To this I would propose to make the horse path of the Leading Canals Sufficiently wide for a Road; which would Indeed be of Little use but for horsemen or Light Carriages; And this union of the Canal and Road would produce numerous Advantages.

"First the Canal would Convey materials to mend the Road at Little expence: *Second* In the Winter Season one part might be frozen and Another open, And as the Inns would be on the banks of the Canals; the Inhabitant would Learn of the various travelars, the State of the Stages of Canal; hence the traveler might take either Canal or Road, whichever the weather And his time Rendered most Convenient; And thus he would be accommodated with an easy passage through the Country.

"Having now Communicated the whole of my thoughts Reletive to Conveyence by Canals; and exhibited the mode by which they will become General and penetrate Into every District, the mind begins to muse over that period when the whole Country will be Intersected with Canals, And every acre Receiving their Assistan[c]e: It will be Unnecessery to Construct more Consequently the tolls which was for the purpose of Raising a Sum to extend Navigations may be Abolished and this will further Reduce the Expence of Carriage, Or the Tolls may be applied to Numerous purposes Such as Paying the expences of Gove[rn]ment; Building semenaries for education; or Errecting Academies for promoting Scientific Knowledge.

"But to Return to that period when Infinate Canals will Spread ore all the Country—Here the Comprehensive mind Views as it Ware a Vast Body full of health and Vigor fed by its Million Veins. Here it finds the Rivers Arrested In their Journey and Industry Conveying their waters through Infinate ducts; Seems to demand that they perform an Important office In facilitating the Labours of Men ere they descend Into Mother Ocean.

"Therefore having Given nourishment to the Various Canals It now becomes a Consideration what further Advantage Can be derived In Addition to that of Carriage and this I Conceive will Come under the following heads.

First. Irrigating or Watering Lands.

Second Working Machinery.

Third, Watering Cities and Towns.

"To Irrigation the Canals will be particularly Favourable, for as they will take In a Supply, where there is a Profusion of Water; they will Conduct it along the high Levels of the Country through numerous Situations which Require nourishment; Here In Irrigation the Canals will become the Conductors of the Streams. from Which Sufficient may be drawn to water the Grounds beneath; And Render them the most Prolific and Luxurient Pastures. Thus the Canal would bear on the means of facilitating Agriculture, And dispen[c]e it to the needy husbandman. And the Easy means of Cultivation being obtained the Application would follow hence the Sunburnt hills would put on a Lively Green; and animate the Fields with Infinate Herds and Flocks.

"Nor would this Injure the Canal for Canals now Collect the Waters of the Waters of the higher Country which they Conduct to their was[t]e Wear; where it Passes off without performing any good office, Whereas it aught to be Convoyed to Such Situations as Require Irregation; And There by a tube of Given demensions: placed at a Certain depth In the Canal, the Farmer Should pay a Stipulated Sum, per hour or day while water Could be spared; of Which the Canal Keepers or Agents would Judge.

"Having hinted at what may be performed by Irrigation, Extracted from Canals; I Leave it to Ingenious Men to determin the mode of Introducing It into practice According to the Local Circumstances: And I now Come to the Consideration of Combining Machinery with Canals.

"When we View the Various Mechanic operations and Contemplate with what Facility we obtain the numerous Conveniences by their Aid, when we examine how much more Manual Labour will produce by being familiar with Machinery, we Should do every thing to encourage and promote so usefull a Science and diffuse the Knowledge.

"It is an unfortunate prejudice which prevails in this Country that by mechanics expediting the Labours of Men; the Labour Is Reduced and the Poor are out of employ But the fact is the Quantity of Labour Is not Reduced, nor are the Poor unemployed. But by the Same Quantity of Labour there is more produce, Which Produce by being Rendered more abundent and Cheap, Comes within the Reach of the Mass of Society. Thus by the Invention of the Stocking Loom there are more people employed in the fabric of Stockings then if they were Knit; the hose is also produced Easy. Consequently Cheap By which means Millions now wear Stockings that would otherwise be necessitated to go Bare Legged.

"The Same Idea extends to every operation of Society to which mechanics Can be applied. Which being expedited by machinary will Give a polish to the Whole Country.

"Yet among All the Mechanic Improvements; the Convenience of the Farmer Appears not to have been Sufficiently Attended to although his Labour might be Rendered much more productive By mechanic Aid; But In all the Farmers operations one of the first Considerations Is to obtain Power At a Little expence And the difficulty of doing this is perhaps the Reason Why Machines have not been much More Introduced, But by the Canal the Requisite power may be obtained, hen[c]e the Farmer who finds a Canal pass through his estate or meander near its margin, Should Consider how to Combine his advantages. For this Purpose his Barn should be so Situated as to Conduct a feeder from the Canal to turn a Small water Wheel: By Which the Following Work might be performed

1st Thrashing and Winnowing Corn,

2 Cut Straw,

3 Break and Clean hemp and Flax,

4 Grind Apples,

5 Mash Turnips, & &c:

"In the department of the Women it might assist in Washing[—]Washing Machines are Becoming very General, and are found of great use In this Country—And be of much use In *Churning* of Which the Labour would be Considerable As the System of Irrigation would produce numerous Dairies, Thus The Canals would facilitate the operations of the Farmers and give Life to numerous other works.

"Nor would the Canal Thus be Injured for as In the System of Irrigation the water would be guaged, Which water might first be applied to machinery and then Irrigation or pass from one farm to another over Numerous machines, Hence As America is abundant In Water the Canals would Receive the Streams of Nature, Conduct them through the Country and distribute them In every Direction. In their Passage the[y] Would Water the Cities and towns, Clens them of Filth and Sprinkle them In Seasons of dirth—When a Canal has a Sufficient feeder there Can be no Injury In drawing Water for all the above purposes provided a Current is not Created, Which may be avoided by digging the Canal one foot deeper, It will then become a Reservoir, for Irrigation and Machinery.

"Thus we See the Infinate Advantages to be derived from a Juditious use of the Streams which Nature has Lifted to our Mountains; Streams by which the demand for horses may be much deminished If the Quick and Long Carriage of a Country Is performed by Canals, Oxen will be best for Agricultural purposes As they may ultimately be fattened for Beef And America Rendered Like one Continued Garden of which every acre would Mentain its Man. Stream which would produce Abundence and every one having the necessaries and Conveniences of Life within their easy Reach would be Left to their discretion to use them like Rational Beings.

"Thus while I Contemplat this hive of Industry, and muse ore a Scene of National Improvement, by domestic application, I Cannot Resist Calling on Common Sense to Testify how Infinately Superior it is. To the Furo of Conquest which enervates Society In a Mad Contest for additional acres, While those In possession Lie Waste and Unimproved."

2. GW replied to Fulton from Philadelphia on 14 Dec.: "By the hands of Doctr Edwards, I was favoured with your Tr⟨ea⟩tise on the improvement of Canal Navigation. For your goodness in sending it to me, I pray you to accept my best thanks.

"The subject is interesting, and I dare presume is well treated; but as the Book came to me in the midst of busy preparatory scenes for Congress, I have not had leisure yet to give it the perusal which the importance of such a work would merit. I shall do it, with pleasure I am persuaded, when I have" (ALS [letterpress copy], DLC:GW; LB, DLC:GW).

To Charles Cotesworth Pinckney

My dear Sir,   Philadelphia 12th Sept. 1796.

After furnishing you with the following copies of Letters, it is scarcely necessary to add any thing by way of explanation of my motives for doing it.[1]

However, I will briefly add that, from the arrival of Mr Gouvr Morris in Europe, up to the date of his last letter to me in June of the present year,[2] I have received much interesting and useful information from him, relative to the political state of things on the other side of the Atlantic: That from the multiplicity of business with which I have been continually overwhelmed, I very rarely acknowledged the receipt of his letters: But upon receiving that of the 3d of July 1795 (copy of which follows) I was struck, forcibly with the idea, as well from the style and manner, as from its being to a single subject, that it had, or was intended to have passed under the eye of Lord Grenville; although no intimation thereof was given to me.

Under this impression, it was natural to suppose that my answer, or the result of it would also be communicated to that Minister; I resolved therefore to frame it accordingly, that Lord Grenville might find from *that* mode, as well as from ordinary course of official communications, in what light the people of this Country viewed the conduct of his towards it.

I little expected indeed, that a private letter of mine, to a friend, would have found a place in the Bureau of the French Directory. Less should I have suspected, that any exception would, or could have been taken at the Sentiments expressed in the one that has got there. But as intimations of the contrary have been given in Colonel Monroes letter, I have thought it expedient to furnish you with *all* the documents relative thereto, with this short history of the rise & progress of it; that you might be enabled, if more is said on the Subject, and occasion should require it, to set the matter right by a plain and simple statement of facts. With very great esteem & regard I am—my dear Sir Your Obedt & Affecte

Go: Washington

ALS, PHi: Gratz Collection; LB, DLC:GW.

1. According to a note following the letter-book copy, GW enclosed Gouverneur Morris to GW, 3 July 1795; GW to Morris, 22 Dec. 1795; James Monroe to GW, 24 March 1796; and GW to Monroe, 25 Aug. 1796.

2. See Morris to GW, 5 June.

From William Augustine Washington

My Dr Unkle   Haywood[1] [Va.] Sept. 12th 1796

Wishing to make a remittance to Judge Phillips, for the use of my Sons, I dispatched my Steward with the inclosed Letters to Fredericksbg with 150 Dollars Alexandria Bank Notes, desiring him to exchange them for Bank Notes of the United States, which he was not able to accomplish in the Towns of Port Royal, Fredericksbg, Falmouth or Dumfries, he brought back my Letter & Money—As you were so obliging as to say you would make Remittances for me, "the means being put into your hands"; I have taken the Liberty of Inclosing you, with the inclosed Letters, 150 Dollars Notes of the Bank of Alexandria, and shall esteem it a particular favr if you will exchange them for United States, or a Bill on Boston, and remit it with the inclosed Letter to Judge Phillips—I have in my Letter to Judge Phillips taken the Liberty of mentioning that the remittance would now be made thro' you, mentioning at the same time my disappointment—I do not know whether he is in advance or not for me, having made a remittance of 200 Dollars this Spring—& when I left Boston I had paid up in advance for their schooling & Board, & left some Money with Judge Phillips for their necessary supplys, but I would allways wish to keap Money in his hands, so that he should never be in advance for me.[2]

Our relation Mrs Mildred Lee, is no more, I have just recd a Letter from Mr Corbin Washington informing me that she expired the 8th Inst.

It give me much pleasure to hear that you & Mrs Washington enjoy good health, which may you long continue to do is the fervent prayer of My Dr sir Your Affectionate Nephew

Wm Augt. Washington

ALS, MAnP.

1. Haywood was William Augustine Washington's estate in Westmoreland County.

2. Augustine Washington (c.1780–1797) and Bushrod Washington, Jr. (1785–1830) attended Phillips Academy at Andover, Massachusetts.

William Augustine Washington had written Samuel Phillips from Haywood on 2 Sept.: "Your favr of the 30th of May I recd about five weeks past, and the one of July the 20th with a Copy of the former about five days since, the first would have been answered before this; but my old & Cruel companion the Gout has confined me to my Room & Bed for about five weeks past so that I am but just able now to hobble a little upon my Crutches.

"I have to return you many thanks, and shall ever consider myself under the strongest obligations to you for your care, and earnest solicitude for the welfare of my Sons . . .

"With this you will receive One Hundred and fifty Dollars. . . .

"P.S. being disappointed in Exchanging Alexandria Notes for United States—I have inclosed them with Letter to the President and requested of him to make the remittance" (MAnP).

GW replied to William Augustine Washington on 28 Sept. (PPRF); see also GW to Phillips, same date (MAnP).

To James Wood

Dear Sir   Philadelphia 12th Septr 1796

By a recurrence to the Acts of the last Session of Congress, you will find one for disposing of the ungranted lands No. Wt of the Ohio; and for appointing a Surveyor General for the purposes therein mentioned.[1] And you may have heard, that Mr DeWitt, who was Geographer to the Army at the close of the War, after the decease of Mr Erskine, and at present the Surveyor General of the State of New York (a man of profound knowledge in Mathematics, and sufficiently skilled in Astronomy) was nominated to that Office, and has declined the acceptance of it.[2]

It is yet vacant; and you have been mentioned to me, as a Gentleman to whom it might be acceptable.

Without taking then a circuitous rout to ascertain this fact, I shall apply immediately to yourself, for information: and will frankly ask, because I am sure you will candidly answer (if the appointment should meet your wishes) whether your knowledge in Mathematics; practical Surveying; and so much of Astronomy as is useful to a skilful exercise of the latter, for discovering the Latitude, Meridian &ca now are, or easily could be made familiar to you.

These questions are propounded, because affirmative qualifications are essential; for it will readily occur to you, that he who is to examine & employ others—⟨d⟩irect their proceedings— and to inspect their works—ought not to be ignorant of the principles which are to be the rule for their conduct.

It is a very honorable and important Office; none perhaps that requires more integrity and vigilance in the execution, to prevent improper speculations and abuse. The Officer holding it must reside in the Country where the business will be chiefly transacted.

As the Season & circumstances begin now to press for an Appointment, and as my continuance here, and the road I shall travel back to Virginia (for the purpose of returning with my family for the winter) are somewhat uncertain, I request the favor of you, to put your answer to this letter under cover to the Secretary of State, who will be directed to open it, and to fill up the blank Commission which I shall deposit in his Office with your name if you are disposed to accept it; or with that of another Gentleman who is held in contemplation if you do not. You may, if it is not too troublesome, address a duplicate to me, at Mount Vernon, to remain in the Post Office at Alexandria until called for.[3] With great esteem & regard I am—Dear Sir Your Very Hble Servant

Go: Washington

ALS, MA; LB, DLC:GW. Forgeries of this document are addressed to Wood, but others are addressed to James Baldwin, James Barnard, James Brooks, James Camp, James Jewett, or James Overton. The forgeries typically omit most of the fourth and all of the fifth paragraphs.

1. GW meant "An Act providing for the Sale of the Lands of the United States, in the territory northwest of the river Ohio, and above the mouth of Kentucky river," approved 18 May (1 *Stat.* 464–69).

2. See GW to the U.S. Senate, 28 May (second letter), and Timothy Pickering to GW, 27 June, and n.2.

3. Wood replied to GW from Richmond on 19 Sept.: "I have had the honor to receive the Letter you were pleased to write me the 12th Instant. while I am highly gratified by your approbation and polite attention, in making me a tender of the Office of Surveyor General; I am Constrained to decline the acceptance of it; from a thorough Conviction that I am not Competent to an honorable discharge of the duties of so important an Office; Candor Obliges me to Confess, that I am Unacquainted with Astronomy or a Knowledge in Mathematics, and that I am superficial in practical surveying. Unfortunately for me, my father died when in my seventeenth year, and immediately after I had Commenced, under him, the study of the Mathematics; before his death I was well grounded in Arithmetic, and had become a good County Court Clerk, having been employed in his office some years previous to that event; since that period, I have been Strugling through the world with a very limited fortune, and after more than thirty years employment in public service, I find myself rather poorer than the day I began. I have Continued in the Office I now fill about thirteen years, for the last three or four years, it has been extremely painful to me, and no Consideration wou'd have induced me to Continue in it, but the Difficulty of working my Farm to advantage, as I had emancipated all my slaves soon after the Conclusion of the war.

"I embrace with pleasure the Occasion which is Offered me of assuring you of the Sentiments of sincere respect and attachment" (ALS, MHi: Pickering Papers; ALS [duplicate], DNA: RG 59, Miscellaneous Letters). Secretary of State Timothy Pickering docketed the ALS as "sent to me to be opened by the President's direction in his absence." Wood sent a brief letter to Pickering with the duplicate that Pickering docketed as "inclosing one open to the President, by whose verbal directions I read it, and sent the Commission of Surveyor General, to Rufus Putnam, seeing Govr Wood declined the office" (see also Pickering to GW, 29 Sept., in DNA: RG 59, Miscellaneous Letters).

Wood's father, James Wood (1707–1759), had founded Winchester, Virginia. He served as county surveyor and the first clerk of the Frederick County Court.

James Wood joined the council of the state of Virginia in June 1784. As president of that body starting in December 1788, he acted as lieutenant governor of the state.

From "A Friend to the People"

Sir,   Baltimore Septr 13th 1796
    Have we not a *right* as a nation, to demand the Marquis La' Fayette as a Citizen of our Country. The People love him—we all love him—and our God knows his goodness and virtue.
                                       A Friend to the People

ALS, DNA: RG 59, Miscellaneous Letters.
    For efforts to free Lafayette from prison, see Justus Erick Bollman to GW, 1 April, and La Rochefoucauld-Liancourt to GW, 25 July; see also GW to La Rochefoucauld-Liancourt, 8 August.

From John Searson

                                       Philada 13 Sepr 1796
    The misfortunes of an honest man Struggling with dire distress, has in all ages been look'd upon, by Compassionate and Benevolent minds with noted Commisseration, Scenes of a truly afflictive nature (tho' Innocent of the Cause of them) has fallen to my Lot, notwithstanding my formerly being a Reputable Wholesale merchant in this City. from such vicissitude in Human affairs, Have made application to the Humane for Relief, And Since my late arrival in this City, your Excellency was pointed out to me by Some friends as most Suitable, from your Excellency's Humane and Charitable Character—I was lately Informed there was a vacancy for the place of Clerk at the War office—Two of my friends viz. Blair McClenaghan & John Taylor Esqr. accompanied me to Willm Symmonds Esqr. first or disposing Clerk in that office, But alas! Could not Succeed. Nothing therefore offering, that I can yet see for a Support, beg leave to throw my Self at the feet of your Excellency's Humanity for such Relief as to your Humane Breast may Seem meet. Should my application meet notice, I Lodge at No. 22 Carter's alley near 2nd Street—I have the Honor to be, (may it please your Excellency) with the most profound Regard, Humility and Respect, and with Prayer to Heaven for long Life prosperity and every Earthly Bliss—Your Excellency's Most Devoted and Humble Servant
                                       Jno. Searson

ALS, DLC:GW.

Searson previously had written GW from Philadelphia on 19 Aug. to explain that he "formerly Intermarried a Reputable female of the City of Philadelphia" and "liv'd in the Character of accomptant with a principal Merchant of that City." After his wife's death, "he took to the Education of youth" and "hath been Reputably Employd both in America & Ireland" (DNA: RG 59, Miscellaneous Letters; see also Searson to GW, 9 April 1798, in *Papers, Retirement Series*, 2:232–34).

According to the various statements in his books and letters, John Searson was a native of Ireland who apprenticed briefly in the West Indies before coming to America while quite young and spending more than twenty years as a tutor, bookkeeper, and merchant at New York and Philadelphia. Meeting with financial misfortunes during the Revolutionary War, he returned to Ireland, spent about fifteen years as schoolmaster at Colerain, issued poems in 1794 and 1795, and then returned to the United States. Searson subsequently issued three more books of poetry, dedicating the latter two volumes to GW: *Poems on Various Subjects and Different Occasions, Chiefly Adapted to Rural Entertainment in the United States of America* (Philadelphia, 1797); *Art of Contentment; With Several Entertaining Pieces of Poetry, Descriptive of the Present Times, in the U. States of America* (Baltimore, [1797]); and *Mount Vernon, A Poem: Being the seat of his excellency George Washington, in the State of Virginia; Lieutenant-general and commander in chief of the land forces of the United States of America* (Philadelphia, [1800]).

In the dedicatory letter to GW in the *Art of Contentment*, Searson reminded GW: "I did myself the honor to wait upon your Excellency, in September, 1796, before your resignation of the Presidency of the United States. . . .

"Your Excellency was so humane and condescending, as to countenance my intention of publishing by subscription, a Poem, suited to the then present state of America, for which I obtained above 1200 subscribers. And your Excellency's condescending and polite letter, for transmitting a Poem to you at Mount Vernon, merits [m]y most sincere gratitude" (see also GW to Searson, 20 Aug. 1797, in *Papers, Retirement Series*, 1:311).

Although *Mount Vernon* was printed after GW's death and included "Elegiac Verses, on the Decease of His Late Excellency, the Illustrious and Ever-Memorable, Great and Good General George Washington, of Immortal Memory," Searson presumably wrote the dedicatory letter to GW before his decease. Searson again mentioned his 1796 visit to GW and added that he had "the honor to visit your Excellency 15th May last, so as to obtain an adequate idea of Mount-Vernon; wishing to compose a poem on that beautiful seat."

From William Thornton

Washington, D.C., 13 September 1796. Thornton supported GW's desire to construct and fund a national university in the Federal City. He discussed practical challenges related to such an institution and its best location.

Df, DLC: William Thornton Papers. For a full transcription, see Harris, *William Thornton Papers*, 395–97; see also Thornton's two letters to GW, 1 Oct., in DLC: William Thornton Papers.

To the Cabinet

Sir,   Philadelphia 14th Sept. 1796
   As I cannot, without peculiar inconvenience to my private concerns, remain in this City beyond sunday next,[1] I desire that all the business in your department which calls for my immediate attention, may be presented to me in the course of this week.
                                        Go: Washington

LB, DNA: RG 59, GW's Correspondence with His Secretaries of State.
   1. The next Sunday was 18 September.

From James McHenry

(private)
Sir   War Office 14 Septr 1796
   If you have a few minutes to spare I could wish you to examine the within conditions for a new contract for cannon. The old contract was too defective to serve as a model or guide in any one respect. The public must be a considerable looser by it; and the cannon which we shall be obliged to recive by no means to be relied on.[1] With the greatest respect I have the honour to be Sir your most ob. st
                                        James McHenry

The mail to Pittsburg is altered. Letters must be in the office on friday before sun down.[2]

ALS, DNA: RG 59, Miscellaneous Letters; ADf, PWacD: Sol Feinstone Collection, on deposit at PPAmP. The postscript appears only on the ALS.
   1. McHenry presumably enclosed a copy of the twelve conditions he listed when he wrote Secretary of the Treasury Oliver Wolcott, Jr., on 13 Sept. regarding cannon for "the frigate destined for the Mediterranean" (see GW to the Dey of Algiers, 13 June, and n.4). The first condition reads: "That the guns be cast in the solid, and bored." The second and third conditions specify that the smaller guns should "conform exactly in weight, bore, caliber and length, to British ship guns of the same dimensions now in use" and that the larger guns "be formed agreeably to the dimensions laid down" in instructions. Conditions

four through eleven detail procedures for proving the quality of the cannon in an examination "by one or two persons, to be appointed by the President of the United States, in the presence of such other persons as shall be named by the owner of the works." The twelfth condition reads: "That the weight of each cannon received, shall be marked on the left trunnion" (DNA: RG 107, Secretary of War Letters, Procurement).

GW replied to McHenry the same day: "The enclosed Conditions appear proper—but as there are certain principles I practice that govern in such cases—it would be too hazardous to Give an opinion without consulting them—and it is impossible for me to go into such detail" (ALS [photocopy], DLC: James McHenry Papers).

2. The following Friday was 16 September.

From Timothy Pickering

Sir,   Department of State Sept. 14. 1796.

I submit to your consideration the inclosed draught of instructions for Messrs Ellicott & Freeman, for running the boundary line between the U. States and the Spanish colonies of East & West Florida;[1] and am, most repectfully, your obedt servant

T. Pickering

I have just heard that Capt. German is arrived, & consequently Mr Pinckney, from Charleston.[2]

ALS, DNA: RG 59, Miscellaneous Letters; LB, DNA: RG 59, GW's Correspondence with His Secretaries of State.

1. The draft instructions have not been identified, but see Pickering to GW, 15 Sept. (first letter).

2. Charles Cotesworth Pinckney, new U.S. minister to France, had sailed from Charleston, S.C. (see Pinckney to GW, 12 Aug., and n.2).

To Robert Brooke

Sir,   Philadelphia 15th Sept: 1796

The Commonwealth of Virginia, having manifested their approbation of my design, to apply the hundred shares in the James River Company, which they had before put at my disposal, to the use of a Siminary to be erected in such part of the State as they should deem most proper; and in consequence of this reference to their opinion, the Legislature having requested me to appropriate them to a Siminary at such place in the upper

Country as I should think most convenient to a majority of its Inhabitants:[1] After careful enquiries, to ascertain that place, I have, upon the fullest consideration of all circumstances, destined those Shares to the use of Liberty-Hall Academy, in Rockbridge County.

It would seem to me proper that this determination should be promulgated by some official act of the Executive of Virginia; and the Legislature may expect it; for the purpose of general information. With due consideration & respect I am—Sir Your Most Obedt Hble Servt

Go: Washington

ALS, Vi; LB, DLC:GW.

1. For the Virginia General Assembly's resolutions adopted on 1 Dec. 1795, see Brooke to GW, 9 Jan. 1796, n.2.; see also GW to Brooke, 16 March 1795.

From Timothy Pickering

Thursday evening Sept. 15. 1796.

The Secretary of State respectfully lays before the President the instructions for Mr Ellicott, altered to conform to the President's idea.[1] If approved, they will be delivered this evening to Mr Ellicott, as he wishes to start very early in the morning.[2]

The Secretary also submits a draught of instructions for General Pinckney—corrected & enlarged.[3]

T. Pickering.

ALS, DNA: RG 59, Miscellaneous Letters; LB, DNA: RG 59, GW's Correspondence with His Secretaries of State.

1. For the initial draft of these instructions, see Pickering to GW, 14 September.

2. GW replied to Pickering on the same evening: "The enclosed Instructions for Mr Ellicot (as now amended) are approved—I was out when they came, or they would have been returned sooner" (ALS, MHi: Pickering Papers).

Pickering gave Andrew Ellicott and Thomas Freeman instructions on 14 Sept. "for running and marking the Southern boundary line, which divides their Territory from the Spanish Colonies of East and west Florida." Pickering continued: "it has been considered that the Country through which the line is to be run, belongs, for the most part, to the native Indians, and is of course a wilderness. Hence many difficulties may attend an attempt to run and mark one continued boundary line from the Missis[s]ippi to the St Mary's. Nevertheless, if the Indians will allow it to be done, and the nature of the Country admits of it, you are to run and mark such a continued boundary line. If the

Indians are adverse to the measure, and oppose your proceeding, you must stop as soon as you find a further advance would hazard your safety, or a breach of our friendship with any tribe. But the Creeks have expressly stipulated a free passage of the Commissioners and their followers to run and mark the boundary line through their Territory; and the Choctaws probably may on the application of the Commissioners also give the like permission as it respects their Country. However, if either the opposition of the Indians or the impracticability of the Country itself through which you must pass, should render the running a continued line impossible or extremely tedious and difficult; then the next best thing must be attempted; that is, accurately to fix the latitude of the boundary line, at the Eastern Bank of the Mississippi, and to run and mark the line thence as far Eastward as the Indian title has been by any regular and lawful means extinguished either under the British or Spanish Governments. If the Indians and the nature of the Country permit you to proceed further, you will go on as far as it shall be practicable. And if from any cause you are obliged to leave any part of the line unsurveyed and unmarked, you will at least ascertain where it strikes the great rivers, from the Mississippi to the Apalachicola.

"From the junction of the Flint River with the Apalachicola, the boundary line ceasing to be a parrallel of latitude, must if possible be run and marked through its whole course, to the head of the River St Mary's.

"So far as the boundary line is a parrallel of latitude, you will ascertain the same with all practicable accuracy, and erect permanent monuments, of Stone where attainable, and at other places, of earth. And in the latter case, it may be eligible to plant in the ground large posts of Cedar, or other durable wood, two or three at each monument, in the range of the line, and to bury them up with several feet of earth, so that by being concealed they may not be removed, and by an exclusion of the air, they may not be liable to rot."

Ellicott and Freeman also needed to "make plats and keep journals of their proceedings . . . made with accuracy and precision, and the latitudes, longitudes, courses and distances expressed in words at length as well as figures." Treaty stipulations required Ellicott and Freeman "to be at the Natches before the 25th of October next" (DNA: RG 59, Domestic Letters; another copy of these instructions is in MHi: Pickering Papers). Ellicott arrived at Natchez on 24 Feb. 1797 (see *Journal of Ellicott*).

3. The enclosed draft has not been identified, but Pickering provided elaborate instructions to Charles Cotesworth Pinckney, new U.S. minister to France, dated 14 Sept., that outlined the complexities of his post because of political and diplomatic complications arising from the French Revolution and the challenge of maintaining U.S. neutrality: "Under such circumstances, the best interests of the two nations may be injured by mutual jealousies: for distrust on one side begets suspicion on the other. Unhappily, as was natural, the distrusts and jealousies of the [French] ministers have been communicated to their nation; or to the Government of their nation: and while they consider the *people* of the United States as the warm and invariable friends of France, they have been persuaded to believe that the *Government* is hostile to their interests, and perhaps even to the principles of the revolution. Nothing can be more un-

founded than this opinion concerning the Government of the United States; and nothing is more important to the interests of the two Countries than its eradication; than the restoration of mutual confidence as the basis of mutual goodwill, and of the exercise of offices highly and reciprocally beneficial.

"Faithfully to represent the disposition of the Government and people of the United States (for their disposition is one); to remove jealousies and obviate complaints, by shewing that they are groundless; to restore that mutual confidence which has been so unfortunately and injuriously impaired; and to explain the relative interests of both Countries, and the real sentiments of your own; are the immediate objects of your mission.

"To enable you satisfactorily to perform this task, you will receive herewith, copies of all the important correspondencies with the French Ministers, from the commencement of Mr Genet's agency to this day; together with copies of such parts of the communications between the Department of State and the Ministers of the United States at Paris, or between the latter and the French Government, as are pertinent to the objects in view. This being accomplished (and the liberal and upright views of the American Government authorize the hope of its accomplishment) a happy foundation will be laid for negociating those friendly and Commercial regulations which our mutual wants require, and which our reciprocal interests and prosperity will strongly enforce."

The instructions urged Pinckney's particular attention to the claims of "our merchants whose property to the probable amount of several millions, has been unlawfully captured or seized." Complaints about Fulwar Skipwith, who had been supervising the merchant claims as U.S. consul general for France, caused GW to authorize Pinckney "to employ, for a reasonable compensation which you will fix, some American Citizen of competent skill and fair reputation, to make the necessary investigations, under your direction; and to report to you, from time to time, the result of his examinations." Pinckney also was to give "constant information of all important occurrences" in Europe. It was deemed best that he communicate to the French government in English (DNA: RG 59, Diplomatic and Consular Instructions).

From Timothy Pickering

Sir   Thursday Evening [15 September 1796]
The paper you put into my hands to-day was attentively perused by us all.[1] I am now going over it by myself, but it will not be possible to get thro' in time to return it before bed-time. Before breakfast in the morning I will wait upon you with it. I am most respectfully your obt servt

T. Pickering

ALS, DLC:GW. The date is taken from the docket.

1. Pickering probably commented on a copy of GW's farewell address. Richard Peters later claimed that GW showed the draft to Pickering, "who

returned it without any Correction exactly as it is printed" (Peters to John Jay, 14 April 1811, in Paltsits, *Farewell Address,* 273–76; quote on 275).

From Jonathan Williams

Sir   Mount pleasant [Pa.] Sept. 16. 1796.
My Servant informs me that you desire to know at what price I would sell my Horse Leopard.[1]

He cost me 300 Dollars about 2 Years since, when I was well assured that he was but 7 years old. Considering the extraordinary Expence of keeping a studd Horse I think 400 Dollars would barely replace my money. I have not found any defect in him, and I beleive him to be at this moment perfectly sound. This price is certainly low for a Stallion, yet that is the reason of my selling him, for I never mounted a more agreeable saddle Horse.

As the animal is a natural curiosity I had rather sell him to you than to any person who did not set a value on that circumstance, & if you think the 400 Dollars too much, I leave him at your own price between that sum and the first cost.

As this note may arrive when you are not at leisure, I have directed my man to leave the Horse in your stables, and to take your orders when to call for an answer. With the greatest Deference & Respect I am sir your obedient & faithful Servant

Jona. Williams

ALS, DLC:GW.

1. *Dunlap and Claypoole's American Daily Advertiser* (Philadelphia) for 23 May 1795 ran an advertisement for stud services: "The curious Horse *Leopard* . . . is a fine well shaped Black Horse, five years old, his hinder parts are most beautifully variegated like the skin of a Leopard, and he is equally remarkable for his spirit and good temper."

From Joseph Barnes

London Sept. 17th 1796
General Washington—I address you thus because to this name are annexed the greatest possible Virtues. When I reflect, that you were the first and *great* Patron of my deceased friend Mr Rumsey, my feelings *revolt* at the Idea, nor could any thing other than the peculiar circumstances under which I have been *excuse,*

my *not* having Since in England written to you on the Subject of his objects: A history of which will *apologize* for my long Silence this I mean to prepare.

At present I can only give you a general Idea—When the arbitrators appointed by the proprietors of Mr Rumseys Patents to Settle all matter between me, being the Legal representative of Mr Rumsey, And Rogers & Parker made their Award in March 1795—by which the *payment* of £2500 which R. & P. had Acknowledged due on one of Rumsey's Machines having performed, as they conceived, as pr agreement, & which of course I expected was *Suspended,* neither *they* nor *I* had the means or money to advance to prosecute the *Rumseian objects*; of consequence they have necessarily Since remained Stationary.[1]

However having, from a course of experiments, made for the purpose, Satisfied ourselves, that if proper means be used the most important of Sd objects will Succeed, particularly the *Steam* Navigation, which was Mr Rumsey's hobby horse—we agreed, as Soon as money requisite could be raised to recommence the prosecution & determine the fate or demonstrate the Utility of the objects in question, by practical experiment: Indeed, I Shall *never* rest Satisfied till this is done. Parker has Since made a Large fortune in France, where he yet is, on his return I mean to consult him on this business.

Being thus necessarily detained & not wishing to Lose time, a Gentln, who came over with me, and myself purchased about 140000 Acres of Land, Situated in the States of Kentuckey & Virginia, at 1/3 Stirg pr Acre; 100000 Acres of which we contracted with a person to Settle on perpetual Lease at 1/ Stirg pr Acre, pr Annum, to commence the third year after the respective residence of the People, Who are chiefly on the Same: the remaining 40000 Acres we allotted to Sell to defray the necessary expences, part of which is Sold at 6/ pr Acre, & I have no doubt but the remainder will Sell for more.

To *facilitate* the Sale of these Lands, & others, by exchange for goods and the Last for cash, I have Long Since opened a commercial house in this City; 36 Queen St. cheapsides.

A friend of mine, General, Mr Nicholson having made application in favor of me to Succeed Mr Johnson as *Consul,* and as the obtainment of this object would So establish my respectability as to enable me to effect all my objects here, and knowing that General Washington ever wishes to distinguish, or prefer a man *only* from merit, & that his merit is in proportion to the *Service* he has rendered to Society, I conceive it proper to observe, that when you consider general, that I have Spent ten years upward & many thousand pounds in the constant pursuit of Philosophical & Mechanical Enquiries & experiments the *objects* of which is *Public Utility*; And that Some years more must necessarily be devoted to *effect* the objects of Sd pursuit, I flatter myself General you will give the application of my friends *due* consideration, & that *these* circumstances will tend to preponderate the Scale in my favor, for the office in question, or any other which you may conceive I merit, or am qualified for.[2] I can have any recommendation from Robt Barclay, Wm Vaughan Esqre & others of this city. With grateful esteem I remain General Washington yours most respectfully

Jos. Barnes

P.S. I have not yet Published my Manuscript Book on Hydraulics, Hydrostatics & Mechanics, which contains more new matter and demonstration & will be of greater Utility than any Book extant on these objects—to my knowledge—When Published you shall have the first copy.[3]

J.B.

ALS, DLC:GW.

Joseph Barnes (Barns; d. 1818) acted as a mechanic for his brother-in-law James Rumsey, a noted steamboat inventor.

1. The arbiters issued their reward on 9 March 1795 (see "Letters of Rumsey, Inventor," 25:21–25).

Originally a merchant in Watertown, Mass., Daniel Parker supplied the Continental army during the latter stages of the Revolutionary War and associated with Robert Morris in a China trade venture, but he fled to Europe in 1784 to escape creditors. Parker agreed in 1790 with Samuel Rogers, another American businessman residing in London, to provide Rumsey with funds in exchange for a share of his steamboat patent.

2. The application from Barnes for a consular appointment has not been identified.

Barnes had written John Nicholson from London on 16 May 1795 that Joshua Johnson, then consul at London, "means to return to America in course of this Summer—Pray Who is proposed to Succeed him?" (PHarH: Nicholson Papers). Johnson continued as consul beyond GW's presidency.

3. Barnes apparently never published this manuscript, but see his *Treatise on the Justice, Policy, and Utility of Establishing an Effectual System for Promoting the Progress of Useful Arts, by Assuring Property in the Products of Genius. . . .* (Philadelphia, 1792). GW owned a copy of this work (see Griffin, *Catalogue of the Washington Collection*, 17).

From Bernard McMahon

(No. 6 North Front Street) [Philadelphia]
Sir   17th Septr 1796.
If my Services in any thing I am capable of, could be useful to you, at the Salary of One Hundred pounds a yea⟨r⟩ and Board at your expence, I would be happy to rendre them, and to endeavour to merit your approbation, I remain with the most profound respect, Sir, your Excellency's Most Obedient And Hble Servant
Berd McMahon.

ALS, DNA: RG 59, Miscellaneous Letters.
     The correspondent, presumably Bernard McMahon (c.1775–1816), apparently wanted to become farm manager at Mount Vernon (see GW to James Anderson, 18 Aug.). Born in Ireland, McMahon came to Philadelphia in 1796 and later established a seed and nursery business in that city. Thomas Jefferson prized McMahon's book, *The American Gardener's Calendar; Adapted to the Climates and Seasons of the United States. . . .* (Philadelphia, 1806).

To the Commissioners for the District of Columbia

Gentlemen,   Philadelphia 18th Septr 1796
     More than once, the Spanish Minister expressed, with pleasing solicitude, the intentions of his Government to erect in the Federal City a suitable Building for the accommodation of its Representative, near the Government of the United States; provided a convenient & agreeable Site could be obtained for the purpose. I always answered that this measure would be very pleasing & agreeable to me; & that I was sure the Commissioners of the Federal City would feel happy in accommodating him with ground for these Buildings.
     But on Tuesday last he told me, that application had been made to you through, or by Mr Barry, and difficulties (which he was not able to explain to me) had occurred.[1] I hope they can be removed, for in my opinion, a precedent of this sort may influence other foreign Governments to follow the example, which would, I conceive, contribute much more to the advancement of the City than any pecuniary consideration to be derived from the Sale of the Lots.[2]
     I shall not dwell however on the subject in this letter, as I expect in eight or ten days to be in the City, and will renew the

matter then. With very great esteem & regard I am—Gentlemen
Your Obedt Servt

G: Washington

Copy, in GW's secretary George Washington Craik's writing, DLC:GW; copy,
DLC:GW; LB, DLC:GW.

1. Spanish minister Carlos Martinez Yrujo spoke to GW on Tuesday,
13 September.

2. The D.C. commissioners wrote Yrujo on 23 Sept.: "It was with great pleasure, we heard from Mr Barry that the Court of Spain were desirous of erecting
a house in this City, for the residence of it's Minister; but as the proposition
was new, in it's kind and required arrangements which the President of the
United States alone, is competent to we suspended taking any measures till he
should return, which we then expected would take place in a shorter time than
has since elapsed. By last post, we had a Letter from the President on the subject, and, in consequence, assure you, that a site for a house, for the purpose
abovementioned, will be appropriated in such a situation as will be agreeable
to you. We take the liberty of suggesting the propriety of making the Selection,
by yourself, or some friend, whom you may authorise for the purpose, while
the President remains in this City, where we daily expect him, that the business
may be completed before his return to Philadelphia—We cannot conclude,
without assuring you that this Instance of the friendly disposition of the King
of Spain, towards these States, excites in our minds, the most pleasing sensations, and the opportunity it affords of expressing our regard for the Spanish
nation, and our high respect for your personal character, gives us peculiar
satisfaction" (DNA: RG 42, Records of the Commissioners for the District of
Columbia, Letters Sent).

Yrujo replied to the D.C. commissioners from Philadelphia on 28 Sept. that
he would "take proper measures respecting the Selection of a Site" (DNA:
RG 42, Records of the Commissioners for the District of Columbia, Letters
Received; see also Commissioners for the District of Columbia to GW, 1 Oct.,
in DNA: RG 42, Records of the Commissioners for the District of Columbia,
Letters Sent).

GW's Farewell Address

Editorial Note

In the preparation of his farewell address to the American
people, GW, as he often did for important documents, sought
the assistance of others he thought were superior in literary ability. When he had considered resignation in 1792, he turned to
James Madison.[1] In 1796 his primary collaborator was Alexander
Hamilton.

The starting point for the 1796 address was Madison's earlier draft. By February 1796, GW had written a new draft that consisted of a brief introduction, a full quotation of Madison's draft, and a somewhat longer section of additional thoughts inspired by the "considerable changes having taken place both at home & abroad" during his second term. While Hamilton was at Philadelphia in February to argue before the Supreme Court, GW showed the draft to him and mentioned a wish that Hamilton should edit the final document. He did not, however, give the address to Hamilton at that time. On 10 May, Hamilton wrote GW, noting that if he was to have sufficient time to edit, he should have GW's final draft as soon as it was completed. Upon receiving Hamilton's letter, GW sent him the draft, by this time slightly altered.[2]

In his instructions to Hamilton, GW expressed his fondness for the structure of the draft, because he hoped that quoting an address written by Madison, who was now a leading opponent of his policies, might shield him from some criticism. Nonetheless, he authorized Hamilton "to throw the *whole* into a different form," requesting, however, that even in that case, Hamilton should revise GW's original draft to perfect it as well.

After receiving the draft, Hamilton enlisted the assistance of John Jay. The two agreed to meet at Jay's house to discuss the address. By the time of that meeting, Hamilton had decided to avail himself of GW's authorization. He used GW's draft to compile an abstract of points to include[3] and then wrote out a new address embodying those points in a new structure without the quotation. Setting GW's draft aside, Hamilton and Jay considered the new draft "paragraph by paragraph, until the whole met with our mutual approbation. Some amendments were made during the interview, but none of much importance."[4] Hamilton transmitted the result to GW on 30 July.[5]

As requested, Hamilton then turned to revising GW's original draft without altering its structure, and he submitted that draft to GW on 10 August.[6]

After considering the various drafts, GW concluded that he preferred the reorganized document to his first draft or to Hamilton's revision in that form. He returned the preferred draft to Hamilton on 25 Aug. for further revision, adding, "I shall expunge all that is marked in the paper as unimportant &ca &ca

and as you perceive some marginal notes, written with a pencil, I pray you to give the sentiments so noticed mature consideration." He also requested that any change be clearly marked so as to prevent mistakes "in copying it for the Press."

Before Hamilton could respond, GW wrote him again on 1 Sept. suggesting the addition of a section on education. Hamilton thought that subject better reserved for GW's annual address to Congress, and so informed GW in a letter of 4 September. However, when he returned the draft on 5 Sept., "corrected agreeably to your intimations," it included "a short paragraph added respecting *Education*." Feeling too ill to rewrite the address in a fair copy, Hamilton contented himself with marking corrections on the draft he had received from GW.

The draft once again in hand, GW wrote out, in his own hand, the final copy for the printer. On 15 Sept. he submitted that copy to his cabinet, who recommended few, if any, changes and none of substance.[7] That same day, he summoned David C. Claypoole, editor of *Claypoole's American Daily Advertiser*, and the two made arrangements for the publication of the address in that paper on 19 September. As the final copy was then in Secretary of State Timothy Pickering's possession, GW promised that it would be delivered to Claypoole the next morning. Claypoole received the copy and later submitted proof sheets and revises to GW, who, he noted, made "but few alterations from the original, except in the punctuation, in which he was very minute." The address was printed on 19 Sept., but given a date of 17 Sept., for reasons not entirely clear (perhaps GW returned the final revise on that date). After Claypoole published the letter, he expressed a wish, which GW granted, to retain the manuscript original from which the printed version was prepared.[8] That document is presented below.

Although the process of composition is quite clear from the existing correspondence, relating that record to the surviving drafts is problematic. The specific problem is with the item that GW sent to Hamilton on 25 Aug. and Hamilton returned on 5 Sept., as there are substantial discrepancies between the surviving version of Hamilton's reorganized draft and the description of the draft in those letters. Horace Binney, the earliest writer to attempt *An Inquiry into the Formation of Washington's Farewell Address*, posited, not unreasonably, that on 30 July Hamilton had sent to GW not the surviving draft, but a fair copy thereof. The surviving draft, Binney thought, was Hamilton's retained copy.[9] He did not know, however, that the surviving draft had on it some pencil notes in GW's writing.

The existence of those notes (which seemed to fit the reference in GW's letter of 25 Aug. to marginal notes in pencil) and the large number of corrections on the surviving draft, encouraged Victor H. Paltsits to conclude that Binney was wrong to search for a missing draft when "there is none."[10] Paltsits, however, did not address the discrepancy between those notes and what GW had written in the letter. GW informed Hamilton that there were certain paragraphs marked as "unimportant &ca &ca" that would be omitted and other marginal notes in pencil to be considered. The penciled notes on the surviving draft are present only at paragraphs that were eventually deleted from the address, and they all state only "omitted in address." Oddly, the final draft that GW sent to the printer includes those same paragraphs (although struck out) with marginal notations (also struck out) that better match the description given to Hamilton.[11] Nor did Paltsits address the fact that the many revisions on the surviving draft are purely stylistic not substantive—exactly the sort of changes that Jay remembered being made to the manuscript during his interview with Hamilton.

To believe that there was only a single draft copy sent by Hamilton on 30 July, returned by GW on 25 Aug., and revised by Hamilton in accordance with GW's suggestions and returned again to GW on 5 Sept. is to believe that GW did not (as he wrote) mark anything on the draft as "unimportant &c &c" although he included such notes in his final copy; that the additional pencil notations were so thoroughly erased that no one who has later examined the surviving draft has reported any traces of them; that in the completely erased notations, GW, who had turned to Hamilton to perfect his language, made suggestions entirely about matters of style (and then made substantive alterations as well as many more stylistic changes in the transition from that draft to the final copy);[12] that Hamilton was unable to fit the "short" paragraph on education in the margins of the draft, but wrote it on a separate paper that has now been lost;[13] that despite GW's instructions about marking the draft, Hamilton returned his corrections in a form where their placement is not always clear;[14] and that GW, who was concerned enough about the security of the mails to send the draft under cover to Jay rather than to Hamilton, was willing to send by mail his only copy of the preferred text. Surely it is reasonable to consider alternatives.

The hypothesis that best fits the known facts is that on 30 July Hamilton sent the draft that he and Jay had marked up in their interview, without making a fair copy, thus placing that document in GW's possession. Before responding to Hamilton on 25 Aug., however, GW had a fair copy made on which he wrote the marginal notations he described and which he sent to Hamilton, retaining the original Hamilton draft as his copy.[15] This copy, which Hamilton revised and returned on 5 Sept., has not been found. Once GW received Hamilton's revisions, he made a new copy, incorporating those revisions and any others that he desired but retaining the paragraphs to be deleted with their corresponding marginal notes, so that the cabinet could consider them. When the cabinet suggested no changes, he struck out those paragraphs and submitted that copy to the printer. At that time he also marked the corresponding paragraphs on the surviving draft as "omitted in address."[16]

This hypothesis with its assumption of a missing draft does not alter the basic conclusion reached by Binney, Paltsits, and most others who have examined the Farewell Address: the ideas are GW's, the structure is Hamilton's, and the language is some indeterminable combination of the two, with contributions from Jay and Madison, all subject to GW's final approval. It does suggest that the editorial changes on the surviving draft provide no information about GW's contributions to the address, since they most likely were made before he received that document. More importantly, historians should be reluctant to attribute differences between the final copy and the surviving draft solely to GW. It is more likely that Hamilton altered much of the language in accordance with GW's intimations on the missing draft. Only the changes marked as corrections on the final copy may be presumed to come from GW alone.

1. See Madison's Conversations with Washington, 5–25 May 1792; GW to James Madison, 20 May 1792; Madison to GW, 20 June 1792 and enclosed draft.

2. GW to Alexander Hamilton, 15 May 1796, and enclosure.

3. See *Hamilton Papers*, 20:178–83, or Paltsits, *Farewell Address*, 174–78.

4. John Jay to Richard Peters, 29 March 1811, in Paltsits, *Farewell Address*, 264–71. Jay recollected that Hamilton had said that GW had requested "our opinion" on the address (p. 270). Although Jay is not mentioned in the letter transmitting the draft to Hamilton, GW might have suggested consulting him in the February 1796 conversation or in his letter to Hamilton written on 29 May (not found). Hamilton also might have taken the request in GW's letter dated 26 June that Jay be consulted on an unrelated matter "and other interesting matters as they occur" as applicable to the farewell address.

5. See *Hamilton Papers*, 20:265–88, or Paltsits, *Farewell Address*, 179–99.

6. See *Hamilton Papers*, 20:294–303, or Paltsits, *Farewell Address*, 200–208. Horace Binney assumed that Jay had assisted on this draft rather than the reorganizing draft sent on 30 July (see Binney, *Farewell Address*, 74). However, Jay recollected that he had later written GW on the subject, and that letter, dated 19 Sept., referenced language present in Hamilton's reorganizing draft and the final address but not in this draft or in GW's initial draft.

7. Timothy Pickering to GW, 15 Sept. (third letter); Peters to Jay, 14 April 1811, in Paltsits, *Farewell Address*, 273–76; Pickering to James A. Hamilton, 16 Jan. 1829, in *Reminiscences of James A. Hamilton*, 33.

8. Certification of David C. Claypoole, 22 Feb. 1826, in Paltsits, *Farewell Address*, 290–92.

9. Binney, *Farewell Address*, 53–55

10. Paltsits, *Farewell Address*, 35–36.

11. See notes 3, 12, 17, and 26 in the document following.

12. See, for example, notes 9, 11, 15, 18, and 25 in the document following.

13. Several marginal notes on the surviving draft are longer than the paragraph on education that appears in the final copy of the address, and there is ample room for the paragraph's insertion on the draft page corresponding to its final position. For an alternative location that is more crowded and so inferior that it is hard to believe that Hamilton would have preferred to place the paragraph there, see Paltsits, *Farewell Address*, 183, and *Hamilton Papers*, 20:271.

14. The editors of the *Hamilton Papers*, for example, disagreed with Paltsits on the proper placement of a phrase written at the bottom of one page (see note 13 to their text of the surviving draft in *Hamilton Papers*, 20:272).

15. If GW had received the surviving draft as it now appears, he would likely have preferred to send a cleaner copy so that additional alterations would stand out.

16. This hypothesis does not explain how the surviving draft found its way into Hamilton's papers, but neither does the single draft hypothesis, since the back and forth ends with the document in GW's possession. Similarly, the single draft hypothesis also requires the existence of a lost text, albeit a draft paragraph on education rather than a full copy of the address.

Farewell Address

Friends & Fellow-Citizens   United States 19th September 1796

The period for a new election of a Citizen, to Administer the Executive government of the United States, being not far distant, and the time actually arrived, when your thoughts must be employed in designating the person, who is to be cloathed with that important trust, it appears to me proper, especially as it may conduce to a more distinct expression of the public voice, that I should now apprise you of the resolution I have formed, to decline being considered among the number of those, out of whom a choice is to be made.

I beg you, at the same time, to do me the justice to be assured, that this resolution has not been taken, without a strict regard to all the considerations appertaining to the relation, which binds a dutiful citizen to his country—and that, in withdrawing the tender of service which silence in my situation might imply, I am influenced by no diminution of zeal for your future interest; no deficiency of grateful respect for your past kindness; but am supported by a full conviction that the step is compatible with both.

The acceptance of, & continuance hitherto in, the office to which your Suffrages have twice called me, have been a uniform sacrifice of inclination to the opinion of duty, and to a deference for what appeared to be your desire. I constantly hoped, that it would have been much earlier in my power, consistently with motives, which I was not at liberty to disregard, to return to that retirement, from which I had been reluctantly drawn. The strength of my inclination to do this, previous to the last Election, had even led to the preparation of an address to declare it to you;[1] but mature reflection on the then perplexed & critical posture of our Affairs with foreign Nations, and the unanimous advice of persons entitled to my confidence, impelled me to abandon the idea.

I rejoice, that the state of your concerns, external as well as internal, no longer renders the pursuit of inclination incompatible with the sentiment of duty, or propriety; & am persuaded whatever partiality may be retained for my services, that in the present circumstances of our country, you will not disapprove my determination to retire.

The impressions with which I first undertook the arduous trust, were explained on the proper occasion.[2] In the discharge of this trust, I will only say, that I have with good intentions, contributed towards the Organization and administration of the government, the best exertions of which a very fallible judgment was capable. Not unconscious, in the out set, of the inferiority of my qualifications, experience in my own eyes, perhaps still more in the eyes of others, has strengthened the motives to diffidence of myself; and every day the encreasing weight of years admonishes me more and more, that the shade of retirement is as necessary to me as it will be welcome. Satisfied that if any circumstances have given peculiar value to my services, they were temporary, I have the consolation to believe, that while choice and prudence invite me to quit the political scene, patriotism does not forbid it.[3]

In looking forward to the moment, which is intended to terminate the career of my public life, my feelings do not permit me to suspend the deep acknowledgement of that debt of gratitude which I owe to my beloved country, for the many honors it has conferred upon me; still more for the stedfast confidence with which it has supported me; and for the opportunities I have thence enjoyed of manifesting my inviolable attachment, by services faithful & persevering, though in usefulness unequal to my zeal. If benefits have resulted to our country from these services, let it always be remembered to your praise, and as an instructive example in our annals, that, under circumstances in which the Passions agitated in every direction were liable to mislead,[4] amidst appearances sometimes dubious, viscissitudes of fortune often discouraging, in situations in which not unfrequently want of Success has countenanced the spirit of criticism, the constancy of your support was the essential prop of the efforts, and a guarantee of the plans by which they were effected. Profoundly penetrated with this idea, I shall carry it with me to my grave, as a strong incitement to unceasing vows[5] that Heaven may continue to you the choicest tokens of its beneficence—that your Union & brotherly affection my be perpetual—that the free constitution, which is the work of your hands, may be sacredly maintained— that its Administration in every department may be stamped with wisdom and virtue—that, in fine, the happiness of the people of these States, under the auspices of liberty, may be made complete, by so careful a preservation and so prudent a use of this blessing as will acquire to them the glory of recommending it to the applause, the affection—and adoption of every nation which is yet a stranger to it.

Here, perhaps, I ought to stop. But a solicitude for your welfare, which cannot end but with my life, and the apprehension of danger, natural to that solicitude, urge me on an occasion like the present, to offer to your solemn contemplation, and to recommend to your frequent review, some sentiments; which are the result of much reflection, of no inconsiderable observation, and which appear to me all important to the permanency of your felicity as a People. These will be offered to you with the more freedom, as you can only see in them the disinterested warnings of a parting friend, who can possibly have no personal motive to biass his counsel. Nor can I forget, as an encouragement to it, your endulgent reception of my sentiments on a former and not dissimilar occasion.[6]

Interwoven as is the love of liberty with every ligament of your hearts, no recommendation of mine is necessary to fortify or confirm the attachment.

The Unity of Government which constitutes you one people is also now dear to you. It is justly so; for it is a main Pillar in the Edifice of your real independence, the support of your tranquility at home, your peace abroad; of your safety; of your prosperity; of that very Liberty which you so highly prize. But as it is easy to foresee, that from different causes & from different quarters, much pains will be taken, many artifices employed, to weaken in your minds the conviction of this truth; as this is the point in your political fortress against which the batteries of internal and external enemies will be most constantly and actively (though often covertly & insidiously) directed, it is of infinite moment, that you should properly estimate the immense value of your national Union, to your collective & individual happiness; that you should cherish a cordial, habitual & immoveable attachment[7] to it; accustoming yourselves to think and speak of it as of the Palladium of your political safety and prosperity; watching for its preservation with jealous anxiety; discountenancing whatever may suggest even a suspicion that it can in any event be abandoned; and indignantly frowning upon the first dawning of every attempt to alienate any portion of our Country from the rest, or to enfeeble the sacred ties which now link together the various parts.

For this you have every inducement of sympathy and interest. Citizens by birth or choice, of a common country, that country has a right to concentrate your affections. The name of AMERICAN, which belongs to you, in your national capacity, must always exalt the just pride of Patriotism, more than any appellation derived from local discriminations. With slight shades of difference, you have the same Religion, Manners, Habits & political Principles. You have in a common cause fought and triumphed together—the independence & Liberty you possess are the work of joint councils, and joint efforts—of common dangers, sufferings and successes.

But these considerations, however powerfully they address themselves to your sensibility are greatly outweighed by those which apply more immediately to your Interest. Here every portion of our country finds the most commanding motives for carefully guarding & preserving the Union of the whole.

The *North*, in an unrestrained intercourse with the *South*, protected by the equal Laws of a common government, finds in the productions of the latter,[8] great additional resources of maritime & commercial enterprise and precious materials of manufacturing industry. The *South* in the same Intercourse, benefitting by the Agency of the *North*, sees its agriculture grow & its commence expand. Turning partly into its own channels the seamen of the *North*, it finds its particular navigation envigorated; and while it contributes, in different ways, to nourish & increase the general mass of the national navigation, it looks forward to the protection of a maritime strength, to which itself is unequally adapted. The *East*, in a like intercourse with the *West*, already finds, and in the progressive improvement of interior communications, by land & water, will more & more find a valuable vent for the commodities which it brings from abroad, or manufactures at home. The *West* derives from the *East* supplies requisite to its growth & comfort—and what is perhaps of still greater consequence, it must of necessity owe the *secure* enjoyment of indispensable *outlets* for its own productions to the weight, influence, and the future maritime strength of the Atlantic side of the Union, directed by an indissoluble community of Interest as *one Nation*. Any other tenure by which the *West* can hold this essential advantage, whether derived from its own seperate strength, or from an apostate & unnatural connection with any foreign Power, must be intrinsically precarious.[9]

While then every part of our country thus feels an immediate & particular Interest in Union, all the parts combined cannot fail to find in the united mass of means & efforts greater strength, greater resource, proportionably greater security from external danger, a less frequent interruption of their Peace by foreign Nations; and, what is of inestimable value! they must derive from Union an exemption from those broils and Wars between themselves, which so frequently[10] afflict neighbouring countries, not tied together by the same government; which their own rivalships alone would be sufficient to produce, but which opposite foreign alliances, attachments & intriegues would stimulate and imbitter. Hence likewise they will avoid the necessity of those overgrown military establishments, which under any form of Government are inauspicious to liberty, and which are to be regarded as particularly hostile to Republican Liberty: In this sense it is, that your Union ought to be considered as a main prop of your liberty, and that the love of the one ought to endear to you the preservation of the other.

These considerations speak a persuasive language to every reflecting & virtuous mind, and exhibit the continuance of the UNION as a primary object of Patriotic desire. Is there a doubt, whether a common government can embrace so large a sphere? Let experience solve it. To listen to mere speculation in such a case were criminal. We are authorized to hope that a proper organization of the whole, with the auxiliary agency of governments for the respective Subdivisions, will afford a happy issue to the experiment. 'Tis well worth a fair and full experiment.[11] With such powerful and obvious motives to Union, affecting all parts of our country, while experience shall not have demonstrated its impracticability, there will always be reason to distrust the patriotism of those, who in any quarter may endeavor to weaken its bands.[12]

In contemplating the causes wch may disturb our Union, it occurs as matter of serious concern, that any ground should have been furnished for characterizing parties by *Geographical* discriminations—*Northern* and *Southern*—*Atlantic* and *Western;*[13] whence designing men may endeavour to excite a belief that there is a real difference of local interests and views. One of the expedients of party to acquire influence, within particular districts, is to misrepresent the opinions & aims of other Districts. You cannot shield yourselves too much against the jealousies and heart burnings which spring from these misrepresentations. They tend to render alien to each other those who ought to be bound together by fraternal affection. The Inhabitants of our Western country have lately had a useful lesson on this head. They have seen, in the Negociation by the Executive, and in the unanimous ratification by the Senate, of the Treaty with Spain, and in the universal satisfaction at that event, throughout the United States, a decisive proof how unfounded were the suspicions propagated among them of a policy in the General Government and in the Atlantic states unfriendly to their Interests in regard to the MISSISSIPPI. They have been witnesses to the formation of two Treaties, that with G: Britain and that with Spain, which secure to them every thing they could desire, in respect to our Foreign relations, towards confirming their prosperity.[14] Will it not be their wisdom to rely for the preservation of these advantages on the UNION by wch they were procured? Will they not henceforth be deaf to those advisers, if such there are, who would sever them from their Brethren and connect them with Aliens?

To the efficacy and permanency of Your Union, a Government for the whole is indispensable. No Alliances however strict between the parts can be an adequate substitute. They must inevitably experience the infractions & interruptions which all Alliances in all times have experienced. Sensible of this momentous truth, you have improved upon your first essay, by the adoption of a Constitution of Government, better calculated than your former for an intimate Union, and for the efficacious management of your common concerns. This government, the offspring of our own choice uninfluenced and unawed, adopted upon full investigation and mature deliberation, completely free in its principles, in the distribution of its powers, uniting security with energy, and containing within itself a provision for its own amendment, has a just claim to your confidence and your support. Respect for its authority, compliance with its Laws, acquiescence in its measures, are duties enjoined by the fundamental maxims of true Liberty. The basis of our political systems is the right of the people to make and to alter their Constitutions of Government. But the Constitution which at any time exists, 'till changed by an explicit and authentic act of the whole People, is sacredly obligatory upon all. The very idea of the power and the right of the People to establish Government presupposes the duty of every Individual to obey the established Government.

All obstructions to the execution of the Laws, all combinations and associations, under whatever plausible character, with the real design to direct, controul counteract, or awe the regular deliberation and action of the Constituted authorities are distructive of this fundamental principle and of fatal tendency. They serve to organize faction, to give it an artificial and extraordinary force—to put in the place of the delegated will of the Nation, the will of a party; often a small but artful and enterprizing minority of the Community; and, according to the alternate triumphs of different parties, to make the public administration the Mirror of the ill concerted and incongruous projects of faction, rather than the Organ of consistent and wholesome plans digested by common councils and modefied by mutual interests. However combinations or Associations of the above description may now & then answer popular ends, they are likely, in the course of time and things, to become potent engines, by which cunning, ambitious and unprincipled men will be enabled to subvert the Power of the People, & to usurp for themselves the reins of Government; destroying afterwards the very engines which have lifted them to unjust dominion.

Towards the preservation of your Government and the permanency of your present happy state, it is requisite, not only that you steadily discountenance irregular oppositions to its acknowledged authority, but also that you resist with care the spirit of innovation upon its principles however specious the pretexts. One method of assault may be to effect, in the forms of the Constitution, alterations which will impair the energy of the system, and thus to undermine what cannot be directly overthrown. In all the changes to which you may be invited, remember that time and habit are at least as necessary to fix the true character of Governments, as of other human institutions—that experience is the surest standard, by which to test the real tendency of the existing Constitution of a country—that facility in changes upon the credit of mere hypotheses & opinion exposes to perpetual change, from the endless variety of hypotheses and opinion: and remember, especially, that for the efficient management of your common interests, in a country so extensive as ours, a Government of as much vigour as is consistent with the perfect security of Liberty is indispensable—Liberty itself will find in such a Government, with powers properly distributed and adjusted, its surest Guardian. It is indeed little else than a name, where the Government is too feeble to withstand the enterprises of faction, to confine each member of the Society within the limits prescribed by the laws, and to maintain all in the secure and tranquil enjoyment of the rights of person and property.[15]

I have already intimated to you the danger of Parties in the State, with particular reference to the founding of them on Geographical discriminations. Let me now take a more comprehensive view, & warn you in the most solemn manner against the baneful effects of the Spirit of Party, generally.

This spirit, unfortunately, is inseperable from our nature, having its root in the strongest passions of the human Mind. It exists under different shapes in all Governments, more or less stifled, controuled, or repressed; but in those of the popular form it is seen in its greatest rankness and is truly their worst enemy.[16]

The alternate domination of one faction over another, sharpened by the spirit of revenge natural to party dissention, which in different ages & countries has perpetrated the most horrid enormities, is itself a frightful despotism. But this leads at length to a more formal and permanent despotism. The disorders & miseries, which result, gradually incline the minds of men to seek security & repose in the absolute power of an Individual: and sooner or later the chief of some prevailing faction more able or more fortunate than his competitors, turns this disposition to the purposes of his own elevation, on the ruins of Public Liberty.

Without looking forward to an extremity of this kind (which nevertheless ought not to be entirely out of sight) the common & continual mischiefs of the spirit of Party are sufficient to make it the interest and the duty of a wise People to discourage and restrain it.

It serves always to distract the Public Councils and enfeeble the Public Administration. It agitates the Community with ill founded jealousies and false alarms, kindles the animosity of one part against another, foments occasionally riot & insurrection. It opens the door to foreign influence & corruption, which find a facilitated access to the government itself through the channels of party passions. Thus the policy and the will of one country, are subjected to the policy and will of another.

There is an opinion that parties in free countries are useful checks upon the Administration of the Government and serve to keep alive the spirit of Liberty. This within certain limits is probably true—and in Governments of a Monarchical cast Patriotism may look with endulgence, if not with favour, upon the spirit of party. But in those of the popular character, in Governments purely elective, it is a spirit not to be encouraged. From their natural tendency, it is certain there will always be enough of that spirit for every salutary purpose. And there being constant danger of excess, the effort ought to be, by force of public opinion, to mitigate & assuage it. A fire not to be quenched; it demands a uniform vigilance to prevent its bursting into a flame, lest instead of warming it should consume.

It is important, likewise, that the habits of thinking in a free Country should inspire caution, in those entrusted with its administration, to confine themselves within their respective Constitutional spheres, avoiding in the exercise of the Powers of one department to encroach upon another. The spirit of encroachment tends to consolidate the powers of all the departments in one, and thus to create whatever the form of government, a real despotism. A just estimate of that love of power, and proneness to abuse it, which predominates in the human heart is sufficient to satisfy us of the truth of this position. The necessity of reciprocal checks in the exercise of political power; by dividing and distributing it into different depositories, & constituting each the Guardian of the Public Weal against invasions by the others, has been evinced by experiments ancient & modern; some of them in our country & under our own eyes. To preserve them must be as necessary as to institute them. If in the opinion of the People, the distribution or modification of the Constitutional powers be in any particular wrong, let it be corrected by an amendment in the way which the Constitution designates. But let there be no change by usurpation; for though this, in one instance, may be the instrument of good, it is the customary weapon by which free governments are destroyed. The precedent must always greatly overbalance in permanent evil any partial or transient benefit which the use can at any time yield.

Of all the dispositions and habits which lead to political prosperity, Religion and morality are indispensable supports. In vain would that man claim the tribute of Patriotism, who should labour to subvert these great Pillars of human happiness, these firmest props of the duties of Men & citizens. The mere Politician, equally with the pious man ought to respect & to cherish them. A volume could not trace all their connections with private & public felicity. Let it simply be asked where is the security for property, for reputation, for life, if the sense of religious obligation *desert* the oaths, which are the instruments of investigation in Courts of Justice? And let us with caution indulge the supposition, that morality can be maintained without religion. Whatever may be conceded to the influence of refined education on minds of peculiar structure—reason & experience both forbid us to expect that National morality can prevail in exclusion of religious principle.

'Tis substantially true, that virtue or morality is a necessary spring of popular government. The rule indeed extends with more or less force to every species of free Government. Who that is a sincere friend to it can look with indifference upon attempts to shake the foundation of the fabric?[17]

Promote then as an object of primary importance, Institutions for the general diffusion of knowledge. In proportion as the structure of a government gives force to public opinion, it is essential that public opinion should be enlightened.

As a very important source of strength & security cherish public credit. One method of preserving it is to use it as sparingly as possible: avoiding occasions of expence by cultivating peace, but remembering also that timely disbursements to prepare for danger frequently prevent much greater disbursements to repel it—avoiding likewise the accumulation of debt, not only by shunning occasions of expence, but by vigorous exertions in time of Peace to discharge the Debts which unavoidable wars may have occasioned, not ungenerously throwing upon posterity the burthen which we ourselves ought to bear. The execution of these maxims belongs to your Representatives, but it is necessary that public opinion should cooperate.[18] To facilitate to them the performance of their duty, it is essential that you should practically bear in mind, that towards the payment of debts there must be Revenue—that to have Revenue there must be taxes—that no taxes can be devised which are not more or less inconvenient & unpleasant—that the intrinsic embarrassment inseperable from the selection of the proper objects (which is always a choice of difficulties) ought to be a decisive motive for a candid construction of the conduct of the Government in making it, and for a spirit of acquiescence in the measures for obtaining Revenue which the public exigencies may at any time dictate.

Observe good faith & justice towds all Nations cultivate peace & harmony with all—Religion & morality enjoin this conduct; and can it be that good policy does not equally enjoin it? It will be worthy of a free, enlightened, and, at no distant period, a great Nation, to give to mankind the magnanimous and too novel example of a People always guided by an exalted justice & benevolence. Who can doubt that in the course of time and things the fruits of such a plan would richly repay any temporary advantages wch might be lost by a steady adherence to it? Can it be, that Providence has not connected the permanent felicity of a Nation with its virtue? The experiment, at least, is recommended by every sentiment which ennobles human Nature. Alas! is it rendered impossible by its vices?

In the execution of such a plan, nothing is more essential than that permanent, inveterate antipathies against particular Nations and passionate attachments for others should be excluded; and that in place of them just & amicable feelings towards all should be cultivated. The Nation, which indulges towards another an habitual hatred, or an habitual fondness, is in some degree a slave. It is a slave to its animosity or to its affection, either of which is sufficient to lead it astray from its duty and its interest. Antipathy in one Nation against another[19] disposes each more readily to offer insult and injury, to lay hold of slight causes of umbrage, and to be haughty and intractable, when accidental or trifling occasions of dispute occur. Hence frequent collisions, obstinate envenomed and bloody contests. The Nation, prompted by ill will & resentment sometimes impels to War the Government, contrary to the best calculations of policy. The Government sometimes participates in the national propensity, and adopts through passion what reason would reject; at other times, it makes the animosity of the nation subservient to projects of hostility instigated by pride, ambition and other sinister & pernicious motives. The peace often, sometimes perhaps the Liberty, of Nations has been the victim.

So likewise, a passionate attachment of one Nation for another produces a variety of evils. Sympathy for the favourite nation, facilitating the illusion of an imaginary common interest, in cases where no real common interest exists, and infusing into one the enmities of the other, betrays the former into a participation in the quarrels & Wars of the latter, without adequate inducement or justification: It leads also to concessions to the favourite Nation of priviledges denied to others, which is apt doubly to injure the Nation making the concessions—by unnecessarily parting with what ought to have been retained—& by exciting jealousy, ill will, and a disposition to retaliate, in the parties from whom eql priviledges are withheld: And it gives to ambitious, corrupted, or deluded citizens (who devote themselves to the favourite Nation) facility to betray, or sacrifice the interests of their own country, without odium, sometimes even with popularity; gilding with the appearances of a virtuous sense of obligation a commendable deference for public opinion, or a laudable zeal for public good, the base or foolish compliances of ambition, corruption or infatuation.

As avenues to foreign influence in innumerable ways, such attachments are particularly alarming to the truly enlightened and independent Patriot. How many opportunities do they afford to tamper with domestic factions, to practice the arts of seduction, to mislead public opinion, to influence or awe the public Councils! Such an attachment of a small or weak, towards a great & powerful Nation, dooms the former to be the satellite of the latter.

Against the insidious wiles of foreign influence (I conjure you to believe me fellow citizens) the jealousy of a free people ought to be *constantly* awake; since history and experience prove that foreign influence is one of the most baneful foes of Republican Government. But that jealousy to be useful must be impartial; else it becomes the instrument of the very influence to be avoided, instead of a defence against it. Excessive partiality for one foreign nation and excessive dislike of another, cause those whom they actuate to see danger only on one side, and serve to veil and even second the arts of influence on the other. Real Patriots, who may resist the intrigues of the favourite, are liable to become suspected and odious; while its tools and dupes usurp the applause & confidence of the people, to surrender their interests.

The great rule of conduct for us, in regard to foreign Nations is in extending our commercial relations to have with them as little *political* connection as possible. So far as we have already formed engagements let them be fulfilled with[20] perfect good faith. Here let us stop.

Europe has a set of primary interests, which to us have none, or a very remote relation. Hence she must be engaged in frequent controversies, the causes of which are essentially foreign to our concerns. Hence therefore it must be unwise in us to implicate ourselves, by artificial ties, in the ordinary vicissitudes of her politics, or the ordinary combinations & collisions of her friendships, or enmities.

Our detached & distant situation invites and enables us to pursue a different course. If we remain one People, under an efficient government, the period is not far off, when we may defy material injury from external annoyance; when we may take such an attitude as will cause the neutrality we may at any time resolve upon to be scrupulously respected; when[21] belligerent nations, under the impossibility of making acquisitions upon us, will not lightly hazard the giving us provocation;[22] when we may choose peace or War, as our interest guided by justice shall counsel.

Why forego the advantages of so peculiar a situation? Why quit our own to stand upon foreign ground? Why, by interweaving our destiny with that of any part of Europe, entangle our peace and prosperity in the toils of European ambition, Rivalship, Interest, Humour or Caprice?

'Tis our true policy to steer clear of permanent Alliances, with any portion of the foreign world—So far, I mean, as we are now at liberty to do it—for let me not be understood as capable of patronising infidility to existing engagements. (I hold the maxim no less applicable to public than to private affairs, that honesty is always the best policy). I repeat it therefore, let those engagements be observed in their genuine sense. But in my opinion, it is unnecessary and would be unwise to extend them.

Taking care always to keep ourselves, by suitable establishments, on a respectably defensive posture, we may safely trust to temporary alliances for extraordinary emergencies.

Harmony, liberal intercourse with all Nations, are recommended by policy, humanity and interest. But even our Commercial policy should hold an equal and impartial hand: neither seeking nor granting exclusive favours or preferences; consulting the natural course of things; diffusing & diversifying by gentle means the streams of Commerce, but forcing nothing; establishing, with Powers so disposed—in order to give trade a stable course, to define the rights of our merchants, and to enable the Government to support them—conventional rules of intercourse, the best that present circumstances and mutual opinion will permit, but temporary, & liable to be from time to time abandoned or varied, as experience and circumstances shall dictate; constantly keeping in view; that 'tis folly in one Nation to look for disinterested favors from another—that it must pay with a portion of its Independence for whatever it may accept under that character—that by such acceptance, it may place itself in the condition of having given equivalents for nominal favours and yet of being reproached with ingratitude for not giving more. There can be no greater error than to expect, or calculate upon real favours from Nation to Nation. 'Tis an illusion which experience must cure, which a just pride ought to discard.

In offering to you, my Countrymen, these counsels of an old and affectionate friend, I dare not hope they will make the strong and lasting impression, I could wish—that they will controul the usual current of the passions, or prevent our Nation from running the course which has hitherto marked the Destiny of Nations: But if I may even flatter myself, that they may be productive of some partial benefit, some occasional good, that they may now & then recur to moderate the fury of party spirit, to warn against the mischiefs of foreign Intriegue, to guard against the Impostures of pretended patriotism—this hope will be a full recompence for the solicitude for your welfare, by which they have been dictated.

How far in the discharge of my Official duties, I have been guided by the principles which have been delineated, the public Records and other evidences of my conduct must witness to You and to the world. To myself, the assurance of my own conscience is, that I have at least believed myself to be guided by them.

In relation to the still subsisting War in Europe, my Proclamation of the 22d of April 1793 is the index to my Plan. Sanctioned by your approving voice and by that of your Representatives in both Houses of Congress, the spirit of that measure has continually governed me; uninfluenced by any attempts to deter or divert me from it.[23]

After deliberate examination with the aid of the best lights I could obtain[24] I was well satisfied that our country, under all the circumstances of the case, had a right to take, and was bound in duty and interest, to take a Neutral position. Having taken it, I determined, as far as should depend upon me, to maintain it, with moderation, perseverence & firmness.

The considerations which respect the right to hold this conduct, it is not necessary on this occasion to detail. I will only observe, that according to my understanding of the matter, that right, so far from being denied by any of the Belligerent Powers has been virtually admitted by all.[25]

The duty of holding a Neutral conduct may be inferred, without any thing more, from the obligation which justice and humanity impose on every Nation, in cases in which it is free to act, to maintain inviolate the relations of Peace and amity towards other Nations.

The inducements of interest for observing that conduct will best be referred to your own reflections & experience. With me, a predominant motive has been to endeavour to gain time to our country to settle & mature its yet recent institutions, and to progress without interruption, to that degree of strength & consistency, which is necessary to give it, humanly speaking, the command of its own fortunes.

Though in reviewing the incidents of my Administration, I am unconscious of intentional error—I am nevertheless too sensible of my defects not to think it probable that I may have committed many errors. Whatever they may be I fervently beseech the Almighty to avert or mitigate the evils to which they may tend. I shall also carry with me the hope that my Country will never cease to view them with indulgence; and that after forty five years of my life dedicated to its Service, with an upright zeal, the faults of incompetent abilities will be consigned to oblivion, as myself must soon be to the mansions of rest.[26]

Relying on its kindness in this as in other things, and actuated by that fervent love towards it, which is so natural to a man, who views in it the native soil of himself and his progenitors for several Generations; I anticipate with pleasing expectation that retreat, in which I promise myself to realize, without alloy, the sweet enjoyment of partaking, in the midst of my fellow Citizens, the benign influence of good Laws under a free Government— the ever favourite object of my heart, and the happy reward, as I trust, of our mutual cares, labours and dangers.[27]

Go: Washington

ADS, NN; LB (dated 17 Sept.), DLC:GW. The address was first printed in *Claypoole's American Daily Advertiser* for 19 Sept. 1796, where it was given a date of 17 September. Except for the date change and variations in capitalization, punctuation, and spelling, the published version reproduced the ADS.

The most important of the various deletions and alterations on the manuscript are indicated in the notes below. For the other changes, see Paltsits, *Farewell Address*, 105–36 (facsimile), and 139–59 (transcription).

On a copy of *Claypoole's American Daily Advertiser* now at NNGL, GW wrote a note, apparently providing directions for its entry into a letter book: "The Letter contain in this Gazette—Addressed to the People of the United States is to be Recorded and in the Order of its da⟨te⟩.

"Let it have a blan⟨k⟩ Page before & after so as to stand distinct as it were. Let it be wrote with a letter larger & fully than the common recordi⟨n⟩g hand—And where words are Printed with capital letters it is to be done so in Recording ⟨th⟩is ⟨letter⟩ and those other wo⟨rd⟩s that are printed in Italicks, must ⟨be d⟩rew underneath and streight by a Ruler."

1. For that draft, see the enclosure printed with James Madison to GW, 20 June 1792.

2. GW alluded to his first inaugural address, 30 April 1789.

3. At this point GW struck out eleven lines of text and a marginal note with an explanation: "obliterated to avoid the imputation of affected modesty." The deleted text reads: "May I also have that of knowing in my retreat, that the involuntary errors, I have probably committed, have been the sources of no serious or lasting mischief to our country. I may then expect to realise, without alloy, the sweet enjoyment of partaking, in the midst of my fellow citizens, the benign influence of good laws under a free government; the ever favorite object of my heart, and the happy reward, I trust, of our mutual cares, dangers & labours."

4. The preceding word replaced three words—"wander & fluctuate"—that GW had struck out.

5. At this point GW struck a parenthetical phrase: "the only return I can henceforth make."

6. GW is referring to his circular letter to the states announcing his resignation from the army in June 1783 (see GW's Draft for a Farewell Address, n.8, printed as an enclosure with GW to Alexander Hamilton, 15 May).

7. The remainder of this paragraph replaced text that read: "that you

should accustom yourselves to reverance it as the palladium of your political safety and prosperity, adapting constantly your words and actions to that momentous idea that you should watch for its preservation with jealous anxiety, discountenance whatever may suggest a suspicion that it can in any event be abandoned; and frown upon the first dawning of any attempt to alienate any portion of our Country from the rest, or to enfeeble the sacred ties which now link together the several parts."

8. GW struck out "many of them peculiar" at this point.

9. Here GW struck the following elaboration: "liable every moment to be disturbed by the fluctuating combinations of the primary interests of Europe, which must be expected to regulate the conduct of the Nations of which it is composed."

10. GW inserted the preceding two words to replace "inevitably," which he struck out.

11. Here GW struck the following sentences: "It may not impossibly be found, that the spirit of party, the machinations of foreign powers, the corruption and ambition of individual citizens, are more formidable adversaries to the unity of our Empire, than any inherent difficulties in the scheme. Against these, the mounds of national opinion, national sympathy and national jealousy ought to be raised."

12. At this point GW struck the following paragraph and a marginal note with an explanation: "not important enough." The paragraph reads: "Besides the more serious causes already hinted as threatening our Union, there is one less dangerous, but sufficiently dangerous to make it prudent to be upon our guard against it. I allude to the petulence of party differences of opinions. It is not uncommon to hear the irritations which these excite vent themselves in declarations, that the different parts of the United States are ill affected to each other in menaces, that the Union will be dissolved by this or that measure. Intimations like these are as indiscreet as they are intemperate. Though frequently made with levity, & without any really evil intention, they have a tendency to produce the consequence which they indicate. They teach the minds of men to consider the Union as precarious—as an object to which they ought not to attach their hopes and fortunes, and thus chill the sentiment in its favor. By alarming the pride of those to whom they are addressed, they set ingenuity at work to depreciate the value of the thing and to discover reasons of indifference towards it. This is not wise. It will be much wiser to habituate ourselves to reverence the Union as the palladium of our national happiness—to accomodate constantly our words and actions to that idea—and to discountenance whatever may suggest a suspicion that it can in any event be abandoned."

The surviving draft in Hamilton's writing continued with another sentence at this point, preceding the paragraph deleted by GW. That omitted sentence reads: "And by all the love I bear you My fellow Citizens I conjure you as often as it appears to frown upon the attempt."

13. GW completed this sentence with words inserted to replace two struck-out sentences: "These discriminations, the mere contrivance of the spirit of Party, (always dexterous to seize every handle by which the passions can be wielded, and too skilful not to turn to account the sympathy of neighbour-

hood), have furnished an argument against the Union, as evidence of a real difference of local interests and views; and serve to hazard it, by organizing large districts of country under the leaders of contending factions, whose rivalships, prejudices & schemes of ambition, rather than the true Interests of the Country, will direct the use of their influence. If it be possible to correct this poison in the habit of our body politic, it is worthy the endeavors of the moderate and the good to effect it."

14. In Article IV of the 27 Oct. 1795 Treaty of San Lorenzo, Spain agreed that navigation of the Mississippi River "in its whole breadth from it source to the Occean" would be free to U.S. citizens, and in Article XXII of the treaty Spain granted to U.S. citizens for three years the right to deposit their merchandise at New Orleans and reship it "without paying any other duty than a fair price for the hire of the stores" with a further promise to continue that right or to offer "an equivalent establishment" on the Mississippi (Miller, *Treaties*, 321–22, 337). For the Jay Treaty of 19 Nov. 1794 with Great Britain, GW may have been referring to Article II, promising British withdrawal from frontier posts, and Article III, reaffirming that navigation of the Mississippi River would remain open to citizens of both countries with the right to cross borders and freely carry on commerce, except within the limits of Hudson's Bay Company (Miller, *Treaties*, 246–48).

15. GW inserted this sentence to replace one that he struck out: "Owing to you as I do, a frank and free disclosure of my heart, I shall not conceal from you the belief I entertain, that your Government as at present constructed is far more likely to prove too feeble than too powerful."

16. Here GW struck six sentences: "In Republics of narrow extent, it is not difficult for those who at any time hold the reins of Power, and command the ordinary public favor, to overturn the established Constitution, in favor of their own aggrandisement. The same thing may likewise be too often accomplished in such Republics, by partial combinations of men, who though not in Office, from birth, riches or other sources of distinction, have extraordinary influence & numerous adherents. By debauching the military force, by surprising some commanding citadel, or by some other sudden & unforeseen movement, the fate of the Republic is decided. But in Republics of large extent, usurpations can scarcely make its way through these avenues. The powers and opportunities of resistance of a wide extended and numerous nation, defy the successful efforts of the ordinary military force, or of any Collections which wealth and patronage may call to their aid. In such Republics, it is safe to assert, that the conflicts of popular factions are the chief, if not the only inlets, of usurpation and Tyranny."

17. At this point GW struck out a paragraph and a marginal note with an explanation: "not sufficiently important." The paragraph reads (text in angle brackets is from the transcription by Paltsits): "Cultivate industry and frugality, as auxiliaries to good morals ⟨& sources of private & public prosperity. Is there no room to regret that our propensity to expence exceeds our means for it? Is there not more luxury among us, and more diffusively, than suits the actual stage of our national progress?⟩ Whatever may be the apology for luxury in a country, mature in the arts which are its ministers, and the ⟨cause⟩ of national

opulence—Can it promote the advantage of a young country, almost wholly Agricultural, in the infancy of the Arts, and certainly not in the maturity of wealth?" The portion of the deleted text following the word "frugality" was at the top of a page, and GW used wafers to attach over that deleted text the paragraph that now follows.

18. The preceding sentence does not appear in the surviving Hamilton draft. It may, however, have been influenced by a marginal note that Hamilton had written beside an earlier paragraph: "ordinary management of affairs to be left to Represent" (*Hamilton Papers*, 20:275).

19. GW struck text reading "begets of course a similar sentiment in that other" at this point.

20. GW struck out a qualifying phrase—"circumspection indeed, but with"—at this point.

21. GW struck out "neither of two" at this point.

22. GW struck out "to throw our weight into the opposite scale" at this point.

23. GW is referring to the Neutrality Proclamation.

24. At this point, GW struck a parenthetical phrase: "and from men disagreeing in their impressions of the origin progress and nature of that war."

25. This paragraph was attached by wafers above a paragraph on the original page. A marginal note explains: "This is the first draught and it is questionable which of the two is to be preferred." The final text includes two minor edits made by GW: the insertion of "it is not necessary" to replace "some of them of a delicate nature, would be improperly the subject of explanation," which he struck out, and the insertion of the words "to detail" after "this occasion." On the original page, GW had started with the same base text and edited it more extensively to read: "The considerations, which respect the right to hold this conduct, would be improperly the subject of particular discussion on this occasion.—I will barely observe, that to me they appeared warranted by well established principles of the Laws of Nations, as applicable to the nature of our alliance with France in connection with the circumstances of the War and the relative situations of the contracting parties" (the transcription is taken from Paltsits).

This paragraph and the two paragraphs following do not appear on the surviving draft in Hamilton's writing.

26. Following this paragraph, GW deleted a paragraph and a marginal note with an explanation: "This paragraph may have the appearance of self distrust and mere vanity." To draw the printer to the final paragraph of the address, he wrote here "Relying &a" with a bracketed note "see the other side." The deleted paragraph reads: "May I, without the charge of ostentation, add, that neither ambition nor interest has been the impelling cause of my actions— that I have never designedly misused any power confided to me, nor hesitated to use one, where I thought it could redound to your benefit? May I, without the appearance of affectation, say that the fortune with which I came into office is not bettered otherwise than by that improvement in the value of property, which the quick progress & uncommon prosperity of our country have produced? May I still further add, without breach of delicacy, that I shall retire without cause for a blush, with sentiment alien to the fervor of those vows for

the happiness of his country so natural to a citizen who sees in it the native soil of his progenitors and himself for four generations."

27. This paragraph has a bracketed note in the right margin that reads: "continuation of the paragraph preceeding the last, ending with the word rest."

From John Jay

Dear Sir   New York 19 Septr 1796

It occurs to me that it may not be perfectly prudent to say that we are never to *expect* Favors from a nation, for that assertion seems to imply that nations always *are*, or always *ought* to be moved *only* by interested motives.[1] It is true that disinterested Favors are so rare, that on *that account* they are not to be expected between nations; and if that Sentiment turned on that Reason vizt their being so *uncommon*, the assertion would then be so limited by that Reason, as not to be liable to misconstruction— I think it would be more safe to omit the word *expected*, and retain only the words *not to be calculated upon*, which appear to me to be quite sufficient—Permit me to submit this to your Consideration and believe me to be with perfect Respect Esteem & attachment Dear Sir your obliged & obt Servt

John Jay

ALS, DLC:GW.

1. Jay is referring to text from the draft for GW's farewell address that Alexander Hamilton had sent with his letter to GW of 30 July. The relevant text reads: "tis folly in one nation to expect disinterested favour in another. . . . There can be no greater error in national policy than to desire expect or calculate upon real favours" (*Hamilton Papers*, 20:285–86).

Jay wrote Richard Peters on 29 March 1811 that he had discussed the draft with Hamilton before it was sent to GW, "paragraph by paragraph, until the whole met our mutual approbation. Some amendments were made during the interview, but none of much importance.

"Although this business had not been hastily dispatched, yet aware of the consequence of such a paper, I suggested the giving it a further critical examination; but he declined it, saying he was pressed for time, and was anxious to return the draft to the President without delay.

"It afterwards occurred to me that a certain proposition was expressed in terms too general and unqualified, and I hinted it in a letter to the President" (Paltsits, *Farewell Address*, 264–71; quote on 271; see also Jay to Peters, 23 April 1811, in Paltsits, *Farewell Address*, 276–77).

From John Lee

Philadelphia September 19th 1796.
Sir,   No. 23 North Eighth Street
Having observed in Claypoole's Paper of this morning your
intention of declining to stand a Candidate for the Chief Magistracy of the Executive of the United States at the ensuing election, for which, as one of your sincere friends, I cannot help
regretting; therefore, Sir, permit me to lay before your Excellency my present situation, and the services which I formerly did
towards supporting the Independence of the United States at a
time when in the greatest danger, and, as a token of your friendship and respect for what I had then done, I received the enclosed letter from you for the same;[1] but within a few years past
I have met with some considerable misfortunes by a long and
tedious lawsuit in New Jersey (which is not yet determined) for
the recovering some very valuable Lands there, which I bought
in England many years since; through these disapppointments,
and having a wife and four children to support, I am induced, by
the advice of a few friends, to take the liberty of reminding your
Excellency that I am the Person your letter above mentioned
was directed to "at Mount Pleasant near Mount Holly," and as
I have formerly been an Agent for several Members of Parliament, before the Revolution, in the Floridas, where at that time
they held great quantities of land, and were under contract by
Treaty with tne upper and Lower Creek Nations of Indians to
supply their necessities annually according to the said Treaty;[2]
should your Excellency think me worthy of being employed as
an Agent, or in any other Department under the Indian Trading-
House Bill, which passed the last Sessions of Congress,[3] or in any
other service of the United States, it will be received by me with
gratitude from your Excellency's hands, and any Security for the
Trust reposed in me, my friends are ready and willing to give.
My recommendation was delivered to Tench Francis Esqr. (the
Purveyor &c.) several months past, and filed in his Office with
others at that time, a Copy of which is herewith enclosed,[4] as also
a Certificate of the time I took the oath of fidelity to the States,
which was within two months after my arrival from England with
the packet of Letters &ca from your old Friend and Neighbour

Coll Fairfax, which I forwarded to you at West Point so soon as I got out from New York to Elizabeth Town which was about the sixteenth of September '78; I had the parcel seven days in New York but to preserve the contents, I was obliged to break open the whole and tear them up in small pieces, which I put into separate sheets of paper numbered with directions how your Excellency should understand to read them which *circumstance* I have no doubt you may now well recollect.[5]

I conclude with my most sincere wishes for your health, and that you may end your days in that rural comfort and happiness of a domestic life, which you once enjoyed with great pleasure before you undertook the arduous task to obtain and support the Independence of your native Country, and for which every good Citizen will remember your name and services to the latest posterity. I have the Honor to be, (with the utmost respect) Your Excellency's obedient & very humble Servant

John Lee

ALS, DNA: RG 59, Miscellaneous Letters.

Lee recently had moved to Philadelphia from his farm, Mount Pleasant, in Burlington County, N.J., about twenty miles from Philadelphia.

1. The enclosed letter has not been found.

2. At the Treaty of Picolata with the Upper and Lower Creek Nations, 18 Nov. 1765, the British engaged to "encourage Proper Persons to supply and furnish the said Indian Nations with all sorts of Goods which have usually been carried amongst them, in the manner which they are now supplied, and in such quantitys as shall be sufficient to answer all their wants" (*Early American Indian Documents*, 12:464–66).

3. For others seeking appointment under this legislation, see Isaac Levan to GW, 26 April, and n.1 to that document.

4. This enclosure has not been identified.

5. The contents of the packet have not been identified.

From Edward Lynch

Sir   Baltimore Septr 20th 1796

Having seen a Publication in the Baltimore newspaper of your intended resignation of being President of the United states[1] I observed it with great regret and so did many others that you shold resign being the chief Majistrate of our Country. My Father who fought with others under you feel very unhappy on the occasion in the late happy Revolution in support of the Liberty of our country. The reason I thus write to you is that I am a student in the College called after your name Washington College. Although as young as I am I feel in my breast your intended Resignation. A vocation having taken place I came to see my father. One Great happiness we have and never will forget is that you sir in all sitiations was all perfection. May God as I hope he will when you die Recieve you in his blessed Mansion but yet I pray that he may Prolong your life to give advice to those that fill your place. with tears and yet pleasure I have the honour of subscribeing myself Although a boy your Humble servant

Edward Lynch
son of Major John Lynch

ALS, DLC:GW.

1. The *Federal Gazette & Baltimore Daily Advertiser* issued a supplement edition on this date with a notice at the top of the first column: "*The first important article that strikes us is, the resignation of the* FATHER *of* AMERICA. *His paternal address to his Children, though lengthy, will appear in this Gazette in the morning.*"

From Timothy Pickering

Sir, Department of State Sept. 20. 1796.

Yesterday I received from Mr Monroe a letter dated the 12th of June, from which we may conclude that the complaints of the French Republic, which had been the subject of his former letters, will not be renewed. But it may be more satisfactory to read Mr Monroes own words at length; and therefore I inclose an extract from his letter, being the only thing interesting in it.[1]

Mr Craik will present you my request for your order on the Secretary of the Treasury for 2000 dollars for occasional demands on the contingent fund.[2] I have the honor to be with the greatest respect sir, your most obt servt

T. Pickering

ALS, DNA: RG 59, Miscellaneous Letters; LB, DNA: RG 59, Domestic Letters; LB, DNA: RG 59, GW's Correspondence with His Secretaries of State. GW replied to this letter on 28 Sept. (DNA: RG 59, Miscellaneous Letters).

1. The enclosed extract reads: "I have the pleasure to inform you that in a late informal conference with one of the Members of the Directoire, I was advised by him that the Directoire had done nothing in regard to us upon the subject communicated to you in several of my preceding letters, and that he presumed they would do nothing, upon that subject. I trust therefore that

their councils are thus settled upon this interesting topic, and that I shall hear nothing further from them on it: but should they take a different turn of which at present there is no particular sympto[m] (for the probability of such a course was greatest in the commencement, and whilst the first impressions were at their height) I shall not fail to apprize you of it, and without delay. As yet no successor is appointed to Mr Adet, nor can I say what the intention of his Government is, in that respect. I presume however upon the authority of the above communication, that in case one is appointed, it will be merely in consequence of Mr Adet's request, and be of course only an ordinary official measure of no particular importance to us" (DNA: RG 59, Miscellaneous Letters). For the full letter from James Monroe, U.S. minister to France, to Pickering, dated 12 June, see *Papers of James Monroe*, 4:34–35.

2. Pickering had written GW on 17 Sept.: "Demands on the fund for the contingent expences of government will doubtless arise in your absence. I request your order to the Secretary of the Treasury to cause two thousand dollars to be paid to me to answer such demands" (ALS, DNA: RG 59, Miscellaneous Letters; LB, DNA: RG 59, Domestic Letters; LB, DNA: RG 59, GW's Correspondence with His Secretaries of State). The account enclosed with GW's report to Congress dated 15 Feb. 1797 shows the requested warrant issued to Pickering on 1 Oct. 1796 (DNA: RG 46, entry 47).

From Timothy Pickering

Sir,   Department of State Sept. 20. 1796.

I have just received a letter dated the 17th from Judge Benson: He accepts the place of third Commissioner under the fifth article of the British treaty, and was to set out yesterday for Passamaquoddy, to meet there the other Commissioners on the third of October. The trust, he remarks, is not incompatible with his present office; and interfering with it only for a short time, his acceptance of it appeared to him indispensable. He concludes with these words—"That my own judgement has coincided with the wishes of the President, certainly affords me a very sensible satisfaction."[1] I am with the highest respect, sir, your most obt servt

                                          Timothy Pickering.

P.S. Amos Marsh, the District Attorney has desired to resign his office, & to have a successor speedily appointed.[2] He recommends no one. It shall be a subject of enquiry.

ALS, DNA: RG 59, Miscellaneous Letters; LB, DNA: RG 59, Domestic Letters; LB, DNA: RG 59, GW's Correspondence with His Secretaries of State. GW replied to this letter on 28 Sept. (DNA: RG 59, Miscellaneous Letters).

1. The letter from Egbert Benson, then an associate justice on the New York Supreme Court, to Pickering has not been identified.

For the persons already selected as commissioners under Article V of the Jay Treaty, see Pickering's second letter to GW on 20 May, and n.6, and GW's first letter to the U.S. Senate, same date; see also GW to Henry Knox, 4 April.

2. Amos Marsh was the federal district attorney for Vermont. For the nomination of Charles Marsh as his replacement, see GW to the U.S. Senate, 30 Dec. (DNA: RG 46, entry 52).

Index

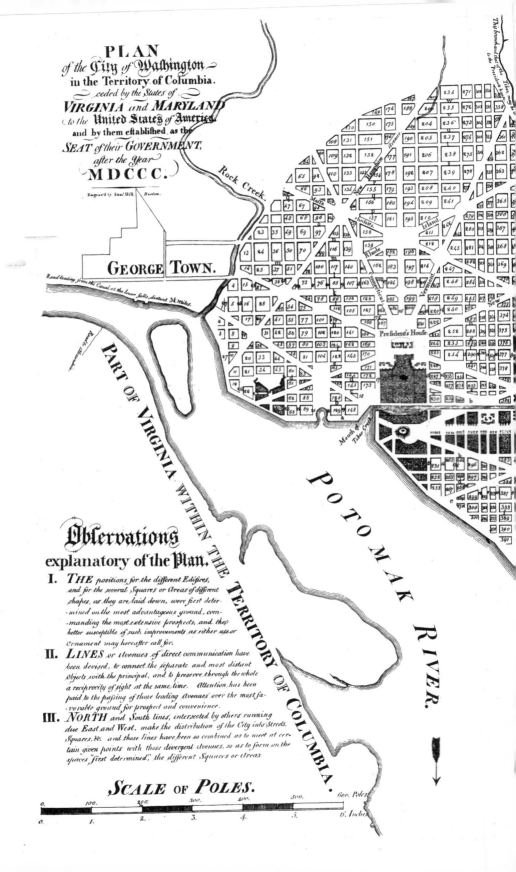

PLAN
of the City of Washington
in the Territory of Columbia.
ceded by the States of
VIRGINIA *and* **MARYLAND**
to the **United States of America**
and by them established as the
SEAT *of their* **GOVERNMENT,**
after the Year
MDCCC.

Engrav'd by Sam¹ Hill. Boston.

GEORGE TOWN.

Rock Creek.

Road leading from the Canal at the lower falls, distant 3½ Miles.

President's House

PART OF VIRGINIA WITHIN THE TERRITORY OF COLUMBIA.

Mouth of Tiber Creek

P O T O M A K   R I V E R.

Observations
explanatory of the **Plan.**

I. THE *positions for the different Edifices,
and for the several Squares or Areas of different
shapes, as they are laid down, were first deter-
-mined on the most advantageous ground, com-
-manding the most extensive prospects, and the
better susceptible of such improvements as either use or
ornament may hereafter call for.*

II. LINES *or avenues of direct communication have
been devised, to connect the separate and most distant
objects with the principal, and to preserve through the whole
a reciprocity of sight at the same time. Attention has been
paid to the passing of those leading Avenues over the most fa-
-vorable ground for prospect and convenience.*

III. NORTH *and South lines, intersected by others running
due East and West, make the distribution of the City into Streets,
Squares, &c. and those lines have been so combined as to meet at certain given points with those divergent avenues, so as to form on the
spaces "first determined," the different Squares or Areas.*

SCALE OF POLES.

0.   100.   200.   300.   400.   500.   600. Poles.

0.   1.   2.   3.   4.   5.   6. Inches.